Education at a Glance

OECD INDICATORS 2003

OECD
ORGANISATION FOR ECONOMIC CO-OPERATION AND DEVELOPMENT

ORGANISATION FOR ECONOMIC CO-OPERATION AND DEVELOPMENT

Pursuant to Article 1 of the Convention signed in Paris on 14th December 1960, and which came into force on 30th September 1961, the Organisation for Economic Co-operation and Development (OECD) shall promote policies designed:
- to achieve the highest sustainable economic growth and employment and a rising standard of living in member countries, while maintaining financial stability, and thus to contribute to the development of the world economy;
- to contribute to sound economic expansion in member as well as non-member countries in the process of economic development; and
- to contribute to the expansion of world trade on a multilateral, non-discriminatory basis in accordance with international obligations.

The original member countries of the OECD are Austria, Belgium, Canada, Denmark, France, Germany, Greece, Iceland, Ireland, Italy, Luxembourg, the Netherlands, Norway, Portugal, Spain, Sweden, Switzerland, Turkey, the United Kingdom and the United States. The following countries became members subsequently through accession at the dates indicated hereafter: Japan (28th April 1964), Finland (28th January 1969), Australia (7th June 1971), New Zealand (29th May 1973), Mexico (18th May 1994), the Czech Republic (21st December 1995), Hungary (7th May 1996), Poland (22nd November 1996), Korea (12th December 1996) and Slovak Republic (14th December 2000). The Commission of the European Communities takes part in the work of the OECD (Article 13 of the OECD Convention).

The Centre for Educational Research and Innovation was created in June 1968 by the Council of the Organisation for Economic Co-operation and Development and all member countries of the OECD are participants.

The main objectives of the Centre are as follows:
- *analyse and develop research, innovation and key indicators in current and emerging education and learning issues, and their links to other sectors of policy;*
- *explore forward-looking coherent approaches to education and learning in the context of national and international cultural, social and economic change; and*
- *facilitate practical co-operation among member countries and, where relevant, with non-member countries, in order to seek solutions and exchange views of educational problems of common interest.*

The Centre functions within the Organisation for Economic Co-operation and Development in accordance with the decisions of the Council of the Organisation, under the authority of the Secretary-General. It is supervised by a Governing Board composed of one national expert in its field of competence from each of the countries participating in its programme of work.

Publié en français sous le titre :

Regards sur l'éducation
Les indicateurs de l'OCDE 2003

FOREWORD

Changing economic and social conditions have given education an increasingly central role in the success of individuals and nations. Human capital has long been identified as a key factor in combating unemployment and low pay but there is now also robust evidence that it is an important determinant of economic growth and emerging evidence that it is associated with a wide range of non-economic benefits, including improvements in health and a greater sense of well-being.

These benefits have driven increased participation in a widening range of learning activities – by people of all ages, from earliest childhood to advanced adulthood. As the demand for learning grows and becomes more diverse, the challenge for governments is to ensure that the learning opportunities provided respond to real, dynamic needs in a cost-effective manner.

In searching for education policies that enhance individuals' social and economic prospects, provide incentives for greater efficiency in schooling and help to mobilise resources to meet rising demands, governments are paying increasing attention to international comparisons. As part of the drive to enhance the OECD's work in this area and to better respond to the needs of citizens and governments, the Directorate for Education, therefore, devotes a major effort to the development and analysis of quantitative indicators. These enable governments to see their education system in the light of other countries' performances. Together with OECD's country policy reviews, the indicators are designed to support and review efforts which governments are making towards policy reform.

Education at a Glance – OECD Indicators 2003 reflects a consensus among professionals on how to measure the current state of education internationally. It provides a rich, comparable and up-to-date array of indicators and is a key instrument for disseminating these indicators to a range of users, from governments seeking to learn policy lessons, academics requiring data for further analysis, to the general public wanting to monitor how its nation's schools are progressing in producing world-class students.

The focus of the 2003 edition of *Education at a Glance* is on the quality of learning outcomes, the policy levers and contextual factors that shape these outcomes, and the broader private and social returns that accrue to investments in education. This includes a comparative picture of student performance near the beginning and end of compulsory education that extends to knowledge and skills in important subject areas as well as learning strategies and engagement with learning. The picture is not limited to aggregate country performance, but also includes variations within countries that allow an examination of equity in the provision and outcomes of education, on dimensions such as gender, age, socio-economic background, type of institution, or field of education. New information on student learning conditions, including the integration of information and communication technologies in the instructional process, as well as on teacher qualifications, teacher working conditions and other factors affecting teacher demand and supply, provide a better understanding of some of the determinants of educational success. Finally, for many indicators, a larger number of OECD countries are now providing data. Through the World Education Indicators programme, a wide range of non-OECD countries are also contributing to *Education at a Glance,* extending the coverage of some of the indicators to almost two-thirds of the world population.

The publication is the product of a longstanding, collaborative effort between OECD governments, the experts and institutions working within the framework of OECD's education indicators programme (INES), and the OECD Secretariat. The publication was drafted by the Division for Education Indicators and Analysis, under the responsibility of Andreas Schleicher, in co-operation with Eric Charbonnier,

Michael Davidson, Ritsuko Doko, Catherine Duchêne, Jean-Luc Heller, Judit Kadar-Fülop, Claire Shewbridge, Karine Tremblay and Hannah v. Ahlefeld. The development of the publication was steered by INES National Co-ordinators in Member countries and facilitated by the financial and material support of the three countries responsible for co-ordinating the INES Networks - the Netherlands, Sweden and the United States. In addition, work on the publication has been aided by a grant from the National Center for Education Statistics (NCES) in the United States. The Annex lists the members of the various bodies as well as the individual experts who have contributed to this publication and the OECD education indicators more generally.

While much progress has been accomplished in recent years, significant further work is needed to link better a broad range of policy needs with the best available data. In developing this programme of work, various challenges and tradeoffs must be faced. First, the indicators need to respond to educational issues that are high on national policy agendas, and where the international comparative perspective can offer important added value to what can be accomplished through national analysis and evaluation. Second, while the indicators need to be as comparable as possible, they also need to be as country-specific as is necessary to allow for historical, systemic and cultural differences between countries. Third, the indicators need to be presented in as straightforward a manner as possible, but remain sufficiently complex to reflect multi-faceted educational realities. Fourth, there is a general desire to keep the indicator set as small as possible, but it needs to be large enough to be useful to policy-makers across countries that face different educational challenges.

The OECD provides the framework to address these challenges more vigorously and to pursue not just the development of indicators in areas where it is feasible and promising to develop data, but also to advance in areas where a considerable investment still needs to be made in conceptual work.

The report is published on the responsibility of the Secretary-General of the OECD.

Barry McGaw
Director for Education
OECD

TABLE OF CONTENTS

INTRODUCTION

ORGANISING FRAMEWORK FOR THE 2003 EDITION OF EDUCATION AT A GLANCE

Education at a Glance – OECD Indicators 2003 provides a rich, comparable and up-to-date array of indicators that reflect a consensus among professionals on how to measure the current state of education internationally. The indicators provide information on the human and financial resources invested in education, on how education and learning systems operate and evolve, and on the returns to educational investments. The indicators are organised thematically, and each is accompanied by relevant background information. The education indicators are presented within an organising framework which:

- distinguishes between the actors in education systems: individual learners, instructional settings and learning environments, educational service providers, and the education system as a whole;

- groups the indicators according to whether they speak to learning outcomes for individuals and countries, policy levers or circumstances that shape these outcomes, or to antecedents or constraints that set policy choices into context; and

- identifies the policy issues to which the indicators relate, with three major categories distinguishing between the quality of educational outcomes and educational provision, issues of equity in educational outcomes and educational opportunities, and the adequacy and effectiveness of resource management.

The following matrix describes the first two dimensions. References between the individual indicators and the cells in this matrix are provided in the section *Contents and Highlights* of this introduction.

		(1) Education and learning outputs and outcomes	(2) Policy levers and contexts shaping educational outcomes	(3) Antecedents or constraints that contextualise policy
(A)	Individual participants in education and learning	(1.A) The quality and distribution of individual educational outcomes	(2.A) Individual attitudes, engagement, and behaviour	(3.A) Background characteristics of the individual learners
(B)	Instructional settings	(1.B) The quality of instructional delivery	(2.B) Pedagogy and learning practices and classroom climate	(3.B) Student learning conditions and teacher working conditions
(C)	Providers of educational services	(1.C) The output of educational institutions and institutional performance	(2.C) School environment and organisation	(3.C) Characteristics of the service providers and their communities
(D)	The education system as a whole	(1.D) The overall performance of the education system	(2.D) System-wide institutional settings, resource allocations, and policies	(3.D) The national educational, social, economic, and demographic context

CONTENTS AND HIGHLIGHTS

This section describes the contents of the volume and summarises key findings. It also highlights new features of this year's edition of *Education at a Glance* and relates the indicators to the organising framework described above.

Chapter A examines the outcomes of education and learning, in terms of...
...the current output of educational institutions and the educational attainment of the adult population,...

Chapter A begins by examining graduation rates at the upper secondary level of education which is often considered the baseline qualification in modern societies (**Indicator A1**). The indicator speaks both to the current output of educational institutions (**Framework Cells 1.C and 1.D**). To gauge progress in educational output, current graduation rates are compared to the educational attainment of older persons who left the education system at different points in time.

The educational attainment of the adult population is not only a measure of the output of education systems, but adult qualifications also provide an important context for education systems (**Framework Cell 3.D**) as witnessed by the close interrelationships between student performance and parental levels of educational attainment (OECD, 2001). Finally, an analysis by gender provides an assessment of gender equity in upper secondary qualifications.

- In 15 out of 17 OECD countries for which comparable data are available, the ratio of upper secondary graduates to the population at the typical age of graduation exceeds 70 per cent. In Denmark, Finland, Germany, Japan and Poland, graduation rates exceed 90 per cent. The challenge now is to ensure that the remaining fraction is not left behind, with the risk of social exclusion that this may entail.

- Comparing the attainment of the population aged 25 to 34 years with that of the population aged 45 to 54 shows that the proportion of individuals who have not completed upper secondary education has been shrinking in almost all OECD countries, and in some rapidly. Many countries with traditionally low levels of education are catching up.

- Among older age groups, females have lower levels of education than males, but for younger people the pattern has reversed and today, graduation rates for females exceed those for males in most countries.

Indicators A2 and A3 on tertiary graduation and attainment extend the picture with an assessment of the supply of advanced skills in different fields of study (**Framework Cells 1.C and 1.D**). Attainment levels for different generations show how the supply of high skills qualifications has evolved and provides an important context for current educational policies (**Framework Cell 3.D**). *New:* For the first time, the indicator also provides trend data on tertiary attainment for the period 1999 to 2001. Finally, the indicator reviews countries' progress in closing the gender gap in tertiary attainment and graduation rates, both overall and across different fields of education.

Indicator A2 also compares drop-out rates which provide some indication of the internal efficiency of education systems (**Framework Cell 1.C**). Students leave educational programmes before their completion for many reasons - they realise that they have chosen the wrong subject or educational programme, they fail to meet the standards set by their educational institution, or they may want to work before completing their programme. Nevertheless, high dropout rates indicate that the education system is not meeting the needs of its clients. Students may find that the educational programmes do not meet their expectations or their needs in order to enter the labour market, or that the programmes require more time outside the labour market than they can justify.

- On average across OECD countries, 30 per cent of persons at the typical age of graduation currently complete the tertiary-type A level of education – but the figure ranges from around 40 per cent in Australia, Finland, Iceland and New Zealand to 20 per cent or below in Austria, the Czech Republic, Germany, Italy and Switzerland.

- On average, one third of OECD students "drop out" before they complete their first degree, regardless of whether they are following tertiary-type A or tertiary-type B programmes.

- As measured by educational attainment, there has been an increase in the stock of university-level skills in the adult population. But most of that increase is due to significant increases in tertiary graduation rates in a comparatively small number of countries.

- On average across OECD countries, every third tertiary-type A graduate obtains a degree in the social sciences, business or law. The second most popular fields are science-related, from which one in four students graduate, on average.

- In the humanities, arts, education, health and welfare, on average in OECD countries more than two thirds of the tertiary-type A graduates are females, whereas there are less than one third in mathematics and computer science and less than one quarter in engineering, manufacturing and construction. Males are also more likely than females to earn advanced research qualifications, such as doctorates.

…the quality of learning outcomes,…

Counting the numbers of graduates alone does not provide information about the quality of learning outcomes. To address this, Chapter A also compares the knowledge and skills attained by students across countries. *New:* **Indicator A4** has been newly introduced and assesses reading literacy skills of students around the age of 9 years.

While Indicator A4 looks at reading skills at the beginning of schooling, **Indicators A5** and **A6** compare the reading, mathematics and science knowledge and skills of students at age 15, *i.e.* towards the end of their compulsory schooling period. These indicators are essential indicators for gauging the quality of educational performance as they assess to what extent societies have succeeded in equipping young adults with key foundation skills at an age when the transition to work is becoming a key concern for many. *New:* Interpreting Indicators A4 and A5 together provides some indication of the progress achieved by education systems between primary and secondary education.

Indicators A4, A5 and A6 not only benchmark the overall performance of countries (**Framework Cell 1.D**), but devote much attention also to the distribution of knowledge and skills in the student population, with the aim to assess to what extent countries succeed in combining high overall performance with an equitable distribution of learning outcomes (**Framework Cell 1.A**).

- 4th-grade students in Sweden perform significantly higher in reading than their counterparts in all other OECD countries. Seven other countries (the Czech Republic, England, Germany, Hungary, Italy, the Netherlands and the United States) still perform significantly above the OECD average.

- On average among OECD countries, 10 per cent of 15-year-olds have acquired Level 5 reading literacy skills, which involve evaluation of information and building of hypotheses, drawing on specialised knowledge, and accommodating concepts contrary to expectations. However, this percentage varies from 19 per cent in Finland and New Zealand to below 1 per cent in Mexico. An average of 12 per cent of 15-year-olds have only acquired the most basic literacy skills at Level 1 and a further 6 per cent fall even below that.

- Six countries (the Czech Republic, Germany, Greece, Hungary, Italy and the United States) performed relatively better in PIRLS than in PISA. In the former four cases, scores were above the OECD average in PIRLS and are below the OECD average in PISA. Three countries performed relatively better in PISA than in PIRLS, Iceland, New Zealand and Norway. France and Sweden performed similarly relative to other countries on both assessments.

- 15-year-olds in Japan display the highest mean scores in mathematical literacy, although their scores cannot be distinguished statistically from students in two other top-performing countries, Korea and New Zealand. On the scientific literacy scale, students in Japan and Korea demonstrate the highest average performance.

- While there are large differences in mean performance among countries, the variation of performance among 15-year-olds within each country is many times larger. However, wide disparities in performance are not a necessary condition for a country to attain a high level of overall performance. On the contrary, five of the countries with the smallest variation in performance on the mathematical literacy scale, namely Canada, Finland, Iceland, Japan and Korea, all perform significantly above the OECD average, and four of them, Canada, Finland, Japan and Korea, are among the six best-performing countries in mathematical literacy.

...and how this varies between genders,...

Recognising the impact that education has on participation in labour markets, occupational mobility and the quality of life, policymakers and educators emphasise the importance of reducing educational differences between males and females. Significant progress has been achieved in reducing the gender gap in educational attainment (see Indicators A1 and A2), although in certain fields of study, such as mathematics and computer science, gender differences favouring males still exist (see Indicator A3).

As females have closed the gap and then surpassed males in many aspects of education, there are now many instances in which there is concern about the underachievement of males in certain areas, such as reading. Gender differences in student performance, as well as in attitudes toward and strategies for learning, therefore need to receive close attention from policymakers if greater gender equity in educational outcomes is to be achieved. Furthermore, students' perceptions of what occupations lie ahead for them can affect their academic decisions and performance. An important policy objective should therefore be to strengthen the role that the education system can play in moderating gender differences in occupational expectations to help reduce performance gaps in different subject areas. *New:* This indicator begins by examining data from OECD's PISA study on gender differences in the occupations which 15-year old students expect to have by the age of 30 and then the newly introduced **Indicator A11** examines gender differences in performance, attitudes, and learning strategies in primary and secondary schools **(Framework Cells 1.A and 2.A)**.

- Already at 4th-grade level, females tend to outperform males in reading literacy, on average, and at age 15 the gender gap in reading tends to be large. In mathematics, 15-year-old males tend to be at a slight advantage in most countries whereas in science, gender patterns are less pronounced and uneven.

- Despite these overall patterns, countries differ, however, widely in the magnitude of gender differences in the different subject areas.

- Gender differences also exist in attitudes and approaches to learning. In the majority of countries, 15-year-old females tend to emphasise memorisation strategies, while males tend to be stronger on elaboration strategies. In all countries, females express greater interest in reading than males while males tend to express more interest in mathematics. Both differences are closely mirrored in performance patterns.

• Gender differences are also observed with regard to the confidence that students express in their abilities and whether they believe in the benefits of learning. In almost all countries, females express a higher self-concept than do males in reading while, in mathematical literacy, males tend to express a higher self-concept than females. In terms of their general self-efficacy males score significantly higher than females, overall and in most countries.

• In about half the countries, females preferred co-operative learning more than males did, whereas males in most countries tended to prefer competitive learning more than females did.

...how performance varies between schools and students,...

Indicators A5 and A6 show that, in most countries, there are considerable differences in performance within each education system. This variation may reflect differences in school and student backgrounds, the human and financial resources available to schools, curricular differences, selection policies and practices, or the way that teaching is organised and delivered. Some countries have non-selective school systems that seek to provide all students with the same opportunities for learning, and allow each school to cater to all levels of student performance. Other countries respond to diversity explicitly by forming groups of students of similar performance levels through selection either within or between schools, with the aim of serving students according to their specific needs. Other countries combine the two approaches. Even in comprehensive school systems, schools may vary significantly in response to the socio-economic and cultural characteristics of the communities that they serve or their geography.

Indicator A7 sheds light on performance differences between schools **(Framework Cells 1.B and 1.C)** and some of the factors associated with these differences **(Framework Cells 3.A, 3.B and 3.C)**.

• On average, differences in the performance of 15-year-olds between schools account for 36 per cent of the OECD average variation in student performance, but this proportion varies from below 10 per cent in Iceland and Sweden to more than 50 per cent in Austria, Belgium, the Czech Republic, Germany, Greece, Hungary, Italy and Poland.

• Some of the variation between schools is attributable to geography, institutional factors or the selection of students by ability. The differences are often compounded by family background, particularly in countries with differentiated school systems, since students' results are associated not only with their own individual backgrounds but – to a greater extent – with the backgrounds of others at their school.

• High overall variation can result from high within-school differences, high between-school differences or a combination of the two.

• In school systems with differentiated school types, the clustering of students with particular socio-economic characteristics in certain schools is greater than in systems where the curriculum does not vary significantly between schools.

...important factors associated with student performance,...

It is well established that students who choose to spend a lot of time reading tend to be better readers than those who do not. However, in examining students' reading practices, it is important to consider not just the amount of time that students spend reading, but also how they invest this time. While some students may choose to read only one type of material (*e.g.*, magazines) frequently, others read a diversity of materials. Understanding what students read frequently and how these choices are related to reading performance can prompt educators and policymakers to devise early-intervention strategies to foster certain reading behaviours in order to promote literacy. *New:* To shed light on this, the newly introduced **Indicator A8** profiles students' reading practices according to the materials they read frequently and demonstrates the relationship between these profiles and their performance in reading literacy. *New:* Furthermore, the newly introduced **Indicator A9** takes this further to explore a broader concept of "engagement" in reading, which encompasses both reading practices and attitudes toward reading.

New: Finally, the newly introduced **Indicator A10** reports data on students' learning strategies, motivational preferences, self-related competencies, and learning preferences as important capacities of students to regulate their own learning. In societies that increasingly depend on the capacity and motivation of their citizens to continue learning throughout life, these capacities are an important outcome of education in themselves and may have an impact on students' success both in school and in their future lives.

Indicators A8, A9 and A10 do not only reflect on learning activities and engagement as important outcomes of education **(Framework Cell 1.A)** but also as important policy levers that can help to both raise overall performance and counter social disadvantage **(Framework Cells 2.A and 2.B)**.

- Females and males show different profiles of reading. Among the two profiles of students poorly diversified in reading, mainly readers of newspapers and magazines, males and females are more or less equally distributed. The third profile, of readers more oriented towards comics, comprises a majority of males, while the profile oriented towards reading books, especially fiction, comprises a majority of females.

- Not surprisingly, 15-year-olds reading a diversity of print material are more proficient in reading than those reading a limited set of print material. Daily engagement in reading magazines, newspapers and comics – a kind of reading that is perhaps less valued by school than fiction books – seems, at least in some cultural contexts, to be a fruitful way of becoming a proficient reader.

- Engagement in reading, as defined in Indicator A9 (time spent reading for pleasure, time spent reading a diversity of material, high motivation and interest in reading), varies widely from country to country with Finland, at the high end, and Spain, at the low end, the extremes. On average, females tend to be substantially stronger engaged in reading than males.

- Fifteen-year-olds whose parents have the lowest occupational status but who are highly engaged in reading achieve better reading scores than students whose parents have high or medium occupational status but who are poorly engaged in reading. All students who are highly engaged in reading achieve reading literacy scores that, on average, are significantly above the OECD mean, whatever their parents' occupational background.

- The extent to which students monitor their own learning is closely related to performance in reading literacy and that students' beliefs that a goal is feasible, that the resources necessary to achieve it are accessible and that it is worth expending energy to achieve the goal are strong predictors of student performance in reading literacy.

...and the returns to investments in education for individuals and the society.

As levels of skill tend to rise with educational attainment, the social costs incurred when those with higher levels of education do not work also rise; and as populations in OECD countries age, higher and longer participation in the labour force can lower dependency ratios and help to alleviate the burden of financing public pensions. **Indicators A12** and **A13** examine the relationship between educational attainment and labour force activity, comparing rates of participation in the labour force first, and then rates of unemployment. Measuring the relationship between labour force activity and educational attainment, these are, first and foremost, indicators of the long-term outcomes of education systems **(Framework Cell 1.D)**. The adequacy of workers' skills and the capacity of the labour market to supply jobs that match those skills are, however, also important contexts for national education policy making **(Framework Cell 3.D)**. Unemployment rates can also influence student decisions to continue in education and therefore can shed light on differing participation rates in education across countries.

- Labour force participation rates rise with educational attainment in most OECD countries. With very few exceptions, the participation rate for graduates of tertiary education is markedly higher than that for upper secondary graduates. The gap in male participation rates is particularly wide between upper secondary graduates and those without an upper secondary qualification.

- The labour force participation rate for females with less than upper secondary attainment is particularly low. Rates for females with tertiary attainment approach or exceed 80 per cent in all but four countries, but remain below those of males in all countries except one.

- The gender gap in labour force participation decreases with increasing educational attainment. Although a gender gap in labour force participation remains among those with the highest educational attainment, it is much narrower than among those with lower qualifications.

- On average among countries, a young person aged 15 in 2001 can expect to be in formal education for as little as under six and a half years. In 16 of the 28 countries studied, this period ranges from six to seven and a half years.

- In addition to the number of years spent in education, a young person aged 15 can expect to hold a job for 6.4 of the 15 years to come, to be unemployed for a total of 0.8 years and to be out of the labour market for 1.4 years. It is in the average duration of spells of unemployment that countries vary most, which primarily reflects differences in youth employment rates.

- In absolute terms, young people today can expect to spend less time in unemployment after completing their initial education than they did ten years ago.

Markets also provide incentives to individuals to develop and maintain appropriate levels of skills through wage differentials, especially through higher earnings for persons completing additional education. Acquiring higher levels of education can also be viewed as an investment in human capital, which includes the stock of skills that individuals maintain or develop, through education or training and then offer, in return for earnings, on the labour market. The higher the earnings from increased human capital, the higher the returns on the investment and the premium paid for enhanced skills and/or higher productivity. *New:* **Indicator A14** and the newly introduced **Indicator A15** seek to measure the returns to education for individuals **(Framework Cell 1.A)**, in terms of higher earnings; for taxpayers, in terms of higher fiscal income from better educated individuals; and for societies more generally **(Framework Cell 1.D)**, in terms of the relationship between education and labour productivity. Together, these indicators shed light on the longer-term impact of education for individuals and societies. Indicator A14 also sheds light on an important national context **(Framework Cell 3.D)** for policy making and can influence public funding policies in general and policies on financial aid to students in particular. It can also provide context for individual students' decisions to engage in education at different levels **(Framework Cell 3.A)**.

- Education and earnings are positively linked. Upper secondary and post-secondary non-tertiary education form a break point in many countries beyond which additional education attracts a particularly high premium. In all countries, graduates of tertiary-level education earn substantially more than upper secondary and post-secondary non-tertiary graduates. Earnings differentials between tertiary and upper secondary education are generally more pronounced than those between upper secondary and lower secondary or below.

• Earnings of people with below upper secondary education tend to be 60 to 90 per cent of those of upper secondary and post-secondary non-tertiary graduates.

• Females still earn less than males with similar levels of educational attainment.

• An analysis of the driving factors of economic growth shows that rising labour productivity accounted for at least half of GDP per capita growth in most OECD countries.

• Labour productivity can be increased in several ways and human capital plays a pivotal role in this equation, not just as an input linking aggregate output to the stocks of productive inputs, but also as a determinant of the rate of technological progress.

• The estimated long-run effect on economic output of one additional year of education in the OECD area is in the order of 6 per cent.

Chapter B considers the financial and human resources invested in education, in terms of...

Financial resources are a central policy lever for improving educational outcomes. As an investment in human skills, education can help to foster economic growth and enhance productivity, contribute to personal and social development, and reduce social inequality. But like any investment, education needs to be financed. After Chapter A examined the returns to education, Chapter B provides a comparative examination of spending patterns in OECD countries. By giving more emphasis to trends in educational spending, the 2003 edition of *Education at a Glance 2003* seeks to analyse how different demand and supply factors interact and how spending on education, compared to spending on other social priorities, has changed.

...the resources that each country invests in education relative to its number of students enrolled,...

Effective schools require the right combination of trained and talented personnel, adequate facilities, state-of-the-art equipment, and motivated students ready to learn. The demand for high-quality education, however, can translate into higher costs per student, and must therefore be weighed against undue burdens for taxpayers. No absolute standards exist for measuring the per student resources needed to ensure optimal returns for individual students or society as a whole. Nonetheless, international comparisons can provide a starting point for discussion by evaluating the variation that exists between OECD countries in educational investment. **Indicator B1** examines direct public and private expenditure on educational institutions in relation to the number of their full-time equivalent (FTE) students. It also reviews how OECD countries apportion per capita education expenditure between different levels of education.

Expenditure per student is a key policy measure which most directly impacts on the individual learner as it acts as a constraint on the learning environment in schools and student learning conditions in the classroom **(Framework Cells 2.A, 3.C and 3.B)**.

However, relating Indicator B1 to Indicators A5 and A6 also shows, that lower expenditure cannot automatically be equated with a lower quality of educational services. Australia, Finland, Ireland, Korea and the United Kingdom, for example, which have moderate expenditure on education per student at primary and lower secondary levels, are among the OECD countries with the highest levels of performance by 15-year-old students in key subject areas.

• In the OECD area, annual public and private expenditure on educational institutions per student between primary and tertiary education is equal to US$ 6 361 but ranges from US$ 3 000 per student or less in the Czech Republic, Hungary, Mexico, Poland, the Slovak Republic, and Turkey to more than US$ 8 000 per student in Austria, Denmark, Norway, Sweden, Switzerland and the United States.

• OECD countries spend US$ 4 470 per primary student, US$ 5 501 per secondary student and US$ 11 109 per tertiary student, but these averages mask a broad range of expenditure across countries. On average, OECD countries spend 2.2 times as much per student at the tertiary level than at the primary level.

• In some OECD countries, low annual expenditure per tertiary student still translates into high overall costs per tertiary student because the duration of tertiary studies is long.

• Expenditure per primary, secondary and post-secondary non-tertiary student increased between 1995 and 2000 by over 25 per cent in Australia, Greece, Ireland, Portugal and Spain whereas at the terti-ary level, spending on education has not always kept pace with the rapid expansion of enrolments. In eight out of 22 OECD countries expenditure on educational institutions per tertiary student decreased between 1995 and 2000 whereas GDP per capita increased.

...and relative to national income,...

Indicator B2 examines the proportion of national resources that goes to educational institutions and the levels of education to which they go. The proportion of national financial resources allocated to education is one of the key choices made by each OECD country; it is an aggregate choice made by governments, enterprises, and individual students and their families. Indicator B2 also shows how the amount of educa-tional spending relative to the size of national wealth and in absolute terms has evolved over time in OECD countries. National resources devoted to education are a key national policy lever *(Framework Cell 2.D)* but also act as an antecedent to the activities of schools, classrooms and individual learners *(Framework Cells 3.C, 3.B and 3.A)*.

• OECD countries spend 5.9 per cent of their collective GDP on their educational institutions.

• In 14 out of 19 OECD countries, public and private spending on educational institutions increased between 1995 and 2000 by more than 5 per cent but, in contrast to the early 1990s, increases in spend-ing on educational institutions tended to fall behind the growth in national income.

• Two-thirds of expenditure on educational institutions, or 3.6 per cent of combined OECD GDP, is devoted to primary, secondary and post-secondary non-tertiary education, although Canada, Korea and the United States spend more than 2 per cent of their GDP on tertiary education.

...the ways in which education systems are financed, and the sources of the funds,...

Cost-sharing between the participants in education and society as a whole is an issue that is under discus-sion in many OECD countries. This is a particularly relevant question at the early and late stages of educa-tion − pre-primary and tertiary − where full or nearly full public funding is less common. As new client groups participate in education, the range of educational opportunities, programmes and providers is growing, and governments are forging new partnerships to mobilise the necessary resources. Public fund-ing is now being looked upon increasingly as providing only a part, albeit a very substantial part, of the investment in education. Private funding is playing an increasingly important role.

New funding strategies aim not only at mobilising the required resources from a wider range of public and private sources, but also at providing a broader range of learning opportunities and improving the efficiency of schooling. In the majority of OECD countries, publicly funded primary and secondary educa-tion is also organised and delivered by public institutions. However, in a fair number of OECD countries the public funds are then transferred to private institutions or given directly to households to spend in the institution of their choice. In the former case, the final spending and delivery of education can be regarded as subcontracted by governments to non-governmental institutions, whereas in the latter instance, students and their families are left to decide which type of institution best meets their requirements. To the extent that private financing of education creates barriers for the participation of learners from lower income groups, this may reflect in variation of performance between institutions (see also Indicator A7).

To shed light on these issues, **Indicator B3** examines the relative proportions of funds for educational institutions from public and private sources, and how these figures have evolved since 1995. As with Indicator B2, national resources devoted to education are a key national policy lever **(Framework Cell 2.D)** as well as an antecedent to the activities of schools, classrooms and individual learners **(Framework Cells 3.C, 3.B and 3.A)**.

- Education institutions are still mainly funded from public sources: 88 per cent of all funds for educational institutions comes directly from public sources. Private funding is however significant in Korea (where it represents 40 per cent of the total), the United States (approaching one third of the total), Australia and Japan (almost one quarter of the total).

- In a number of OECD countries, governments pay most of the costs of primary, secondary and post-secondary non-tertiary education but leave the management of educational institutions to the private sector, to provide a wider range of learning opportunities without creating barriers to the participation of students from low-income families.

- Tertiary institutions tend to mobilise a much higher proportion of their funds from private sources than primary, secondary and post-secondary non-tertiary institutions. The private share ranges from less than 3 per cent in Denmark, Finland and Greece to 77 per cent in Korea but includes private payments that are subsidised from public sources.

- Across the education levels the trend in the public/private share of education expenditure is a mixed one with shifts towards public spending as much in evidence as shifts towards private expenditure. In most cases where there have been shifts towards private expenditure this did not lead to a decrease in the real level of public-sector spending.

…relative to the size of public budgets,…

All governments are involved in education, funding or directing the provision of services. Since markets offer no guarantee of equal access to educational opportunities, governments fund educational services to ensure that they are within the reach of their populations. Public expenditure on education as a percentage of total public expenditure indicates the value of education relative to the value of other public investments such as health care, social security, defence and security. **Indicator B4** completes the picture of the volume of resources invested in education by examining changes in public spending on education in absolute terms and relative to changes in overall public spending.

Since the second half of the 1990s, most OECD countries made serious efforts to consolidate public budgets. Education had to compete for public financial support against a wide range of other areas covered in government budgets. *New:* To portray this, a newly introduced feature of the indicator is to evaluate changes in educational expenditure in absolute terms and relative to changes in the size of public budgets.

Finally, the level of government that has responsibility for, and control over, the funding of education is often thought to have a strategic advantage in influencing decisions regarding educational governance. An important question in educational policy is, therefore, the extent to which the division of responsibility for educational funding between national, regional and local authorities translates into responsibility for educational decision-making. *New:* To shed light on this, a newly introduced feature of Indicator B4 is an examination of the source of public funds by level of government. Important decisions regarding educational funding are made both at the level of government where the funds originate and at the level of government by which they are finally spent or distributed. In illustrating each countries policy for centralisation or decentralisation of funding, this indicator provides, along with other indicators, some context for the educational performance of the system as a whole.

As with Indicators B2 and B3, national resources devoted to education are a key national policy lever **(Framework Cell 2.D)** as well as an antecedent to the activities of schools, classrooms and individual learners **(Framework Cells 3.C, 3.B and 3.A)**.

- On average, OECD countries devote 13.0 per cent of total public expenditure to educational institutions.

- Public funding of education is a social priority, even in OECD countries with little public involvement in other areas.

- Public expenditure on education tended to grow faster than total public spending, but not as fast as GDP. Education's share of public expenditure grew fastest in Denmark, Greece and Sweden. In the Czech Republic, Germany, Italy, the Netherlands, the Slovak Republic and Sweden, public expenditure on education increased between 1995 and 2000 despite public budgets falling in real terms.

- In virtually every OECD country, public funding of primary, secondary and post-secondary non-tertiary education is more decentralised than public funding for tertiary education.

...different financing instruments,...

The primary financing mechanism of education in most OECD countries remains direct spending on educational institutions. However, governments are looking increasingly towards greater diversity in financing instruments. Comparing these instruments helps to identify policy alternatives. Subsidies to students and their families, the subject of **Indicator B5,** constitute one such alternative to direct spending on institutions. They are used as incentives to engage individuals or groups of individuals in education or to open opportunities for them in different types of institutions **(Framework Cells 2.A and 2.C)**.

Governments subsidise the costs of education and related expenditure in order to increase access to education and reduce social inequalities. Furthermore, public subsidies play an important role in indirectly funding educational institutions. Channelling institutional funding through students may heighten institutional competition and therefore the efficiency of education funding. Since aid for student living costs can also serve as a substitute for work as a financial resource, public subsidies may enhance educational attainment by enabling students to study full-time and to work fewer hours or not at all.

Public subsidies come in many forms: means-based subsidies, family allowances for all students, tax allowances for students or parents, or other household transfers. Should household subsidies take the form of grants or loans? Do loans effectively help increase the efficiency of financial resources invested in education and shift some of the costs to the beneficiaries? Or are student loans less appropriate than grants for encouraging low-income students to pursue their education? **Indicator B5** cannot answer these questions, but it does provide a useful overview of the subsidy policies being pursued in different OECD countries.

- Public subsidies for students and households are mainly a feature at the tertiary level.

- An average of 17 per cent of public spending on tertiary education is devoted to supporting students, households and other private entities. In Australia, Denmark, New Zealand, Sweden and the United Kingdom, public subsidies account for about 30 per cent or more of public tertiary education budgets.

- Subsidies are generally more evident in systems where students are expected to pay for at least part of the cost of their education.

- Subsidised student loan systems tend to operate in countries with high levels of participation at the tertiary level.

- In most OECD countries, the beneficiaries of public subsidies have considerable discretion regarding the spending of subsidies. In all reporting OECD countries, subsidies are spent mainly outside educational institutions, and almost half of these countries, exclusively outside.

...and how the money is invested and apportioned among different resource categories.

Chapter B concludes with an examination of how financial resources are invested and apportioned among resource categories (**Indicator B6**). The allocation of resources can influence the quality of instruction (through the relative expenditure on teachers' salaries, for example), the condition of educational facilities (through expenditure on school maintenance), and the ability of the education system to adjust to changing demographic and enrolment trends. A comparison of how OECD countries apportion their educational expenditure among resource categories can provide some insight into the differences in organisational structure and operation of educational institutions. Systemic budgetary and structural decisions on allocating resources eventually make themselves felt in the classroom; they affect teaching and the conditions under which teaching takes place. A system-wide description of decisions on how educational funding is spent which will influence system level outputs (**Framework Cell 2.D**).

- On average, one quarter of expenditure on tertiary education is attributable to R&D at tertiary educational institutions. Significant differences between OECD countries in the emphasis on R&D in tertiary institutions explain part of the large differences in expenditure per tertiary student.

- In primary, secondary, and post-secondary non-tertiary education combined, current expenditure accounts, on average across all OECD countries, for 92 per cent of total spending. In all but three OECD countries, 70 per cent or more of primary, secondary and post-secondary non-tertiary current expenditure is spent on staff salaries.

Chapter C looks at access to education, participation and progression, in terms of...

A well-educated population has become a defining feature of a modern society. Education is seen as a mechanism for instilling civic values, and as a means for developing individuals' productive and social capacity. Early childhood programmes prepare young children socially and academically for primary education. Primary and secondary education provides basic skills that serve as a foundation for young people to become productive members of society. Tertiary education provides opportunities for acquiring advanced knowledge and skills, either immediately after initial schooling or later. Many employers encourage ongoing training, and assist workers in upgrading or re-orienting their skills to meet the demands of changing technologies. Chapter C sketches a comparative picture of access, participation and progression in education across OECD countries.

...the expected duration of schooling, overall and at the different levels of education,...

Virtually all young people in OECD countries can expect to go to school for 11 years. However, participation patterns and progression through education vary widely. Both the timing and participation rate in pre-school and after the end of compulsory education differ considerably between countries. Some countries have extended participation in education, for example, by making pre-school education almost universal by the age of three, by retaining the majority of young people in education until the end of their teens, or by maintaining 10 to 20 per cent participation among up to the late 20s.

Indicator C1 sheds light on these issues by portraying enrolment rates and the expected duration of schooling. It can help to elucidate the structure of education systems and access to educational opportunities in them. Enrolment patterns indicate overall outcomes of educational policy (**Framework Cell 1.D**) but, in the form of school expectancy, also outcomes at the individual level (**Framework Cell 1.A**).

- In 25 out of 28 OECD countries, individuals participate in formal education for between 16 and 20 years, on average. Most of the variation between countries on this measure derives from differences in enrolments in upper secondary education.

- School expectancy increased between 1995 and 2001 in 20 out of 21 OECD countries reporting comparable data.

- In half of the OECD countries, more than 70 per cent of children aged three to four are enrolled in either pre-primary or primary programmes. At the other end of the spectrum, a 17-year-old can expect to spend an average of 2.6 years in tertiary education.

- In the majority of OECD countries, females can expect to receive 0.5 more years, on average, of education than males.

…entry to and participation in different types of educational programmes and institutions,…

While the successful graduation from upper secondary education is becoming the norm in most OECD countries, routes to it are becoming increasingly varied. Upper secondary programmes can differ in their curricular content, often depending on the type of further education or occupation for which the programmes are intended to prepare students. Most upper secondary programmes in OECD countries are primarily designed to prepare students for further studies at the tertiary level. The orientation of these programmes can be general, pre-vocational or vocational. Besides the programmes primarily preparing students for further education, in most OECD countries there are also upper secondary programmes designed to prepare students for direct entry to the labour market. Enrolment in these different types of educational programmes is examined in **Indicator C2**.

Indicator C2 also sheds light on rates of entry to tertiary education, that provide an important indication of the degree to which a population is acquiring those high-level skills and knowledge that labour markets in knowledge societies value.

Like Indicator C1, Indicator C2 reflects on overall outcomes of educational policy (**Framework Cell 1.D**) as well as on outcomes at the individual level (**Framework Cell 1.A**).

- Today, four out of ten school leavers are likely to attend tertiary programmes leading to the equivalent of a bachelors' or higher tertiary-type A degree. In some OECD countries, every second school leaver is likely to attend such a programme.

- On average in OECD countries, a 17-year-old can now expect to receive 2.6 years of tertiary-type A education, of which 2 years will be full-time.

- With the exception of France and Germany, participation in tertiary education grew in all OECD countries between 1995 and 2001.

- The majority of tertiary students are enrolled in public institutions, but in Belgium, Japan, Korea, the Netherlands and the United Kingdom, most students are enrolled in privately managed institutions.

- The majority of primary and secondary students are enrolled in public institutions. However, privately managed schools now enrol, on average, 10 per cent of primary students, 13 per cent of lower secondary students and 20 per cent of upper secondary students.

…cross-border movements of students,…

Access to and participation in tertiary education is no longer limited to national boundaries. One way for students to expand their knowledge is to attend higher educational institutions in countries other than their own. Such international student mobility involves costs and benefits to students and institutions in sending and host countries alike. While the direct short-term monetary costs and benefits of this mobility are relatively easy to measure, the long-term social and economic benefits to students, institutions and countries are more difficult to quantify. The number of students studying in other countries (**Indicator C3**), however, provides some idea of the extent of student mobility.

The indicator reflects on students' motivation to study in other countries and hence raise their labour market prospects (**Framework Cell 2.A**) but is also indicative of the national policy on student mobility (**Framework Cell 2.D**). The policy itself is, of course, a condition under which students' mobility takes place (**Framework Cell 3.A**) and the extent of student mobility is a context for the learning environment in school and teaching and learning practices in the classroom (**Framework Cells 3.C and 3.B**).

- Five countries (Australia, France, Germany, the United Kingdom and the United States) receive 71 per cent of all foreign students studying in the OECD area.

- In absolute numbers, students from Greece, Japan, Korea and Turkey represent the largest sources of intakes from OECD countries. Students from China and Southeast Asia comprise the largest numbers of foreign students from non-OECD countries.

- In relative terms, the percentage of foreign students enrolled in OECD countries ranges from below one to almost 17 per cent in Switzerland. Proportional to their size, Australia, Austria, Belgium, Switzerland and the United Kingdom take in the most foreign students, when measured as a percentage of their tertiary enrolments.

…and learning beyond initial education.

All OECD countries are experiencing rapid social and economic changes that are making the transition to working life more uncertain. Entering the labour market is often a difficult period of transition. While the length of time spent in education has increased, a significant proportion of young people still remain marginal if they are neither in education or working, *i.e.*, they are either unemployed or in non-employment. **Indicators C4** and **C5** examine the education and employment status of young men and women and provide information on how successfully the transition from school to work is made. Indicator C4 focuses on the combination of work and study and Indicator C5 on the work status young people who are no longer in education. Both indicators reflect outcomes not only for the individual student (**Framework Cell 1.A**) but also for the education system as whole as it interacts with the labour market (**Framework Cell 1.D**). They also provides a context for current participation rates and patterns both individually and collectively within the system (**Framework Cells 3.A and 3.D**).

- The percentage of 20 to 24-year-olds not in education ranges from 50 to 70 per cent in most OECD countries.

- In some countries, education and work largely occur consecutively, while in other countries they are concurrent. Work-study programmes, relatively common in European countries, offer coherent vocational education routes to recognised occupational qualifications.

- In some countries, many young people also combine paid work out of school hours with education. In other countries, initial education and work are rarely associated.

- Most persons aged 15 to 19 are still in school. In many OECD countries, a high percentage of those who are not are either unemployed or not in the labour force.

- In Austria, Italy, Mexico, the Slovak Republic and Turkey, over 10 per cent of persons aged 15 to 19 are neither at school nor in the workforce.

- This situation is true mainly for young males in Austria, Finland, the Slovak Republic and Sweden, and young females in Greece, Mexico, Portugal and Turkey.

Chapter D examines the learning environment and organisation of schools, in terms of...

Chapters A, B and C examined financial resources invested in education, patterns of participation, and the results of education in terms of student achievement and the labour market outcomes of education. Chapter D concludes the publication with an examination of student learning conditions, teacher working conditions in education systems and aspects of teacher demand and supply more generally.

...student learning conditions,...

How effectively learning time is used depends on how appropriate study programmes are, and on how much instruction time a student receives. Instruction time is a policy lever which acts most directly on the individual learner **(Framework Cell 2.A)** but also as a context for teaching and learning practices in the classroom and school **(Framework Cells 3.B and 3.C)**.

Indicator D1 examines instruction time available for various study areas for students. *New:* A newly introduced feature of the indicator is the extension of the age range covered from 7 to 15 years.

- Students between the ages of 9 and 11 receive, on average across OECD countries, 813 hours per year of compulsory instruction time and 840 hours per year of intended instruction time in the classroom, while students between the ages of 12 and 14 spend nearly 100 hours more per year. However, these figures vary significantly across countries.

- On average among countries, reading and writing in the language of instruction, mathematics and science comprise about half of the compulsory curriculum for 9 to 11-year-olds and 41 per cent for 12 to 14-year-olds.

- The degree to which schools and local and regional authorities can specify curricular content and timetables varies widely from country to country.

The size of the learning group that shares teacher time is another variable that impacts on the use of classroom learning time. **Indicator D2** looks at the variation in average class size, and the ratio of students to teaching staff across OECD countries to estimate the human resources available for individual students. Both measures are factors which on the whole schools can influence **(Framework Cell 2.C)**, though in some cases these can constrained by system level policies. They are also important contexts which shape student learning **(Framework Cell 3.A)** and classroom instruction **(Framework Cell 3.B)**. *New:* A newly introduced feature of the indicator is the examination of a wider range of categories of educational staff, including both pedagogical and other personnel.

- The average class size in primary education is 22, but varies between countries from 36 students in Korea per class to less than half of that number in Greece, Iceland and Luxembourg.

- The number of students per class increases by an average of two students between primary and lower secondary education but ratios of students to teaching staff tend to decrease with increasing levels of education due to more annual instruction time.

- Teaching and non teaching staff employed in primary and secondary schools ranges from less than 80 persons per 1000 students enrolled in Canada, Japan, Korea and Mexico to 119 persons or more per 1 000 students in France, Hungary , Iceland and Italy.

...the availability and use of information technology at school and at home,...

In addition to classroom time and human resources, new technologies assume an increasingly important role in education. They not only equip students with important skills to participate effectively in the modern world, but also foster the development of self-regulated learning strategies and skills, as part of an essential foundation for lifelong learning. However, the mere presence of modern information and communication technology (ICT) in schools does not guarantee its effective use. *New:* The newly introduced **Indicator D3** presents information on the use of ICT in upper secondary schools and analyses some of the perceived obstacles to the effective integration of ICT in the learning process, including teachers' professional development in ICT. The availability of ICT in schools can strongly influence the school environment (**Framework Cell 2.C**) and sets a context in which instruction can be delivered (**Framework Cell 3.B**). The use of ICT in teaching and learning practices is also within the influence of instructional settings (**Framework Cell 2.B**) and shapes the learning environment for individual students (**Framework Cell 3.A**).

- Among the 14 countries with comparable data represented in indicator D3, a typical student in upper secondary education attends schools where there is one computer for every 9 students. This ratio varies widely among countries, from three students per computer in Denmark and Sweden to more than 15 students per computer in Mexico and Spain.

- On average, 63 per cent of upper secondary students attend schools where principals reported that teachers' lack of knowledge and skills was an obstacle to successful ICT implementation: more than three quarters of principals reported this in France and Norway.

- On average, one third of upper secondary teachers participated in ICT-related professional development in the school year 2000/2001, compared to one half of teachers who participated in non-ICT related professional development in the same period.

- From a list of 22 obstacles to the use of ICT in teaching - including obstacles related to computer hardware and infrastructure, computer software, teachers and school and classroom organisation – insufficient number of computers for students to use tended to be reported by the principals of upper secondary students as the *most serious obstacle* to the use of ICT in teaching. A shortage of maintenance and technical support, as well as teachers' lack of knowledge/skills in using computers for instructional purposes were other frequently reported obstacles.

...teacher training and professional development of teachers,...

Among a wide range of factors influencing the quality of instruction are teachers' preparation for providing quality instruction. *New:* The newly introduced **Indicator D4** examines the qualification requirements for new teachers for pre-primary, primary, lower secondary and upper secondary education (general programmes) in the public sector as well as measures to support professional development. Where available, the percentage of the current stock of teachers with the required qualification level is also provided.

Levels of teacher qualifications influence the quality of teaching practice (**Framework Cell 2.B**) and act as an antecedent to the quality of instructional delivery and to student learning (**Framework Cells 3.B and 3.A**). Measures to support school policy in supporting professional development can also influence the learning environment in schools (**Framework Cell 2.C**) and act as antecedents to teaching and learning practices (**Framework Cell 3.B**).

- All OECD countries now require a tertiary-type A or tertiary-type B qualification (ISCED 5A or 5B) in order to enter the teaching profession at the primary level and beyond.

- The duration of pre-service training for primary teachers varies from three years in Austria, Belgium (both Flemish and French Communities), Iceland, Ireland, New Zealand and Spain to five years or more in Finland, France and Germany.

- Over 90 per cent of upper secondary students attend schools where the principal organises staff development activities (including research) in Denmark, Norway and Sweden.

- Observational visits to other upper secondary schools is a frequent practice in Denmark, Finland, Korea, Norway, Portugal and Sweden. Formal peer observation or mentoring is more often used in Denmark, France, Italy, Korea, Mexico and Switzerland.

... and teachers' working conditions.

Chapter D concludes with a comparative review of teachers' working conditions. Education systems employ a large number of professionals in increasingly competitive market conditions. Ensuring a sufficient number of skilled teachers is a key concern in all OECD countries. Key determinants of the supply of qualified teachers are the salaries and working conditions of teachers, including starting salaries and pay scales, and the costs incurred by individuals to become teachers, compared with salaries and costs in other occupations. Both affect the career decisions of potential teachers and the types of people attracted to the teaching profession. At the same time, teachers' salaries are the largest single factor in the cost of providing education. Teacher compensation is thus a critical consideration for policy-makers seeking to maintain the quality of teaching and a balanced education budget. The size of education budgets naturally reflects trade-offs between a number of interrelated factors, including teachers' salaries, the ratio of students to teaching staff, the quantity of instruction time planned for students, and the designated number of teaching hours. To shed light on these issues, **Indicator D5** shows the starting, mid-career and maximum statutory salaries of teachers in public primary and secondary education, and incentive schemes and bonuses used in teacher rewards systems.

Together with class size and ratios of students to teaching staff (Indicator D2), hours of instruction for students (Indicator D1) and teachers' salaries (Indicator D5), the amount of time that teachers spend in the classroom teaching influences the financial resources which countries need to invest in education. While the number of teaching hours and the extent of non-teaching responsibilities are important parts of a teacher's working conditions, they also affect the attractiveness of the profession itself. To shed light on this, **Indicator D6** examines the statutory working time of teachers at different levels of education, as well as the statutory teaching time, *i.e.,* the time that full-time teachers are expected to spend teaching students. Although working time and teaching time only partly determine the actual workload of teachers, they do give some insight into differences between countries in what is demanded of teachers.

Teacher salaries and working hours not only impact on recruitment and retention of teachers within institutions (**Framework Cell 2.C**), but as a feature of teacher working conditions, they also provide a context to the quality of instruction in instructional settings and for the learning outcomes of individual learners (**Framework Cells 3.A and 3.B**).

- The mid-career salaries of lower secondary teachers range from less than US$ 10 000 in Hungary and the Slovak Republic to US$ 40 000 and more in Germany, Japan, Korea, Switzerland and the United States.

- An upper secondary teacher's salary per teaching hour is, on average, 40 per cent higher than that of a primary teacher, but the difference varies from 10 per cent or less in Australia, New Zealand, Scotland, the Slovak Republic, Turkey and the United States to around 60 per cent or more in the Flemish Community of Belgium, France, Hungary, Iceland, Korea, the Netherlands and Spain.

- In lower secondary education, teachers in Australia, Denmark, England, New Zealand and Scotland reach the highest step on the salary scale in 11 years or less, while a teacher in Austria, the Czech Republic, France, Greece, Hungary, Italy, Japan, Korea and Spain must teach for more than 30 years before reaching the maximum.

- In most countries, allowances are paid to all or most teachers for taking on management responsibilities; teaching more classes or hours than are required under a full-time contract (*e.g.*, acting duties); and involvement in special tasks such as guidance counselling or training student teachers.

- The number of teaching hours per year in public primary schools averages 792 hours but ranges from 605 to 1 139 hours among OECD countries.

- The average number of teaching hours in the lower secondary education is 714 hours but ranges from 553 to 1 182 hours among OECD countries.

- Regulations of teachers' working time vary across countries. In most countries, teachers are formally required to work a specific number of hours; while in others just teaching time in lessons per week is specified.

It also provides a more general picture of teacher supply and demand, including teacher demographics.

Ensuring an adequate supply of qualified teachers is a major tasks school managers and school authorities are facing. On the system level, provisions for teacher training and teacher licensing, recruitment policies, statutory salary and bonus schemes, and statutory work conditions constitute the basic policy framework for teacher supply. At the local level, demand for and supply of teachers with specific subject matter expertise depends on a series of other factors as well. Local labour market conditions influence teachers' career decisions, *e.g.* industries competing for skills and expertise that teachers dispose of can play a role in the 'brain drain' from schools and conversely, the absence of other local labour opportunities may influence the choice of a teaching career. Teacher flow in a school may also depend on the age composition of the teaching staff, and on the social composition of the student population as well as on the school's working climate. *New:* The newly introduced **Indicator D7** provides general information on teacher supply and demand issues at the upper secondary level and, where there are shortages, how they are coped with at the level of schools (**Framework Cell 2.C**). These issues and the policies that they give rise to are also antecedents at school, class and student level (**Framework Cells 3.A, 3.B and 3.C**) as they will impact on the school learning environment, classroom climate and pupil engagement.

Finally, an important factor influencing teacher demand and supply is the age distribution of the teaching force. *New:* The newly introduced **Indicator D8** analyses the age and gender mix in countries' teaching force and thus reflects on a resource available system-wide (**Framework Cell 2.D**). The gender and age mix of the teaching force also represent antecedents at school, class and student level (**Framework Cells 3.A, 3.B and 3.C**) as they will impact on the school learning environment, classroom climate and pupil engagement.

- The percentages of less than fully qualified teachers ranges from 0.4 per cent in Ireland to 20 per cent or more in Mexico, Norway, Portugal, and Sweden.

- On average, about 12 per cent of teaching posts (full-time equivalents) were vacant and were to be covered at the beginning of school year 2001/2002 in the countries for which upper secondary schools were surveyed.

- Nearly two thirds of the teachers in Mexico and Switzerland, but only less than 1 per cent in Korea are employed on a part-time basis.

- In upper secondary education, teacher shortage is most pressing in computer science, mathematics, foreign languages, science, and technology, whereas it appears less problematic in arts, physical education, social studies and language of instruction.

- In 15 out of 19 OECD countries, most primary teachers are at least 40 years old, and in Germany, Italy and Sweden, more than one third of teachers are older than 50 years.

- Compared with 1998, the average proportion of teachers aged 50 years or over increased on average by 6.2 per cent (1.8 percentage points) in secondary education. In Finland, Germany, Ireland and the United Kingdom, this proportion rose by more than 4 percentage points.

- The proportion of young teachers increased in 10 out of 14 OECD countries for which data are available. In France, Korea, Luxembourg, New Zealand and Sweden, the proportion of teachers aged under 30 years increased by more than 3 percentage points whereas Ireland and Japan are the only two countries showing significant decrease between 1998 and 2001 in the proportion of teachers under 30 years.

FURTHER RESOURCES

The web site *www.oecd.org/edu/eag2003* provides a rich source of information on the methods employed for the calculation of the indicators, the interpretation of the indicators in the respective national contexts and the data sources involved. The web site also provides access to the data underlying the indicators.

The web site *www.pisa.oecd.org* provides information on the OECD Programme for International Student Assessment (PISA), on which many of the indicators in this publication draw.

Education Policy Analysis is a companion volume to *Education at a Glance*, which takes up selected themes of key importance for governments. The 2003 edition contains four chapters that draw together key findings and policy developments: Diversity, equity and inclusion; career guidance: new ways forward; changing patterns of governance in higher education; and strategies for sustainable investment in lifelong learning.

READER'S GUIDE

Coverage of the statistics

Although a lack of data still limits the scope of the indicators in many countries, the coverage extends, in principle, to the entire national education system regardless of the ownership or sponsorship of the institutions concerned and regardless of education delivery mechanisms. With one exception described below, all types of students and all age groups are meant to be included: children (including students with special needs), adults, nationals, foreigners, as well as students in open distance learning, in special education programmes or in educational programmes organised by ministries other than the Ministry of Education, provided the main aim of the programme is the educational development of the individual. However, vocational and technical training in the workplace, with the exception of combined school and work-based programmes that are explicitly deemed to be parts of the education system, is not included in the basic education expenditure and enrolment data.

Educational activities classified as "adult" or "non-regular" are covered, provided that the activities involve studies or have a subject matter content similar to "regular" education studies or that the underlying programmes lead to potential qualifications similar to corresponding regular educational programmes. Courses for adults that are primarily for general interest, personal enrichment, leisure or recreation are excluded.

Calculation of international means

For many indicators a country mean is presented and for some an OECD total.

The *country mean* is calculated as the unweighted mean of the data values of all countries for which data are available or can be estimated. The country mean therefore refers to an average of data values at the level of the national systems and can be used to answer the question of how an indicator value for a given country compares with the value for a typical or average country. It does not take into account the absolute size of the education system in each country.

The *OECD total* is calculated as a weighted mean of the data values of all countries for which data are available or can be estimated. It reflects the value for a given indicator when the OECD area is considered as a whole. This approach is taken for the purpose of comparing, for example, expenditure charts for individual countries with those of the entire OECD area for which valid data are available, with this area considered as a single entity.

Note that both the country mean and the OECD total can be significantly affected by missing data. Given the relatively small number of countries, no statistical methods are used to compensate for this. In cases where a category is not applicable (code "a") in a country or where the data value is negligible (code "n") for the corresponding calculation, the value zero is imputed for the purpose of calculating country means. In cases where both the numerator and the denominator of a ratio are not applicable (code "a") for a certain country, this country is not included in the country mean.

For financial tables using 1995 data, both the country mean and OECD total are calculated for countries providing both 1995 and 2000 data. This allows comparison of the country mean and OECD total over time with no distortion due to the exclusion of certain countries in the different years.

Classification of levels of education

The classification of the levels of education is based on the revised International Standard Classification of Education (ISCED-97). The biggest change between the revised ISCED and the former ISCED (ISCED-76) is the introduction of a multi-dimensional classification framework, allowing for the alignment of the educational content of programmes using multiple classification criteria. ISCED is an instrument for compiling statistics on education internationally and distinguishes among six levels of education. The *Glossary and the notes in Annex 3 (Indicator A2)* describe in detail the ISCED levels of education, and Annex 1 shows corresponding theoretical graduation ages of the main educational programmes by ISCED level.

Symbols for missing data

Five symbols are employed in the tables and graphs to denote missing data:

a   Data not applicable because the category does not apply.

c   There are too few observations to provide reliable estimates *(i.e.,* there are fewer than five schools or fewer than 30 students with valid data for this cell).

m   Data not available.

n   Magnitude is either negligible or zero.

x   Data included in another category or column of the table *(e.g., x*(2) means that data included in column 2 of the table).

Country codes

OECD Member countries

Australia	AUS	Japan	JPN
Austria	AUT	Korea	KOR
Belgium	BEL	Luxembourg	LUX
Belgium (Flemish Community)	BFL	Mexico	MEX
Belgium (French Community)	BFR	Netherlands	NLD
Canada	CAN	New Zealand	NZL
Czech Republic	CZE	Norway	NOR
Denmark	DNK	Poland	POL
England	ENG	Portugal	PRT
Finland	FIN	Scotland	SCO
France	FRA	Slovak Republic	SVK
Germany	DEU	Spain	ESP
Greece	GRC	Sweden	SWE
Hungary	HUN	Switzerland	CHE
Iceland	ISL	Turkey	TUR
Ireland	IRL	United Kingdom	UKM
Italy	ITA	United States	USA

Countries participating in the OECD/UNESCO World Education Indicators programme

Argentina, Brazil, Chile, China, Egypt, India, Indonesia, Jamaica, Jordan, Malaysia, Paraguay, Peru, Philippines, Russian Federation, Thailand, Tunisia, Uruguay and Zimbabwe participate in the OECD/ UNESCO World Education Indicators (WEI) programme. Data for these countries are collected using the same standards and methods that are applied for OECD countries and therefore are included in this publication. Israel has observer status in OECD's activities on education and has contributed to the OECD indicators on educational finance.

THE OUTPUT OF EDUCATIONAL INSTITUTIONS AND THE IMPACT OF LEARNING

OVERVIEW

Indicator A1: Current upper secondary graduation rates and attainment of the adult population

Chapter A examines the outcomes of education and learning, in terms of…

Indicator A2: Current tertiary graduation and survival rates and attainment of the adult population

…the current output of educational institutions and educational attainment of the adult population,…

Indicator A3: Graduates by field of study

Indicator A4: Reading literacy of 4th-grade students

…the quality of learning outcomes and how this varies among schools and students,…

Indicator A5: Reading literacy of 15-year-olds

Indicator A6: Mathematical and scientific literacy of 15-year-olds

Indicator A7: How student performance varies between schools

Indicator A8: Profiles of 15-year-old readers

...and the returns to education for individuals and society.

INDICATOR A1: CURRENT UPPER SECONDARY GRADUATION RATES AND ATTAINMENT OF THE ADULT POPULATION

A₁

- In 15 out of 17 OECD countries for which comparable data are available, the ratio of upper secondary graduates to the population at the typical age of graduation exceeds 70 per cent. In Denmark, Finland, Germany, Japan and Poland, graduation rates exceed 90 per cent. The challenge now is to ensure that the remaining fraction is not left behind, with the risk of social exclusion that this may entail.

- Comparing the attainment of the population aged 25 to 34 years with that of the population aged 45 to 54 shows that the proportion of individuals who have not completed upper secondary education has been shrinking in almost all OECD countries, and in some rapidly. Many countries with traditionally low levels of education are catching up.

- Among older age groups, females have lower levels of education than males, but for younger people the pattern has reversed and today, graduation rates for females exceed those for males in most countries.

Chart A1.1

Upper secondary graduation rates (2001)

Ratio of unduplicated count of all upper secondary graduates to population at typical age of graduation

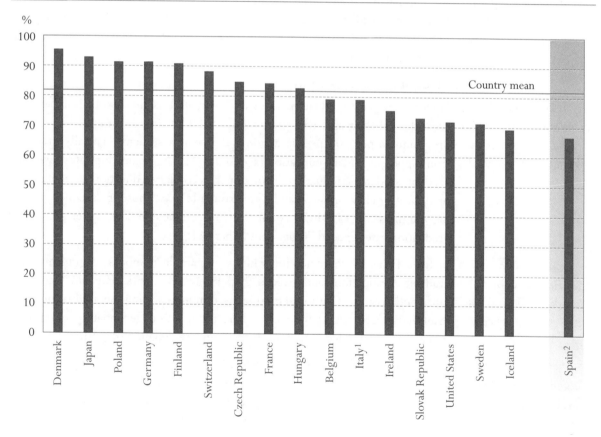

1. Year of reference 2000.
2. A significant proportion of the youth cohort is not covered by this indicator.
Countries are ranked in descending order of total upper secondary graduation rates.
Source: OECD. Table A1.1. See Annex 3 for notes (www.oecd.org/edu/eag2003).

A1

To gauge the share of the population that has obtained the minimum credentials for successfully entering the labour market ...

Policy context

Rising skill demands in OECD countries have made qualifications at the upper secondary level of education the minimum credential for successful labour market entry. Upper secondary education serves as the foundation for advanced learning and training opportunities, as well as preparation for direct entry into the labour market. Although many countries do allow students to leave the education system at the end of the lower secondary level, young people in OECD countries who leave without an upper secondary qualification tend to face severe difficulties in entering the labour market (see Indicators A12 to A15).

...this indicator shows the current upper secondary graduate output of educational institutions...

The upper secondary graduation rate reflects the current output of education systems, *i.e.*, the percentage of the typical upper secondary school-age population that follow and successfully complete upper secondary programmes. Although high upper secondary graduation rates do not guarantee that an education system has adequately equipped its graduates with the basic skills and knowledge necessary to enter the labour market – this indicator does not capture the quality of educational outcomes – it is one indication of the extent to which education systems succeed in meeting the minimum requirements of the labour market.

...as well as historical patterns of upper secondary completion.

By comparing educational attainment levels between different generations one can identify the evolution of education levels within the population, reflecting both changing demands of the labour market and changing educational policies.

Evidence and explanations

In 15 out of 17 OECD countries with comparable data, upper secondary graduation rates exceed 70 per cent...

Upper secondary graduation rates are estimated as the number of persons, regardless of their age, who graduate for the first time from upper secondary programmes per 100 people at the age at which students typically graduate from upper secondary education (see Annex 1). The graduation rates take into account students graduating from upper secondary education at the modal or typical graduation ages, and older students (*e.g.*, those in "second chance" programmes). In 15 OECD countries with comparable data, upper secondary graduation rates exceed 70 per cent (Chart A1.1).

...and in Denmark, Finland, Germany, Japan and Poland exceed 90 per cent.

In five of the 17 countries for which comparable numbers of graduates are available, graduation rates exceed 90 per cent (Denmark, Finland, Germany, Japan and Poland). Caution should be used in interpreting the graduation rates displayed in Chart A1.1 for Spain where the length of secondary programmes was recently extended, which leads to an underestimation of graduation rates.

Upper secondary attainment levels have increased in almost all countries...

A comparison of the levels of educational attainment between older and younger age groups indicates marked progress with regard to the percentage of the population graduating from upper secondary education (Chart A1.2). On average, only 60 per cent of 45 to 54 year-olds has attained upper secondary level of education, compared to 74 per cent of 25 to 34 year-olds.

This is especially striking in countries whose adult population generally has a lower attainment level. In younger age groups, differences among countries in the level of educational attainment are less pronounced. As a result, many countries currently showing low attainment in the adult population are expected to move closer to those with higher attainment levels. In Korea, Portugal and Spain, the proportion of individuals aged 25 to 34 with at least upper secondary attainment is around twice as high as that in the age group 45 to 54. Improvement is significant as well in Belgium, France, Greece and Ireland, while progress remains slow in Mexico and Turkey.

...and many countries with traditionally low levels of education are catching up.

Gender differences in graduation rates

The balance of educational attainment between males and females in the adult population is unequal in most OECD countries: historically females did not have sufficient opportunities and/or incentives to reach the same level of education as males. Females are generally over-represented among those who did not proceed to upper secondary education and under-represented at the higher levels of education.

Among older age groups, females have lower levels of education than males...

Chart A1.2

Percentage of the population that has attained at least upper secondary education[1], by age group (2001)

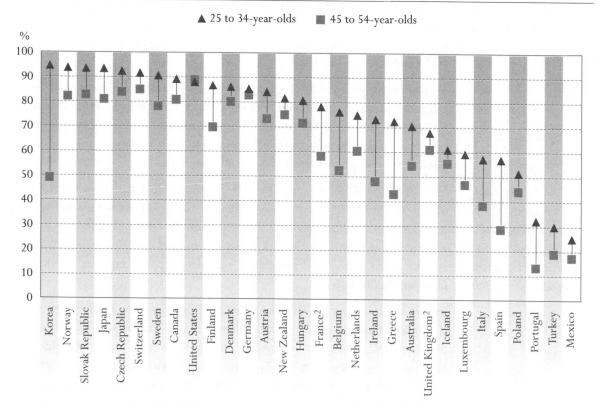

▲ 25 to 34-year-olds   ■ 45 to 54-year-olds

1. Excluding ISCED 3C short programmes.
2. Not all ISCED 3 programmes meet minimum requirements for ISCED 3C long programmes.
Countries are ranked in descending order of the percentage of 25 to 34-year-olds who have attained at least upper secondary education.
Source: OECD. Table A1.2. See Annex 3 for notes (www.oecd.org/edu/eag2003).

A1

*...but for younger people
the pattern is now
reversing.*

However, these differences are mostly attributable to the large gender differences in the attainment of older age groups and have been significantly reduced or reversed among younger age groups.

*Today, graduation
rates for females exceed
those for males in most
countries.*

Today, graduation rates no longer show significant differences between males and females in half of the countries with available data (Table A1.1). Further, in 15 out of 16 OECD countries for which total upper secondary graduation rates can be compared between the genders, graduation rates for females exceed those for males, and in Finland, Iceland, Ireland and Spain by 13 percentage points or more. In the majority of OECD countries, the gender ratio for general upper secondary programmes strongly favours females, only in Korea and Turkey do more males graduate than females, and here the difference between the genders is negligible. Conversely, in most OECD countries, more males than females graduate from pre-vocational and vocational upper secondary programmes.

Graduation from post-secondary non-tertiary programmes

*In some countries, a
significant proportion of
students broaden their
knowledge at the upper
secondary level after
completing a first upper
secondary programme.*

Post-secondary non-tertiary programmes are offered in 27 of the OECD countries and straddle the boundary between upper secondary and post-secondary education from a comparative point of view, even though they might clearly be considered upper secondary or post-secondary programmes in a national context. Although the content of post-secondary non-tertiary programmes may not be significantly more advanced than upper secondary programmes, they serve to broaden the knowledge of participants who have already gained an upper secondary qualification. The students tend to be older than those enrolled at the upper secondary level.

Typical examples of such programmes would be trade and vocational certificates in Canada and the United States, nursery teacher training in Austria and Switzerland or vocational training in the dual system for holders of general upper secondary qualifications in Germany. In most countries, post-secondary non-tertiary programmes are vocationally oriented.

*In Austria, Hungary,
Ireland and New
Zealand 21 per cent or
more of a typical age
cohort complete a post-
secondary non-tertiary
programme.*

In 8 out of 20 OECD countries reporting comparable data, 11 per cent or more of upper secondary graduates also graduate from a post-secondary non-tertiary programme, either instead of or in addition to tertiary education (OECD average 9.5 per cent). In Austria, Hungary, Ireland and New Zealand, 21 per cent or more of a typical age cohort complete a post-secondary non-tertiary programme (Table A1.3).

In just over half of OECD countries with available data, the majority of, if not all, post-secondary non-tertiary students graduate from ISCED 4C programmes, which are designed primarily to prepare graduates for direct entry into the labour market. Apprenticeships that are designed for students who have already graduated from an upper secondary programme are also included in this category. However, in 9 out of 20 OECD countries, the majority of post-secondary non-tertiary graduates have completed programmes, that are designed to provide direct access to either tertiary-type A or B edu-

A1

cation. In Austria, 20 per cent graduate from ISCED 4A programmes and in Switzerland 17 per cent graduate from ISCED 4B programmes.

Definitions and methodologies

Upper secondary graduates are those who successfully complete the final year of upper secondary education, regardless of their age. In some countries, successful completion requires a final examination; in others it does not.

Gross graduation rates for ISCED 3A, 3B and 3C programmes cannot be added, as some individuals graduate from more than one upper secondary programme and would thus be counted twice. The same applies for graduation rates by programme orientation, *i.e.*, general or vocational. The unduplicated total count of graduates is calculated by netting out those students who graduated from another upper secondary programme in a previous year.

For some countries, an unduplicated count of post-secondary non-tertiary graduates is unavailable and graduation rates may be overestimated because graduates complete multiple programmes at the same level. These countries are marked with a footnote in Table A1.3.

Pre-vocational and vocational programmes include both school-based programmes and combined school and work-based programmes that are recognised as part of the education system. Entirely work-based education and training that is not overseen by a formal education authority is not taken into account.

Data on population and educational attainment are taken from OECD and EUROSTAT databases, which are compiled from National Labour Force Surveys. See Annex 3 at *www.oecd.org/edu/eag2003* for national sources.

The attainment profiles are based on the percentage of the population aged 25 to 64 years that has completed a specified level of education. The International Standard Classification of Education (ISCED-97) is used to define the levels of education. See Annex 3 at *www.oecd.org/edu/eag2003* for a description of ISCED-97 education programmes and attainment levels and their mappings for each country.

Graduate data refer to the school year 2000-2001 and are based on the UOE data collection on education statistics that is administered annually by the OECD.

Educational attainment data derive from National Labour Force Surveys and levels are based upon the International Standard Classification of Education (ISCED-97).

A1

Table A1.1
Upper secondary graduation rates (2001)
Ratio of upper secondary graduates to total population at typical age of graduation (multiplied by 100) in public and private institutions,
by programme destination, programme orientation and gender

	Total (unduplicated)			ISCED 3A (designed to prepare for direct entry to tertiary-type A education)		ISCED 3B (designed to prepare for direct entry to tertiary-type B education)		ISCED 3C (long) similar to duration of typical 3A or 3B programmes		ISCED 3C (short) shorter than duration of typical 3A or 3B programmes		General programmes		Pre-vocational/ Vocational programmes	
	M + F	Males	Females	M + F	Females	M + F	Females	M + F	Females	M + F	Females	M + F	Females	M + F	Females
	(1)	(2)	(3)	(4)	(5)	(6)	(7)	(8)	(9)	(10)	(11)	(12)	(13)	(14)	(15)
Australia[1]	m	m	m	68	74	m	m	m	m	m	m	m	m	m	m
Austria	m	m	m	16	20	53	41	n	n	1	1	16	20	54	42
Belgium	79	76	83	60	65	a	a	19	18	17	24	36	42	60	65
Canada	m	m	m	m	m	m	m	m	m	m	m	m	m	m	m
Czech Republic	85	83	87	53	63	n	n	a	a	32	24	16	20	71	69
Denmark	96	m	m	54	65	a	a	64	71	a	a	54	65	64	71
Finland	91	85	97	91	97	a	a	a	a	a	a	54	66	73	78
France	85	82	87	51	59	10	9	3	2	37	32	32	38	69	64
Germany	92	89	94	32	35	59	58	a	a	a	a	32	35	59	58
Greece	m	m	m	20	24	a	a	7	7	x(8)	x(9)	20	24	7	7
Hungary[1]	83	80	86	57	65	x(4)	x(5)	x(10)	x(11)	24	18	m	m	m	m
Iceland	70	61	78	48	60	1	2	24	15	15	18	49	61	38	33
Ireland	76	69	83	72	78	a	a	5	5	a	a	55	58	22	25
Italy[1]	79	76	83	69	74	2	3	a	a	20	18	29	38	62	56
Japan	93	91	95	69	73	1	n	24	22	x(8)	x(9)	69	73	24	23
Korea	m	m	m	63	62	a	a	37	38	a	a	63	62	37	38
Luxembourg*	m	m	m	42	48	8	8	22	17	a	a	27	31	42	41
Mexico	m	m	m	29	31	a	a	4	4	x(8)	x(9)	29	31	4	4
Netherlands	m	m	m	62	69	a	a	16	17	18	14	34	37	61	61
New Zealand	m	m	m	63	67	25	29	28	32	x(8)	x(9)	m	m	a	a
Norway	m	m	m	72	89	a	a	43	37	m	m	72	89	43	37
Poland	92	88	95	74	81	a	a	a	a	27	19	36	47	65	55
Portugal	m	m	m	m	m	m	m	m	m	m	m	m	m	m	m
Slovak Republic	73	72	74	63	69	n	n	1	1	21	15	16	20	69	66
Spain[2,]*	67	59	75	47	55	n	n	11	11	13	15	47	55	24	27
Sweden	71	68	75	71	75	n	n	n	n	a	a	42	46	29	28
Switzerland	88	91	86	25	26	50	41	15	21	n	n	28	32	62	57
Turkey*	m	m	m	36	31	a	a	m	m	a	a	19	18	17	13
United Kingdom	m	m	m	m	m	m	m	m	m	m	m	m	m	m	m
United States	72	70	73	m	m	m	m	m	m	m	m	m	m	m	m
Country mean	*82*	*78*	*85*	*54*	*60*	*8*	*8*	*13*	*13*	*9*	*8*	*38*	*44*	*44*	*42*
Argentina[1]	m	m	m	40	47	a	a	a	a	a	a	21	28	19	19
Brazil[1]	m	m	m	57	64	m	m	a	a	a	a	x(4)	x(5)	m	m
Chile[1]	m	m	m	35	40	29	29	a	a	a	a	35	40	29	29
China[1]	m	m	m	16	14	a	a	13	13	3	2	16	14	15	15
India	m	m	m	18	16	n	n	m	m	n	n	18	16	n	n
Indonesia	m	m	m	23	24	13	11	a	a	a	a	x(4)	x(5)	m	m
Israel	m	m	m	60	66	25	22	3	1	a	a	60	66	28	23
Jamaica	m	m	m	71	71	n	n	a	a	a	a	71	71	n	n
Malaysia[1]	m	m	m	14	18	a	a	72	81	m	m	m	m	2	1
Paraguay[1]	m	m	m	36	39	a	a	m	m	a	a	29	31	8	8
Peru[1]	m	m	m	59	58	x(4)	x(5)	a	a	a	a	49	49	10	9
Philippines[1]	m	m	m	65	70	a	a	a	a	a	a	65	70	a	a
Russian Federation	m	m	m	53	x(4)	a	a	a	a	a	a	53	x(12)	a	a
Thailand	m	m	m	29	33	20	18	a	a	a	a	29	33	19	17
Tunisia	m	m	m	27	30	7	8	7	8	a	a	27	30	14	16
Zimbabwe[3]	m	m	m	4	3	a	a	12	9	a	a	16	12	m	m

Note: x indicates that data are included in another column. The column reference is shown in brackets after "x". *e.g.,* x(2) means that data are included in column 2.
1. Year of reference 2000.
2. Significant proportion of the youth cohort is missing.
3. Year of reference 2002.
* See Annex 3 for notes (*www.oecd.org/edu/eag2003*).
Source: OECD.

Table A1.2
Population that has attained at least upper secondary education (2001)
Percentage of the population that has attained at least upper secondary education[1], by age group

| | Age group | | | | |
	25-64	25-34	35-44	45-54	55-64
OECD COUNTRIES					
Australia	59	71	60	55	44
Austria	77	84	81	73	65
Belgium	59	76	64	53	39
Canada	82	89	85	81	67
Czech Republic	86	92	90	84	76
Denmark	80	86	80	80	72
Finland	74	87	84	70	51
France[2]	64	78	67	58	46
Germany	83	85	86	83	76
Greece	51	73	60	43	28
Hungary	70	81	79	72	44
Iceland	57	61	60	56	46
Ireland	58	73	62	48	35
Italy	43	57	49	39	22
Japan	83	94	94	81	63
Korea	68	95	77	49	30
Luxembourg	53	59	57	47	42
Mexico	22	25	25	17	11
Netherlands	65	75	69	61	50
New Zealand	76	82	80	75	60
Norway	86	94	91	82	71
Poland	46	52	48	44	36
Portugal	20	32	20	14	9
Slovak Republic	85	94	90	83	66
Spain	40	57	45	29	17
Sweden	81	91	86	78	65
Switzerland	87	92	90	85	81
Turkey	24	30	24	19	13
United Kingdom[2]	63	68	65	61	55
United States	88	88	89	89	83
Country mean	*64*	*74*	*69*	*60*	*49*
NON-OECD COUNTRIES					
Argentina[3]	42	51	43	38	28
Brazil[3]	26	31	29	23	14
Chile[3]	46	58	48	40	27
China	15	16	22	9	7
Indonesia	21	33	22	15	7
Jamaica	37	61	31	12	8
Malaysia[3]	38	52	40	22	12
Paraguay[3]	22	30	23	16	11
Peru[1]	44	56	47	36	22
Philippines	36	m	m	m	m
Thailand[3]	18	27	18	10	6
Uruguay[3]	31	37	34	29	21

1. Excluding ISCED 3C short programmes.
2. Not all ISCED 3 programmes meet minimum requirements for ISCED 3C long programmes.
3. Year of reference 2000.
Source: OECD. See Annex 3 for notes *(www.oecd.org/edu/eag2003)*.

A1

Table A1.3
Post-secondary non-tertiary graduation rates (2001)
Ratio of post-secondary non-tertiary graduates to total population at typical age of graduation (multiplied by 100) in public and private institutions, by programme destination and gender

	Total (unduplicated)			ISCED 4A (designed to prepare for direct entry to tertiary-type A education)		ISCED 4B (designed to prepare for direct entry to tertiary-type B education)		ISCED 4C (designed to prepare for direct entry to the labour market)	
	M + F	Males	Females	M + F	Females	M + F	Females	M + F	Females
	(1)	(2)	(3)	(4)	(5)	(6)	(7)	(8)	(9)
Australia	m	m	m	m	m	m	m	m	m
Austria	21.8	18.3	25.4	19.7	21.8	2.4	4.2	0.1	0.2
Belgium[1]	16.5	15.1	18.0	9.8	9.8	a	a	6.8	8.2
Canada	m	m	m	m	m	m	m	m	m
Czech Republic	8.6	8.6	8.7	6.4	6.6	a	a	2.2	2.1
Denmark[1]	0.3	0.4	0.2	0.3	0.2	a	a	n	a
Finland	1.7	1.5	1.8	a	a	a	a	2.7	3.1
France[1]	1.2	0.8	1.7	0.7	0.9	a	a	0.6	0.8
Germany	15.0	16.2	13.8	9.5	8.8	5.5	5.0	a	a
Greece	m	m	m	a	a	a	a	m	m
Hungary[1,2]	34.1	30.9	37.5	7.3	7.6	a	a	26.6	29.7
Iceland	4.1	4.7	3.4	n	n	n	n	4.1	3.4
Ireland	32.1	16.9	48.1	a	a	a	a	32.1	48.1
Italy[2]	3.7	2.9	4.4	a	a	a	a	3.7	4.4
Japan	m	m	m	m	m	m	m	m	m
Korea	a	a	a	a	a	a	a	a	a
Luxembourg[1]	3.3	4.9	1.5	a	a	a	a	3.3	1.5
Mexico	a	a	a	a	a	a	a	a	a
Netherlands[1]	1.0	1.7	0.4	a	a	a	a	1.0	0.4
New Zealand	21.3	18.0	24.8	1.3	1.7	7.5	9.0	12.4	14.1
Norway[1]	8.0	11.2	4.6	2.7	2.0	a	a	5.2	2.6
Poland[1]	11.3	7.3	15.5	a	a	a	a	11.3	15.5
Portugal	m	m	m	m	m	m	m	m	m
Slovak Republic	2.9	2.0	3.9	2.9	3.9	n	n	n	n
Spain	5.8	5.5	6.2	5.4	5.6	0.5	0.6	n	n
Sweden	m	m	m	m	m	m	m	0.4	0.2
Switzerland	19.7	22.3	17.1	2.9	1.9	17.2	15.5	n	n
Turkey	a	a	a	a	a	a	a	a	a
United Kingdom	m	m	m	m	m	m	m	m	m
United States[1]	6.9	6.3	7.6	a	a	a	a	6.9	7.6
Country mean	*9.5*	*8.5*	*10.6*	*2.9*	*3.0*	*1.4*	*1.4*	*5.0*	*5.9*

OECD COUNTRIES

Note: x indicates that data are included in another column. The column reference is shown in brackets after "x". *e.g.*, x(2) means that data are included in column 2.
1. Gross graduation rate may include some double counting.
2. Year of reference 2000.
Source: OECD. See Annex 3 for notes *(www.oecd.org/edu/eag2003)*.

INDICATOR A2: CURRENT TERTIARY GRADUATION AND SURVIVAL RATES AND ATTAINMENT OF THE ADULT POPULATION

- On average across OECD countries, 30 per cent of persons at the typical age of graduation currently complete the tertiary-type A level of education - a figure that ranges from around 40 per cent in Australia, Finland, Iceland and New Zealand to 20 per cent or below in Austria, the Czech Republic, Germany, Italy and Switzerland.

- On average, one third of OECD students "drop out" before they complete their first degree, regardless of whether they are following tertiary-type A or tertiary-type B programmes.

- As measured by educational attainment, there has been an increase in the stock of university-level skills in the adult population. However, most of that increase is due to significant increases in tertiary graduation rates in a comparatively small number of countries.

Chart A2.1

Tertiary-type A graduation rates, by duration of programme (2001)
Ratio of number of graduates to the population at the typical age of graduation (multiplied by 100)

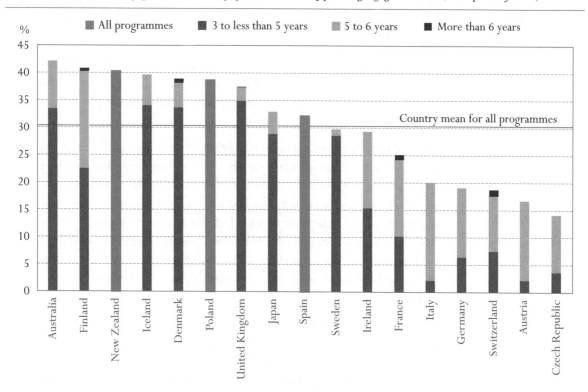

Countries are ranked in descending order of total tertiary-type A graduation rates.
Source: OECD. Table A2.1. See Annex 3 for notes *(www.oecd.org/edu/eag2003).*

A₂

This indicator shows tertiary graduation rates as well as historical patterns of tertiary educational attainment…

…and sheds light on the internal efficiency of tertiary education systems.

Policy context

Tertiary graduation rates are an indicator of the current production rate of advanced knowledge by each country's education system. Countries with high graduation rates at the tertiary level are the most likely to be developing or maintaining a highly skilled labour force. Measures of educational attainment show the evolution of advanced knowledge in the population.

Tertiary level dropout and survival rates can be useful indicators of the internal efficiency of tertiary education systems but the specific reasons for leaving a tertiary programme are varied: students may realise that they have chosen the wrong subject or educational programme; they may fail to meet the standards set by their educational institution, particularly in tertiary systems that provide broader access; or they may find attractive employment before completing their programme. "Dropping out" is not necessarily an indication of failure by individual students, but high dropout rates may well indicate that the education system is not meeting the needs of its clients. Students may not find that the educational programmes offered meet their expectations or their labour market needs. It may also be that students find that programmes take longer than the number of years which they can justify being outside the labour market.

Evidence and explanations

Graduation rates at the tertiary level

Tertiary programmes vary widely in structure and scope among countries.

Tertiary graduation rates are influenced both by the degree of access to tertiary programmes and by the demand for higher skills in the labour market. They are also affected by the way in which the degree and qualification structures are organised within countries.

This indicator distinguishes between different categories of tertiary qualifications: *i)* degrees at tertiary-type B level (ISCED 5B); *ii)* degrees at tertiary-type A level (ISCED 5A); and *iii)* advanced research qualifications at the doctorate level (ISCED 6).

Tertiary-type A programmes are largely theoretically-based and designed to provide qualifications for entry to advanced research programmes and professions with high skill requirements. Countries differ in the way in which tertiary-type A studies are organised. The institutional framework may be universities but it can also be other institutions. The duration of programmes leading to a first type-A qualification ranges from three years (*e.g.*, the Bachelor's degree in most colleges in Ireland and the United Kingdom in most fields of study and the *Licence* in France) to five years or more (*e.g.*, the *Diplom* in Germany and the *Laurea* in Italy).

Whereas, in many countries, there is a clear distinction between first and second university degrees, *i.e.*, undergraduate and graduate programmes, this distinction is not made in other countries, where degrees that are comparable internationally at the "Master's" level are obtained through a single programme of long duration. To ensure international comparability, it is therefore neces-

A2

sary to compare degree programmes of similar cumulative duration, as well as completion rates for first-degree programmes.

To allow for comparisons that are independent of differences in national degree structures, tertiary-type A degrees are subdivided in accordance with the total theoretical duration of studies at the tertiary level. Specifically, the OECD classification divides degrees into those of medium (three to less than five years), long (five to less than six years) and very long duration (more than six years). Degrees obtained from short programmes of less than three years' duration are not considered equivalent to the completion of the tertiary-type A level of education and are therefore not included in this indicator. Second-degree programmes are classified according to the cumulative duration of the first and second-degree programme and individuals who already hold a first degree are netted out of these.

Tertiary-type A programmes are subdivided in accordance with the theoretical duration of studies to allow for comparisons that are independent of differences in national degree structures.

On average in OECD countries, 30 per cent of persons at the typical age of graduation complete tertiary-type A education. This figure ranges from around 40 per cent in Australia, Finland, Iceland and New Zealand to 20 per cent or below in Austria, the Czech Republic, Germany, Italy and Switzerland (Chart A2.1).

On average in OECD countries, 30 per cent of persons at the typical age of graduation complete tertiary-type A education…

Chart A2.2

Graduation rates for advanced research programmes (2001)
Sum of graduation rates over single years of age (multiplied by 100)

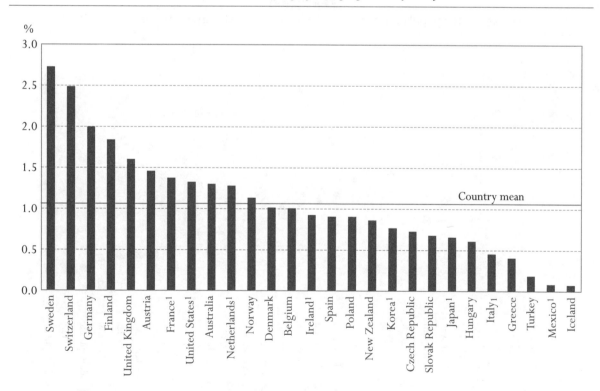

1. Gross graduation rates were used for these countries, which were calculated as the ratio of the number of graduates to the population at the typical age of graduation, multiplied by 100.
Countries are ranked in descending order of graduation rates for advanced research programmes.
Source: OECD. Table A2.1. See Annex 3 for notes *(www.oecd.org/edu/eag2003).*

A2

In general, in countries with higher graduation rates the majority of students complete medium length programmes (three to less than five years). A notable exception to this rule is Finland where 45 per cent of students complete longer programmes. The pattern for countries with lower tertiary-type A graduation rates is more obvious. In Austria, the Czech Republic, Germany, Italy and Switzerland, the majority of students complete longer programmes (of at least five years' duration), and graduation rates are 20 per cent or below.

...while the graduation rate at the tertiary–type B level is 11 per cent...

Tertiary-type B programmes are classified at the same level of competencies as tertiary-type A programmes but are more occupationally-oriented and lead to direct labour market access. The programmes are typically of shorter duration than type A programmes (typically two to three years). Generally they are not deemed to lead to university-level degrees. Graduation rates for tertiary-type B programmes account, on average in OECD countries, for 11 per cent of an age cohort (Table A2.1). In Japan, 27 per cent of the population at the typical age of graduation complete the tertiary-type B level of education, and this figure is between 16 and 19 per cent in France, Ireland, New Zealand and Switzerland.

... and 1.1 per cent obtain an advanced research qualification.

On average across OECD countries, 1.1 per cent of the population obtain an advanced research qualification, such as a Ph.D. In Sweden and Switzerland this is around 2.5 per cent and in Germany 2 per cent (Chart A2.2).

Chart A2.3

Percentage of the population that has attained tertiary education, by age group (2001)

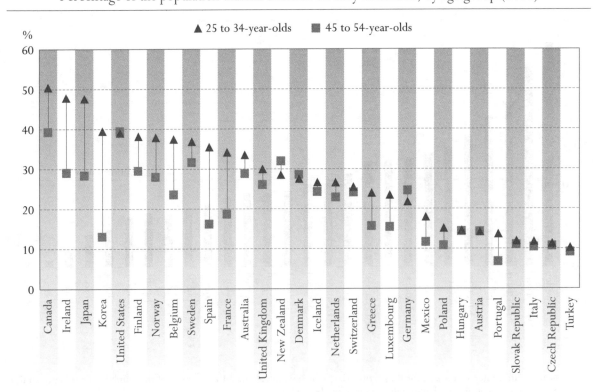

▲ 25 to 34-year-olds ■ 45 to 54-year-olds

Countries are ranked in descending order of the percentage of 25 to 34-year-olds who have attained tertiary education.
Source: OECD. Table A2.3. See Annex 3 for notes (*www.oecd.org/edu/eag2003*).

The rising skill requirements of labour markets, an increase in unemployment during recent years and higher expectations by individuals and society have influenced the proportion of young people who obtain at least a tertiary qualification. As measured by tertiary qualifications, there has been a general increase in the stock of higher-level skills in the adult population. Among OECD countries, only 14 per cent of 45 to 54 year-olds hold tertiary-type A and advanced research qualifications, whereas 18 per cent of 25 to 34 year-olds do so (Table A2.3). In some countries this increase has been marked. In Korea and Spain, for example, only 11 and 13 per cent of 45 to 54-year-olds, respectively, have obtained a tertiary qualification compared to 25 and 24 per cent among 25 to 34-year-olds. In Belgium, France, Ireland and Japan the increase is less marked but still significant (Chart A2.3).

There has been an increase in the proportion of young people who have attained a qualification equivalent to tertiary-type A and advanced research programmes.

Trends in tertiary attainment

An overview of the level of educational attainment at the tertiary level (Table A2.4) over the last ten years confirms the strong trend of increases in the proportion of the adult population attaining tertiary education. For the 19 OECD countries where data are available for both 1991 and 2001, the average increase is of 10 percentage points, with notable increases in Canada and Spain (19 percentage points) and in Ireland (28 percentage points).

Chart A2.4

Difference between females and males in levels of tertiary attainment, by year

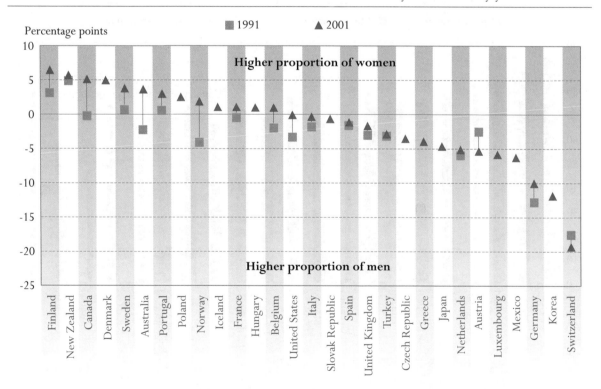

Countries are ranked in descending order of the difference between female and male 25 to 64-year-olds who have attained tertiary education in 2001.
Source: OECD. See Annex 3 for notes *(www.oecd.org/edu/eag2003).*

Increased participation in tertiary education has moderated differences among countries...

The result of this increased participation in tertiary education has been a reduction of the differences among countries. With the exception of Canada and Ireland at the upper side of the distribution and of Austria, Italy, Portugal and Turkey at the lower side, OECD countries enjoyed an increased proportion of highly skilled people in the population, so that levels are now more similar.

...but some countries have been left behind.

However, the proportion of people holding tertiary qualifications remains rather low in Austria, Italy, Portugal and Turkey, where there seems to have been limited improvement over the last ten years. Other countries that have seen very limited increases in tertiary graduation rates include Germany, the Netherlands and Switzerland (Table A2.4).

The gender gap in tertiary graduation is sometimes reversing.

The increase in the stock of tertiary graduates has not been equal for both males and females. In 1991, the levels of tertiary attainment were about the same for males and females. Ten years later, the advantage is clearly in favour of females. On average in the OECD, 29 percent of females have attained tertiary qualifications, whereas only 26 percent of males have. The relative increase of tertiary qualifications for females is especially noticeable in Canada, Ireland and Spain, showing an increase of 23, 31 and 21 percentage points respectively. By contrast, in both Germany and Switzerland where the stock of females hold-

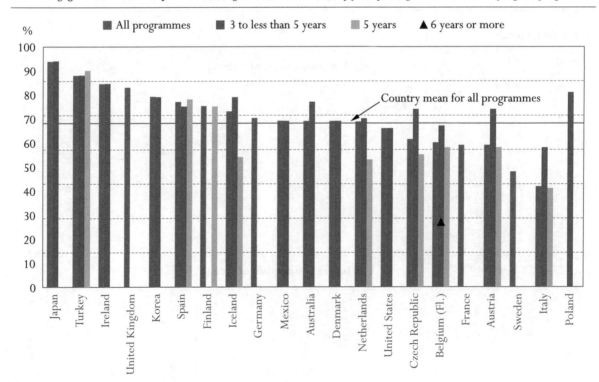

Chart A2.5

Survival rates in tertiary-type A education, by duration of programme (2000)

Number of graduates divided by the number of new entrants in the typical year of entrance to the specified programme

Countries are ranked in descending order of tertiary-type A survival rate for all programmes.
Source: OECD. Table A2.2. See Annex 3 for notes *(www.oecd.org/edu/eag2003).*

ing tertiary qualifications is comparatively low, there has been very limited improvement over the past ten years (increases of one and four percentage points respectively).

Survival rates at the tertiary level

Tertiary-type A survival rates differ widely among OECD countries, ranging from above 80 per cent in Ireland, Japan, Turkey and the United Kingdom to below 60 per cent in Austria, France, Italy and Sweden (Chart A2.5). In both Austria and Italy the majority of students who do successfully complete a first tertiary-type A programme have followed longer programmes lasting five to six years. In contrast, the majority of students in Ireland, Japan, Korea and Turkey, where survival rates are around 80 per cent or above, have completed a medium first tertiary-type A programme (three to five years long) (see Table A2.2).

Tertiary-type A survival rates are generally higher in countries with more flexible qualification structures…

Tertiary-type B survival rates range from above 80 per cent in Denmark, the Flemish Community of Belgium, Japan, Mexico, Poland and Sweden, to around 50 per cent in Ireland and Italy. In general, tertiary-type B programmes are of a shorter duration than tertiary-type A programmes. In the majority of countries with available data, most, if not all, students successfully complete short programmes (two to three years). It is however interesting to note that both Denmark and the Flemish Community of Belgium have the majority of students graduating from medium length type B programmes (in the Flemish Community the only tertiary-type B programme option) and the highest survival rates at the tertiary-type B level (see Table A2.2).

…a pattern that is not as clearly visible at the tertiary-type B level.

In Italy, Japan and Korea, survival rates for students following advanced research programmes are 85 per cent or higher. Conversely, students are far likelier to drop out of such programmes in France and Iceland (36 and 50 per cent survival rate, respectively).

For advanced research programmes, survival rates are high in Italy, Japan and Korea.

Definitions and methodologies

Tertiary graduates are those who obtain a tertiary qualification in the specified reference year. This indicator distinguishes between different categories of tertiary qualifications: *i)* qualifications at the tertiary-type B level (ISCED 5B); *ii)* tertiary-type A qualifications (ISCED 5A); and *iii)* advanced research degrees of doctorate standard (ISCED 6). For some countries, data are not available for the categories requested. In such cases, the OECD has assigned graduates to the most appropriate category. See Annex 3 at *www.oecd.org/edu/eag2003* for a list of programmes included for each country at the tertiary-type A and type B levels. Tertiary-type A degrees are also subdivided in accordance with the total theoretical duration of studies at the level of ISCED 5A, to allow for comparisons that are independent of differences in national degree structures.

Data on graduates refer to the academic year 2000–2001 and are based on the UOE data collection on education statistics that is administered annually by the OECD.

Graduation rates for first tertiary programmes (tertiary-type A and type B) are calculated as gross graduation rates. In order to calculate gross graduation rates, countries identify the age at which graduation typically occurs (see Annex 1). The graduates themselves, however, may be of any age. The number of graduates is then divided by the population at the typical graduation age. In many coun-

A₂

tries, defining a typical age of graduation is difficult, however, because graduates are dispersed over a wide range of ages.

A net graduation rate is calculated for advanced tertiary programmes (where duplication of certificates awarded does not pose a problem) as the sum of age-specific graduation rates. The net graduation rate can be interpreted as the percentage of persons within a virtual age cohort who obtain a tertiary qualification, and is thus unaffected by changes in population size or typical graduation age. Gross graduation rates are presented for those countries that cannot provide such detailed data.

Survival rate at the tertiary level is defined as the proportion of new entrants to the specified level of education who successfully complete a first qualification. Dropouts are defined as those students who leave the specified level in the educational system without obtaining a first qualification. The first qualification refers to any degree, regardless of the duration of study, obtained at the end of a programme which does not have as a prerequisite a previous degree at the same level. The survival rate is calculated as the ratio of the number of students who are awarded an initial degree to the number of new entrants to the level *n* years before, *n* being the number of years of full-time study required to complete the degree.

Educational attainment data are derived from National Labour Force Surveys and levels are based upon the International Standard Classification of Education (ISCED-97).

Data on population and education attainment are taken from OECD and EUROSTAT databases, which are compiled from National Labour Force Surveys. See Annex 3 at *www.oecd.org/edu/eag2003* for national sources.

The attainment profiles are based on the percentage of the population aged 25 to 64 years that has completed a specified level of education. The International Standard Classification of Education (ISCED-97) is used to define the levels of education. See Annex 3 at *www.oecd.org/edu/eag2003* for a description of ISCED-97 education programmes and attainment levels and their mappings for each country.

Table A2.1
Tertiary graduation rates (2001)
Ratio of tertiary graduates to the population at the typical age of graduation, multiplied by 100, by programme destination and duration of programme

A₂

| | Tertiary-type B programmes (first-time graduation) | Tertiary-type A programmes (first-time graduation) | | | | Advanced research programmes[1] |
		All programmes	3 to less than 5 years (excluding students who subsequently completed a longer programme)	5 to 6 years	More than 6 years	
	(1)	(2)	(3)	(4)	(5)	(6)
Australia[2]	m	42.0	33.3	8.7	a	1.3
Austria	m	16.6	2.1	14.5	n	1.5
Belgium	m	m	m	m	m	1.0
Canada	m	m	m	m	m	m
Czech Republic*	5.0	14.1	3.6	10.5	a	0.7
Denmark	8.0	38.8	33.5	4.5	0.8	1.0
Finland*	7.3	40.7	22.4	17.7	0.5	1.8
France	17.9	25.0	10.2	14.0	0.9	1.4
Germany	10.7	19.0	6.4	12.7	a	2.0
Greece	m	m	m	m	m	0.4
Hungary	m	m	m	m	m	0.6
Iceland*	7.6	39.5	33.9	5.6	n	0.1
Ireland*	19.0	29.3	15.3	14.0	x(4)	0.9
Italy	0.3	20.0	2.1	17.8	n	0.5
Japan	27.4	32.8	28.8	4.0	a	0.7
Korea	m	m	m	m	m	0.8
Luxembourg	m	m	m	m	m	m
Mexico	m	m	m	m	m	0.1
Netherlands	m	m	m	m	m	1.3
New Zealand	17.6	40.2	m	m	m	0.9
Norway	m	m	m	m	m	1.1
Poland	m	38.6	m	m	m	0.9
Portugal	m	m	m	m	m	m
Slovak Republic	2.3	m	m	m	m	0.7
Spain	10.9	32.1	m	m	m	0.9
Sweden	4.0	29.6	28.5	1.2	a	2.7
Switzerland	16.1	18.7	7.4	10.1	1.1	2.5
Turkey	m	m	m	m	m	0.2
United Kingdom	11.5	37.4	34.8	2.5	0.1	1.6
United States	m	m	m	m	m	1.3
Country mean	*11.0*	*30.3*	*18.7*	*9.8*	*0.3*	*1.1*

OECD COUNTRIES

Note: x indicates that data are included in another column. The column reference is shown in brackets after "x". *e.g.,* x(2) means that data are included in column 2.
1. Net graduation rate is calculated by summing the graduation rates by single year of age, except for France, Italy, Japan, Korea, Mexico, the Netherlands and the United States.
2. Year of reference 2000
* See Annex 3 for notes (*www.oecd.org/edu/eag2003*).
Source: OECD.

A₂

Table A2.2
Survival rates in tertiary education (2000)

Number of graduates divided by the number of new entrants in the typical year of entrance, by programme destination, and distribution of graduates by duration of programme

		Tertiary-type A education			Tertiary-type B education				
		Survival rate for all tertiary-type A programmes	Survival rate for programmes of duration:			Survival rate for all tertiary-type B programmes	Survival rate for programmes of duration:			Advanced research programmes
			3 to less than 5 years	5 to less than 6 years	6 years or more		2 to less than 3 years	3 to less than 5 years	5 years or more	
		(1)	(2)	(3)	(4)	(5)	(6)	(7)	(8)	(9)
OECD COUNTRIES	Australia*	69	77	m	n	m	m	a	a	m
	Austria	59	74	58	n	m	m	m	m	m
	Belgium (Fl.)*	60	67	58	27	88	a	88	a	m
	Czech Republic	61	74	55	a	77	75	78	a	m
	Denmark	69	69	a	a	84	65	90	a	m
	Finland	75	m	75	a	m	m	m	m	m
	France*	59	m	m	m	72	72	n	a	36
	Germany	70	a	a	a	75	a	a	a	m
	Iceland	73	79	54	n	55	73	31	n	50
	Ireland	85	85	x(2)	x(2)	50	50	x(6)	a	m
	Italy	42	58	41	a	51	a	51	a	89
	Japan	94	94	x(2)	x(2)	86	86	x(6)	x(6)	85
	Korea	79	79	x(2)	a	74	73	78	a	95
	Mexico	69	69	x(2)	a	81	81	x(6)	a	54
	Netherlands	69	70	53	a	58	59	50	a	m
	Poland	m	81	m	a	84	84	a	a	m
	Spain	77	75	78	n	74	74	n	n	m
	Sweden	48	m	m	a	85	m	m	a	m
	Turkey	88	88	90	a	77	77	a	a	a
	United Kingdom*	83	m	m	m	m	m	m	m	m
	United States*	66	66	a	a	62	62	x(6)	x(6)	m
	Country mean	*70*	*76*	*62*	*2*	*73*	*72*	*67*	*n*	*58*
NON-OECD COUNTRY	Israel	70	m	m	m	91	m	m	m	m

Note: x indicates that data are included in another column. The column reference is shown in brackets after "x". *e.g.*, x(2) means that data are included in column 2.
* See Annex 3 for notes (*www.oecd.org/edu/eag2003*).
Source: OECD.

Table A2.3
Population that has attained tertiary education (2001)
Percentage of the population that has attained tertiary-type B education or tertiary-type A and advanced research programmes, by age group

A2

	Tertiary-type B education					Tertiary-type A and advanced research programmes				
	25-64	25-34	35-44	45-54	55-64	25-64	25-34	35-44	45-54	55-64
	(1)	(2)	(3)	(4)	(5)	(6)	(7)	(8)	(9)	(10)
Australia	10	10	10	10	9	19	24	19	19	12
Austria	7	7	8	8	6	7	7	8	7	5
Belgium	15	20	16	13	10	13	18	13	11	8
Canada	21	25	23	20	15	20	25	20	20	15
Czech Republic	x(6)	x(7)	x(8)	x(9)	x(10)	11	11	13	11	9
Denmark	5	6	6	5	4	22	22	23	23	17
Finland	17	20	21	16	12	15	18	16	13	11
France	11	17	12	9	6	12	18	11	10	8
Germany	10	8	11	10	10	13	14	15	15	10
Greece	5	7	7	4	3	12	17	14	12	6
Hungary	x(6)	x(7)	x(8)	x(9)	x(10)	14	15	15	14	12
Iceland	6	6	8	6	4	19	21	21	19	11
Ireland	22	28	23	18	13	14	20	14	11	8
Italy	x(6)	x(7)	x(8)	x(9)	x(10)	10	12	11	10	6
Japan	15	23	19	11	5	19	24	25	17	10
Korea	7	15	6	2	1	17	25	20	11	8
Luxembourg	7	8	6	6	5	11	15	11	10	8
Mexico	2	3	2	1	n	13	15	15	11	7
Netherlands	2	2	3	2	2	21	24	21	21	16
New Zealand	15	12	16	18	17	14	17	15	14	7
Norway	3	3	3	3	2	28	35	28	25	19
Poland	x(6)	x(7)	x(8)	x(9)	x(10)	12	15	11	11	10
Portugal	2	3	3	2	2	7	11	7	5	3
Slovak Republic	1	1	1	1	n	10	11	11	10	8
Spain	7	12	7	3	2	17	24	18	13	8
Sweden	15	17	17	14	10	17	20	16	17	15
Switzerland	10	10	11	9	8	16	16	18	15	13
Turkey	x(6)	x(7)	x(8)	x(9)	x(10)	9	10	8	9	6
United Kingdom	8	9	9	8	7	18	21	18	18	12
United States	9	9	10	10	7	28	30	28	30	24
Country mean	*8*	*9*	*8*	*7*	*5*	*15*	*18*	*16*	*14*	*10*
Argentina[1]	5	6	5	4	2	9	9	10	10	6
Brazil[1]	x(6)	x(7)	x(8)	x(9)	x(10)	8	7	9	9	6
Chile[1]	1	2	1	1	n	9	11	9	9	6
China	3	4	3	2	2	1	2	1	1	2
Indonesia	2	3	3	2	1	2	4	3	2	1
Jamaica[1]	1	1	1	1	1	3	3	4	3	2
Malaysia[1]	x(6)	x(7)	x(8)	x(9)	x(10)	9	13	9	6	4
Paraguay[1]	2	2	2	1	2	9	11	9	7	4
Peru[1]	8	10	8	6	3	8	8	9	9	6
Philippines	10	m	m	m	m	m	m	m	m	m
Thailand[1]	2	4	2	1	1	8	9	10	6	3
Uruguay[1]	9	9	11	9	7	x(1)	x(2)	x(3)	x(4)	x(5)

Note: x indicates that data are included in another column. The column reference is shown in brackets after "x". *e.g.*, x(2) means that data are included in column 2.
1. Year of reference 2000.
Source: OECD. See Annex 3 for notes *(www.oecd.org/edu/eag2003)*.

A₂

Table A2.4
Trends in educational attainment at tertiary level (1991 - 2001)
Percentage of the population of 25 to 34-year-olds that has attained tertiary education, by gender.

		Year										
		1991	1992	1993	1994	1995	1996	1997	1998	1999	2000	2001
Australia	Males	22	m	22	23	24	25	23	25	26	28	29
	Females	24	m	24	25	25	26	28	32	32	35	38
	M+F	23	m	23	24	25	25	26	28	29	31	34
Austria	Males	8	8	m	8	8	9	12	12	12	16	15
	Females	8	8	m	9	9	9	13	13	13	14	14
	M+F	8	8	m	9	9	9	12	13	13	15	14
Belgium	Males	25	25	26	27	28	29	29	30	30	33	34
	Females	29	29	32	33	33	36	37	38	38	39	41
	M+F	27	27	29	30	30	32	33	34	34	36	38
Canada	Males	30	31	32	35	37	38	40	41	42	43	45
	Females	33	35	37	41	44	46	48	50	52	54	56
	M+F	32	33	35	38	40	42	44	45	47	48	51
Czech Republic	Males	m	m	m	13	13	12	12	11	12	12	12
	Females	m	m	m	11	10	10	10	10	10	11	11
	M+F	m	m	m	12	12	11	11	10	11	11	11
Denmark	Males	m	m	m	m	m	m	m	27	28	26	25
	Females	m	m	m	m	m	m	m	27	29	31	34
	M+F	m	m	m	m	m	m	m	27	29	29	29
Finland	Males	28	28	m	28	29	29	30	29	30	30	30
	Females	39	39	m	40	41	41	43	43	45	46	46
	M+F	33	33	m	34	35	35	36	36	37	38	38
France	Males	19	21	22	23	23	24	26	27	29	30	32
	Females	21	22	24	26	27	28	30	32	33	35	37
	M+F	20	22	23	24	25	26	28	30	31	32	34
Germany	Males	23	22	m	22	23	22	23	23	23	24	23
	Females	19	19	m	19	19	18	19	20	20	20	20
	M+F	21	20	m	20	21	20	21	22	22	22	22
Greece	Males	m	m	m	24	25	26	21	22	22	22	21
	Females	m	m	m	26	27	30	24	27	27	26	27
	M+F	m	m	m	25	26	28	22	24	25	24	24
Hungary	Males	m	m	m	m	m	11	11	12	11	12	13
	Females	m	m	m	m	m	17	14	16	16	17	16
	M+F	m	m	m	m	m	14	12	14	14	15	15
Iceland	Males	m	m	m	m	m	19	20	21	25	24	24
	Females	m	m	m	m	m	28	26	27	30	31	29
	M+F	m	m	m	m	m	24	23	24	28	28	26
Ireland	Males	20	21	m	24	27	31	33	30	40	44	45
	Females	19	22	m	24	28	32	32	29	43	49	50
	M+F	20	21	m	24	27	31	33	29	41	47	48
Italy	Males	7	7	m	8	8	8	m	8	9	9	10
	Females	6	7	m	8	9	9	m	10	11	12	13
	M+F	7	7	m	8	8	8	m	9	10	10	12
Japan	Males	m	m	m	m	m	m	45	45	44	46	46
	Females	m	m	m	m	m	m	45	46	46	49	49
	M+F	m	m	m	m	m	m	45	45	45	47	48
Korea	Males	m	m	m	m	33	34	m	38	39	41	42
	Females	m	m	m	m	24	26	m	30	31	34	37
	M+F	m	m	m	m	29	30	m	34	35	37	40
Luxembourg	Males	m	m	m	m	m	m	m	m	22	24	25
	Females	m	m	m	m	m	m	m	m	20	22	22
	M+F	m	m	m	m	m	m	m	m	21	23	23
Mexico	Males	m	m	m	m	m	m	19	19	19	19	20
	Females	m	m	m	m	m	m	15	14	14	16	16
	M+F	m	m	m	m	m	m	17	17	16	17	18
Netherlands	Males	23	24	m	25	25	26	m	28	25	27	26
	Females	22	23	m	23	24	24	m	27	25	26	27
	M+F	22	24	m	24	25	25	m	27	25	27	27
New Zealand	Males	21	21	m	18	23	m	23	24	24	25	26
	Females	25	25	m	24	26	m	27	28	28	29	31
	M+F	23	23	m	21	24	m	25	26	26	27	29
Norway	Males	26	27	m	29	29	27	27	29	30	30	33
	Females	28	29	m	33	35	33	33	36	39	40	44
	M+F	27	28	m	31	32	30	30	33	35	35	38
Poland	Males	m	m	m	m	9	m	9	10	10	11	12
	Females	m	m	m	m	11	m	12	14	15	17	18
	M+F	m	m	m	m	10	m	10	12	12	14	15
Portugal	Males	7	m	m	10	11	11	m	8	9	10	10
	Females	10	m	m	16	16	17	m	14	14	15	17
	M+F	9	m	m	13	14	14	m	11	11	12	14
Slovak Republic	Males	m	m	m	13	12	12	10	11	11	11	11
	Females	m	m	m	12	11	13	11	11	11	12	12
	M+F	m	m	m	13	12	12	10	11	11	11	12
Spain	Males	15	22	m	24	25	26	28	29	31	31	32
	Females	18	23	m	27	28	31	33	35	36	37	39
	M+F	16	22	m	25	27	29	30	32	33	34	36
Sweden	Males	26	26	m	26	27	28	29	30	29	31	34
	Females	28	27	m	29	30	29	30	32	34	36	39
	M+F	27	27	m	27	29	28	29	31	32	34	37
Switzerland	Males	29	29	m	31	29	31	33	34	36	34	35
	Females	13	13	m	13	13	14	16	15	16	17	17
	M+F	21	21	m	22	22	23	25	25	26	26	26
Turkey	Males	7	7	m	7	8	m	9	9	10	10	11
	Females	5	4	m	6	7	m	6	7	7	8	9
	M+F	6	6	m	7	8	m	7	8	8	9	10
United Kingdom	Males	19	22	m	24	24	25	26	27	29	30	30
	Females	18	19	m	22	22	23	23	25	26	27	29
	M+F	19	21	m	23	23	24	25	26	27	29	29
United States	Males	29	29	m	31	33	34	34	34	36	36	36
	Females	31	31	m	33	35	37	37	38	39	40	42
	M+F	30	30	m	32	34	35	36	36	37	38	39
Country mean	*Males*									25	26	26
	Females									27	28	29
	M+F									26	27	28

Source: OECD. See Annex 3 for notes *(www.oecd.org/edu/eag2003).*

OECD COUNTRIES

INDICATOR A3: GRADUATES BY FIELD OF STUDY

- On average across OECD countries, every third tertiary-type A graduate obtains a degree in the social sciences, business or law. The second most popular fields are science-related, from which one in four students graduate, on average.

- In the humanities, arts, education, health and welfare, on average in OECD countries more than two thirds of the tertiary-type A graduates are females, whereas female graduates are less than one-third in mathematics and computer science and less than one-quarter in engineering, manufacturing and construction.

- In OECD countries, males are still more likely than females to earn advanced research qualifications, such as doctorates.

- Science related fields, closely followed by social sciences, business and law, are the most popular fields of study at the tertiary-type B level.

A3

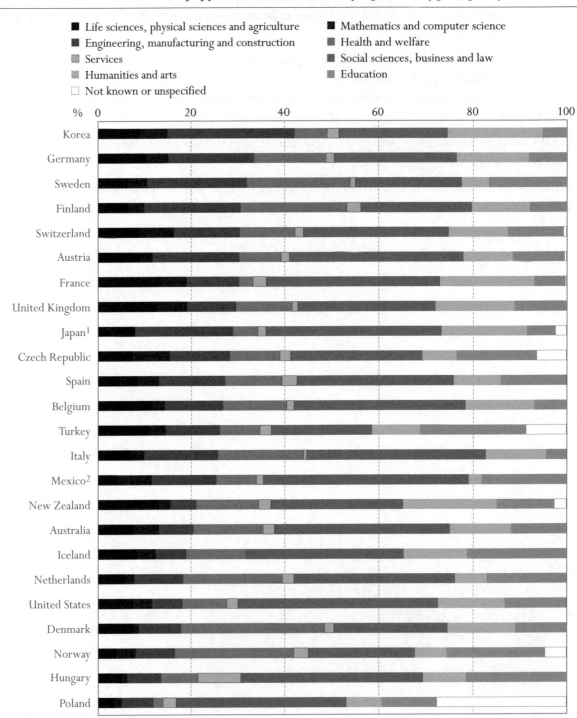

Chart A3.1

Graduates by field of study (2001)

Graduates with tertiary-type A and advanced research qualifications, by field of study

■ Life sciences, physical sciences and agriculture   ■ Mathematics and computer science
■ Engineering, manufacturing and construction   ■ Health and welfare
■ Services   ■ Social sciences, business and law
■ Humanities and arts   ■ Education
□ Not known or unspecified

Countries are ranked in descending order of the proportion of qualifications in life sciences, physical sciences and agriculture, mathematics and computer science, and engineering, manufacturing and construction.
1. Mathematics and computer science are included in the category "life sciences, physical sciences and agriculture".
2. Excludes tertiary-type A second degree programmes.
Source: OECD. Table A3.1. See Annex 3 for notes *(www.oecd.org/edu/eag2003).*

Policy context

Changing opportunities in the job market, relative earnings in different occupations and sectors, and admission policies and practices among tertiary education institutions may affect the fields which students choose to study. In turn, the relative popularity of the various fields of study affects the demand for courses and teaching staff, as well as the supply of new graduates. This indicator sheds light on the distribution of tertiary graduates across different fields of study, as well as on the relative share of females among graduates in those fields.

This indicator shows the distribution of tertiary graduates across fields of study.

Evidence and explanations

Graduates by field of study

In 21 of the 25 countries providing data, the largest concentration of tertiary-type A and advanced research qualifications awarded is in the combined fields of social sciences, business and law (Table A3.1). On average in OECD countries, every third tertiary-type A graduate obtains a degree in the social sciences, business or law. The percentage of tertiary-type A qualifications awarded in the social sciences, business and law ranges from under 23 per cent in Norway, Sweden and Turkey, to over 40 per cent in Mexico and the United States. In Turkey the largest concentration of tertiary-type A and advanced research qualifications awarded is in the field of education, and in Norway in the fields of health and welfare.

On average in OECD countries, every third tertiary-type A graduate obtains a degree in the social sciences, business or law.

The percentage of tertiary-type A and advanced research students receiving qualifications in science-related fields (engineering, manufacturing and construction, life sciences, physical sciences and agriculture, mathematics and computing, but not including health and welfare) is 26 per cent on average in OECD countries and ranges from less than 17 per cent in Hungary, Norway and Poland, to around one-third in Germany and Sweden, and 42 per cent in Korea. Slightly less popular on average in OECD countries are the fields of humanities, arts and education from which 25 per cent of tertiary-type A and advanced research students graduate.

The second largest concentration of tertiary-type A and advanced research qualifications awarded is in the science-related fields.

The distribution of qualifications awarded by field of study is driven by the relative popularity of these fields among students, the relative number of students admitted to these fields in universities and equivalent institutions, and the degree structure of the various disciplines in a particular country.

Individual preferences, admission policies and degree structures influence the prevalence of the different fields of study.

Part of the variation in graduation rates between countries (Table A2.1) can also be accounted for by differences in the number of tertiary-type A degrees earned in the fields of education and the humanities. Countries with high graduation rates, on average, have a higher proportion of graduates in education and humanities and a lower proportion of graduates in science-related fields. In other words, there is less variation in graduation rates in science-related fields among countries than in overall graduation rates.

A₃

The majority of OECD graduates at the tertiary-type B level are from science-related fields.

Although the same three combined fields of study yield the majority of graduates, the picture is slightly different for tertiary-type B education, where programmes are more occupationally oriented: science-related fields have the largest concentration of graduates (25 per cent), followed by the combined field of the social sciences, business and law (24 per cent), and then the combined field of the humanities, arts and education (22 per cent). However, health and welfare graduates are more common at this level than engineering, manufacturing and construction graduates (18 and 16 per cent respectively) (see Table A3.1).

The selection of a field of study at this level is heavily dependent on opportunities to study similar subject matter, or to prepare for similar occupations at the post-secondary non-tertiary or tertiary-type A level. For example, if nurses in a particular country were trained primarily in tertiary-type B programmes, the proportion of students graduating with qualifications in medical sciences from that level would be higher than if nurses were primarily trained in upper secondary or tertiary-type A programmes.

Chart A3.2

Proportion of tertiary qualifications awarded to females (2001)

For all fields of study for females with tertiary-type A first and second degrees and advanced research qualifications

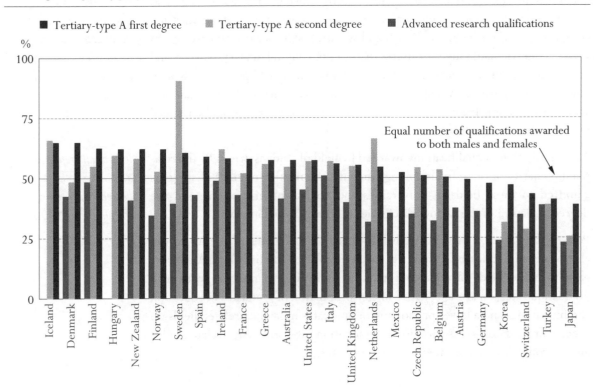

Countries are ranked in descending order of the percentage of tertiary-type A first degrees that are awarded to females.
Source: OECD. Table A3.2. See Annex 3 for notes (www.oecd.org/edu/eag2003).

EDUCATION AT A GLANCE © OECD 2003

A3

Gender differences in tertiary graduation

Overall, tertiary-type A graduation rates for females equal or exceed those for males in 20 out of 26 OECD countries. On average in OECD countries, 55 per cent of all first tertiary-type A graduates are females. However, major differences remain between fields of study. In the humanities, arts, education, health and welfare, more than two thirds of the tertiary-type A graduates are females, on average in OECD countries, whereas less than one third of mathematics and computer science graduates and less than one-fifth of engineering, manufacturing and construction graduates are females (Table A3.2).

Tertiary-type A graduation rates for females equal or exceed those for males in most countries...

In Denmark, Finland, Hungary, Iceland, New Zealand, Norway and Poland, the proportion of females obtaining a first tertiary-type A qualification is above 60 per cent but it is 43 per cent or below in Japan, Switzerland and Turkey (Table A3.2).

...but are 43 per cent of below in Japan, Switzerland and Turkey.

Males remain more likely than females to obtain advanced research qualifications in OECD countries (Table A3.2). Graduation rates from advanced research, *e.g.,* Ph.D. programmes, are lower for females than for males in all countries except Italy. On average in OECD countries, nearly two-thirds of all graduates at this level are males. In Japan and Korea, just over three-quarters of advanced research qualifications are awarded to males.

In OECD countries, males are still more likely than females to earn advanced research qualifications, such as doctorates.

Definitions and methodologies

Tertiary graduates are those who obtain a tertiary qualification in the specified reference year. This indicator distinguishes between different categories of tertiary qualifications: *i)* qualifications at the tertiary-type B level (ISCED 5B); and *ii)* qualifications at the tertiary-type A level (ISCED 5A) and *iii)* advanced research qualifications (ISCED 6). For some countries, data are not available for the categories requested. In such cases, the country has assigned graduates to the most appropriate category.

Data on graduates refer to the academic year 2000-2001 and are based on the UOE data collection on education statistics that is annually administered by the OECD.

Data in tables A3.1 and A3.2 cover graduates from all tertiary degrees reported in Table A2.1. Tertiary graduates who receive their qualification in the reference year are divided into categories based on their subject of specialisation.

Table A3.2 shows the percentage distribution of qualifications among females by subject category.

A3

Table A3.1
Tertiary graduates, by field of study and level of education (2001)

		Education	Humanities and arts	Social sciences, business and law	Services	Engineering, manufacturing and construction	Agriculture	Health and welfare	Life sciences	Physical sciences	Mathematics and statistics	Computing	Not known or unspecified
		(1)	(2)	(3)	(4)	(5)	(6)	(7)	(8)	(9)	(10)	(11)	(12)	(13)
Australia[1]	A	11.9	13.0	37.3	2.4	7.5	1.3	14.8	5.3	1.0	0.4	5.2	a
	B	m	m	m	m	m	m	m	m	m	m	m	m
Austria	A	11.1	10.5	36.9	1.8	18.7	2.6	8.9	3.4	2.8	0.7	2.2	0.5
	B	42.1	3.4	3.4	6.5	24.9	4.5	13.7	n	1.1	0.1	0.4	a
Belgium[2]	A	6.9	14.7	36.4	1.6	12.5	3.5	13.5	5.8	2.4	0.8	2.0	a
	B	21.0	7.3	26.8	2.1	9.1	0.6	27.4	0.5	0.4	n	4.7	0.1
Canada	A	m	m	m	m	m	m	m	m	m	m	m	m
	B	m	m	m	m	m	m	m	m	m	m	m	m
Czech Republic	A	17.1	7.2	28.0	2.3	12.8	3.7	10.6	1.7	2.0	0.8	7.3	6.4
	B	a	7.5	36.2	8.2	6.2	3.0	34.1	a	a	a	4.8	a
Denmark	A	11.0	14.4	24.2	2.0	9.0	1.8	30.8	3.0	2.8	0.5	0.8	a
	B	n	5.2	24.0	9.3	40.0	5.2	n	n	n	n	16.3	a
Finland	A	7.9	12.4	23.4	3.1	20.8	2.6	22.6	1.6	2.2	0.9	2.5	n
	B	0.6	7.0	19.1	20.5	18.4	3.2	21.8	a	a	a	9.4	a
France	A	6.6	20.1	36.8	2.9	11.2	0.8	3.0	6.9	5.8	2.9	2.6	0.3
	B	a	1.5	39.6	5.6	25.1	n	20.3	1.8	2.4	0.4	3.2	a
Germany	A	8.2	15.3	25.9	1.8	18.4	1.9	15.3	3.2	5.2	1.7	3.1	a
	B	9.7	1.0	10.3	8.8	13.9	3.0	51.9	n	a	a	0.3	0.9
Greece	A	m	m	m	m	m	m	m	m	m	m	m	m
	B	m	m	m	m	m	m	m	m	m	m	m	m
Hungary[2]	A	21.5	9.1	38.7	9.2	7.4	3.7	7.9	0.4	0.8	0.1	1.1	a
	B	n	n	44.2	32.4	15.9	n	1.2	n	n	6.2	n	a
Iceland	A	21.3	13.3	33.5	n	6.5	1.5	12.9	4.4	2.5	0.3	3.9	a
	B	21.6	11.9	39.3	n	n	n	n	n	n	n	27.1	a
Ireland	A	m	m	m	m	m	m	m	m	m	m	m	m
	B	m	m	m	m	m	m	m	m	m	m	m	m
Italy	A	4.2	12.9	38.0	0.6	15.9	2.0	18.2	3.4	1.6	2.1	0.8	0.2
	B	31.4	68.6	a	a	a	a	a	a	a	a	a	a
Japan[1]	A	6.1	18.3	37.2	1.7	21.2	3.3	5.3	4.6	x(9)	x(9)	x(9)	2.4
	B	8.0	15.9	7.9	25.3	16.2	0.7	20.2	n	x(9)	x(9)	x(9)	5.9
Korea	A	5.2	20.2	23.0	2.5	27.2	2.8	7.0	2.1	4.1	2.3	3.7	a
	B	9.0	15.1	17.9	5.0	38.0	1.5	9.0	4.8	0.1	n	3.4	a
Luxembourg	A	m	m	m	m	m	m	m	m	m	m	m	m
	B	m	m	m	m	m	m	m	m	m	m	m	m
Mexico[4]	A	18.2	2.7	43.5	1.5	13.8	2.0	8.6	0.8	1.3	0.3	7.2	a
	B	a	2.5	28.0	10.0	38.0	1.5	6.9	0.4	a	0.1	12.7	a
Netherlands	A	17.0	6.7	34.3	2.5	10.5	2.5	21.2	1.0	2.3	0.2	1.6	0.1
	B	10.0	a	38.6	8.1	2.6	a	34.6	a	a	a	6.1	a
New Zealand	A	12.4	19.8	28.1	2.5	5.5	1.5	13.4	11.7	n	0.1	2.3	2.6
	B	25.1	13.2	21.1	14.1	3.4	2.6	11.0	0.5	0.4	n	7.8	0.9
Norway	A	20.9	6.8	22.6	3.2	8.3	1.4	25.4	1.2	1.3	0.2	4.1	4.6
	B	a	5.8	60.6	4.9	3.8	a	0.9	0.1	a	a	23.1	0.8
Poland	A	11.6	7.4	36.3	2.9	7.0	1.7	1.9	1.1	0.7	0.6	0.9	27.6
	B	100.0	a	a	a	a	a	a	a	a	a	a	a
Portugal	A	m	m	m	m	m	m	m	m	m	m	m	m
	B	m	m	m	m	m	m	m	m	m	m	m	m
Slovak Republic	A	18.0	5.4	28.8	7.2	17.8	4.2	9.2	2.2	2.2	0.6	4.4	a
	B	2.8	9.9	5.5	7.7	7.1	1.2	64.9	n	n	n	0.9	a
Spain	A	14.1	9.9	33.3	3.2	14.2	2.7	12.1	2.6	3.2	1.3	3.4	0.1
	B	4.8	7.7	27.4	13.2	23.8	0.6	11.5	n	n	n	10.7	0.2
Sweden	A	16.7	5.7	22.5	1.1	21.5	1.1	22.0	2.8	2.5	0.6	3.5	a
	B	2.5	12.8	12.6	13.7	26.0	4.1	11.8	0.1	0.1	n	16.2	a
Switzerland	A	11.9	12.6	30.8	1.8	14.1	1.4	11.7	3.5	3.9	1.0	6.5	0.7
	B	13.9	3.5	39.2	10.8	12.1	1.7	11.9	n	n	n	6.9	n
Turkey	A	22.5	10.1	21.5	2.4	11.6	4.2	8.6	2.0	4.9	2.8	0.8	8.7
	B	a	2.3	28.3	4.7	27.5	4.8	4.0	a	0.1	a	4.3	24.2
United Kingdom	A	11.2	16.8	29.2	1.3	10.5	1.1	11.9	6.5	5.2	1.4	5.0	a
	B	7.9	9.8	15.9	1.6	10.6	1.9	39.7	1.8	2.2	0.4	8.2	a
United States	A	13.1	14.2	42.6	2.4	6.4	2.3	9.5	3.9	1.5	0.9	3.2	0.1
	B	2.7	0.2	32.8	8.8	18.3	2.2	27.0	a	a	a	7.8	0.2
Country mean	*A*	*13.1*	*12.0*	*31.7*	*2.6*	*13.2*	*2.3*	*13.0*	*3.4*	*2.6*	*1.0*	*3.3*	*2.2*
	B	*13.0*	*8.8*	*24.1*	*9.2*	*15.8*	*1.8*	*17.7*	*n*	*n*	*n*	*7.5*	*1.4*
Israel	A	18.0	12.9	41.8	a	9.6	0.8	5.4	3.2	1.9	6.5	x(11)	a
	B	m	m	m	m	m	m	m	m	m	m	m	m

Note: Column 1 specifies the level of education, where A equals tertiary-type A and advanced research programmes, and B equals tertiary-type B programmes.
Note: x indicates that data are included in another column. The column reference is shown in brackets after "x". *e.g.,* x(2) means that data are included in column 2.
1. Year of reference 2000.
2. Excludes tertiary-type B second degree programmes.
3. All sciences included in life sciences.
4. Excludes tertiary-type A second degree programmes.
* See Annex 3 for notes (*www.oecd.org/edu/eag2003*).
Source: OECD.

Table A3.2

Percentage of tertiary qualifications awarded to females, by type of tertiary education and by subject category (2001)

A3

	All fields of study					Health and welfare		Life sciences, physical sciences and agriculture		Mathematics and computer science		Humanities, arts and education		Social sciences, business, law and services		Engineering, manufacturing and construction	
	Tertiary-type B (First degree)	Tertiary-type B (Second degree)	Tertiary-type A (First degree)	Tertiary-type A (Second degree)	Advanced research degrees	Tertiary-type B education	Tertiary-type A and advanced research programmes	Tertiary-type B education	Tertiary-type A and advanced research programmes	Tertiary-type B education	Tertiary-type A and advanced research programmes	Tertiary-type B education	Tertiary-type A and advanced research programmes	Tertiary-type B education	Tertiary-type A and advanced research programmes	Tertiary-type B education	Tertiary-type A and advanced research programmes
	(1)	(2)	(3)	(4)	(5)	(6)	(7)	(8)	(9)	(10)	(11)	(12)	(13)	(14)	(15)	(16)	(17)
Australia[1]	m	m	57	54	41	m	76	m	51	m	26	m	71	m	52	m	22
Austria	58	79	49	n	37	80	61	21	52	28	18	80	67	80	51	11	17
Belgium	62	m	50	53	32	80	59	42	42	13	24	70	65	60	53	15	20
Canada	m	m	m	m	m	m	m	m	m	m	m	m	m	m	m	m	m
Czech Republic	72	a	51	54	35	90	70	58	46	49	11	60	71	71	52	21	30
Denmark	35	94	65	48	42	n	82	29	46	13	30	68	69	47	43	31	23
Finland	63	a	63	55	48	89	86	53	52	50	35	74	78	68	67	26	19
France	54	a	58	52	43	81	61	47	50	19	32	57	74	68	60	13	24
Germany	63	a	48	a	35	81	58	14	41	19	24	88	68	51	44	7	21
Greece	a	a	57	56	a	m	m	m	m	m	m	m	m	m	m	m	m
Hungary	a	m	62	59	m	73	77	m	45	60	21	m	74	70	59	24	28
Iceland	47	a	65	66	a	a	87	a	60	26	19	56	80	53	57	a	21
Ireland	m	m	m	m	m	m	m	m	m	m	m	m	m	m	m	m	m
Italy	57	a	56	57	51	a	61	a	52	a	52	56	81	a	55	a	28
Japan	67	a	39	25	23	78	53	51	31	x(8)	x(9)	84	67	76	31	16	10
Korea	54	37	47	31	24	82	56	46	43	35	44	71	70	56	41	32	22
Luxembourg	m	m	m	m	m	m	m	m	m	m	m	m	m	m	m	m	m
Mexico	42	a	52	m	35	81	62	43	48	47	43	66	65	52	56	21	24
Netherlands	61	a	54	66	31	83	74	a	37	12	16	85	71	49	49	3	12
New Zealand	62	68	62	58	41	84	80	44	47	27	29	70	72	63	54	25	32
Norway	49	a	62	53	34	97	82	a	46	33	19	67	73	55	48	1	22
Poland	84	a	63	70	42	a	67	a	64	a	45	84	77	a	65	a	24
Portugal	m	m	m	m	m	m	m	m	m	m	m	m	m	m	m	m	m
Slovak Republic	80	a	52	a	40	92	69	96	46	a	15	64	70	64	52	39	31
Spain	53	a	59	m	43	82	76	25	52	25	32	70	72	67	60	18	28
Sweden	53	a	60	90	39	95	79	65	53	42	39	50	75	68	59	26	28
Switzerland	44	40	43	28	34	79	55	7	36	15	14	68	60	38	36	7	12
Turkey	47	a	41	39	38	57	55	52	45	31	40	76	46	55	38	26	24
United Kingdom	61	x(1)	55	55	40	86	73	43	53	26	28	60	67	54	54	13	19
United States	59	a	57	57	45	87	75	36	52	40	33	77	69	64	54	14	21
Country mean	58	64	55	51	38	79	69	43	48	31	29	70	70	60	52	18	22
Israel	m	a	61	60	47	m	71	m	56	m	34	m	81	m	58	m	23

Note: x indicates that data are included in another column. The column reference is shown in brackets after "x". *e.g.,* x(2) means that data are included in column 2.
1. Year of reference 2000.
* See Annex 3 for notes *(www.oecd.org/edu/eag2003)*.
Source: OECD.

OECD COUNTRIES

NON-OECD COUNTRY

INDICATOR A4: READING LITERACY OF 4TH-GRADE STUDENTS

A4

- Fourth-grade students in Sweden perform significantly higher than their counterparts in all other OECD countries. Seven other countries (the Czech Republic, England, Germany, Hungary, Italy, the Netherlands and the United States) still perform significantly above the OECD mean of 529 points, with scores ranging from 537 to 554 points.

- With England and the United States as notable exceptions, the data show that high mean scores can be achieved along with relatively small differences among students within countries.

Chart A4.1

Multiple comparisons of mean performance of 4th-grade students on the PIRLS reading literacy scale (2001)

	Mean	S.E.	Years of formal schooling	Average age	Sweden	Netherlands[1]	England[1]	Hungary	United States[1]	Italy	Germany	Czech Republic	New Zealand	Scotland[1]	France	Greece[2]	Slovak Republic	Iceland	Norway	Turkey
Mean					561	554	553	543	542	541	539	537	529	528	525	524	518	512	499	449
S.E.					(2.2)	(2.5)	(3.4)	(2.2)	(3.8)	(2.4)	(1.9)	(2.3)	(3.6)	(3.6)	(2.4)	(3.5)	(2.8)	(1.2)	(2.9)	(3.5)
Years of formal schooling					4	4	5	4	4	4	4	4	5	5	4	4	4	4	4	4
Average age					10.8	10.3	10.2	10.7	10.2	9.8	10.5	10.5	10.1	9.8	10.1	9.9	10.3	9.7	10.0	10.2
Sweden	561	(2.2)	4	10.8	□	▲	▲	▲	▲	▲	▲	▲	▲	▲	▲	▲	▲	▲	▲	▲
Netherlands[1]	554	(2.5)	4	10.3	▽	□	○	▲	▲	▲	▲	▲	▲	▲	▲	▲	▲	▲	▲	▲
England[1]	553	(3.4)	5	10.2	▽	○	□	▲	▲	▲	▲	▲	▲	▲	▲	▲	▲	▲	▲	▲
Hungary	543	(2.2)	4	10.7	▽	▽	▽	□	○	○	○	○	▲	▲	▲	▲	▲	▲	▲	▲
United States[1]	542	(3.8)	4	10.2	▽	▽	▽	○	□	○	○	○	▲	▲	▲	▲	▲	▲	▲	▲
Italy	541	(2.4)	4	9.8	▽	▽	▽	○	○	□	○	○	▲	▲	▲	▲	▲	▲	▲	▲
Germany	539	(1.9)	4	10.5	▽	▽	▽	○	○	○	□	○	▲	▲	▲	▲	▲	▲	▲	▲
Czech Republic	537	(2.3)	4	10.5	▽	▽	▽	○	○	○	○	□	▲	▲	▲	▲	▲	▲	▲	▲
New Zealand	529	(3.6)	5	10.1	▽	▽	▽	▽	▽	▽	▽	▽	□	○	○	○	▲	▲	▲	▲
Scotland[1]	528	(3.6)	5	9.8	▽	▽	▽	▽	▽	▽	▽	▽	○	□	○	○	▲	▲	▲	▲
France	525	(2.4)	4	10.1	▽	▽	▽	▽	▽	▽	▽	▽	○	○	□	○	○	▲	▲	▲
Greece[2]	524	(3.5)	4	9.9	▽	▽	▽	▽	▽	▽	▽	▽	○	○	○	□	○	▲	▲	▲
Slovak Republic	518	(2.8)	4	10.3	▽	▽	▽	▽	▽	▽	▽	▽	▽	▽	○	○	□	○	▲	▲
Iceland	512	(1.2)	4	9.7	▽	▽	▽	▽	▽	▽	▽	▽	▽	▽	▽	▽	○	□	▲	▲
Norway	499	(2.9)	4	10.0	▽	▽	▽	▽	▽	▽	▽	▽	▽	▽	▽	▽	▽	▽	□	▲
Turkey	449	(3.5)	4	10.2	▽	▽	▽	▽	▽	▽	▽	▽	▽	▽	▽	▽	▽	▽	▽	□

Instructions:
Read across the row for a country to compare performance with the countries listed along the top of the chart. The symbols indicate whether the mean performance of the country in the row is significantly higher than that of the comparison country, significantly lower than that of the comparison country, or if there is no statistically significant difference between the mean performance of the two countries.

▲ Mean performance statistically significantly higher than in comparison country.
○ No statistically significant difference from comparison country.
▽ Mean performance statistically significantly lower than in comparison country.

Mean performance statistically significantly above the country mean
Not statistically significantly different from the country mean
Mean performance statistically significantly below the country mean

1. Met guidelines for sample participation rates only after replacement schools were included.
2. National defined population covers less than 95 per cent of national desired population.
Countries are ranked in descending order of mean performance on the PIRLS reading literacy scale.
Source: IEA Progress in Reading Literacy Study (PIRLS) 2001. See Annex 3 for notes (*www.oecd.org/edu/eag2003*).

Policy context

The ability to read, understand and use information is at the heart of academic and personal development. Reading literacy is the foundation for learning across school subjects, and it equips individuals with the ability to participate more fully in their communities and society, which is fundamental for the well being of nations. It is one of the most important abilities that students acquire and develop as they progress through their school years. Data from the International Association for the Evaluation of Educational Achievement's (IEA) Progress in Reading Literacy Study (PIRLS) provide a profile of reading literacy skills of students during the early years of schooling, at the 4th-grade level. Indicator A5 complements this profile with information on reading literacy skills among 15-year-olds.

This indicator provides a profile of the reading literacy of 4th-grade students in terms of mean performance and variation in performance.

Evidence and explanations

PIRLS and PISA define reading literacy as an interactive, constructive process and emphasise the importance of students' ability to use reading for different purposes (see also Box A4.1). This indicator profiles 4th-grade students' performance in reading literacy in several ways: by examining countries' mean performance, distribution of performance within countries, and performance differences between males and females.

Mean performance of countries

Examining countries' mean scores in a given subject can be useful for obtaining an overall indication of how an education system is performing at a certain grade and in a certain area.

Already at the 4th grade level, countries differ significantly in the reading performance of their students...

At the same time, if one country's scores are higher than those of another country, it cannot automatically be inferred that the schools in the former are more effective, since learning starts well before school and occurs in a range of institutional and out-of-school settings. Nonetheless, if a country's scores are higher, one can legitimately conclude that the cumulative impact of all learning experiences in that country, from early childhood until the point in testing, has resulted in more desirable outcomes in the subject areas assessed.

On the PIRLS reading literacy scale, 4th-grade students in Sweden perform significantly higher than their counterparts in all other OECD countries, with a mean score that is 32 points higher than the OECD average (Chart A4.1 and Table A4.1). Seven other countries (the Czech Republic, England, Germany, Hungary, Italy, the Netherlands and the United States) still perform significantly above the OECD mean of 529 points, with scores ranging from 537 to 554 points. Four countries (France, Greece, New Zealand and Scotland) have average scores that are not significantly different from the OECD mean, and another four (Iceland, Norway, the Slovak Republic and Turkey) score significantly below the OECD mean.

In interpreting these results, it needs to be taken into account that, unlike in PISA, the samples for PIRLS were grade-based and resulted in considerable differences in the average age of students across participating OECD countries.

Box A4.1. Reading literacy in PISA and PIRLS – Definitions

PISA and PIRLS both seek to inform about the reading literacy performance of students. However, differences in curricular demands and developmental expectations placed on 9-year-olds and 15-year-olds result in differences in the approach. As 9-year-olds commonly have just reached the end of their early reading instruction, PIRLS focuses on the acquisition of reading literacy. By contrast the focus of PISA is on the extent to which students who are approaching the end of compulsory education have acquired the capacity to access, manage, integrate, evaluate and reflect on written information, as the foundation for further learning and their active and full participation in modern societies. In short, while the focus at the beginning of schooling is on learning to read, the focus towards the end of compulsory education is on using reading for learning.

Similarities and distinctions in definitions of reading literacy

Both PISA and PIRLS view reading as an interactive, constructive process and emphasise the importance of students' ability to reflect on reading and to use reading for different purposes.

PISA defines reading literacy as *understanding, using and reflecting on written texts, in order to achieve one's goals, to develop one's knowledge and potential and to participate in society.* This implies the active and interactive role of the reader in gaining meaning from written texts. It also recognises the full scope of situations in which reading literacy plays a role for young adults, from private to public, from school to work, from active citizenship to lifelong learning. It spells out the idea that literacy enables the fulfilment of individual aspirations – from defined aspirations such as gaining an educational qualification or obtaining a job, to those less immediate goals which enrich and extend one's personal life.

In a similar way, PIRLS defines reading literacy as: …*the ability to understand and use those written language forms required by society and/or valued by the individual. Young readers can construct meaning from a variety of texts. They read to learn, to participate in a community of readers, and for enjoyment.*

Both definitions take into account the range of material students choose and are required to read. By doing so, they suggest that reading is not a unitary skill, but rather a set of processes, approaches, and skills that vary among readers, text types, and purposes or situations for reading. While social, personal, and curricular elements of reading literacy are also emphasised in both definitions, the developmental differences between the two age groups are apparent. For 9-year-olds, PIRLS emphasises the typical environment in which students read. While PISA stresses students' readiness to participate in larger society, PIRLS emphasises students' ability to participate in "communities of readers…."

Similarities and distinctions in the reporting of reading literacy

The reporting scales in PISA emphasise the type of reading tasks, requiring students to demonstrate their proficiency in retrieving information, understanding texts, interpreting them, reflecting on the content and form of texts in relation to their own knowledge of the world, and evaluating and arguing their own point of view. The reporting scales in PIRLS emphasise purposes for reading and identify two of the most common for this age group: reading for literary experience and reading to acquire and use information.

Source: Knowledge and Skills for Life – A New Framework For Assessment (OECD, 1999) and Framework and Specifications for PIRLS Assessment 2001 (International Study Center at Boston College, 2nd edition, March 2001).

For example, students in the best performing country, Sweden, were a year older than students in Iceland and Italy and almost a year older than students in France, Greece, New Zealand and Norway. Among the 11 countries that participated in both PISA and PIRLS, the average age of students explains 49 per cent of the cross-country performance differences on the PIRLS scale which is considerable and must be accounted for when comparing performance levels across countries.

In addition to the overall reading literacy scale, data from PIRLS also are reported in terms of two subscales, which are based on the *purposes* dimension of the PIRLS assessment framework: reading for literary purposes and reading for informational purposes. Examining countries' mean performance on these subscales is important in that it can shed light on countries' relative strengths

...as well as in terms of performance patterns across two subscales of reading.

Chart A4.2

Mean performance of 4th-grade students on the overall PIRLS reading literacy scale and the PIRLS reading literacy subscales (2001)

▨ Mean performance statistically significantly above the country mean
▨ Not statistically significantly different from the country mean
▨ Mean performance statistically significantly below the country mean

Overall PIRLS reading literacy scale			PIRLS reading for literary purposes subscale			PIRLS reading for informational purposes subscale		
Sweden	561	(2.2)	Sweden	559	(2.4)	Sweden	559	(2.2)
Netherlands[1]	554	(2.5)	England[1]	559	(3.9)	Netherlands[1]	553	(2.6)
England[1]	553	(3.4)	Netherlands[1]	552	(2.5)	England[1]	546	(3.6)
Hungary	543	(2.2)	United States[1]	550	(3.8)	Germany	538	(1.9)
United States[1]	542	(3.8)	Hungary	548	(2.0)	Hungary	537	(2.2)
Italy	541	(2.4)	Italy	543	(2.7)	Czech Republic	536	(2.7)
Germany	539	(1.9)	Germany	537	(1.9)	Italy	536	(2.4)
Czech Republic	537	(2.3)	Czech Republic	535	(2.3)	France	533	(2.5)
New Zealand	529	(3.6)	New Zealand	531	(3.9)	United States[1]	533	(3.7)
Country mean	*529*	*(0.7)*	*Country mean*	*531*	*(0.7)*	Scotland[1]	527	(3.6)
Scotland[1]	528	(3.6)	Scotland[1]	529	(3.5)	*Country mean*	*527*	*(0.7)*
France	525	(2.4)	Greece[2]	528	(3.3)	New Zealand	525	(3.8)
Greece[2]	524	(3.5)	Iceland	520	(1.3)	Slovak Republic	522	(2.7)
Slovak Republic	518	(2.8)	France	518	(2.6)	Greece[2]	521	(3.7)
Iceland	512	(1.2)	Slovak Republic	512	(2.6)	Iceland	504	(1.5)
Norway	499	(2.9)	Norway	506	(2.7)	Norway	492	(2.8)
Turkey	449	(3.5)	Turkey	448	(3.4)	Turkey	452	(3.8)

1. Met guidelines for sample participation rates only after replacement schools were included.
2. National defined population covers less than 95 per cent of national desired population.
Countries are ranked in descending order of mean performance of each reading literacy scale.
Source: IEA Progress in Reading Literacy Study (PIRLS) 2001. See Annex 3 for notes (*www.oecd.org/edu/eag2003*).

A4

and weaknesses. While most countries perform similarly relative to the OECD mean on both subscales, there are a few exceptions (Chart A4.2). In the United States, on items related to reading for literary purposes, students perform significantly above the OECD mean, whereas on items related to reading for informational purposes, their performance is not significantly different from the OECD mean. In France and the Slovak Republic, the situation is reversed. In these countries, students perform relatively better when reading for informational purposes. This is particularly pronounced in France, where students are significantly below the mean on the literary purposes subscale, but significantly above the mean on the informational purposes subscale.

Chart A4.3

Distribution of performance of 4th-grade students on the PIRLS reading literacy scale (2001)

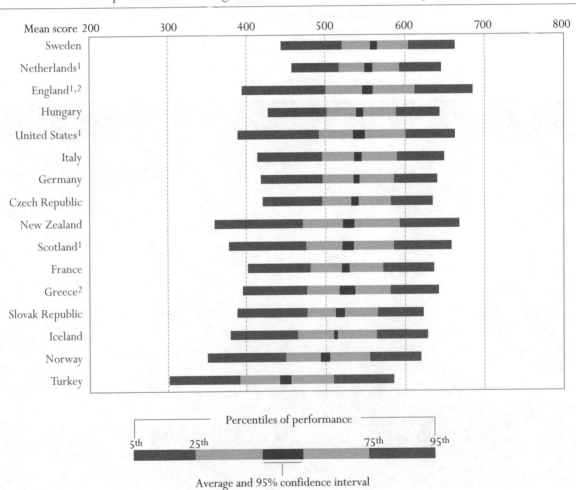

1. Met guidelines for sample participation rates only after replacement schools were included.
2. National defined population covers less than 95 per cent of national desired population.
Countries are ranked in descending order of mean performance on the PIRLS reading literacy scale.
Source: IEA Progress in Reading Literacy Study (PIRLS) 2001. Table A4.1. See Annex 3 for notes *(www.oecd.org/edu/eag2003).*

Distribution of performance

While mean scores are useful for obtaining a general picture of performance, they often mask significant variation in the performance of students within countries. In this indicator, within-country variation is measured by the inter-quartile range, or the difference between the mean scores of students at the 75th percentile and those of students at the 25th percentile *i.e.* the range of scores which covers the performance of the middle 50 per cent of students.

In PIRLS, the degree of within-country variation in performance in reading literacy varies among countries, with the interquartile range varying from 76 points in the Netherlands to 121 points in New Zealand (Table A4.1 and Chart A4.3). In the latter country, as well as in Turkey and England, the difference between students in the top quarter and those in the bottom quartile is greater than or equal to the difference between the averages of students in the highest- and lowest-performing countries.

It also is useful to compare a country's range of performance with its average performance, as education systems do not only seek to achieve high performance overall, but to do so for all students. With a few notable exceptions (*e.g.,* England and the United States), the data show that high mean scores can be achieved along with relatively small differences among students within countries. Three countries (Hungary, the Netherlands and Sweden) have among the highest relative means in reading literacy and lowest relative interquartile ranges. Conversely, among the countries performing significantly below the OECD mean, only the Slovak Republic has an interquartile range that is relatively small, below the OECD mean.

Definitions and methodologies

The PIRLS target population was students in the upper of the two adjacent grades that contained the largest proportion of nine year-old students at the time of testing. Beyond the age criterion embedded in the definition, the target population should represent that point in the curriculum where students have essentially finished learning the basic reading skills and will focus more on "reading to learn" in the subsequent grades. Thus the PIRLS target grade was expected to be the 4th grade.

Note that the OECD average, as presented in this indicator, is based only on the 16 OECD countries that participated in PIRLS. The Canadian provinces of Ontario and Quebec also took part in the study but as these represent less than 65 per cent of Canada as a whole, Canada is not shown in the tables and charts. The OECD mean is equal to 529 score points on the PIRLS scale. The average age of the students assessed ranges from 9.7 years in Iceland to 10.8 years in Sweden.

For additional notes on methodology, see *www.oecd.org/edu/eag2003* .

Some countries achieve high performance standards for the vast majority of students...

...while in other countries there are large disparities in the performance of students.

The performance scores are based on the Progress in Reading Literacy Study (PIRLS) that was undertaken by the International Association for the Evaluation of Educational Achievement (IEA) during 2001.

Table A4.1
Mean performance and variation in performance in reading literacy of 4th-grade students (2001)
Performance of 4th-grade students on the PIRLS reading literacy scale, by percentile

| | | Mean | | Years of formal schooling | Average age | Percentiles | | | | | | | | Inter-quartile range[1] |
| | | | | | | 5th | | 25th | | 75th | | 95th | | |
		Mean score	S.E.			Score	S.E.	Score	S.E.	Score	S.E.	Score	S.E.	
Czech Republic	▲	537	(2.3)	4	10.5	421	(5.2)	496	(1.9)	582	(3.0)	634	(4.7)	86
England[2,3]	▲	553	(3.4)	5	10.2	395	(6.3)	501	(4.4)	612	(4.5)	685	(5.3)	112
France		525	(2.4)	4	10.1	403	(5.2)	481	(2.8)	573	(1.8)	636	(4.5)	91
Germany	▲	539	(1.9)	4	10.5	419	(3.9)	497	(3.1)	586	(1.9)	640	(1.9)	90
Greece[3]		524	(3.5)	4	9.9	396	(4.0)	477	(5.3)	582	(3.1)	642	(4.1)	105
Hungary	▲	543	(2.2)	4	10.7	428	(4.4)	502	(2.4)	589	(2.9)	643	(3.8)	87
Iceland	▼	512	(1.2)	4	9.7	380	(3.3)	466	(2.8)	564	(2.3)	629	(5.4)	99
Italy	▲	541	(2.4)	4	9.8	415	(6.5)	496	(3.2)	590	(3.1)	649	(2.7)	94
Netherlands[2]	▲	554	(2.5)	4	10.3	458	(4.1)	517	(3.8)	593	(2.9)	645	(3.6)	76
New Zealand		529	(3.6)	5	10.1	360	(4.7)	472	(5.9)	593	(4.5)	668	(5.1)	121
Norway	▼	499	(2.9)	4	10.0	351	(5.0)	450	(4.1)	556	(6.4)	620	(4.4)	105
Scotland[2]		528	(3.6)	5	9.8	378	(5.1)	476	(6.0)	586	(2.7)	658	(6.1)	110
Slovak Republic	▼	518	(2.8)	4	10.3	389	(9.7)	477	(2.7)	566	(1.8)	623	(3.9)	88
Sweden	▲	561	(2.2)	4	10.8	445	(4.5)	521	(4.7)	605	(1.7)	663	(2.1)	84
Turkey	▼	449	(3.5)	4	10.2	302	(3.9)	392	(4.0)	510	(4.1)	586	(6.0)	118
United States[2]	▲	542	(3.8)	4	10.2	389	(8.9)	492	(4.7)	601	(4.2)	663	(2.8)	108
Country mean		*529*	*(0.7)*	*4*	*10.2*	*396*		*482*		*581*		*643*		*98*

▲ Mean performance statistically significantly above the country mean

▼ Mean performance statistically significantly below the country mean

1. Difference between the scores at the 25th and 75th percentiles.
2. Met guidelines for sample participation rates only after replacement schools were included.
3. National Defined Population covers less than 95 per cent of National Desired Population.
Source: IEA Progress in Reading Literacy Study (PIRLS) 2001.

INDICATOR A5: READING LITERACY OF 15-YEAR-OLDS

A5

- On average among OECD countries, 10 per cent of 15-year-olds have acquired Level 5 literacy skills, which involve evaluation of information and building of hypotheses, drawing on specialised knowledge, and accommodating concepts contrary to expectations. However, this percentage varies from 19 per cent in Finland and New Zealand to below 1 per cent in Mexico.

- Six countries (the Czech Republic, Germany, Greece, Hungary, Italy and the United States) performed relatively better in PIRLS than in PISA. In the first four cases, scores were above the OECD average in PIRLS and are below the OECD average in PISA. Three countries performed relatively better in PISA than in PIRLS: Iceland, New Zealand and Norway. France and Sweden performed similarly relative to other countries on both assessments.

Chart A5.1

Proficiency of 15-year-olds on the PISA reading literacy scale (2000)
Percentage of 15-year-olds at each level of proficiency on the PISA reading literacy scale

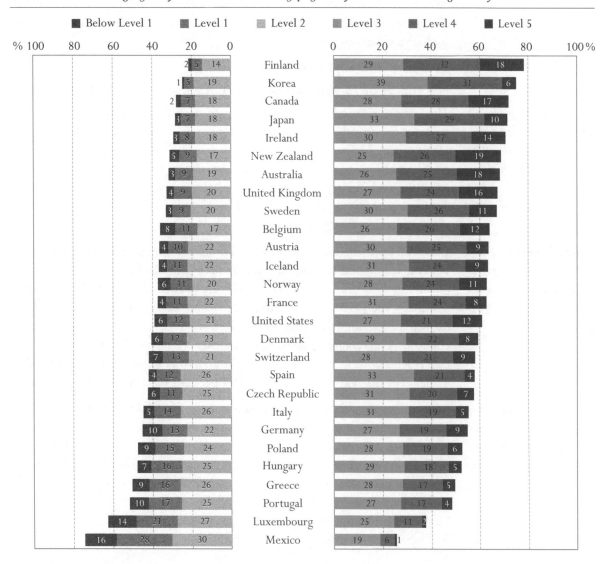

Countries are ranked in descending order of the percentage of students at Levels 3, 4 and 5 on the PISA reading literacy scale.
Source: OECD PISA database, 2001. Table A5.1. See Annex 3 for notes on methodology *(www.oecd.org/edu/eag2003)* and *www.pisa.oecd.org.*

A5

This indicator shows the performance of 15-year-olds in reading literacy.

Policy context

The capacity of students approaching the end of compulsory education to access, manage, integrate, evaluate and reflect on written information is a foundation for further learning as well as their full participation in modern societies.

This indicator shows the performance of 15-year-olds on tasks based on a concept of reading literacy that goes beyond the notion of decoding written material and literal comprehension. Reading in PISA incorporates understanding and reflecting on texts. Literacy involves the ability to use written information to fulfil goals, and the consequent ability of complex modern societies to use written information effectively.

When Indicators A4 and A5 are examined together, they provide a context for examining improvements in reading literacy performance between the primary school age and the end of compulsory education, even if the PISA and PIRLS studies are somewhat different in orientation and even if the measurement of performance at two age levels at a single point in time can only be a rough proxy for longitudinal progress.

Evidence and explanations

Percentage of 15-year-olds proficient at each level of reading literacy

PISA provides an interpretative framework for performance levels in reading literacy.

This indicator examines reading literacy in several ways (see Box A5.1 for an explanation of reading literacy in PISA). First, it describes proficiency in terms of the range of scores that 15-year-olds achieve in each country. Proficiency in reading is examined at five levels, each representing tasks of increasing complexity, with Level 5 being the highest. Second, this indicator describes performance in terms of the mean scores achieved by 15-year-olds and the distribution of scores among student populations.

Ten per cent of 15-year-olds in OECD countries have acquired Level 5 literacy skills …

Chart A5.1 presents an overall profile of proficiency on the reading literacy scale with the length of the coloured components of the bars showing the percentage of 15-year-olds proficient at each level (see Box A5.2). As can be seen from the chart, the percentage of students reaching each level of literacy and the patterns of distribution among the levels varies from country to country. Across countries, on average, 10 per cent of students reach proficiency Level 5, 32 per cent reach at least Level 4 (*i.e.*, Levels 4 and 5), 61 per cent reach at least Level 3, 82 per cent reach at least Level 2, and 94 per cent reach at least Level 1.

…but this proportion ranges across countries from 19 to less than 1 per cent.

Examining individual countries' performance by proficiency level is revealing: In five countries (Australia, Canada, Finland, New Zealand and the United Kingdom), 15 per cent or more of students reach the highest level of proficiency in reading literacy. In Belgium, Ireland and the United States, a significant percentage of students also reach proficiency level 5 (between 12 and 15 per cent). However, only five per cent or less of the students in Brazil, Greece, Latvia, Luxembourg, Mexico, Portugal, Spain and the Russian Federation reach the highest level of proficiency.

A5

Box A5.1. What is reading literacy in PISA?

Reading literacy is the ability to understand, use and reflect on written texts in order to achieve one's goals, to develop one's own knowledge and potential, and to participate effectively in society. This definition goes beyond the notion that reading means decoding written material and literal comprehension. Rather, reading also incorporates understanding and reflecting on texts, for a variety of reasons and in a variety of contexts. PISA's assessment of reading literacy reflects three dimensions: aspect of reading task; form of reading material; and the use for which the text is constructed.

What scales are reported? PISA's assessment of reading literacy is reported on three scales. A "retrieving information" scale is based on students' ability to locate information in a text. An "interpreting" scale is based on the ability to construct meaning and draw inferences from written information. A "reflection and evaluation" scale is based on students' ability to relate a text to their knowledge, ideas and experiences. In addition, a reading literacy scale summarises the results from the three reading scales. Indicator A5 focuses on the latter scale only which is referred to as the "reading literacy scale".

What do the scale scores mean? The scores on each scale represent degrees of proficiency in each dimension or aspect of reading literacy. For example, a low score on a scale indicates that a student has limited skills, whereas a high score indicates that a student has advanced skills in this area.

What are proficiency levels? In an attempt to capture this progression of difficulty, each of the reading literacy scales is divided into five levels based on the type of knowledge and skills students need to demonstrate at a particular level. Students at a particular level not only demonstrate the knowledge and skills associated with that level but also the proficiencies defined by lower levels. For instance, all students proficient at Level 3 are also proficient at Levels 1 and 2.

Although there is a general tendency among countries with a high proportion of 15-year-olds scoring at Level 5 to have fewer students below the lowest level of proficiency (see Finland, for example), this is not always the case. Belgium and the United States, for example, stand out in showing an above-average share of performers at the highest proficiency level while, at the same time, showing an above-average proportion of students scoring below Level 1 (Table A5.1).

A large proportion of high performers typically means fewer low performers, but in some countries, there are large disparities.

Half of all 15-year-olds in Finland and at least 40 per cent of students in five other countries reach at least Level 4 on the reading literacy scale. With the exception of Luxembourg and Mexico, at least one in five students in each OECD country reaches at least Level 4. In Brazil, the country with the lowest overall performance in reading literacy, only about 4 per cent of students score at Level 4 or above.

A5

Box A5.2. What can students at each proficiency level do and what scores are associated with the levels?

Students proficient at *Level 5 (over 625 points)* are capable of completing sophisticated reading tasks, such as managing information that is difficult to find in unfamiliar texts; showing detailed understanding of such texts and inferring which information in the text is relevant to the task; and being able to evaluate critically and build hypotheses, draw on specialised knowledge, and accommodate concepts that may be contrary to expectations.

Students proficient at *Level 4 (553 to 625 points)* are capable of difficult reading tasks, such as locating embedded information, construing meaning from nuances of language and critically evaluating a text.

Students proficient at *Level 3 (481 to 552 points)* are capable of reading tasks of moderate complexity, such as locating multiple pieces of information, drawing links between different parts of the text, and relating it to familiar everyday knowledge.

Students proficient at *Level 2 (408 to 480 points)* are capable of basic reading tasks, such as locating straightforward information, making low-level inferences of various types, deciding what a well-defined part of the text means, and using some outside knowledge to understand it.

Students proficient at *Level 1 (335 to 407 points)* are capable of completing only the least complex reading tasks developed for PISA, such as locating a single piece of information, identifying the main theme of a text or making a simple connection with everyday knowledge.

Students performing *below Level 1 (below 335 points)* are not able to show routinely the most basic type of knowledge and skills that PISA seeks to measure. These students may have serious difficulties in using reading literacy as an effective tool to advance and extend their knowledge and skills in other areas.

In one third of OECD countries, more than two thirds of 15-year-olds reach at least Level 3.

In one third of OECD countries, between 67 and 79 per cent of 15-year-old students are proficient at least at Level 3 on the reading literacy scale: Australia, Canada, Finland, Ireland, Japan, Korea, New Zealand, Sweden and the United Kingdom. Using these nine countries to explore the question "is the pattern of proficiency similar across countries?" several patterns emerge. In Canada and Finland, for instance, relatively large proportions of students reach Level 5 and at least 90 per cent of students in each country reach at least Level 2 - these countries show strong results across the reading literacy scale. In Australia, Ireland, New Zealand and the United Kingdom, there are large numbers of students at the highest level, but over 10 per cent of students perform at or below Level 1. These countries perform well in getting students to higher levels of proficiency but succeed less well than Canada or Finland in reducing the proportion with low skills. The opposite is true in Korea, where less than 6 per cent of students are at Level 1 or below, but where a below-average proportion (6 per cent) reach the highest level of proficiency (Table A5.1).

A5

In every OECD country, at least half of all students are at Level 2 or higher. Interestingly, in Spain, where only 4 per cent of students reach Level 5, an above-average 84 per cent reach at least Level 2. However, over 40 per cent of students in Spain have Level 2 as their highest proficiency level (Table A5.1).

Reading literacy, as defined in PISA, focuses on the knowledge and skills required to apply "reading to learn" rather than on the technical skills acquired in "learning to read". Since comparatively few young adults in OECD countries have not acquired technical reading skills, PISA does not therefore seek to measure such things as the extent to which 15-year-old students are fluent readers or how well they spell or recognise words. In line with most contemporary views about reading literacy, PISA focuses on measuring the extent to which individuals are able to construct, expand and reflect on the meaning of what they have read in a wide range of texts both within and beyond school. The simplest reading tasks that can still be associated with this notion of reading literacy are those at Level 1. Students proficient at this level are capable of completing only the least complex reading tasks developed for PISA, such as locating a single piece of information, identifying the main theme of a text or making a simple connection with everyday knowledge.

The simplest tasks in PISA require students to do more than just read words fluently.

Students performing below 335 points, *i.e.,* below Level 1, are not capable of the most basic type of reading that PISA seeks to measure. This does not mean that they have no literacy skills. In fact, most of these students can probably read in a technical sense, and the majority of them (54 per cent on average among OECD countries) are able to solve successfully at least 10 per cent of the non-multiple choice reading tasks in PISA 2000 (and 6 per cent correctly solve one-quarter of them). Nonetheless, their pattern of answers in the assessment is such that they would be expected to solve fewer than half of the tasks in a test made up of items drawn solely from Level 1, and therefore perform below Level 1. Such students show serious difficulties in using reading literacy as an effective tool to advance and extend their knowledge and skills in other areas. Students with literacy skills below Level 1 may, therefore, be at risk not only of difficulties in their initial transition from education to work but also of failure to benefit from further education and learning opportunities throughout life.

While students below Level 1 may have the technical capacity to read, they may face serious difficulties in future life…

Education systems with large proportions of students performing below, or even at, Level 1 should be concerned that significant numbers of their students may not be acquiring the necessary literacy knowledge and skills to benefit sufficiently from their educational opportunities. This situation is even more troublesome in light of the extensive evidence suggesting that it is difficult in later life to compensate for learning gaps in initial education. Adult literacy skills and participation in continuing education and training are strongly related, even after controlling for other characteristics affecting participation in training.

…and, along with those at Level 1, may not acquire the necessary literacy skills to sufficiently benefit from educational opportunities.

In the combined OECD area, 12 per cent of students perform at Level 1, and 6 per cent below Level 1, but there are wide differences among countries. In Finland and Korea, only around 5 per cent of students perform at Level 1, and less than 2 per cent below it, but these countries are exceptions. In all other

The percentage of students at or below Level 1 varies widely, from a few per cent to nearly half…

OECD countries, between 9 and 44 per cent of students perform at or below Level 1. Over 2 per cent and, in half of the OECD countries over 5 per cent, perform below Level 1 (Table A5.1).

...and, in some countries, a considerable minority do not reach Level 1.

The countries with 20 per cent or more of students at Level 1 or below are, respectively, Brazil, Hungary, Germany, Greece, Latvia, Liechtenstein, Luxembourg, Mexico, Poland, Portugal, the Russian Federation and Switzerland. In Brazil, Germany, Latvia, Luxembourg, Mexico and Portugal, between close to 10 and 23 per cent of students do not reach Level 1, *i.e.,* are unable routinely to show the most basic skills that PISA seeks to measure. This is most remarkable in the case of Germany, which has the relatively high figure of 9 per cent of its students performing at Level 5 (Table A5.1).

National means and distribution of performance in reading literacy

Average scores can usefully summarise country performances...

Another way to summarise student performance and to compare the relative standing of countries in terms of student performance in PISA 2000 is to display the mean scores for students in each country. To the extent that high average performance at age 15 can be considered predictive of a highly skilled future workforce, countries with high average performance will have an important economic and social advantage. It should be noted, however, that average performance charts often mask significant variation in performance within countries, reflecting different performance among many different groups of students.

...but mask wide differences in student performance within countries.

As in previous international studies of student performance, such as the Third International Mathematics and Science Study (TIMSS), only around one-tenth of PISA's total variation in student performance lies between countries and can, therefore, be captured through a comparison of country averages. The remaining variation of student performance occurs within countries, *i.e.,* between educational programmes, between schools, and between students within schools. Thus, this indicator also presents information on the distribution of reading literacy scores, examining the range of performance between the top and bottom quarter of students in each country.

Finland shows unparalleled overall performance, almost two-thirds of a proficiency level ahead of the OECD average.

On the reading literacy scale, students from Finland perform on average higher than students from any other country participating in the study (see Chart A5.2). Their mean score, 546 points, is almost two-thirds of a proficiency level above the OECD average of 500 points (or in statistical terms, almost half the international standard deviation above the mean). Twelve other countries, Australia, Austria, Belgium, Canada, Iceland, Ireland, Japan, Korea, the Netherlands, New Zealand, Sweden and the United Kingdom, score significantly above the OECD mean. Five countries perform at or about the OECD mean, and 14 countries, including the four non-OECD countries, perform significantly below the OECD mean.

Chart A5.2

Multiple comparisons of mean performance on the PISA reading literacy scale (2000)

A5

	Mean	S.E.	Finland	Canada	New Zealand	Australia	Ireland	Korea	United Kingdom	Japan	Sweden	Austria	Belgium	Iceland	Norway	France	United States	Denmark	Switzerland	Spain	Czech Republic	Italy	Germany	Liechtenstein	Hungary	Poland	Greece	Portugal	Russian Federation	Latvia	Luxembourg	Mexico	Brazil
			546	534	529	528	527	525	523	522	516	507	507	507	505	505	504	497	494	493	492	487	484	483	480	479	474	470	462	458	441	422	396
			(2.6)	(1.6)	(2.8)	(3.5)	(3.2)	(2.4)	(2.6)	(5.2)	(2.2)	(2.4)	(3.6)	(1.5)	(2.8)	(2.7)	(7.0)	(2.4)	(4.2)	(2.7)	(2.4)	(2.9)	(2.5)	(4.1)	(4.0)	(4.5)	(5.0)	(4.5)	(4.2)	(5.3)	(1.6)	(3.3)	(3.1)
Finland	546	(2.6)	□	▲	▲	▲	▲	▲	▲	▲	▲	▲	▲	▲	▲	▲	▲	▲	▲	▲	▲	▲	▲	▲	▲	▲	▲	▲	▲	▲	▲	▲	▲
Canada	534	(1.6)	▽	□	○	○	○	▲	▲	○	▲	▲	▲	▲	▲	▲	▲	▲	▲	▲	▲	▲	▲	▲	▲	▲	▲	▲	▲	▲	▲	▲	▲
New Zealand	529	(2.8)	▽	○	□	○	○	○	○	○	▲	▲	▲	▲	▲	▲	▲	▲	▲	▲	▲	▲	▲	▲	▲	▲	▲	▲	▲	▲	▲	▲	▲
Australia	528	(3.5)	▽	○	○	□	○	○	○	○	○	▲	▲	▲	▲	▲	▲	▲	▲	▲	▲	▲	▲	▲	▲	▲	▲	▲	▲	▲	▲	▲	▲
Ireland	527	(3.2)	▽	○	○	○	□	○	○	○	○	▲	▲	▲	▲	▲	▲	▲	▲	▲	▲	▲	▲	▲	▲	▲	▲	▲	▲	▲	▲	▲	▲
Korea	525	(2.4)	▽	▽	○	○	○	□	○	○	○	▲	▲	▲	▲	▲	▲	▲	▲	▲	▲	▲	▲	▲	▲	▲	▲	▲	▲	▲	▲	▲	▲
United Kingdom	523	(2.6)	▽	▽	○	○	○	○	□	○	○	▲	▲	▲	▲	▲	▲	▲	▲	▲	▲	▲	▲	▲	▲	▲	▲	▲	▲	▲	▲	▲	▲
Japan	522	(5.2)	▽	○	○	○	○	○	○	□	○	○	○	○	○	○	○	▲	▲	▲	▲	▲	▲	▲	▲	▲	▲	▲	▲	▲	▲	▲	▲
Sweden	516	(2.2)	▽	▽	▽	○	○	○	○	○	□	▲	○	▲	○	○	○	▲	▲	▲	▲	▲	▲	▲	▲	▲	▲	▲	▲	▲	▲	▲	▲
Austria	507	(2.4)	▽	▽	▽	▽	▽	▽	▽	○	▽	□	○	○	○	○	○	○	○	▲	▲	▲	▲	▲	▲	▲	▲	▲	▲	▲	▲	▲	▲
Belgium	507	(3.6)	▽	▽	▽	▽	▽	▽	▽	○	○	○	□	○	○	○	○	○	○	▲	▲	▲	▲	▲	▲	▲	▲	▲	▲	▲	▲	▲	▲
Iceland	507	(1.5)	▽	▽	▽	▽	▽	▽	▽	○	▽	○	○	□	○	○	▲	▲	▲	▲	▲	▲	▲	▲	▲	▲	▲	▲	▲	▲	▲	▲	▲
Norway	505	(2.8)	▽	▽	▽	▽	▽	▽	▽	○	○	○	○	○	□	○	○	○	○	▲	▲	▲	▲	▲	▲	▲	▲	▲	▲	▲	▲	▲	▲
France	505	(2.7)	▽	▽	▽	▽	▽	▽	▽	○	○	○	○	▽	○	□	○	○	○	▲	▲	▲	▲	▲	▲	▲	▲	▲	▲	▲	▲	▲	▲
United States	504	(7.0)	▽	▽	▽	○	○	○	○	○	○	○	○	○	○	○	□	○	○	○	○	○	○	○	○	○	▲	▲	▲	▲	▲	▲	▲
Denmark	497	(2.4)	▽	▽	▽	▽	▽	▽	▽	▽	▽	○	○	▽	○	○	○	□	○	○	○	▲	▲	▲	▲	▲	▲	▲	▲	▲	▲	▲	▲
Switzerland	494	(4.2)	▽	▽	▽	▽	▽	▽	▽	○	○	○	○	▽	○	○	○	○	□	○	○	○	▲	▲	▲	▲	▲	▲	▲	▲	▲	▲	▲
Spain	493	(2.7)	▽	▽	▽	▽	▽	▽	▽	▽	▽	○	○	▽	▽	▽	○	○	○	□	○	○	○	○	○	▲	▲	▲	▲	▲	▲	▲	▲
Czech Republic	492	(2.4)	▽	▽	▽	▽	▽	▽	▽	▽	▽	○	○	▽	▽	▽	○	○	○	○	□	○	○	○	○	○	▲	▲	▲	▲	▲	▲	▲
Italy	487	(2.9)	▽	▽	▽	▽	▽	▽	▽	▽	▽	▽	▽	▽	▽	▽	○	▽	○	○	○	□	○	○	○	○	○	▲	▲	▲	▲	▲	▲
Germany	484	(2.5)	▽	▽	▽	▽	▽	▽	▽	▽	▽	▽	▽	▽	▽	▽	○	▽	○	○	○	○	□	○	○	○	○	▲	▲	▲	▲	▲	▲
Liechtenstein	483	(4.1)	▽	▽	▽	▽	▽	▽	▽	▽	▽	▽	▽	▽	▽	▽	○	▽	○	○	○	○	○	□	○	○	○	○	▲	▲	▲	▲	▲
Hungary	480	(4.0)	▽	▽	▽	▽	▽	▽	▽	▽	▽	▽	▽	▽	▽	▽	○	▽	○	○	○	○	○	○	□	○	○	○	▲	▲	▲	▲	▲
Poland	479	(4.5)	▽	▽	▽	▽	▽	▽	▽	▽	▽	▽	▽	▽	▽	▽	○	▽	○	○	○	○	○	○	○	□	○	○	▲	▲	▲	▲	▲
Greece	474	(5.0)	▽	▽	▽	▽	▽	▽	▽	▽	▽	▽	▽	▽	▽	▽	▽	▽	▽	▽	▽	○	○	○	○	○	□	○	▲	▲	▲	▲	▲
Portugal	470	(4.5)	▽	▽	▽	▽	▽	▽	▽	▽	▽	▽	▽	▽	▽	▽	▽	▽	▽	▽	▽	○	○	○	○	○	○	□	▲	▲	▲	▲	▲
Russian Federation	462	(4.2)	▽	▽	▽	▽	▽	▽	▽	▽	▽	▽	▽	▽	▽	▽	▽	▽	▽	▽	▽	▽	▽	▽	▽	▽	▽	▽	□	○	▲	▲	▲
Latvia	458	(5.3)	▽	▽	▽	▽	▽	▽	▽	▽	▽	▽	▽	▽	▽	▽	▽	▽	▽	▽	▽	▽	▽	▽	▽	▽	▽	▽	○	□	▲	▲	▲
Luxembourg	441	(1.6)	▽	▽	▽	▽	▽	▽	▽	▽	▽	▽	▽	▽	▽	▽	▽	▽	▽	▽	▽	▽	▽	▽	▽	▽	▽	▽	▽	▽	□	▲	▲
Mexico	422	(3.3)	▽	▽	▽	▽	▽	▽	▽	▽	▽	▽	▽	▽	▽	▽	▽	▽	▽	▽	▽	▽	▽	▽	▽	▽	▽	▽	▽	▽	▽	□	▲
Brazil	396	(3.1)	▽	▽	▽	▽	▽	▽	▽	▽	▽	▽	▽	▽	▽	▽	▽	▽	▽	▽	▽	▽	▽	▽	▽	▽	▽	▽	▽	▽	▽	▽	□
Upper rank[1]			1	2	2	2	3	4	5	3	9	11	11	11	11	11	10	16	16	17	17	19	21	20	21	21	23	24	27	27	30	31	32
Lower rank[1]			1	4	8	9	9	9	9	10	11	16	16	15	16	16	20	19	21	21	21	24	25	26	26	27	28	28	29	29	30	31	32

Statistically significantly above the country mean
Not statistically significantly different from the country mean
Statistically significantly below the country mean

▲ Mean performance statistically significantly higher than in comparison country.
○ No statistically significant difference from comparison country.
▽ Mean performance statistically significantly lower than in comparison country.

Instructions

Read across the row for a country to compare performance with the countries listed along the top of the chart. The symbols indicate whether the mean performance of the country in the row is statistically significantly lower than that of the comparison country, statistically significantly higher than that of the comparison country, or if there is no statistically significant difference between the mean performance of the two countries.

Note: Countries are presented in descending order of mean performance on the PISA reading literacy scale. Due to low response rates, the Netherlands is excluded from the figure. Assuming negligible to moderate levels of bias due to non-response, the position of the Netherlands may be expected, with 95 per cent confidence, to lie between 2nd and 14th place among countries.

1. Because data are based on samples, it is not possible to report exact rank order positions for countries. However, it is possible to report the range of rank order positions within which the country mean lies with 95 per cent likelihood.

Source: OECD PISA database, 2001. See Annex 3 for notes on methodology *(www.oecd.org/edu/eag2003)* and *www.pisa.oecd.org.*

A5

High average scores are not enough: countries also look to raise the level of performance of poor performers.

Looking at the distribution in student performance (Table A5.2), shows that the variation in student performance on the reading literacy scale within countries is large. The variation within every country far exceeds the range of country mean scores. The difference between the 75th and 25th percentiles, which covers the middle half of the national performance distribution, exceeds the magnitude of one proficiency level (72 score points) in all countries, and about two times the magnitude of one proficiency level in Australia, Belgium, Germany and New Zealand. (The OECD average on this measure is 1.8 times the magnitude of one proficiency level.)

Are these observed disparities inevitable?

Together, these findings suggest that educational systems in many countries face significant challenges in addressing the needs of all students, including those most in need as well as those performing exceptionally well.

That is hard to say, but some countries contain them within a far narrower range than others…

One can also observe that countries with similar levels of average performance show considerable variation in disparities of student performance. For example, Korea and the United Kingdom both show above-average mean performance on the reading literacy scale at around 525 score points. The difference between the 75th and 25th percentile in Korea is 92 points, significantly below the OECD average, but in the United Kingdom it is 137 score points, similar to the OECD average. A similar result can be observed for countries scoring below average. Italy and Germany each perform at around 485 score points, significantly below the OECD average. In Italy the difference between the 75th and 25th percentile is 124 points, but in Germany, it is 146 points. Bringing the bottom quarter of students closer to the mean is one way for countries with wide internal disparities to raise overall performance.

…and some countries succeed in combining high average performance with low disparities.

Finally, comparing the range of performance within a country with its average performance shows that some countries attain both relatively low differences between top and bottom-performing students and relatively high levels of overall performance. There is a tendency for high performing countries to show relatively small disparities. For example, the three countries with the smallest differences between the 75th and 25th percentiles - Finland, Japan and Korea - are also among the best performing countries in reading literacy. By contrast, one of the three countries with the highest performance differences, Germany, scores significantly below the OECD average (Table A5.2).

Box A5.3. Reading literacy performance in PISA and PIRLS

As shown in Box A4.1, there are significant similarities in the way that reading literacy is defined and measured in the PISA and PIRLS assessments. While direct comparisons of the results between the two studies are not possible – as PIRLS and PISA are different assessments with different approaches to defining their target population – it is in interesting to make some comparisons at a general level for the 11 countries for which there are country-wide data for both assessments.

Standing relative to OECD mean

Six countries (the Czech Republic, Germany, Greece, Hungary, Italy and the United States) performed relatively better in PIRLS than in PISA. In the first four cases, scores were above the OECD average in PIRLS and are below the OECD average in PISA. Three countries performed relatively better in PISA than in PIRLS: Iceland, New Zealand and Norway. France and Sweden performed similarly relative to other countries on both assessments (Table A5.3).

Distribution of performance

In the Czech Republic and Sweden, variation in reading literacy performance is low among both 4th graders and at age 15. However, in Sweden average performance is above OECD level in both age groups whereas in the Czech Republic, average performance among 4th graders is above the OECD level but at an age below the OECD average (Tables A4.1 and A5.2). German 4th graders perform well on average and with low disparities. By contrast, 15-year-olds perform below average and show some of the largest disparities in student performance. Students in New Zealand show some of the largest disparities in both age groups.

The comparison is based on the Czech Republic, France, Germany, Greece, Hungary, Iceland, Italy, New Zealand, Norway, Sweden and the United States. Canada and the United Kingdom are not considered in this comparison because only certain jurisdictions participated in PIRLS. The Netherlands is not considered because their mean reading score is not published due to low response rates. The Slovak Republic and Turkey, which participated in PIRLS, did not participate in PISA 2000.

In interpreting these results, it needs to be taken into account that, unlike in PISA, the samples for PIRLS were grade-based and resulted in considerable differences in the average age of students across participating countries. For example, students in the best performing country, Sweden, were a year older than students in Iceland and Italy and almost a year older than students in France, Greece, New Zealand and Norway. Among the 11 countries that participated in both PISA and PIRLS, the average age of students explains 49 per cent of the cross-country performance differences which is considerable. These differences need to be taken into account not only when interpreting average performance in PIRLS, but also when comparing performance differences in countries between PISA and PIRLS.

A5

The performance scores are based on assessments administered as part of the Programme for International Student Assessment (PISA) undertaken by the OECD during 2000.

Definitions and methodologies

The target population studied for this indicator was 15-year-old students. Operationally, this refers to students aged between 15 years and 3 (completed) months and 16 years and 2 (completed) months at the beginning of the testing period, and enrolled in an educational institution, regardless of the grade level or type of institution and of whether they participated in school full-time or part-time.

To facilitate the interpretation of the scores assigned to students in PISA, the mean score for reading literacy performance among OECD countries was set at 500 and the standard deviation at 100, with the data weighted so that each OECD country contributed equally. These reference points anchor PISA's measurement of student proficiency.

For notes on standard errors, significance tests, and multiple comparisons see Annex 3 at *www.oecd.org/edu/eag2003*.

A5

Table A5.1
Reading proficiency of 15-year-olds (2000)
Percentage of 15-year-olds at each level of proficiency on the PISA reading literacy scale

		Proficiency levels											
		Below Level 1 *(less than 335 score points)*		**Level 1** *(from 335 to 407 score points)*		**Level 2** *(from 408 to 480 score points)*		**Level 3** *(from 481 to 552 score points)*		**Level 4** *(from 553 to 625 score points)*		**Level 5** *(above 625 score points)*	
		%	S.E.	%	S.E.	%	S.E.	%	S.E.	%	S.E.	%	S.E.
OECD COUNTRIES	Australia	3.3	(0.5)	9.1	(0.8)	19.0	(1.1)	25.7	(1.1)	25.3	(0.9)	17.6	(1.2)
	Austria	4.4	(0.4)	10.2	(0.6)	21.7	(0.9)	29.9	(1.2)	24.9	(1.0)	8.8	(0.8)
	Belgium	7.7	(1.0)	11.3	(0.7)	16.8	(0.7)	25.8	(0.9)	26.3	(0.9)	12.0	(0.7)
	Canada	2.4	(0.3)	7.2	(0.3)	18.0	(0.4)	28.0	(0.5)	27.7	(0.6)	16.8	(0.5)
	Czech Republic	6.1	(0.6)	11.4	(0.7)	24.8	(1.2)	30.9	(1.1)	19.8	(0.8)	7.0	(0.6)
	Denmark	5.9	(0.6)	12.0	(0.7)	22.5	(0.9)	29.5	(1.0)	22.0	(0.9)	8.1	(0.5)
	Finland	1.7	(0.5)	5.2	(0.4)	14.3	(0.7)	28.7	(0.8)	31.6	(0.9)	18.5	(0.9)
	France	4.2	(0.6)	11.0	(0.8)	22.0	(0.8)	30.6	(1.0)	23.7	(0.9)	8.5	(0.6)
	Germany	9.9	(0.7)	12.7	(0.6)	22.3	(0.8)	26.8	(1.0)	19.4	(1.0)	8.8	(0.5)
	Greece	8.7	(1.2)	15.7	(1.4)	25.9	(1.4)	28.1	(1.7)	16.7	(1.4)	5.0	(0.7)
	Hungary	6.9	(0.7)	15.8	(1.2)	25.0	(1.1)	28.8	(1.3)	18.5	(1.1)	5.1	(0.8)
	Iceland	4.0	(0.3)	10.5	(0.6)	22.0	(0.8)	30.8	(0.9)	23.6	(1.1)	9.1	(0.7)
	Ireland	3.1	(0.5)	7.9	(0.8)	17.9	(0.9)	29.7	(1.1)	27.1	(1.1)	14.2	(0.8)
	Italy	5.4	(0.9)	13.5	(0.9)	25.6	(1.0)	30.6	(1.0)	19.5	(1.1)	5.3	(0.5)
	Japan	2.7	(0.6)	7.3	(1.1)	18.0	(1.3)	33.3	(1.3)	28.8	(1.7)	9.9	(1.1)
	Korea	0.9	(0.2)	4.8	(0.6)	18.6	(0.9)	38.8	(1.1)	31.1	(1.2)	5.7	(0.6)
	Luxembourg	14.2	(0.7)	20.9	(0.8)	27.5	(1.3)	24.6	(1.1)	11.2	(0.5)	1.7	(0.3)
	Mexico	16.1	(1.2)	28.1	(1.4)	30.3	(1.1)	18.8	(1.2)	6.0	(0.7)	0.9	(0.2)
	New Zealand	4.8	(0.5)	8.9	(0.5)	17.2	(0.9)	24.6	(1.1)	25.8	(1.1)	18.7	(1.0)
	Norway	6.3	(0.6)	11.2	(0.8)	19.5	(0.8)	28.1	(0.8)	23.7	(0.9)	11.2	(0.7)
	Poland	8.7	(1.0)	14.6	(1.0)	24.1	(1.4)	28.2	(1.3)	18.6	(1.3)	5.9	(1.0)
	Portugal	9.6	(1.0)	16.7	(1.2)	25.3	(1.0)	27.5	(1.2)	16.8	(1.1)	4.2	(0.5)
	Spain	4.1	(0.5)	12.2	(0.9)	25.7	(0.7)	32.8	(1.0)	21.1	(0.9)	4.2	(0.5)
	Sweden	3.3	(0.4)	9.3	(0.6)	20.3	(0.7)	30.4	(1.0)	25.6	(1.0)	11.2	(0.7)
	Switzerland	7.0	(0.7)	13.3	(0.9)	21.4	(1.0)	28.0	(1.0)	21.0	(1.0)	9.2	(1.0)
	United Kingdom	3.6	(0.4)	9.2	(0.5)	19.6	(0.7)	27.5	(0.9)	24.4	(0.9)	15.6	(1.0)
	United States	6.4	(1.2)	11.5	(1.2)	21.0	(1.2)	27.4	(1.3)	21.5	(1.4)	12.2	(1.4)
	OECD total	*6.2*	*(0.4)*	*12.1*	*(0.4)*	*21.8*	*(0.4)*	*28.6*	*(0.4)*	*21.8*	*(0.4)*	*9.4*	*(0.4)*
	Country mean	*6.0*	*(0.1)*	*11.9*	*(0.2)*	*21.7*	*(0.2)*	*28.7*	*(0.2)*	*22.3*	*(0.2)*	*9.5*	*(0.1)*
NON-OECD COUNTRIES	Brazil	23.3	(1.4)	32.5	(1.2)	27.7	(1.3)	12.9	(1.1)	3.1	(0.5)	0.6	(0.2)
	Latvia	12.7	(1.3)	17.9	(1.3)	26.3	(1.1)	25.2	(1.3)	13.8	(1.1)	4.1	(0.6)
	Liechtenstein	7.6	(1.5)	14.5	(2.1)	23.2	(2.9)	30.1	(3.4)	19.5	(2.2)	5.1	(1.6)
	Russian Federation	9.0	(1.0)	18.5	(1.1)	29.2	(0.8)	26.9	(1.1)	13.3	(1.0)	3.2	(0.5)

Source: OECD PISA database, 2001. See Annex 3 for notes on methodology (*www.oecd.org/edu/eag2003*) and *www.pisa.oecd.org*.

A5

Table A5.2
Variation in performance in reading literacy of 15-year-olds (2000)
Performance of 15-year-olds on the PISA reading literacy scale, by percentile

		Mean		Standard deviation		Percentiles													
						5th		10th		25th		75th		90th		95th	
		Mean score	S.E.	S.D.	S.E.	Score	S.E.	Score	S.E.	Score	S.E.	Score	S.E.	Score	S.E.	Score	S.E.
OECD COUNTRIES	Australia	528	(3.5)	102	(1.6)	354	(4.8)	394	(4.4)	458	(4.4)	602	(4.6)	656	(4.2)	685	(4.5)
	Austria	507	(2.4)	93	(1.6)	341	(5.4)	383	(4.2)	447	(2.8)	573	(3.0)	621	(3.2)	648	(3.7)
	Belgium	507	(3.6)	107	(2.4)	308	(10.3)	354	(8.9)	437	(6.6)	587	(2.3)	634	(2.5)	659	(2.4)
	Canada	534	(1.6)	95	(1.1)	371	(3.8)	410	(2.4)	472	(2.0)	600	(1.5)	652	(1.9)	681	(2.7)
	Czech Republic	492	(2.4)	96	(1.9)	320	(7.9)	368	(4.9)	433	(2.8)	557	(2.9)	610	(3.2)	638	(3.6)
	Denmark	497	(2.4)	98	(1.8)	326	(6.2)	367	(5.0)	434	(3.3)	566	(2.7)	617	(2.9)	645	(3.6)
	Finland	546	(2.6)	89	(2.6)	390	(5.8)	429	(5.1)	492	(2.9)	608	(2.6)	654	(2.8)	681	(3.4)
	France	505	(2.7)	92	(1.7)	344	(6.2)	381	(5.2)	444	(4.5)	570	(2.4)	619	(2.9)	645	(3.7)
	Germany	484	(2.5)	111	(1.9)	284	(9.4)	335	(6.3)	417	(4.6)	563	(3.1)	619	(2.8)	650	(3.2)
	Greece	474	(5.0)	97	(2.7)	305	(8.2)	342	(8.4)	409	(7.4)	543	(4.5)	595	(5.1)	625	(6.0)
	Hungary	480	(4.0)	94	(2.1)	320	(5.6)	354	(5.5)	414	(5.3)	549	(4.5)	598	(4.4)	626	(5.5)
	Iceland	507	(1.5)	92	(1.4)	345	(5.0)	383	(3.6)	447	(3.1)	573	(2.2)	621	(3.5)	647	(3.7)
	Ireland	527	(3.2)	94	(1.7)	360	(6.3)	401	(6.4)	468	(4.3)	593	(3.6)	641	(4.0)	669	(3.4)
	Italy	487	(2.9)	91	(2.7)	331	(8.5)	368	(5.8)	429	(4.1)	552	(3.2)	601	(2.7)	627	(3.1)
	Japan	522	(5.2)	86	(3.0)	366	(11.4)	407	(9.8)	471	(7.0)	582	(4.4)	625	(4.6)	650	(4.3)
	Korea	525	(2.4)	70	(1.6)	402	(5.2)	433	(4.4)	481	(2.9)	574	(2.6)	608	(2.9)	629	(3.2)
	Luxembourg	441	(1.6)	100	(1.5)	267	(5.1)	311	(4.4)	378	(2.8)	513	(2.0)	564	(2.8)	592	(3.5)
	Mexico	422	(3.3)	86	(2.1)	284	(4.4)	311	(3.4)	360	(3.6)	482	(4.8)	535	(5.5)	565	(6.3)
	New Zealand	529	(2.8)	108	(2.0)	337	(7.4)	382	(5.2)	459	(4.1)	606	(3.0)	661	(4.4)	693	(6.1)
	Norway	505	(2.8)	104	(1.7)	320	(5.9)	364	(5.5)	440	(4.5)	579	(2.7)	631	(3.1)	660	(4.6)
	Poland	479	(4.5)	100	(3.1)	304	(8.7)	343	(6.8)	414	(5.8)	551	(6.0)	603	(6.6)	631	(6.0)
	Portugal	470	(4.5)	97	(1.8)	300	(6.2)	337	(6.2)	403	(6.4)	541	(4.5)	592	(4.2)	620	(3.9)
	Spain	493	(2.7)	85	(1.2)	344	(5.8)	379	(5.0)	436	(4.6)	553	(2.6)	597	(2.6)	620	(2.9)
	Sweden	516	(2.2)	92	(1.2)	354	(4.5)	392	(4.0)	456	(3.1)	581	(3.1)	630	(2.9)	658	(3.1)
	Switzerland	494	(4.2)	102	(2.0)	316	(5.5)	355	(5.8)	426	(5.5)	567	(4.7)	621	(5.5)	651	(5.3)
	United Kingdom	523	(2.6)	100	(1.5)	352	(4.9)	391	(4.1)	458	(2.8)	595	(3.5)	651	(4.3)	682	(4.9)
	United States	504	(7.1)	105	(2.7)	320	(11.7)	363	(11.4)	436	(8.8)	577	(6.8)	636	(6.5)	669	(6.8)
	OECD total	*499*	*(2.0)*	*100*	*(0.8)*	*322*	*(3.4)*	*363*	*(3.3)*	*433*	*(2.5)*	*569*	*(1.6)*	*622*	*(2.0)*	*653*	*(2.1)*
	Country mean	*500*	*(0.6)*	*100*	*(0.4)*	*324*	*(1.3)*	*366*	*(1.1)*	*435*	*(1.0)*	*571*	*(0.7)*	*623*	*(0.8)*	*652*	*(0.8)*
NON-OECD COUNTRIES	Brazil	396	(3.1)	86	(1.9)	255	(5.0)	288	(4.5)	339	(3.4)	452	(3.4)	507	(4.2)	539	(5.5)
	Latvia	458	(5.3)	102	(2.3)	283	(9.7)	322	(8.2)	390	(6.9)	530	(5.3)	586	(5.8)	617	(6.6)
	Liechtenstein	483	(4.1)	96	(3.9)	310	(15.9)	350	(11.8)	419	(9.4)	551	(5.8)	601	(7.1)	626	(8.2)
	Russian Federation	462	(4.2)	92	(1.8)	306	(6.9)	340	(5.4)	400	(5.1)	526	(4.5)	579	(4.4)	608	(5.3)

Source: OECD PISA database, 2001. See Annex 3 for notes on methodology (*www.oecd.org/edu/eag2003*) and *www.pisa.oecd.org*.

A5

Table A5.3
Mean performance in reading literacy of 4th-grade students and 15-year-olds (2000, 2001)
Performance of 4th -grade students on the PIRLS reading literacy scale and of 15-year-olds on the PISA reading literacy scale

<table>
<tr><th rowspan="2">OECD COUNTRIES</th><th></th><th colspan="2">Performance of 15-year-olds
on the PISA reading literacy scale</th><th colspan="3">Performance of 4th-grade students
on the PIRLS reading literacy scale</th></tr>
<tr><th></th><th></th><th></th><th></th><th></th><th></th></tr>
<tr><td>Czech Republic</td><td>▼</td><td>492</td><td>(2.4)</td><td>Δ</td><td>537</td><td>(2.3)</td></tr>
<tr><td>France</td><td></td><td>505</td><td>(2.7)</td><td></td><td>525</td><td>(2.4)</td></tr>
<tr><td>Germany</td><td>▼</td><td>484</td><td>(2.5)</td><td>Δ</td><td>539</td><td>(1.9)</td></tr>
<tr><td>Greece</td><td>▼</td><td>474</td><td>(5.0)</td><td></td><td>524</td><td>(3.5)</td></tr>
<tr><td>Hungary</td><td>▼</td><td>480</td><td>(4.0)</td><td>Δ</td><td>543</td><td>(2.2)</td></tr>
<tr><td>Iceland</td><td>▲</td><td>507</td><td>(1.5)</td><td>∇</td><td>512</td><td>(1.2)</td></tr>
<tr><td>Italy</td><td>▼</td><td>487</td><td>(2.9)</td><td>Δ</td><td>541</td><td>(2.4)</td></tr>
<tr><td>New Zealand</td><td>▲</td><td>529</td><td>(2.8)</td><td></td><td>529</td><td>(3.6)</td></tr>
<tr><td>Norway</td><td></td><td>505</td><td>(2.8)</td><td>∇</td><td>499</td><td>(2.9)</td></tr>
<tr><td>Sweden</td><td>▲</td><td>516</td><td>(2.2)</td><td>Δ</td><td>561</td><td>(2.2)</td></tr>
<tr><td>United States</td><td></td><td>504</td><td>(7.1)</td><td>Δ</td><td>542</td><td>(3.8)</td></tr>
</table>

▲ Mean performance statistically significantly above the PISA country mean

▼ Mean performance statistically significantly below the PISA country mean

Δ Mean performance statistically significantly above the PIRLS country mean

∇ Mean performance statistically significantly below the PIRLS country mean

Source: IEA Progress in Reading Literacy Study (PIRLS) 2001 and OECD PISA database, 2001.

INDICATOR A6: MATHEMATICAL AND SCIENTIFIC LITERACY OF 15-YEAR-OLDS

• 15-year-olds in Japan display the highest mean scores in mathematical literacy, although their scores cannot be distinguished statistically from students in two other top-performing countries, Korea and New Zealand. On the scientific literacy scale, students in Japan and Korea demonstrate the highest average performance.

• While there are large differences in mean performance among countries, the variation of performance among 15-year-olds within each country is many times larger. However, wide disparities in performance are not a necessary condition for a country to attain a high level of overall performance. On the contrary, five of the countries with the smallest variation in performance on the mathematical literacy scale, namely Canada, Finland, Iceland, Japan and Korea, all perform significantly above the OECD average, and four of them, Canada, Finland, Japan and Korea, are among the six best-performing countries in mathematical literacy.

Chart A6.1
Multiple comparisons of mean performance on the PISA mathematical literacy scale (2000)

A6

Column headers (left→right): Japan, Korea, New Zealand, Finland, Australia, Canada, Switzerland, United Kingdom, Belgium, France, Austria, Denmark, Iceland, Liechtenstein, Sweden, Ireland, Norway, Czech Republic, United States, Germany, Hungary, Russian Federation, Spain, Poland, Latvia, Italy, Portugal, Greece, Luxembourg, Mexico, Brazil

Column means: 557 547 537 536 533 533 529 529 520 517 515 514 514 514 510 503 499 498 493 490 488 478 476 470 463 457 454 447 446 387 334

Column S.E.: (5.5) (2.8) (3.1) (2.1) (3.5) (1.4) (4.4) (2.5) (3.9) (2.7) (2.5) (2.4) (2.3) (7.0) (2.5) (2.7) (2.8) (2.8) (7.6) (2.5) (4.0) (5.5) (3.1) (5.5) (4.5) (2.9) (4.1) (5.6) (2.0) (3.4) (3.7)

Country	Mean	S.E.	Jpn	Kor	NZ	Fin	Aus	Can	Swi	UK	Bel	Fra	Aut	Den	Ice	Lie	Swe	Ire	Nor	Cze	USA	Ger	Hun	Rus	Spa	Pol	Lat	Ita	Por	Gre	Lux	Mex	Bra
Japan	557	(5.5)	□	○	○	▲	▲	▲	▲	▲	▲	▲	▲	▲	▲	▲	▲	▲	▲	▲	▲	▲	▲	▲	▲	▲	▲	▲	▲	▲	▲	▲	▲
Korea	547	(2.8)	○	□	○	○	○	▲	▲	▲	▲	▲	▲	▲	▲	▲	▲	▲	▲	▲	▲	▲	▲	▲	▲	▲	▲	▲	▲	▲	▲	▲	▲
New Zealand	537	(3.1)	○	○	□	○	○	○	○	○	▲	▲	▲	▲	▲	▲	▲	▲	▲	▲	▲	▲	▲	▲	▲	▲	▲	▲	▲	▲	▲	▲	▲
Finland	536	(2.1)	▽	○	○	□	○	○	○	○	▲	▲	▲	▲	▲	▲	▲	▲	▲	▲	▲	▲	▲	▲	▲	▲	▲	▲	▲	▲	▲	▲	▲
Australia	533	(3.5)	▽	○	○	○	□	○	○	○	▲	▲	▲	▲	▲	▲	▲	▲	▲	▲	▲	▲	▲	▲	▲	▲	▲	▲	▲	▲	▲	▲	▲
Canada	533	(1.4)	▽	▽	○	○	○	□	○	○	▲	▲	▲	▲	▲	▲	▲	▲	▲	▲	▲	▲	▲	▲	▲	▲	▲	▲	▲	▲	▲	▲	▲
Switzerland	529	(4.4)	▽	▽	○	○	○	○	□	○	○	○	○	○	○	○	▲	▲	▲	▲	▲	▲	▲	▲	▲	▲	▲	▲	▲	▲	▲	▲	▲
United Kingdom	529	(2.5)	▽	▽	○	○	○	○	○	□	○	○	○	○	○	○	▲	▲	▲	▲	▲	▲	▲	▲	▲	▲	▲	▲	▲	▲	▲	▲	▲
Belgium	520	(3.9)	▽	▽	▽	▽	▽	▽	○	○	□	○	○	○	○	○	○	○	▲	▲	▲	▲	▲	▲	▲	▲	▲	▲	▲	▲	▲	▲	▲
France	517	(2.7)	▽	▽	▽	▽	▽	▽	○	○	○	□	○	○	○	○	○	○	▲	▲	▲	▲	▲	▲	▲	▲	▲	▲	▲	▲	▲	▲	▲
Austria	515	(2.5)	▽	▽	▽	▽	▽	▽	○	○	○	○	□	○	○	○	○	○	○	○	▲	▲	▲	▲	▲	▲	▲	▲	▲	▲	▲	▲	▲
Denmark	514	(2.4)	▽	▽	▽	▽	▽	▽	▽	▽	○	○	○	□	○	○	○	○	○	○	▲	▲	▲	▲	▲	▲	▲	▲	▲	▲	▲	▲	▲
Iceland	514	(2.3)	▽	▽	▽	▽	▽	▽	▽	▽	○	○	○	○	□	○	○	○	○	○	▲	▲	▲	▲	▲	▲	▲	▲	▲	▲	▲	▲	▲
Liechtenstein	514	(7.0)	▽	▽	○	○	○	○	○	○	○	○	○	○	○	□	○	○	○	○	○	○	○	▲	▲	▲	▲	▲	▲	▲	▲	▲	▲
Sweden	510	(2.5)	▽	▽	▽	▽	▽	▽	▽	▽	○	○	○	○	○	○	□	○	○	○	○	▲	▲	▲	▲	▲	▲	▲	▲	▲	▲	▲	▲
Ireland	503	(2.7)	▽	▽	▽	▽	▽	▽	▽	▽	○	○	○	○	○	○	○	□	○	○	○	○	○	▲	▲	▲	▲	▲	▲	▲	▲	▲	▲
Norway	499	(2.8)	▽	▽	▽	▽	▽	▽	▽	▽	▽	▽	○	○	○	○	○	○	□	○	○	○	○	○	▲	▲	▲	▲	▲	▲	▲	▲	▲
Czech Republic	498	(2.8)	▽	▽	▽	▽	▽	▽	▽	▽	▽	▽	○	○	○	○	○	○	○	□	○	○	○	○	▲	▲	▲	▲	▲	▲	▲	▲	▲
United States	493	(7.6)	▽	▽	▽	▽	▽	▽	▽	▽	▽	▽	▽	○	○	○	○	○	○	○	□	○	○	○	○	○	▲	▲	▲	▲	▲	▲	▲
Germany	490	(2.5)	▽	▽	▽	▽	▽	▽	▽	▽	▽	▽	▽	▽	▽	▽	○	○	○	○	○	□	○	○	○	○	▲	▲	▲	▲	▲	▲	▲
Hungary	488	(4.0)	▽	▽	▽	▽	▽	▽	▽	▽	▽	▽	▽	▽	▽	○	○	○	○	○	○	○	□	○	○	○	○	▲	▲	▲	▲	▲	▲
Russian Federation	478	(5.5)	▽	▽	▽	▽	▽	▽	▽	▽	▽	▽	▽	▽	▽	▽	▽	○	○	○	○	○	○	□	○	○	○	○	▲	▲	▲	▲	▲
Spain	476	(3.1)	▽	▽	▽	▽	▽	▽	▽	▽	▽	▽	▽	▽	▽	▽	▽	▽	▽	▽	○	○	○	○	□	○	○	○	▲	▲	▲	▲	▲
Poland	470	(5.5)	▽	▽	▽	▽	▽	▽	▽	▽	▽	▽	▽	▽	▽	▽	▽	▽	▽	▽	○	○	○	○	○	□	○	○	○	○	▲	▲	▲
Latvia	463	(4.5)	▽	▽	▽	▽	▽	▽	▽	▽	▽	▽	▽	▽	▽	▽	▽	▽	▽	▽	▽	▽	○	○	○	○	□	○	○	○	○	▲	▲
Italy	457	(2.9)	▽	▽	▽	▽	▽	▽	▽	▽	▽	▽	▽	▽	▽	▽	▽	▽	▽	▽	▽	▽	▽	○	○	○	○	□	○	○	○	▲	▲
Portugal	454	(4.1)	▽	▽	▽	▽	▽	▽	▽	▽	▽	▽	▽	▽	▽	▽	▽	▽	▽	▽	▽	▽	▽	○	○	○	○	○	□	○	○	▲	▲
Greece	447	(5.6)	▽	▽	▽	▽	▽	▽	▽	▽	▽	▽	▽	▽	▽	▽	▽	▽	▽	▽	▽	▽	▽	▽	▽	○	○	○	○	□	○	▲	▲
Luxembourg	446	(2.0)	▽	▽	▽	▽	▽	▽	▽	▽	▽	▽	▽	▽	▽	▽	▽	▽	▽	▽	▽	▽	▽	▽	▽	▽	○	○	○	○	□	▲	▲
Mexico	387	(3.4)	▽	▽	▽	▽	▽	▽	▽	▽	▽	▽	▽	▽	▽	▽	▽	▽	▽	▽	▽	▽	▽	▽	▽	▽	▽	▽	▽	▽	▽	□	▲
Brazil	334	(3.7)	▽	▽	▽	▽	▽	▽	▽	▽	▽	▽	▽	▽	▽	▽	▽	▽	▽	▽	▽	▽	▽	▽	▽	▽	▽	▽	▽	▽	▽	▽	□

	Jpn	Kor	NZ	Fin	Aus	Can	Swi	UK	Bel	Fra	Aut	Den	Ice	Lie	Swe	Ire	Nor	Cze	USA	Ger	Hun	Rus	Spa	Pol	Lat	Ita	Por	Gre	Lux	Mex	Bra
Upper rank[1]	1	2	4	4	4	5	4	6	9	10	10	10	11	9	13	16	17	17	16	20	20	21	23	23	25	26	26	27	29	31	32
Lower rank[1]	3	3	8	7	9	8	10	10	15	15	16	16	16	18	17	19	20	20	23	22	23	25	25	26	28	28	29	30	30	31	32

Legend (row shading):
Statistically significantly above the country mean
Not statistically significantly different from the country mean
Statistically significantly below the country mean

▲ Mean performance statistically significantly higher than in comparison country.
○ No statistically significant difference from comparison country.
▽ Mean performance statistically significantly lower than in comparison country.

Instructions

Read across the row for a country to compare performance with the countries listed along the top of the chart. The symbols indicate whether the mean performance of the country in the row is statistically significantly lower than that of the comparison country, statistically significantly higher than that of the comparison country, or if there is no statistically significant difference between the mean performance of the two countries.
Note: Countries are presented in descending order of mean performance on the PISA mathematical literacy scale. Due to low response rates, the Netherlands is excluded from the figure. Assuming negligible to moderate levels of bias due to non-response, the position of the Netherlands may be expected, with 95 per cent confidence, to lie between 1st and 4th place among countries.
1. Because data are based on samples, it is not possible to report exact rank order positions for countries. However, it is possible to report the range of rank order positions within which the country mean lies with 95 per cent likelihood.
Source: OECD PISA database, 2001. See Annex 3 for notes on methodology (www.oecd.org/edu/eag2003) and www.pisa.oecd.org.

A6

Policy context

Mathematics and science today need to be used by the many, not just the few…

The need to provide the foundations for the professional training of a small number of mathematicians, scientists and engineers dominated the content of school mathematics and science curricula for much of the past century. With the growing role of science, mathematics and technology in modern life, however, the objectives of personal fulfilment, employment and full participation in society increasingly require all adults to be mathematically, scientifically and technologically literate.

…if people are to understand and participate in the modern world.

Deficiencies in mathematical and scientific literacy can have grave consequences not only on the labour market and earnings prospects of individuals but also on the competitiveness of nations. Conversely, the performance of a country's best students in mathematics and science-related subjects can have implications for the part that country will play in tomorrow's advanced technology sector. Aside from workplace requirements, mathematical and scientific literacy also are important for understanding the environmental, medical, economic and other issues that confront modern societies and that rely heavily on technological and scientific advances.

This indicator shows the performance of 15-year-olds in mathematical and scientific literacy.

Consequently, policy-makers and educators alike attach great importance to mathematics and science education. Addressing the increasing demand for mathematical and scientific skills requires excellence throughout educational systems, and it is important to monitor how well nations provide young adults with fundamental skills in these areas. The Programme for International Student Assessment (PISA) provides information about how well 15-year-olds perform in these areas with a focus on assessing the knowledge and skills that prepare students for life and lifelong learning (Box A6.1).

Evidence and explanations

Charts A6.1 and A6.2 order countries by the mean performance of their students on the mathematical and scientific literacy scales. The charts also show which countries perform above, below, or about the same as the OECD average and how their students perform in comparison with students in every other country.

Japan shows the highest mean score in mathematical literacy…

Students in Japan display the highest mean scores in mathematical literacy, although their scores cannot be distinguished statistically from students in three other top-performing countries: Korea, the Netherlands and New Zealand. Other countries that score significantly above the OECD average include Australia, Austria, Belgium, Canada, Denmark, Finland, France, Iceland, Liechtenstein, Sweden, Switzerland and the United Kingdom (Chart A6.1).

…and Korea in scientific literacy.

On the scientific literacy scale, students in Korea and Japan demonstrate the highest average performance compared to students in other OECD countries. Australia, Austria, Canada, the Czech Republic, Finland, Ireland, New Zealand, Sweden and the United Kingdom are among other countries that score significantly above the OECD average (Chart A6.2).

A6

Box A6.1. What are mathematical and scientific literacy in PISA?

What is *mathematical* **literacy?** Mathematical literacy in PISA concerns students' ability to recognise and interpret mathematical problems encountered in their world, to translate these problems into a mathematical context, to use mathematical knowledge and procedures to solve the problems within their mathematical context, to interpret the results in terms of the original problem, to reflect upon the methods applied, and to formulate and communicate the outcomes.

What do different points along the mathematical literacy scale mean? The scale can be described in terms of the knowledge and skills students need to demonstrate at various points along the mathematical literacy scale.

- Towards the top end of the mathematical literacy scale, around 750 score points, students typically take a creative and active role in their approach to mathematical problems.

- Around 570 score points on the scale, students are typically able to interpret, link and integrate different representations of a problem or different pieces of information; and/or use and manipulate a given model, often involving algebra or other symbolic representations; and/or verify or check given propositions or models.

- At the lower end of the scale, around 380 score points, students are usually able to complete only a single processing step consisting of reproducing basic mathematical facts or processes or applying simple computational skills.

What is *scientific* **literacy?** Scientific literacy reflects students' ability to use scientific knowledge, to recognise scientific questions and to identify what is involved in scientific investigations, to relate scientific data to claims and conclusions, and to communicate these aspects of science.

What do different points along the scientific literacy scale mean? The scale can be described in terms of increasingly difficult tasks required for students:

- Towards the top end of the scientific literacy scale, around 690 score points, students generally are able to create or use simple conceptual models to make predictions or give explanations; analyse scientific investigations in relation to, for example, experimental design or the identification of an idea being tested; relate data as evidence to evaluate alternative viewpoints or different perspectives; and communicate scientific arguments and/or descriptions in detail and with precision.

- Around 550 score points, students typically are able to use scientific concepts to make predictions or provide explanations; recognise questions that can be answered by scientific investigation and/or identify details of what is involved in a scientific investigation; and select relevant information from competing data or chains of reasoning in drawing or evaluating conclusions.

- Towards the lower end of the scale, around 400 score points, reached by at least three-quarters of the students in almost all countries, students are able to recall simple scientific factual knowledge (*e.g.,* names, facts, terminology, simple rules); and use common science knowledge in drawing or evaluating conclusions.

A6

As can be inferred by reading the lists of above-average performers in the previous paragraphs, in general, countries that perform well in one subject area also perform well in the other subject area (*i.e.*, mean mathematics and science scores are highly correlated). However, there are some exceptions. For example, the scores for mathematical literacy of the Czech Republic and Ireland are not significantly different from the OECD average, but their students perform significantly above the OECD average on the scientific literacy scale. Conversely, students in Belgium, France, Iceland, and Switzerland perform significantly above the OECD average on the mathematical literacy scale, but their score in scientific literacy is not statistically different than the OECD average. Students in Denmark and Liechtenstein, while above the OECD mean in mathematical literacy, are below the OECD mean in scientific literacy.

While there are large differences in mean performance among countries, the variation of performance among students within each country is many times larger.

While there are large differences in mean performance among countries, the variation of performance among students within each country is many times larger. Tables A6.1 and A6.2 show how students perform at the 5th, 25th, 75th and 95th percentiles in each county. The distributions of student performance on the mathematical literacy scale in Belgium, Germany, Greece, Hungary, New Zealand, Poland, Switzerland and the United States, show a relatively large gap between the 75th and 25th percentiles — between 135 and 149 score points. Finland, Iceland, Ireland, Japan and Korea show comparatively smaller disparities, with 113 score points or less separating the 75th and 25th percentiles.

In scientific literacy, Belgium, Denmark, France, Germany, Hungary, New Zealand, Switzerland and the United States exhibit relatively large gaps between students at the 75th and 25th percentiles — between 140 and 154 score points each — while Finland, Japan Korea and Mexico exhibit relatively small differences between these groups of students, with less than 118 score point differences.

Disparities in performance are not a necessary condition for a country to attain a high level of overall performance.

It is useful to relate the range of performance to average performance. This comparison shows that wide disparities in student performance are not a necessary condition for a country to attain a high level of overall performance. On the contrary, it is striking to see that five of the countries with the smallest differences between the 75th and 25th percentiles on the mathematical literacy scale, namely Canada, Finland, Iceland, Japan and Korea, all perform significantly above the OECD average (Table A6.1). Furthermore, four of them, Canada, Finland, Japan and Korea are among the six best-performing countries in mathematical literacy. A similar pattern is observed for scientific literacy. Again, Canada, Finland, Japan and Korea are among the six countries with the smallest differences between 75th and 25th percentiles, as well as among the six best performing countries.

Conversely, the countries with the largest internal disparities tend to perform below the OECD mean. In mathematical literacy, for example, among the five countries (Belgium, Germany, Greece, Hungary and Poland) with the largest differences between the students at the 75th and 25th percentiles, only two (Belgium and the United States) do not perform significantly below the OECD average.

Chart A6.2

Multiple comparisons of mean performance on the PISA scientific literacy scale (2000)

A6

Column headers (countries, left to right) with Mean and S.E.:

Country	Mean	S.E.
Korea	552	(2.7)
Japan	550	(5.5)
Finland	538	(2.5)
United Kingdom	532	(2.7)
Canada	529	(1.6)
New Zealand	528	(2.4)
Australia	528	(3.5)
Austria	519	(2.5)
Ireland	513	(3.2)
Sweden	512	(2.5)
Czech Republic	511	(2.4)
France	500	(3.2)
Norway	500	(2.7)
United States	499	(7.3)
Hungary	496	(4.2)
Iceland	496	(2.2)
Belgium	496	(4.3)
Switzerland	496	(4.4)
Spain	491	(3.0)
Germany	487	(2.4)
Poland	483	(5.1)
Denmark	481	(2.8)
Italy	478	(3.1)
Liechtenstein	476	(7.1)
Greece	461	(4.9)
Russian Federation	460	(4.7)
Latvia	460	(5.6)
Portugal	459	(4.0)
Luxembourg	443	(2.3)
Mexico	422	(3.2)
Brazil	375	(3.3)

Rank ranges (across the bottom, in column order as above):

	Korea	Japan	Finland	United Kingdom	Canada	New Zealand	Australia	Austria	Ireland	Sweden	Czech Republic	France	Norway	United States	Hungary	Iceland	Belgium	Switzerland	Spain	Germany	Poland	Denmark	Italy	Liechtenstein	Greece	Russian Federation	Latvia	Portugal	Luxembourg	Mexico	Brazil
Upper rank[1]	1	1	3	3	4	4	4	8	9	9	10	13	13	11	13	14	13	13	16	19	19	21	22	20	25	26	25	26	30	31	32
Lower rank[1]	2	2	4	7	8	8	8	10	12	13	13	18	18	21	21	20	21	21	22	23	25	25	25	26	29	29	29	29	30	31	32

Legend:

Statistically significantly above the country mean

Not statistically significantly different from the country mean

Statistically significantly below the country mean

▲ Mean performance statistically significantly higher than in comparison country.

○ No statistically significant difference from comparison country.

▽ Mean performance statistically significantly lower than in comparison country.

Instructions

Read across the row for a country to compare performance with the countries listed along the top of the chart. The symbols indicate whether the mean performance of the country in the row is statistically significantly lower than that of the comparison country, statistically significantly higher than that of the comparison country, or if there is no statistically significant difference between the mean performance of the two countries.

Note: Countries are presented in descending order of mean performance on the PISA scientific literacy scale. Due to low response rates, the Netherlands is excluded from the figure. Assuming negligible to moderate levels of bias due to non-response, the position of the Netherlands may be expected, with 95 per cent confidence, to lie between 3rd and 14th place among countries.

1. Because data are based on samples, it is not possible to report exact rank order positions for countries. However, it is possible to report the range of rank order positions within which the country mean lies with 95 per cent likelihood.

Source: OECD PISA database, 2001. See Annex 3 for notes on methodology *(www.oecd.org/edu/eag2003)* and *www.pisa.oecd.org.*

A6

The performance scores are based on assessments administered as part of the Programme for International Student Assessment (PISA) undertaken by the OECD during 2000.

Definitions and methodologies

The target population studied for this indicator was 15-year-old students. Operationally, this refers to students aged between 15 years and 3 (completed) months and 16 years and 2 (completed) months at the beginning of the testing period and enrolled in an educational institution, irrespective of the grade level or type of institution and of whether they participated in school full-time or part-time.

To facilitate the interpretation of the scores assigned to students in PISA, the mean score for mathematical and scientific literacy performance among OECD countries was set at 500 and the standard deviation at 100, with the data weighted so that each OECD country contributed equally.

For notes on standard errors, significance tests, and multiple comparisons see Annex 3 at *www.oecd.org/edu/eag2003*.

A6

Table A6.1
Variation in performance in mathematical literacy of 15-year-olds (2000)
Performance of 15-year-olds on the PISA mathematical literacy scale, by percentile

		Mean		Percentiles											
				5th		10th		25th		75th		90th		95th	
		Mean score	S.E.	Score	S.E.	Score	S.E.	Score	S.E.	Score	S.E.	Score	S.E.	Score	S.E.
OECD COUNTRIES	Australia	533	(3.5)	380	(6.4)	418	(6.4)	474	(4.4)	594	(4.5)	647	(5.7)	679	(5.8)
	Austria	515	(2.5)	355	(5.3)	392	(4.6)	455	(3.5)	581	(3.8)	631	(3.6)	661	(5.2)
	Belgium	520	(3.9)	322	(11.0)	367	(8.6)	453	(6.5)	597	(3.0)	646	(3.9)	672	(3.5)
	Canada	533	(1.4)	390	(3.2)	423	(2.5)	477	(2.0)	592	(1.7)	640	(1.9)	668	(2.6)
	Czech Republic	498	(2.8)	335	(5.4)	372	(4.2)	433	(4.1)	564	(3.9)	623	(4.8)	655	(5.6)
	Denmark	514	(2.4)	366	(6.1)	401	(5.1)	458	(3.1)	575	(3.1)	621	(3.7)	649	(4.6)
	Finland	536	(2.2)	400	(6.5)	433	(3.6)	484	(4.1)	592	(2.5)	637	(3.2)	664	(3.5)
	France	517	(2.7)	364	(6.4)	399	(5.4)	457	(4.7)	581	(3.1)	629	(3.2)	656	(4.6)
	Germany	490	(2.5)	311	(7.9)	349	(6.9)	423	(3.9)	563	(2.7)	619	(3.6)	649	(3.9)
	Greece	447	(5.6)	260	(9.0)	303	(8.1)	375	(8.1)	524	(6.7)	586	(7.8)	617	(8.6)
	Hungary	488	(4.0)	327	(7.1)	360	(5.7)	419	(4.8)	558	(5.2)	615	(6.4)	648	(6.9)
	Iceland	514	(2.3)	372	(5.7)	407	(4.7)	459	(3.5)	572	(3.0)	622	(3.1)	649	(5.5)
	Ireland	503	(2.7)	357	(6.4)	394	(4.7)	449	(4.1)	561	(3.6)	606	(4.3)	630	(5.0)
	Italy	457	(2.9)	301	(8.4)	338	(5.5)	398	(3.5)	520	(3.5)	570	(4.4)	600	(6.1)
	Japan	557	(5.5)	402	(11.2)	440	(9.1)	504	(7.4)	617	(5.2)	662	(4.9)	688	(6.1)
	Korea	547	(2.8)	400	(6.1)	438	(5.0)	493	(4.2)	606	(3.4)	650	(4.3)	676	(5.3)
	Luxembourg	446	(2.0)	281	(7.4)	328	(4.2)	390	(3.8)	509	(3.4)	559	(3.2)	588	(3.9)
	Mexico	387	(3.4)	254	(5.5)	281	(3.6)	329	(4.1)	445	(5.2)	496	(5.6)	527	(6.6)
	New Zealand	537	(3.1)	364	(6.1)	405	(5.4)	472	(3.9)	607	(4.0)	659	(4.2)	689	(5.2)
	Norway	499	(2.8)	340	(7.0)	379	(5.2)	439	(4.0)	565	(3.9)	613	(4.5)	643	(4.5)
	Poland	470	(5.5)	296	(12.2)	335	(9.2)	402	(7.0)	542	(6.8)	599	(7.7)	632	(8.5)
	Portugal	454	(4.1)	297	(7.3)	332	(6.1)	392	(5.7)	520	(4.3)	570	(4.3)	596	(5.0)
	Spain	476	(3.1)	323	(5.8)	358	(4.3)	416	(5.3)	540	(4.0)	592	(3.9)	621	(3.1)
	Sweden	510	(2.5)	347	(5.8)	386	(4.0)	450	(3.3)	574	(2.6)	626	(3.3)	656	(5.5)
	Switzerland	529	(4.4)	353	(9.1)	398	(6.0)	466	(4.8)	601	(5.2)	653	(5.8)	682	(4.8)
	United Kingdom	529	(2.5)	374	(5.9)	412	(3.6)	470	(3.2)	592	(3.2)	646	(4.3)	676	(5.9)
	United States	493	(7.6)	327	(11.7)	361	(9.6)	427	(9.7)	562	(7.5)	620	(7.7)	652	(7.9)
	OECD total	*498*	*(2.1)*	*318*	*(3.1)*	*358*	*(3.4)*	*429*	*(3.0)*	*572*	*(2.1)*	*628*	*(1.9)*	*658*	*(2.1)*
	Country mean	*500*	*(0.7)*	*326*	*(1.5)*	*367*	*(1.4)*	*435*	*(1.1)*	*571*	*(0.8)*	*625*	*(0.9)*	*655*	*(1.1)*
NON-OECD COUNTRIES	Brazil	334	(3.7)	179	(5.5)	212	(5.2)	266	(4.2)	399	(5.5)	464	(7.5)	499	(8.9)
	Latvia	463	(4.5)	288	(9.0)	328	(8.9)	393	(5.7)	536	(6.2)	593	(5.6)	625	(6.6)
	Liechtenstein	514	(7.0)	343	(19.7)	380	(18.9)	454	(15.5)	579	(7.5)	635	(16.9)	665	(15.0)
	Russian Federation	478	(5.5)	305	(9.0)	343	(7.4)	407	(6.6)	552	(6.6)	613	(6.8)	648	(7.8)

Source: OECD PISA database, 2001. See Annex 3 for notes on methodology (*www.oecd.org/edu/eag2003*) and *www.pisa.oecd.org*.

A6

Table A6.2
Variation in performance in scientific literacy of 15-year-olds (2000)
Performance of 15-year-olds on the PISA scientific literacy scale, by percentile

		Mean		Percentiles											
				5th		10th		25th		75th		90th		95th	
		Mean score	S.E.	Score	S.E.	Score	S.E.	Score	S.E.	Score	S.E.	Score	S.E.	Score	S.E.
OECD COUNTRIES	Australia	528	(3.5)	368	(5.1)	402	(4.7)	463	(4.6)	596	(4.8)	646	(5.1)	675	(4.8)
	Austria	519	(2.6)	363	(5.7)	398	(4.0)	456	(3.8)	584	(3.5)	633	(4.1)	659	(4.3)
	Belgium	496	(4.3)	292	(13.5)	346	(10.2)	424	(6.6)	577	(3.5)	630	(2.6)	656	(3.0)
	Canada	529	(1.6)	380	(3.7)	412	(3.4)	469	(2.2)	592	(1.8)	641	(2.2)	670	(3.0)
	Czech Republic	511	(2.4)	355	(5.6)	389	(4.0)	449	(3.6)	577	(3.8)	632	(4.1)	663	(4.9)
	Denmark	481	(2.8)	310	(6.0)	347	(5.3)	410	(4.8)	554	(3.5)	613	(4.4)	645	(4.7)
	Finland	538	(2.5)	391	(5.2)	425	(4.2)	481	(3.5)	598	(3.0)	645	(4.3)	674	(4.3)
	France	500	(3.2)	329	(6.1)	363	(5.4)	429	(5.3)	575	(4.0)	631	(4.2)	663	(4.9)
	Germany	487	(2.4)	314	(9.5)	350	(6.0)	417	(4.9)	560	(3.3)	618	(3.5)	649	(4.7)
	Greece	461	(4.9)	300	(9.3)	334	(8.3)	393	(7.0)	530	(5.3)	585	(5.3)	616	(5.8)
	Hungary	496	(4.2)	328	(7.5)	361	(4.9)	423	(5.5)	570	(4.8)	629	(5.1)	659	(8.5)
	Iceland	496	(2.2)	351	(7.0)	381	(4.3)	436	(3.7)	558	(3.1)	607	(4.1)	635	(4.8)
	Ireland	513	(3.2)	361	(6.5)	394	(5.7)	450	(4.4)	578	(3.4)	630	(4.6)	661	(5.4)
	Italy	478	(3.1)	315	(7.1)	349	(6.2)	411	(4.4)	547	(3.5)	602	(4.0)	633	(4.4)
	Japan	550	(5.5)	391	(11.3)	430	(9.9)	495	(7.2)	612	(5.0)	659	(4.7)	688	(5.7)
	Korea	552	(2.7)	411	(5.3)	442	(5.3)	499	(4.0)	610	(3.4)	652	(3.9)	674	(5.7)
	Luxembourg	443	(2.3)	278	(7.2)	320	(6.8)	382	(3.4)	510	(2.8)	563	(4.4)	593	(4.0)
	Mexico	422	(3.2)	303	(4.8)	325	(4.6)	368	(3.1)	472	(4.7)	525	(5.5)	554	(7.0)
	New Zealand	528	(2.4)	357	(5.6)	392	(5.2)	459	(3.8)	600	(3.4)	653	(5.0)	683	(5.1)
	Norway	500	(2.8)	338	(7.3)	377	(6.6)	437	(4.0)	569	(3.5)	619	(3.9)	649	(6.2)
	Poland	483	(5.1)	326	(9.2)	359	(5.8)	415	(5.5)	553	(7.3)	610	(7.6)	639	(7.5)
	Portugal	459	(4.0)	317	(5.0)	343	(5.1)	397	(5.2)	521	(4.7)	575	(5.0)	604	(5.3)
	Spain	491	(3.0)	333	(5.1)	367	(4.3)	425	(4.4)	558	(3.5)	613	(3.9)	643	(5.5)
	Sweden	512	(2.5)	357	(5.7)	390	(4.6)	446	(4.1)	578	(3.0)	630	(3.4)	660	(4.5)
	Switzerland	496	(4.4)	332	(5.8)	366	(5.4)	427	(5.1)	567	(6.4)	626	(6.4)	656	(9.0)
	United Kingdom	532	(2.7)	366	(6.8)	401	(6.0)	466	(3.8)	602	(3.9)	656	(4.7)	687	(5.0)
	United States	499	(7.3)	330	(11.7)	368	(10.0)	430	(9.6)	571	(8.0)	628	(7.0)	658	(8.4)
	OECD total	*502*	*(2.0)*	*332*	*(3.3)*	*368*	*(3.1)*	*431*	*(2.8)*	*576*	*(2.1)*	*631*	*(1.9)*	*662*	*(2.3)*
	Country mean	*500*	*(0.7)*	*332*	*(1.5)*	*368*	*(1.0)*	*431*	*(1.0)*	*572*	*(0.8)*	*627*	*(0.8)*	*657*	*(1.2)*
NON-OECD COUNTRIES	Brazil	375	(3.3)	230	(5.5)	262	(5.9)	315	(3.7)	432	(4.9)	492	(7.8)	531	(8.2)
	Latvia	460	(5.6)	299	(10.1)	334	(8.8)	393	(7.7)	528	(5.7)	585	(7.2)	620	(8.0)
	Liechtenstein	476	(7.1)	314	(23.5)	357	(20.0)	409	(12.3)	543	(12.7)	595	(12.4)	629	(24.0)
	Russian Federation	460	(4.7)	298	(6.5)	333	(5.4)	392	(6.2)	529	(5.8)	591	(5.9)	625	(5.7)

Source: OECD PISA database, 2001. See Annex 3 for notes on methodology (*www.oecd.org/edu/eag2003*) and *www.pisa.oecd.org*.

INDICATOR A7: HOW STUDENT PERFORMANCE VARIES BETWEEN SCHOOLS

- On average, differences in the performance of 15-year-olds between schools account for 36 per cent of the OECD average variation in student performance, but this proportion varies from below 10 per cent in Iceland and Sweden to more than 50 per cent in Austria, Belgium, the Czech Republic, Germany, Greece, Hungary, Italy and Poland.

- Some of the variation between schools is attributable to geography, institutional factors or the selection of students by ability. The differences are often compounded by family background, particularly in countries with differentiated school systems, since students' results are associated not only with their own individual backgrounds but – to a greater extent – with the backgrounds of others at their school.

- High overall variation can result from high within-school differences, high between-school differences or a combination of the two.

- In school systems with differentiated school types, the clustering of students with particular socio-economic characteristics in certain schools is greater than in systems where the curriculum does not vary significantly between schools.

A7

Variation in student performance between and within schools on the PISA reading literacy scale (2000)
Expressed as a percentage of the average variation in student performance in OECD countries

■ Between-school variation   Within-school variation

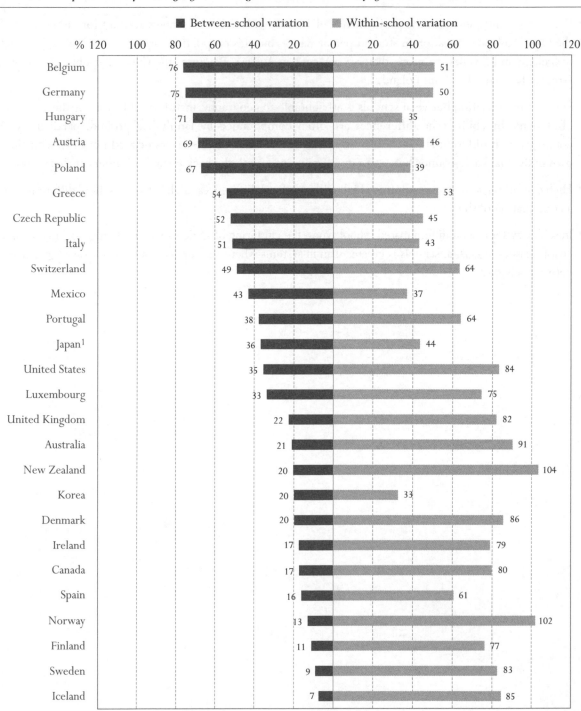

Country	Between-school variation	Within-school variation
Belgium	76	51
Germany	75	50
Hungary	71	35
Austria	69	46
Poland	67	39
Greece	54	53
Czech Republic	52	45
Italy	51	43
Switzerland	49	64
Mexico	43	37
Portugal	38	64
Japan[1]	36	44
United States	35	84
Luxembourg	33	75
United Kingdom	22	82
Australia	21	91
New Zealand	20	104
Korea	20	33
Denmark	20	86
Ireland	17	79
Canada	17	80
Spain	16	61
Norway	13	102
Finland	11	77
Sweden	9	83
Iceland	7	85

Countries are ranked in descending order of the total between-school variation in student performance on the PISA reading literacy scale.
1. Due to sampling methods used, the between-school variance in Japan includes variation between classes within schools.
Source: OECD PISA database, 2001. Table A7.1. See Annex 3 for notes on methodology *(www.oecd.org/edu/eag2003)* and *www.pisa.oecd.org.*

A7

Policy context

Indicators A5 and A6 have shown that, in most countries, there are considerable differences in performance within each education system. This variation may result from the background of students and schools, from the human and financial resources available to schools, from curricular differences, from selection policies and practices and from the way in which teaching is organised and delivered.

Many factors account for the performance differences observed by PISA…

Some countries have non-selective school systems that seek to provide all students with the same opportunities for learning and that allow each school to cater to the full range of student performance. Other countries respond to diversity explicitly by forming groups of students of similar performance levels through selection either within or between schools, with the aim of serving students according to their specific needs. And in yet other countries, combinations of the two approaches occur. Even in comprehensive school systems, there may be significant variation between schools due to the socio-economic and cultural characteristics of the communities that the schools serve or due to geographical differences (such as differences between regions, provinces or states in federal systems, or differences between rural and urban areas). Finally, there may be significant variation between individual schools that cannot be easily quantified or otherwise described, part of which could result from differences in the quality or effectiveness of the teaching that those schools provide.

…and the organisation of the education system can play a significant part in this equation.

To examine the impact of such policies and practices, this indicator examines differences between schools in reading literacy performance. The results for mathematical and scientific literacy are broadly similar and therefore not shown in this indicator.

To shed light on this, this indicator examines performance differences between schools.

Evidence and explanations

Chart A7.1 and Table A7.1 show the extent of variation attributable to different factors in each country. The length of the bars indicates the total observed variation in student performance on the reading literacy scale. Note that the values are expressed as percentages of the average variation between OECD countries in student performance on the reading literacy scale. If the sum of the two bars for each country is larger than 100, this indicates that variation in student performance is greater in the corresponding country than in a typical OECD country. Similarly, a combined value smaller than 100 indicates below-average variation in student performance.

Chart A7.1 compares the extent of variation in student performance within countries…

The bar for each country is aligned so that variation between schools is represented by the length to the left of the vertical line down the centre of the chart, and variation within schools is represented by the length to the right of that vertical line. Longer segments to the left of the vertical line indicate greater variation in the mean performance of schools. Longer segments to the right of the vertical line indicate greater variation among students within schools.

…and breaks it down into between-school and within-school differences.

On average, differences between schools account for 36 per cent of the OECD average between-student variation, but this proportion varies widely across countries.

As shown in Chart A7.1, in most countries a considerable portion of the variation in student performance lies between schools. On average, among the 26 OECD countries included in this comparison, differences between schools account for 36 per cent of the OECD average between-student variation. In Austria, Belgium, the Czech Republic, Germany, Greece, Hungary, Italy and Poland, more than 50 per cent of the OECD average between-student variation is between schools (see Column 3 in Table A7.1). Where there is substantial variation between schools and less variation between students within schools, students will generally be in schools in which other students perform at levels similar to their own. This selectivity may reflect family choice of school or residential location, or policies on school enrolment, allocation of students or the curriculum.

Some countries have low variation between schools and within schools…

In Korea, overall variation in student performance on the reading literacy scale is about half the OECD average variation in that category, and Korea's variation between schools is only about 20 per cent of the OECD average variation between schools. Korea thus not only achieves high average performance in reading and low overall disparity between students, but does so with relatively little variation in mean performance between schools. Spain also shows low overall variation (around three-quarters of the OECD average) and low between-school variation (16 per cent of the OECD average variation in student performance) but, unlike Korea, has a mean score significantly below the OECD average.

…particularly those with the lowest overall variation.

The smallest variation in reading performance between schools occurs in Finland, Iceland and Sweden, where the differences account for only between 7 and 11 per cent of the average between-student variation in OECD countries. In these countries performance is largely unrelated to the schools in which students are enrolled. They are thus likely to encounter a similar learning environment in terms of the ability distribution of students. It is noteworthy that overall variation in student performance in these countries is below the OECD average. These education systems succeed both in minimising differences between schools and in containing the overall variation in student performance in reading literacy.

High overall variation can result from high within-school differences,…

Australia, New Zealand and Norway (with 112, 126 and 116 per cent of the OECD average between-student variation, respectively) are among the countries with the highest overall variation in reading performance, but only a comparatively small proportion (21, 20 and 13 per cent of the OECD average of student performance) results from differences between schools. In these countries, most variation occurs within schools, suggesting that individual schools need to cater to a more diverse client base.

…high between-school differences…

Belgium, Germany and Switzerland (124, 133 and 112 per cent of the average between-student variation in OECD countries) are also countries with comparatively high overall variation in student performance, but a large proportion (76, 75 and 49 per cent of the OECD average variation in student performance) results from differences in performance between schools.

The United States, another country with comparatively large overall variation in student performance (118 per cent of the average variation between students in OECD countries), is somewhere in the middle, with 35 per cent of the average OECD variation in student performance between schools.

…or a combination of the two.

The fuller analysis in the report *Knowledge and Skills for Life* (OECD, 2001) suggests that, in school systems with differentiated school types, the clustering of students with particular socio-economic characteristics in certain schools is greater than in systems where the curriculum does not vary significantly between schools. In Austria, Belgium, the Czech Republic, Germany, Italy and the Netherlands, for example, the between-school variation associated with the fact that students attend different types of school is considerably compounded by differences in social and family background. This may be a consequence of selection or self-selection: when the school market provides some differentiation, students from lower social backgrounds may tend to be directed to, or choose for themselves, less demanding study programmes, or may opt not to participate in the selection procedures of the education system.

Some of the variation between schools is attributable to geography, institutional factors or selection of students by ability.

The fuller analysis also suggests that the effect of the overall social background of a school's intake on student performance tends to be greater than the impact of the individual student's social background. Students from a lower socio-economic background attending schools in which the average socio-economic background is high tend to perform much better than when they are enrolled in a school with a below-average socio-economic intake – and the reverse is true for more advantaged students in less advantaged schools. This suggests that institutional differentiation in education systems, often compounded by the social background of a school's intake, self-selection by students and/or their parents as well as judgements on prior performance, can have a major impact on an individual student's success at school.

Definitions and methodologies

The target population studied for this indicator was 15-year-old students. Operationally, this refers to students aged between 15 years and 3 (completed) months and 16 years and 2 (completed) months at the beginning of the testing period and enrolled in an educational institution, irrespective of the grade level or type of institution and of whether they participated in school full-time or part-time.

The performance scores are based on assessments administered as part of the Programme for International Student Assessment (PISA) undertaken by the OECD during 2000.

To facilitate the interpretation of the scores assigned to students in PISA, the mean score for reading literacy performance among OECD countries was set at 500 and the standard deviation at 100, with the data weighted so that each OECD country contributed equally. These reference points anchor PISA's measurement of student proficiency.

Variation in Table A7.1 is expressed by statistical variance. This is obtained by squaring the standard deviation referred to earlier in this chapter. The statistical variance rather than the standard deviation is used for this comparison to allow for the decomposition of the components of variation in student performance.

The average is calculated over the OECD countries included in the table. Owing to the sampling methods used in Japan, the between-school variation in Japan includes variation between classes within schools.

For notes on standard errors, significance tests, and multiple comparisons see Annex 3 at *www.oecd.org / edu / eag2003*.

A7

Table A7.1
Sources of variation in performance in reading literacy of 15-year-old students (2000)
Between-school and within-school variation in student performance on the PISA reading literacy scale

		Variation expressed as a percentage of the average variation in student performance (SP) across the OECD countries							Total variation between schools expressed as a percentage of the total variation within the country[2]
		Total variation in SP expressed as a percentage of the average variation in student performance across OECD countries			Variation explained by the international socio-economic index of occupational status of students		Variation explained by the international socio-economic index of occupational status of students and schools		
	Total variation in SP[1]		Total variation in SP between schools	Total variation in SP within schools	Between-school variation explained	Within-school variation explained	Between-school variation explained	Within-school variation explained	
Australia	10 357	111.6	20.9	90.6	8.3	6.7	14.2	6.9	18.8
Austria	8 649	93.2	68.6	45.7	10.4	0.4	42.6	0.3	60.0
Belgium	11 455	123.5	76.0	50.9	11.0	1.8	44.2	1.9	59.9
Canada	8 955	96.5	17.1	80.1	4.6	5.0	7.8	5.1	17.6
Czech Republic	9 278	100.0	51.9	45.3	8.8	1.8	34.4	1.8	53.4
Denmark	9 614	103.6	19.6	85.9	10.2	8.0	11.6	8.1	18.6
Finland	7 994	86.2	10.7	76.5	1.5	4.6	1.7	4.6	12.3
France	m	m	m	m	m	m	m	m	m
Germany	12 368	133.3	74.8	50.2	11.7	2.3	51.5	2.3	59.8
Greece	9 436	101.7	53.8	52.9	7.0	1.1	25.0	1.1	50.4
Hungary	8 810	95.0	71.2	34.8	8.3	0.3	49.4	0.2	67.2
Iceland	8 529	91.9	7.0	85.0	1.6	5.0	1.7	5.0	7.6
Ireland	8 755	94.4	17.1	79.2	5.5	5.7	10.1	5.7	17.8
Italy	8 356	90.1	50.9	43.4	3.4	0.5	23.8	0.5	54.0
Japan[3]	7 358	79.3	36.5	43.9	m	m	m	m	45.4
Korea	4 833	52.1	19.7	33.0	1.0	0.2	7.1	0.2	37.4
Luxembourg	10 088	108.7	33.4	74.9	11.1	8.3	26.7	8.2	30.8
Mexico	7 370	79.4	42.9	37.4	5.2	0.1	25.7	0.1	53.4
New Zealand	11 701	126.1	20.1	103.9	7.3	10.9	11.6	11.0	16.2
Norway	10 743	115.8	12.6	102.4	3.7	8.7	4.9	8.7	10.9
Poland	9 958	107.3	67.0	38.9	6.3	1.1	42.4	1.1	63.2
Portugal	9 436	101.7	37.5	64.3	10.6	4.6	23.8	4.6	36.8
Spain	7 181	77.4	15.9	60.9	5.4	3.0	9.1	3.1	20.7
Sweden	8 495	91.6	8.9	83.0	4.5	6.9	5.8	6.9	9.7
Switzerland	10 408	112.2	48.7	63.7	12.7	4.0	24.3	3.9	43.4
United Kingdom	10 098	108.9	22.4	82.3	9.6	8.4	16.0	8.7	21.4
United States	10 979	118.3	35.1	83.6	12.0	5.6	25.5	5.8	29.6
Brazil	7 427	80.1	35.8	47.1	6.5	1.9	19.7	2.1	43.1
Latvia	10 435	112.5	35.1	77.5	4.9	4.4	16.7	4.5	31.2
Liechtenstein	m	m	m	m	m	m	m	m	43.9
Russian Federation	8 466	91.3	33.6	57.1	4.8	2.4	15.4	2.3	37.1

OECD COUNTRIES (Australia through United States)
NON-OECD COUNTRIES (Brazil through Russian Federation)

1. The total variation in student performance is obtained as the square of the standard deviation shown in Table A5.2. The statistical variance and not the standard deviation is used for this comparison to allow for the decomposition of the components of variation in student performance. For reasons explained in the *PISA 2000 Technical Report*, the sum of the between and within-school variance components may, for some countries, differ slightly from the square of the standard deviation shown in Table A5.2.
2. This index is often referred to as the intra-class correlation (rho).
3. Due to the sampling methods used in Japan, the between-school variance in Japan includes variation between classes within schools.
Source: OECD PISA database, 2001. See Annex 3 for notes on methodology (*www.oecd.org/edu/eag2003*) and *www.pisa.oecd.org*.

INDICATOR A8: PROFILES OF 15-YEAR-OLD READERS

A8

- PISA identifies several profiles of readers. Some 15-year-olds focus their reading on a limited set of print material; magazines only, or magazines and newspapers. Others, more diversified in their reading interests, choose a broader range of print content. Some choose to read comics in addition to magazines and newspapers while others prefer books, either fiction or non-fiction, to comics.

- Profiles of readers differ perceptibly from one country to another. In some countries, such as Finland and Japan, a high proportion of the students who read a variety of print content mainly read newspapers, magazines and comics. In other countries, such as Australia, New Zealand and the United Kingdom, students who read a diverse range of materials tend to choose newspapers, magazines and books (fiction and non-fiction).

- Females and males show clearly different profiles of reading. Among the two profiles of students poorly diversified in reading, mainly readers of newspapers and magazines, males and females are more or less equally distributed. The third profile, of readers more oriented towards comics, comprises a majority of males, while the profile oriented towards reading books, especially fiction, comprises a majority of females.

- Not surprisingly, 15-year-olds reading a diversity of print material are more proficient in reading than those reading a limited set of print material. But the gap in reading proficiency between those reading comics and those reading fiction is not huge. Daily engagement in reading magazines, newspapers and comics – a kind of reading that is perhaps less valued by school than fiction books – seems, at least in some cultural contexts, to be a fruitful way of becoming a proficient reader.

Chart A8.1

Performance and profiles of 15-year-old readers (2000)

Performance of 15-year-olds on the PISA combined reading literacy scale and percentage of students by reading profile cluster

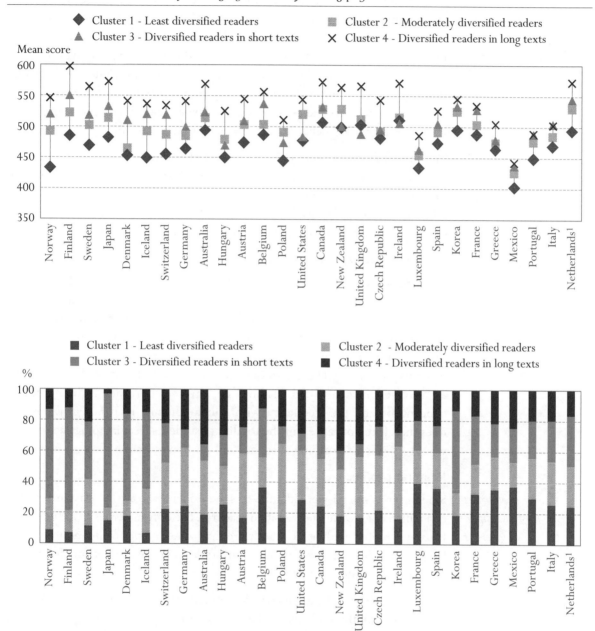

1. Response rate is too low to ensure comparability.

Countries are ranked in descending order of the difference between mean scores on the PISA combined reading literacy scale in Cluster 1- Least diversified readers and Cluster 4 - Diversified readers in long texts.

Source: OECD PISA database, 2001. Table A8.2. See Annex 3 for notes *(www.oecd.org/edu/eag2003).*

A8

This indicator examines the reading literacy skills of 15-year-old students in relation to the frequency and diversity of print materials that they read.

Policy context

Students' reading practices outside of the classroom are associated with their reading literacy performance. It is well established that students who choose to spend a lot of time reading tend to be better readers than those who do not. In examining students' reading practices, it is important to consider not just the amount of time that students spend reading, but also how they invest this time. While some students may choose to read only one type of material (*e.g.*, magazines) frequently, others read a diversity of materials. Understanding what students read frequently and how these choices are related to reading performance can prompt educators and policymakers to devise early-intervention strategies to foster certain reading behaviours in order to promote literacy.

This indicator, drawn from PISA, profiles students' reading practices according to the materials they read frequently and demonstrates the relationship between these profiles and their performance in reading literacy. Indicator A9 builds on these findings to explore a broader concept of "engagement" in reading, which encompasses both reading practices and attitudes toward reading.

Evidence and explanations

Students can be grouped according to their reading patterns of different material.

In PISA, students were asked to rate how frequently they chose to read different kinds of print materials, including magazines, newspapers, comics, and fiction and non-fiction books. Based on their responses, students were grouped into four distinct reading profiles, or *clusters*. The distribution of these clusters is based on two dimensions: the frequency of reading, and the diversity of reading. These two dimensions are reflected in such expressions as "involved in diversified reading" or "diversified reader". This indicator concentrates on the frequency with which students read *for enjoyment* and does therefore not represent the totality of students' reading practices, which would also include reading at school and for homework.

Reading profiles

Cluster 1 comprises the least diversified readers…

Students in Cluster 1 were identified as the readers who are the least involved in diversified reading (least diversified readers). The only materials that students in Cluster 1 report reading frequently are magazines; 38 per cent read magazines frequently. Much smaller percentages of students in Cluster 1 report frequently reading other materials (Table A8.1).

…Cluster 2 moderately diversified readers…

Students in Cluster 2 can be considered modestly diversified readers. While a vast majority of the students in Cluster 2 report frequently reading newspapers (89 per cent) as well as magazines (70 per cent), very small percentages of students report reading other print materials.

…Cluster 3 readers that are diversified in short texts …

In Cluster 3, the overwhelming majority of students frequently read magazines (85 per cent) and newspapers (81 per cent) – as in Cluster 2 – but they also frequently read comics (89 per cent). By comparison with Clusters 1 and 2, these students are more involved in diversified reading, but their focus is on relatively short and undemanding texts.

Likewise, Cluster 4 includes students who are diversified readers, but the focus of these students is on more demanding and longer texts, namely books. A majority of these students report frequently reading magazines (71 per cent), newspapers (76 per cent), and fiction (72 per cent), while almost half (48 per cent) report frequently reading non-fiction books (Table A8.1).

...and Cluster 4 readers that are diversified in long and complex texts...

Reading profiles and performance

Grouping students by their involvement in diversified reading can provide insight into the relationship between reading practices and reading literacy. Performance on the combined reading literacy scale is related among OECD countries to the frequency with which students report reading a diversity of materials. Students in Cluster 1, the least diversified readers, had the lowest mean score (468 points) on the combined reading literacy scale compared to students in other clusters, and score significantly below the OECD average. The modestly diversified readers in Cluster 2 had a mean score of 498 points, which is statistically similar to the OECD average and significantly higher than the mean score for students in Cluster 1. By contrast, the diversified readers of shorter texts (Cluster 3) scored higher than the OECD average (514 points versus 500 points), while the diversified readers of longer texts in Cluster 4 scored significantly higher, with 539 points, than both the OECD average and the average of students in Cluster 3. The average difference between scores of the least diversified readers (Cluster 1) and the diversified readers of longer texts (Cluster 4) was 71 points, almost an entire proficiency level (Table A8.2).

Reading patterns are closely associated with performance...

The relationship between diversified reading of longer texts and reading literacy scores is evident *within* most countries as well. In all countries except Italy, students who are diversified readers of longer texts (Cluster 4) obtain the highest average reading literacy scores. At the other extreme, in all countries except Ireland and the United Kingdom, students who are among the least diversified readers (Cluster 1) have the lowest mean scores within their respective countries compared to the other clusters. The difference between scores of the least diversified readers (Cluster 1) and the diversified readers of longer texts (Cluster 4) ranged from 34 points in Italy to 112 and 113 points in Finland and Norway, respectively (Chart A8.1).

...both overall as well as within each country.

The relationship between reading profiles and performance among students in Clusters 2 and 3 is somewhat less consistent among countries. For example, in several English-speaking countries (Ireland, New Zealand, the United Kingdom, and the United States) and in certain Eastern European countries (Hungary and Poland), students in Cluster 2 obtain higher reading literacy scores than students in Cluster 3. This result is interesting in that it suggests that, in these countries, students who report reading a more diverse array of reading materials, especially comics and to a lesser extent books, perform less well than students who report reading only newspapers and magazines (Table A8.2).

Another way of exploring the relationship between reading practices and reading literacy is to examine the distribution of readers across the PISA reading proficiency levels (for the definition of the proficiency levels, see Indicator A5).

A8

As would be expected, among countries, Cluster 1 has the largest share of students reading at or below Level 1 relative to the other clusters (27 per cent versus 16, 13, and 10 per cent respectively for Clusters 2, 3, and 4). By contrast, Cluster 4 has the largest share of students reading at the two highest levels of proficiency (Levels 4 or 5) – 47 per cent compared with 35, 28, and 21 for Clusters 3, 2, and 1, respectively (Chart A8.2 and Table A8.3).

Reading profiles among countries

Reading patterns differ widely among countries…

Although the relationship between diversified reading and reading literacy appears to be somewhat similar among countries, the actual patterns of reading practices are not. The countries that have the lowest proportion of students in Cluster 1 are Finland (7 per cent), Iceland (7 per cent), Norway (8 per cent), and Sweden (11 per cent). By contrast, more than 30 per cent of students in six countries are in Cluster 1: Belgium, France, Greece, Luxembourg, Mexico and Spain.

…and some of these differences are reflected in performance patterns.

Four of these countries with high proportions of the least diversified readers (Greece, Luxembourg, Mexico and Spain) have overall mean reading scores that are significantly below the OECD average of 500, while one (France) scores similar to the OECD average and another (Belgium) scores significantly above the OECD average (Table A8.2 and Chart A8.1).

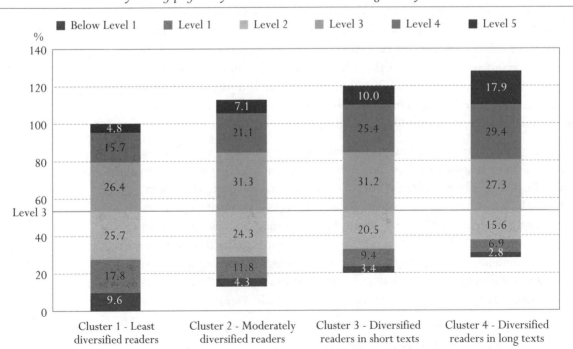

Chart A8.2

Percentage of 15-year-olds in each PISA reading profile cluster (2000)
by level of proficiency on the PISA combined reading literacy scale

Source: OECD PISA database, 2001. Table A8.3. See Annex 3 for notes *(www.oecd.org/edu/eag2003).*

Not surprisingly, there is also a large range among countries in the proportions of students who are diversified readers of longer texts (Cluster 4). The proportions of students in Cluster 4 ranged from 3 per cent in Japan and 12 per cent in Belgium and Finland to more than one-third of the students in Australia, New Zealand, and the United Kingdom. As one would expect, countries that have a high proportion of students who are diversified readers of longer texts have mean scores that are significantly above the OECD average. The converse, however, is not necessarily true. For instance, although Finland and Japan have low proportions of students in Cluster 4, these two countries also have mean reading scores that are well above the OECD mean. This may in part be explained by the fact that, in both of these countries, two-thirds to three quarters of the students are diversified readers of shorter texts (Cluster 3).

Reading profiles and gender

Patterns of diversity of reading practices also vary by gender. Numerous studies in various countries have demonstrated that females, on average, spend more time reading and also tend to read different types of materials than do males. Indeed, the concentration of males in certain clusters shows this to be the case. On average, 34 per cent of males, compared to 23 per cent of females, are grouped in Cluster 3. The majority of students in Cluster 3 report frequently reading shorter texts such as newspapers, magazines, and comics, but not books. Conversely, in Cluster 4, females outnumber males (29 per cent versus 16 per cent on average). Students in Cluster 4 tend to frequently read newspapers, magazines, and books (especially fiction), but not comics. Thus, the more involved readers of fiction are clearly females, a trend that is observed in every OECD country. The distinction between males and females is more balanced among the less diversified readers (Clusters 1 and 2), and varies more by country (Table A8.4).

Females tend to be not just better performers but also more diversified readers.

Definitions and methodologies

The target population studied for this indicator was 15-year-old students. Operationally, this referred to students who were from 15 years and 3 (completed) months to 16 years and 2 (completed) months at the beginning of the testing period and who were enrolled in an educational institution, regardless of the grade level or type of institution and or whether they participated in school full-time or part-time.

The performance scores are based on assessments administered as part of the Programme for International Student Assessment (PISA) undertaken by the OECD during 2000.

In PISA, students were asked to rate how frequently they read different kinds of materials. For the cluster analysis in this indicator, reading one kind of material 'several times a month' or 'several times a week' is considered as frequent reading, 'a few times a year' and 'once a month' as moderate reading, and 'never or hardly ever' as no reading.

For notes on standard errors, significance tests, and multiple comparisons see Annex 3 at *www.oecd.org/edu/eag2003*.

Table A8.1
Profiles of 15-year-old readers (2000)
Cross-country mean percentage of 15-year-olds reading each kind of print material, by PISA reading profile cluster

	No reading	Moderate reading	Frequent reading
Cluster 1 - Least diversified readers **(22.4 per cent of students)**			
Magazines	15.6	46.0	38.4
Newspapers	47.6	52.2	0.2
Comics	49.6	37.4	12.9
Fiction	40.6	47.1	12.3
Non-fiction	53.7	40.7	5.7
Cluster 2 - Moderately diversified readers **(27.1 per cent of students)**			
Magazines	4.6	25.4	69.9
Newspapers	-	11.4	88.6
Comics	60.7	38.9	0.4
Fiction	45.3	51.9	2.7
Non-fiction	51.7	45.3	3.1
Cluster 3 - Diversified readers in short texts **(28.3 per cent of students)**			
Magazines	1.8	13.5	84.7
Newspapers	2.4	16.1	81.4
Comics	-	10.6	89.4
Fiction	18.2	51.3	30.5
Non-fiction	24.5	54.4	21.0
Cluster 4 - Diversified readers in long texts **(22.2 per cent of students)**			
Magazines	3.2	26.3	70.5
Newspapers	2.2	21.7	76.1
Comics	46.0	48.4	5.6
Fiction	0.7	27.4	71.9
Non-fiction	4.3	47.5	48.3

Source: OECD PISA database, 2001.

Table A8.2

Performance and profiles of 15-year-old readers (2000)

Performance of 15-year-olds on the PISA combined reading literacy scale and percentage of students, by PISA reading profile cluster

	All students		Cluster 1 - Least diversified readers				Cluster 2 - Moderately diversified readers				Cluster 3 - Diversified readers in short texts				Cluster 4 - Diversified readers in long texts			
	Mean score	S.E.	Mean score	S.E.	%	S.E.	Mean score	S.E.	%	S.E.	Mean score	S.E.	%	S.E.	Mean score	S.E.	%	S.E.
Australia	528	(3.5)	494	(4.9)	18.5	(0.9)	514	(3.7)	35.0	(1.1)	522	(6.3)	10.8	(0.6)	569	(4.4)	35.7	(1.2)
Austria	507	(2.4)	474	(4.6)	16.6	(0.7)	503	(2.4)	41.9	(0.9)	509	(3.5)	17.0	(0.5)	545	(3.6)	24.6	(0.8)
Belgium	507	(3.6)	487	(4.4)	36.3	(0.6)	503	(5.4)	19.6	(0.6)	537	(3.4)	31.8	(0.7)	556	(5.5)	12.3	(0.5)
Canada	534	(1.6)	507	(2.3)	24.3	(0.4)	528	(1.7)	30.8	(0.5)	531	(2.5)	16.2	(0.3)	572	(1.9)	28.7	(0.5)
Czech Republic	492	(2.4)	482	(3.5)	22.0	(0.7)	492	(2.8)	35.6	(0.9)	494	(3.4)	18.7	(0.6)	543	(2.9)	23.8	(0.7)
Denmark	497	(2.4)	453	(5.0)	17.5	(0.8)	464	(6.0)	10.1	(0.6)	511	(2.3)	56.2	(1.0)	541	(5.2)	16.2	(0.6)
Finland	546	(2.6)	485	(14.6)	6.9	(0.5)	522	(4.4)	14.2	(0.6)	550	(2.2)	66.6	(0.9)	597	(3.5)	12.3	(0.5)
France	505	(2.7)	488	(4.1)	32.6	(0.9)	503	(3.4)	19.2	(0.7)	528	(2.9)	31.3	(0.9)	534	(4.1)	16.8	(0.7)
Germany	484	(2.5)	464	(4.2)	24.1	(0.8)	485	(2.8)	38.0	(0.8)	499	(5.9)	11.6	(0.6)	541	(3.1)	26.3	(0.7)
Greece	474	(5.0)	464	(5.3)	35.4	(0.9)	474	(6.6)	21.3	(0.8)	478	(5.8)	21.5	(0.7)	505	(5.2)	21.8	(0.9)
Hungary	480	(4.0)	450	(4.8)	25.1	(1.0)	479	(4.3)	25.1	(0.8)	470	(4.7)	20.1	(0.7)	525	(4.7)	29.6	(1.0)
Iceland	507	(1.5)	449	(6.5)	6.6	(0.5)	492	(2.6)	28.6	(0.7)	520	(2.1)	49.7	(0.8)	537	(4.3)	15.1	(0.6)
Ireland	527	(3.2)	510	(5.9)	16.3	(0.7)	515	(3.3)	47.0	(0.8)	507	(5.9)	8.9	(0.6)	571	(3.6)	27.8	(1.0)
Italy	487	(2.9)	469	(4.7)	25.8	(0.9)	485	(3.3)	27.9	(0.7)	505	(3.3)	26.5	(0.8)	503	(4.1)	19.8	(0.7)
Japan	522	(5.2)	482	(8.2)	14.5	(0.9)	514	(7.2)	8.1	(0.5)	532	(4.6)	74.4	(0.9)	573	(7.7)	3.0	(0.3)
Korea	525	(2.4)	495	(3.9)	18.8	(0.6)	525	(3.7)	14.6	(0.6)	531	(2.4)	53.1	(1.1)	545	(3.8)	13.6	(0.7)
Luxembourg	441	(1.6)	434	(2.5)	39.4	(0.8)	454	(4.3)	21.3	(0.6)	461	(4.0)	19.2	(0.7)	486	(3.8)	20.0	(0.6)
Mexico	422	(3.3)	403	(3.6)	37.5	(1.3)	426	(5.9)	15.6	(0.8)	438	(4.3)	22.3	(5.9)	443	(4.9)	24.7	(0.7)
New Zealand	529	(2.8)	499	(4.8)	18.0	(0.7)	529	(3.1)	30.1	(0.9)	500	(6.4)	12.4	(0.6)	564	(3.7)	39.4	(1.0)
Norway	505	(2.8)	433	(7.1)	8.5	(0.6)	492	(4.2)	20.2	(0.7)	520	(2.7)	58.0	(0.9)	546	(4.3)	13.3	(0.5)
Poland	479	(4.5)	445	(7.0)	16.7	(0.9)	491	(4.2)	48.0	(1.1)	474	(6.6)	11.4	(0.7)	511	(6.3)	24.0	(1.1)
Portugal	470	(4.5)	449	(5.8)	29.8	(0.9)	477	(4.1)	25.9	(0.7)	487	(5.8)	24.4	(0.6)	489	(5.9)	19.8	(0.6)
Spain	493	(2.7)	474	(3.4)	36.2	(1.1)	492	(3.6)	23.0	(0.7)	503	(3.4)	17.5	(0.7)	526	(2.9)	23.3	(0.7)
Sweden	516	(2.2)	469	(4.8)	11.1	(0.5)	502	(2.8)	30.3	(0.8)	518	(2.8)	37.3	(0.8)	564	(3.6)	21.3	(0.7)
Switzerland	494	(4.3)	455	(4.6)	22.1	(0.9)	487	(4.3)	30.3	(0.8)	519	(5.1)	25.4	(0.8)	534	(5.2)	22.2	(0.8)
United Kingdom	523	(2.6)	503	(4.3)	17.1	(0.6)	512	(2.7)	39.4	(0.9)	488	(5.3)	8.4	(0.5)	566	(3.7)	35.1	(1.0)
United States	504	(7.1)	478	(7.6)	28.4	(1.3)	520	(5.8)	32.1	(1.5)	482	(10.9)	10.8	(1.1)	544	(6.0)	28.7	(1.5)
Country mean	*500*	*(0.6)*	*468*	*(1.0)*	*22.4*	*(0.2)*	*498*	*(0.7)*	*27.1*	*(0.1)*	*514*	*(0.9)*	*28.3*	*(0.2)*	*539*	*(0.9)*	*22.2*	*(0.2)*
Brazil	396	(3.1)	370	(4.4)	29.5	(1.1)	407	(5.1)	15.1	(0.8)	413	(4.3)	27.5	(1.0)	418	(3.6)	27.9	(1.1)
Latvia	458	(5.3)	412	(8.2)	13.8	(0.8)	464	(5.3)	39.9	(1.3)	433	(8.7)	15.2	(0.9)	499	(5.7)	31.1	(1.4)
Liechtenstein	483	(4.1)	442	(11.0)	21.9	(2.1)	478	(8.0)	40.7	(2.5)	524	(12.6)	14.3	(2.1)	526	(11.7)	23.2	(2.5)
Russian Federation	462	(4.2)	426	(6.3)	11.5	(0.5)	451	(5.1)	17.1	(0.6)	432	(4.8)	21.6	(1.2)	495	(3.9)	49.7	(1.1)
Netherlands[1]	-	-	494	(5.4)	24.7	(1.3)	530	(4.5)	25.8	(1.0)	544	(4.0)	33.1	(1.2)	573	(4.9)	16.5	(0.9)

OECD COUNTRIES (Australia through United States)
NON-OECD COUNTRIES (Brazil through Netherlands)

1. Response rate is too low to ensure comparability.
Source: OECD PISA database, 2001.

A8

Table A8.3
Cross-country mean percentage of 15-year-olds in each PISA reading profile cluster (2000)
by level of proficiency on the PISA combined reading literacy scale

	Below Level 1 (less than 335 score points)	Level 1 (from 335 to 407 score points)	Level 2 (from 408 to 480 score points)	Level 3 (from 481 to 552 score points)	Level 4 (from 553 to 625 score points)	Level 5 (above 625 score points)
Cluster 1 - Least diversified readers	9.6	17.8	25.7	26.4	15.7	4.8
Cluster 2 - Moderately diversified readers	4.3	11.8	24.3	31.3	21.1	7.1
Cluster 3 - Diversified readers in short texts	3.4	9.4	20.5	31.2	25.4	10
Cluster 4 - Diversified readers in long texts	2.8	6.9	15.6	27.3	29.4	17.9

Source: OECD PISA database, 2001.

Table A8.4
Profiles of 15-year-old readers and gender (2000)
Percentage of 15-year-olds in each PISA reading profile cluster, by gender

		Cluster 1 - Least diversified readers		Cluster 2 - Moderately diversified readers		Cluster 3 - Diversified readers in short texts		Cluster 4 - Diversified readers in long texts	
		Males	Females	Males	Females	Males	Females	Males	Females
OECD COUNTRIES	Australia	17.4	19.7	39.0	30.7	15.5	5.7	28.2	43.9
	Austria	16.9	16.0	42.1	42.0	23.6	10.9	17.4	31.2
	Belgium	34.2	38.5	22.1	16.9	36.3	26.9	7.4	17.6
	Canada	24.7	23.9	34.3	27.2	19.4	13.1	21.6	35.8
	Czech Republic	19.4	24.3	44.8	27.3	22.9	14.9	12.9	33.5
	Denmark	18.2	16.8	11.7	8.4	60.3	52.1	9.7	22.8
	Finland	8.1	5.8	12.2	15.9	74.1	59.7	5.6	18.6
	France	31.7	33.5	16.7	21.6	41.2	22.2	10.4	22.8
	Germany	23.3	24.8	42.6	33.3	16.7	6.7	17.4	35.2
	Greece	24.7	46.0	29.6	12.9	27.4	15.7	18.3	25.3
	Hungary	25.8	24.3	28.3	22.0	21.6	18.7	24.3	35.0
	Iceland	6.5	6.8	29.0	28.2	55.2	44.3	9.4	20.7
	Ireland	15.7	16.9	53.7	40.6	11.2	6.7	19.5	35.8
	Italy	23.4	28.0	30.0	25.9	31.0	21.9	15.5	24.3
	Japan	12.2	16.7	6.4	9.7	79.5	69.5	1.9	4.0
	Korea	16.6	21.5	13.1	16.4	60.3	44.1	10.0	18.1
	Luxembourg	36.2	42.5	23.6	19.1	27.4	11.3	12.8	27.1
	Mexico	36.9	38.0	15.4	15.8	26.8	17.7	20.9	28.5
	New Zealand	18.2	17.9	33.9	26.5	17.6	7.2	30.4	48.4
	Norway	8.6	8.3	19.6	20.7	66.0	49.9	5.8	21.0
	Poland	21.0	12.3	48.1	48.0	14.6	8.2	16.3	31.6
	Portugal	22.9	36.0	37.2	15.7	27.8	21.4	12.1	26.9
	Spain	30.7	41.5	27.9	18.4	25.1	10.4	16.4	29.8
	Sweden	11.9	10.2	29.5	31.1	45.0	29.5	13.6	29.2
	Switzerland	20.2	23.9	34.2	26.5	32.7	18.2	13.0	31.3
	United Kingdom	13.9	20.2	46.0	33.1	12.5	4.4	27.6	42.3
	United States	30.4	26.5	33.2	31.1	15.0	7.0	21.4	35.4
	Country mean	*20.9*	*23.6*	*29.8*	*24.7*	*33.8*	*22.9*	*15.5*	*28.8*
NON-OECD COUNTRIES	Brazil	33.4	26.2	19.5	11.4	29.4	25.9	17.7	36.5
	Latvia	17.0	10.8	42.3	37.5	16.7	13.8	23.9	37.8
	Liechtenstein	17.3	24.8	51.1	31.1	17.9	10.9	13.7	33.2
	Russian Federation	15.4	7.7	21.4	13.0	22.1	21.3	41.0	58.1
	Netherlands[1]	24.5	25.0	27.2	24.3	41.4	24.3	6.9	26.3

1. Response rate is too low to ensure comparability.
Source: OECD PISA database, 2001.

INDICATOR A9: ENGAGEMENT IN READING OF 15-YEAR-OLDS

A9

- Engagement in reading, as defined in this chapter (time spent reading for pleasure, time spent reading a diversity of material, high motivation and interest in reading), varies widely from country to country with Finland, at the high end, and Spain, at the low end, the extremes.

- On average, females tend to be far more strongly engaged in reading than males.

- Fifteen-year-olds whose parents have the lowest occupational status but who are highly engaged in reading achieve better reading scores than students whose parents have high or medium occupational status but who are poorly engaged in reading. All students who are highly engaged in reading achieve reading literacy scores that, on average, are significantly above the OECD mean, whatever their parents' occupational background. This suggests that student engagement with reading may be an important policy lever to counter social disadvantage.

Chart A9.1

Engagement in reading (2000)

Performance of 15-year-olds on the PISA index of engagement in reading, by gender

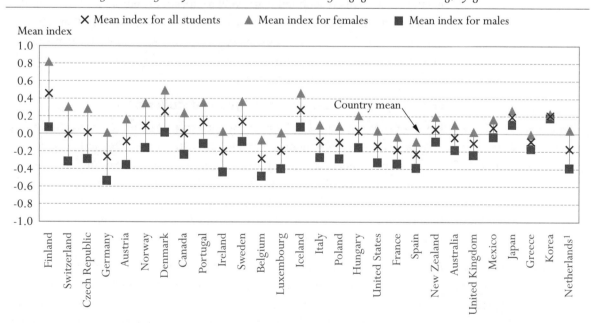

1. Response rate is too low to ensure comparability.

Countries are ranked in descending order of the difference between females and males on the PISA index of engagement in reading.
Source: OECD PISA database, 2001. Table A9.1. See Annex 3 for notes *(www.oecd.org/edu/eag2003).*

A9

This indicator examines 15-year-old students' engagement in reading, as measured by their reading practices and their attitudes towards reading...

Policy context

Most current models of reading acquisition consider both reading practices and reading attitudes to be key factors related to reading performance. While reading practices encompass behavioural attributes related to reading (the amount of time students spend reading and, as described in Indicator A8, the diversity of materials they read), reading attitudes encompass students' interest in reading and their motivation to read. When considered together, these two factors – practices and attitudes – provide a composite of overall engagement in reading.

In societies that increasingly depend on the capacity and motivation of their citizens to continue learning throughout life, engagement is an important outcome of education in itself. In addition, it is also an important predictor of student performance as students who are highly engaged in reading tend to perform better on assessments of reading literacy than those who are less engaged.

...as well as the impact of engagement and socio-economic status on performance in reading literacy.

Indicator A9 examines the level of reading engagement for 15-year-olds, using data from PISA. Importantly, this indicator explores the potential role of engagement in moderating the impact of social background on student performance in reading literacy.

Evidence and explanations

In addition to assessing their performance, PISA also asked students about their reading practices and attitudes.

In PISA 2000, students were asked questions about both their reading practices (see also Indicator A8) and their attitudes toward reading (interest in reading and motivation to read). Based on these questions, an index of reading engagement was created. The index scale ranges from –1 to 1, with 0 as the mean value for the combined OECD student population. Negative values do not necessarily mean that students responded negatively to questions, but instead that students in this particular country as a whole responded less positively than students among the OECD countries. Conversely, a positive value indicates that students in a particular country responded more favourably, on average, than did students among the OECD countries.

How engaged in reading are 15-year-old students?

Overall levels of student engagement in reading vary widely between the two extremes – Finland and Belgium.

Levels of engagement in reading vary by country. The country that has the highest average level of engagement is Finland, at 0.46 on the PISA index of reading engagement. Other countries where levels of engagement in reading are relatively high are Denmark (0.26), Iceland (0.27), Japan (0.20) and Korea (0.21). By comparison, countries where the levels of engagement are relatively low are Belgium (-0.28), Germany (-0.26), Ireland (-0.20), Luxembourg (-0.19) and Spain (-0.23) (Table A9.1).

Females tend to be substantially more engaged in reading than males.

Among countries, levels of engagement in reading also vary by gender. In fact, females are substantially more engaged in reading than males, with an average gap of 0.38 on the reading engagement index. The reasons why males are less engaged in reading and the solutions to improve their engagement are much debated issues. Discrimination at school, gender stereotyped reading material, and social norms of masculinity that may discourage commitment to school-

A9

work are all potential explanations that have been offered for the lower levels of engagement among males. Whatever the reasons may be for this pattern, it is clear that fostering engagement in reading will necessitate actions targeted at males.

In every OECD country, females have a higher average engagement in reading than males. In some countries, such as Switzerland and Finland, the gap between females and males is more pronounced (0.62 and 0.74, respectively), while in other countries it is relatively low, such as in Greece (0.17), Japan (0.17), Korea (0.04) and Mexico (0.20). However, there are some interesting differences when males and females are compared between different countries. Males from some countries are more engaged in reading than females from other countries. For instance, males from Denmark, Finland, Iceland, Japan, and Korea report being either as engaged or more engaged in reading than females from Belgium, France and Spain (Table A9.1 and Chart A9.1).

Can engagement in reading moderate the effects of social background on reading literacy?

Previous studies have shown that engagement in reading can "compensate" for low family income and educational background. In order to explore this, PISA students were distributed into groups based on two variables: their level of engagement in reading and their parents' occupational status. For each of these two indices, three separate groups were created: the low group (below the 25th percentile), the middle group (from the 25th percentile to the 75th percentile) and the high group (above the 75th percentile). These two variables were then combined and nine categories of students were identified (Table A9.2).

PISA assesses the extent to which both engagement in reading and social background relate to performance.

Students who are less engaged readers are somewhat more numerous than expected among the group of students whose parents have the lowest occupational status. (The "expected percentage" refers to the percentage of students that one would expect to see in any of the nine categories if they were evenly distributed according to the parameters of the categories). Likewise, highly engaged students are more numerous than expected among the group of students whose parents have the highest occupational status. Approximately 8 per cent of all students are in the low group on both indices, while another 8 per cent are in the high group on both indices. However, engagement is not completely predicted by parents' occupational status. There are students from less privileged social backgrounds who are highly engaged in reading as well as students from more privileged backgrounds who are the least engaged readers.

Not surprisingly, students who have parents with the highest occupational status and who are highly engaged in reading obtain the highest average scores (583 points) on the combined reading literacy scale. Conversely, students who have parents with the lowest occupational status and who are the least engaged in reading had the lowest average scores (423 points) among the 9 groups.

Not surprisingly, students from more advantaged social backgrounds tend to be more engaged in reading…

A9

...but highly engaged students from disadvantaged backgrounds tend to perform as well as students in the middle engagement groups of students from advantaged backgrounds...

...which suggests that student engagement with reading may be an important policy lever to counter social disadvantage.

Perhaps more importantly, however, 15-year-old students who are highly engaged readers and whose parents have the lowest occupational status achieved a significantly higher average reading score (540 points) than students whose parents have the highest occupational status but who are poorly engaged in reading (491 points). In fact, the highly engaged students whose parents have low occupational status performed as well on average as those students who are in the middle engagement group but whose parents have high status occupations (Table A9.2 and Chart A9.2).

All students who are highly engaged in reading achieve reading literacy scores that, on average, are significantly above the OECD mean (500 points), whatever their parents' occupational background. Conversely, students who are poorly engaged in reading score below the OECD mean, regardless of their parents' occupational background. Within each grouping of occupational status, students who are in the group of least engaged readers register average scores that range from 85 to 117 points lower than those who are in the highly engaged reading group, with the largest difference seen among students whose parents have the lowest occupational status (Table A9.2).

Chart A9.2

Reading literacy performance and socio-economic background of 15-year-olds, by level of reading engagement (2000)

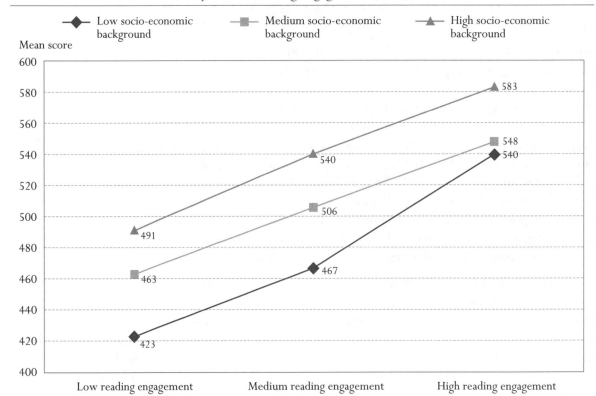

Source: OECD PISA database, 2001. Table A9.2. See Annex 3 for notes *(www.oecd.org/edu/eag2003)*.

Definitions and methodologies

The target population studied for this indicator was 15-year-old students. Operationally, this referred to students who were from 15 years and 3 (completed) months to 16 years and 2 (completed) months at the beginning of the testing period and who were enrolled in an educational institution, regardless of the grade level or type of institution and of whether they participated in school full-time or part-time.

The concept of engagement in reading, as presented in this indicator, is built on three components: frequency of reading, diversity and content of reading, and interest in reading. The first two components address students' reading practices, while the final component addresses their attitudes. To assess the first component, students were asked about how much time they usually spent on reading for enjoyment each day. They were asked to respond by indicating which one of five descriptions best represented the time they spent reading, ranging from 'I do not read for enjoyment' to 'more than two hours a day'. To assess the second component, students were asked to indicate the kinds of materials they choose to read from a list that included newspapers, magazines, fiction, non-fiction, comics, e-mails and web pages. They were also asked to indicate the frequency with which they read each type of material – from 'never' to 'several times a week'. To assess the third component, a reading attitude scale comprising nine statements about reading, either positive or negative, was included in the questionnaire. Students were asked to indicate their degree of agreement with each statement on a four-point scale ranging from 'strongly disagree' to 'strongly agree'.

The information on occupational status in this indicator is based on the PISA International Socio-Economic Index of Occupational Status (ISEI). Students were asked to report their mothers' and fathers' occupation, and to state whether each parent was in full-time paid work; part-time paid work; not working but looking for a paid job; or 'other'. The open-ended responses were then coded in accordance with the International Standard Classification of Occupations (ISCO 1988). The index captures the attributes of occupations that convert parents' education into income. The index was derived by the optimal scaling of occupation groups to maximise the indirect effect of education on income through occupation, and to minimise the direct effect of education on income, net of occupation (both effects being net of age). The index is based on either the father's or mother's occupations, whichever is the higher. Values on the index range from 0 to 90; low values represent low socio-economic status and high values represent high socio-economic status.

For notes on standard errors, significance tests, and multiple comparisons see Annex 3 at *www.oecd.org/edu/eag2003*.

The performance scores are based on assessments administered as part of the Programme for International Student Assessment (PISA) undertaken by the OECD during 2000.

A9

Table A9.1
Engagement in reading (2000)
Mean scores of 15-year-olds on the index of engagement in reading, overall and by gender

	All students		Females	Males	Difference between females and males
	Mean index	S.E.	Mean index	Mean index	
Australia	-0.04	(0.03)	0.11	-0.18	0.28
Austria	-0.08	(0.03)	0.17	-0.35	0.52
Belgium	-0.28	(0.02)	-0.07	-0.48	0.41
Canada	0.01	(0.01)	0.24	-0.23	0.47
Czech Republic	0.02	(0.02)	0.29	-0.29	0.57
Denmark	0.26	(0.02)	0.50	0.02	0.48
Finland	0.46	(0.02)	0.82	0.08	0.74
France	-0.18	(0.02)	-0.03	-0.33	0.30
Germany	-0.26	(0.02)	0.01	-0.53	0.55
Greece	-0.09	(0.02)	0.00	-0.17	0.17
Hungary	0.03	(0.02)	0.21	-0.15	0.36
Iceland	0.27	(0.01)	0.46	0.08	0.39
Ireland	-0.20	(0.02)	0.03	-0.43	0.46
Italy	-0.08	(0.02)	0.10	-0.27	0.37
Japan	0.20	(0.03)	0.28	0.11	0.17
Korea	0.21	(0.02)	0.23	0.19	0.04
Luxembourg	-0.19	(0.02)	0.01	-0.39	0.40
Mexico	0.07	(0.01)	0.17	-0.03	0.20
New Zealand	0.05	(0.02)	0.20	-0.09	0.29
Norway	0.09	(0.02)	0.35	-0.16	0.51
Poland	-0.10	(0.02)	0.09	-0.28	0.36
Portugal	0.13	(0.02)	0.36	-0.11	0.47
Spain	-0.23	(0.02)	-0.09	-0.38	0.29
Sweden	0.14	(0.02)	0.37	-0.08	0.45
Switzerland	0.00	(0.01)	0.31	-0.31	0.62
United Kingdom	-0.10	(0.02)	0.03	-0.24	0.26
United States	-0.14	(0.03)	0.04	-0.32	0.36
Country mean	*0.00*	*(0.00)*	*0.19*	*-0.19*	*0.38*
Brazil	0.11	(0.02)	0.36	-0.17	0.53
Latvia	-0.04	(0.02)	0.17	-0.27	0.44
Liechtenstein	-0.13	(0.05)	0.13	-0.36	0.49
Russian Federation	0.17	(0.02)	0.37	-0.02	0.39
Netherlands[1]	-0.17	(0.04)	0.04	-0.38	0.42

OECD COUNTRIES

NON-OECD COUNTRIES

1. Response rate is too low to ensure comparability.
Source: OECD PISA database, 2001.

Table A9.2
Expected and observed percentages of 15-year-olds and performance on the PISA index of reading engagement (2000)
by level of reading engagement and socio-economic background (Cross-country means)

	Low reading engagement			Medium reading engagement			High reading engagement		
	Expected (%)	Observed (%)	Mean score	Expected (%)	Observed (%)	Mean score	Expected (%)	Observed (%)	Mean score
Low socio-economic background	6.3	7.6	423	12.5	12.6	467	6.3	4.9	540
Medium socio-economic background	12.3	12.9	463	25.0	25.1	506	12.3	12.0	548
High socio-economic background	6.3	4.5	491	12.5	12.3	540	6.3	8.2	583

Source: OECD PISA database, 2001.

INDICATOR A10: FIFTEEN-YEAR-OLDS'
SELF-REGULATED LEARNING

A10

- The indicator reveals four clusters of student approaches to learning which are associated with student performance in reading literacy.

- A closer look also shows that the extent to which students monitor their own learning is closely related to performance in reading literacy. Furthermore, it shows that students' beliefs that a goal is feasible, that the resources necessary to achieve it are accessible and that it is worth expending energy to achieve the goal are strong predictors of student performance in reading literacy.

A10

Chart A10.1

Mean performance of 15-year-olds on the PISA combined reading literacy scale and
percentage of students by PISA self-regulated learning cluster (2000)

◆ Cluster 1 - Low-level prerequisites for self-regulated learning
■ Cluster 2 - Medium-level prerequisites for self-regulated learning
▲ Cluster 3 - Medium-level prerequisites for self-regulated learning
✕ Cluster 4 - High-level prerequisites for self-regulated learning

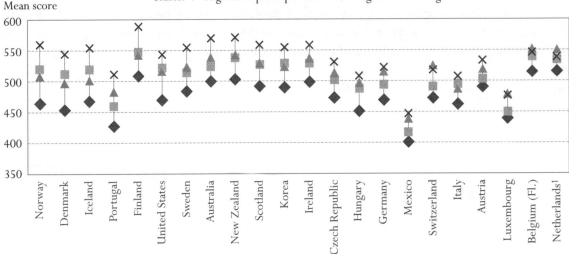

■ Cluster 1 - Low-level prerequisites for self-regulated learning
■ Cluster 2 - Medium-level prerequisites for self-regulated learning
■ Cluster 3 - Medium-level prerequisites for self-regulated learning
■ Cluster 4 - High-level prerequisites for self-regulated learning

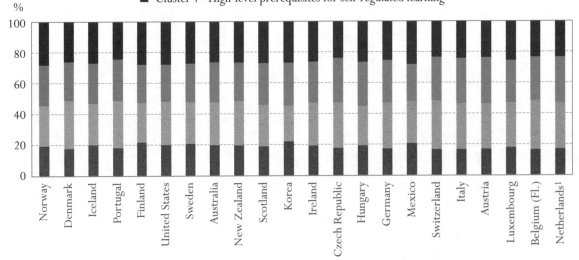

1. Response rate is too low to ensure comparability.
*Countries are ranked in descending order of the difference between mean scores on the PISA combined reading literacy scale in Cluster 4 -
High-level prerequisites for self-regulated learning and Cluster 1 - Low-level prerequisites for self-regulated learning.*
Source: OECD PISA database, 2001. Table A10.2. See Annex 3 for notes *(www.oecd.org/edu/eag2003).*

Policy context

Although many scholastic competencies are learned in subject areas (such as reading, mathematics and science), other relevant competencies are developed "between the lines" of the curriculum. Often, these cross-curricular competencies are neither precisely defined nor firmly embedded in a specific area of the curriculum. Nevertheless, they are important outcomes of education systems because they contribute to the development of personal skills needed for full and active participation in societies and economies. PISA places great importance on such competencies, and devotes time in each PISA assessment to cross-curricular competencies that participating countries have identified as important.

This indicator examines patterns of results between and within countries on measures of 15 - year-old students' self-regulated learning…

PISA 2000 collected self-report data on students' learning strategies, motivational preferences, self-related competencies, and learning preferences. This indicator examines 13 measures that underlie these broad categories in order to gain a picture of students' abilities to regulate their own learning. In societies that increasingly depend on the capacity and motivation of their citizens to continue learning throughout life, these abilities are an important outcome of education in themselves and may have an impact on students' success both in school and in their future lives.

…as well as the relationship of selected self-regulated learning scales to performance in reading literacy.

Evidence and explanations

In PISA 2000, students were asked a series of questions related to self-regulated learning, including on their:

Self-regulated learning includes many aspects, including…

- uses of cognitive and metacognitive learning strategies (*e.g.*, memorisation, elaboration, and control strategies);

…uses of cognitive and meta-cognitive learning strategies…

- motivational preferences and volition (*e.g.*, instrumental motivation, verbal interest, math interest, and effort and persistence in learning);

…motivational preferences and volition…

- self-related cognitions (*e.g.*, self-efficacy, verbal self-concept, math self-concept, and academic self-concept); and

…self-related cognitions…

- preferences for learning situations (*e.g.*, preference for cooperative learning and preference for competitive learning).

…and preferences for learning situations.

For each of the 13 scales on self-regulated learning (listed in parentheses above), indices were created based on students' self-reports to related questions. The index scales range from −1 to 1, with 0 as the mean value for the combined OECD student population. Negative values do not necessarily mean that students responded negatively to questions, but instead that students in this particular country as a whole responded less positively than students among the OECD countries. Conversely, a positive value indicates that students in a particular country responded more favourably, on average, than students among the OECD countries as a whole (Table A10.1).

This indicator first considers the patterns of responses on the 13 self-regulated learning scales in combination, by means of a cluster analysis. Then it examines

A10

select self-regulated learning scales, students' use of control strategies and self-efficacy, and their relationship to reading literacy.

Profiles of self-regulated learning

Through cluster analysis, students were grouped in accordance with their approaches to learning.

In general, cluster analysis groups individuals based on how similar they are with respect to a number of defining characteristics. Students belonging to one cluster have relatively similar characteristics and students belonging to different clusters have relatively dissimilar characteristics. In the present cluster analysis, the 13 scales of self-regulated learning were used as defining characteristics. Each student was allocated to one cluster in accordance with the specific combination of scores he or she displayed on the scales of self-regulated learning.

Students in Cluster 4 are characterised by high scores on all aspects of self-regulated learning...

Table A10.1 illustrates the mean index scores on each of the 13 self-regulated learning scales for the four clusters, or profiles, identified in the analysis. Students in Cluster 4 are characterised by the highest scores in all aspects of self-regulated learning, while their peers in Cluster 1 have the lowest scores on almost all of the scales.

...while students in Cluster 1 show the lowest scores, particularly as concerning comprehension-oriented learning strategies and self-evaluation.

Students in these two extreme clusters display particularly marked differences in their use of comprehension-oriented learning strategies (*e.g.*, elaboration). Similarly, the self-evaluative perspective on learning characterised by control of one's own learning processes (*i.e.*, control strategies) is particularly strong among students in Cluster 4, but weak among students in Cluster 1. Large gaps between these two clusters are also found for effort and persistence put into learning and confidence in being able to achieve even difficult goals (self-efficacy). Indeed, it is on these two scales that students in Cluster 4 report the highest scores.

Students in Clusters 2 and 3 report moderate use of self-regulated learning behaviours and attitudes.

By contrast, students in Clusters 3 and 2 report more moderate use of self-regulated learning behaviours and attitudes, with students in Cluster 3 generally scoring slightly above the mean and students in Cluster 2 generally scoring slightly below the mean on the individual scales. The main exceptions are the mathematics-specific scales (interest in mathematics and mathematical self-concept), on which students in Cluster 2 significantly outscore their generally higher-scoring counterparts in Cluster 3. This domain-specific aspect distinguishes students in Clusters 3 and 2 from one another, as well as from students in other clusters, who display relatively more uniform results across the scales (Table A10.1).

Among countries, students are distributed fairly equally among the four clusters. Between 25 and 28 percent of students are in each of the top three clusters (*e.g.*, 2 through 4). Only Cluster 1 is somewhat smaller, with 19.6 percent of the students (Table A10.2).

Grouping students by how they score on the self-regulated learning scales can provide insight into the relationship between these behaviours and attitudes and students' performance in school. Focusing on performance on the reading literacy scale reveals a clear hierarchy. Overall, students in each cluster score significantly higher than their counterparts in the respective lower clusters.

Such differences are also found within countries (Chart A10.1 and Table A10.2). In general, the pattern within a country is the same as the pattern among countries. Students in Cluster 4 outperform their peers in all other clusters on the combined reading literacy scale, and as a rule, the higher the number of the cluster, the higher the performance on the reading literacy scale.

Students in Cluster 4 tend to outperform their peers in all other clusters in reading literacy...

However, there are some exceptions. In the Flemish Community of Belgium, Luxembourg, the Netherlands and Switzerland, students in Cluster 3 tend to outperform their peers in Cluster 4. In these countries, the reading-specific pattern of Cluster 3 seems to foster reading performance just as well as the generally high values across the self-regulated learning scales displayed by Cluster 4 students. Additionally, in Denmark, Finland, Iceland, Italy, Korea, Norway, and the United States, the performance of students in Cluster 2 is as good as – or better than – the performance of students in Cluster 3.

...but there are exceptions to this pattern.

The performance of students in Cluster 1 on the combined reading literacy scale is generally comparatively low within countries. The difference in performance of students in Cluster 1 and those in Cluster 4 ranges from a low of 23 points on the combined reading literacy scale in the Netherlands to a high of 91 points in Denmark and Norway. The mean difference between students in these two clusters is 62 points, nearly a full proficiency level.

When interpreting these results, it is important to bear in mind that students' cluster membership cannot be seen as a competence indicator *per se*. The moderate use of learning strategies as in Cluster 2, for example, might also be seen as an indicator for adaptive learning. In other words, if the tasks at hand are of minor difficulty for the students, there is less need to use strategies to monitor learning. Still, the general consistency of results among and within countries indicates that specific configurations of the behaviours and attitudes related to self-regulated learning are associated with high performance in reading literacy.

Chart A10.1 shows the percentage of students in each cluster in each country. In some countries (Finland, Mexico, Norway and the United States), 28 per cent of the 15 year-olds in PISA belong to the cluster with the highest scores on the self-regulated learning scales (Cluster 4).

In Finland, Mexico, Norway and the United States 28 per cent of students belong to Cluster 4...

The percentage of students in this Cluster, however, is smaller in the Flemish Community of Belgium and Switzerland, where only 23 per cent of fall into this category.

...while it is just 23 per cent in the Flemish Community of Belgium and Switzerland.

Within each country, there is a significant percentage of students in Cluster 1. The size of this cluster ranges from 17 per cent in Austria, the Flemish Community of Belgium, Germany, Italy, the Netherlands and Switzerland to 22 per cent in Korea. This group of students may require particular attention, as they may not yet have succeeded in acquiring the prerequisites for lifelong learning and, in the absence of additional support, they may be unlikely to succeed either in school or in their future undertakings (Chart A10.1 and Table A10.2).

A10

Self-regulated learning and performance in reading literacy

A closer look shows that...

As this indicator has shown, self-regulated learning can contribute to performance in school, specifically with respect to reading literacy. Students with the necessary disposition and attitudes for self-regulated learning (*e.g.*, metacognitive learning strategies, sufficient interest in learning, and a positive self-regard) are more likely to outperform their peers who lack these attributes. In the following, the indicator examines the relationship of two of the self-regulated learning scales to performance in reading literacy.

Control strategies

...the extent to which students monitor their own learning is closely related to performance in reading literacy.

Students may apply a variety of cognitive (e.g., memorisation, elaboration, transformation) and metacognitive strategies (e.g., planning, monitoring) during the learning process. One metacognitive strategy measured in PISA 2000 is students' use of control strategies, the extent to which they attempt to monitor their own learning. The index of control strategies was derived from responses to questions about the frequency with which students chart out exactly what they need to learn, work out as they go what concepts they have not really understood, look for additional information when they do not understand, force themselves to check whether they remember what they have learned, and make sure they have remembered the most important things.

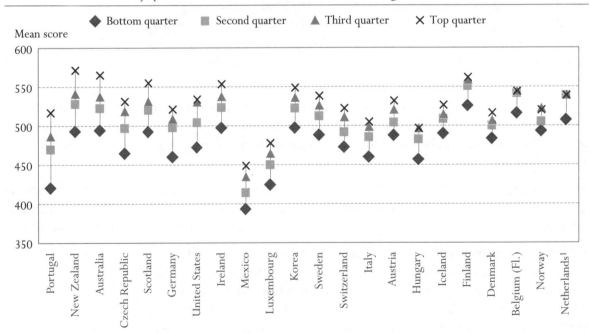

Chart A10.2

Performance of 15-year-olds on the PISA combined reading literacy scale, by quarters of the PISA index of control strategies (2000)

1. Response rate is too low to ensure comparability.
Countries are ranked in descending order of the difference between performance on the PISA combined reading literacy scale of students in the top quarter of the PISA index of control strategies and those at the bottom quarter of the index.
Source: OECD PISA database, 2001. Table A10.3. See Annex 3 for notes *(www.oecd.org/edu/eag2003).*

EDUCATION AT A GLANCE © OECD 2003

The use of control strategies is closely related to performance in the reading literacy assessment in almost all of the participating countries (Chart A10.2 and Table A10.3). The connection is particularly strong in Portugal, where students who report frequent use of control strategies (top quarter of the control strategy scale) outperform those who rarely use control strategies (bottom quarter) by almost one standard deviation (96 points). Australia, the Czech Republic, Germany, New Zealand, Scotland and the United States also display large differences in performance (60 points or more) between students in the two extreme quarters on this index. In the Flemish Community of Belgium and Norway, the gap between the reading literacy scores of students who report frequent use of control strategies and those who report using them only rarely is only half that magnitude, at just under 30 points.

The use of control strategies is closely related to performance in the reading literacy assessment.

An additional finding is that, in many countries, the mean reading scores of students in the second and third quarters of the control strategy scale – and, in some countries, students in the top quarter – are close together. On average, the gap between the two middle groups is of 13 points on the performance scale. With the exception of the Czech Republic, Mexico and the United States, where there is 20-point gap or more between the middle two quarters, it is not possible to distinguish notable performance differences in any of the countries. Rather, there are considerable differences in the performance of students reporting frequent (top quarter), medium (second and third quarters), and infrequent (bottom quarter) use of control strategies.

For many countries the mean reading scores of students in the second and third quarters of the control strategy scale are close together…

In six countries, the mean performance of students who report using control strategies about half the time (second and third quarters) is similar to those of students who report regular use of control strategies (top quarter). Thus, in Finland, the Flemish Community of Belgium, Germany, Hungary, Italy and the Netherlands, it is only students who rarely use control strategies (bottom quarter) who clearly lag behind their peers in reading proficiency. In these six countries, use of control strategies seems to be a minimum requirement, and how often the students use (or perceive they use) these strategies makes little difference in terms of reading proficiency (Chart A10.2 and Table A10.3).

… and in six countries, only students who rarely use control strategies clearly lag behind in reading proficiency.

In interpreting these differences, it is important to bear in mind that the reading performance of students from the top quarter of the control strategies scale varies considerably among the participating countries. Comparison of Mexico and New Zealand, for example, shows that students who use control strategies frequently in Mexico (top quarter) achieve far lower scores on the reading literacy scale than New Zealand students who use control strategies only rarely (bottom quarter). Even if there are strong correlations within a country, it does not follow that the frequent use of control strategies (top quarter) leads to an equally high performance and gives students the same relative advantage in all countries. The countries differ in a number of features that impact student performance, and the frequency of use of control strategies is just one of these. Within countries, however, the use of control strategies gives students a considerable relative advantage.

The use of control strategies does not guarantee high performance in comparison to other countries, but gives students a considerable relative advantage within their countries.

A10

Self-efficacy

Furthermore, students' beliefs that a goal is feasible ...

Self-efficacy beliefs are characterised by the confidence of being able to successfully orchestrate an action, even in the face of difficulties. The belief that a goal is essentially feasible, that the resources necessary to achieve it are accessible, and in turn, that it is worth expending a great deal of energy to pursue, are important for successful learning.

...is important for successful learning and closely related to student performance in reading literacy.

PISA shows a relationship between students' self-efficacy beliefs and performance in reading literacy (Chart A10.3 and Table A10.4). In all the OECD countries, the largest performance gaps are found between students who are very confident in being able to meet learning challenges in the face of difficulties (top quarter) and students who express very little confidence in this respect (bottom quarter). This corresponds to an average difference of 56 points on the proficiency scale, or just over half a standard deviation on the international reading literacy scale. The relative advantage of positive self-efficacy beliefs is particularly strong in Denmark, Iceland and Sweden where the students in the top quarter of the self-efficacy scale outperform their peers in the bottom quarter by at least 79 points. By contrast, in the Flemish Community of Belgium, Hungary, Italy, and the Netherlands, the difference in performance between students in the top and bottom quarter of the self-efficacy scale is relatively small, at less than 40 points.

Chart A10.3

Performance of 15-year-olds on the PISA combined reading literacy scale,
by quarters of the PISA index of self-efficacy (2000)

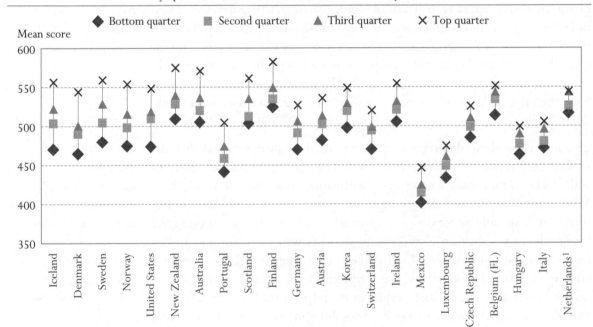

1. Response rate is too low to ensure comparability.
Countries are ranked in descending order of the difference between performance on the PISA combined reading literacy scale of students in the top quarter of the PISA index of self-efficacy and those at the bottom quarter of the index.
Source: OECD PISA database, 2001. Table A10.4. See Annex 3 for notes (www.oecd.org/edu/eag2003).

Definitions and methodologies

The target population studied for this indicator was 15-year-old students. Operationally, this referred to students who were from 15 years and 3 (completed) months to 16 years and 2 (completed) months at the beginning of the testing period and who were enrolled in an educational institution, regardless of the grade level or type of institution and of whether they participated in school full-time or part-time.

Twenty-six of the 32 countries that participated in PISA 2000 administered the self-regulated learning component on which this indicator is based: Australia, Austria, the Flemish Community of Belgium, Brazil, the Czech Republic, Denmark, Finland, Germany, Hungary, Ireland, Iceland, Italy, Korea, Latvia, Liechtenstein, Luxembourg, Mexico, the Netherlands, New Zealand, Norway, Portugal, the Russian Federation, Scotland, Sweden, Switzerland and the United States. Note that Belgium and the United Kingdom, countries that did participate in the main PISA assessments, are represented in the self-regulated learning option only by participating jurisdictions: the Flemish Community of Belgium and Scotland, respectively. Canada, France, Greece, Ireland, Japan, and Spain, as well as the French Community of Belgium and England, did not participate in this option.

The PISA index on *memorisation* was derived from the frequency with which students used the following strategies when studying: I memorise everything that might be covered; I memorise as much as possible; I memorise all new material so I that I can recite it; and I practice saying the material to myself over and over. A four-point scale with the response categories 'almost never', 'sometimes', 'often' and 'almost always' was used.

The PISA index on *elaboration* was derived from the frequency with which students used the following strategies when studying: I try to relate new material to things I have learned in other subjects; I chart out how the information might be useful in the real world; I try to understand the material better by relating it to things I already know; and, I chart out how the material fits in with what I have already learned. A four-point scale with the response categories 'almost never', 'sometimes', 'often' and 'almost always' was used.

The PISA index on *control strategies* was derived from the frequency with which students used the following strategies when studying: I start by figuring out exactly what I need to learn; I force myself to check to see if I remember the most important things; and, when I study and don't understand something, I look for additional information to clarify this. A four-point scale with the response categories 'almost never', 'sometimes', 'often' and 'almost always' was used.

The PISA index on *interest in reading* was derived from students' level of agreement with the following statements: because reading is fun, I wouldn't want to give it up; I read in my spare time; and, when I read, I sometimes get totally absorbed.

The performance scores are based on assessments administered as part of the Programme for International Student Assessment (PISA) undertaken by the OECD during 2000.

A10

A10

A four-point scale with the response categories 'disagree', 'disagree somewhat', 'agree somewhat' and 'agree' was used.

The PISA index on *interest in mathematics* was derived from students' level of agreement with the following statements: when I do mathematics, I sometimes get totally absorbed; mathematics is important to me personally; and because doing mathematics is fun, I wouldn't want to give it up. A four-point scale with the response categories 'disagree', 'disagree somewhat', 'agree somewhat' and 'agree' was used.

The PISA index on *student self-concept in reading* was derived from students' level of agreement with the following statements: I'm hopeless in <classes of the language of assessment>; I learn things quickly in the <classes of the language of assessment>; and, I get good marks in the <language of assessment>. A four-point scale with the response categories 'disagree', 'disagree somewhat', 'agree somewhat' and 'agree' was used. Similarly, the PISA index on *self-concept in mathematics* was derived from students' level of agreement with the following statements: I get good marks in mathematics; mathematics is one of my best subjects; and, I have always done well in mathematics. A four-point scale with the response categories 'disagree', 'disagree somewhat', 'agree somewhat' and 'agree' was used.

The PISA index on *co-operative learning* was derived from students' level of agreement with the following statements: I like to work with other students; I like to help other people do well in a group; and, it is helpful to put together everyone's ideas when working on a project. A four-point scale with the response categories 'disagree', 'disagree somewhat', 'agree somewhat' and 'agree' was used. Similarly, the PISA index on *competitive learning* was derived from students' level of agreement with the following statements: I like to try to be better than other students; trying to be better than others makes me work well; I would like to be the best at something; and, I learn faster if I'm trying to do better than the others. A four-point scale with the response categories 'disagree', 'disagree somewhat', 'agree somewhat' and 'agree' was used.

The cluster analysis for this indicator is based on scale scores that are standardised within countries. The aim of standardisation is to reduce or eliminate unwanted between-group differences such as those due to response sets.

For more information of the theoretical underpinnings of this model of self-regulated learning, see *Approaches to Learning: Strategies and Motivation* (OECD, 2003).

For notes on standard errors, significance tests, and multiple comparisons see Annex 3 at *www.oecd.org/edu/eag2003*.

Table A10.1
Cross-country mean index of 15-year-olds on the PISA indices of self-regulated learning (2000)
by PISA self-regulated learning cluster

	Cluster 1 - Low-level prerequisites for self-regulated learning (19.6 per cent of students)	Cluster 2 - Medium-level prerequisites for self-regulated learning (27.2 per cent of students)	Cluster 3 - Medium-level prerequisites for self-regulated learning (25.4 per cent of students)	Cluster 4 - High-level prerequisites for self-regulated learning (27.8 per cent of students)
Use of cognitive and meta-cognitive learning strategies				
Memorisation strategies	-0.87	-0.34	0.29	0.70
Elaboration strategies	-1.02	-0.30	0.16	0.89
Control strategies	-1.14	-0.34	0.26	0.94
Motivation and interest				
Instrumental motivation	-0.92	-0.25	0.26	0.70
Interest in reading	-0.62	-0.15	0.13	0.48
Interest in mathematics	-0.81	0.43	-0.63	0.75
Effort and perseverance	-1.13	-0.30	0.17	0.97
Self-concept				
Perceived self-efficacy	-1.08	-0.19	-0.01	0.99
Self concept in reading	-0.61	-0.23	0.23	0.48
Self-concept in mathematics	-0.77	0.53	-0.76	0.74
Academic self concept	-1.03	0.11	-0.19	0.83
Preference for learning situations				
Co-operative learning	-0.37	0.01	0.03	0.21
Competitive learning	-0.78	0.08	-0.15	0.63

Source: OECD PISA database, 2001.

Table A10.2
Performance of 15–year-olds on the PISA combined reading literacy scale and percentage of students (2000)
by PISA self-regulated learning cluster

	Cluster 1 - Low-level prerequisites for self-regulated learning		Cluster 2 - Medium-level prerequisites for self-regulated learning		Cluster 3 - Medium-level prerequisites for self-regulated learning		Cluster 4 - High-level prerequisites for self-regulated learning	
	Mean score	%	Mean score	%	Mean score	%	Mean score	%
Australia	499	19.8	522	28.0	538	25.8	569	26.4
Austria	490	16.9	502	29.6	519	29.8	533	23.7
Belgium (Fl.)	514	16.5	539	32.2	550	28.0	545	23.3
Czech Republic	472	17.5	501	30.0	511	28.5	531	23.9
Denmark	453	17.6	511	31.5	497	24.7	544	26.2
Finland	508	21.4	547	26.0	544	24.5	588	28.0
Germany	469	17.1	493	30.3	516	27.4	522	25.2
Hungary	450	19.2	487	25.9	495	28.5	508	26.4
Iceland	467	19.9	518	27.1	501	25.8	554	27.2
Ireland	498	19.1	527	28.4	533	26.3	558	26.2
Italy	462	16.6	494	30.0	488	29.2	507	24.1
Korea	489	21.9	528	23.4	525	27.9	554	26.8
Luxembourg	439	17.8	448	29.4	479	27.3	476	25.6
Mexico	400	20.6	416	27.7	440	23.9	447	27.9
New Zealand	502	19.4	536	29.3	541	24.7	570	26.6
Norway	463	19.3	519	26.5	509	25.9	559	28.3
Portugal	427	18.1	459	30.8	483	26.8	511	24.3
Scotland	491	18.7	525	27.3	528	26.9	558	27.1
Sweden	483	20.5	513	27.4	522	24.8	554	27.2
Switzerland	472	16.7	490	31.9	525	27.9	517	23.4
United States	469	19.8	520	28.6	518	23.6	543	28.0
Country mean	*465*	*19.6*	*496*	*27.2*	*506*	*25.4*	*527*	*27.8*
Brazil	374	18.7	397	25.6	415	26.3	430	29.4
Latvia	421	18.3	457	30.9	473	23.9	495	26.8
Liechtenstein	469	20.8	470	28.3	503	25.4	516	25.5
Russian Federation	426	21.9	468	25.4	472	23.4	496	29.3
Netherlands[1]	515	16.9	533	30.3	551	29.5	538	23.3

OECD COUNTRIES / NON-OECD COUNTRIES

1. Response rate is too low to ensure comparability.
Source: OECD PISA database, 2001.

Table A10.3
Performance of 15-year-olds on the PISA combined reading literacy scale (2000)
by quarters of the PISA index of control strategies

A10

	Bottom quarter		Second quarter		Third quarter		Top quarter	
	Mean score	S.E.	Mean score	S.E.	Mean score	S.E.	Mean score	S.E.
Australia	494	(4.5)	525	(4.6)	540	(4.3)	564	(5.8)
Austria	485	(4.3)	502	(3.1)	517	(3.9)	531	(3.5)
Belgium (Fl.)	512	(7.2)	543	(4.2)	542	(5.3)	545	(5.0)
Czech Republic	464	(3.1)	497	(3.0)	518	(3.3)	532	(2.9)
Denmark	481	(3.8)	497	(3.6)	507	(3.3)	514	(3.3)
Finland	527	(3.8)	546	(2.9)	556	(3.6)	562	(3.6)
Germany	459	(4.3)	495	(4.0)	508	(3.6)	519	(3.3)
Hungary	456	(5.8)	483	(4.4)	495	(4.3)	496	(5.6)
Iceland	490	(3.2)	509	(3.2)	513	(3.1)	526	(3.6)
Ireland	499	(4.3)	525	(5.1)	537	(4.0)	553	(3.8)
Italy	461	(5.1)	485	(3.8)	499	(3.4)	505	(3.2)
Korea	496	(3.4)	521	(2.9)	534	(3.1)	548	(3.0)
Luxembourg	424	(3.3)	453	(3.0)	456	(3.3)	475	(3.3)
Mexico	394	(3.4)	415	(3.9)	432	(4.3)	449	(4.7)
New Zealand	494	(4.2)	531	(3.7)	540	(3.6)	572	(5.0)
Norway	494	(5.2)	505	(3.5)	521	(4.4)	518	(4.1)
Portugal	419	(5.6)	464	(5.0)	483	(4.4)	515	(4.4)
Scotland	493	(5.4)	521	(5.2)	531	(5.7)	555	(4.6)
Sweden	491	(3.2)	515	(3.2)	527	(3.9)	539	(3.0)
Switzerland	469	(4.9)	492	(4.9)	503	(4.8)	522	(6.1)
United States	477	(7.4)	505	(8.3)	528	(5.7)	534	(8.3)
Country mean	*474*	*(1.0)*	*500*	*(1.0)*	*512*	*(0.8)*	*526*	*(1.0)*
Brazil	368	(4.4)	395	(4.0)	414	(4.0)	425	(4.3)
Latvia	430	(6.4)	465	(6.3)	463	(6.7)	482	(5.6)
Liechtenstein	462	(9.9)	479	(10.9)	477	(9.7)	520	(9.7)
Russian Federation	431	(5.0)	462	(4.9)	476	(4.7)	485	(4.7)
Netherlands[1]	511	(5.6)	542	(4.2)	541	(3.7)	536	(4.9)

OECD COUNTRIES / *NON-OECD COUNTRIES*

1. Response rate is too low to ensure comparability.
Source: OECD PISA database, 2001.

Table A10.4
Performance of 15-year-olds on the PISA combined reading literacy scale (2000)
by quarters of the PISA index of self-efficacy

	Bottom quarter		Second quarter		Third quarter		Top quarter	
	Mean score	S.E.	Mean score	S.E.	Mean score	S.E.	Mean score	S.E.
OECD COUNTRIES								
Australia	506	(4.5)	520	(5.2)	536	(4.1)	571	(4.7)
Austria	483	(4.0)	503	(4.0)	513	(3.1)	536	(3.7)
Belgium (Fl.)	514	(8.4)	535	(4.4)	543	(4.6)	552	(6.5)
Czech Republic	486	(2.7)	499	(3.5)	510	(3.2)	526	(3.8)
Denmark	465	(3.6)	490	(4.0)	500	(3.2)	544	(2.6)
Finland	525	(3.1)	535	(3.7)	549	(3.0)	583	(4.1)
Germany	470	(4.2)	492	(3.5)	506	(3.8)	527	(4.9)
Hungary	464	(5.5)	477	(4.5)	490	(6.1)	500	(5.1)
Iceland	471	(3.0)	504	(3.3)	522	(3.7)	556	(3.5)
Ireland	506	(4.3)	521	(4.6)	531	(4.0)	555	(4.3)
Italy	472	(4.9)	481	(3.4)	496	(3.3)	506	(4.4)
Korea	498	(3.4)	520	(3.3)	528	(2.8)	549	(3.0)
Luxembourg	434	(2.9)	449	(3.9)	461	(3.1)	475	(3.3)
Mexico	402	(3.3)	415	(4.1)	425	(4.3)	447	(5.4)
New Zealand	509	(4.8)	529	(3.9)	538	(4.1)	575	(5.3)
Norway	475	(4.2)	499	(3.8)	515	(5.7)	554	(3.6)
Portugal	442	(5.3)	459	(5.5)	473	(5.3)	505	(4.9)
Scotland	504	(5.6)	513	(5.8)	535	(4.4)	562	(5.6)
Sweden	480	(3.1)	505	(3.3)	528	(3.3)	560	(3.4)
Switzerland	471	(4.4)	495	(5.2)	499	(5.5)	520	(5.1)
United States	474	(7.4)	510	(7.1)	518	(6.9)	548	(8.3)
Country mean	*478*	*(21.5)*	*500*	*(7.1)*	*510*	*(13.9)*	*534*	*(14.8)*
NON-OECD COUNTRIES								
Brazil	376	(3.8)	395	(3.8)	411	(4.3)	432	(4.7)
Latvia	434	(5.7)	457	(6.2)	467	(6.2)	494	(6.6)
Liechtenstein	446	(11.0)	475	(7.4)	514	(8.8)	507	(11.8)
Russian Federation	435	(4.9)	458	(4.9)	470	(3.5)	492	(5.0)
Netherlands[1]	517	(5.4)	526	(3.9)	543	(5.4)	545	(4.5)

1. Response rate is too low to ensure comparability.
Source: OECD PISA database, 2001.

INDICATOR A11: GENDER DIFFERENCES IN STUDENT PERFORMANCE

- Already at the 4th-grade level, females tend to outperform males in reading literacy, on average, and at age 15 the gender gap in reading tends to be large.

- In mathematics, 15-year-old males tend to be at a slight advantage in most countries whereas in science, gender patterns are less pronounced and uneven.

- In civics knowledge, few gender differences emerge among 14-year-olds.

- Despite these overall patterns, countries differ, however, widely in the magnitude of gender differences in the different subject areas.

- In about half the countries, females preferred co-operative learning more than males did, whereas males in most countries tended to prefer competitive learning more than females did.

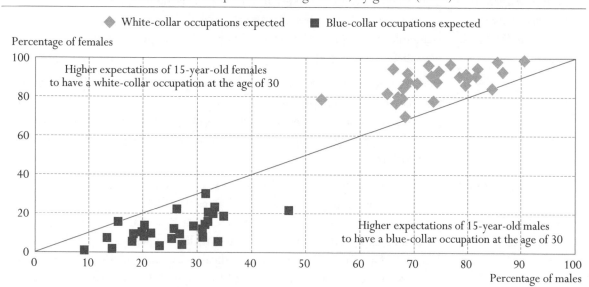

Chart A11.1

Expectations of 15-year-old students to have a white-collar or blue-collar occupation at the age of 30, by gender (2000)

Source: OECD PISA database, 2001. Table A11.1. See Annex 3 for notes *(www.oecd.org/edu/eag2003).*

A11

This indicator examines gender differences in students' performance in various subject areas, as well as on various other attitudinal scales.

Policy context

Recognising the impact that education has on participation in labour markets, occupational mobility and the quality of life, policymakers and educators emphasise the importance of reducing educational differences between males and females. Significant progress has been achieved in reducing the gender gap in educational attainment (see Indicators A1 and A2), although in certain fields of study, such as mathematics and computer science, gender differences favouring males still exist (see Indicator A3).

As females have closed the gap and then surpassed males in many aspects of education, there are now many instances in which there is concern about the under-achievement of males in certain areas, such as reading. Gender differences in student performance, as well as in attitudes toward and strategies for learning, therefore need to receive close attention from policymakers if greater gender equity in educational outcomes is to be achieved. Furthermore, students' perceptions of what occupations lie ahead for them can affect their academic decisions and performance. An important policy objective should therefore be to strengthen the role that the education system can play in moderating gender differences in performance in different subject areas. This indicator begins by examining data from OECD's PISA study on gender differences in the occupations which 15-year old students expect to have by the age of 30 and then goes on to analyse gender differences in performance, attitudes, and learning strategies by drawing upon findings from PISA as well as the International Association for the Evaluation of Educational Achievement's (IEA) PIRLS and Civic Education Studies.

Evidence and explanations

Students' aspirations and expectations for the future can affect their academic performance and choices...

PISA explored students' expected occupations at the age of 30 in order to understand the future aspirations and expectations for their own future. These expectations are likely to affect their academic performance as well as the courses and educational pathways that they pursue. Students with higher academic aspirations are also more likely to be engaged with school and related activities.

Perhaps not surprisingly, PISA suggests that students' expected occupations are associated with their parents' professions, although the correlations are only weak to moderate. On average across countries the correlation of students' expected occupations with fathers' occupations is 0.19 and that of mothers' occupations is 0.15.

The occupations they expect to have by age 30 seem to be predictive of their future career choices.

More importantly, the occupations that students expect to have at the age of 30 seem to be predictive for the career choices that they make later on. For example, female students in the participating countries are far more likely than males to report expected occupations related to life sciences and health, including biology, pharmacy, medicine and medical assistance, dentistry, nutrition and nursing, as well as professions related to teaching: Twenty per cent of females expect to be in life sciences or health related professions compared to only 7 per cent of males; 9 per cent of females compared to 3 per cent of males expect to be in occupations associated with teaching. Male students, on the other hand, more often expect careers associated with physics, mathematics or engineering (18 per cent of males versus 5 per cent of females) or occupations related to metal, machinery and related trades (6 per cent of males versus less than 1 per cent of females).

PISA classified students' expected professions at the age of 30 into four socio-economic categories, namely white-collar high-skilled, white-collar low-skilled, blue-collar high-skilled and blue-collar low-skilled . This taxonomy shows that in 40 out of the 42 countries females seem to have higher expectation towards their future occupations than males. Chart A11.1 indicates this relationship. Each symbol represents one country, with diamonds representing the percentage of students expecting a white-collar occupation at the age of 30 and the squares representing the percentage of students expecting to have a blue-collar occupation at the age of 30. In Belgium, the Czech Republic and Denmark 25 per cent more females than males expect to have a white-collar occupation at the age of 30. Mexico and Korea are countries where large percentages of males and females seem to have high expectations for a white-collar occupation (more than 80 per cent), with small differences found in this expectation between males and females (less than 10 per cent) (see Table A11.1).

Females seem to have higher expectation towards future occupations than males....

Chart A11.2 provides further detail on this by showing the percentage of male and female students who expect to have a white-collar profession, either high- or low-skilled. The left side of the chart shows the percentage of males and the right side the percentage for females. The percentages of females expecting to hold a white-collar position at the age of 30 range from around 95 per cent in Belgium, Poland and the United States to 66 per cent in Japan. Similar patterns are found for males ranging from more than 80 per cent Korea, Mexico and the United States to 51 per cent in Japan (see Table A11.1).

.....but there is considerable variation in expectations between countries for both genders.

These results are of significance for policy development. Combining the PISA data on the occupations that 15-year-olds males and females expect to have at age 30 with data on today's gender patterns in choices relating to educational pathways and occupations suggests that gender differences in occupational expectations at age 15 are likely to persist and to have a significant influence on the future of students. An important policy objective should be to strengthen the role that education systems play in moderating gender differences in occupational expectations and - to the extent that these are related to gender patterns in student performance and student interest - to reduce performance gaps in different subject areas.

On average, and in all countries, 4th-grade females outperform 4th-grade males on the reading literacy scale (Chart A11.3). The difference between females' scores and males' scores ranges from 8 points in Italy to over 20 points in England, Greece, New Zealand, Norway and Sweden, and in all countries, the differences are statistically significant.

Already at 4th-grade level, females tend to outperform males in reading literacy...

A11

Chart A11.2

15-year-olds' expectation of having a white-collar occupation at age 30
Percentage of 15-year-olds expecting to have a white-collar low-skilled or
white-collar high skilled occupation, by gender

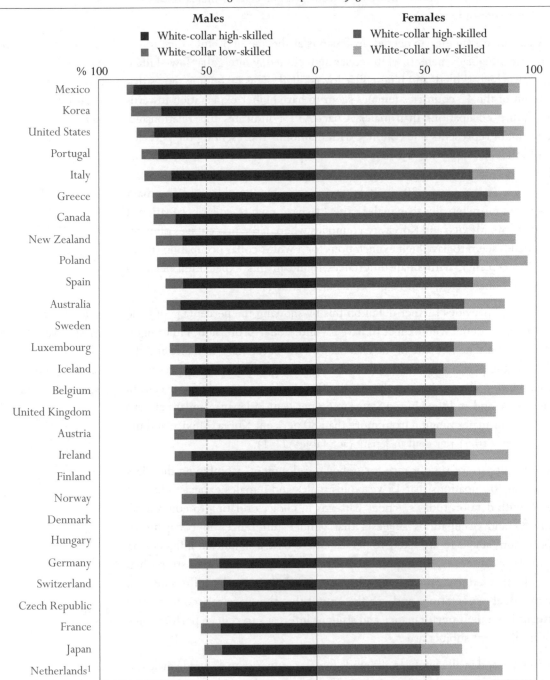

1. Response rate is too low to ensure comparability.
Source: OECD PISA database, 2001. Table A11.1. See Annex 3 for notes *(www.oecd.org/edu/eag2003).*

EDUCATION AT A GLANCE © OECD 2003

Among 15-year-olds, PISA shows even larger differences in reading literacy performance. In every country and on average, females reach higher levels of performance in reading literacy than do males. This difference is not only universal but also large: 32 points on average (Table A11.3 and Chart A11.4).

...and age 15, the gender gap in reading tends to be large.

Although gender differences appear to be more pronounced among 15-year-olds, the measures from the PISA and PIRLS assessments are highly correlated among countries (r=0.81).

In mathematical literacy, there are statistically significant differences in about half the countries, in all of which males perform better. The average gap between males and females in mathematical literacy is 11 points (Table A11.3 and Chart A11.4).

In mathematics, 15-year-old males tend to be at a slight advantage...

Measures of scientific literacy from PISA 2000 show fewer disparities between males and females than measures of reading and mathematical literacy, and the pattern of the differences is not as consistent among countries. Twenty-five OECD countries show no statistically significant gender differences in science performance (Table A11.3 and Chart A11.4).

...whereas in science, gender patterns are less pronounced and uneven...

Chart A11.3

Gender differences in performance of 4th-grade students on the PIRLS reading literacy scale (2001)

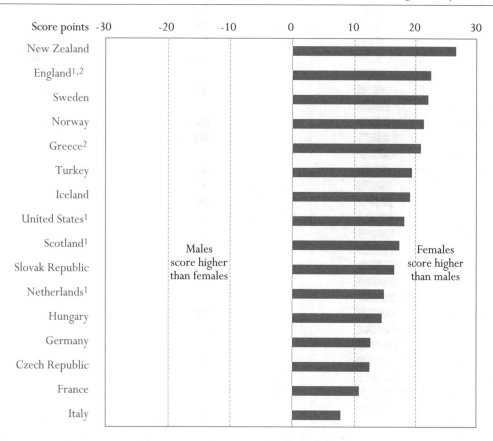

1. Met guidelines for sample participation rates only after replacement schools were included.
2. National defined population covers less than 95 per cent of national desired population.
Countries are presented in descending order of magnitude of difference betweeen females' and males' mean scores on the reading literacy scale.
Source: IEA Progress in Reading Literacy Study (PIRLS) 2001. Table A11.2. See Annex 3 for notes *(www.oecd.org/edu/eag2003)*.

A11

...and the IEA Civic Education Study shows few gender differences in civic knowledge.

Also gender differences in civic knowledge, as measured by the IEA Civic Education Study, are relatively small (Table A11.4). The civic knowledge test, which was administered to 14-year-olds in 28 countries in 1999, was designed to test students' knowledge of fundamental democratic principles and their skills in interpreting material with civic or political content. The study found that, without controlling for other variables, both civic content knowledge and skills in interpreting political communication are unrelated to gender among 14-year-olds in most countries. When other factors related to civic knowledge

Chart A11.4

Gender differences in performance of 15-year-olds on the PISA reading, mathematical and scientific literacy scales (2000)

■ Difference between males' and females' scores is statistically significant
■ Difference between males' and females' scores is not statistically significant

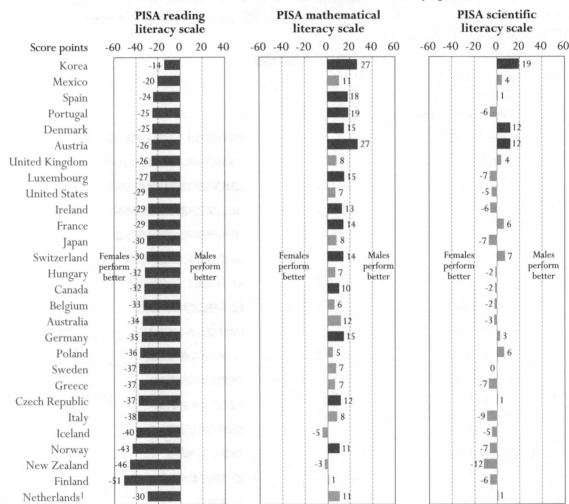

1. Response rate is too low to ensure comparability.
Countries are ranked in ascending order of the difference between the mean performance of females and males on the PISA reading literacy scale.
Source: OECD PISA database, 2001. Table A11.3. See Annex 3 for notes *(www.oecd.org/edu/eag2003).*

EDUCATION AT A GLANCE © OECD 2003

A11

(such as students' predicted level of educational attainment and home literacy resources) are held constant, slight differences arise favouring males, but only in about one-third of the 28 countries surveyed.

Countries differ, however, widely in the magnitude of gender differences in the different subject areas.

The fact that the direction of gender differences in reading and mathematics tends to be somewhat consistent among countries suggests that there are underlying features of education systems or societies and cultures that may foster such gender gaps. However, the wide variation between countries in the magnitude of gender differences suggests that current differences may be the result of variations in students' learning experiences and are thus amenable to changes in policy.

The gap between scores of 15-year-old males and females in reading literacy in PISA ranged from 25 points or less in Denmark, Korea, Mexico, Portugal, and Spain to about twice that amount in Finland. The gap in mathematical literacy ranged from statistically insignificant differences in 14 OECD countries to 27 points in Austria and Korea. Thus, some countries do appear to provide a learning environment that benefits both genders equally, either as a direct result of educational efforts or because of a more favourable social context. In reading literacy, Korea, and to a lesser extent Ireland, Japan, and the United Kingdom, achieve both high mean scores and below average gender differences. In mathematical literacy, Belgium, Finland, Japan, New Zealand and the United Kingdom similarly achieve both high mean performance and relatively small gender differences (Table A11.3 and Indicators A5 and A6).

Box A11.1 Gender differences among low performers

Fostering high performance and gender parity in education will require that attention be paid to students who are among the lowest performers. In all OECD countries, 15-year-old males are more likely to be among the lowest-performing students in reading literacy (*i.e.* to perform at or below Level 1 on the combined reading literacy scale); the average ratio of males to females at this level is 1.7 among OECD countries, ranging from 1.3 in Mexico to 3.5 in Finland.

Because 15-year-old males tend to perform better than females on the mathematical literacy scale, one might expect that females would be more represented among the lowest performing students in mathematics. However, much of the gender difference in mathematical literacy scores is attributable to larger differences in favour of males among the better students, not a relative absence of males among the poorer performers. In 15 of the OECD countries in PISA, 15-year-old males are more likely to be among the best performing students, while in no country is the same true for females. However, among students who perform at least 100 points below the OECD mean on the mathematical literacy scale, the proportion of females and males is roughly equal. These findings suggest that the underachievement of young males across subject domains is a significant challenge for education policy that will need particular attention if the proportion of students at the lowest levels of proficiency is to be reduced.

For more information and data on low performers, see the *Knowledge and Skills for Life – First Results from PISA 2000* (OECD, 2001).

A11

Gender differences exist not only in student performance, but also in attitudes, habits and approaches to learning.

Self-regulated learning scales

Gender differences exist not only on measures of proficiency in different subjects, but in attitudinal and other measures related to learning habits. As described in Indicator A9, PISA 2000 collected data on a variety of skills and attitudes that are considered prerequisites for students' abilities to manage the learning process, or their self-regulated learning. These 13 self-regulated learning scales address students' uses of learning strategies, motivation, self-related cognitions, and learning preferences (see *Approaches to Learning: Strategies and Motivation*, OECD, 2003). By identifying differences between males and females in the self-regulated learning scales (Tables A11.5a and A11.5b), this indicator pinpoints their relative strengths and weaknesses. Targeting interventions to account for differences in students' learning strategies or attitudes could have important impacts on pedagogy.

Learning strategies.

In the majority of countries, 15-year-old females tend to emphasise memorisation strategies…

Differences in the learning strategies that males and females use may provide information on possible strategies to reduce gender differences in performance. In the majority of countries, 15-year-old females report emphasising memorisation strategies (*e.g.*, reading material aloud several times and learning key facts) more than males do (Table A11.5a).

…while males tend to be stronger on elaboration strategies.

Conversely, males report using elaboration strategies (*e.g.*, exploring how material relates to things one has learned in other contexts) more than females. However, in almost all countries with statistically significant gender differences, females report using control strategies (*i.e.*, strategies that allow them to control the learning process) more often than do males. This suggests that females are more likely to adopt a self-evaluating perspective during the learning process (see OECD, 2001). Males, on the other hand, perhaps could benefit from more general assistance in planning, organizing, and structuring learning activities (Table A11.5a).

Motivation.

In all countries, females express greater interest in reading…

In all countries, females express greater interest in reading than males. And as shown in Indicators A8 and A9, they also tend to be more involved readers of books, particularly fiction, and to be more engaged in reading than males.

…while males tend to express more interest in mathematics…

By contrast, males express more interest in mathematics than do females in almost every country in the study. In fact, Portugal and Mexico are the only countries where females and males report similar levels of interest in mathematics.

…and both differences are closely mirrored in performance patterns.

Gender differences in performance in reading and mathematical literacy are closely mirrored in student interest in their respective subjects. These gender differences in attitudes may reveal inequalities in the effectiveness with which schools and societies promote motivation and interest in different subject areas.

Self-related cognitions

The confidence that students have in their abilities and their beliefs about the benefits of learning are also factors that have a close relationship to performance and also vary by gender. In all countries except Korea, females express a higher self-concept than do males in reading. These differences are especially pronounced in Finland, Germany, Italy and the United States. In mathematical literacy, males tend to express a higher self-concept than females, particularly in Germany, Norway, and Switzerland. In terms of their general self-efficacy, or belief that one's goals can be achieved, males score significantly higher than females, overall and in most countries. The differences between males and females are particularly pronounced in Denmark, Sweden and Norway (Table A11.5b).

Gender differences are also observed with regard to confidence that students have in their abilities and whether they believe in the benefits of learning…

Learning styles

In about half the countries, females preferred co-operative learning more than males did, whereas males in most countries tended to prefer competitive learning more than females did. On the co-operative learning scale, these gender differences are most pronounced in Ireland, Italy and the United States. On the competitive learning scale, they are most evident in Ireland, Portugal and Scotland (Table A11.5b).

…as well as in student attitudes to co-operative and competitive learning.

Definitions and methodologies

The reading performance scores of 4th graders are based on the Progress in Reading Literacy Study (PIRLS) that was undertaken by the International Association for the Evaluation of Educational Achievement (IEA) during 2001. The PIRLS target population was students in the upper of the two adjacent grades that contained the largest proportion of nine year-old students at the time of testing. Beyond the age criterion embedded in the definition, the target population should represent that point in the curriculum where students have essentially finished learning the basic reading skills and will focus more on "reading to learn" in the subsequent grades. Thus the PIRLS target grade was expected to be the 4th grade (Table A11.2).

The reading performance scores of 4th graders are based on the Progress in Reading Literacy Study (PIRLS).

The scores on the civics knowledge test are based on assessments of students during the second phase of the International Association for the Evaluation of Educational Achievement's (IEA) Civic Education Study. The internationally desired population includes all students enrolled on a full-time basis in that grade in which most students aged 14 years to 14 years and 11 months are found at the time of testing. Time of testing for most countries was the first week of the 8th month of the school year (Table A11.4).

The civics knowledge scores are based on the Civics Education Study that was undertaken by the IEA during 1999.

The PISA target population studied for this indicator was 15-year-old students. Operationally, this referred to students who were from 15 years and 3 (completed) months to 16 years and 2 (completed) months at the beginning of the testing period and who were enrolled in an educational institution, regardless of the grade level or type of institution and of whether they participated in school full-time or part-time.

Twenty-six of the 32 countries that participated in PISA 2000 administered the self-regulated learning component on which this indicator is based: Australia, Austria, the Flemish Community of Belgium, Brazil, the Czech Republic, Denmark, Finland, Germany, Hungary, Ireland, Iceland, Italy, Korea, Latvia, Liechtenstein, Luxembourg, Mexico, the Netherlands, New Zealand, Norway, Portugal, the Russian Federation, Scotland, Sweden, Switzerland and the United States. Note that Belgium and the United Kingdom, countries that did participate in the main

The reading, mathematics and science performance scores for 15–year-olds are based on assessments administered as part of the Programme for International Student Assessment (PISA) undertaken by the OECD during 2000.

PISA assessments, are represented in the self-regulated learning option only by participating jurisdictions: the Flemish Community and Scotland, respectively. Canada, France, Greece, Ireland, Japan, and Spain, as well as the French Community of Belgium and England did not participate in this option.

For the definition of the indices referred to in this indicator, see Indicator A10.

For notes on standard errors, significance tests, and multiple comparisons see Annex 3 at *www.oecd.org/edu/eag2003*.

Table A11.1
15 year-olds' occupational expectations by age 30, by gender
Percentage of 15 year-olds expecting to have a white- or blue-collar occupation, by gender

A11

	All students				Males				Females			
	White-Collar High-Skilled	White-Collar Low-Skilled	Blue-Collar High-Skilled	Blue-Collar Low-Skilled	White-Collar High-Skilled	White-Collar Low-Skilled	Blue-Collar High-Skilled	Blue-Collar Low-Skilled	White-Collar High-Skilled	White-Collar Low-Skilled	Blue-Collar High-Skilled	Blue-Collar Low-Skilled
	%	%	%	%	%	%	%	%	%	%	%	%
Australia	65.0	11.7	10.4	12.9	62.4	6.0	19.0	12.7	67.8	17.9	1.2	13.1
Austria	55.3	17.2	11.7	15.8	56.3	8.6	21.9	13.3	54.8	25.1	2.2	17.9
Belgium	65.6	14.2	15.4	4.9	58.5	7.6	27.9	6.0	73.1	21.3	1.8	3.7
Canada	70.9	10.2	7.1	11.8	64.6	9.7	13.0	12.8	77.1	10.8	1.2	10.8
Czech Republic	44.5	22.0	16.2	17.3	41.1	11.9	28.3	18.7	47.6	31.1	5.3	16.0
Denmark	58.5	17.5	19.6	4.3	50.5	10.9	34.1	4.5	67.7	25.1	2.9	4.2
Finland	60.4	15.8	12.2	11.5	55.5	9.1	21.4	14.0	65.0	22.0	3.7	9.2
France	48.9	14.7	9.9	26.5	44.1	8.5	18.7	28.7	53.4	20.5	1.7	24.4
Germany	48.8	20.9	17.2	13.2	44.7	13.3	30.1	11.9	53.1	28.0	4.6	14.3
Greece	72.3	11.7	9.4	6.6	66.0	8.6	17.9	7.6	78.5	14.6	1.3	5.6
Hungary	52.7	19.0	16.6	11.7	50.3	9.5	28.0	12.2	55.3	28.5	5.1	11.1
Iceland	59.2	12.6	7.9	20.3	60.3	6.4	13.5	19.8	58.4	18.5	2.4	20.7
Ireland	64.1	12.2	11.7	12.1	57.5	7.2	22.6	12.7	70.3	16.9	1.3	11.5
Italy	69.1	15.2	5.8	9.9	66.6	11.9	10.6	10.9	71.6	18.7	0.9	8.8
Japan	45.8	12.9	4.0	37.4	43.3	7.7	7.3	41.7	48.2	17.9	0.7	33.2
Korea	71.2	13.2	1.6	13.9	71.1	13.4	2.4	13.0	71.4	13.0	0.6	15.0
Luxembourg	59.6	14.3	8.7	17.4	55.7	11.3	15.4	17.6	63.0	16.9	2.8	17.2
Mexico	86.0	3.6	2.1	8.2	84.0	2.5	3.4	10.1	88.0	4.7	0.8	6.4
New Zealand	67.0	15.1	8.5	9.4	61.3	11.8	16.5	10.4	72.4	18.3	0.8	8.4
Norway	57.4	12.7	12.9	17.1	55.0	6.4	23.2	15.4	60.1	18.9	2.3	18.7
Poland	68.8	15.4	14.2	1.7	63.3	9.4	24.4	2.9	74.5	21.7	3.5	0.4
Portugal	76.5	9.5	5.1	9.0	72.7	7.0	9.8	10.5	79.8	11.7	0.8	7.7
Spain	66.6	12.2	8.2	13.1	61.2	7.7	16.1	15.0	71.7	16.6	0.7	11.0
Sweden	63.2	10.3	8.1	18.5	62.0	5.8	13.6	18.6	64.5	14.8	2.4	18.3
Switzerland	45.3	16.4	15.0	23.3	42.7	11.5	26.9	18.8	47.6	21.0	3.9	27.4
United Kingdom	57.1	16.3	7.6	19.0	51.0	14.0	14.5	20.5	63.0	18.6	0.8	17.6
United States	80.5	8.2	5.1	6.2	74.4	7.5	9.8	8.4	85.8	8.8	1.0	4.3
Country mean	*62.2*	*13.9*	*10.1*	*13.8*	*58.4*	*9.1*	*18.2*	*14.4*	*66.1*	*18.6*	*2.1*	*13.2*
Argentina	79.7	7.2	1.9	11.2	74.3	7.3	4.4	14.1	83.6	7.1	0.1	9.1
Brazil	87.4	7.8	2.4	2.3	86.0	4.7	4.5	4.8	88.6	10.4	0.7	0.2
Chile	68.9	10.2	7.6	13.3	64.8	5.7	14.5	15.0	72.6	14.2	1.5	11.8
Hong Kong-China	58.6	17.2	0.6	23.7	54.1	19.5	0.6	25.8	63.1	14.9	0.5	21.5
Indonesia	76.2	6.8	3.8	13.2	78.2	1.3	6.0	14.5	74.2	12.1	1.7	12.0
Israel	63.7	5.6	1.1	29.7	64.8	3.5	2.2	29.5	62.9	7.0	0.3	29.8
Latvia	63.1	18.0	13.4	5.5	55.0	13.8	22.7	8.5	70.5	21.8	5.0	2.7
Liechtenstein	36.3	17.1	14.2	32.4	40.6	13.9	24.4	21.1	32.2	20.4	3.1	44.2
Peru	84.1	7.9	6.2	1.8	82.9	2.6	11.0	3.4	85.2	13.1	1.4	0.2
Russian Federation	58.6	6.9	11.0	23.5	47.6	4.8	15.9	31.7	69.1	9.0	6.2	15.7
Thailand	43.3	17.4	10.9	28.4	33.5	12.5	22.0	32.0	49.8	20.8	3.4	26.0
Netherlands[1]	57.6	18.6	8.4	15.5	58.6	9.4	15.7	16.3	56.4	28.1	0.8	14.7

1. Response rate is too low to ensure comparability.
Source: OECD PISA database, 2001.

OECD COUNTRIES

NON-OECD COUNTRIES

A11

Table A11.2
Performance of 4ᵗʰ-grade students and gender (2001)
Mean performance of 4ᵗʰ-grade students on the PIRLS reading literacy scale, by gender

	Females		Males		Difference[1]	
	Mean score	**S.E.**	**Mean score**	**S.E.**	**Score difference**	**S.E.**
Czech Republic	543	(2.8)	531	(2.6)	**12**	(2.8)
England[2,3]	564	(3.9)	541	(3.7)	**22**	(3.3)
France	531	(2.7)	520	(3.0)	**11**	(3.3)
Germany	545	(2.2)	533	(2.5)	**13**	(2.7)
Greece[3]	535	(3.8)	514	(4.0)	**21**	(3.9)
Hungary	550	(2.4)	536	(2.5)	**14**	(3.8)
Iceland	522	(1.9)	503	(1.5)	**19**	(2.4)
Italy	545	(2.6)	537	(2.7)	**8**	(2.5)
Netherlands[2]	562	(2.7)	547	(2.8)	**15**	(2.2)
New Zealand	542	(4.7)	516	(4.2)	**27**	(5.4)
Norway	510	(3.5)	489	(3.4)	**21**	(3.9)
Scotland[2]	537	(3.9)	519	(4.2)	**17**	(4.0)
Slovak Republic	526	(3.0)	510	(3.3)	**16**	(3.0)
Sweden	572	(2.6)	550	(2.5)	**22**	(2.6)
Turkey	459	(4.0)	440	(3.7)	**19**	(3.1)
United States[2]	551	(3.8)	533	(4.9)	**18**	(4.1)
Country mean	*538*	*(0.8)*	*521*	*(0.8)*	*17*	*(0.8)*

OECD COUNTRIES

1. Positive differences indicate that females perform better than males while negative differences indicate that males perform better than females. Differences that are statistically significant are indicated in bold.
2. Met guidelines for sample participation rates only after replacement schools were included.
3. National Defined Population covers less than 95 per cent of National Desired Population.
Source: IEA Progress in Reading Literacy Study (PIRLS) 2001.

Table A11.3
Performance of 15-year-old students and gender (2000)
Mean performance of 15-year-olds on the PISA reading, mathematical, and scientific literacy scales, by gender

A11

	Reading literacy						Mathematical literacy						Scientific literacy					
	Males		Females		Difference[1]		Males		Females		Difference[1]		Males		Females		Difference[1]	
	Mean Score	S.E.	Mean Score	S.E.	Score dif.	S.E.	Mean Score	S.E.	Mean Score	S.E.	Score dif.	S.E.	Mean Score	S.E.	Mean Score	S.E.	Score dif.	S.E.
Australia	513	(4.0)	546	(4.7)	**-34**	(5.4)	539	(4.1)	527	(5.1)	12	(6.2)	526	(3.9)	529	(4.8)	-3	(5.3)
Austria	495	(3.2)	520	(3.6)	**-26**	(5.2)	530	(4.0)	503	(3.7)	**27**	(5.9)	526	(3.8)	514	(4.3)	**12**	(6.3)
Belgium	492	(4.2)	525	(4.9)	**-33**	(6.0)	524	(4.6)	518	(5.2)	6	(6.1)	496	(5.2)	498	(5.6)	-2	(6.7)
Canada	519	(1.8)	551	(1.7)	**-32**	(1.6)	539	(1.8)	529	(1.6)	**10**	(1.9)	529	(1.9)	531	(1.7)	-2	(1.9)
Czech Republic	473	(4.1)	510	(2.5)	**-37**	(4.7)	504	(4.4)	492	(3.0)	**12**	(5.2)	512	(3.8)	511	(3.2)	1	(5.1)
Denmark	485	(3.0)	510	(2.9)	**-25**	(3.3)	522	(3.1)	507	(3.0)	**15**	(3.7)	488	(3.9)	476	(3.5)	**12**	(4.8)
Finland	520	(3.0)	571	(2.8)	**-51**	(2.6)	537	(2.8)	536	(2.6)	1	(3.3)	534	(3.5)	541	(2.7)	-6	(3.8)
France	490	(3.5)	519	(2.7)	**-29**	(3.4)	525	(4.1)	511	(2.8)	**14**	(4.2)	504	(4.2)	498	(3.8)	6	(4.8)
Germany	468	(3.2)	502	(3.9)	**-35**	(5.2)	498	(3.1)	483	(4.0)	**15**	(5.1)	489	(3.4)	487	(3.4)	3	(4.7)
Greece	456	(6.1)	493	(4.6)	**-37**	(5.0)	451	(7.7)	444	(5.4)	7	(7.4)	457	(6.1)	464	(5.2)	-7	(5.7)
Hungary	465	(5.3)	496	(4.3)	**-32**	(5.7)	492	(5.2)	485	(4.9)	7	(6.2)	496	(5.8)	497	(5.0)	-2	(6.9)
Iceland	488	(2.1)	528	(2.1)	**-40**	(3.1)	513	(3.1)	518	(2.9)	-5	(4.0)	495	(3.4)	499	(3.0)	-5	(4.7)
Ireland	513	(4.2)	542	(3.6)	**-29**	(4.6)	510	(4.0)	497	(3.4)	**13**	(5.1)	511	(4.2)	517	(4.2)	-6	(5.5)
Italy	469	(5.1)	507	(3.6)	**-38**	(7.0)	462	(5.3)	454	(3.8)	8	(7.3)	474	(5.6)	483	(3.9)	-9	(7.7)
Japan	507	(6.7)	537	(5.4)	**-30**	(6.4)	561	(7.3)	553	(5.9)	8	(7.4)	547	(7.2)	554	(5.9)	-7	(7.2)
Korea	519	(3.8)	533	(3.7)	**-14**	(6.0)	559	(4.6)	532	(5.1)	**27**	(7.8)	561	(4.3)	541	(5.1)	**19**	(7.6)
Luxembourg	429	(2.6)	456	(2.3)	**-27**	(3.8)	454	(3.0)	439	(3.2)	**15**	(4.7)	441	(3.6)	448	(3.2)	-7	(5.0)
Mexico	411	(4.2)	432	(3.8)	**-20**	(4.3)	393	(4.5)	382	(3.8)	11	(4.9)	423	(4.2)	419	(3.9)	4	(4.8)
New Zealand	507	(4.2)	553	(3.8)	**-46**	(6.3)	536	(5.0)	539	(4.1)	-3	(6.7)	523	(4.6)	535	(3.8)	-12	(7.0)
Norway	486	(3.8)	529	(2.9)	**-43**	(4.0)	506	(3.8)	495	(2.9)	**11**	(4.0)	499	(4.1)	505	(3.3)	-7	(5.0)
Poland	461	(6.0)	498	(5.5)	**-36**	(7.0)	472	(7.5)	468	(6.3)	5	(8.5)	486	(6.1)	480	(6.5)	6	(7.4)
Portugal	458	(5.0)	482	(4.6)	**-25**	(3.8)	464	(4.7)	446	(4.7)	**19**	(4.9)	456	(4.8)	462	(4.2)	-6	(4.3)
Spain	481	(3.4)	505	(2.8)	**-24**	(3.2)	487	(4.3)	469	(3.3)	**18**	(4.5)	492	(3.5)	491	(3.6)	1	(4.0)
Sweden	499	(2.6)	536	(2.5)	**-37**	(2.7)	514	(3.2)	507	(3.0)	7	(4.0)	512	(3.5)	513	(2.9)	0	(3.9)
Switzerland	480	(4.9)	510	(4.5)	**-30**	(4.2)	537	(5.3)	523	(4.8)	**14**	(5.0)	500	(5.7)	493	(4.7)	7	(5.4)
United Kingdom	512	(3.0)	537	(3.4)	**-26**	(4.3)	534	(3.5)	526	(3.7)	8	(5.0)	535	(3.4)	531	(4.0)	4	(5.2)
United States	490	(8.4)	518	(6.2)	**-29**	(4.1)	497	(8.9)	490	(7.3)	7	(5.4)	497	(8.9)	502	(6.5)	-5	(5.3)
Country mean	*485*	*(0.8)*	*517*	*(0.7)*	*-32*	*(0.9)*	*506*	*(1.0)*	*495*	*(0.9)*	*11*	*(1.2)*	*501*	*(0.9)*	*501*	*(0.8)*	*0*	*(1.0)*
Brazil	388	(3.9)	404	(3.4)	**-17**	(4.0)	349	(4.7)	322	(4.7)	**27**	(5.6)	376	(4.8)	376	(3.8)	0	(5.6)
Latvia	432	(5.5)	485	(5.4)	**-53**	(4.2)	467	(5.3)	460	(5.6)	6	(5.8)	449	(6.4)	472	(5.8)	**-23**	(5.4)
Liechtenstein	468	(7.3)	500	(6.8)	**-31**	(11.5)	521	(11.5)	510	(11.1)	12	(17.7)	484	(10.9)	468	(9.3)	16	(14.7)
Russian Federation	443	(4.5)	481	(4.1)	**-38**	(2.9)	478	(5.7)	479	(6.2)	-2	(4.8)	453	(5.4)	467	(5.2)	**-14**	(4.5)
Netherlands[2]	517	(4.8)	547	(3.8)	**-30**	(5.7)	569	(4.9)	558	(4.6)	11	(6.2)	529	(6.3)	529	(5.1)	1	(8.1)

OECD COUNTRIES
NON-OECD COUNTRIES

1. Positive differences indicate that males perform better than females while negative differences indicate that females perform better than males.
   Differences that are statistically significant are indicated in bold.
2. Response rate is too low to ensure comparability.
Source: OECD PISA database, 2001.

Table A11.4
Civic knowledge of 14-year-old students and gender (1999)
Mean performance of 14-year-olds on the civic knowledge scale, by gender

	Males		Females		Difference[1]	
	Mean score	S.E.	Mean score	S.E.	Score difference	S.E.
Australia	101	(1.1)	103	(0.9)	-2	(1.4)
Belgium (Fr.)[2]	93	(1.3)	97	(1.1)	-5	(1.7)
Czech Republic	104	(1.0)	102	(0.8)	2	(1.3)
Denmark[2]	102	(0.7)	99	(0.7)	3	(1.0)
England[1]	100	(1.0)	99	(0.8)	0	(1.3)
Finland	108	(0.8)	110	(0.9)	-2	(1.2)
Germany[4]	101	(0.7)	99	(0.6)	1	(0.9)
Greece	107	(0.9)	109	(0.8)	-2	(1.2)
Hungary	101	(0.8)	102	(0.7)	-1	(1.0)
Italy	104	(1.1)	106	(0.9)	-2	(1.4)
Norway[2]	103	(0.7)	103	(0.6)	1	(0.9)
Poland	109	(1.5)	112	(2.2)	-3	(2.6)
Portugal[5]	97	(0.9)	96	(0.8)	1	(1.2)
Slovak Republic	105	(0.9)	105	(0.8)	0	(1.1)
Sweden[3]	99	(1.1)	100	(0.8)	-1	(1.3)
Switzerland	100	(0.9)	97	(0.8)	2	(1.2)
United States[3]	106	(1.3)	107	(1.2)	-2	(1.8)

1. Positive differences indicate that males perform better than females while negative differences indicate that females perform better than males.
   Differences that are statistically significant are indicated in bold.
2. Countries' overall participation rate after replacement less than 85 per cent.
3. Countries with testing date at beginning of school year.
4. Does not cover all of the national population.
5. Grade 8 selected instead of Grade 9 due to average age.
Source: IEA Civic Education Study (2001).

Table A11.5a
Gender differences among 15-year-olds on the PISA self-regulated learning scales (2000)
Difference between male and female 15-year-olds' scores on PISA indices of self-regulated learning

A11

		Index of memorisa-tion strategies		Index of elabora-tion strategies		Index of control strategies		Index of instru-mental motivation		Index of interest in reading		Index of interest in mathematics		Index of effort and perseverance	
		Differ-ence[1]	Effect size	Differ-ence[1]	Effect size	Differ-ence[1]	Effect size	Differ-ence[1]	Effect size	Differ-ence[1]	Effect size	Differ-ence[1]	Effect size	Differ-ence[1]	Effect size
OECD COUNTRIES	Australia	-0.07	0.07	0.10	0.12	-0.15	0.14	0.10	0.12	-0.29	0.36	0.22	0.28	-0.05	0.08
	Austria	-0.29	0.28	0.14	0.14	-0.17	0.19	-0.35	0.05	-0.61	0.62	0.39	0.38	-0.05	0.08
	Belgium (Fl.)	-0.15	0.14	0.19	0.19	-0.14	0.16	0.04	0.05	-0.47	0.54	0.10	0.16	-0.13	0.21
	Czech Republic	-0.31	0.31	0.04	0.05	-0.31	0.34	-0.09	0.12	-0.79	0.79	0.22	0.26	-0.12	0.20
	Denmark	0.07	0.09	0.12	0.13	-0.02	0.04	0.19	0.25	-0.52	0.53	0.31	0.28	-0.07	0.12
	Finland	-0.08	0.09	0.12	0.14	-0.10	0.12	-0.01	0.02	-0.87	0.96	0.25	0.28	-0.15	0.25
	Germany	-0.28	0.28	0.08	0.08	-0.19	0.21	0.00	0.00	-0.63	0.60	0.34	0.38	-0.10	0.16
	Hungary	-0.28	0.33	0.10	0.11	-0.24	0.27	-0.03	0.05	-0.52	0.49	0.03	0.05	-0.10	0.17
	Iceland	0.00	0.02	0.10	0.11	-0.02	0.01	-0.01	0.01	-0.40	0.45	-0.03	0.02	-0.14	0.21
	Ireland	-0.26	0.26	-0.05	0.05	-0.33	0.31	0.08	0.08	-0.56	0.53	0.14	0.13	-0.17	0.23
	Italy	0.00	0.01	0.04	0.04	-0.36	0.38	0.20	0.22	-0.57	0.58	0.06	0.09	-0.17	0.26
	Korea	-0.07	0.07	0.02	0.01	-0.06	0.04	0.04	0.04	-0.03	0.02	0.04	0.07	0.02	0.03
	Luxembourg	-0.40	0.36	-0.06	0.06	-0.29	0.29	-0.21	0.15	-0.42	0.43	0.25	0.27	-0.16	0.24
	Mexico	0.04	0.03	-0.07	0.08	-0.19	0.20	0.00	0.01	-0.21	0.32	-0.02	0.02	-0.13	0.20
	New Zealand	-0.12	0.12	0.02	0.01	-0.20	0.19	0.05	0.05	-0.35	0.37	0.21	0.24	-0.06	0.09
	Norway	0.26	0.29	0.20	0.21	0.16	0.18	0.07	0.09	-0.63	0.60	0.47	0.38	-0.02	0.03
	Portugal	-0.03	0.02	-0.03	0.03	-0.31	0.34	-0.08	0.11	-0.71	0.80	-0.11	0.02	-0.18	0.29
	Scotland	-0.09	0.14	0.07	0.11	-0.13	0.22	0.01	0.02	-0.43	0.43	0.14	0.17	-0.08	0.14
	Sweden	0.09	0.11	0.28	0.29	0.02	0.02	0.06	0.07	-0.34	0.47	0.26	0.35	-0.01	0.01
	Switzerland	-0.16	0.17	0.02	0.03	-0.22	0.24	-0.03	0.04	-0.65	0.68	0.46	0.51	-0.10	0.16
	United States	-0.21	0.17	-0.10	0.08	-0.35	0.31	-0.04	0.05	-0.35	0.36	0.05	0.08	-0.22	0.31
	Country mean	*-0.11*	*0.10*	*0.06*	*0.06*	*-0.18*	*0.18*	*0.02*	*0.02*	*-0.50*	*0.53*	*0.18*	*0.20*	*-0.11*	*0.16*
NON-OECD COUNTRIES	Brazil	-0.10	0.10	-0.11	0.11	-0.18	0.17	-0.10	0.13	-0.34	0.42	0.10	0.08	-0.12	0.19
	Latvia	-0.13	0.18	0.03	0.03	-0.19	0.25	-0.10	0.14	-0.54	0.61	0.03	0.03	-0.09	0.15
	Liechtenstein	-0.15	0.18	0.21	0.21	-0.11	0.12	0.06	0.08	-0.43	0.42	0.48	0.71	-0.07	0.11
	Russian Federation	-0.15	0.20	0.09	0.09	-0.17	0.19	-0.11	0.16	-0.42	0.41	-0.03	0.02	-0.12	0.18
	Netherlands[2]	-0.03	0.03	0.17	0.19	-0.04	0.05	0.25	0.17	-0.70	0.70	0.58	0.48	-0.05	0.08

1. Positive differences indicate that males perform better than females while negative differences indicate that females perform better than males.
2. Response rate is too low to ensure comparability.
Source: OECD PISA database, 2001.

Table A11.5b
Gender differences among 15-year-olds on the PISA self-regulated learning scales (2000) (continued)
Difference between male and female 15-year-olds' scores on PISA indices of self-regulated learning

		Index of co-operative learning		Index of competitive learning		Index of self-efficacy		Index of self-concept in reading		Index of self-concept in mathematics		Index of academic self-concept	
		Difference[1]	Effect size	Difference[1]	Effect size	Difference[1]	Effect size	Difference[1]	Effect size	Difference[1]	Effect size	Difference[1]	Effect size
OECD COUNTRIES	Australia	-0.14	0.03	0.20	0.32	0.13	0.22	-0.17	0.21	0.23	0.29	0.03	0.05
	Austria	-0.30	0.17	0.12	0.15	0.20	0.32	-0.35	0.34	0.29	0.30	-0.06	0.10
	Belgium (Fl.)	-0.22	0.14	0.19	0.23	0.14	0.24	-0.13	0.18	0.18	0.27	0.04	0.08
	Czech Republic	-0.33	0.15	0.00	0.01	0.17	0.30	-0.36	0.37	0.26	0.31	-0.04	0.05
	Denmark	-0.11	0.02	0.29	0.25	0.28	0.45	-0.32	0.31	0.39	0.40	0.10	0.16
	Finland	-0.29	0.11	0.22	0.30	0.21	0.34	-0.42	0.45	0.35	0.36	-0.03	0.04
	Germany	-0.24	0.10	0.13	0.16	0.13	0.21	-0.45	0.43	0.42	0.42	0.00	0.00
	Hungary	-0.23	0.01	-0.06	0.02	0.11	0.19	-0.32	0.33	0.12	0.13	-0.06	0.08
	Iceland	-0.18	0.08	0.22	0.28	0.18	0.26	-0.20	0.20	0.20	0.19	-0.04	0.05
	Ireland	-0.42	0.23	0.41	0.39	0.12	0.17	-0.15	0.12	0.09	0.13	-0.02	0.03
	Italy	-0.49	0.27	0.13	0.14	0.12	0.19	-0.44	0.40	0.18	0.11	-0.15	0.21
	Korea	0.09	0.14	0.09	0.12	0.10	0.15	0.02	0.03	0.15	0.16	0.09	0.12
	Luxembourg	-0.36	0.19	0.04	0.13	0.12	0.18	-0.21	0.18	0.28	0.28	-0.04	0.06
	Mexico	0.20	0.11	0.10	0.13	0.00	0.01	-0.21	0.25	0.05	0.09	-0.04	0.06
	New Zealand	-0.23	0.08	0.23	0.28	0.12	0.19	-0.29	0.27	0.26	0.26	0.04	0.05
	Norway	-0.34	0.15	0.31	0.34	0.22	0.33	-0.38	0.37	0.50	0.44	0.04	0.05
	Portugal	-0.35	0.14	0.35	0.38	0.08	0.14	-0.31	0.32	0.14	0.16	0.01	0.02
	Scotland	-0.03	0.05	0.35	0.42	0.19	0.32	-0.10	0.14	0.22	0.24	0.02	0.03
	Sweden	-0.05	0.05	0.21	0.27	0.24	0.37	-0.30	0.37	0.36	0.41	0.05	0.08
	Switzerland	-0.28	0.14	0.24	0.30	0.13	0.22	-0.31	0.35	0.50	0.55	0.03	0.05
	United States	-0.42	0.21	0.05	0.13	0.04	0.06	-0.39	0.36	0.09	0.13	-0.08	0.11
	Country mean	*-0.27*	*0.10*	*0.18*	*0.21*	*0.14*	*0.22*	*-0.29*	*0.29*	*0.25*	*0.25*	*-0.02*	*0.02*
NON-OECD COUNTRIES	Brazil	-0.24	0.11	0.21	0.21	0.06	0.08	0.28	0.30	0.25	0.21	0.03	0.05
	Latvia	-0.31	0.15	-0.11	0.11	0.03	0.05	0.51	0.51	0.18	0.18	-0.07	0.11
	Liechtenstein	-0.17	0.09	0.27	0.36	0.07	0.12	0.37	0.37	0.39	0.58	0.00	0.01
	Russian Federation	-0.20	0.05	-0.15	0.10	0.07	0.11	0.52	0.48	0.02	0.00	-0.08	0.11
	Netherlands[2]	-0.33	0.20	0.36	0.34	0.24	0.44	0.25	0.26	0.65	0.57	0.12	0.20

1. Positive differences indicate that males perform better than females while negative differences indicate that females perform better than males.
2. Response rate is too low to ensure comparability.
Source: OECD PISA database, 2001.

INDICATOR A12: LABOUR FORCE PARTICIPATION BY LEVEL OF EDUCATIONAL ATTAINMENT

A12

- Labour force participation rates rise with educational attainment in most OECD countries. With very few exceptions, the participation rate for graduates of tertiary education is markedly higher than that for upper secondary graduates. The gap in male participation rates is particularly wide between upper secondary graduates and those without an upper secondary qualification.

- The labour force participation rate for females with less than upper secondary attainment is particularly low. Rates for females with tertiary attainment approach or exceed 80 per cent in all but four countries, but remain below those of males in all countries except one.

- The gender gap in labour force participation decreases with increasing educational attainment. Although a gender gap in labour force participation remains among those with the highest educational attainment, it is much narrower than among those with lower qualifications.

A12

Chart A12.1

Differences between labour force participation rates of males and females, by level of educational attainment for 25 to 64-year-olds (2001)

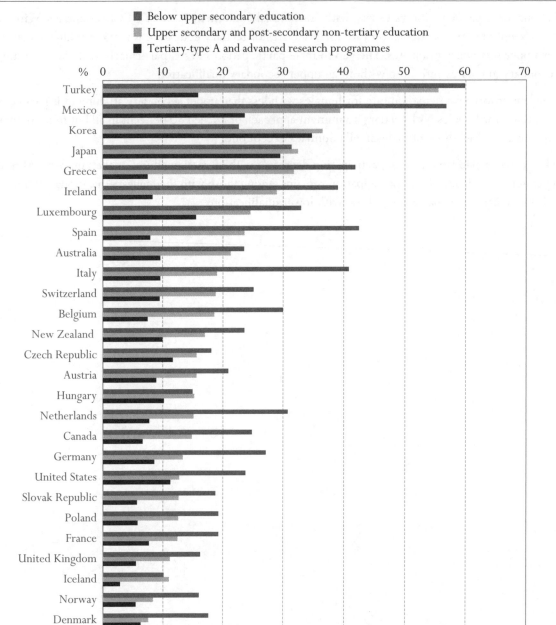

■ Below upper secondary education
■ Upper secondary and post-secondary non-tertiary education
■ Tertiary-type A and advanced research programmes

Countries are ranked in descending order of the difference in participation rates of males and females who have completed upper secondary and post-secondary non-tertiary education.
Source: OECD. Table A12.1. See Annex 3 for notes *(www.oecd.org/edu/eag2003)*.

Policy context

OECD economies and labour markets are becoming increasingly dependent on a stable supply of well-educated workers to further their economic development and to maintain their competitiveness. As levels of skill tend to rise with educational attainment, the costs incurred when those with higher levels of education do not work also rise; and as populations in OECD countries age, higher and longer participation in the labour force can lower dependency ratios and help to alleviate the burden of financing public pensions.

This indicator examines the relationship between educational attainment and labour force activity, comparing rates of participation in the labour force first, and then rates of unemployment. The adequacy of workers' skills and the capacity of the labour market to supply jobs that match those skills are important issues for policy-makers.

This indicator examines the relationship between educational attainment and labour-market status.

A12

Evidence and explanations

Labour force participation

Variation between countries in labour force participation by females is a primary factor in the differences in overall participation rates between OECD countries. The overall labour force participation rates for males aged 25 to 64 range from 81 per cent or less in Belgium, Hungary, Italy and Poland to 94 per cent and above in Iceland, Japan, Mexico and Switzerland (Table A12.1). By contrast, reflecting very different cultural and social patterns, labour force participation among females ranges from 55 per cent or less in Greece, Italy, Mexico, Spain and Turkey, to over 77 per cent in the Nordic countries. Prolonged education and non-employment are two factors which contribute to these disparities, generally increasing the number of people not in the labour force.

Labour force participation rates for males vary less between countries than those for females.

Labour force participation rates for males are generally higher among those with higher educational qualifications. With the exception of Ireland, Mexico, Spain and Turkey, where the trend is less pronounced, the participation rate for graduates of tertiary education is markedly higher than that for upper secondary graduates. The difference ranges from a few percentage points to between 8 and 9 percentage points in Austria, Denmark, Germany and Poland. It is very small between the ages of 35 and 44, when most people are in employment, and may stem mainly from the fact that the less skilled leave the labour market earlier. After 55, those with higher educational attainment tend to remain in employment longer than others (Table A12.1).

Labour force participation rates for males rise with educational attainment in most OECD countries.

The gap in participation rates of males aged 25 to 64 years is particularly wide between upper secondary graduates and those who have not completed an upper secondary qualification. In 18 out of 30 OECD countries, the difference in the rate of participation between upper secondary graduates and those without such a qualification exceeds ten percentage points. The most extreme case is Hungary, where only half of the male population without upper secondary education, but over 80 per cent with such attainment, participate in the labour force. The gap in participation rates between males with low and males with

The gap in male participation rates is particularly wide between those with and those without an upper secondary qualification.

A12

Among females, the difference in labour force participation by level of educational attainment is even wider.

Labour force participation among females with qualifications below upper secondary is particularly low…

…but the gender gap in labour force participation decreases with increasing educational attainment.

The education gap in male participation in the labour force is strongly influenced by differences among the older population.

high educational attainment is less than five percentage points in Iceland, Korea, Mexico, Portugal and Turkey (Table A12.1).

Labour force participation rates for females aged 25 to 64 years show yet more marked differences, not only between those with below upper secondary and those with upper secondary attainment (20 percentage points or more in 15 out of the 30 OECD countries) but also between those with upper secondary and those with tertiary-type A attainment (around 10 percentage points or more in 23 countries). Particular exceptions are Japan, Korea and Sweden where participation rates for females with upper secondary qualifications approach those for females with a tertiary qualification (a difference of around 3 to 7 percentage points) (Table A12.1).

Participation rates for females with less than upper secondary attainment are particularly low, averaging 50 per cent over all OECD countries and around 40 per cent or below in Belgium, Greece, Hungary, Ireland, Italy and Turkey. Rates for females with tertiary attainment exceed 80 per cent everywhere except Hungary, Japan, Korea, Luxembourg, Mexico and Turkey, but remain below those of males in all countries (Table A12.1).

Although the gender gap in labour force participation remains among those with the highest educational attainment, it is much narrower than among those with lower qualifications. On average among OECD countries, with each additional level attained, the difference between the participation of males and females decreases significantly: from 26 percentage points at below upper secondary level, to 19 percentage points at upper secondary and 10 percentage points at tertiary level (Table A12.1).

Much of the overall gap between the labour force participation rates of males with differing educational attainment is explained by larger differences in the older populations, particularly among males between the ages of 55 and 64 (Table A12.1). At least 70 per cent of males aged 55 to 64 with a tertiary-level qualification are active in the labour force in 18 out of 30 countries. Only Greece, Korea, Mexico and Turkey have participation rates as high among those who have not completed upper secondary education. By contrast, the education gap in female labour force participation is relatively wide in all age groups.

The patterns observed here reflect a number of underlying causes. Since earnings tend to increase with educational attainment, the monetary incentive to participate is greater for individuals with higher qualifications. In addition, those individuals often work on more interesting and stimulating tasks, and hold functions of higher responsibility, which increase their motivation to remain in the labour force. Conversely, hard physical work, generally associated with rather low levels of education, can lead to a need for early retirement. Moreover, industrial restructuring in many countries has reduced job opportunities for unskilled workers, or for workers with skills that have been made obsolete by new technologies. A sizeable number of these people have left the labour market either through early retirement schemes or because there are only limited job opportunities. The educational attainment of females and their participation

A12

rates in the labour market have been lower historically than those of males, and in spite of considerable advances over the last few decades, current participation rates continue to show the impact of these historical factors.

Unemployment rates by level of educational attainment

The unemployment rate is a measure of a particular economy's ability to supply a job to everyone who wants one. To the extent that educational attainment is assumed to be an indicator of skill, it can signal to employers the potential knowledge, capacities and workplace performance of candidates for employment. The employment prospects of individuals of varying educational attainment will depend both on the requirements of labour markets and on the supply of workers with differing skills. Those with low educational qualifications are at particular risk of economic marginalisation since they are both less likely to be labour force participants and more likely to be without a job if they are actively seeking one.

Those with low educational attainment are both less likely to be labour force participants and more likely to be unemployed.

In 18 out of the 30 OECD countries, male labour force participants aged 25 to 64 with a qualification below upper secondary education are more than 1.5 times as likely to be unemployed as their counterparts who have completed upper secondary education. In 17 countries, the unemployment rate for male upper secondary graduates is at least 1.5 times the unemployment rate among tertiary-type A graduates. At the tertiary level, completion of shorter vocationally-oriented programmes (ISCED 5B) is associated with higher unemployment rates than those for graduates of more theoretical, longer programmes at ISCED level 5A in about two thirds of the countries (Table A12.2).

Unemployment rates fall with higher educational attainment.

In most countries, the disparities in unemployment rates between levels of educational attainment are particularly strong among males between 30 and 44 years of age. The association between unemployment rates and educational attainment is similar among females, although the gap between upper secondary and tertiary attainment is even wider in many countries. The disadvantage for females is visible for one-third of countries, but the unemployment rates are similar in the others, independently of the levels of attainment. At the tertiary level, the gap is much less obvious, even in the countries where a large gender disparity is a general phenomenon (Chart A12.2).

The wide variation between countries in unemployment rates observed among those with low educational attainment is attributable to a number of factors. In some countries (especially those facing a transition process: the Czech Republic, Hungary, Poland and the Slovak Republic), the high unemployment rates of the poorly educated reflect generally difficult labour market conditions, which affect these individuals in particular. To a lesser extent, this is also the case in Finland, France and Germany. Unemployment rates among those without an upper secondary qualification are also relatively high in some countries where labour markets are less regulated (Canada, the United Kingdom and the United States). On the other hand, in countries where agriculture is still an important sector of employment (Mexico and Portugal), unemployment rates of persons without upper secondary education tend to be low. Finally, where overall

A number of factors contribute to the variation between countries in the association between unemployment rates and educational attainment.

A12

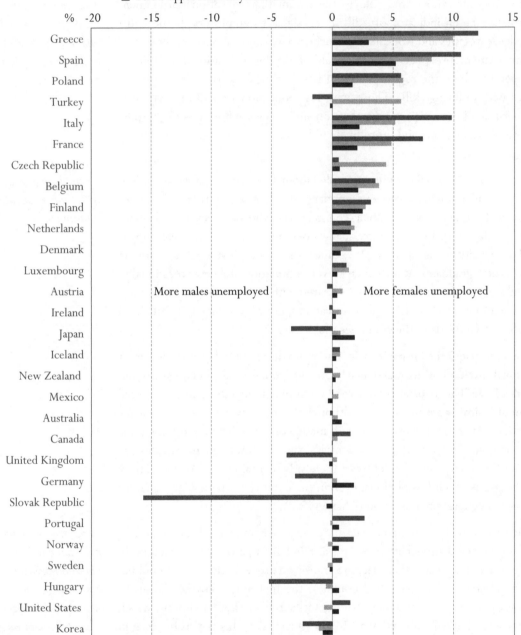

Chart A12.2

Differences between unemployment rates of females and males,
by level of educational attainment, for 30 to 44-year-olds (2001)

■ Tertiary education
■ Upper secondary and post-secondary non-tertiary education
■ Below upper secondary education

Countries are ranked in descending order of the difference in unemployment rates of females to males who have completed upper secondary education or post-secondary non-tertiary education.
Source: OECD. Table A12.2. See Annex 3 for notes *(www.oecd.org/edu/eag2003).*

A12

labour market conditions are particularly favourable in 2000/2001 (Austria, Iceland, Luxembourg, the Netherlands and Norway), jobs appear to be available for workers with low as well as high educational attainment (Table A12.2). Generally the lower skilled are among the first victims of negative changes in the economic climate.

Definitions and methodologies

The labour force participation rate for a particular age group is equal to the percentage of individuals in the population of the same age group who are either employed or unemployed, as defined according to the guidelines of the International Labour Office (ILO).

Data are derived from national labour force surveys.

The unemployed are defined as individuals who are without work, actively seeking employment and currently available to start work. The employed are defined as those who during the survey reference week: *i)* work for pay (employees) or profit (self-employed and unpaid family workers) for at least one hour, or *ii)* have a job but are temporarily not at work (through injury, illness, holiday, strike or lock-out, educational or training leave, maternity or parental leave, etc.) and have a formal attachment to their job.

The unemployment rate is the number of unemployed persons divided by the number of labour force participants (expressed as a percentage). The level of educational attainment is based on the definitions of ISCED-97.

A12

Table A12.1
Labour force participation rates (2001)
by level of educational attainment and gender for 25 to 64-year-olds and 55 to 64-year-olds

		25 to 64-year-olds					55 to 64-year-olds			
		Below upper secondary education	Upper secondary and post-secondary non-tertiary education	Tertiary-type B education	Tertiary-type A and advanced research programmes	All levels of education	Below upper secondary education	Upper secondary and post-secondary non-tertiary education	Tertiary education	All levels of education
		(1)	(2)	(3)	(4)	(5)	(6)	(7)	(8)	(9)
Australia	Males	79	89	89	92	86	54	67	74	62
	Females	55	68	77	83	66	30	42	61	38
Austria	Males	70	84	88	94	83	30	40	64	41
	Females	49	69	83	85	65	15	19	40	18
Belgium	Males	69	87	91	92	81	25	44	58	36
	Females	39	69	81	84	60	11	21	31	16
Canada	Males	73	88	91	90	86	52	64	66	61
	Females	48	73	81	83	72	28	46	51	41
Czech Republic	Males	70	88	x(4)	94	87	35	55	79	55
	Females	52	73	x(4)	83	70	13	27	61	25
Denmark	Males	75	87	91	96	86	55	65	81	66
	Females	57	79	88	90	77	31	60	67	52
Finland	Males	70	86	90	93	83	43	54	65	51
	Females	61	79	86	88	77	40	53	67	49
France	Males	76	88	92	92	85	36	44	66	44
	Females	57	76	85	84	70	29	36	51	34
Germany	Males	77	84	88	92	84	44	49	67	53
	Females	50	70	81	83	67	26	35	53	34
Greece	Males	82	88	85	90	85	60	48	57	57
	Females	40	57	79	83	52	25	16	30	24
Hungary	Males	50	83	x(4)	89	75	22	46	64	36
	Females	35	67	x(4)	79	58	8	21	43	16
Iceland	Males	95	95	97	98	96	91	92	99	93
	Females	85	84	91	95	87	81	83	82	82
Ireland	Males	79	93	95	94	87	61	72	80	66
	Females	40	64	74	85	60	21	35	50	29
Italy	Males	74	86	x(4)	91	80	36	49	71	41
	Females	34	67	x(4)	81	50	12	29	41	16
Japan	Males	87	95	98	97	95	80	86	86	84
	Females	56	63	66	68	63	48	49	47	49
Korea	Males	84	89	94	91	88	74	67	70	71
	Females	61	53	58	56	57	51	25	42	48
Luxembourg	Males	78	86	92	92	84	22	34	73	36
	Females	45	62	80	77	56	7	20	48	14
Mexico	Males	94	96	97	94	94	81	78	79	80
	Females	37	56	61	70	43	27	37	37	28
Netherlands	Males	77	89	89	91	86	44	54	61	52
	Females	47	73	82	83	65	20	33	46	27
New Zealand	Males	80	91	89	93	89	66	79	80	75
	Females	56	74	77	83	71	41	58	65	52
Norway	Males	74	89	92	94	88	59	74	88	74
	Females	58	81	90	88	80	47	66	84	63
Poland	Males	64	83	x(4)	92	81	35	41	68	41
	Females	45	71	x(4)	86	67	20	24	45	24
Portugal	Males	87	87	94	94	87	63	57	78	64
	Females	66	84	88	95	71	41	32	60	42
Slovak Republic	Males	62	88	89	93	86	25	46	64	43
	Females	43	76	90	88	71	3	12	52	11
Spain	Males	83	90	93	91	86	59	62	73	61
	Females	41	66	77	83	54	20	38	58	24
Sweden	Males	79	88	89	91	87	68	74	82	74
	Females	66	83	86	90	82	56	69	82	68
Switzerland	Males	87	93	96	96	94	78	82	85	83
	Females	62	74	85	86	74	41	58	68	54
Turkey	Males	82	87	x(4)	87	84	52	25	43	49
	Females	22	32	x(4)	71	27	14	5	15	14
United Kingdom	Males	67	88	93	93	86	51	67	73	64
	Females	51	77	85	87	74	44	65	69	58
United States	Males	75	86	90	92	87	55	66	77	68
	Females	52	73	80	81	73	33	54	66	54
Country mean	*Males*	*77*	*88*	*92*	*93*	*86*	*52*	*59*	*72*	*59*
	Females	*50*	*70*	*81*	*83*	*65*	*29*	*39*	*54*	*37*

Note: x indicates that data are included in another column. The column reference is shown in brackets after "x". *e.g.,* x(2) means that data are included in column 2.
Source: OECD. See Annex 3 for notes *(www.oecd.org/edu/eag2003).*

Table A12.2
Unemployment rates (2001)
by level of educational attainment and gender of 25 to 64-year-olds and 30 to 44-year-olds

A12

		25 to 64-year-olds					30 to 44-year-olds			
		Below upper secondary education	Upper secondary and post-secondary non-tertiary education	Tertiary-type B education	Tertiary-type A and advanced research programmes	All levels of education	Below upper secondary education	Upper secondary and post-secondary non-tertiary education	Tertiary education	All levels of education
		(1)	(2)	(3)	(4)	(5)	(6)	(7)	(8)	(9)
Australia	Males	8.1	4.5	4.5	2.5	5.2	8.6	4.6	2.8	5.3
	Females	7.0	5.2	3.9	2.6	5.1	8.4	5.0	3.5	5.7
Austria	Males	7.2	2.9	1.4	1.3	3.2	6.5	2.4	1.2	2.7
	Females	5.7	3.3	2.0	1.5	3.6	6.0	3.2	1.6	3.5
Belgium	Males	7.4	4.4	2.5	2.5	4.8	8.8	3.7	2.1	4.9
	Females	10.4	6.9	2.5	3.8	6.3	12.3	7.5	2.6	6.8
Canada	Males	10.2	6.2	4.8	4.4	6.2	10.8	6.3	4.8	6.3
	Females	10.2	6.2	4.5	4.4	5.8	12.3	6.7	4.8	6.2
Czech Republic	Males	19.3	4.7	x(4)	1.9	5.4	23.4	4.5	1.8	5.3
	Females	19.1	8.0	x(4)	2.2	8.9	24.0	8.9	2.4	9.7
Denmark	Males	4.0	2.7	3.3	3.5	3.1	4.0	2.3	3.2	2.8
	Females	6.2	4.0	3.1	3.1	4.1	7.2	3.9	3.9	4.3
Finland	Males	10.5	7.9	4.7	3.0	7.2	11.9	7.1	2.8	6.5
	Females	12.7	9.2	5.9	3.6	8.1	15.0	9.8	5.3	8.2
France	Males	9.7	5.1	4.3	4.1	6.2	10.7	4.7	3.5	6.1
	Females	14.4	9.3	5.0	5.6	9.8	18.1	9.5	5.5	10.6
Germany	Males	15.6	8.1	4.4	3.4	7.7	14.2	7.0	2.6	6.5
	Females	11.5	8.4	5.8	4.4	8.1	11.2	7.4	4.4	7.2
Greece	Males	4.9	6.2	4.9	4.5	5.3	4.7	5.1	4.2	4.7
	Females	12.3	15.1	8.3	9.6	12.5	16.7	14.9	7.1	13.2
Hungary	Males	12.5	4.8	x(4)	1.1	5.5	15.1	4.6	0.7	5.6
	Females	7.6	4.2	x(4)	1.3	4.3	9.9	4.1	1.2	4.5
Iceland	Males	2.3	1.2	0.8	1.0	1.5	1.7	1.4	0.6	1.3
	Females	2.4	2.8	2.4	0.2	2.1	2.3	2.0	0.9	1.8
Ireland	Males	5.5	2.3	1.9	1.1	3.3	6.3	2.0	1.6	3.4
	Females	5.1	2.8	2.3	1.0	2.9	6.1	2.7	1.9	3.1
Italy	Males	6.9	4.9	x(4)	3.8	5.8	7.1	3.8	3.9	5.4
	Females	14.0	9.3	x(4)	7.2	10.7	16.8	8.9	6.1	11.1
Japan	Males	6.9	4.8	3.2	2.8	4.4	7.5	3.6	2.0	3.1
	Females	4.3	4.7	3.8	3.1	4.2	4.2	4.2	3.8	4.0
Korea	Males	4.3	3.7	5.0	3.2	3.8	4.9	3.5	2.7	3.4
	Females	1.8	2.7	3.3	2.0	2.3	2.5	2.4	1.9	2.3
Luxembourg	Males	1.6	0.8	0.9	1.1	1.1	1.0	0.6	1.2	0.9
	Females	2.4	1.5	0.4	2.6	1.8	2.2	2.0	1.6	1.9
Mexico	Males	1.4	1.9	2.1	2.2	1.6	1.3	1.2	2.0	1.5
	Females	1.4	1.6	1.8	2.2	1.6	1.3	1.7	1.7	1.5
Netherlands	Males	2.5	1.1	0.0	0.7	1.6	2.6	0.8	0.6	1.2
	Females	3.5	2.3	1.2	2.1	2.7	4.1	2.6	2.1	2.8
New Zealand	Males	7.4	3.0	4.4	2.8	4.0	8.1	3.2	3.4	4.1
	Females	5.9	3.6	2.9	3.2	3.9	7.5	3.8	3.6	4.4
Norway	Males	3.4	2.9	0.7	1.7	2.6	4.2	3.2	1.5	2.8
	Females	3.3	2.5	1.9	1.8	2.4	5.9	2.9	2.0	2.7
Poland	Males	21.7	14.0	x(4)	4.0	13.9	26.3	13.5	1.8	13.7
	Females	23.7	18.3	x(4)	5.9	17.0	31.9	19.3	3.4	18.1
Portugal	Males	2.7	3.1	2.6	2.0	2.7	2.4	3.0	1.4	2.4
	Females	4.6	3.3	2.9	3.3	4.3	5.0	2.8	1.9	4.2
Slovak Republic	Males	44.3	14.8	5.3	4.5	15.7	55.1	14.8	3.9	16.1
	Females	34.6	14.8	11.0	3.4	15.7	39.5	14.8	3.4	15.8
Spain	Males	7.3	5.4	4.1	4.7	6.2	7.6	4.6	3.4	5.8
	Females	16.1	12.8	13.0	8.8	13.3	18.1	12.7	8.6	13.5
Sweden	Males	5.6	5.0	3.4	2.6	4.5	6.3	4.7	2.9	4.3
	Females	6.4	4.2	2.5	2.2	3.8	7.0	4.3	2.7	3.9
Switzerland	Males	m	1.1	m	m	1.1	m	m	m	m
	Females	m	2.9	m	m	3.1	m	3.4	m	3.4
Turkey	Males	9.2	8.0	x(4)	5.6	8.6	9.3	5.5	3.4	7.9
	Females	6.9	13.5	x(4)	6.1	7.7	7.7	11.2	3.2	7.3
United Kingdom	Males	9.4	4.1	2.7	2.0	4.1	11.9	3.9	2.2	4.2
	Females	5.7	3.7	1.7	1.9	3.4	8.2	4.3	2.0	4.0
United States	Males	7.5	4.2	2.5	1.9	3.7	7.4	4.4	1.8	3.7
	Females	8.9	3.4	2.3	2.0	3.3	8.9	3.7	2.3	3.6
Country mean	Males	8.9	4.8	3.3	2.8	5.0	9.9	4.5	2.4	4.9
	Females	9.4	6.4	4.0	3.5	6.1	11.1	6.3	3.3	6.3

Note: x indicates that data are included in another column. The column reference is shown in brackets after "x". *e.g.*, x(2) means that data are included in column 2.
Source: OECD. See Annex 3 for notes *(www.oecd.org/edu/eag2003)*.

INDICATOR A13: EXPECTED YEARS IN EDUCATION, EMPLOYMENT AND NON-EMPLOYMENT BETWEEN THE AGES OF 15 AND 29

- On average among countries, a young person aged 15 in 2001 can expect to be in formal education for a little under six and a half years. In 16 of the 28 countries studied, this period ranges from six to seven and a half years.

- In addition to the expected number of years spent in education, a young person aged 15 can expect to hold a job for 6.4 of the 15 years to come, to be unemployed for a total of 0.8 years and to be out of the labour market for 1.4 years. It is in the average duration of spells of unemployment that countries vary most, which primarily reflects differences in youth employment rates.

- In absolute terms, young people today can expect to spend less time in unemployment after completing their initial education than they did ten years ago.

Chart A13.1

Expected years in education and not in education, by work status of 15 to 29-year-olds (2001)

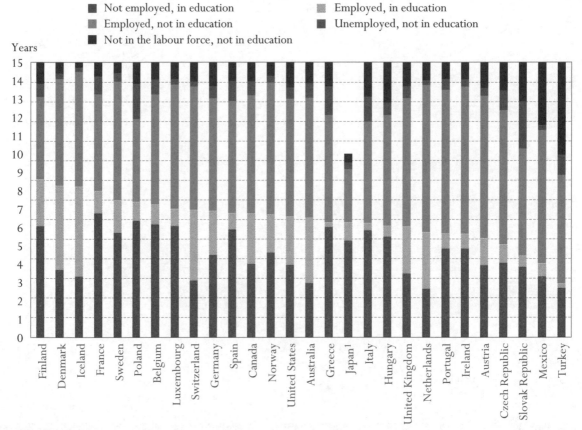

1. Data refer to 15 to 24-year-olds.
Countries are ranked in descending order of the expected years in education of the youth population.
Source: OECD. Table A13.1. See Annex 3 for notes *(www.oecd.org/edu/eag2003).*

EDUCATION AT A GLANCE © OECD 2003

Expected years in education, employment and non-employment between the ages of 15 and 29   **CHAPTER A** ■ ················

A13

Policy context

During the past decade, young people have spent longer in initial education, with the result that they delay their entry into the world of work (see *Education at a Glance*, OECD, 1998). Some of this additional time is spent combining work and education, a practice that is widespread in some countries. Once young people have completed their education, access to the labour market is often impeded by spells of unemployment or non-employment, although this situation affects males and females differently. In absolute terms, however, young people today can expect to spend less time in unemployment after completing initial education than they did ten years ago.

This indicator shows the expected years young people spend in education, employment and non-employment.

Evidence and explanations

On the basis of the current situation of persons between the ages of 15 and 29, this indicator gives a picture of the major trends affecting the transition from school to work.

On average, a young person aged 15 in 2001 can expect to be in education for around six and a half years (Table A13.1). Between 1985 and 1996, this value rose by almost 1.5 years. Since 1996, the overall increase has been slower. Countries where young people used to spend relatively little time in education have made up some ground, whereas those in which they stayed in education longest are now recording little increase.

On average, a 15-year-old can expect to be in the education system for about another six and a half years.

In 16 of the 28 countries studied, a 15-year-old can expect to spend from six to seven and a half years in education. There is, however, a gap of around four years separating the two extreme groups: Denmark, Finland, France and Iceland (eight years or more) on the one hand and Mexico, the Slovak Republic and Turkey (four years on average) on the other.

The average overall number of expected years in education is marginally higher for females (6.5 compared with 6.3 years). In many countries, the figures are about the same, but Turkey stands out as an exception, with only 2.4 years of expected education for young females aged 15 years. At the other end of the scale, a longer average period of education often goes hand in hand with a relatively higher average for females (Table A13.1).

The figure for expected years of education covers some very different combinations of education and work. Employment combined with education includes both work-study programmes and part-time jobs. While such combinations are rare in half of the countries studied, in the other half they account for between one and four of the additional years that young people expect to spend in education.

The figure for expected years of education covers some very different combinations of education and work.

In addition to the average six and a half years spent in education, a young person aged 15 can expect to hold a job for 6.4 of the 15 years to come, to be unemployed for a total of 0.8 years and to be out of the labour market for 1.4 years, neither in education nor seeking work (Table A13.1). It is worth noting that, in absolute terms, young people can expect to spend less time in unemployment after completion of initial education than they could ten years ago.

Today, a 15-year-old can expect to hold a job for 6.4 years, to be unemployed for almost one year and to be out of the labour force for 1.4 years until the age of 29.

A13

It is in the average duration of spells of unemployment that countries vary most, which mainly reflects differences in youth employment rates. The cumulative average duration of unemployment is four months or below in Denmark, Iceland, Luxembourg, Mexico, the Netherlands and Switzerland, but more than 18 months in Greece, Poland, and the Slovak Republic.

By and large, males and females differ very little in terms of the expected number of years in unemployment. However, while the situation is similar for both genders in many countries, females appear to be at a disadvantage in Greece, Portugal and Spain and at an advantage in Australia, Canada, Germany, Hungary, the Slovak Republic, Turkey and the United Kingdom (Table A13.1). In some of the latter countries, however, notably in Australia, the United Kingdom, and in particular Turkey, the lower expectancy for females is largely influenced by the fact that many females leave the labour market, thereby reducing pressure on jobs.

Whereas young males can expect to spend little more than eight months neither in education nor in the labour force between the ages of 15 and 29, the average figure for females is more than two years. In Austria, Finland and Sweden, young males and young females do not differ much in this measure. Conversely, in the Czech Republic, Hungary, Mexico and Turkey there is a much stronger tendency for young females to leave the labour market. In all of the other countries, females between the ages of 15 and 29 spend an average of about one year more than males outside the labour market.

Definitions and methodologies

Data are derived from national labour force surveys.

The statistics presented here are calculated from labour force survey data on age-specific proportions of young people in each of the specified categories. These proportions are then totalled over the 15 to 29 age group to yield the expected number of years spent in various situations. For countries providing data from the age of 16 only, it is assumed that the 15 year-olds are all in education and out of the labour force. This improvement in the calculation tends to increase the average number of expected years in education compared to the last edition of *Education at a Glance*. The calculation thus assumes that young persons currently aged 15 years will show the same pattern of education and work between the ages of 15 and 29 as the population between those age limits in the given data year.

Persons in education include those attending part-time as well as full-time. The definitions of the various labour force statuses are based on the guidelines of the International Labour Office (ILO), except for the category 'youth in education and employed', which includes all work-study programmes whatever their classification according to the ILO guidelines. The data for this indicator were obtained from a special collection with a reference period in the early part of the calendar year, usually the first quarter or the average of the first three months.

Table A13.1
Expected years in education and not in education for 15 to 29-year-olds (2001)
by gender and work status

		Expected years in education			Expected years not in education			
		Not employed	Employed (including work study programmes)	Sub-total	Employed	Unemployed	Not in the labour force	Sub-total
Australia	Males	3.0	3.6	6.6	6.9	0.9	0.5	8.4
	Females	2.9	3.5	6.4	6.1	0.7	1.8	8.6
	M+F	3.0	3.5	6.5	6.5	0.8	1.2	8.5
Austria	Males	3.6	1.8	5.4	7.9	0.5	1.3	9.6
	Females	4.3	1.1	5.4	7.6	0.4	1.6	9.6
	M+F	3.9	1.5	5.4	7.7	0.4	1.4	9.6
Belgium	Males	5.9	1.3	7.3	6.4	0.8	0.5	7.7
	Females	6.4	0.8	7.2	5.6	0.8	1.4	7.8
	M+F	6.2	1.1	7.2	6.0	0.8	0.9	7.8
Canada	Males	4.0	2.5	6.5	6.8	1.0	0.7	8.5
	Females	4.0	3.0	7.0	6.0	0.5	1.4	8.0
	M+F	4.0	2.8	6.8	6.4	0.8	1.0	8.2
Czech Republic	Males	3.7	1.2	5.0	8.6	1.1	0.3	10.0
	Females	4.4	0.7	5.1	6.0	1.1	2.8	9.9
	M+F	4.1	1.0	5.1	7.3	1.1	1.6	9.9
Denmark	Males	3.4	4.7	8.1	6.2	0.3	0.3	6.9
	Females	4.0	4.5	8.4	5.3	0.3	0.9	6.6
	M+F	3.7	4.6	8.3	5.8	0.3	0.6	6.7
Finland	Males	5.8	2.3	8.1	5.0	0.7	1.1	6.9
	Females	6.3	2.8	9.1	3.9	0.7	1.2	5.9
	M+F	6.1	2.6	8.6	4.5	0.7	1.2	6.4
France	Males	6.6	1.3	7.8	5.9	0.9	0.3	7.2
	Females	7.0	1.2	8.1	4.6	1.0	1.2	6.9
	M+F	6.8	1.2	8.0	5.3	1.0	0.8	7.0
Germany	Males	4.4	2.5	6.9	6.6	0.8	0.8	8.1
	Females	4.6	2.3	6.9	5.7	0.5	1.9	8.1
	M+F	4.5	2.4	6.9	6.1	0.6	1.3	8.1
Greece	Males	6.0	0.3	6.2	6.9	1.3	0.6	8.8
	Females	6.1	0.2	6.3	4.8	1.8	2.1	8.7
	M+F	6.0	0.2	6.3	5.8	1.6	1.3	8.7
Hungary	Males	5.4	0.6	5.9	7.0	0.9	1.2	9.1
	Females	5.6	0.6	6.2	5.1	0.5	3.2	8.8
	M+F	5.5	0.6	6.1	6.0	0.7	2.2	8.9
Iceland	Males	3.2	4.4	7.6	7.0	0.2	0.1	7.4
	Females	3.5	5.4	8.8	5.5	0.2	0.5	6.2
	M+F	3.3	4.9	8.2	6.3	0.2	0.3	6.8
Ireland	Males	4.5	0.7	5.2	8.8	0.5	0.5	9.8
	Females	5.2	0.9	6.0	7.2	0.3	1.4	9.0
	M+F	4.8	0.8	5.6	8.0	0.4	0.9	9.4
Italy	Males	5.6	0.4	6.0	6.4	1.3	1.3	9.0
	Females	6.1	0.4	6.5	4.6	1.4	2.5	8.5
	M+F	5.8	0.4	6.2	5.5	1.4	1.9	8.8
Japan[1]	Males	5.6	1.0	6.6	2.8	0.4	0.3	3.4
	Females	5.0	0.9	5.9	3.0	0.4	0.7	4.1
	M+F	5.3	1.0	6.3	2.9	0.4	0.5	3.7
Luxembourg	Males	6.1	1.1	7.2	7.1	0.4	0.4	7.8
	Females	6.1	0.8	6.8	6.4	0.2	1.5	8.2
	M+F	6.1	0.9	7.0	6.8	0.3	0.9	8.0
Mexico	Males	3.3	0.9	4.2	9.9	0.3	0.6	10.8
	Females	3.3	0.5	3.9	4.9	0.2	6.1	11.1
	M+F	3.3	0.7	4.0	7.3	0.3	3.4	11.0
Netherlands	Males	2.8	3.0	5.8	8.4	0.2	0.5	9.2
	Females	2.5	3.1	5.7	7.6	0.3	1.5	9.3
	M+F	2.7	3.1	5.7	8.0	0.2	1.0	9.3
Norway	Males	4.4	1.8	6.2	7.8	0.5	0.5	8.8
	Females	4.8	2.4	7.2	6.5	0.3	1.0	7.8
	M+F	4.6	2.1	6.7	7.2	0.4	0.7	8.3
Poland	Males	6.2	1.0	7.2	5.2	2.0	0.6	7.8
	Females	6.5	1.0	7.5	3.8	1.9	1.8	7.5
	M+F	6.4	1.0	7.4	4.5	1.9	1.2	7.6
Portugal	Males	4.5	0.8	5.3	8.7	0.4	0.6	9.7
	Females	5.2	0.8	6.0	7.0	0.7	1.3	9.0
	M+F	4.8	0.8	5.6	7.8	0.6	0.9	9.4
Slovak Republic	Males	3.6	0.8	4.3	6.2	3.0	1.5	10.7
	Females	4.1	0.4	4.5	5.5	2.1	2.9	10.5
	M+F	3.8	0.6	4.4	5.9	2.6	2.2	10.6
Spain	Males	5.5	0.8	6.3	7.2	1.0	0.5	8.7
	Females	6.3	0.9	7.2	5.0	1.2	1.5	7.8
	M+F	5.9	0.9	6.8	6.1	1.1	1.0	8.2
Sweden	Males	5.6	1.6	7.1	6.8	0.5	0.5	7.9
	Females	5.8	2.0	7.8	6.1	0.4	0.7	7.2
	M+F	5.7	1.8	7.5	6.5	0.5	0.6	7.5
Switzerland	Males	3.0	4.3	7.3	6.7	0.2	0.8	7.7
	Females	3.2	3.4	6.6	6.7	0.3	1.4	8.4
	M+F	3.1	3.9	7.0	6.7	0.3	1.1	8.0
Turkey	Males	3.1	0.3	3.4	8.2	1.5	1.9	11.6
	Females	2.3	0.2	2.4	3.4	0.6	8.6	12.6
	M+F	2.7	0.2	2.9	5.9	1.1	5.0	12.1
United Kingdom	Males	3.4	2.4	5.8	7.7	0.8	0.6	9.2
	Females	3.5	2.7	6.2	6.2	0.5	2.0	8.8
	M+F	3.5	2.6	6.0	7.0	0.6	1.3	9.0
United States	Males	4.1	2.4	6.5	7.1	0.7	0.8	8.5
	Females	3.8	2.9	6.7	5.8	0.5	2.0	8.3
	M+F	3.9	2.6	6.6	6.4	0.6	1.4	8.4
Country mean	*Males*	*4.5*	*1.8*	*6.3*	*7.2*	*0.8*	*0.7*	*8.7*
	Females	*4.7*	*1.8*	*6.5*	*5.7*	*0.7*	*2.1*	*8.5*
	M+F	*4.6*	*1.8*	*6.4*	*6.4*	*0.8*	*1.4*	*8.6*

1. Data refer to 15 to 24-year-olds.

Source: OECD. See Annex 3 for notes *(www.oecd.org/edu/eag2003)*.

INDICATOR A14: THE RETURNS TO EDUCATION: EDUCATION AND EARNINGS

A14

- Education and earnings are positively linked. Upper secondary and post-secondary non-tertiary education form a break point in many countries beyond which additional education attracts a particularly high premium. In all countries, graduates of tertiary-level education earn substantially more than upper secondary and than post-secondary non-tertiary graduates. Earnings differentials between tertiary and upper secondary education are generally more pronounced than those between upper secondary and lower secondary or below.

- Earnings of people with below upper secondary education tend to be 60 to 90 per cent of those of upper secondary and post-secondary non-tertiary graduates.

- Females still earn less than males with similar levels of educational attainment.

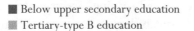

Relative earnings with income from employment (2001)
by level of educational attainment and gender for 25 to 64-year-olds (upper secondary education=100)

A14

■ Below upper secondary education
■ Tertiary-type B education
■ Tertiary-type A and advanced research programmes

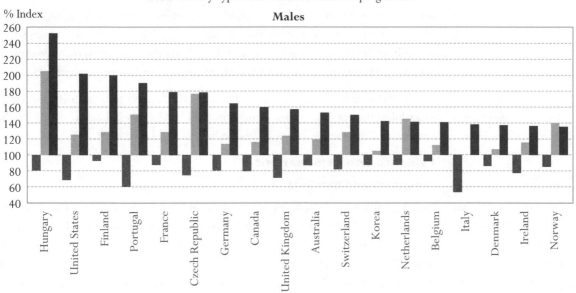

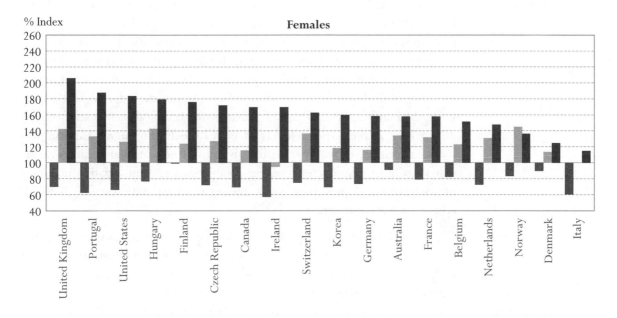

Countries are ranked in descending order of relative earnings for the population having attained the level of tertiary-type A and advanced research programmes.
Source: OECD. Table A14.1. See Annex 3 for national data sources *(www.oecd.org/edu/eag2003).*

A14

This indicator examines the earnings of workers with differing educational attainment...

Policy context

One way in which markets provide incentives for individuals to develop and maintain appropriate levels of skills is through wage differentials, in particular through the enhanced earnings accorded to persons completing additional education. The pursuit of higher levels of education can also be viewed as an investment in human capital. Human capital includes the stock of skills that individuals maintain or develop, usually through education or training, and then offer in return for earnings in the labour market. The higher the earnings that result from increases in human capital, the higher the returns on that investment and the premium paid for enhanced skills and/or for higher productivity.

...as well as the returns to educational investment.

At the same time, education involves costs which need to be considered when examining the returns to investment in education. This indicator examines the returns and the various costs and benefits that influence them.

Evidence and explanations

Education and earnings

Earnings differentials are a measure of the current financial incentives in a particular country for an individual to invest in further education.

Earnings differentials according to educational attainment are a measure of the current financial incentives in a particular country for an individual to invest in further education. Earnings differentials may also reflect differences in the supply of educational programmes at different levels or the barriers in access to those programmes. The earnings benefit of completing tertiary education can be seen by comparing the ratio of the mean annual earnings of those who graduated from tertiary education with the mean annual earnings of upper secondary or post-secondary non-tertiary graduates. The earnings disadvantage from not completing upper secondary is apparent from a similar comparison. Variations in relative earnings (before taxes) between countries reflect a number of factors, including skill demands in the labour force, minimum wage legislation, the strength of unions, the coverage of collective bargaining agreements, the supply of workers at the various levels of educational attainment, the range of work experience of workers with high and low educational attainment, the distribution of employment among occupations and the relative incidence of part-time and part-year work among workers with varying levels of educational attainment.

Education and earnings are positively linked, whatever the type of socio-economic system or the degree of economic development.

Chart A14.1 shows a strong positive relationship between educational attainment and earnings. In all countries, graduates of tertiary-level education earn substantially more than upper secondary and post-secondary non-tertiary graduates. Earnings differentials between tertiary and upper secondary education are generally more pronounced than those between upper secondary and lower secondary or below, suggesting that upper secondary and post-secondary non-tertiary education form a break-point in many countries, beyond which additional education attracts a particularly high premium. Among those countries which report gross earnings, the earnings premium for males aged 25 to 64 years with tertiary-level education ranges from 32 per cent or less in Belgium, Denmark, Ireland, Korea and New Zealand, to 78 per cent or more in the Czech Republic, Hungary, Portugal and United States.

The earnings data shown in this indicator differ among countries in a number of ways. Caution should therefore be exercised in interpreting the results. In particular, in countries reporting annual earnings, differences in the incidence of part-year work among individuals with different levels of educational attainment will have an effect on relative earnings that is not reflected in the data for countries reporting weekly or monthly earnings (see definitions below).

Education and gender disparity in earnings

Tertiary education enhances earnings relative to upper secondary and post-secondary non-tertiary education more for females than for males in Australia, Belgium, Canada, Ireland, Korea, the Netherlands, New Zealand, Norway, Switzerland and the United Kingdom, whereas the reverse is true in the remaining countries (Table A14.1).

Although both males and females with upper secondary, post-secondary non-tertiary or tertiary attainment have substantial earnings advantages compared with those of the same gender who do not complete upper secondary education, earnings differentials between males and females with the same educational attainment remain substantial, reinforced by the frequency of part-time work for females.

Earnings differentials between males and females with the same educational attainment remain substantial…

When all levels of education are taken together, the earnings of females between 30 and 44 range from less than 55 per cent of those of males in Switzerland and the United Kingdom to over 75 per cent of those of males in Hungary and Spain (Table A14.2).

Some of the gap in earnings between males and females may be explained by different choices of career and occupation, differences in the amount of time that males and females spend in the labour force, and the relatively high incidence of part-time work among females. Furthermore, earnings data by age suggest that there may be a movement towards more equality of average earnings between males and females across all levels of education, a result which might also be influenced by the increased proportion of females among younger tertiary graduates. In four out of 18 countries with available data, the ratio of female to male earnings at the tertiary-type A and advanced research programmes levels is at least 10 percentage points higher among 30 to 44-year-olds than among 55 to 64-year-olds (Table A14.2).

…with some of the differences explained by career and occupational choices, the amount of time that males and females spend in the labour force, and the relatively high incidence of part-time work among females.

Private internal rates of return to investment in education

The overall incentives to invest in human capital that are embedded in labour market benefits and financing arrangements can be summarised in estimates of the private internal rates of return (Chart A14.2 and Table A14.3). The rate of return represents a measure of the returns obtained, over time, relative to the cost of the initial investment in education. It is expressed as a percentage and is analogous to percentage returns from investing in a savings account (see Annex 3 at *www.oecd.org/edu/eag2003* for an explanation of the methodology). In its most comprehensive form, the costs equal tuition fees, foregone earnings net of taxes adjusted for the probability of being in employment less the resources

The overall incentives to invest in human capital that are embedded in labour market benefits can be summarised in the private rate of return.

A14

made available to students in the form of grants and loans. The benefits are the gains in posttax earnings adjusted for higher employment probability less the repayment, if any, of public support during the period of study. The calculations assume that the student is fulltime in education and has no work activity, hence no earnings while studying. The calculated rates of return are, however, likely to be biased upwards as unemployment, retirement and early retirement benefits are not taken into account. The rate of return calculations reported in this indicator do not take into account the nonmonetary benefits of education.

Chart A14.2

Comprehensive private internal rates of return to education (1999-2000)

*Impact of pretax earnings, taxes, unemployment risk, tuition fees and
public student support in upper secondary and tertiary education, by gender (in percentage points)*

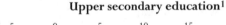

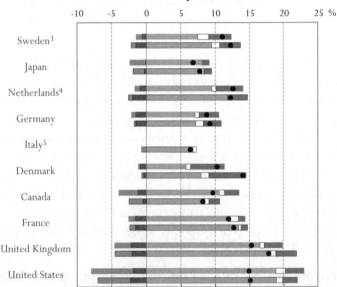

1. The rate of return to upper secondary education is calculated by comparing the benefits and costs with those of lower secondary education.
2. The rate of return to tertiary education is calculated by comparing the benefits and costs with those of upper secondary education.
3. In tertiary education, the theoretical length of standard tertiary courses is used in the calculations rather than the average theoretical length of different programmes for males and females. For females, earnings differential between upper and lower secondary levels are not large enough to permit a positive rate of return calculation.
4. Year of reference 1997.
5. Data for males derive from 1998 post-tax earnings data.
Countries are ranked in descending order of the total comprehensive rates of return to education of males in upper secondary education.
Source: OECD. Table A14.3.

A14

The estimated private internal rates of return to upper secondary and university education differ significantly across the countries listed in Table A14.3 but are higher in all cases than the real interest rate, and often significantly so, suggesting that human capital investment is an attractive way for the average person to build up wealth. For tertiary studies, three groups of countries can be identified depending on the estimated values of the internal rate of return, which includes the combined effect of earnings, length of studies, taxation, unemployment risk, tuition fees and public student support.

In all countries, the private rate of return is higher than real interest rates, and often significantly so.

• First, with its very high rewards from tertiary education, the United Kingdom is in a group of its own.

• Second, Denmark, France, the Netherlands, Sweden and the United States have relatively high internal rates of return, ranging from 10 to 15 per cent.

• Third, in the remaining countries, rates are below 10 per cent, with the lowest rates recorded for Italy and Japan.

In upper secondary education, the internal rate is calculated to exceed 10 per cent in countries listed in Table A14.3 with the exceptions of Germany (females), Japan, the Netherlands and Sweden.

At the tertiary level, the gender differential in rates of return calculations is limited in most countries. However, at the upper secondary level, gender differences are more marked in Germany and in the United States with returns cut by one-quarter to one-third for females, due to relatively narrow earnings differentials.

As can be seen from Table A13.3, earnings differentials and the length of education are generally the prime determinants of the private internal rates of return. Thus, countries with strong overall incentives to invest in human capital are typically characterised by high educationearnings differentials and/or relatively short education programmes, and *vice versa*. The calculated high rates of return to tertiary education in the United Kingdom, for example, are to an important extent due to relatively short standard university studies, whereas the low rates of return in Germany are strongly influenced by comparatively long study periods. Indeed, if the average length of tertiary studies were to be shortened by one year without compromising quality, the internal rate of return for males in the countries under review would increase by 1 to 5 percentage points, if all other factors were held constant. To put such a hypothetical shortening of tertiary studies into perspective, it should be noted that to achieve the same increase via wider wage differentiation would require an increase in the tertiary wage premium by 5 to 14 percentage points.

Earnings differentials and the length of education tend to be the prime determinants of the returns…

There are, however, notable exceptions to this general pattern. Despite narrow wage differentials and long study periods, Denmark and, to a lesser extent, Sweden offer comparatively strong incentives to acquire university education. And France has strong incentives for young people to invest in upper secondary education despite relatively small wage gains compared to the length of such education.

A14

...but there are other factors, including...

The contribution of the various factors to the difference between the narrow internal rate of return, comprising only earnings differentials and the length of education, and the comprehensive rate can be evaluated by adding them successively to the rate of return formula:

...taxes, which reduce the returns,...

Taxes reduce the internal rate of return derived from pretax earnings and study periods by 1.3 percentage points on average for tertiary education and 1.1 percentage point for upper secondary education in the countries under review. At the tertiary level, the impact of taxes is particularly strong in the United Kingdom and in the United States, mainly reflecting large education earnings differentials combined with progressive tax systems, but also in the Netherlands and France. At the upper secondary level, the depressing effect of the tax system is most notable in Germany, due to the strong degree of progressivity of the tax system over the relevant earnings range, and in Denmark, while it is the smallest in Japan.

...lower risks of unemployment, which increase the returns,...

Unemployment risk differentials increase the internal rate of return compared with rates based only on pretax earnings and the length of study. Reflecting the large differential in unemployment rates between people with lower and upper secondary education, the increase in the internal rate is particularly large for upper secondary education, averaging 3.6 percentage points for males and females for the countries under review. The relatively high unemployment differential in France adds as much as 8.3 to 9.4 percentage points to the internal rate of return. For tertiary education, the differential employment prospects have much less effect on the rates of return, adding on average 0.7 to 0.9 percentage points for males and females, respectively, in the countries included in Table A14.3.

...tuition fees, which reduce the returns...

Tuition fees have a particularly important negative impact on rates of return to tertiary education in the United States, and, to a lesser extent, in Canada and the United Kingdom. In the continental European countries, the impact is significantly smaller due to the much lower level of tuition fees.

...and public grant or loan arrangements, which boost returns.

Public student grant and loan arrangements at the tertiary level give a significant boost to incentives, averaging 2.5 to 3 percentage points in the countries under review, compared with rates of returns excluding such support. The impact is particularly strong in Denmark, the Netherlands and Sweden, while it is weak in France, and absent in Italy.

Social rates of return of investment in education

The benefits to society of additional education can be assessed on the basis of a social rate of return...

The benefits to society of additional education can be assessed on the basis of social rates of return. The social internal rate of return needs to reflect the costs and benefits to society of investment in education, which can differ significantly from private costs and benefits. The social cost includes the opportunity cost of having people not participating in the production of output and the full cost of the provision of education rather than only the cost borne by the individual. The social benefit includes the increased productivity associated with the investment in education and a host of possible noneconomic benefits, such as lower crime, better health, more social cohesion and more informed and effective citizens. While data on social costs are available for most OECD countries, information about the full range of social benefits is less readily available. To the extent that productivity gains are reflected in labour cost differentials, the latter can be used as a measure of the economic gains for society of education activity. However, the possibility of externalities associated with education suggests that the observed earnings differentials might not fully account for the economy-wide efficiency gains. On the other hand, studies suggest that a (small) part of the wage premia received by better educated individuals is due to educational attainments, signalling inherent abilities to employers rather than productivity differentials due to investment in human capital. And while the non-economic benefits of education are found to be important, it is often difficult to translate them into monetary values for inclusion in rateofreturn calculations.

In view of the difficulty of constructing comprehensive social rates of return, Table A14.4 presents estimates of a "narrow" definition that abstracts from any externality effects and noneconomic benefits. To the extent that there are sizeable positive externalities related to human capital investment by the average student, these estimates will thus be biased downwards.

...which can, however, currently only be estimated in a narrow sense excluding non-economic benefits.

The estimates suggest that the social internal rate of return is particularly high at both the upper secondary and tertiary levels in the United Kingdom and the United States, while it is the lowest in Denmark at both of these education levels. In France, it is moderate for upper secondary education but comparatively high at the tertiary level.

Primarily reflecting that the social cost of education is typically much higher than the private cost, the "narrow" social internal rates of return are significantly lower than the private internal rates of return. At the tertiary level, the differences are particularly large in Denmark and Sweden, with gaps ranging from 4 to almost 7.5 percentage points. At the upper secondary level, differentials between the private and social rates of return are notably wide in France, but comparatively small in Germany and the Netherlands.

Social returns are still well above risk-free real interest rates, but tend to be lower than private returns, due to the significant social costs of education.

The interpretation of the internal rates of return

The private and social internal rates of return reported above are generally well above the riskfree real interest rate. Given that the return on human capital accumulation is subject to considerable uncertainty (as indicated by the wide dispersion of earnings among the better educated), investors are likely to require a compensating risk premium. However, the size of the premium of the internal rates of return over the real interest rate is higher than would seem to be warranted by considerations of risk alone. The high internal rates of return can be interpreted in two different ways.

The high rates of return can be interpreted as indicating...

One interpretation is that the high rates indicate a serious shortage of better educated workers driving up their earnings. This might imply a transitory situation, where high returns to education would subsequently generate enough supply response to push the rates into line with returns available on other

...a dis-equilibrium in the market for educated workers, which calls for increasing educational capacity...

productive assets. However, the adjustment period could be protracted and the speed of adjustment would depend largely on the capacity of the education system to respond to the derived increase in demand and the capacity of the labour market to absorb the changing relative supplies of labour. The rebalancing mechanism could also be accelerated by better availability of information to students about the returns to different courses of study, thereby helping them to make more informed choices.

...or significantly lower marginal returns than average returns...

Part of the high returns may also be compatible with a market equilibrium. This would be the case if the marginal rates are significantly lower than the average rates. The marginal rate would indeed be lower than the average rate if the students at the margin are of lower ability and motivation than the average students, and thus unlikely to be able to command the average wage premium. According to this interpretation, the high internal rates of return would partly reflect economic rents on a scarce resource, namely ability and motivation.

...which would lessen the case for public intervention.

If the returns to education at the margin are lower, the case for public intervention to stimulate human capital accumulation is lessened if the quality of the marginal student cannot be improved. On the other hand, to the extent that the education system can improve cognitive and noncognitive skills of young people, education policy could make a significant contribution to efficiency and equity in the longer run.

Definitions and methodologies

Data are derived from national labour force surveys and other surveys.

Relative earnings from employment are defined as the mean earnings (income from work before taxes) of persons at a given level of educational attainment divided by the mean earnings of persons with upper secondary education. This ratio is then multiplied by 100. The estimates are restricted to individuals with income from employment during the reference period.

Earnings data in Table A14.1 are annual for most countries but for France, Spain and Switzerland they are monthly. In Belgium and France, data cover the earnings of employees only. The Spanish data exclude people who work fewer than fifteen hours a week. The observed differences in relative earnings between countries therefore reflect variations not only in wage rates but also in coverage, in the number of weeks worked per year and in hours worked per week. Since lower educational attainment is associated with fewer hours of work (in particular with part-time work) and with less stable employment (more likelihood of temporary employment or more susceptibility to unemployment over the course of a year), the relative earnings charts shown for higher educational attainment in the tables and charts will be greater than what would be evident from an examination of relative rates of pay. The observed differences in relative earnings of males and females within a country can likewise be affected by some of these factors.

For the methods employed for the calculation of the rates of return in Tables A14.3 and A14.4, see Annex 3 at *www.oecd.org/edu/eag2003*.

Table A14.1
Relative earnings of the population with income from employment
by level of educational attainment and gender for 25 to 64-year-olds and 30 to 44-year-olds (upper secondary education =100)

A14

			Below upper secondary education		Post-secondary non-tertiary education		Tertiary-type B education		Tertiary-type A and advanced research programmes		All tertiary education	
			25-64	30-44	25-64	30-44	25-64	30-44	25-64	30-44	25-64	30-44
			(1)	(2)	(3)	(4)	(5)	(6)	(7)	(8)	(9)	(10)
Australia	1999	Males	87	85	111	116	120	122	153	152	141	142
		Females	91	89	116	113	134	132	158	158	150	148
		M+F	81	79	112	118	118	118	146	146	136	136
Belgium	2000	Males	93	x(1)	99	x(3)	113	x(5)	141	x(7)	128	x(9)
		Females	83	x(1)	112	x(3)	123	x(5)	152	x(7)	133	x(9)
		M+F	92	x(1)	102	x(3)	112	x(5)	147	x(7)	128	x(9)
Canada	1999	Males	80	78	102	101	116	117	160	159	138	137
		Females	70	67	98	89	115	115	170	184	139	144
		M+F	80	79	102	100	113	113	163	167	136	137
Czech Republic	1999	Males	75	77	a	a	177	182	178	176	178	177
		Females	72	75	a	a	127	124	172	176	170	174
		M+F	68	70	a	a	151	151	180	182	179	181
Denmark	2000	Males	86	83	91	94	107	107	137	134	131	128
		Females	90	89	92	109	114	112	125	122	123	121
		M+F	87	85	100	106	110	111	127	123	124	121
Finland	1999	Males	93	90	m	m	129	125	200	188	167	159
		Females	99	96	m	m	124	123	176	172	145	141
		M+F	96	94	m	m	120	115	190	179	153	144
France	1999	Males	88	86	130	118	129	137	179	182	159	163
		Females	80	81	133	108	132	139	158	165	145	152
		M+F	84	84	130	112	125	133	169	174	150	155
Germany	2000	Males	81	88	114	117	114	112	164	163	143	141
		Females	74	73	128	127	116	118	159	158	141	142
		M+F	76	80	115	114	117	116	165	163	145	143
Hungary	2001	Males	81	81	140	137	205	182	252	253	252	253
		Females	77	80	128	124	143	128	180	174	179	174
		M+F	77	78	131	126	164	144	210	203	210	202
Ireland	1998	Males	78	83	80	55	116	125	136	142	130	135
		Females	58	59	80	82	95	81	170	166	140	133
		M+F	77	79	69	68	108	114	153	153	138	137
Italy	1998	Males	54	55	m	m	x(7)	x(8)	138	142	138	142
		Females	61	56	m	m	x(7)	x(8)	115	114	115	114
		M+F	58	57	m	m	x(7)	x(8)	127	126	127	126
Korea	1998	Males	88	90	m	m	105	109	143	136	132	129
		Females	69	75	m	m	118	138	160	181	141	164
		M+F	78	80	m	m	106	113	147	142	135	134
Netherlands	1997	Males	88	86	126	121	145	130	141	133	142	132
		Females	73	73	120	124	131	136	148	154	146	152
		M+F	85	84	121	119	139	131	144	139	144	138
New Zealand	2001	Males	76	74	m	m	x(9)	x(10)	x(9)	x(10)	130	122
		Females	72	72	m	m	x(9)	x(10)	x(9)	x(10)	136	135
		M+F	74	75	m	m	x(9)	x(10)	x(9)	x(10)	133	128
Norway	1999	Males	85	89	118	116	140	143	136	138	136	138
		Females	84	88	121	118	145	151	136	138	137	139
		M+F	85	90	124	120	155	155	132	133	135	135
Portugal	1999	Males	60	57	m	m	150	155	190	194	180	185
		Females	63	58	m	m	133	139	188	206	170	185
		M+F	62	58	m	m	141	146	192	202	178	187
Sweden	1999	Males	87	86	m	m	x(9)	x(10)	x(9)	x(10)	138	140
		Females	88	87	m	m	x(9)	x(10)	x(9)	x(10)	126	122
		M+F	89	88	m	m	x(9)	x(10)	x(9)	x(10)	131	131
Switzerland	2001	Males	82	82	113	109	129	130	150	146	141	139
		Females	75	76	122	124	137	146	163	171	154	162
		M+F	79	79	114	116	147	150	167	165	159	159
United Kingdom	2001	Males	72	67	m	m	124	126	157	162	147	151
		Females	70	74	m	m	142	133	206	216	183	183
		M+F	67	68	m	m	128	124	174	181	159	161
United States	2001	Males	69	69	123	125	125	125	202	199	193	190
		Females	67	66	120	123	126	129	183	189	176	180
		M+F	70	69	121	122	123	122	195	192	186	183

OECD COUNTRIES

Note: x indicates that data are included in another column. The column reference is shown in brackets after "x". *e.g.*, x(2) means that data are included in column 2.
Source: OECD. See Annex 3 for national data sources (*www.oecd.org/edu/eag2003*).

Table A14.2
Differences in earnings between females and males
Average annual earnings of females as a percentage of males by level of educational attainment of 30 to 44-year-olds and 55 to 64-year-olds

		Below upper secondary education		Upper secondary and post-secondary non-tertiary education		Tertiary-type B education		Tertiary-type A and advanced research programmes		All levels of education	
		30-44	55-64	30-44	55-64	30-44	55-64	30-44	55-64	30-44	55-64
		(1)	(2)	(3)	(4)	(5)	(6)	(7)	(8)	(9)	(10)
Australia	1999	66	67	63	75	68	66	65	58	65	66
Canada	1999	51	61	58	66	59	57	69	65	63	62
Czech Republic	1999	66	58	67	64	45	62	67	63	63	61
Denmark	2000	76	67	71	69	74	75	65	63	72	66
Finland	1999	74	78	69	77	68	73	63	65	70	70
France	1999	70	62	75	69	76	72	68	64	74	60
Germany	2000	51	49	62	59	64	65	59	62	60	53
Hungary	2001	83	81	84	94	59	48	58	69	77	78
Ireland	1998	50	36	70	55	46	43	83	60	66	43
Italy	1998	71	70	69	43	x(7)	x(8)	56	45	73	57
Korea	1998	57	62	69	70	87	96	92	99	67	50
Netherlands	1997	46	43	55	50	57	39	63	50	55	45
New Zealand	2001	59	57	61	70	x(7)	x(8)	68	54	62	62
Norway	1999	60	61	61	63	64	65	61	61	62	61
Portugal	1999	72	70	70	67	63	57	75	68	73	66
Spain	1998	61	x(1)	81	x(3)	70	x(5)	73	x(7)	79	x(9)
Sweden	1999	74	73	74	69	x(9)	x(10)	x(9)	x(10)	71	70
Switzerland	2001	50	50	55	52	61	42	63	66	54	47
United Kingdom	2001	55	43	50	53	53	81	66	66	54	54
United States	2001	58	65	60	54	62	57	57	50	60	51

Note: x indicates that data are included in another column. The column reference is shown in brackets after "x". *e.g.,* x(2) means that data are included in column 2.
Source: OECD. See Annex 3 for national data sources (*www.oecd.org/edu/eag2003*).

Table A14.3
Private internal rates of return to education (1999-2000)
The impact of higher pre-tax earnings (accounting for length of studies), taxes, unemployment risk, tuition fees and public student support)
in upper secondary and tertiary education, by gender (in percentage points)

	Return to upper secondary education (in percentage points)[1]								Return to tertiary education (in percentage points)[2]												
	Comprehensive private internal rate of return		Impact of						Comprehensive private internal rate of return		Impact of										
			Higher pre-tax earnings		Higher taxes		Lower unemployment risk				Higher pre-tax earnings		Higher taxes		Lower unemployment risk		Tuition fees		Public student support	
	Males	Females	Males	Females	Males	Females	Males	Females	Males	Females	Males	Females	Males	Females	Males	Females	Males	Females	Males	Females
Canada	13.6	12.7	11.9	10.8	-1.6	-1.2	3.6	3.1	8.1	9.4	8.4	10.6	-0.5	-1.3	0.6	0.6	-2.0	-2.7	1.6	2.2
Denmark	11.3	10.5	11.3	8.3	-2.2	-1.4	2.2	3.6	13.9	10.1	7.9	5.7	-0.4	-1.0	1.1	0.7	-0.1	-0.2	5.4	4.9
France	14.8	19.2	7.5	10.5	-1.0	-0.7	8.3	9.4	12.2	11.7	13.3	12.1	-1.6	-1.7	0.4	1.2	-0.8	-0.9	0.9	1.0
Germany	10.8	6.9	10.0	6.1	-2.1	-1.7	2.9	2.5	9.0	8.3	7.1	7.0	-1.5	-1.6	1.1	0.6	-0.3	-0.6	2.6	2.9
Italy[3]	11.2	m	9.5	m	m	m	1.7	m	6.5	m	6.7	m	m	m	0.5	m	-0.7	m	n	m
Japan	6.4	8.5	4.4	6.6	-0.2	-0.2	2.2	2.1	7.5	6.7	8.0	8.0	-0.3	-0.2	0.3	0.0	-1.6	-2.2	1.1	1.1
Netherlands[4]	7.9	8.4	6.9	7.9	-0.2	-1.6	1.2	2.1	12.0	12.3	11.7	9.4	-2.0	-1.0	n	0.7	-0.6	-0.7	2.9	3.9
Sweden[5]	6.4	m	3.9	m	-0.6	m	3.1	m	11.4	10.8	9.4	7.4	-1.5	-0.7	1.2	1.6	-0.7	-0.8	3.0	3.3
United Kingdom	15.1	m	12.4	m	-1.5	m	4.2	m	17.3	15.2	18.1	16.4	-2.1	-2.3	0.7	0.7	-2.4	-2.3	3.0	2.7
United States	16.4	11.8	14.4	10.6	-0.9	-1.3	2.9	2.5	14.9	14.7	18.9	18.8	-2.3	-2.0	0.9	1.4	-4.7	-6.0	2.1	2.7
Country mean[6]	*11.4*	*11.1*	*9.2*	*8.7*	*-1.1*	*-1.1*	*3.6*	*3.6*	*11.8*	*11.3*	*11.4*	*10.6*	*-1.3*	*-1.3*	*0.7*	*0.9*	*-1.5*	*-1.8*	*2.5*	*2.9*

OECD COUNTRIES

1. The rate of return to upper secondary education is calculated by comparing the benefits and costs with those of lower secondary education.
2. The rate of return to tertiary education is calculated by comparing the benefits and costs with those of upper secondary education.
3. Data for males derive from 1998 post-tax earnings data.
4. Year of reference 1997.
5. In tertiary education, the theoretical length of standard tertiary courses is used in the calculations rather than the average theoretical length of different programmes for males and females. For females, earnings differential between upper and lower secondary levels are not large enough to permit a positive rate of return calculation.
6. Data for males exclude Italy; data for females in upper secondary education exclude Sweden and the United Kingdom.
Source: OECD.

Table A14.4
Social rates of return to education (1999-2000)
Rates of return to upper secondary and tertiary education, by gender (in percentage points)

| | Social return to upper secondary education[1] | | Social return to tertiary education[2] | |
	Males	Females	Males	Females
Canada[3]	m	m	6.8	7.9
Denmark	9.3	8.7	6.3	4.2
France	9.6	10.6	13.2	13.1
Germany	10.2	6.0	6.5	6.9
Italy[4]	8.4	m	7.0	m
Japan	5.0	6.4	6.7	5.7
Netherlands	6.2	7.8	10.0	6.3
Sweden	5.2	m	7.5	5.7
United Kingdom	12.9	m	15.2	13.6
United States	13.2	9.6	13.7	12.3

OECD COUNTRIES

1. The rate of return to upper secondary education is calculated by comparing the benefits and costs with those of lower secondary education.
2. The rate of return to tertiary education is calculated by comparing the benefits and costs with those of upper secondary education.
3. In Canada, no data were available on expenditure per student in upper secondary education.
4. In Italy, the sample size of earnings for females was not large enough to allow for the calculation of rates of return.
Source: OECD.

INDICATOR A15: THE RETURNS TO EDUCATION: LINKS BETWEEN HUMAN CAPITAL AND ECONOMIC GROWTH

- An analysis of the driving factors of economic growth shows that rising labour productivity accounted for at least half of GDP per capita growth in most OECD countries.

- Labour productivity can be increased in several ways and human capital plays a pivotal role in this equation, not just as an input linking aggregate output to the stocks of productive inputs, but also as a determinant of the rate of technological progress.

- The estimated long-run effect on economic output of one additional year of education in the OECD area is in the order of 6 per cent.

Chart A15.1

Large differentials in GDP per capita (2000)

Percentage point differences in trend, PPP-based, GDP per capita with respect to the United States

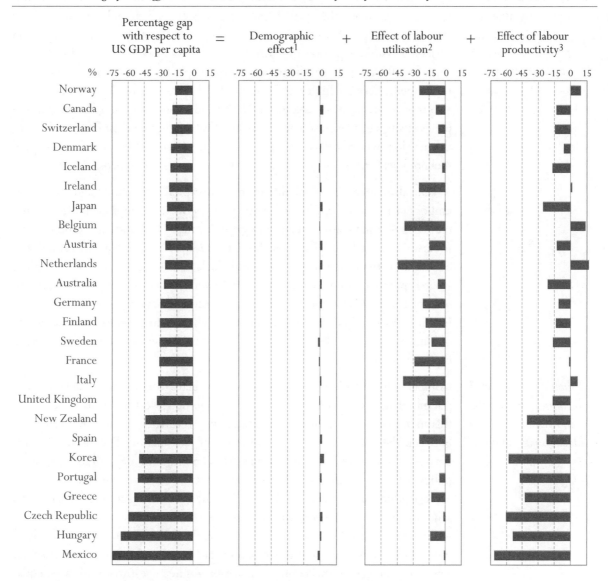

| | Percentage gap with respect to US GDP per capita | = | Demographic effect[1] | + | Effect of labour utilisation[2] | + | Effect of labour productivity[3] |

1. Based on the ratio of working age population (15-64 years) to total population.
2. Based on employment rates and average hours worked.
3. GDP per hour worked.
Source: OECD. See Annex 3 for notes *(www.oecd.org/edu/eag2003).*

A15

This indicator estimates the effect of changes in explanatory variables, including human capital, on changes in output per capita growth rates.

Policy context

What makes some countries seemingly able to thrive on new technological opportunities while others are held back? One of the most important lessons that emerges from the "OECD growth project" is that policies that ensure stable macroeconomic conditions are important for growth, as high and variable inflation depresses investment and excessive tax burdens distort proper resource allocation. Also, the importance of capital – in the broadest sense – is reaffirmed; there are high returns not only to physical capital accumulation but also to investment in education and R&D. In addition, institutional structures and policy settings that favour competition and flexibility in capital and labour markets, the development of new technologies and the dissemination of innovations and technological change also make a key difference to growth prospects.

A central element in all of this is "human capital" the knowledge and skills embodied in workers. This indicator focuses on the role that human capital plays in fostering output per capita growth rates. The indicator complements Indicator A14 which examines the relationship between human capital and economic returns at the level of individuals. While Indicator A14 examines what happens to the earnings of an individual as his or her schooling rises, holding constant factor prices and the economy-wide average level of education, Indicator A15 seeks to capture the effects of changes in a country's overall stock of human capital on labour productivity holding the aggregate stock of physical capital constant.

It should be interpreted in connection with the individual returns to education as examined in Indicator A14.

Comparisons of micro-level estimates of returns to education (such as those portrayed in IndicatorA14) and macro-econometric estimates as reflected in this indicator, are potentially of great policy relevance because discrepancies between them can point to the existence of externalities that drive a wedge between the private and public returns to schooling and may call for corrective policy action. For instance, if the productivity of each worker increases with average education at the aggregate level of the economy as it does with his own school attainment, the first of these effects will constitute an externality and will generate a tendency for underinvestment in education because individuals will fail to take into account the indirect social benefits that can arise from their schooling choices. In this context, micro-econometric estimates of wage equations with individual cross-section data for a given country will only pick up the own-education effects of schooling (because the indirect aggregate effect does not vary across individuals within a given country), whereas macro-econometric estimates with cross-country data should also capture the social externality.

Evidence and explanations

In the last decade, productivity has accelerated in some countries but slowed down in others.

In the last decade, per capita growth rates in OECD countries have ceased to converge. Productivity has accelerated in some of the most affluent economies, most notably the United States, and slowed down substantially in others, such as continental Europe and Japan, while signs of what has been named a "New Economy", driven by the upsurge of new technologies, have emerged.

A15

Data for 2000 show the United States well at the top of the OECD income distribution, followed by Norway, Canada and Switzerland with GDP per capita about 15-20 percentage points below the United States' figure. The bulk of the OECD countries, including all other major economies lagged behind per capita GDP in the United States by 25-35 percentage points (Chart A15.1).

Labour-force participation rates tended to remain stable over the last decade, with rising prime-age female participation rates largely compensated by falling participation rates among older workers and youngsters. However, participation rates only provide a partial proxy for the actual labour input in production, and the utilisation of supplied labour needs to be taken into account as well. A number of countries (*e.g.* the United States or Japan) have high employment rates and higher than average hours worked. While most of the Nordic countries have even higher employment rates, but this is offset by lower hours worked. By contrast, low employment rates in some countries (*e.g.* Belgium, France, Italy, the Netherlands and Spain) combined with relatively low hours, explain more than 20 percentage points of the gap between their per capita GDP and that of the United States. Chart A15.1 suggests that labour utilisation (employment rates combined with hours worked) is an important factor in accounting for differences in the GDP per capita levels between countries.

Employment rates combined with hours worked explain significant differences in levels of GDP per capita.

These differences in levels have caused renewed interest in the main factors driving economic growth and the policies that might influence it. The "OECD growth project", from which this indicator presents selected findings, shows that the observed growth patterns are a reflection of structural shifts in the factors and policies that drive economic growth. Understanding them better provides valuable lessons for policymaking, even if some OECD economies may be slowing down

An analysis of the driving factors of economic growth shows that...

A first approach to reviewing growth in GDP per capita over the past decade is to break it down into three major components, comprising growth rates of: *i)* the ratio of persons of working-age (15-64 years) to the total population; *ii)* the ratio of employed persons to the working age population (the "employment rate"); and *iii)* labour productivity (Chart A15.2).

Chart A15.2 shows that, for the vast majority of OECD countries, demographic trends were a relatively minor component of growth in GDP per capita over the 1990s. The only countries where demographic change made a positive and significant contribution to growth in GDP per capita were Ireland, Korea, Mexico and Turkey, the former having experienced a reversal in traditional migration flows in the 1990s. However, in some OECD countries, demographic trends have begun (in this accounting sense) to act as a slight drag on growth in GDP per capita. This tendency is set to strengthen in the future due to more rapid increase in the share of older persons in total population.

...changes in demography have not yet become a major drag on growth...

A15

Chart A15.2
The driving forces of GDP per capita growth (1990-2000)
Trend series, average annual percentage change

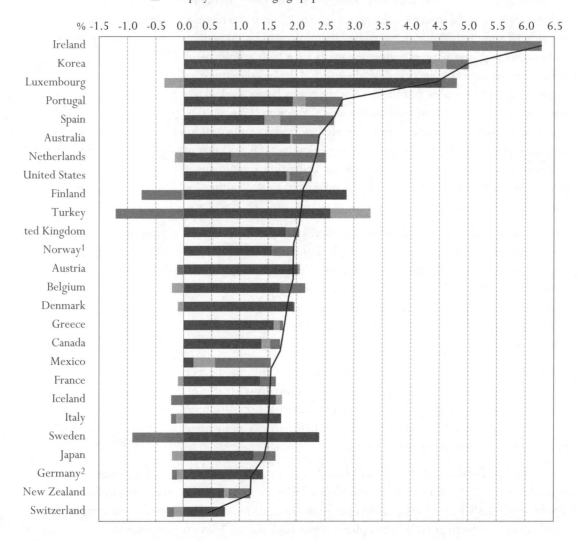

—— GDP per capita growth
Contribution to GDP per capita growth from trend changes in:
■ GDP per person employed
■ Working-age population/total population
■ Employment/working-age population

land only.
-2000.
OECD. See Annex 3 for notes *(www.oecd.org/edu/eag2003)*.

Rising labour productivity, defined as GDP per person employed, accounted for at least half of GDP per capita growth in most OECD countries over the 1990s. Since hours worked fell in most countries during the 1990s, especially in continental Europe, labour productivity growth was higher on an hourly basis than when measured on a head-count basis. Declines in hours worked reflect both shorter statutory (or collectively agreed) working weeks as well as, especially in a number of European countries, a substantial increase in part-time work.

...and rising labour productivity accounted for at least half of GDP per capita growth in most OECD countries.

Compared with the previous decade, hourly labour productivity picked up in a number of countries, including Australia, Finland, Germany, Norway, Portugal, Sweden and the United States, while it declined in the other countries. However, these changes in productivity trends were accompanied by different employment patterns across countries. Among the G-7 economies, significant employment increase in the United States (as well as in Canada and Japan with no acceleration in productivity) contrasted sharply with declines in Germany and Italy. Even stronger contrasts in employment patterns were found amongst some smaller countries, where strong upward trends in employment rates in Ireland, the Netherlands and Spain compare with declines in Finland, Sweden and Turkey.

Labour productivity can be increased in several ways: by improving the quality of labour used in the production process, by increasing the use of capital per worker and improving its quality, or by attaining greater overall efficiency in how these factors of production are used together, which economists call multi-factor productivity. Multi-factor productivity reflects many types of efficiency improvements, such as improved managerial practices, organisational changes and innovative ways of producing goods and services. Multi-factor productivity can rise because better skills and better technology may cause the blend of labour and capital to produce more efficiently, organisational and managerial changes may help to improve operations, and innovation may lead to more valuable output being produced with a given combination of capital and labour.

Labour productivity can be increased in several ways...

The skills and competencies embodied in workers - in short the quality of labour or "human capital" - plays a fundamental role in labour productivity growth. The rise in the educational attainment among workers over the 1990s is only one sign of this role. Increases in the level of post-educational skills may be even more important, although few hard measures are available. Consequently, as empirical studies have found, human capital is a significant determinant of economic growth.

...and human capital plays a pivotal role in this equation...

Chart A15.3 shows that growth in output per employed person is partly attributable to increases in "human capital" of those in employment. The chart displays the impact of changes in the average human capital of workers on growth in cyclically adjusted GDP per hour worked. Essentially, the chart decomposes average annual percentage changes in GDP per capita over the period 1990 to 2000 into the components that are due to: *i)* changes in the average hours worked, *ii)* changes in the average years of formal education (used here as a proxy for changes in the quality of labour), and *iii)* changes in

...not just as an input linking aggregate output to the stocks of productive inputs and technical efficiency...

A15

the hourly GDP per efficient unit of labour, which is equivalent to changes in GDP per worker once changes in working hours and changes in the average quality of labour are accounted for. The latter is based on a measure of labour input that sums up shares of workers with different levels of formal education, each weighted by their relative wage. The rationale behind this measure is first, that educational attainment accounts for a good proportion of human capital embodied in workers; and second, that relative wages between different levels of education provide a reasonable quantitative proxy for the relative productivity of workers with different levels of education (see Box A15.1).

OECD countries have invested heavily in education over past decades and this has resulted in a positive contribution of human capital enhancement in growth rates of GDP per person employed, or labour productivity. Over the past decade, skill upgrading amongst workers was particularly marked in Europe,

Chart A15.3

Enhancements in human capital contribute to labour productivity growth (1990-2000)
Average annual percentage change

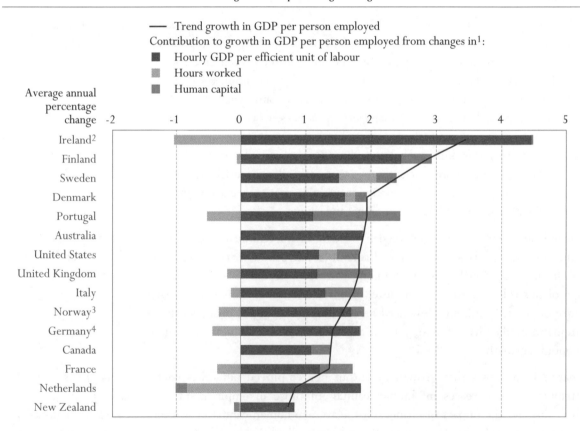

1. Based on the following decomposition: growth in GDP per person employed = (changes in hourly GDP per efficient unit of labour) + (changes in average hours worked) + (changes in human capital).
2. 1990-1999 for Ireland.
3. Mainland only.
4. 1991-2000 for Germany.
Source: OECD. See Annex 3 for notes *(www.oecd.org/edu/eag2003).*

although it was accompanied by sluggish employment growth because productivity gains were achieved in part by dismissals or not employing workers with low skills. By contrast, in the United States, Australia, Canada, the Netherlands and New Zealand, skill upgrading has played, at best, a modest role in GDP growth per employed person. Improving labour-market conditions in these countries has widened the employment base, especially in the 1990s, allowing low-skilled workers to get a foothold in employment.

However, education plays an important role in this equation, not only as an input linking aggregate output to the stocks of productive inputs and technical efficiency, but as a key determinant of the rate of technological progress that affects the output per worker. In fact, one reason for the renewed interest in the productivity-enhancing role of human capital is that human capital complements new technologies. For technologies to be developed and used effectively, and network externalities of new technology to materialise, the right skills and competencies must be in place. One of the factors behind the good growth record of some countries has been the availability of a large pool of qualified personnel, and skilled labour shortages are rightly considered as a constraint on the growth process.

…but also as a determinant of the rate of technological progress.

During the 1990s, in the OECD countries for which data are available, the rise in the number of knowledge workers (scientists, engineers and others, such as ICT specialists and technicians who generate knowledge) accounted for nearly 30 per cent of the net employment gains recorded during this period. Wages have followed a similar pattern. For example in the United States, the wage of knowledge workers has risen much faster than wages of other occupations. Between 1985 and 1998, real earnings of knowledge-intensive workers grew by almost 17 per cent, cumulatively, compared with 5.3 per cent for the average employee in the United States. During the same period "goods-producing" occupations suffered a cut in their real earnings of nearly 2.5 per cent.

Summing up the different influences of education on economic growth, the "OECD growth project" concludes that the estimated long-run effect on output of one additional year of education in the adult population is in the order of 6 per cent in the OECD area.

As a result, an additional year of education has, on average, a long-term impact on economic output of 6 per cent.

A15

Box 14.1. Estimating changes in the quality of factor inputs: the example of the labour input

In order to assess the impact of labour and capital inputs on output and productivity growth rates, proper account should be taken of the role that each factor plays as input in the production process. In the case of labour input, the simple count of hours worked is only a crude approximation, insofar as workers show great differences in education, experience, sector of activity and other attributes that greatly affect their marginal productivity. In particular, a measure of labour input in efficiency units can be obtained by weighting different types of labour by their marginal contribution to the production activity in which they are employed. Since these productivity measures are generally not observable, information on relative wages by characteristics is used to derive the required weights to aggregate different types of labour.

The difference between the weighted and unweighted series yields an index for the compositional change of labour input, or its quality. To take into account the effect of changes in the composition of labour input, six different types of workers were considered, based on gender and three different educational levels: below upper-secondary; upper secondary and tertiary education. It is assumed that: *i)* workers with different levels of education work the same (average) number of hours; and *ii)* relative wage rates are constant over the sample period. Compared with other proxies available in the literature (largely for the United States) this decomposition is rather crude, but it does shed light on the role of compositional changes in labour input consistently for a range of OECD countries, thereby permitting cross-country comparisons. (For more details on this procedure, see OECD, 2003).

Definitions and methodologies

Human capital is estimated on the basis of completed levels of education and average years of schooling at each level in the working-age population. It should be borne in mind that educational attainment is a crude and somewhat narrow proxy for skills and competencies, taking little account of the quality of formal education or of other important dimensions of human capital. It is derived from OECD data combined with data from de la Fuente and Doménech (2000).

For further information on definitions, methods and sources see *The Sources of Economic Growth in OECD Countries* (OECD, 2003) and *The New Economy: Beyond the Hype* (OECD 2001) from which the material for this indicator has been derived. The figures shown are as published in these reports and do not take account of the subsequent revisions that have been made to some countries' GDP data. These revisions do not however affect the general messages from the analysis.

FINANCIAL AND HUMAN RESOURCES INVESTED IN EDUCATION

OVERVIEW

Chapter B reviews the financial and human resources invested in education, in terms of…

…the resources that each country invests in education, relative to the number of students enrolled, national income and the size of public budgets,…

B

…the ways in which education systems are financed, and the sources from which the funds originate,…

…different financing instruments,…

...and how the money is invested and apportioned between different resource categories.

Indicator B6: Expenditure on institutions by service category and by resource category

Table B6.1.   Expenditure on institutions by service category as a percentage of GDP (2000)

Table B6.2.   Expenditure per student on instruction, ancillary services and research and development (R&D) (2000)

Table B6.3.   Expenditure on educational institutions by resource category (2000)

B

Classification of educational expenditure

Educational expenditure in this indicator are classified through three dimensions:

• The first dimension – represented by the horizontal axis in the diagram below – relates to the location where spending occurs. Spending on schools and universities, education ministries and other agencies directly involved in providing and supporting education is one component of this dimension. Spending on education outside these institutions is another.

• The second dimension – represented by the vertical axis in the diagram below – classifies the goods and services that are purchased. Not all expenditure on educational institutions can be classified as direct educational or instructional expenditure. Educational institutions in many OECD countries not only offer teaching services but also various ancillary services to support students and their families, such as meals, transport, housing, etc. In addition, at the tertiary level spending on research and development can be significant. Not all spending on educational goods and services occurs within educational institutions. For example, families may purchase textbooks and materials themselves or seek private tutoring for their children.

• The third dimension – represented by the colours in the diagram below – distinguishes between the sources from which the funds originate. These include the public sector and international agencies (indicated by the light blue colour) and households and other private entities (indicated by the mid-blue colour). Where private expenditure on education is subsidised by public funds, this is indicated by cells in dark blue colour. The diagram is reported at the beginning of each indicator to signal its coverage.

B

	Spending on educational institutions (e.g., schools, universities, educational administration and student welfare services)	Spending on education outside educational institutions (e.g., private purchases of educational goods and services, including private tutoring)
Spending on educational core services	e.g., public spending on instructional services in educational institutions	e.g., subsidised private spending on books
	e.g., subsidised private spending on instructional services in institutions	e.g., private spending on books and other school materials or private tutoring
	e.g., private spending on tuition fees	
Spending on research and development	e.g., public spending on university research	
	e.g., funds from private industry for research and development in educational institutions	
Spending on educational services other than instruction	e.g., public spending on ancillary services such as meals, transport to schools, or housing on the campus	e.g., subsidised private spending on student living costs or reduced prices for transport
	e.g.., private spending on fees for ancillary services	e.g., private spending on student living costs or transport

■ Public sources of funds   ■ Private sources funds   ■ Private funds publicly subsidised

INDICATOR B1: EDUCATIONAL EXPENDITURE PER STUDENT

B1

- In the OECD area, annual public and private expenditure on educational institutions per student between primary and tertiary education are equal in average to US$ 6 361 but ranges from around US$ 3 000 per student or less in Czech Republic, Hungary, Mexico, Poland, the Slovak Republic, and Turkey to more than US$ 8 000 per student in Austria, Denmark, Norway, Switzerland and United States.

- OECD countries spend US$ 4 470 per primary student, US$ 5 501 per secondary student and US$ 11 109 per tertiary student, but these averages mask a broad range of expenditure across countries. On average, as represented by the simple mean across all OECD countries, countries spend 2.2 times as much per student at the tertiary level than at the primary level.

- Lower expenditure cannot automatically be equated with a lower quality of educational services. Australia, Finland, Ireland, Korea and the United Kingdom, for example, which have moderate expenditure on education per student at primary and lower secondary levels, are among the OECD countries with the highest levels of performance by 15-year-old students in key subject areas.

- In some OECD countries, low annual expenditure per tertiary student still translates into high overall costs per tertiary student because the duration of tertiary studies is long.

- Expenditure per primary, secondary and post-secondary non-tertiary student increased between 1995 and 2000 by over 25 per cent in Australia, Greece, Ireland, Portugal and Spain whereas at the tertiary level, spending on education has not always kept pace with the rapid expansion of enrolments.

- In eight out of 22 OECD countries expenditure on educational institutions per tertiary student decreased between 1995 and 2000 whereas GDP per capita increased.

Chart B1.1

Expenditure on educational institutions per student (2000)
Annual expenditure on educational institutions per student in equivalent US dollars converted using PPPs, for primary to tertiary education, based on full-time equivalents

Expenditure per student (equivalent US dollars converted using PPPs)

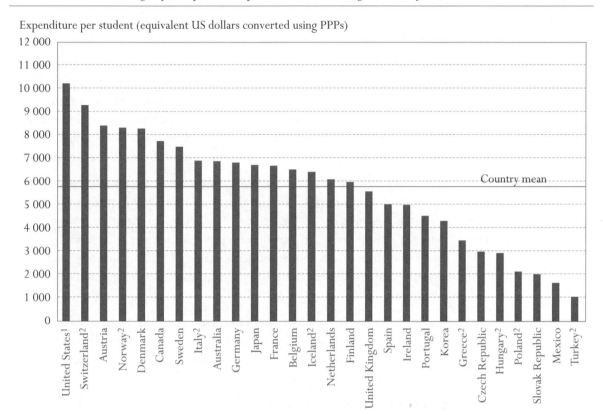

B1

1. Public and independent private institutions only.
2. Public institutions only.
Countries are ranked in descending order of expenditure per student.
Source: OECD. Table B1.1. See Annex 3 for notes *(www.oecd.org/edu/eag2003).*

B1

Policy context

This indicator shows annual and cumulative expenditure on education per student in absolute terms...

Effective schools require the right combination of trained and talented personnel, adequate facilities, state-of-the-art equipment and motivated students ready to learn. The demand for high-quality education, which can translate into higher costs per student, needs to be balanced against placing undue burdens on taxpayers.

...and relative to GDP per capita.

As a result, the question of whether the resources devoted to education yield adequate returns to the investments made figures prominently in the public debate. Although the optimal volume of resources required to prepare each student for life and work in modern societies is difficult to assess, international comparisons of spending on education per student can provide a starting point for evaluating the effectiveness of different models of educational provision.

It also compares trends in the development of expenditure on education per student.

Policy-makers must also balance the importance of improving the quality of educational services with the desirability of expanding access to educational opportunities, notably at the tertiary level. The comparative review in this indicator of how trends in expenditure on education per student have evolved shows how the expansion of enrolments in many OECD countries, particularly in tertiary education, has not always been paralleled by changes in educational investment.

Finally, decisions on the allocation of funds to the various levels of education are also important. For example, some OECD countries emphasise broad access to higher education while others invest in near-universal education for children as young as three or four years of age.

Evidence and explanations

What this indicator covers and what it does not cover

The indicator shows direct public and private expenditure on educational institutions in relation to the number of full-time equivalent students enrolled in these institutions.

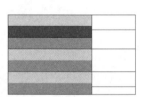

Coverage diagram (see page 181 for explanations)

Public subsidies for students' living expenses have been excluded to ensure international comparability of the data. Expenditure data for students in private educational institutions are not available for certain OECD countries, and some other countries do not report complete data on independent private institutions. Where this is the case, only the expenditure on public and government-dependent private institutions has been taken into account. Note that variation in expenditure on education per student may reflect not only variation in the material resources provided to students (*e.g.,* variations in the ratio of students to teaching staff) but also variation in relative salary levels.

While educational expenditure is dominated below the tertiary level by spending on instructional services, at the tertiary level, other services, particularly those related to R&D activities, can account for a significant proportion of educational spending. Indicator B6 provides further information on how spending is distributed by different types of services provided.

Expenditure on education per student in equivalent US dollars

Annual expenditure on educational institutions per student between primary and tertiary education provides an assessment of the investment that is made in each student. OECD countries as a whole spend US$ 6 361 per student between primary and tertiary education. Spending on education at this level ranges from around US$ 3 000 per student or less in Czech Republic, Hungary, Mexico, Poland, the Slovak Republic, and Turkey to more than US$ 8 000 per student in Austria, Denmark, Norway, Switzerland and the United States. In nine out of 28 countries, spending on education varies between US$ 6 000 and 7 000 per student.

Among nine out of 28 countries, spending on education between primary and tertiary education lies between US$ 6 000 and 7 000 per student.

However, even if overall spending per student is similar in some OECD countries, the ways in which resources are allocated across the different levels of education varies widely. OECD countries as a whole spend US$ 4 470 per student at the primary level, US$ 5 501 per student at the secondary level and US$ 11 109 per student at the tertiary level. At the tertiary level, these averages are influenced by high expenditure in a few large OECD countries, most notably the United States. Spending on education per student in the "typical" OECD country, as represented by the simple mean across all OECD countries, amounts to US$ 4 381 at the primary level, US$ 5 957 at the secondary level and US$ 9 571 at the tertiary level of education (Table B1.1)

As a whole, OECD countries spend US$ 4 470 per primary student, US$ 5 501 per secondary student and US$ 11 109 per tertiary student...

B1

These averages mask a broad range of expenditure on education per student across OECD countries. At the primary level, expenditure on educational institutions ranges from US$ 1 291 per student in Mexico to US$ 7 074 per student in Denmark. Differences between OECD countries are even greater at the secondary level, where spending on education per student varies by a factor of 6, from US$ 1 615 in Mexico to US$ 9 780 in Switzerland. Expenditure on education per tertiary student ranges from US$ 3 222 in Poland to US$ 20 358 in the United States (Table B1.1).

...but these averages mask a broad range of expenditure across OECD countries.

These comparisons are based on purchasing power parities, not market exchange rates, and therefore reflect the amount of a national currency that will buy the same basket of goods and services in a given country as that bought by the US dollar in the United States.

On average, expenditure on Research and Development (R&D) in tertiary institutions represents 27 per cent of all tertiary expenditure. In six out of 21 OECD countries for which tertiary expenditure are separated by type of services, R&D expenditure in tertiary institutions represents more than 35 per cent of tertiary expenditure. On a per student-basis this can translate into significant amounts, as in Australia, Austria, Belgium, Canada, Denmark, Germany, the Netherlands, Sweden and the United Kingdom, where expenditure for R&D in tertiary institutions amounts to over US$ 3 000 per student (Chart B1.2 and Table B6.2).

R&D expenditure in tertiary institutions amounts to over US$ 3 000 per student in Australia, Belgium, Germany, the Netherlands, Sweden and the United Kingdom.

R&D spending in tertiary educational institutions not only depends on total R&D expenditure in a country, but also on the national infrastructure for R&D activities. OECD countries in which most R&D is performed by tertiary

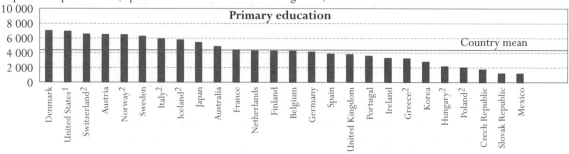

Chart B1.2

Expenditure on educational institutions per student by level of education (2000)
Annual expenditure on educational institutions per student in equivalent US dollars converted using PPPs, by level of education, based on full-time equivalents

■ Total expenditure per student ■ Research and development in tertiary institutions
■ Ancillary services (transport, meals, housing provided by institutions) ■ Educational core services

Expenditure per student (equivalent US dollars converted using PPPs)

◆ Lower secondary education ◆ Upper secondary education

Expenditure per student (equivalent US dollars converted using PPPs)

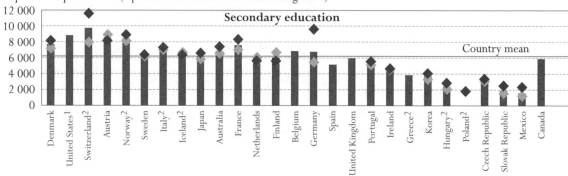

Expenditure per student (equivalent US dollars converted using PPPs)

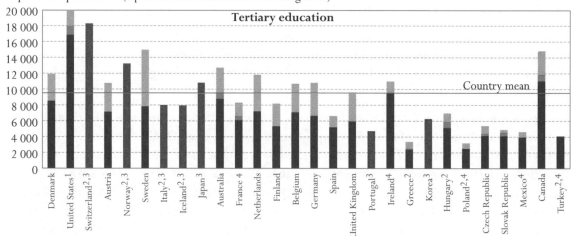

1. Public and independent private institutions only.
2. Public institutions only.
3. The bar represents total expenditure at tertiary level and includes research and development expenditure.
4. Research and development expenditure at tertiary level and thus total expenditure are underestimated.
Countries are ranked in descending order of expenditure per student in primary education. Data for primary education are missing for Canada and Turkey.
Source: OECD. Tables B1.1 and B6.2. See Annex 3 for notes *(www.oecd.org/edu/eag2003).*

B1

educational institutions tend to report higher expenditure per tertiary student than countries in which a large part of R&D is performed in other public institutions or by industry.

The labour intensiveness of the traditional model of classroom education accounts for the predominance of teachers' salaries in overall costs. Differences in the average class size and in the ratio of students to teaching staff (Indicator D2), in staffing patterns, in teachers' salaries (Indicator D5) and in teaching materials and facilities influence the differences in cost between levels of education, types of programme and types of school.

The labour intensiveness of education accounts for the predominance of teachers' salaries in overall costs.

It would be misleading to equate lower unit expenditure generally with lower quality of educational services. Australia, Finland, Ireland, Korea and the United Kingdom, for example, which have moderate expenditure on education per student at primary and lower secondary levels, are among the OECD countries with the highest levels of performance by 15-year-old students in key subject areas (see Indicators A5 and A6)

Lower unit expenditure cannot simply be equated with lower student performance.

B1

Differences in educational expenditure per student between levels of education

Expenditure on education per student exhibits a common pattern throughout the OECD: in each OECD country it rises sharply from primary to tertiary education. This pattern can be understood by looking at the main determinants of expenditure, particularly the location and mode of educational provision. The vast majority of education still takes place in traditional school settings with – despite some differences – similar organisation, curriculum, teaching style and management. These shared features are likely to lead to similar patterns of unit expenditure.

Expenditure on education per student consistently rises with the level of education.

Comparisons of the distribution of expenditure between levels of education are an indication of the relative emphasis placed on education at different levels in various OECD countries, as well as of the relative costs of providing education at those levels.

However, even though expenditure on education per student rises with the level of education in almost all OECD countries from primary to tertiary, the relative sizes of the differentials vary markedly between countries (Chart B1.3). At the secondary level, expenditure on education per student is, on average, 1.4 times that at the primary level, although the difference ranges from one time the expenditure per primary student in Sweden to more than 1.6 times in the Czech Republic, France and Germany.

Although OECD countries spend, on average, 2.2 times as much on education per student at the tertiary level as at the primary level, spending patterns vary widely between countries. For example, whereas Italy and Portugal only spend around 1.3 times as much on a tertiary student as on a primary student, Mexico and the Slovak Republic spend respectively 3.6 and 3.8 times as much (Chart B1.3)

On average, OECD countries spend 2.2 times as much on education per student at the tertiary level as at the primary level.

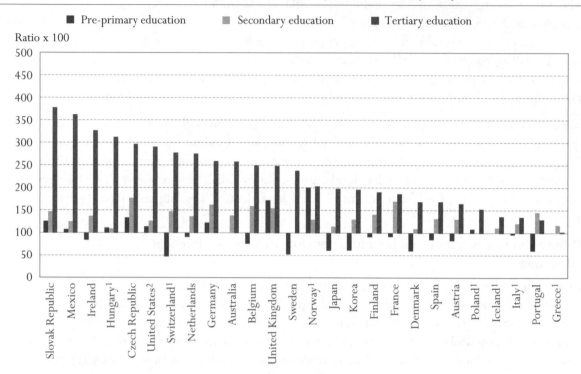

Chart B1.3

Differences in expenditure on educational institutions per student relative to primary education (2000)
Ratio of expenditure on educational institutions per student at various levels of education to expenditure on educational institutions per student in primary education, multiplied by 100

■ Pre-primary education   ▨ Secondary education   ■ Tertiary education

Notes: A ratio of 500 for tertiary education means that expenditure on educational institutions per tertiary student in a particular country is 5 times the expenditure on educational institutions per primary student.
A ratio of 50 for pre-primary education means that expenditure on educational institutions per pre-primary student in a particular country is half the expenditure on educational institutions per primary student.
1. Public institutions only.
2. Public and independent private institutions only.
Countries are ranked in descending order of expenditure on educational institutions per student in tertiary education relative to expenditure on educational institutions per student in primary education.
Source: OECD. Table B1.1. See Annex 3 for notes *(www.oecd.org/edu/eag2003).*

Educational expenditure per student over the average duration of tertiary studies

Annual expenditure on education per student does not always reflect the full cost of tertiary studies.

Since both the typical duration and the intensity of tertiary education vary between OECD countries, the differences between countries in annual expenditure on education per student on educational services as shown in Chart B1.2 do not necessarily reflect the variation in the total cost of educating the typical tertiary student.

Students can choose from a range of institutions and enrolment options.

Today, students can choose from a range of institutions and enrolment options in order to find the best fit between their degree objectives, abilities and personal interests. Many students enrol on a part-time basis while others work while studying, or attend more than one institution before graduating. These varying enrolment patterns can affect the interpretability of expenditure on education per student.

In particular, comparatively low annual expenditure on education per student can result in comparatively high overall costs of tertiary education if the typical duration of tertiary studies is long. Chart B1.4 shows the average expenditure that is incurred per student throughout the course of tertiary studies. The figures account for all students for whom expenditure is incurred, including those who do not finish their studies. Although the calculations are based on a number of simplified assumptions and therefore should be treated with some caution (see Annex 3 at *www.oecd.org/edu/eag2003*), some striking shifts in the rank order of OECD countries between the annual and aggregate expenditure can be noted.

Low annual expenditure may translate into high overall costs of tertiary education if the duration of tertiary studies is long.

For example, annual spending per tertiary student in Ireland is about the same as in Austria (US$ 11 083 in Ireland compared with US$ 10 851 in Austria) (Table B1.1). But because of differences in the tertiary degree structure (Indicator A2), the average duration of tertiary studies is a little bit less than two times longer in Austria than in Ireland (6.2 years in Austria, compared with 3.2 years in Ireland). As a consequence, the cumulative expenditure for each tertiary student is almost two times higher in Austria than in the Ireland (US$ 66 948 compared with US$ 35 909) (Chart B1.4 and Table B1.3).

B1

Chart B1.4

Cumulative expenditure on educational institutions per student over the average duration of tertiary studies (2000)

Annual expenditure on educational institutions per student multiplied by average duration of studies, in equivalent US dollars converted using PPPs

Each segment of the bar represents the annual expenditure on educational institutions per student.
The number of segments represents the number of years a student remains on average in tertiary education.

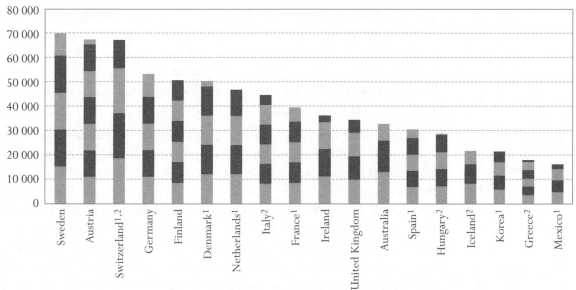

Equivalent US dollars converted using PPPs

Countries are ranked in descending order of expenditure on educational institutions per student over the average duration of tertiary studies.
1. The duration of tertiary studies is obtained by a special survey conducted in 1997 for the academic year 1995.
2. Public institutions only.
Source: OECD. Table B1.3. See Annex 3 for notes *(www.oecd.org/edu/eag2003)*.

The total cost of tertiary-type A studies in Switzerland (US$106 282) is more than twice as high as in the other reporting countries, except Germany (Table B1.3). These differences must, of course, be interpreted in the light of differences in national degree structures as well as possible differences between OECD countries in the academic level of the qualifications of students leaving university. While similar trends are observed in tertiary-type B studies, the total cost of these studies tends to be much lower than those of tertiary type-A programmes, largely because of their shorter duration.

Educational expenditure per student in relation to national GDP

OECD countries spend an average of 19 percent of GDP per capita on each primary student, 25 per cent per secondary student and 42 per cent per tertiary student.

Expenditure on education per student relative to GDP per capita is a spending measure that takes OECD countries' relative wealth into account. Since education is universal at lower levels, spending on education per student relative to GDP per capita at the lower levels of education can be interpreted as the resources spent on young people relative to a country's ability to pay. At higher levels of education, this measure is affected by a combination of national income, spending and enrolment rates.

At the tertiary level, for example, OECD countries can be relatively high on this measure if a relatively large proportion of their wealth is spent on educating a relatively small number of students. For the OECD as a whole, expenditure on education per student averages 19 per cent of GDP per capita at the primary level, 25 per cent at the secondary level and 42 per cent at the tertiary level (Table B1.2).

Beneath a certain level of GDP per capita, poorer OECD countries tend to spend less per student ...

The relationship between GDP per capita and expenditure per student is complex. Chart B1.3 shows the co-existence of two different relationships between two distinct groups of countries (see ovals in Chart B1.5). Countries with a GDP per capita equivalent to 25 000 US dollars or less demonstrate a clear positive relationship between spending on education per student and GDP per capita. In this group, including the Czech Republic, Greece, Hungary, Korea, Mexico, Poland, Portugal, the Slovak Republic, Spain and Turkey, poorer OECD countries tend to spend less per student than richer OECD countries. This trend can also be observed when looking at spending as a percentage of GDP per capita (Table B1.2).

...but the trend can not be generalised.

However, on the other hand, there is a considerable variation in spending on education per student among OECD countries with a GDP per capita greater than 25 000 US dollars (see ovals in Chart B1.5). The higher GDP per capita, the greater the variation in expenditure devoted to students. Thus, Austria, Canada and Ireland for example, are countries with similar levels of GDP per capita which spend very different proportions of their GDP per capita per student in secondary education. The proportion of national income spent per secondary student in Canada and Ireland - 21 and respectively 16 per cent of GDP per capita - is below the OECD average. By contrast, Austria spends 31 per cent of GDP per capita per secondary student, which is one of the highest proportions (Table B1.2).

Expenditure on educational institutions per student relative to GDP per capita (2000)
Annual expenditure on educational institutions per student relative to GDP per capita,
in equivalent US dollars converted using PPPs, by level of education

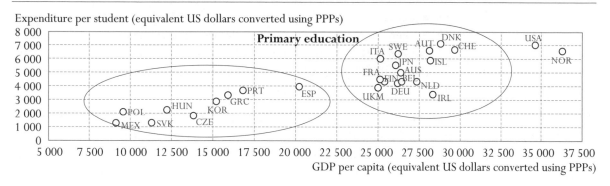

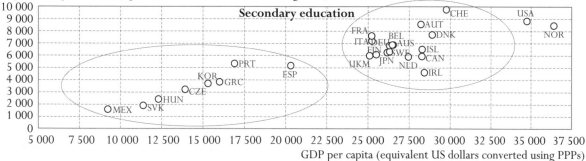

B1

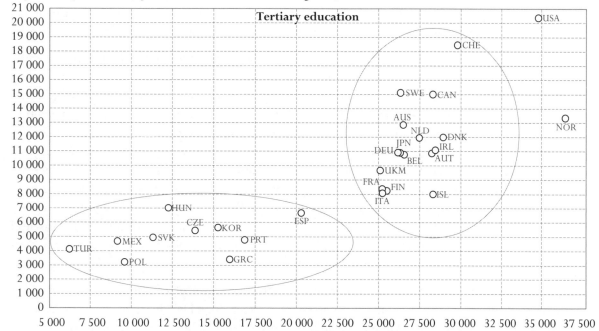

Note: Please refer to the Reader's Guide for list of country codes and country names used in this chart.
Source: OECD. Tables B1.1, B1.2 and Annex 2. See Annex 3 for notes *(www.oecd.org/edu/eag2003).*

Changes in expenditure on education per student between 1995 and 2000

The number of young people in a population influences both the enrolment rate and the amount of resources and organisational effort which a country must invest in its education system. Thus, the size of the youth population in a given country shapes the potential demand for initial education and training. The higher the number of young people, the greater the potential demand for educational services. Chart B1.6 shows in absolute terms and at 2000 constant prices the effects of changes in enrolment and in expenditure between 1995 and 2000 on spending on education per student.

Expenditure on education per primary, secondary and post-secondary non-tertiary student increased by over 25 per cent in Australia, Greece, Ireland, Portugal and Spain.

Expenditure per primary, secondary and post-secondary non-tertiary student increased between 1995 and 2000 by over 25 per cent in Australia, Greece, Ireland, Portugal and Spain. On the other hand, the Czech Republic and Norway saw a decline in expenditure on education per primary, secondary and post-secondary non-tertiary student by over 5 per cent. In eight out of the 20 OECD countries, changes remained within plus or minus 6 per cent compared with 1995 (Chart B1.6)

At primary and secondary levels, changes in enrolments were not the main factor driving expenditure...

Although institutional arrangements often adapt to changing demographic conditions only with a considerable time lag, changes in enrolments do not seem to have been the main factor driving changes in expenditure per primary, secondary and post-secondary non-tertiary student Japan and Spain are exceptions to this pattern , where a drop of more than 9 per cent in enrolments combined with a slight rise in expenditure on education has led to a significant increase in spending on education per student. In contrast, in France, Greece, Ireland and Portugal, an increase of more than 10 per cent in education budgets, coupled with a slight decrease in enrolments, has emphasized the increase in spending per primary, secondary and post-secondary non-tertiary student.

Other exceptions are Norway, Sweden and the United Kingdom, the three OECD countries with the highest increase in the number of primary, secondary and post-secondary non-tertiary students between 1995 and 2000. These however present different patterns. In Sweden , increases in expenditure out-paced the rising enrolment leading to a slight increase in expenditure per student, whereas in the United Kingdom the increase in enrolments was broadly matched by the increase in expenditure. In contrast, in Norway, an increase in student numbers due partly to the expansion of primary education from six to seven years, implemented in the school year 1997-1998 has not been counterbalanced by a similar increase in educational spending. This has lead to a decrease in expenditure per primary, secondary and post-secondary non-tertiary student between 1995 and 2000.

...while at the tertiary level, spending on education has not always kept pace with the rapid expansion of enrolments.

The pattern is different at the tertiary level of education. In six out of 22 OECD countries —Austria, the Czech Republic, Finland, Hungary, Norway and the United Kingdom — tertiary expenditure on education per student declined between 1995 and 2000 by 4.5 per cent or more. In all of these countries except Norway, this was mainly the result of the rapid increase in the number of tertiary students of more than 10 per cent during the same period

B1

Change in expenditure on educational institutions per student in comparison to underlying factors,
by level of education (1995, 2000)

*Indices of change in expenditure on educational institutions, enrolment and expenditure on educational institutions
per student between 1995 and 2000 (1995=100, 2000 constant prices)*

■ Change in expenditure   ■ Change in the number of students   ■ Change in expenditure per student

Index of change (1995=100)

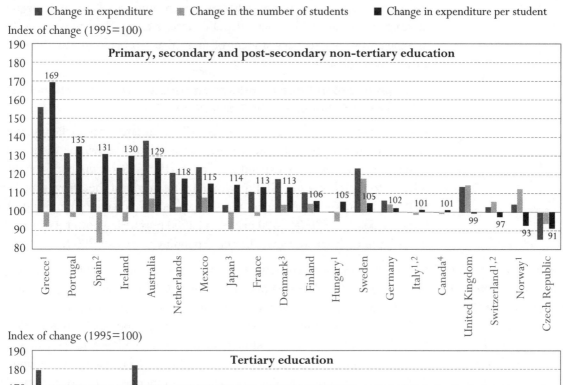

Index of change (1995=100)

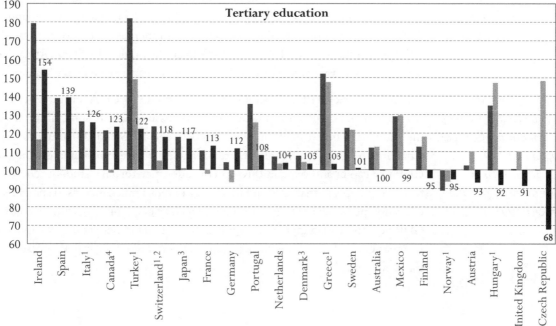

B1

1. Public institutions only.
2. Public expenditure only.
3. Post-secondary non-tertiary included in both upper secondary and tertiary education.
4. Post-secondary non-tertiary included in tertiary education.
Countries are ranked in descending order of change in expenditure on educational institutions per student.
Source: OECD. Table B2.2. See Annex 3 for notes *(www.oecd.org/edu/eag2003).*

(Chart B1.6). On the other hand, expenditure per tertiary student rose significantly in Greece, Ireland and Portugal despite a growth in enrolment of 48, 17 and 26 per cent, respectively. Germany and Norway were the only OECD countries in which the number of tertiary students actually declined by more than 4 per cent, although in Germany, this decline occurred mainly in the earlier years of this period whereas student numbers have lately begun to increase significantly. All other OECD countries except Turkey with increases in expenditure per tertiary student of more than 10 per cent saw little or no change in enrolments.

Changes in expenditure on education per student versus changes in GDP per capita between 1995 and 2000

Does growing national income necessarily translate into higher spending on education per student? The arrows in Chart B1.7 show, for each OECD country, the changes in expenditure on tertiary education per student in relation to the changes in GDP per capita. The origin of the arrow represents GDP per capita (horizontal axis) and the expenditure on education per student (vertical axis) in 1995 (at 2000 prices and 2000 purchasing power parities), and the point of each arrow shows the corresponding values for 2000.

In eight out of 22 OECD countries expenditure on educational institutions per tertiary student decreased between 1995 and 2000 whereas GDP per capita increased.

In general, changes in expenditure on education per student are linked to changes in GDP per capita. However, in eight out of 22 OECD countries expenditure on educational institutions per tertiary student decreased between 1995 and 2000 whereas GDP per capita increased over the same period (see arrows in blue on Chart B1.7). Expenditure per student increased in all other countries. In nine of these – Canada, France, Germany, Ireland, Italy, Japan, Spain, Switzerland and Turkey – expenditure on education per student increased at a greater rate than GDP per capita between 1995 and 2000. In all the other OECD countries, GDP per capita increased at a greater rate than expenditure per tertiary student.

Countries with comparable levels of expenditure and GDP per capita in 2000 display different patterns of investment in education between 1995 an 2000.

Among countries with comparable levels of expenditure on education per tertiary student and GDP per capita in 2000, it is possible to note some differences in the patterns of investment on education between 1995 and 2000. For example, while for the year 2000, Finland, France and Italy have approximately the same GDP per capita and expenditure on education per tertiary student, compared to 1995, it appears that Italy and to a lesser extent France increased spending on education per student at a greater rate than GDP per capita growth. By contrast, GDP per capita also increased significantly in Finland between 1995 and 2000 whereas expenditure on education per tertiary student slightly decreased over the same period.

B1

Chart B1.7.

Changes in expenditure on educational institutions per student in tertiary education and national income
Changes between 1995 and 2000 in expenditure on educational institutions per tertiary student compared with GDP per capita (2000 constant US dollars and 2000 constant PPPs)

——▶ Index of change between 1995 and 2000 in GPD per capita is higher than in expenditure on educational institutions per student over the same period

——▶ Expenditure on educational institutions per student decreased between 1995 and 2000 whereas GDP per capita increased over the same period

——▶ Index of change between 1995 and 2000 in expenditure on educational institutions per student is higher than change in GPD per capita over the same period

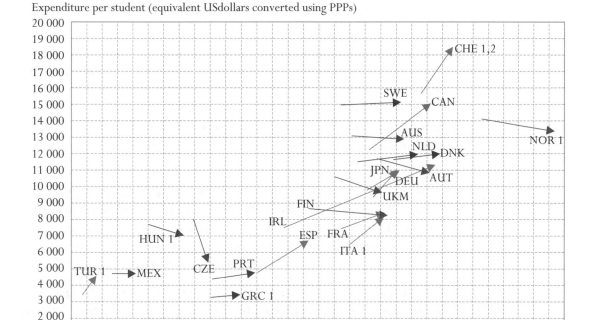

Expenditure per student (equivalent USdollars converted using PPPs)

GDP per capita (equivalent US dollars converted using PPPs)

Note: Please refer to the Reader's Guide for list of country codes and country names used in this chart.
The beginning of the arrow indicates spending per student and GPD per capita in 1995. The end of the arrow indicates the corresponding values for 2000.
1. Public institutions only.
2. Public expenditure only.
Source: OECD. Table B1.1 and Annex 2. See Annex 3 for notes *(www.oecd.org/edu/eag2003).*

Definitions and methodologies

Expenditure on education per student on a particular level of education is calculated by dividing the total expenditure on educational institutions at that level by the corresponding full-time equivalent enrolment. Only those educational institutions and programmes are taken into account for which both enrolment and expenditure data are available. Expenditure in national currency is converted into equivalent US dollars by dividing the national currency figure by the purchasing power parity (PPP) index. The PPP exchange rate gives the amount of a national currency that will buy the same basket of goods and services

Data refer to the financial year 2000 and are based on the UOE data collection on educational statistics administered by the OECD in 2002 (for details see Annex 3).

in a given OECD country as that bought by the US dollar in the United States. The PPP exchange rate is used because the market exchange rate is affected by many factors (interest rates, trade policies, expectations of economic growth, etc.) that have little to do with current relative domestic purchasing power in different OECD countries. (Annex 2 gives further details.)

Data for the financial year 1995 are based on a special survey carried out among OECD countries in 2000 and updated in 2002.

Charts B1.6 and B1.7 show expenditure on education per student in the financial year 1995. The data on expenditure for 1995 were obtained by a special survey conducted in 2000 and updated in 2002. OECD countries were asked to collect the 1995 data according to the definitions and the coverage of the UOE 2002 data collection. All expenditure data, as well as the GDP for 1995, are adjusted to 2000 prices using the GDP price deflator.

Expenditure on education per student relative to GDP per capita is calculated by expressing expenditure on education per student in units of national currency as a percentage of GDP per capita, also in national currency. In cases where the educational expenditure data and the GDP data pertain to different reference periods, the expenditure data are adjusted to the same reference period as the GDP data, using inflation rates for the OECD country in question (see Annex 2).

Expected expenditure over the average duration of tertiary studies (Table B1.3) is calculated by multiplying current annual expenditure by the typical duration of tertiary studies. The methodology used for the estimation of the typical duration of tertiary studies is described in Annex 3 at *www.oecd.org/edu/eag2003*. For the estimation of the duration of tertiary education, data are based on a special survey carried out in OECD countries in 1997 and 2000.

The ranking of OECD countries by annual expenditure on education per student on educational services is affected by differences in how countries define full-time, part-time and full-time equivalent enrolment. Some OECD countries count every participant at the tertiary level as a full-time student while others determine a student's intensity of participation by the credits which he or she obtains for successful completion of specific course units during a specified reference period. OECD countries that can accurately account for part-time enrolment will have higher expenditure per full-time equivalent student than OECD countries that cannot differentiate between different modes of student attendance.

Note that data appearing in earlier editions of this publication may not always be comparable to data shown in the 2003 edition due to changes in definitions and coverage that were made as a result of the OECD expenditure comparability study (see Annex 3 at *www.oecd.org/edu/eag2003* for details on changes).

Table B1.1
Expenditure on educational institutions per student (2000)
Annual expenditure on educational institutions per student in equivalent US dollars converted using PPPs , by level of education, based on full-time equivalents

B1

	Pre-primary education (for children 3 years and older)	Primary education	Lower secondary education	Upper secondary education	All secondary education	Post-secondary non-tertiary education	Tertiary education — All tertiary education	Tertiary-type B education	Tertiary-type A and advanced research programmes	Expenditure from primary to tertiary education
	(1)	(2)	(3)	(4)	(5)	(6)	(7)	(8)	(9)	(10)
OECD COUNTRIES										
Australia	m	4 967	6 579	7 424	6 894	6694	12 854	7 260	14 044	6 904
Austria	5 471	6 560	8 934	8 165	8 578	10947	10 851	x(7)	x(7)	8 430
Belgium	3 282	4 310	x(5)	x(5)	6 889	x(5)	10 771	x(7)	x(7)	6 544
Canada	6 120	x(5)	x(5)	x(5)	5 947	x(8)	14 983	12 801	16 690	7 764
Czech Republic	2 435	1 827	3 134	3 360	3 239	1624	5 431	1 970	5 946	3 004
Denmark	4 255	7 074	7 222	8 164	7 726	x(4,7)	11 981	x(7)	x(7)	8 302
Finland	3 944	4 317	6 737	5 641	6 094	x(5)	8 244	4 208	8 426	6 003
France	4 119	4 486	7 076	8 334	7 636	6207	8 373	8 898	8 230	6 708
Germany	5 138	4 198	5 470	9 625	6 826	10148	10 898	5 728	11 754	6 849
Greece[1]	x(2)	3 318	x(5)	x(5)	3 859	1400	3 402	2 889	3 643	3 494
Hungary[1]	2 511	2 245	2 109	2 829	2 446	3223	7 024	3 474	7 098	2 956
Iceland[1]	m	5 854	6 705	6378	6 518	m	7 994	m	7 548	6 446
Ireland	2 863	3 385	4 625	4 655	4 638	4234	11 083	x(7)	x(7)	5 016
Italy[1]	5 771	5 973	7 089	7 308	7 218	m	8 065	4 114	8 136	6 928
Japan	3 376	5 507	5 904	6 615	6 266	x(4,7)	10 914	8 507	11 302	6 744
Korea	1 949	3 155	3 655	4 440	4 069	a	6 118	4 106	7 502	4 294
Luxembourg	m	m	m	m	m	m	m	m	m	m
Mexico	1 385	1 291	1 289	2 317	1 615	a	4 688	x(7)	x(7)	1 666
Netherlands	3 920	4 325	6 100	5 671	5 912	5006	11 934	6 890	12 004	6 125
New Zealand	m	m	m	m	m	m	m	m	m	m
Norway[1]	13 170	6 550	8 185	8 925	8 476	x(5)	13 353	x(7)	x(7)	8 333
Poland[1]	2 278	2 105	x(2)	1 790	m	x(4)	3 222	1 135	3 252	2 149
Portugal	2 237	3 672	5 151	5 563	5 349	a	4 766	x(7)	x(7)	4 552
Slovak Republic	1 644	1 308	1 558	2 488	1 927	x(4)	4 949	x(4)	4 949	2 028
Spain	3 370	3 941	x(5)	x(5)	5 185	x(5)	6 666	6 306	6 712	5 037
Sweden	3 343	6 336	6 238	6 411	6 339	4452	15 097	x(7)	x(7)	7 524
Switzerland[1]	3 114	6 631	8 012	11 622	9 780	7199	18 450	10 516	19 491	9 311
Turkey[1]	m	m	m	m	m	a	4 121	x(7)	x(7)	1 073
United Kingdom	6 677	3 877	x(5)	x(5)	5 991	x(5)	9 657	x(7)	x(7)	5 592
United States[2]	7 980	6 995	x(5)	x(5)	8 855	x(7)	20 358	x(7)	x(7)	10 240
Country mean	*4 137*	*4 381*	*5 575*	*6 063*	*5 957*	*4075*	*9 571*	*~*	*~*	*5 736*
OECD total	*4 477*	*4 470*	*~*	*~*	*5 501*	*~*	*11 109*	*~*	*~*	*6 361*
NON-OECD COUNTRIES										
Argentina	1 653	1 598	2 256	2 579	2 382	a	m	5 382	m	m
Brazil[1,3]	1 243	928	909	851	890	m	11 946	m	11 946	1 142
Chile	1 563	1 940	1 914	2 081	2 016	a	7 483	3 987	8 240	2 629
India[3]	56	268	429	707	540	m	1 831	4 917	1 668	446
Indonesia	85	137	370	494	416	a	1 799	x(7)	x(7)	331
Israel	3 369	4 351	x(5)	x(5)	5 518	4240	11 550	8 115	15 544	5 837
Jamaica[1]	m	m	1 244	1 483	1 327	3171	6 894	2 686	14 588	1 426
Malaysia[1]	491	1 235	x(5)	x(5)	2 238	8256	11 237	6 266	12 759	2 219
Paraguay	x(2)	722	x(5)	x(5)	1 256	m	4 012	2 109	4 969	1 031
Philippines[1]	93	573	581	613	587	m	1 589	x(7)	x(7)	645
Russian Federation[1]	1 297	x(5)	x(5)	x(5)	954	1439	892	763	960	968
Thailand	848	1 111	1 038	858	935	m	2 137	3 398	1 886	1 173
Tunisia[1]	m	2 280	x(2)	x(2)	x(2)	x(2)	m	m	m	1 220
Uruguay[1]	1 039	1 011	1 093	1 379	1 219	a	2 057	x(7)	x(7)	1 228
Zimbabwe	7	780	x(5)	x(5)	1 904		m	m	m	m

Note: x indicates that data are included in another column. The column reference is shown in brackets after "x". *e.g.*, x(2) means that data are included in column 2.
1. Public institutions only.
2. Public and independent private institutions only.
3. Year of reference 1999.
Source: OECD. See Annex 3 for notes (*www.oecd.org/edu/eag2003*).

B1

Table B1.2
Expenditure on educational institutions per student relative to GDP per capita (2000)
Expenditure on educational institutions per student relative to GDP per capita by level of education, based on full-time equivalents

	Pre-primary education (for children 3 years and older)	Primary education	Lower secondary education	Upper secondary education	All secondary education	Post-secondary non-tertiary education	Tertiary education			Expenditure from primary to tertiary education
							All tertiary education	Tertiary-type B education	Tertiary-type A and advanced research programmes	
	(1)	(2)	(3)	(4)	(5)	(6)	(7)	(8)	(9)	(10)
OECD COUNTRIES										
Australia	m	19	26	29	27	26	50	28	55	27
Austria	19	23	32	29	31	39	39	x(7)	x(7)	30
Belgium	12	16	x(5)	x(5)	26	x(5)	41	x(7)	x(7)	25
Canada	22	x(5)	x(5)	x(5)	21	x(8)	53	46	59	28
Czech Republic	18	13	23	24	23	12	39	14	43	22
Denmark	15	25	25	28	27	x(4,7)	42	x(7)	x(7)	29
Finland	16	17	27	22	24	x(5)	33	17	33	24
France	16	18	28	33	30	25	33	35	33	27
Germany	20	16	21	37	26	39	42	22	45	26
Greece[1]	x(2)	21	x(5)	x(5)	24	9	21	18	23	22
Hungary[1]	21	18	17	23	20	26	58	28	58	24
Iceland[1]	m	21	24	23	23	m	28	m	27	23
Ireland	10	12	16	16	16	15	39	x(7)	x(7)	18
Italy[1]	23	24	28	29	29	m	32	16	32	28
Japan	13	21	23	25	24	x(4,7)	42	33	43	26
Korea	13	21	24	29	27	a	40	27	49	28
Luxembourg	m	m	m	m	m	m	m	m	m	m
Mexico	15	14	14	25	18	a	51	x(7)	x(7)	18
Netherlands	14	16	22	21	22	18	44	25	44	22
New Zealand	m	m	m	m	m	m	m	m	m	m
Norway[1]	36	18	23	25	23	x(4)	37	x(7)	x(7)	23
Poland[1]	24	22	x(2)	19	m	x(4)	34	12	34	23
Portugal	13	22	31	33	32	a	28	x(7)	x(7)	27
Slovak Republic	15	12	14	22	17	x(4)	44	x(4)	44	18
Spain	17	20	x(5)	x(5)	26	x(5)	33	31	33	25
Sweden	13	24	24	25	24	17	58	x(7)	x(7)	29
Switzerland[1]	11	22	27	39	33	24	62	36	66	31
Turkey[1]	m	m	m	m	m	a	66	x(7)	x(7)	17
United Kingdom	27	16	x(5)	x(5)	24	x(5)	39	x(7)	x(7)	21
United States[2]	23	20	x(5)	x(5)	26	x(7)	59	x(7)	x(7)	30
Country mean	*17*	*19*	*23*	*26*	*25*	*17*	*42*	*26*	*42*	*25*
NON-OECD COUNTRIES										
Argentina	13	13	18	21	19	a	m	43	m	m
Brazil[1,3]	16	12	11	11	11	m	150	m	150	14
Chile	17	21	20	22	21	a	79	42	88	28
India[3]	2	10	15	25	19	x(7)	65	176	60	16
Indonesia	15	5	16	18	17	a	87	x(7)	x(7)	11
Israel	15	21	x(5)	x(5)	24	20	54	39	58	26
Jamaica[1]	m	m	34	40	36	86	187	73	397	39
Malaysia[1]	5	14	x(5)	x(5)	25	92	125	70	142	25
Paraguay	x(2)	16	x(5)	x(5)	28	m	91	48	112	23
Philippines[1]	2	15	15	16	15	m	41	x(7)	x(7)	17
Russian Federation[1]	15	x(5)	x(5)	x(5)	11	17	11	9	11	11
Thailand	14	19	17	14	16	m	36	57	32	20
Tunisia[1]	m	36	x(2)	x(2)	x(2)	x(2)	m	m	m	19
Uruguay[1]	12	11	12	15	13	a	23	x(7)	x(7)	14
Zimbabwe	n	30	x(5)	x(5)	73	m	m	m	m	m

Note: x indicates that data are included in another column. The column reference is shown in brackets after "x". *e.g.*, x(2) means that data are included in column 2.
1. Public institutions only.
2. Public and independent private institutions only.
3. Year of reference 1999.
Source: OECD. See Annex 3 for notes (*www.oecd.org/edu/eag2003*).

Table B1.3
Cumulative expenditure on educational institutions per student over the average duration of tertiary studies (2000)
Average duration of tertiary studies and expenditure on educational institutions over the average duration of studies
in equivalent US dollars converted using PPPs, by type of programme

	Method[1]	Average duration of tertiary studies (in years)			Cumulative expenditure per student over the average duration of tertiary studies		
		All tertiary education	Tertiary-type B education	Tertiary-type A and advanced research programmes	All tertiary education	Tertiary-type B education	Tertiary-type A and advanced research programmes
		(1)	(2)	(3)	(4)	(5)	(6)
Australia	CM	2.5	1.6	2.6	32 521	11 398	35 953
Austria	AF	6.2	2.5	7.3	66 948	x(4)	x(4)
Canada	CM	m	m	m	m	m	m
Denmark[2]	AF	4.2	2.1	4.4	50 199	x(4)	x(4)
Finland	CM	6.0	a	6.0	50 469	a	50 469
France[2]	AF	4.7	2.8	5.3	39 200	24 629	43 666
Germany	CM	4.9	2.4	6.0	52 962	13 976	70 639
Greece[3]	AF	5.2	3.0	7.3	17 723	8 753	26 633
Hungary[3]	CM	4.1	2.0	4.1	28 448	6 949	28 748
Iceland[3]	CM	2.7	2.0	2.8	21 424	m	21 435
Ireland	CM	3.2	2.2	4.0	35 909	x(4)	x(4)
Italy[3]	CM	5.5	3.3	5.6	44 278	13 453	45 319
Korea[2]	CM	3.4	2.1	4.2	20 985	8 500	31 660
Mexico[2]	AF	3.4	x(3)	3.4	16 044	x(4)	x(4)
Netherlands[2]	CM	3.9	x(1)	x(1)	46 543	x(4)	x(4)
Norway	CM	m	m	m	m	m	m
Poland[3]	CM	m	m	3.7	m	m	11 966
Spain[2]	AF	4.6	1.5	4.7	30 330	9 390	31 593
Sweden	CM	4.6	2.6	4.7	69 561	x(4)	x(4)
Switzerland[2,3]	CM	3.6	2.2	5.5	66 867	22 997	10 6282
United Kingdom	CM	3.5	x(1)	x(1)	34 202	x(4)	x(4)
Country mean		*4.3*	*2.1*	*4.8*	*40 371*		

Note: x indicates that data are included in another column. The column reference is shown in brackets after "x". *e.g.*, x(2) means that data are included in column 2.
1. Either the Chain Method (CM) or an Approximation Formula (AF) was used to estimate the duration of tertiary studies.
2. The duration of tertiary studies is obtained by a special survey conducted in 1997 for the academic year 1995.
3. Public institutions only.
Source: OECD. See Annex 3 for notes *(www.oecd.org/edu/eag2003).*

INDICATOR B2: EXPENDITURE ON EDUCATIONAL INSTITUTIONS RELATIVE TO GROSS DOMESTIC PRODUCT

• OECD countries spend 5.9 per cent of their collective GDP on their educational institutions.

• In 14 out of 19 OECD countries, public and private spending on educational institutions increased between 1995 and 2000 by more than 5 per cent but, in contrast to the early 1990s, increases in spending on educational institutions tended to fall behind the growth in national income.

• Two-thirds of expenditure on educational institutions, or 3.6 per cent of combined OECD GDP, is devoted to primary, secondary and post-secondary non-tertiary education, although Canada, Korea and the United States spend more than 2 per cent of their GDP on tertiary education.

Chart B2.1

Expenditure on educational institutions as a percentage of GDP (1995, 2000)
Direct and indirect expenditure on educational institutions from public and private sources, by level of education, source of funds and year

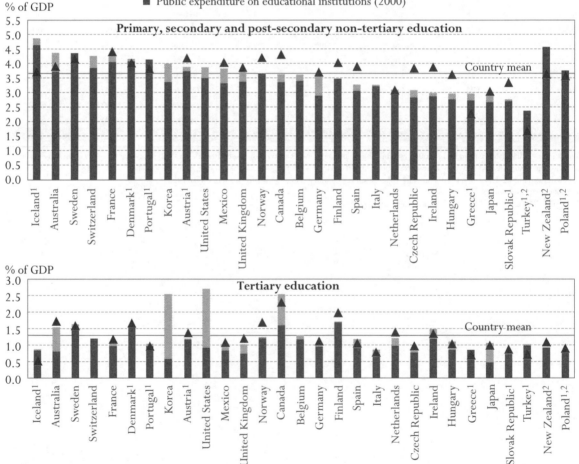

1. Public subsidies included in private expenditure.
2. Private expenditure on educational institutions are missing.
Countries are ranked in descending order of total expenditure on educational institutions from both public and private sources in primary, secondary and post-secondary non-tertiary education. Countries presenting public expenditure only are ranked separately.
Source: OECD. Table B2.1b. See Annex 3 for notes *(www.oecd.org/edu/eag2003).*

Policy context

Expenditure on education is an investment that can help to foster economic growth, enhance productivity, contribute to personal and social development, and reduce social inequality. The proportion of total financial resources devoted to education is one of the key choices made in each OECD country; and is an aggregate choice made by governments, enterprises, and individual students and their families. If the social and private returns on that investment are sufficiently large, there is an incentive for enrolment to expand and total investment to increase.

In appraising how much is spent on education, governments have to assess demands for increased spending in areas such as teachers' salaries and educational facilities. This indicator can provide a point of reference for this as it shows how the volume of educational spending, relative to the size of national wealth and in absolute terms, has evolved over time in various OECD countries.

This indicator provides a measure of the relative proportion of a nation's wealth that is invested in educational institutions.

It also includes a comparative review of changes in educational investment over time.

B2

Evidence and explanations

What this indicator covers and what it does not cover

This indicator covers expenditure on schools, universities and other public and private institutions involved in delivering or supporting educational services. Expenditure on institutions is not limited to expenditure on instructional services but also includes public and private expenditure on ancillary services for students and families, where these services are provided through educational institutions. At the tertiary level, spending on research and development can also be significant and is included in this indicator, to the extent that the research is performed by educational institutions.

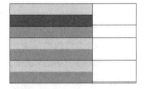

Coverage diagram (see page 181 for explanations)

Not all spending on educational goods and services occurs within educational institutions. For example, families may purchase textbooks and materials commercially or seek private tutoring for their children outside educational institutions. At the tertiary level, student living costs and forgone earnings can also account for a significant proportion of the costs of education. All such expenditure outside educational institutions is excluded from this indicator, even if it is publicly subsidised. Public subsidies for educational expenditure outside institutions are discussed in Indicators B4 and B5.

Overall investment relative to GDP

All OECD countries invest a substantial proportion of national resources in education. Taking into account both public and private sources of funds, OECD countries as a whole spend 5.9 per cent of their collective GDP on their educational institutions at primary, secondary and tertiary levels. Under current conditions of tight constraints on public budgets, such a large spending item is subject to close scrutiny by governments looking for ways to reduce or limit the growth of expenditure.

As a whole, OECD countries spend 5.9 per cent of their combined GDP on their educational institutions.

The highest spending on educational institutions can be observed in Korea and the United States, with around 7.0 per cent of GDP accounted for by public and private spending on educational institutions, followed by Canada, Denmark,

Iceland and Sweden with more than 6.2 per cent. Nine out of 29 OECD countries, however, spend less than 5 per cent of GDP on educational institutions, and in Greece, the Slovak Republic and Turkey this figure is only between 3.4 and 4.2 per cent (Table B2.1a).

The national resources devoted to education depend on a number of inter-related factors of supply and demand.

Many factors influence the relative position of OECD countries on this indicator. For example, OECD countries with high spending levels may be enrolling larger numbers of students, while countries with low spending levels may either be limiting access to higher levels of education or delivering educational services in a particularly efficient manner. The distribution of enrolments between sectors and fields of study may also differ, as may the duration of studies and the scale and organisation of related educational research. Finally, large differences in GDP between OECD countries imply that similar percentages of GDP spent on education can translate into very different absolute amounts per student (see Indicator B1).

Changes in overall educational spending between 1995 and 2000

In 14 out of 19 OECD countries, public and private spending on educational institutions increased between 1995 and 2000 by more than 5 per cent…

In 14 out of the 19 OECD countries for which comparable trend data are available, public and private investment in education increased by 5 per cent or more between 1995 and 2000 in real terms. Increases in expenditure on educational institutions amounted to between 20 and 38 per cent in Australia, Denmark, Ireland, Mexico, Portugal and Sweden and to over 40 per cent in Greece. The trend is similar when public investment is considered separately: direct public expenditure on institutions and public subsidies to households designated for institutions rose by 5 per cent or more in 20 out of 25 OECD countries between 1995 and 2000. New Zealand and Turkey, for which no data on private spending are available, show considerable growth in public spending on educational institutions (Table B2.2).

…but increases in spending on education tended to fall behind the growth in national income.

Spending on educational institutions increased between 1995 and 2000 in real terms but tended to lag behind growth in GDP. Around two-thirds of OECD countries showed a decrease in the proportion of GDP devoted to educational institutions. Most notable are the Czech Republic, Finland, Ireland, Norway and the Slovak Republic where the proportion of GDP spent on education decreased by more than 0.7 percentage points (Table B2.1a).

While the strong growth of GDP in Ireland hides significant increases in spending on educational institutions when spending on education is considered as a proportion of GDP, education in the Czech Republic and the Slovak Republic did not benefit significantly from growth in GDP. Both countries were already among the OECD countries spending a lower proportion of GDP on education in 1995 and have now fallen further behind (Table B2.1a).

Expenditure on educational institutions by level of education

Countries differ markedly in their

High overall spending on education does not necessarily translate into a high level of spending at all levels of education. Differences in spending on educational institutions are most striking at the pre-primary level of education. Here, spending ranges from less than 0.2 per cent of GDP in Australia, Ireland, Korea, Japan and New Zealand, to 0.7 per cent or more in Denmark, France, Hungary and Norway (Table B2.1c). Differences at the pre-primary level can be explained mainly by participation rates among younger children (see Indicator C1).

investment in pre-primary educational institutions.

Investing in early childhood education is of key importance in order to build a strong foundation for lifelong learning and to ensure equitable access to learning opportunities later in school. However, high-quality early childhood education and care are not only provided by the educational institutions covered by this indicator. Inferences on access to and quality of early childhood education and care should therefore be made with caution.

B2

Because of the largely universal enrolment at the primary and lower secondary levels of education in OECD countries, and the high participation rates in upper secondary education (see Indicators C1 and C2), these levels account for the bulk of expenditure on educational institutions, namely 3.6 per cent of the combined OECD GDP (Chart B2.1). At the same time, significantly higher spending on education per student at the upper secondary and tertiary levels of education causes the overall investment in these levels to be higher than enrolment numbers alone would suggest. One-quarter of combined OECD expenditure on educational institutions is accounted for by tertiary education.

Two-thirds of expenditure on educational institutions is devoted to primary, secondary and post-secondary non-tertiary education.

Canada, Korea and the United States spend 2.6 and 2.7 per cent, respectively, of their GDP on tertiary institutions (Chart B2.1). This accounts for more than one-third of all of their expenditure on educational institutions. Denmark, Finland and Sweden also show high spending levels, with 1.6 per cent or more of GDP devoted to tertiary institutions. On the other hand, France, Portugal and Switzerland spend slightly below the average proportion of GDP on tertiary institutions but are among the OECD countries with the highest proportion of GDP spent on primary, secondary and post-secondary non-tertiary education. In Switzerland, nevertheless, a moderate proportion of GDP spent on tertiary institutions translates into one of the highest levels of spending per tertiary student, because of a comparatively low tertiary enrolment rate and a high level of GDP (Tables B2.1b and B1.3).

Canada, Korea and the United States spend more than 2 per cent of their GDP on tertiary education.

Countries vary in the levels of education at which spending has increased. Austria, Finland, France, Germany, Greece, Mexico, Portugal, Sweden and Turkey, OECD countries with a comparably high increase in absolute spending on educational institutions between 1995 and 2000, invested the additional resources in similar proportions in primary, secondary and post-secondary non-tertiary and tertiary education (Chart B2.2). Australia, Denmark, the Netherlands, New Zealand, Poland and the United Kingdom invested most of the increases made between 1995 and 2000 into primary, secondary and post-secondary non-tertiary education. Conversely, in Canada, Hungary, Ireland, Italy, Japan, the Slovak Republic, Spain, and Switzerland spending on tertiary

While some OECD countries have increased spending at all levels of education, others have focused spending increases on specific levels.

Chart B2.2

Changes in total expenditure on educational institutions and in national income (1995, 2000)
*Index of change between 1995 and 2000 in total expenditure on educational institutions
from public and private sources and in national income (1995=100, 2000 constant prices)*

■ Change in total expenditure on educational institutions ■ Change in GDP

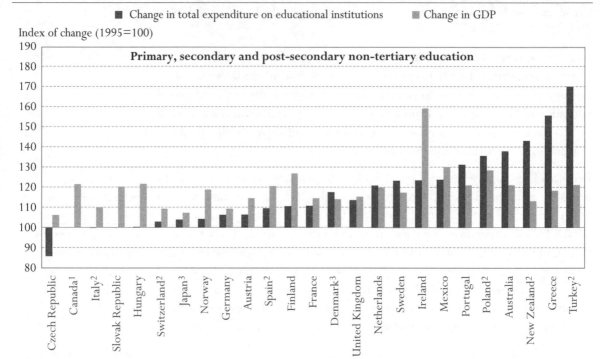

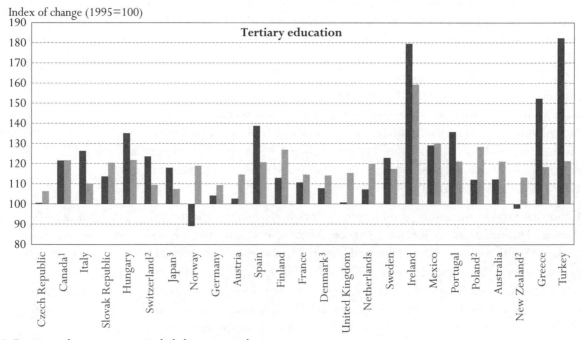

1. Post-secondary non-tertiary included in tertiary education.
2. Public expenditure only.
3. Post-secondary non-tertiary included in both upper secondary and tertiary education.
Countries are ranked in ascending order of change in total expenditure on educational institutions in primary, secondary and post-secondary non-tertiary education between 1995 and 2000.
Source: OECD. Table B2.2 and Annex 2. See Annex 3 for notes *(www.oecd.org/edu/eag2003).*

education increased by more than 10 per cent between 1995 and 2000 while spending on lower levels increased much more slowly (Chart B2.2).

Important factors influencing national expenditure on education

The national resources devoted to education depend on a number of inter-related factors of supply and demand, such as the demographic structure of the population, enrolment rates, income per capita, national levels of teachers' salaries and the organisation and delivery of instruction.

The size of the school-age population in a particular country (see Indicator A1 in the 2001 edition of *Education at a Glance*) shapes the potential demand for initial education and training. The larger the number of young people, the greater the potential demand for educational services. Among OECD countries of comparable national income, a country with a relatively large youth population will have to spend a higher percentage of its GDP on education so that each young person in that country has the opportunity to receive the same quantity of education as young people in other OECD countries. Conversely, if the youth population is relatively small, the same country will be required to spend less of its wealth on education in order to achieve similar results.

The larger the number of young people, the greater the potential demand for educational services.

Although OECD countries generally have little control over the size of their youth populations, the proportion of students participating at various levels of education is indeed a central policy issue. Variations in enrolment rates between OECD countries reflect differences in the demand for education, from pre-primary to tertiary education, as well as the supply of programmes at all levels. Indicator C1 shows that the number of years that a five-year-old child can expect to spend in education ranges among OECD countries from ten to 21. The variation in expected years in tertiary education is even wider, from one year in Mexico to over four years in Finland.

The higher the enrolment rate, the more financial resources will be required.

Definitions and methodologies

Expenditure on educational institutions, as covered by this indicator, includes expenditure on instructional educational institutions as well as expenditure on non-instructional educational institutions. *Instructional educational institutions* are educational institutions which directly provide instructional programmes (*i.e.,* teaching) to individuals in an organised group setting or through distance education. Business enterprises or other institutions providing short-term courses of training or instruction to individuals on a "one-to-one" basis are not included. *Non-instructional educational institutions* provide administrative, advisory or professional services to other educational institutions, although they do not enrol students themselves. Examples include national, state, and provincial ministries or departments of education; other bodies that administer education at various levels of government or analogous bodies in the private sector; and organisations that provide such education-related services as vocational or psychological counselling, placement, testing, financial aid to students, curriculum development, educational research, building operations and maintenance services, transportation of students, and student meals and housing.

Data refer to the financial year 2000 and are based on the UOE data collection on educational statistics administered by the OECD in 2002 (for details see Annex 3).

This broad definition of institutions ensures that expenditure on services, which are provided in some OECD countries by schools and universities and in others by agencies other than schools, are covered on a comparable basis.

The distinction by source of funds is based on the initial source of funds and does not reflect subsequent public-to-private or private-to-public transfers. For this reason, subsidies to households and other entities, such as subsidies for tuition fees and other payments to educational institutions, are included in public expenditure in this indicator. Payments from households and other private entities to educational institutions include tuition and other fees, net of offsetting public subsidies. A detailed discussion of public subsidies can be found in Indicator B5.

Data for the financial year 1995 are based on a special survey carried out among OECD countries.

Tables B2.1a, B2.1b and B2.2 show expenditure on educational institutions for the financial year 1995. The data on expenditure for 1995 were obtained by a special survey in 2000 and updated in 2002 in which expenditure for 1995 was adjusted to methods and definitions used in the 2002 UOE data collection.

Data for 1995 are expressed in 2000 price levels.

Chart B2.2 and Table B2.2 present an index of change in expenditure on institutions and GDP between 1995 and 2000. All expenditure, as well as 1995 GDP, is adjusted to 2000 prices using the GDP deflator.

For comparisons over time, the country mean accounts only for those OECD countries for which data are available for all reported reference years.

Note that data appearing in earlier editions of this publication may not always be comparable to data shown in the 2002 edition due to changes in definitions and coverage that were made as a result of the OECD expenditure comparability study (see Annex 3 at *www.oecd.org/edu/eag2003* for details on changes).

Table B2.1a
Expenditure on educational institutions as a percentage of GDP (1995, 2000)
Expenditure on educational institutions from public and private sources for all levels of education, by source of funds and year

B2

| | | 2000 | | | 1995 | |
	Public[1]	Private[2]	Total	Public[1]	Private[2]	Total
Australia	4.6	1.4	6.0	4.6	1.0	5.6
Austria[3]	5.4	0.3	5.7	5.9	0.3	6.3
Belgium	5.1	0.4	5.5	m	m	m
Canada	5.2	1.2	6.4	6.2	0.8	7.0
Czech Republic	4.2	0.5	4.6	4.9	0.5	5.4
Denmark[3]	6.4	0.3	6.7	6.1	0.2	6.3
Finland	5.5	0.1	5.6	6.3	x	6.3
France	5.7	0.4	6.1	5.9	0.4	6.3
Germany	4.3	1.0	5.3	4.5	1.0	5.5
Greece[3]	3.7	0.2	4.0	2.9	n	3.0
Hungary	4.4	0.6	5.0	4.9	0.6	5.5
Iceland[1]	5.7	0.6	6.3	4.5	0.6	5.1
Ireland	4.1	0.4	4.6	4.7	0.5	5.3
Italy	4.5	0.4	4.9	4.8	m	m
Japan	3.5	1.2	4.6	3.5	1.1	4.7
Korea	4.3	2.8	7.1	m	m	m
Luxembourg	m	m	m	m	m	m
Mexico	4.7	0.8	5.5	4.6	1.0	5.6
Netherlands	4.3	0.4	4.7	4.6	m	4.8
New Zealand	5.8	m	5.8	4.8	m	4.8
Norway	5.8	0.1	5.9	7.0	0.2	7.1
Poland[3]	5.2	m	5.2	5.5	m	5.5
Portugal[3]	5.6	0.1	5.7	5.3	n	5.3
Slovak Republic[3]	4.0	0.2	4.2	4.6	0.4	5.1
Spain	4.3	0.6	4.9	4.6	1.0	5.5
Sweden	6.3	0.2	6.5	6.3	0.1	6.4
Switzerland	5.3	0.4	5.7	5.4	m	m
Turkey[3]	3.4	n	3.4	2.3	n	2.3
United Kingdom	4.5	0.7	5.3	4.6	0.9	5.5
United States	4.8	2.2	7.0	m	m	m
Country mean	*4.8*	*0.6*	*5.5*			
OECD total	*4.6*	*1.3*	*5.9*			
Country mean for countries with 1990, 1995 AND 2000 data (24 countries)	*5.0*	*0.5*	*5.6*	*5.1*	*0.5*	*5.7*
Argentina[3]	4.5	1.4	5.9	m	m	m
Brazil[3,4]	4.2	m	m	m	m	m
Chile	4.2	3.3	7.4	m	m	m
India[4]	4.1	0.2	4.2	m	m	m
Indonesia[3,5]	1.5	0.8	2.3	m	m	m
Israel	6.6	1.6	8.2	6.9	1.5	8.5
Jamaica	6.4	3.3	9.7	m	m	m
Malaysia[3]	5.9	n	5.9	m	m	m
Paraguay	5.0	2.2	7.2	m	m	m
Philippines[4]	3.9	2.5	6.4	m	m	m
Russian Federation[3]	3.0	m	m	m	m	m
Thailand[3]	4.9	0.2	5.1	m	m	m
Tunisia[3]	7.7	m	m	m	m	m
Uruguay[3,5]	2.8	0.1	3.0	m	m	m
Zimbabwe[3]	7.6	m	m	m	m	m

OECD COUNTRIES

NON-OECD COUNTRIES

1. Including public subsidies to households attributable for educational institutions. Including direct expenditure on educational institutions from international sources.
2. Net of public subsidies attributable for educational institutions.
3. Public subsidies to households not included in public expenditure, but in private expenditure.
4. Year of reference 1999.
5. Direct expenditure on educational institutions from international sources exceeds 1.5 per cent of all public expenditure.
Source: OECD. See Annex 3 for notes (*www.oecd.org/edu/eag2003*).

Table B2.1b
Expenditure on educational institutions as a percentage of GDP (1995, 2000)
Expenditure on educational institutions from public and private sources, by level of education, source of funds and year

	Primary, secondary and post-secondary non-tertiary education				Tertiary education			
	2000			1995	2000			1995
	Public [1]	Private [2]	Total	Total	Public [1]	Private [2]	Total	Total
OECD COUNTRIES								
Australia	3.7	0.7	4.4	3.9	0.8	0.7	1.6	1.7
Austria[3]	3.7	0.2	3.9	4.2	1.2	n	1.2	1.3
Belgium[4]	3.4	0.2	3.6	m	1.2	0.1	1.3	m
Canada[5]	3.3	0.3	3.6	4.3	1.6	1.0	2.6	2.3
Czech Republic[4]	2.8	0.3	3.1	3.8	0.8	0.1	0.9	1.0
Denmark[3,6]	4.1	0.1	4.2	4.0	1.5	n	1.6	1.6
Finland	3.5	n	3.5	4.0	1.7	n	1.7	1.9
France	4.0	0.2	4.3	4.4	1.0	0.1	1.1	1.1
Germany	2.9	0.7	3.6	3.7	1.0	0.1	1.0	1.1
Greece[3]	2.7	0.2	3.0	2.3	0.9	n	0.9	0.7
Hungary	2.8	0.2	3.0	3.6	0.9	0.3	1.1	1.0
Iceland[3]	4.6	0.2	4.9	3.7	0.8	n	0.9	0.5
Ireland[4]	2.9	0.1	3.0	3.9	1.2	0.3	1.5	1.3
Italy	3.2	0.1	3.3	m	0.7	0.1	0.9	0.8
Japan[6]	2.7	0.2	2.9	3.0	0.5	0.6	1.1	1.0
Korea	3.3	0.7	4.0	m	0.6	1.9	2.6	m
Luxembourg	m	m	m	m	m	m	m	m
Mexico	3.3	0.5	3.8	4.0	0.8	0.2	1.1	1.1
Netherlands	3.0	0.1	3.1	3.1	1.0	0.2	1.2	1.4
New Zealand	4.6	m	4.6	3.6	0.9	m	0.9	1.1
Norway	3.6	n	3.7	4.2	1.2	n	1.3	1.7
Poland[3]	3.7	m	3.7	3.6	0.8	m	0.8	0.9
Portugal[3]	4.1	n	4.1	3.8	1.0	0.1	1.1	0.9
Slovak Republic[3,4]	2.7	0.1	2.8	3.3	0.7	0.1	0.8	0.8
Spain	3.1	0.2	3.3	3.9	0.9	0.3	1.2	1.0
Sweden[4]	4.4	n	4.4	4.1	1.5	0.2	1.7	1.6
Switzerland	3.8	0.4	4.3	m	1.2	m	1.2	m
Turkey[3]	2.4	m	2.4	1.7	1.0	n	1.0	0.7
United Kingdom	3.4	0.4	3.8	3.9	0.7	0.3	1.0	1.2
United States[5]	3.5	0.4	3.9	m	0.9	1.8	2.7	m
Country mean	*3.4*	*0.3*	*3.6*		*1.0*	*0.3*	*1.3*	
OECD total	*3.3*	*0.4*	*3.6*		*0.9*	*0.9*	*1.7*	
Country mean *for countries with 1995 data only*			*3.6*	*3.7*			*1.2*	*1.2*
NON-OECD COUNTRIES								
Argentina[3]	3.2	0.4	3.7	m	0.8	0.4	1.2	m
Brazil[3,7]	3.0	m	m	m	0.8	m	m	m
Chile	3.2	1.4	4.6	m	0.6	1.7	2.3	m
India[6,7]	2.8	0.2	3.0	m	0.7	n	0.7	m
Indonesia[3,4]	1.1	0.3	1.5	m	0.4	0.4	0.8	m
Israel	4.5	0.2	4.7	5.0	1.1	0.8	1.9	1.9
Jamaica	4.8	2.6	7.4	m	1.3	0.5	1.8	m
Malaysia[3]	4.0	n	m	m	1.7	m	m	m
Paraguay	4.1	1.6	5.7	m	0.9	0.5	1.4	m
Philippines	3.3	1.5	4.8	m	0.5	1.0	1.5	m
Russian Federation	1.7	m	m	m	0.5	m	m	m
Thailand[3]	2.8	0.1	2.9	m	0.7	0.2	0.9	m
Tunisia[3]	5.2	m	m	m	m	m	m	m
Uruguay[3,4]	2.0	0.1	2.1	m	0.6	n	0.6	m
Zimbabwe[6]	7.6	m	m	m	m	m	m	m

1. Including public subsidies to households attributable for educational institutions. Including direct expenditure on educational institutions from international sources.
2. Net of public subsidies attributable for educational institutions.
3. Public subsides to households not included in public expenditure, but in private expenditure.
4. Direct expenditure on tertiary-level educational institutions from international sources exceeds 1.5 per cent of all public expenditure.
   International sources at primary and secondary level exceed 1.5 per cent in Uruguay.
5. Post-secondary non-tertiary included in tertiary education.
6. Post-secondary non-tertiary included in both upper secondary and tertiary education.
7. Year of reference 1999.
Source: OECD. See Annex 3 for notes (www.oecd.org/edu/eag2003).

B2

Table B2.1c
Expenditure on educational institutions as a percentage of GDP (2000)
Expenditure on educational institutions from public and private sources[1], by level of education

| | Pre-primary education (for children 3 years and older) | Primary, secondary and post-secondary non-tertiary education | | | | Tertiary education | | | All levels of education combined (including undistributed and advanced research pro-grammes) |
		All primary, secondary and post-secondary non-tertiary education	Primary and lower secondary education	Upper secondary education	Post-secondary non-tertiary education	All tertiary education	Tertiary-type B education	Tertiary-type A education	
	(1)	(2)	(3)	(4)	(5)	(6)	(7)	(8)	(9)
Australia	0.1	4.4	3.3	0.9	0.1	1.6	0.2	1.4	6.0
Austria	0.5	3.9	2.6	1.2	0.1	1.2	0.2	1.0	5.7
Belgium[2]	0.5	3.6	1.2	2.4	x(4)	1.3	x(6)	x(6)	5.5
Canada	0.2	3.6	x(2)	x(2)	x(7)	2.6	1.1	1.4	6.4
Czech Republic	0.5	3.1	2.0	1.1	n	0.9	n	0.9	4.6
Denmark	0.8	4.2	2.8	1.4	x(4,6)	1.6	x(6)	x(6)	6.7
Finland	0.4	3.5	2.3	1.2	x(4)	1.7	n	1.7	5.6
France	0.7	4.3	2.8	1.5	n	1.1	0.3	0.9	6.1
Germany	0.6	3.6	2.1	1.2	0.2	1.0	0.1	1.0	5.3
Greece[2]	x(2)	3.0	1.1	1.7	0.1	0.9	0.2	0.6	4.0
Hungary	0.7	3.0	1.8	1.1	0.1	1.1	n	1.1	5.0
Iceland[2]	m	4.9	m	m	m	0.9	0.1	0.8	6.3
Ireland	n	3.0	2.2	0.6	0.1	1.5	x(6)	x(6)	4.6
Italy	0.5	3.3	2.0	1.3	n	0.9	n	0.9	4.9
Japan	0.2	2.9	2.0	0.9	x(4,6)	1.1	0.1	1.0	4.6
Korea	0.1	4.0	2.7	1.3	a	2.6	0.7	1.9	7.1
Luxembourg	m	m	m	m	m	m	m	m	m
Mexico	0.5	3.8	3.1	0.8	a	1.1	x(6)	x(6)	5.5
Netherlands	0.3	3.1	2.3	0.8	n	1.2	n	1.2	4.7
New Zealand[3]	0.2	4.6	3.2	1.3	0.1	0.9	0.2	0.8	5.8
Norway	0.7	3.7	2.5	1.2	x(4)	1.3	n	1.3	5.9
Poland[3]	0.5	3.7	2.5	1.3	m	0.8	n	0.8	5.2
Portugal	0.3	4.1	2.9	1.2	a	1.1	x(6)	x(6)	5.7
Slovak Republic	0.4	2.8	1.7	1.1	x(4)	0.8	x(4)	0.8	4.2
Spain[2]	0.5	3.3	1.2	2.0	x(4)	1.2	0.1	1.1	4.9
Sweden	0.5	4.4	3.0	1.3	n	1.7	x(6)	x(6)	6.5
Switzerland	0.2	4.3	2.7	1.5	0.1	1.2	0.1	1.1	5.7
Turkey	m	2.4	1.7	0.7	a	1.0	x(8)	1.0	3.4
United Kingdom[2]	0.4	3.8	1.2	2.5	x(4)	1.0	x(6)	x(6)	5.3
United States	0.4	3.9	x(2)	x(2)	x(6)	2.7	x(6)	x(6)	7.0
Country mean	*0.4*	*3.6*	*2.2*	*1.3*	*0.1*	*1.3*	*0.2*	*1.0*	*5.4*
OECD total	*0.4*	*3.6*	*2.1*	*1.3*	*0.1*	*1.7*	*x(6)*	*x(6)*	*5.9*
Argentina	0.4	3.7	2.9	0.8	a	1.2	0.5	0.7	5.9
Brazil[3,4]	0.4	3.0	2.5	0.5	m	0.8	m	0.8	4.2
Chile	0.5	4.6	3.3	1.3	a	2.3	0.2	2.1	7.4
India[4]	n	3.0	2.1	0.9	n	0.7	0.1	0.6	4.2
Indonesia	n	1.5	1.1	0.4	a	0.8	x(6)	x(6)	2.3
Israel	0.8	4.7	2.4	2.2	n	1.9	x(6)	x(6)	8.2
Jamaica	0.5	7.4	5.4	1.4	0.6	1.8	0.5	1.2	9.7
Malaysia[2]	0.1	4.0	1.7	2.1	0.2	1.7	0.3	1.4	5.9
Paraguay[2]	0.1	5.7	3.3	2.4	m	1.4	0.2	1.1	7.2
Philippines	n	4.8	4.6	0.2	0.1	1.5	x(6)	x(6)	6.4
Russian Federation	0.5	1.7	m	m	0.2	0.5	0.1	0.3	3.0
Thailand	0.6	2.9	2.3	0.6	m	0.9	0.2	0.6	5.1
Tunisia[3]	2.4	5.2	5.2	m	m	m	m	m	7.7
Uruguay	0.3	2.1	1.6	0.5	a	0.6	x(6)	x(6)	3.0
Zimbabwe	n	7.6	7.6	m	m	m	m	m	m

Note: x indicates that data are included in another column. The column reference is shown in brackets after "x". *e.g.*, x(2) means that data are included in column 2.
1. Including international sources.
2. Column 3 only refers to primary education and column 4 refers to all secondary education.
3. Including only direct public expenditure on educational institutions.
4. Year of reference 1999.
Source: OECD. See Annex 3 for notes *(www.oecd.org/edu/eag2003)*.

Table B2.2
Change in expenditure on educational institutions (1995, 2000)
Index of change between 1995 and 2000 in expenditure on educational institutions from public and private sources, by level of education (1995=100, 2000 constant prices)

	All levels of education			Primary, secondary and post-secondary non-tertiary education			Tertiary education		
	Public expenditure on educational institutions	Private expenditure on educational institutions	Total expenditure on educational institutions from both public and private sources	Public expenditure on educational institutions	Private expenditure on educational institutions	Total expenditure on educational institutions from both public and private sources	Public expenditure on educational institutions	Private expenditure on educational institutions	Total expenditure on educational institutions from both public and private sources
	(1)	(2)	(3)	(4)	(5)	(6)	(7)	(8)	(9)
Australia	125	154	131	137	146	138	89	155	112
Austria	106	92	105	106	114	106	103	96	103
Belgium	m	m	m	m	m	m	m	m	m
Canada[1]	107	116	109	99	120	100	126	114	121
Czech Republic	96	61	91	89	59	86	119	49	100
Denmark[2]	120	139	120	118	113	118	106	432	108
Finland	111	x(1)	113	110	x(4)	111	110	x(7)	113
France	111	103	111	111	104	111	112	101	111
Germany	104	106	105	106	107	106	102	119	104
Greece	155	x(1)	160	147	x(4)	156	160	x(7)	152
Hungary	110	118	111	101	88	100	129	160	135
Ireland	139	129	138	123	141	124	206	125	180
Italy	101	m	m	100	m	m	118	165	126
Japan[2]	108	109	108	104	104	104	126	112	118
Mexico	134	109	129	127	106	124	133	118	129
Netherlands	117	115	117	122	107	121	104	120	107
New Zealand	136	m	m	143	m	m	98	m	m
Norway	99	60	98	105	76	104	91	53	89
Poland	122	m	m	136	m	m	112	m	m
Portugal	129	289	130	131	208	131	130	292	136
Slovak Republic	105	43	100	105	34	100	120	67	114
Spain	115	m	m	110	m	m	139	139	139
Sweden	120	216	122	123	83	123	114	225	123
Switzerland	107	m	m	103	m	m	124	m	m
Turkey	175	m	m	174	m	m	180	275	182
United Kingdom	112	102	111	114	112	114	107	90	101
Israel	116	120	117	116	98	115	121	136	127

1. Post-secondary non-tertiary included in tertiary education.
2. Post-secondary non-tertiary included in both upper secondary and tertiary education.
Source: OECD. See Annex 3 for notes (*www.oecd.org/edu/eag2003*).

INDICATOR B3: RELATIVE PROPORTIONS OF PUBLIC AND PRIVATE INVESTMENT IN EDUCATIONAL INSTITUTIONS

- Education institutions are still mainly funded from public sources: just over 88 per cent of all funds for educational institutions comes directly from public sources. Private funding is however significant in Korea (where it represents 40 per cent of the total), the United States (approaching one third of the total), Australia and Japan (almost one quarter of the total).

- In a number of OECD countries, governments pay most of the costs of primary, secondary and post-secondary non-tertiary education but leave the management of educational institutions to the private sector, to provide a wider range of learning opportunities without creating barriers to the participation of students from low-income families.

- Tertiary institutions tend to mobilise a much higher proportion of their funds from private sources than primary, secondary and post-secondary non-tertiary institutions. The private share ranges from less than 3 per cent in Denmark, Finland and Greece to 77 per cent in Korea but includes private payments that are subsidised from public sources.

- Across the education levels the trend in the public/private share of education expenditure is a mixed one with shifts towards public spending as much in evidence as shifts towards private expenditure. In most cases where there have been shifts towards private expenditure this did not lead to a decrease in the real level of public-sector spending.

B3

Chart B3.1

Distribution of public and private expenditure on educational institutions, by level of education (2000)

■ Private expenditure on educational institutions, excluding public subsidies to households and other private entities
■ Total public subsidies to households and other private entities, excluding public subsidies for student living costs
■ Public expenditure on educational institutions

Pre-primary education

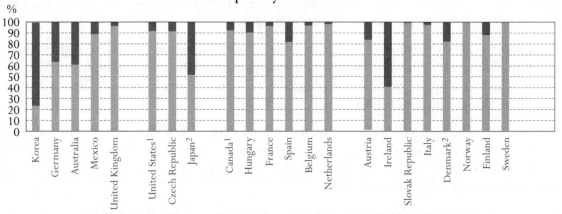

Primary, secondary and post-secondary non-tertiary education

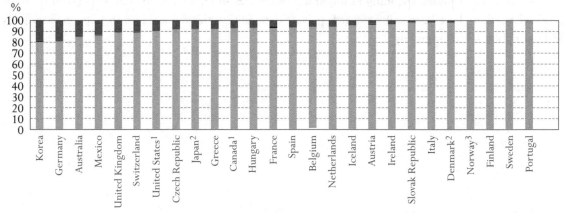

Tertiary education

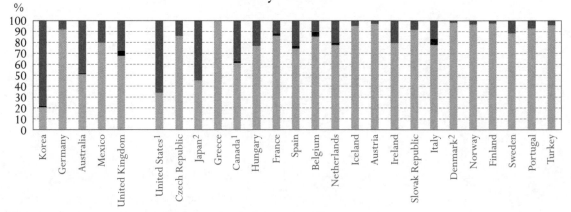

1. Post-secondary non-tertiary included in tertiary education.
2. Post-secondary non-tertiary included in both upper secondary and tertiary education.
3. Total public subsidies to households may be included in private payments.
Countries are ranked in ascending order of the proportion of direct public expenditure in primary, secondary and post-secondary non-tertiary education.
Source: OECD. Table B3.2. See Annex 3 for notes *(www.oecd.org/edu/eag2003).*

Policy context

Cost-sharing between participants in the education system and society as a whole is an issue that is under discussion in many OECD countries. This question is especially relevant at the beginning and ending stages of initial education – pre-primary and tertiary education – where full or nearly full public funding is less common. As well as illustrating the policy for cost-sharing in each country, it can shed light on the influence that public funding, as a policy lever, can and does have on the output of the system as a whole.

This indicator shows the relative proportions of public and private spending on educational institutions...

As new client groups participate increasingly in a wider range of educational programmes and have more opportunities made available by increasing numbers of providers, governments are forging new partnerships to mobilise the necessary resources to pay for education. New policies are designed to allow the different actors and stakeholders to participate more fully and to share costs and benefits more equitably.

...and how these proportions have changed since 1995.

B3

As a result, public funding is now seen increasingly as providing only a part, although a very important part, of investment in education. The role of private sources has become more important in the funding of education. Some stakeholders are concerned that this balance should not become so tilted as to lead potential learners away from learning, instead of towards it. Thus changes in a country's public/private funding share can provide important context to changing patterns and levels of participation within its educational system.

Evidence and explanations

What this indicator covers and what it does not cover

Governments can spend public funds directly on educational institutions or use them to provide subsidies to private entities for the purpose of education. When reporting on the public and private proportions of educational expenditure, it is therefore important to distinguish between the initial sources of funds and the final direct purchasers of educational goods and services.

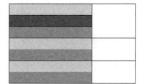

Coverage diagram (see page 181 for explanations)

Initial public spending includes both direct public expenditure on educational institutions and transfers to the private sector. To gauge the level of public expenditure, the components showing direct public expenditure on educational institutions and public subsidies for education therefore need to be added together. Initial private spending includes tuition fees and other student or household payments to educational institutions, less the portion of such payments offset by public subsidies.

The final public and private proportions are the percentages of educational funds spent directly by public and private purchasers of educational services. Final public spending includes direct public purchases of educational resources and payments to educational institutions and other private entities. Final private spending includes tuition fees and other private payments to educational institutions (whether offset or not by public subsidies).

Not all spending on instructional goods and services occurs within educational institutions. For example, families may purchase textbooks and materials commercially or seek private tutoring for their children outside educational institutions. At the tertiary level, student living costs and forgone earnings can also account for a significant proportion of the costs of education. All such expenditure outside educational institutions, even if they are publicly subsidised, are excluded from this indicator. Public subsidies for educational expenditure outside institutions are discussed in Indicators B4 and B5.

Public and private proportions of expenditure on educational institutions

Educational institutions are still mainly funded by public sources…

Schools, universities and other educational institutions are still mainly publicly funded, although there is a substantial and growing degree of private funding. On average across OECD countries, just over 88 per cent of all funds for educational institutions comes directly from public sources. In addition, 0.6 per cent is channelled to institutions via public subsidies to households (Table B3.1).

…but OECD countries vary significantly in the extent to which they draw on private funds.

Among the OECD countries reporting data, the proportion of private payments to educational institutions, including private payments that are subsidies varies widely. In Finland, Norway, Portugal, Sweden and Turkey it is 3 per cent or less, compared with almost one quarter in Australia and Japan, approaching one third in the United States and just over 40 per cent in Korea. (Table B3.1).

In most OECD countries, private expenditure is comprised mainly of household expenditure on tuition and other fees at tertiary institutions, while in Germany and Switzerland nearly all private expenditure is accounted for by contributions from the business sector to the dual system of apprenticeship at the upper secondary and post-secondary non-tertiary levels. In general the reporting of private expenditures on education is problematic and it is likely that some of the reported data are incomplete.

In pre-primary education, the private share of total payments to educational institutions represents on average 17 per cent.

Investment in early childhood education is of key importance in order to build a strong foundation for lifelong learning and to ensure equitable access to learning opportunities later in school. In pre-primary education, the private share of total payments to educational institutions is very variable. It ranges from 5 per cent or less in Belgium, France, Italy, the Netherlands, the Slovak Republic, and the United Kingdom, to well over a third in Australia and Germany, around 50 per cent in Japan, 60 per cent in Ireland and 75 per cent in Korea (Table B3.2).

Public funding dominates at the primary/secondary levels.

Public funding very much dominates primary, secondary and post-secondary non-tertiary levels of education in OECD countries: on average the rate of public funding amongst OECD countries is 93 per cent. There are, nevertheless, significant levels of private funding in some countries, most notably Australia (15 per cent), Germany (20 per cent), Korea (19 per cent), and Mexico (14 per cent) (Chart B3.1).

In some OECD countries, however, significant public funds are given to institutions in the private sector…

Although the vast majority of public funds are directed at public institutions, in a number of OECD countries, significant public funds are in fact transferred to private institutions or given directly to households to spend in the institution of their choice. In the former case, the final spending and delivery of education can be regarded as subcontracted by governments to non-governmental institutions, whereas in the latter instance, students and their families are left to decide which type of institution best meets their requirements.

On average across OECD countries at the primary/secondary level, 12 per cent of the public funds designated for educational institutions is spent in institutions that are privately managed (Table B3.3). In the Netherlands, where the central government is the major final source of funds, 71 per cent of public money for primary, secondary and post-secondary non-tertiary educational institutions is transferred from the government to private institutions and in Belgium it is over 50 per cent.

In Australia, France, Spain and the United Kingdom, the share of public funds transferred to private institutions ranges at the primary/secondary and post-secondary level of education ranges from 12 to 22 per cent.

Public funding transfers to private households (and other private entities) are generally not a significant feature at the primary/secondary level – on average across OECD countries, the proportion of public funds transferred is some 4 per cent and exceeds 10 per cent in only Denmark, Hungary and Sweden (Table B3.3).

Nevertheless, funding strategies such as these not only mobilise the required resources from a wider range of public and private sources, but also provide a broader range of learning opportunities and can improve the efficiency of schooling.

Other than in Austria, Germany and Greece, the private proportion of educational expenditure is far higher at the tertiary level than at the primary, secondary and post-secondary non-tertiary levels. While primary, secondary and post-secondary non-tertiary education are usually perceived as a public good with mainly public returns, at the tertiary level the high private returns in the form of better employment and income opportunities (see Indicators A3 and A13) suggest that a greater contribution by individuals to the costs of tertiary education may be justified, provided, of course, that governments can ensure that funding is accessible to students irrespective of their economic background (see also Indicator B5).

The proportion of expenditure on tertiary institutions covered by individuals, businesses and other private sources including private payments that are subsidies, ranges from less that 3 per cent in Denmark, Finland and Greece, to around one half in Australia and Japan, two-thirds in the United States and over three-quarters in Korea (Chart B3.1). In Korea, over 80 per cent of students are enrolled in private universities, where more than 95 per cent of budgets are derived from tuition fees.

It is more usual, however, for households/students to receive some transfers of public funding at the tertiary level than at other levels. So for instance on average, some 17 per cent of public funds at the tertiary level are transferred to households/students. This proportion is highest in New Zealand (46 per cent), Denmark (39 per cent), Australia (32 per cent), Sweden (30 per cent), Norway (29 per cent) and the Netherlands (27 per cent).

…thus seeking to provide a wider range of learning opportunities without creating barriers to the participation of students from low-income families.

B3

Tertiary institutions tend to mobilise a much higher proportion of their funds from private sources…

…but the private share, including private payments that are subsidies, ranges widely from less than 3 per cent in Denmark, Finland and Greece, to 77 per cent in Korea.

Public funding transfers to households/students are more prevalent at the tertiary level than at other levels.

The amounts paid by students and their families to cover tuition fees and other education-related expenditure differ between OECD countries according to taxation and spending policies, and the willingness of governments to support students. This willingness, in turn, is influenced by students' enrolment status (full-time or part-time), age and residency (whether they are living at home). To some extent, however, the guidelines used in establishing eligibility for these subsidies are breaking down. Mature students, whose numbers are increasing, are more likely to have established their own households and to prefer part-time or distance learning to full-time, on-campus study.

Changes in public and private investment in education

B₃

For education as a whole, the trend in the private share of education funding is a mixed one amongst countries.

A comparison between 1995 and 2000 of the proportion of educational expenditure which was met through private funds, shows that as many countries recorded increases as recorded decreases in the private funding share (Chart B3.2 and Table B3.1). In Australia, the private funding share increased from 20.6 per cent in 1995 to 24.3 per cent in 2000. On the other hand, in the Czech Republic, the Slovak Republic and Spain a decrease of around 5 percentage points in the private share of funding was recorded.

Six countries recorded slight shifts from public to private funding of primary, secondary and post-secondary non-tertiary education.

Six countries for whom comparable data are available recorded shifts from public to private funding of primary, secondary and post-secondary non-tertiary education. In only one of these countries, Canada, was the increase in the private share more than 1 percentage point (private share increasing from 6 per cent to 8 per cent).

Shifts of funding in the opposite direction, towards public funding, were equally evident, most notably in the Czech Republic, the Slovak Republic and Spain and where the public funding share of expenditure increased by between 4 and 6 percentage points (Chart B3.2 and Table B3.2).

At tertiary level there are also some striking changes which at least in part are a response to dramatic growth in participation.

In many OECD countries, the growth in tertiary participation (Indicator C2) represents a response to heavy demand, both individual and social. But, just as many tertiary structures and programmes were designed for a different era, so too were its funding mechanisms. As demand for tertiary education has increased in many OECD countries, so has the share of the financial burden borne by families for a number of countries such as Australia, Hungary, Sweden and Turkey.

In most OECD countries, shifts towards private expenditure have not led to decreases in real terms of public expenditure.

It is important to note that rises in private educational expenditure have not generally been accompanied by falls in real terms of public expenditure on education at the tertiary level or indeed at the primary, secondary and post-secondary non-tertiary level. On the contrary, public investment in education has increased in most of the OECD countries for which 1995 to 2000 data are available, regardless of changes in private spending (Table B2.2). In fact, some of the OECD countries with the highest growth in private spending have also shown the highest increase in public funding of education. This indicates that increasing private spending on tertiary education tends to complement, rather than replace, public investment. A notable exception to this is in Australia where

Share of private expenditure on educational institutions (1995, 2000)

■ Share of private expenditure (1995)   ■ Share of private expenditure (2000)

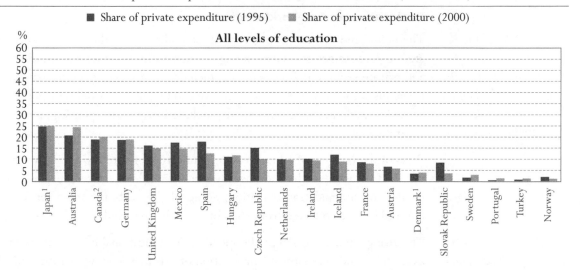

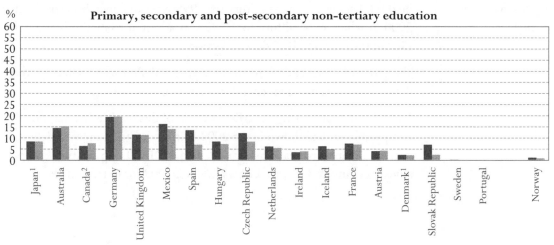

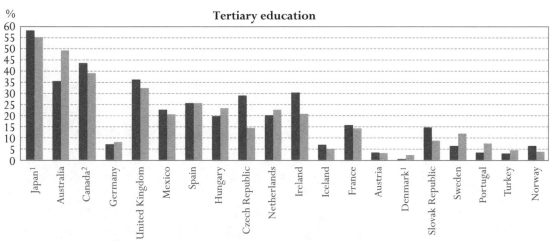

B3

1. Post-secondary non-tertiary included in both upper secondary and tertiary education.
2. Post-secondary non-tertiary included in tertiary education.
Countries are ranked in descending order of the share of private expenditure in 2000 for all levels of education.
Source: OECD. Tables B3.1 and B3.2. See Annex 3 for notes *(www.oecd.org/edu/eag2003)*.

the shift towards private expenditure at tertiary level has been accompanied by a fall in the level of public expenditure in real terms.

Definitions and methodologies

Data refer to the financial year 2000 and are based on the UOE data collection on educational statistics administered by the OECD in 2002 (for details see Annex 3).

The public and private proportions of expenditure on educational institutions are the percentages of total spending originating in, or generated by, the public and private sectors. Private spending includes all direct expenditure on educational institutions, whether partially covered by public subsidies or not. Public subsidies attributable to households, included in private spending, are shown separately.

Parts of the budgets of educational institutions are related to ancillary services offered to students, which are usually student welfare services, such as student meals, housing and transportation. Some of the costs for these services are covered by fees collected from students, which are included.

Data for the financial year 1995 are based on a special survey carried out among OECD countries in 2000.

The change in private and public spending on educational institutions is shown as an index and compares the proportion of private spending in 1995 with that in 2000. The data on expenditure for 1995 were obtained by a special survey in 2000 in which expenditure for 1995 was adjusted to methods and definitions used in the current UOE data collection.

The glossary at the end of this volume gives a definition of public, government-dependent private and independent private institutions.

Note that data appearing in earlier editions of this publication may not always be comparable to data shown in the 2002 edition due to changes in definitions and coverage that were made as a result of the OECD expenditure comparability study (see Annex 3 at *www.oecd.org/edu/eag2003* for details on changes).

Table B3.1

Relative proportions of public and private expenditure on educational institutions for all levels of education (1995, 2000)

Distribution of public and private sources of funds for educational institutions after transfers from public sources, by year

		2000			1995		
		Public sources	Private sources[1]	Private - *of which:* subsidised	Public sources	Private sources[1]	Private - *of which:* subsidised
OECD COUNTRIES	Australia	75.7	24.3	0.3	79.4	20.6	3.0
	Austria	94.2	5.8	2.3	93.4	6.6	1.5
	Belgium	92.1	7.9	1.1	m	m	m
	Canada	79.9	20.1	0.7	81.2	18.8	7.2
	Czech Republic	89.9	10.1	n	85.0	15.0	6.2
	Denmark	96.0	4.0	m	96.5	3.5	n
	Finland	98.0	2.0	n	m	m	m
	France	92.1	7.9	1.7	91.4	8.6	1.9
	Germany	81.1	18.9	a	81.4	18.6	a
	Greece	93.8	6.2	m	m	m	m
	Hungary	88.3	11.7	n	89.0	11.0	n
	Iceland	91.1	8.9	m	88.0	12.0	m
	Ireland	90.5	9.5	n	89.8	10.2	m
	Italy	90.9	9.1	1.3	m	m	m
	Japan	75.2	24.8	m	75.4	24.6	m
	Korea	59.2	40.8	1.0	m	m	m
	Luxembourg	m	m	m	m	m	m
	Mexico	85.3	14.7	0.5	82.6	17.4	m
	Netherlands	90.3	9.7	m	90.1	9.9	m
	New Zealand	m	m	m	m	m	m
	Norway	98.7	1.3	n	97.9	2.1	n
	Poland	m	m	a	m	m	m
	Portugal	98.6	1.4	m	99.4	0.6	m
	Slovak Republic	96.4	3.6	m	91.6	8.4	m
	Spain	87.4	12.6	0.6	82.1	17.9	0.4
	Sweden	97.0	3.0	a	98.3	1.7	m
	Switzerland	91.8	8.2	1.0	m	m	m
	Turkey	98.6	1.4	n	99.1	0.9	0.2
	United Kingdom	85.2	14.8	0.9	83.9	16.1	3.5
	United States	68.2	31.8	m	m	m	m
	Country mean	*88.4*	*11.6*	*0.6*			
NON-OECD COUNTRIES	Argentina	76.3	23.7	m	m	m	m
	Chile	53.8	46.2	2.2	m	m	m
	India[2]	95.5	4.5	m	m	m	m
	Indonesia	64.5	35.5	m	m	m	m
	Israel	80.0	20.0	1.0	80.5	19.5	1.3
	Jamaica	65.0	35.0	1.1	m	m	m
	Paraguay	69.0	31.0	m	m	m	m
	Thailand	95.2	4.8	m	m	m	m
	Uruguay	95.0	5.0	m	m	m	m

1. Including subsidies attributable to payments to educational institutions received from public sources.
2. Year of reference 1999.
Source: OECD. See Annex 3 for notes (*www.oecd.org/edu/eag2003*).

B3

Table B3.2
Relative proportions of public and private expenditure on educational institutions (1995, 2000)
Distribution of public and private sources of funds for educational institutions after transfers from public sources, by level of education and year

		Pre-primary education (for children 3 years and older)			Primary, secondary and post-secondary non-tertiary education						Tertiary education					
		2000			2000			1995			2000			1995		
		Public sources	Private sources[1]	Private- of which: subsi- dised	Public sources	Private sources[1]	Private- of which: subsi- dised	Public sources	Private sources[1]	Private- of which: subsi- dised	Public sources	Private sources[1]	Private- of which: subsi- dised	Public sources	Private sources[1]	Private- of which: subsi- dised
OECD COUNTRIES	Australia	60.7	39.3	n	84.8	15.2	n	85.6	14.4	0.7	51.0	49.0	0.9	64.6	35.4	8.3
	Austria	83.4	16.6	0.5	95.8	4.2	0.9	96.0	4.0	0.6	96.7	3.3	7.7	96.5	3.5	4.6
	Belgium	96.0	4.0	a	93.9	6.1	0.1	m	m	m	85.2	14.8	4.5	m	m	m
	Canada[2]	92.0	8.0	m	92.4	7.6	m	93.7	6.3	m	61.0	39.0	1.7	56.6	43.4	22.3
	Czech Republic	90.8	9.2	n	91.7	8.3	n	87.9	12.1	6.6	85.5	14.5	n	71.0	29.0	8.6
	Denmark[3]	81.8	18.2	m	97.8	2.2	m	97.8	2.2	n	97.6	2.4	n	99.4	0.6	n
	Finland	87.7	12.3	n	99.5	0.5	n	m	m	m	97.2	2.8	n	m	m	m
	France	95.9	4.1	n	93.0	7.0	1.9	92.5	7.5	2.1	85.7	14.3	2.3	84.3	15.7	2.6
	Germany	63.1	36.9	a	80.5	19.5	a	80.6	19.4	a	91.8	8.2	a	92.8	7.2	a
	Greece	m	m	m	91.7	8.3	m	m	m	m	99.7	0.3	m	m	m	m
	Hungary	89.8	10.2	n	92.7	7.3	n	91.7	8.3	n	76.7	23.3	n	80.3	19.7	n
	Iceland	m	m	m	95.1	4.9	m	93.7	6.3	m	94.9	5.1	m	93.0	7.0	m
	Ireland	40.2	59.8	m	96.0	4.0	m	96.5	3.5	m	79.2	20.8	m	69.7	30.3	m
	Italy	97.0	3.0	m	97.8	2.2	0.3	m	m	m	77.5	22.5	6.1	m	m	m
	Japan[3]	51.3	48.7	a	91.7	8.3	m	91.7	8.3	m	44.9	55.1	m	42.0	58.0	m
	Korea	25.9	74.1	0.5	80.8	19.2	0.9	m	m	m	23.3	76.7	1.1	m	m	m
	Luxembourg	m	m	m	m	m	m	m	m	m	m	m	m	m	m	m
	Mexico	88.3	11.7	0.2	86.1	13.9	0.5	83.8	16.2	m	79.4	20.6	0.6	77.4	22.6	m
	Netherlands	97.4	2.6	a	94.6	5.4	1.0	93.9	6.1	m	77.4	22.6	2.4	79.9	20.1	m
	New Zealand	m	m	m	m	m	n	m	m	m	m	m	n	m	m	m
	Norway	100.0	n	n	99.2	0.8	x	98.9	1.1	n	96.2	3.8	a	93.6	6.4	n
	Poland	m	m	a	m	m	a	m	m	m	m	m	a	m	m	m
	Portugal	m	m	m	99.9	0.1	m	100.0	n	m	92.5	7.5	m	96.5	3.5	m
	Slovak Republic	98.5	1.5	a	97.6	2.4	m	93.1	6.9	m	91.2	8.8	m	85.3	14.7	m
	Spain	81.5	18.5	n	93.0	7.0	n	86.6	13.4	n	74.4	25.6	2.5	74.4	25.6	2.0
	Sweden	100.0	a	m	99.9	0.1	m	99.9	0.2	m	88.1	11.9	m	93.6	6.4	a
	Switzerland	m	m	m	89.0	11.0	1.0	m	m	m	m	m	m	m	m	m
	Turkey	m	m	m	m	m	a	100.0	a	a	95.4	4.6	n	97.0	3.0	0.7
	United Kingdom	95.9	4.1	a	88.7	11.3	n	88.5	11.5	n	67.7	32.3	4.6	63.9	36.1	16.0
	United States[2]	91.2	8.8	m	90.0	10.0	m	m	m	m	33.9	66.1	m	m	m	m
	Country mean	*82.7*	*17.3*	*0.1*	*92.8*	*7.2*	*0.4*				*78.6*	*21.4*	*1.9*			
NON-OECD COUNTRIES	Argentina	m	m	m	87.9	12.1	m	m	m	m	66.2	33.8	0.1	m	m	m
	Chile	70.2	29.8	n	70.0	30.0	a	m	m	m	18.3	81.7	7.0	m	m	m
	India[2,4]	93.6	6.4	m	93.6	6.4	m	m	m	m	99.8	0.2	m	m	m	m
	Indonesia	5.3	94.7	m	76.5	23.5	m	m	m	m	43.8	56.2	m	m	m	m
	Israel	74.7	25.3	n	94.1	5.9	1.3	93.1	6.9	0.8	56.5	43.5	n	59.2	40.8	3.0
	Jamaica	61.6	38.4	n	63.6	36.4	0.9	m	m	m	71.5	28.5	2.3	m	m	m
	Malaysia	88.9	11.1	a	100.0	n	m	m	m	m	m	m	m	m	m	m
	Paraguay	m	m	m	71.9	28.1	m	m	m	m	62.6	37.4	m	m	m	m
	Philippines	m	m	a	67.9	32.1	a	m	m	m	34.4	65.6	m	m	m	m
	Thailand	98.0	2.0	m	97.8	2.2	x	m	m	m	80.4	19.6	m	m	m	m
	Uruguay	89.2	10.8	m	94.5	5.5	x	m	m	m	99.7	0.3	m	m	m	m

1. Including subsidies attributable to payments to educational institutions received from public sources.
   To calculate private funds net of subsidies, subtract public subsidies (columns 3,6,9) from private funds (columns 2,5,8).
   To calculate total public funds, including public subsidies, add public subsidies (columns 3,6,9) to direct public funds (columns 1,4,7).
2. Post-secondary non-tertiary included in tertiary education.
3. Post-secondary non-tertiary included in both upper secondary and tertiary education.
4. Year of reference 1999.
Source: OECD. See Annex 3 for notes (*www.oecd.org/edu/eag2003*).

B3

Table B3.3

Distribution of total public expenditure on education (2000)

Public expenditure on education transferred to educational institutions and public transfers to the private sector as a percentage of total public expenditure on education, by level of education

	Primary, secondary and post-secondary non-tertiary education			Tertiary education			All levels of education combined		
	Direct public expenditure on public institutions	Direct public expenditure on private institutions	Indirect public transfers and payments to the private sector	Direct public expenditure on public institutions	Direct public expenditure on private institutions	Indirect public transfers and payments to the private sector	Direct public expenditure on public institutions	Direct public expenditure on private institutions	Indirect public transfers and payments to the private sector
OECD COUNTRIES									
Australia	79.1	17.1	3.8	68.3	n	31.7	75.8	13.0	10.2
Austria	98.0	0.2	1.7	80.7	0.6	18.7	93.0	0.8	6.2
Belgium	45.2	54.5	0.3	35.6	48.1	16.3	44.0	51.8	4.2
Canada[1]	98.3	1.7	m	78.1	0.5	21.4	91.1	1.2	7.7
Czech Republic	91.3	3.1	5.6	90.2	1.2	8.6	92.0	2.5	5.6
Denmark[2]	77.2	6.8	16.0	61.1	n	38.9	72.8	4.2	23.1
Finland	91.5	4.7	3.8	74.8	7.5	17.7	85.8	5.9	8.3
France	83.1	13.4	3.5	88.6	3.3	8.1	85.2	10.9	3.9
Germany	86.4	9.4	4.1	83.6	2.4	14.0	83.0	10.9	6.1
Greece	99.8	a	0.2	94.2	a	5.8	98.5	a	1.5
Hungary	82.2	7.0	10.7	79.0	3.8	17.3	84.0	5.6	10.4
Iceland	97.7	1.1	1.2	77.1	1.0	21.9	94.1	1.1	4.8
Ireland	96.4	n	3.6	87.6	n	12.4	93.7	n	6.3
Italy	97.6	1.4	1.0	79.9	1.6	18.5	93.9	1.8	4.3
Japan[2]	96.3	3.5	0.2	76.3	12.6	11.1	91.9	6.2	1.9
Korea	86.9	11.6	1.5	45.2	45.4	9.4	81.1	16.0	2.9
Luxembourg	m	m	m	m	m	m	m	m	m
Mexico	96.8	n	3.2	95.0	n	5.0	96.8	0.0	3.2
Netherlands	21.7	70.5	7.8	38.0	34.9	27.0	26.8	60.7	12.4
New Zealand	88.6	3.6	7.8	51.8	2.0	46.3	78.6	4.2	17.2
Norway	89.9	4.5	5.6	68.2	3.2	28.6	81.7	5.9	12.4
Poland	m	m	m	m	m	m	m	m	m
Portugal	91.4	7.1	1.5	93.3	n	6.7	91.3	6.5	2.3
Slovak Republic	96.6	3.4	n	96.2	a	3.8	96.9	2.3	0.8
Spain	85.6	13.4	1.0	88.9	2.6	8.5	86.6	10.8	2.6
Sweden	85.9	3.0	11.1	65.7	4.8	29.5	80.6	3.9	15.4
Switzerland	89.8	7.7	2.5	92.0	6.7	1.3	90.0	7.2	2.8
Turkey	99.0	m	1.0	91.6	0.5	7.9	96.7	0.2	3.1
United Kingdom	78.1	21.8	0.1	a	87.1	12.9	66.4	31.3	2.4
United States[1]	99.7	0.3	m	73.2	9.0	17.7	92.8	3.2	4.0
Country mean	*85.1*	*11.9*	*3.7*	*72.5*	*10.7*	*16.8*	*82.3*	*11.1*	*6.6*
NON-OECD COUNTRIES									
Argentina	86.3	13.1	0.6	97.2	2.4	0.4	88.6	10.9	0.5
Brazil[3]	97.8	2.2	n	91.8	0.9	7.3	96.6	1.9	1.5
Chile	66.0	33.6	0.4	38.3	31.3	30.3	62.1	33.2	4.7
India[1, 3]	66.6	33.3	0.1	77.3	22.6	0.2	72.7	27.2	0.1
Indonesia	90.2	6.4	3.4	m	m	m	92.4	5.0	2.6
Israel	74.5	24.2	1.3	6.3	82.1	11.6	63.5	33.2	3.3
Jamaica	98.4	0.1	1.5	90.4	n	9.6	94.1	2.8	3.1
Paraguay	92.8	6.9	0.3	98.7	x	1.3	93.9	5.7	0.4
Philippines	99.2	a	0.8	97.4	a	2.6	99.0	m	1.0
Thailand	93.5	2.4	4.2	62.7	1.0	36.2	87.9	2.1	10.0
Tunisia	m	m	m	m	m	m	m	m	m
Uruguay	99.9	a	0.1	100.0	a	n	100.0	a	n

1. Post-secondary non-tertiary included in tertiary education.
2. Post-secondary non-tertiary included in both upper secondary and tertiary education.
3. Year of reference 1999.
Source: OECD. See Annex 3 for notes (*www.oecd.org/edu/eag2003*).

INDICATOR B4: TOTAL PUBLIC EXPENDITURE ON EDUCATION

- On average, OECD countries devote 13.0 per cent of total public expenditure to educational institutions.

- Public funding of education is a social priority, even in OECD countries with little public involvement in other areas.

- Public expenditure on education tended to grow faster than total public spending, but not as fast as GDP. Education's share of public expenditure grew fastest in Denmark, Greece and Sweden. In the Czech Republic, Germany, Italy, the Netherlands, the Slovak Republic, and Sweden, public expenditure on education increased between 1995 and 2000 despite public budgets falling in real terms.

- In virtually every OECD country, public funding of primary, secondary and post-secondary non-tertiary education is more decentralised than public funding for tertiary education

B4

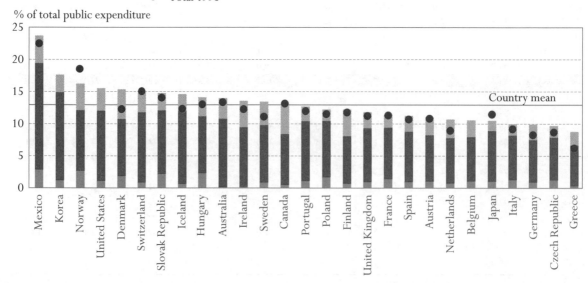

Chart B4.1

Public expenditure on education as a percentage of total public expenditure (2000)
Direct public expenditure on educational institutions plus public subsidies to households (including subsidies for living costs, and public subsidies for other private entities) as a percentage of total public expenditure, by level of education and year

- Tertiary education
- Primary, secondary and post-secondary non-tertiary education
- Below primary education and non-classified
- Total 1995

Countries are ranked in descending order of total expenditure from both public and private sources on educational institutions as a percentage of total public expenditure in 2000.
Source: OECD. Table B4.1. See Annex 3 for notes (www.oecd.org/edu/eag2003).

Policy context

Governments become involved in providing services to the public for different reasons. If the public benefit from a particular service is greater than the private benefit, then markets alone may fail to provide these services adequately. Education is one area where all governments intervene to fund or direct the provision of services. As there is no guarantee that markets will provide equal access to educational opportunities, government funding of educational services ensures that education is not beyond the reach of some members of society. Public expenditure on education as a percentage of total public expenditure indicates the value of education relative to that of other public investments such as health care, social security, defence and security. It thus provides context to the other indicators on expenditure, particularly B3 on the public/private shares of expenditure on education, as well as providing quantification of an important policy lever in its own right.

This indicator focuses on public expenditure on education.

Since the second half of the 1990s, most OECD countries made serious efforts to consolidate public budgets. Education had to compete for public financial support against a wide range of other areas covered in government budgets. To portray this, this indicator also evaluates the change in educational expenditure in absolute terms and relative to changes in the size of public budgets.

It also evaluates how public expenditure has changed over time in absolute terms and relative to total government spending. Finally, the source of public funds by level of government are examined.

The level of government that has responsibility for, and control over, the funding of education is often thought to have a strategic advantage in influencing decisions regarding educational governance. An important question in educational policy is, therefore, the extent to which the division of responsibility for educational funding between national, regional and local authorities translates into responsibility for educational decision-making. Important decisions regarding educational funding are made both at the level of government where the funds originate and at the level of government by which they are finally spent or distributed. In illustrating each country's policy for centralisation or decentralisation of funding, this indicator provides, along with other indicators, some context for the educational performance of the system as a whole.

Evidence and explanations

What this indicator covers and what it does not cover

This indicator shows total public expenditure on education. This expenditure includes direct public expenditure on educational institutions as well as public subsidies to households (*e.g.*, scholarships and loans to students for tuition fees and student living costs) and to other private entities for education (*e.g.*, subsidies to companies or labour organisations that operate apprenticeship programmes). Unlike the preceding indicators, this indicator also includes public subsidies that are not attributable to household payments for educational institutions, such as subsidies for student living costs.

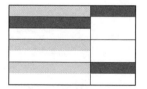

Coverage diagram (see page 181 for explanations)

OECD countries differ in the ways in which they use public money for education. Public funds may flow directly to schools or be channelled to institutions via levels of government or indeed via households; they may also be restricted to the purchase of educational services or be used to support student living costs.

It is important to examine public investment in education in conjunction with private investment, as shown in Indicator B3.

Overall level of public resources invested in education

On average, OECD countries devote 13.0 per cent of total public expenditure to education.

On average, OECD countries devote 13.0 per cent of total public expenditure to education. However, the values for individual countries range from below ten per cent in the Czech Republic, Germany and Greece, to almost 24 per cent in Mexico. (Chart B4.1). As in the case of spending on education in relation to GDP per capita, these values need to be interpreted in the light of student demography and enrolment rates.

On average OECD countries spend three times as much on primary, secondary and post-secondary non-tertiary education than on tertiary education.

The public-sector proportion of the funding of the different levels of education varies widely between OECD countries. In 2000, OECD countries spent between 6.3 (Greece) and 16.5 per cent (Mexico) of total public expenditure on primary, secondary and post-secondary non-tertiary education, and between 1.6 (Japan) and 4.7 per cent (Canada) on tertiary education. On average in OECD countries, reflecting in the main higher student numbers, public funding of primary, secondary and post-secondary non-tertiary education is three times that of tertiary education. This ratio varies by country from less than double in Canada, Denmark and Finland to as high as five times in Korea. The latter is indicative of the relatively high proportion of private funds which go into tertiary education in Korea. (Table B4.1).

When public expenditure on education is examined as a proportion of total public spending, the relative sizes of public budgets (as measured by public spending in relation to GDP) need to be taken into account.

Public funding of education is a social priority, even in OECD countries with little public involvement in other areas.

Across OECD countries, when the size of public budgets relative to GDP is compared with the proportion of public spending that is committed to education, it is evident that even in countries with relatively low rates of public spending, the priority that education is awarded within that spending is very high. For instance, the share of public spending that goes to education in Korea, Mexico and the United States is amongst the highest of OECD countries (Chart B4.1) and yet total public spending accounts for a relatively low proportion of GDP in these countries (Chart B4.2).

Although the overall pattern is not clear cut, there is some evidence to suggest that countries with high rates of public spending spend proportionately less of it on education: only one of the top ten countries for public spending on public services overall, is in the top ten of public spenders on education.

Typically, public expenditure on education grew faster than total public spending, but not as fast as national income.

The process of budget consolidation puts pressure on education as on every other service. Nevertheless, with the exception of Japan and Norway, spending on education grew at least as fast as spending in other public areas; the proportion of public budgets spent on education growing, on average, from 12.1 per cent in 1995 to 13.0 per cent in 2000. The figures suggest that the greatest increases in the share of public expenditure on education took place in Denmark (increasing from 12.2 per cent to 15.3 per cent), Greece (6.2 per cent to 8.8 per cent) and Sweden (11.0 per cent to 13.4 per cent).

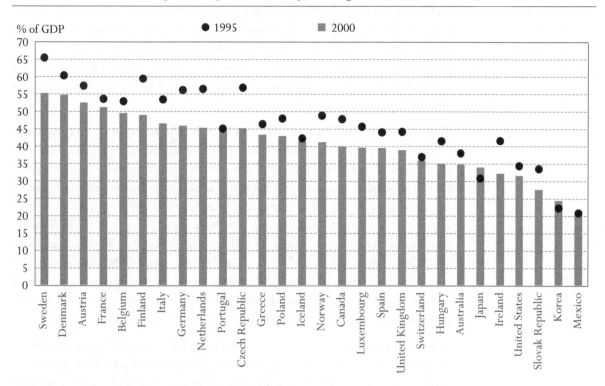

Chart B4.2

Total public expenditure as a percentage of GDP (1995, 2000)

B4

Note: This chart represents public expenditure on all services and not simply public expenditure on education.
Countries are ranked in descending order of total public expenditure as a percentage of GDP in 2000.
Source: OECD. Annex 2. See Annex 3 for notes *(www.oecd.org/edu/eag2003).*

Across OECD countries, funding of primary, secondary and post-secondary non-tertiary education is more decentralised than public funding for tertiary education (Tables B4.2a and B4.2b). On average at the primary, secondary and post-secondary non-tertiary level 49 per cent of the initial funding comes from central rather than regional or local government compared with 77 per cent for tertiary education. Moreover, there are greater levels of transfers of funds from central to regional and local levels of government at the below tertiary level than there are at the tertiary levels, adding to the contrast in decentralisation between the levels of education.

In virtually every OECD country, public funding of primary, secondary and post-secondary non-tertiary education is more decentralised than public funding for tertiary education.

Only two countries - New Zealand and the Slovak Republic - have entirely centralised funding systems below the tertiary level, whilst at the tertiary level, five countries- Hungary, Netherlands, New Zealand, Norway and the Slovak Republic operate such systems. Only Belgium has no central initial or final funding at the primary, secondary and post-secondary non-tertiary level.

Definitions and methodologies

B4

Educational expenditure is expressed as a percentage of a country's total public sector expenditure and as a percentage of GDP. Public educational expenditure includes expenditure on educational institutions and subsidies for students' living costs and for other private expenditure outside institutions. Public expenditure on education includes expenditure by all public entities, including ministries other than the ministry of education, local and regional governments and other public agencies.

Total public expenditure, also referred to as total public spending, corresponds to the non-repayable current and capital expenditure of all levels of government: central, regional and local. Current expenditure includes final consumption expenditure, property income paid, subsidies and other current transfers (*e.g.*, social security, social assistance, pensions and other welfare benefits). Figures for total public expenditure have been taken from the OECD National Accounts Database (see Annex 2) and use the System of National Accounts 1993. In previous editions of *Education at a Glance*, total public expenditure was based on the System of National Accounts 1968. The change in the system of national accounts may explain differences in this indicator in comparison with previous editions of this publication.

The initial educational expenditure of each level of government – also referred to as the expenditure originating at that level – is the total educational expenditure of all public authorities at the level in question (direct expenditure plus transfers to other levels of government and to the private sector), less the transfers received from other levels of government. The proportion of initial expenditure made by a particular level of government is calculated as a percentage of the total, consolidated expenditure of all three levels. Only expenditure specifically designated for education is taken into account in determining the proportion of initial expenditure borne by a particular level. General-purpose transfers between levels of government, which provide much of the revenue of regional and local governments in some countries, have been excluded from the calculations.

The final expenditure of each level of government includes funds spent directly on educational institutions and transfers to households or other private entities (after transfers from other levels of government have occurred).

Note that data appearing in earlier editions of this publication may not always be comparable to data shown in the 2003 edition due to changes in definitions and coverage that were made as a result of the OECD expenditure comparability study (see Annex 3 at *www.oecd.org/edu/eag2003* for details on changes).

Table B4.1
Total public expenditure on education (1995, 2000)
Public expenditure on educational institutions plus public subsidies to households (which includes subsidies for living costs, and other private entities)
as a percentage of GDP and as a percentage of total public expenditure, by level of education and year

	Public expenditure on education as a percentage of total public expenditure				Public expenditure[1] on education as a percentage of GDP			
	2000			1995	2000			1995
	Primary, secondary and post-secondary non-tertiary education	Tertiary education	All levels of education combined	All levels of education combined	Primary, secondary and post-secondary non-tertiary education	Tertiary education	All levels of education combined	All levels of education combined
OECD COUNTRIES								
Australia	10.6	3.2	13.9	13.3	3.9	1.2	5.1	5.2
Austria	7.2	2.7	11.0	10.8	3.8	1.4	5.8	6.2
Belgium	6.9	2.6	10.6	m	3.4	1.3	5.2	m
Canada[2]	7.9	4.7	13.1	13.1	3.3	2.0	5.5	6.5
Czech Republic	6.6	1.8	9.7	8.7	3.0	0.8	4.4	4.9
Denmark[3]	8.8	4.6	15.3	12.2	4.8	2.5	8.4	7.4
Finland	7.4	4.2	12.2	11.7	3.6	2.0	6.0	7.0
France	8.0	2.0	11.4	11.3	4.1	1.0	5.8	6.0
Germany	6.6	2.4	9.9	8.2	3.0	1.1	4.5	4.6
Greece	6.3	2.1	8.8	6.2	2.7	0.9	3.8	2.9
Hungary	8.8	3.0	14.1	12.9	3.1	1.0	4.9	5.4
Iceland	11.3	2.6	14.6	12.2	4.7	1.1	6.0	4.9
Ireland	9.3	4.1	13.5	12.2	3.0	1.3	4.4	5.1
Italy	6.9	1.8	10.0	9.2	3.2	0.8	4.6	4.9
Japan[3]	7.9	1.6	10.5	11.4	2.7	0.5	3.6	3.6
Korea	13.6	2.7	17.6	m	3.3	0.7	4.3	m
Luxembourg	m	m	m	m	m	m	m	m
Mexico	16.5	4.3	23.6	22.4	3.4	0.9	4.9	4.6
Netherlands	7.0	2.9	10.7	8.9	3.2	1.3	4.8	5.0
New Zealand	m	m	m	14.4	4.9	1.7	7.0	5.7
Norway	9.4	4.1	16.2	18.4	3.9	1.7	6.7	9.0
Poland	8.8	1.8	12.2	11.5	3.8	0.8	5.2	5.5
Portugal	9.2	2.3	12.7	11.9	4.2	1.0	5.7	5.4
Slovak Republic	9.8	2.7	14.7	14.0	2.7	0.7	4.1	4.7
Spain	7.8	2.4	11.2	10.6	3.1	1.0	4.4	4.7
Sweden	8.9	3.6	13.4	11.0	4.9	2.0	7.4	7.2
Switzerland	10.9	3.4	15.1	15.0	3.9	1.2	5.4	5.5
Turkey	m	m	m	m	2.4	1.1	3.5	2.4
United Kingdom	8.3	2.5	11.8	11.2	3.4	1.0	4.8	5.1
United States[2]	10.9	3.5	15.5	m	3.5	1.1	5.0	m
Country mean	*8.9*	*2.9*	*13.0*	*12.1*	*3.5*	*1.2*	*5.2*	*5.4*
NON-OECD COUNTRIES								
Argentina	9.8	2.4	13.6	m	3.3	0.8	4.5	m
Brazil[4]	7.3	2.2	10.4	m	3.0	0.9	4.3	m
Chile	13.5	2.5	17.5	m	3.2	0.6	4.2	m
India[2,4]	8.6	2.2	12.7	m	2.8	0.7	4.1	m
Indonesia	7.4	2.2	9.6	m	1.1	0.3	1.5	m
Israel	9.0	2.5	13.7	13.3	4.5	1.2	6.8	6.9
Jamaica	8.1	2.4	11.1	m	4.8	1.4	6.5	m
Malaysia	17.2	8.5	26.7	m	4.0	2.0	6.2	m
Paraguay	9.3	1.9	11.2	m	4.1	0.9	5.0	m
Philippines	11.7	1.9	13.9	m	3.3	0.5	3.9	m
Russian Federation	6.0	1.7	10.6	m	1.7	0.5	3.0	m
Thailand	16.8	6.3	31.0	m	2.9	1.1	5.4	m
Tunisia	13.3	m	19.4	m	5.2	m	7.7	m
Uruguay	8.3	2.4	11.8	m	1.9	0.6	2.8	m
Zimbabwe[2]	m	m	m	m	7.6	m	7.6	m

1. Public expenditure presented in this table includes public subsidies to households for living costs, which are not spent on educational institutions. Thus the figures presented here exceed those on public spending on institutions found in Table B2.1b.
2. Post-secondary non-tertiary is included in tertiary education and excluded from primary, secondary and post-secondary non-tertiary education.
3. Post-secondary non-tertiary included in both upper secondary and tertiary education.
4. Year of reference 1999.
Source: OECD. See Annex 3 for notes (*www.oecd.org/edu/eag2003*).

Table B4.2a
Initial sources of public educational funds and final purchasers of educational resources (2000)
by level of government for primary, secondary and post-secondary non-tertiary education

		Initial funds (before transfers between levels of government)				Final funds (after transfers between levels of government)			
		Central	Regional	Local	Total	Central	Regional	Local	Total
OECD COUNTRIES	Australia	27	73	n	100	19	81	n	100
	Austria	70	8	22	100	34	43	23	100
	Belgium	a	94	6	100	a	94	6	100
	Canada[1]	4	70	26	100	3	10	87	100
	Czech Republic	80	a	20	100	80	a	20	100
	Denmark[2]	32	10	58	100	36	11	53	100
	Finland	41	a	59	100	9	a	91	100
	France	74	12	14	100	73	13	14	100
	Germany	8	75	18	100	7	71	22	100
	Greece	93	7	a	100	82	15	3	100
	Hungary	71	x	29	100	20	x	80	100
	Iceland	m	m	m	m	m	m	m	m
	Ireland	100	a	n	100	82	a	18	100
	Italy	81	5	14	100	81	4	15	100
	Japan[2]	25	57	18	100	1	81	18	100
	Korea	m	m	m	m	m	m	m	m
	Luxembourg	m	m	m	m	m	m	m	m
	Mexico	82	17	n	100	22	78	n	100
	Netherlands	94	n	6	100	74	n	26	100
	New Zealand	100	n	n	100	100	a	n	100
	Norway	34	a	66	100	11	a	89	100
	Poland	5	1	94	100	1	1	97	100
	Portugal	94	6	m	100	94	6	m	100
	Slovak Republic	100	a	a	100	100	a	a	100
	Spain	17	78	5	100	17	78	5	100
	Sweden	m	m	m	m	m	m	m	m
	Switzerland	3	52	45	100	n	58	42	100
	Turkey	m	m	m	m	m	m	m	m
	United Kingdom	26	a	74	100	24	a	76	100
	United States[1]	8	51	41	100	1	1	99	100
	Country mean	*49*	*30*	*26*	*100*	*37*	*30*	*35*	*100*
NON-OECD COUNTRIES	Argentina	9	91	m	100	1	99	m	100
	Brazil[3]	5	58	37	100	4	58	38	100
	Chile	95	a	5	100	48	a	52	100
	India[1,3]	10	84	6	100	10	71	19	100
	Indonesia	m	m	m	m	100	n	x	100
	Israel	90	a	10	100	67	a	33	100
	Jamaica	100	a	a	100	100	a	a	100
	Paraguay	100	n	n	100	98	2	x	100
	Philippines	86	a	14	100	86	a	14	100
	Russian Federation	7	18	75	100	7	18	75	100
	Thailand	94	a	6	100	90	a	10	100
	Tunisia	100	a	a	100	100	a	a	100
	Uruguay	100	a	a	100	100	a	a	100
	Zimbabwe[1]	100	a	a	100	100	a	a	100

1. Post-secondary non-tertiary included in tertiary education.
2. Post-secondary non-tertiary included in both upper secondary and tertiary education.
3. Year of reference 1999.
Source: OECD. See Annex 3 for notes *(www.oecd.org/edu/eag2003)*.

EDUCATION AT A GLANCE © OECD 2003

Table B4.2b
Initial sources of public educational funds and final purchasers of educational resources (2000)
by level of government for tertiary education

	Initial funds (before transfers between levels of government)				Final funds (after transfers between levels of government)			
	Central	Regional	Local	Total	Central	Regional	Local	Total
Australia	91	9	n	100	91	9	n	100
Austria	99	1	n	100	99	1	n	100
Belgium	17	82	1	100	17	82	1	100
Canada[1]	34	66	n	100	23	73	n	100
Czech Republic	97	a	3	100	97	a	3	100
Denmark[2]	88	2	10	100	88	2	10	100
Finland	86	a	14	100	79	a	21	100
France	91	5	4	100	91	5	4	100
Germany	17	80	3	100	11	86	3	100
Greece	99	1	a	100	99	1	a	100
Hungary	100	x	n	100	100	x	n	100
Iceland	m	m	m	m	m	m	m	m
Ireland	100	a	n	100	90	a	10	100
Italy	92	7	n	100	91	8	n	100
Japan[2]	84	16	n	100	84	16	n	100
Korea	m	m	m	m	m	m	m	m
Luxembourg	m	m	m	m	m	m	m	m
Mexico	83	17	n	100	82	18	n	100
Netherlands	100	n	n	100	100	n	n	100
New Zealand	100	n	n	100	100	a	n	100
Norway	100	a	n	100	100	a	a	100
Poland	99	1	n	100	99	1	n	100
Portugal	m	m	m	m	m	m	m	m
Slovak Republic	100	a	a	100	100	a	a	100
Spain	16	83	1	100	16	83	1	100
Sweden	96	4	a	100	95	5	a	100
Switzerland	46	54	1	100	31	69	n	100
Turkey	m	m	m	m	m	m	m	m
United Kingdom	100	a	n	100	87	a	13	100
United States[1]	39	55	6	100	39	55	6	100
Country mean	*77*	*23*	*2*	*100*	*74*	*24*	*3*	*100*
Argentina	31	69	n	100	1	99	n	100
Brazil[3]	64	34	2	100	64	34	2	100
Chile	100	a	a	100	100	a	a	100
India[1,3]	38	62	x	100	38	62	a	100
Israel	98	a	2	100	98	a	2	100
Jamaica	100	a	a	100	100	a	a	100
Malaysia	100	m	n	100	100	m	a	100
Paraguay	100	n	n	100	100	n	n	100
Philippines	100	a	a	100	100	a	a	100
Russian Federation	81	17	2	100	81	17	2	100
Thailand	100	a	a	100	100	a	a	100
Uruguay	100	a	a	100	100	a	a	100

OECD COUNTRIES / *NON-OECD COUNTRIES*

1. Post-secondary non-tertiary included in tertiary education.
2. Post-secondary non-tertiary included in both upper secondary and tertiary education.
3. Year of reference 1999.
Source: OECD. See Annex 3 for notes (*www.oecd.org/edu/eag2003*).

INDICATOR B5: SUPPORT FOR STUDENTS AND HOUSEHOLDS THROUGH PUBLIC SUBSIDIES

B5

- Public subsidies for students and households are mainly a feature at the tertiary level.

- An average of 17 per cent of public spending on tertiary education is devoted to supporting students, households and other private entities. In Australia, Denmark, New Zealand, Sweden and the United Kingdom, public subsidies account for about 30 per cent or more of public tertiary education budgets.

- Subsidies are generally more evident in systems where students are expected to pay for at least part of the cost of their education.

- Subsidised student loan systems tend to operate in countries with high levels of participation at the tertiary level.

- In most OECD countries, the beneficiaries of public subsidies have considerable discretion regarding the spending of subsidies. In all reporting OECD countries, subsidies are spent mainly outside educational institutions, and in almost half of these countries, exclusively outside.

Chart B5.1

Public subsidies for education in tertiary education (2000)
Public subsidies for education to the private sector as a percentage of total public expenditure on education, by type of subsidy

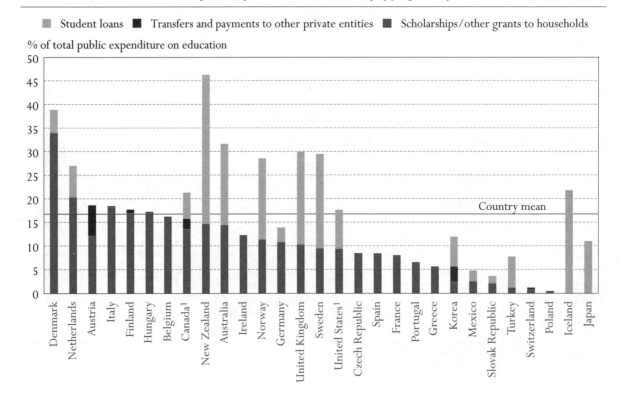

■ Student loans ■ Transfers and payments to other private entities ■ Scholarships/other grants to households

1. Including post-secondary non-tertiary education.
Countries are ranked in descending order of scholarships/other grants to households and transfers and payments to other private entities in tertiary education.
Source: OECD. Table B5.2. See Annex 3 for notes *(www.oecd.org/edu/eag2003).*

Policy context

Subsidies to students and their families are policy levers through which govern-ments can encourage participation in education, particularly among students from low-income families, by covering part of the cost of education and related expenses. They thereby can seek to address issues of access and equality of opportunity. Their success must therefore be judged, at least in part, through examination of indicators of participation, retention and completion. Further-more, public subsidies play an important role in indirectly financing educational institutions.

Channelling funding for institutions through students may also help to increase competition between institutions and result in greater efficiency in the financing of education. Since aid for student living costs can serve as a substitute for work as a financial resource, public subsidies may enhance educational attainment by enabling students to study full-time and to work fewer hours or not at all.

Public subsidies come in many forms: as means-based subsidies, as family allow-ances for all students, as tax allowances for students or their parents, or as other household transfers. Unconditional subsidies such as tax reductions or family allowances may provide less of an incentive for low-income students to partici-pate in education than means-tested subsidies. However, they may still help to reduce disparities between households with and without children in education.

A key question is whether financial subsidies for households should be provided in the form of grants or loans. Are loans an effective means to help increase the efficiency of financial resources invested in education and shift some of the cost of education to the beneficiaries of educational investment? Or are student loans less appropriate than grants in encouraging low-income students to pursue their education? This indicator cannot answer this question but portray the policies for subsidies that the different OECD countries pursue.

Evidence and explanations

What this indicator covers and what it does not cover

This indicator shows the proportion of public spending on education that is transferred to students, families and other private entities. Some of these funds are spent indirectly on educational institutions, for example, when subsidies are used to cover tuition fees. Other subsidies for education do not relate to educa-tional institutions, such as subsidies for student living costs.

The indicator distinguishes between scholarships and grants, which are non-repayable subsidies, on the one hand, and loans on the other. The indicator does not, however, distinguish between different types of grants or loans, such as scholarships versus family allowances and subsidies in kind.

Governments can also support students and their families by providing tax reductions and tax credits. These types of subsidy are not covered by this indicator.

This indicator examines direct and indirect public spending on educational institutions as well as public subsidies to households for student living costs.

B₅

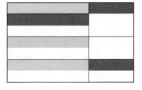

Coverage diagram (see page 181 for explanations)

The indicator reports the full volume of student loans in order to provide information on the level of support which current students receive. Given that repayments to loan programmes are made by former students who took out loans several years previously, it is difficult to estimate the real costs of loan programmes, net of repayments and loans are therefore reported on a gross basis only. International comparisons of total repayments in the same reference period cannot be made, since they are heavily influenced by changes in schemes for the distribution of loans and by changes in the numbers of students receiving loans. Moreover, in most countries, loan repayments do not flow to the education authorities, and thus the money is not available to them to cover other educational expenditure.

It is also common for governments to guarantee the repayment of loans to students made by private lenders. In some OECD countries, this indirect form of subsidy is as significant as, or more significant than, direct financial aid to students. However, for reasons of comparability, the indicator only takes into account the amounts relating to public transfers for private loans that are made to private entities not the total value of loans generated.

Some OECD countries also have difficulties quantifying the amount of loans attributable to students. Therefore, data on student loans should be treated with some caution.

Public subsidies to households and other private entities

OECD countries spend an average of around 0.4 per cent of their GDP on public subsidies to households and other private entities.

OECD countries spend an average of 0.4 per cent of their GDP on public subsidies to households and other private entities for all levels of education combined. The subsidies are largest in relation to GDP in Denmark (1.75 per cent of GDP), followed by New Zealand (1.18 per cent) and Sweden (1.14 per cent). Furthermore, on average across OECD countries, 7.0 per cent of public budgets for education is spent on transfers to the private sector (Tables B5.1 and B5.2). Most of these amounts are devoted to the tertiary level of education, except in the Czech Republic, France, Hungary, Mexico, and Switzerland, where more than 50 per cent of transfers to the private sector are devoted to primary, secondary and post-secondary non-tertiary education.

At the primary, secondary and post-secondary non-tertiary levels, public subsidies account for a comparatively small proportion of public spending on education.

Most OECD countries offer public subsidies to households from upper secondary education onwards. There are usually few subsidies available before the upper secondary level, since in most OECD countries education up to that level is compulsory, free of charge, predominantly provided by the public sector and largely provided at the point of residence of students and their families. In nine out of 28 OECD countries, subsidies to households and private entities therefore account for 1 per cent or less of total public spending on primary, secondary and post-secondary non-tertiary education. However, in Hungary, the Netherlands, New Zealand, and Sweden, public subsidies account for between 8 and 11 per cent of public expenditure on primary, secondary and post-secondary non-tertiary education; and in Denmark for 16 per cent (Chart B5.2). In most of the OECD countries with high proportions of subsi-

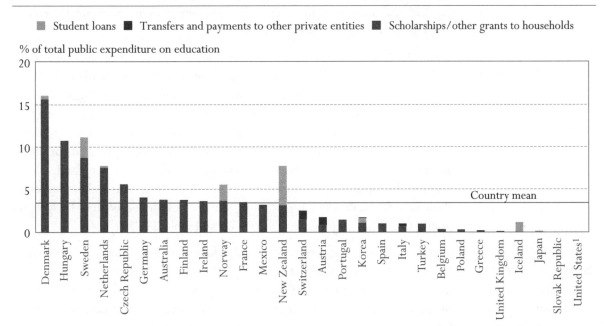

Chart B5.2

Public subsidies for education in primary, secondary and post-secondary non-tertiary education (2000)
Public subsidies for education to the private sector as a percentage of
total public expenditure on education, by type of subsidy

■ Student loans   ■ Transfers and payments to other private entities   ■ Scholarships/other grants to households

% of total public expenditure on education

Country mean

Denmark, Hungary, Sweden, Netherlands, Czech Republic, Germany, Australia, Finland, Ireland, Norway, France, Mexico, New Zealand, Switzerland, Austria, Portugal, Korea, Spain, Italy, Turkey, Belgium, Poland, Greece, United Kingdom, Iceland, Japan, Slovak Republic, United States[1]

B5

1. Excluding post-secondary non-tertiary education.
Countries are ranked in descending order of scholarships/other grants to households and transfers and payments to other private entities for
primary, secondary and post-secondary non-tertiary education.
Source: OECD. Table B5.1. See Annex 3 for notes *(www.oecd.org/edu/eag2003).*

dies at the primary, secondary and post-secondary non-tertiary levels of education, these subsidies are directed at adults re-entering secondary education.

The proportion of educational budgets spent on subsidies to households and private entities is much higher at the tertiary level. OECD countries spend, on average, 17 per cent of their public budgets for tertiary education on subsidies to households and other private entities (Chart B5.1). In Australia, Denmark, New Zealand, Sweden and the United Kingdom, public subsidies account for 30 per cent or more of public spending on tertiary education. Only Poland, the Slovak Republic and Switzerland spend less than 5 per cent of their total public spending on tertiary education on subsidies (Table B5.2).

Australia, Denmark, New Zealand, Sweden and the United Kingdom spend 30 per cent or more of their public education budget at the tertiary level on subsidies to the private sector.

A key question in many OECD countries is whether financial subsidies for households should primarily be provided in the form of grants or loans. Governments choose to subsidise students' living costs or educational costs through different mixtures of grants and loans. Advocates of student loans argue that money spent on loans goes further, that is, if the amount spent on grants were used to guarantee or subsidise loans instead, more aid would be available to students in total, and overall access would be increased. Loans also shift some of the cost of education to those who benefit most from educational investment.

OECD countries use different mixtures of grants and loans to subsidise students' educational costs.

Opponents of loans argue that student loans will be less effective than grants in encouraging low-income students to pursue their education. They also argue that loans may be less efficient than anticipated because of the various subsidies provided to borrowers or lenders, and of the costs of administration and servicing. Cultural differences between and within countries may also affect students' willingness to take out a student loan.

Chart B5.1 presents the proportion of public educational expenditure spent on loans, grants and scholarships and other subsidies to households at the tertiary level. Grants and scholarships include family allowances and other specific subsidies, but exclude tax reductions. 13 out of 29 reporting OECD countries rely exclusively on grants or scholarships and transfers and payments to other private entities. The remaining OECD countries provide both grants or scholarships and loans to students. In general, the highest subsidies to students are provided by those OECD countries which offer student loans and in most cases these countries are spending an above-average proportion of their budgets on grants and scholarships alone (Chart B5.1 and Table B5.2).

The largest subsidies in the form of student loans tend to be in countries with the highest participation rates in tertiary education.

The motivation for governments to introduce a student loan system can often be to better manage the cost of an expanding tertiary sector. It is notable, for instance, that the three countries reporting the largest subsidies in the form of student loans – Iceland, New Zealand and Sweden – also have some of the highest rates of entry into tertiary education of OECD countries (see Indicator C2). There are exceptions to this, however. Finland has the second highest tertiary (type A) entry rates of OECD countries but does not operate a publicly funded student loan system.

Repayments of loans reduce the real cost of loan programmes to the public budget; at the same time they increase the burden on households for education.

Repayments of public loans can be a substantial source of income for governments and can decrease the costs of loan programmes significantly. The current reporting of household expenditure on education, as part of private expenditures (Indicator B4) does not take into account the repayment by previous recipients of public loans. These repayments can be a substantial burden to individuals and have an impact on the decision to participate in tertiary education. However, many OECD countries make the repayment of loans dependent on the later level of income of graduates.

How subsidies are used: student living costs and tuition fees

In most OECD countries, the beneficiaries of subsidies have considerable discretion about how they spend public subsidies.

In most OECD countries, the bulk of public payments to households for education are not earmarked, that is, their use is determined by the beneficiaries, namely the students and their families. In a few OECD countries, however, public subsidies are earmarked for payments to educational institutions. Australia, New Zealand and the United Kingdom, for example, earmark public subsidies for tuition fees. In Australia, loans and tuition fees are closely related through the Higher Education Contribution Scheme (HECS). Under HECS, students can elect to pay their contributions for their university education in advance, semester by semester, and receive a 25 per cent discount, or, they can repay their accumulated contribution through the tax system when their annual income exceeds a minimum threshold. For the purpose of the OECD education indicators, HECS is counted as a loan scheme, although students may not see the delayed payments as a loan. In OECD countries where tuition fees are substantial, a proportion of the public subsidy to households is effectively earmarked for payments to educational institutions, even without an official policy.

Scholarships and other grants attributable to students are largely spent outside educational institutions. They support educational expenses other than tuition fees. In Denmark, Finland, Hungary and the Netherlands, scholarships and other grants not attributable for tuition fees to educational institutions account for more than 15 per cent of the total public spending on tertiary education. Poland and Switzerland are the only OECD countries where scholarships and other grants attributable for expenditure outside institutions amount to less than 1 per cent of total public spending on education (Table B5.2).

In all reporting OECD countries subsidies are spent mainly outside educational institutions, and in one out of three OECD countries exclusively outside.

B5

In OECD countries where students are required to pay tuition fees, access to public subsidies is of particular importance in order to provide students with access to educational opportunities, regardless of their financial situation. Indicator B4 shows what proportion of funding of educational institutions originates from private sources.

Subsidies are particularly important in systems where students are expected to pay at least part of the cost of their education.

In OECD countries with low levels of private involvement in the funding of educational institutions, the level of public subsidies tends to be lower also (Tables B5.2 and B3.2). An exception is Korea, where despite the fact that around 80 per cent of all expenditure on tertiary institutions originates from private sources, the level of subsidies to support tuition payments to institutions is, at 2 per cent, comparatively low (Tables B5.2 and B3.2).

Definitions and methodologies

Public subsidies to households include the following categories: *i)* grants/scholarships; *ii)* public student loans; *iii)* family or child allowances contingent on student status; *iv)* public subsidies in cash or kind specifically for housing, transportation, medical expenses, books and supplies, social, recreational and other purposes; and *v)* interest-related subsidies for private loans.

Data refer to the financial year 2000 and are based on the UOE data collection on educational statistics administered by the OECD in 2002 (for details see Annex 3).

Expenditure on student loans is reported on a gross basis, that is, without subtracting or netting out repayments or interest payments from the borrowers (students or households). This is because the gross amount of loans including scholarships and grants is the relevant variable for measuring financial aid to current participants in education.

Public costs related to private loans guaranteed by governments are included as subsidies to other private entities. Unlike public loans, only the net cost of these loans is included.

The value of tax reductions or credits to households and students is not included.

Note that data appearing in earlier editions of this publication may not always be comparable to data shown in the 2002 edition due to changes in definitions and coverage that were made as a result of the OECD expenditure comparability study (see Annex 3 at *www.oecd.org/edu/eag2003* for details on changes).

Table B5.1

Public subsidies to the private sector as a percentage of total public expenditure on education and GDP for primary, secondary and post-secondary non-tertiary education (2000)

Direct public expenditure on educational institutions and subsidies for households and other private entities as a percentage of total public expenditure on education and GDP

| | | Subsidies for education to private entities | | | | | Subsidies for education to private entities as percentage of GDP |
| | Direct expenditure for institutions | Financial aid to students | | | Transfers and payments to other private entities | Total | |
		Scholarships/ other grants to households	Student loans	Total			
OECD COUNTRIES							
Australia	96.2	3.8	n	3.8	n	3.8	0.15
Austria	98.3	0.8	a	0.8	0.9	1.7	0.07
Belgium	99.7	0.3	n	0.3	n	0.3	0.01
Canada[1]	m	m	m	m	m	m	m
Czech Republic	94.4	5.6	a	5.6	n	5.6	0.17
Denmark	84.0	15.6	0.4	16.0	n	16.0	0.78
Finland	96.2	3.6	n	3.6	0.2	3.8	0.14
France	96.5	3.5	a	3.5	a	3.5	0.15
Germany	95.9	4.1	n	4.1	n	4.1	0.12
Greece	99.8	0.2	m	0.2	a	0.2	0.01
Hungary	89.3	10.7	a	10.7	n	10.7	0.33
Iceland	98.8	m	1.2	1.2	m	1.2	0.05
Ireland	96.4	3.6	n	3.6	n	3.6	0.11
Italy	99.0	0.7	a	0.7	0.3	1.0	0.03
Japan	99.8	m	0.2	0.2	n	0.2	n
Korea	98.5	1.0	0.5	1.5	0.1	1.5	0.05
Luxembourg	m	m	m	m	m	m	m
Mexico	96.8	3.2	a	3.2	a	3.2	0.11
Netherlands	92.2	7.6	0.2	7.8	n	7.8	0.25
New Zealand	92.2	3.1	4.6	7.8	n	7.8	0.38
Norway	94.4	3.6	2.0	5.6	n	5.6	0.22
Poland	99.7	0.3	x	0.3	m	0.3	0.01
Portugal	98.5	1.5	a	1.5	a	1.5	0.06
Slovak Republic	100.0	n	a	n	a	n	n
Spain	99.0	1.0	a	1.0	n	1.0	0.03
Sweden	88.9	8.7	2.4	11.1	m	11.1	0.55
Switzerland	97.5	1.5	n	1.5	1.1	2.5	0.10
Turkey	99.0	1.0	a	1.0	m	1.0	0.02
United Kingdom	99.9	0.1	a	0.1	n	0.1	n
United States[1]	100.0	n	n	n	n	n	n
Country mean	*96.6*	*3.2*	*0.4*	*3.4*	*0.1*	*3.4*	*0.13*
NON-OECD COUNTRIES							
Argentina	99.4	0.6	a	0.6	0.1	0.6	n
Brazil[2]	100.0	n	a	n	a	n	n
Chile	99.6	0.4	a	0.4	a	0.4	n
India[1,2]	99.9	0.1	x	0.1	x	0.1	n
Indonesia	96.6	3.4	m	3.4	m	3.4	n
Israel	98.7	1.3	n	1.3	n	1.3	0.1
Jamaica	98.5	1.5	n	1.5	n	1.5	0.1
Malaysia	99.7	0.3	a	0.3	m	0.3	n
Paraguay	99.7	0.2	a	0.2	0.1	0.3	n
Philippines	99.2	a	a	a	0.8	0.8	n
Thailand	95.8	0.7	3.5	4.2	m	4.2	0.1
Uruguay	99.9	0.1	a	0.1	a	0.1	n

1. Excluding post-secondary non-tertiary education.
2. Year of reference 1999.

Source: OECD. See Annex 3 for notes (*www.oecd.org/edu/eag2003*).

Table B5.2
Public subsidies to the private sector as a percentage
of total public expenditure on education and GDP for tertiary education (2000)
Direct public expenditure on educational institutions and subsidies for households and other private entities as a percentage of total public expenditure on education and GDP

B5

	Direct expenditure for institutions	Subsidies for education to private entities						Subsidies for education to private entities as percentage of GDP
		Financial aid to students			Scholarships/ other grants to households attributable for educational institutions	Transfers and payments to other private entities	Total	
		Scholarships/ other grants to households	Student loans	Total				
OECD COUNTRIES								
Australia	68.3	14.5	17.2	31.7	1.2	n	31.7	0.37
Austria	81.3	12.2	a	12.2	x	6.4	18.7	0.27
Belgium	83.7	16.3	n	16.3	4.4	n	16.3	0.21
Canada[1]	78.6	13.6	5.7	19.2	m	2.2	21.4	0.42
Czech Republic	91.4	8.6	a	8.6	n	n	8.6	0.07
Denmark	61.1	33.9	4.9	38.9	n	n	38.9	0.98
Finland	82.3	16.9	n	16.9	n	0.8	17.7	0.36
France	91.9	8.1	a	8.1	2.5	a	8.1	0.08
Germany	86.0	10.9	3.1	14.0	a	n	14.0	0.15
Greece	94.2	5.8	m	5.8	m	a	5.8	0.05
Hungary	82.7	17.3	a	17.3	n	n	17.3	0.18
Iceland	78.1	m	21.9	21.9	m	m	21.9	0.24
Ireland	87.6	12.4	n	12.4	m	n	12.4	0.16
Italy	81.5	18.3	n	18.3	6.3	0.2	18.5	0.15
Japan	88.9	m	11.1	11.1	m	n	11.1	0.06
Korea	90.6	1.9	5.0	6.9	6.9	2.5	9.4	0.06
Luxembourg	m	m	m	m	m	m	m	m
Mexico	95.0	2.5	2.4	5.0	0.8	n	5.0	0.04
Netherlands	73.0	20.3	6.7	27.0	2.3	n	27.0	0.35
New Zealand	53.7	14.7	31.5	46.3	n	n	46.3	0.80
Norway	71.4	11.5	17.1	28.6	a	n	28.6	0.48
Poland	99.5	0.5	n	0.5	a	m	0.5	0.00
Portugal	93.3	6.7	n	6.7	m	n	6.7	0.07
Slovak Republic	96.2	2.1	1.6	3.8	m	a	3.8	0.03
Spain	91.5	8.5	n	8.5	3.1	n	8.5	0.08
Sweden	70.5	9.6	19.9	29.5	a	a	29.5	0.59
Switzerland	98.7	0.8	n	0.8	m	0.5	1.3	0.02
Turkey	92.1	1.3	6.6	7.9	n	m	7.9	0.08
United Kingdom	70.0	10.4	19.6	30.0	4.7	n	30.0	0.30
United States[1]	82.3	9.5	8.3	17.7	x	a	17.7	0.20
Country mean	*83.2*	*11.0*	*6.4*	*16.4*	*1.7*	*0.5*	*16.8*	*0.24*
NON-OECD COUNTRIES								
Argentina	99.6	0.3	m	0.3	m	0.1	0.4	n
Brazil[2]	92.7	5.1	2.2	7.3	m	n	7.3	0.07
Chile	69.7	13.6	16.7	30.3	26.5	a	30.3	0.19
India[2]	99.8	0.2	x	0.2	x	x	0.2	n
Israel	88.4	9.9	1.6	11.6	n	n	11.6	0.14
Jamaica	90.4	2.8	6.7	9.6	2.8	n	9.6	0.13
Malaysia	83.6	2.5	13.9	16.4	m	m	16.4	0.33
Paraguay	98.7	1.3	a	1.3	x	a	1.3	0.01
Philippines	97.4	2.5	0.1	2.6	x	a	2.6	0.01
Thailand	63.8	0.1	36.1	36.2	x	m	36.2	0.40
Uruguay	100.0	n	a	n	n	a	n	n

1. Including post-secondary non-tertiary education.
2. Year of reference 1999.
Source: OECD. See Annex 3 for notes (*www.oecd.org/edu/eag2003*).

INDICATOR B6: EXPENDITURE ON INSTITUTIONS BY SERVICE CATEGORY AND BY RESOURCE CATEGORY

- On average, one quarter of expenditure on tertiary education is attributable to R&D at tertiary educational institutions. Significant differences between OECD countries in the emphasis on R&D in tertiary institutions explain part of the large differences in expenditure per tertiary student.

- In primary, secondary, and post-secondary non-tertiary education combined, current expenditure accounts, on average across all OECD countries, for 92 per cent of total spending. In all but three OECD countries, 70 per cent or more of primary, secondary and post-secondary non-tertiary current expenditure is spent on staff salaries.

B₆

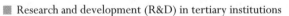

Chart B6.1

Expenditure on instruction, research and development (R&D) and ancillary services in
tertiary educational institutions as a percentage of GDP (2000)

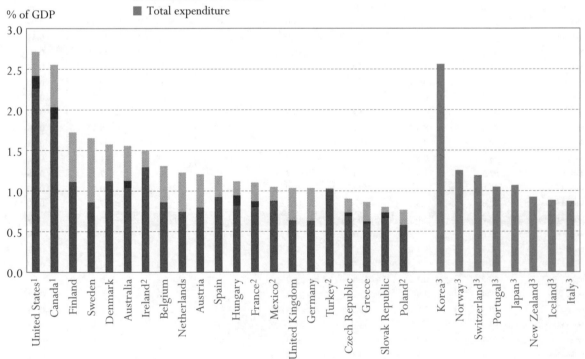

Countries are ranked in descending order of expenditure on instruction, research and development (R&D) and ancillary services in tertiary institutions.
1. Including post-secondary non-tertiary education.
2. Research and development (R&D) expenditure at tertiary level and thus total expenditure are underestimated.
3. The bar represents total expenditure at tertiary level and includes research and development (R&D) expenditure.
Source: OECD. Table B6.1. See Annex 3 for notes *(www.oecd.org/edu/eag2003).*

EDUCATION AT A GLANCE © OECD 2003

Policy context

How spending is apportioned between different categories of expenditure can affect the quality of services (*e.g.*, through teachers' salaries), the condition of educational facilities (*e.g.*, school maintenance) and the ability of the education system to adjust to changing demographic and enrolment trends (as in the construction of new schools).

Comparisons of how different OECD countries apportion educational expenditure between the various resource categories can provide some insight into variation in the organisation and operation of educational institutions. Decisions on the allocation of resources made at the system level, both budgetary and structural, eventually feed through to the classroom and affect the nature of instruction and the conditions under which it is provided.

Educational institutions offer a range of educational services besides instruction. At the primary, secondary and post-secondary non-tertiary levels of education, institutions may offer meals, free transport to and from school or boarding facilities. At the tertiary level, institutions may offer housing and often perform a wide range of research activities as an integral part of tertiary education.

This indicator compares OECD countries with respect to the division of spending between current and capital expenditure and the distribution of current expenditure by resource category.

B6

It also compares how OECD countries' spending is distributed by different functions of educational institutions.

Evidence and explanations

What this indicator covers and what it does not cover

This indicator breaks down educational expenditure by current and capital expenditure and the three main functions which educational institutions typically fulfil. This includes, first, costs directly attributable to instruction, such as teachers' salaries or school materials, and costs indirectly related to the provision of instruction, such as expenditure on administration, instructional support services, development of teachers, student counselling, or on the construction and/or provision of school facilities. Second, it includes spending on ancillary services, such as student welfare services provided by educational institutions. Third, it includes spending attributable to research and development (R&D) performed at tertiary educational institutions, either in the form of separately funded R&D activities or in the form of those proportions of salaries and current expenditure in general education budgets that are attributable to the research activities of staff.

Coverage diagram (see page 181 for explanations)

The indicator does not include public and private R&D spending outside educational institutions, such as R&D spending in industry. A comparative review of R&D spending in sectors other than education is provided in the OECD Science and Technology Indicators. Expenditure on student welfare services at educational institutions only includes public subsidies for those services. Expenditure by students and their families on services that are provided by institutions on a self-funding basis are not included.

Expenditure on instruction, R&D and ancillary services

Below the tertiary level, educational expenditure is dominated by spending on educational core services. At the tertiary level, other services, particularly those related to R&D activities, can account for a significant proportion of educa-

Significant differences among OECD countries in the emphasis on R&D

in tertiary institutions explain part of the variation in expenditure per tertiary student.

tional spending. Differences between OECD countries in expenditure on R&D activities can therefore explain a significant part of the differences between OECD countries in overall educational expenditure per tertiary student (Chart B6.1). High levels of R&D spending in tertiary educational institutions in Australia, Austria, Belgium, Canada, Denmark, Finland, Germany, the Netherlands, Sweden and the United Kingdom (between 0.4 and 0.8 of GDP), for example, imply that spending on education per student in these OECD countries would be considerably lower if the R&D component were excluded (Table B6.1).

Student welfare services are integral functions of schools and universities.

Student welfare services and, sometimes, services for the general public, are integral functions of schools and universities in many OECD countries. Countries finance these ancillary services with different combinations of public expenditure, public subsidies and fees paid by students and their families.

B6

Expenditure on ancillary services at primary, secondary, and post-secondary non-tertiary levels represents 6 per cent of total spending on educational institutions.

On average, OECD countries spend 0.2 per cent of their GDP on subsidies for ancillary services provided by primary, secondary and post-secondary non-tertiary institutions. This represents 6 per cent of total spending on these institutions. At the high end, the Czech Republic, Finland, France, Hungary and the Slovak Republic spend about 10 per cent or more of total spending on educational institutions on ancillary services, which translates into more than US$ 500 (PPP) per student in Finland, France and Sweden and more than US$ 250 (PPP) per student in Canada, the Czech Republic, the Flemish Community of Belgium, Hungary, Italy, the United Kingdom and the United States (Tables B6.1 and B6.2).

In more than two-thirds of OECD countries, the amount spent on ancillary services is higher than the amount spent on subsidies to households at the primary, secondary and post-secondary non-tertiary levels. Exceptions to this pattern are Germany, Ireland, the Netherlands and Sweden, where expenditure on subsidies to households is higher (Tables B5.1 and B6.1).

On average, expenditure on subsidies for ancillary services at the tertiary level amounts to just 0.1 per cent of GDP. Nevertheless, on a per student basis this can translate into significant amounts, as in Australia, Canada, the Flemish community of Belgium, France, Hungary and United States, where subsidies for ancillary services amount to over US$ 500 (PPP). At the tertiary level, ancillary services are more often provided on a self-financed basis (Tables B6.1 and B6.2).

Current and capital expenditure, and the distribution of current expenditure by resource category

Educational expenditure can first be divided into current and capital expenditure. Capital expenditure comprises spending on assets that last longer than one year and includes spending on the construction, renovation and major repair of buildings. Current expenditure comprises spending on school resources used each year for the operation of schools.

Current expenditure can be further sub-divided into three broad functional categories: compensation of teachers, compensation of other staff, and other

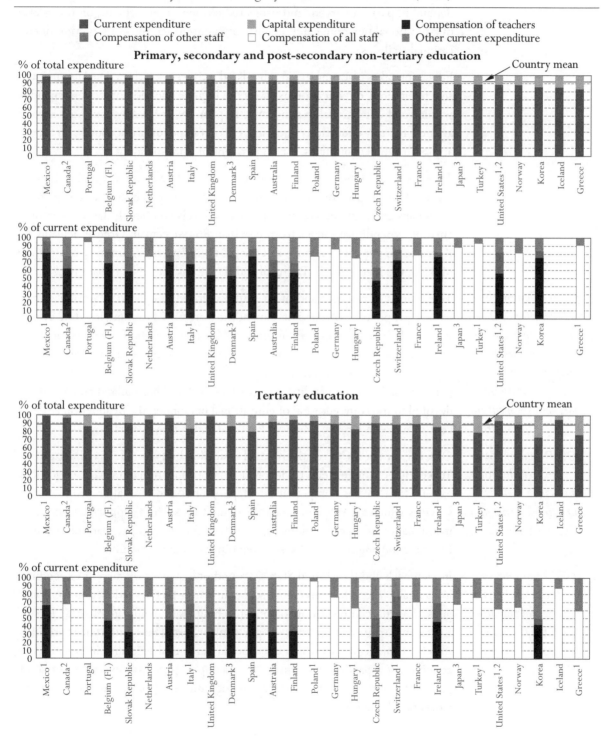

Chart B6.2

Distribution of total and current expenditure on educational institutions, by resource category and level of education (2000)

■ Current expenditure ▨ Capital expenditure ■ Compensation of teachers
▨ Compensation of other staff □ Compensation of all staff ▨ Other current expenditure

Primary, secondary and post-secondary non-tertiary education

% of total expenditure — Country mean

% of current expenditure

Tertiary education

% of total expenditure — Country mean

% of current expenditure

1. Public institutions.
2. Post-secondary non-tertiary included in tertiary education.
3. Post-secondary non-tertiary included in both upper secondary and tertiary education.
Countries are ranked in descending order of current expenditure on primary, secondary and post-secondary non-tertiary education.
Source: OECD. Table B6.3. See Annex 3 for notes *(www.oecd.org/edu/eag2003).*

B6

current expenditure (on, for example, teaching materials and supplies, maintenance of school buildings, preparation of student meals and renting of school facilities). The amount allocated to each of these functional categories will depend in part on current and projected changes in enrolment, on the salaries of educational personnel and on costs of maintenance and construction of educational facilities.

Education takes place mostly in school and university settings. The labour-intensive technology of education explains the large proportion of current spending within total educational expenditure. In primary, secondary, and post-secondary non-tertiary education combined, current expenditure accounts, on average across all OECD countries, for 92 per cent of total spending.

There is some noticeable variation between OECD countries with respect to the relative proportions of current and capital expenditure: at the primary, secondary and post-secondary non-tertiary levels combined, the proportion of current expenditure ranges from less than 86 per cent in Greece, Iceland and Korea to 96 per cent or more in Canada, the Flemish Community of Belgium, Mexico, the Netherlands, Portugal and the Slovak Republic (Chart B6.2).

In all except three OECD countries, 70 per cent or more of current expenditure at the primary, secondary and post-secondary non-tertiary levels is spent on staff salaries.

The salaries of teachers and other staff employed in education account for the largest proportion of current expenditure in OECD countries. On average across OECD countries, expenditure on the compensation of educational personnel accounts for 80 per cent of current expenditure at the primary, secondary and post-secondary non-tertiary levels of education combined. Although 70 per cent or less of expenditure in the Czech Republic, Finland and Sweden is devoted to the compensation of educational personnel, the proportion is 90 per cent or more in Greece, Mexico, Portugal and Turkey (Chart B6.2).

OECD countries with smaller education budgets invest relatively more in personnel and less in other services.

OECD countries with relatively small education budgets (Mexico, Portugal and Turkey, for example) tend to devote a larger proportion of current educational expenditure to the compensation of personnel and a smaller proportion to services which are sub-contracted or bought in, such as support services (*e.g.*, maintenance of school buildings), ancillary services (*e.g.*, preparation of meals for students) and renting of school buildings and other facilities.

OECD countries vary in the proportions of current expenditure which they allocate to the compensation of teachers and other staff.

In Denmark and the United States, around one quarter of current expenditure in primary, secondary and post-secondary non-tertiary education combined goes towards compensation of non-teaching staff, while in Austria, Ireland, Korea and Spain this figure is 10 per cent or less. These differences are likely to reflect the degree to which educational personnel specialise in non-teaching activities in a particular country (for example, principals who do not teach, guidance counsellors, bus drivers, school nurses, janitors and maintenance workers) (Table B6.3).

At the tertiary level, the proportion of total expenditure spent on capital outlays is larger than at the primary, secondary and post-secondary non-tertiary levels, generally because of more differentiated and advanced teaching facilities. In 16 out of 27 OECD countries, the proportion spent on capital expenditure at the tertiary level is 10 per cent or more, and in Greece, Korea, Spain and Turkey it is above 20 per cent (Chart B6.2).

At the tertiary level, the proportion of capital expenditure is generally larger because of differentiated and advanced teaching facilities.

Differences are likely to reflect how tertiary education is organised in each OECD country, as well as the degree to which expansion in enrolments requires the construction of new buildings.

OECD countries, on average, spend 31 per cent of current expenditure at the tertiary level on purposes other than the compensation of educational personnel. This is explained by the higher cost of facilities and equipment in higher education (Chart B6.2).

B6

Definitions and methodologies

The distinction between current and capital expenditure is the standard one used in national income accounting. Current expenditure refers to goods and services consumed within the current year, and must be made recurrently in order to sustain the production of educational services. Capital expenditure refers to assets which last longer than one year, including spending on construction, renovation or major repair of buildings and on new or replacement equipment. The capital expenditure reported here represents the value of educational capital acquired or created during the year in question – that is, the amount of capital formation – regardless of whether the capital expenditure was financed from current revenue or by borrowing. Neither current nor capital expenditure includes debt servicing.

Data refer to the financial year 2000 and are based on the UOE data collection on educational statistics administered by the OECD in 2002 (for details see Annex 3).

Calculations cover expenditure by public institutions or, where available, that of public and private institutions combined.

Current expenditure other than on the compensation of personnel includes expenditure on services which are sub-contracted or bought in, such as support services (*e.g.,* maintenance of school buildings), ancillary services (*e.g.,* preparation of meals for students) and renting of school buildings and other facilities. These services are obtained from outside providers (unlike the services provided by the education authorities or educational institutions themselves using their own personnel).

Expenditure on R&D includes all expenditure on research performed at universities and other tertiary education institutions, regardless of whether the research is financed from general institutional funds or through separate grants or contracts from public or private sponsors. The classification of expenditure is based on data collected from the institutions carrying out R&D rather than on the sources of funds.

"Ancillary services" are services provided by educational institutions that are peripheral to the main educational mission. The two main components of ancillary services are student welfare services and services for the general

B₆

public. At primary, secondary, and post-secondary non-tertiary levels, student welfare services include meals, school health services, and transportation to and from school. At the tertiary level, it includes halls of residence (dormitories), dining halls, and health care. Services for the general public include museums, radio and television broadcasting, sports, and recreational and cultural programmes. Expenditure on ancillary services including fees from students or households are excluded.

Educational core services are estimated as the residual of all expenditure, *i.e.,* total expenditure on educational institutions net of expenditure on R&D and ancillary services.

Note that data appearing in earlier editions of this publication may not always be comparable to data shown in the 2003 edition due to changes in definitions and coverage that were made as a result of the OECD expenditure comparability study (see Annex 3 at *www.oecd.org/edu/eag2003* for details on changes).

Table B6.1
Expenditure on institutions by service category as a percentage of GDP (2000)
Expenditure on instruction, research and development (R&D) and ancillary services in educational institutions
as a percentage of GDP and private expenditure on educational goods purchased outside educational institutions as a percentage of GDP

	Primary, secondary and post-secondary non-tertiary education				Tertiary education				
	Expenditure on educational institutions			Private payments on instructional services/ goods outside educational institutions	Expenditure on educational institutions				Private payments on instructional services/ goods outside educational institutions
	Educational core services	Ancillary services (transport, meals, housing provided by institutions)	Total		Educational core services	Ancillary services (transport, meals, housing provided by institutions)	Research and development at tertiary institutions	Total	
	(1)	(2)	(3)	(4)	(5)	(6)	(7)	(8)	(9)
Australia	4.21	0.16	4.37	0.14	1.04	0.09	0.43	1.56	0.15
Austria	x(3)	x(3)	3.88	m	0.80	x(5)	0.41	1.21	m
Belgium	x(3)	x(3)	3.62	m	0.86	x(5)	0.45	1.31	m
Belgium (Fl.)	3.24	0.22	3.46	0.18	0.76	0.05	0.44	1.26	0.14
Canada[1]	3.44	0.19	3.62	m	1.89	0.14	0.52	2.55	0.41
Czech Republic	2.62	0.46	3.08	m	0.69	0.04	0.17	0.90	m
Denmark[2]	x(3)	x(3)	4.16	0.78	1.12	x(5)	0.45	1.58	0.98
Finland	3.10	0.39	3.48	m	1.11	n	0.61	1.72	m
France[3]	3.68	0.58	4.25	0.14	0.80	0.07	0.23	1.10	0.08
Germany	3.51	0.08	3.59	0.19	0.63	n	0.40	1.03	0.07
Greece[4]	2.87	0.04	2.91	0.75	0.60	0.03	0.24	0.86	0.07
Hungary[4]	2.49	0.34	2.83	m	0.82	0.12	0.18	1.12	m
Iceland	x(3)	x(3)	4.87	m	x(8)	x(8)	x(8)	0.89	m
Ireland[3]	2.93	0.06	2.99	m	1.29	x(5)	0.21	1.50	m
Italy	3.14	0.12	3.26	0.05	0.84	0.04	x(6)	0.87	0.24
Japan[2]	x(3)	x(3)	2.91	0.80	x(8)	x(8)	x(8)	1.07	m
Korea	x(3)	x(3)	4.04	m	x(8)	x(8)	x(8)	2.57	m
Luxembourg	m	m	m	m	m	m	m	m	m
Mexico[3]	x(3)	x(3)	3.83	0.21	0.88	x(5)	0.17	1.05	0.18
Netherlands	3.07	0.03	3.11	0.17	0.74	n	0.48	1.23	0.06
New Zealand	x(3)	x(3)	4.56	m	x(8)	x(8)	x(8)	0.93	m
Norway	x(3)	x(3)	3.67	m	x(8)	x(8)	x(8)	1.25	n
Poland[3,4]	3.52	0.23	3.75	m	0.58	n	0.19	0.77	m
Portugal	x(3)	x(3)	4.13	0.06	x(8)	x(8)	x(8)	1.05	0.07
Slovak Republic	2.53	0.25	2.77	0.24	0.66	0.07	0.07	0.80	0.10
Spain	3.17	0.11	3.28	m	0.92	x(5)	0.26	1.19	m
Sweden	3.93	0.43	4.36	0.55	0.86	a	0.79	1.65	0.59
Switzerland	x(3)	x(3)	4.26	m	x(8)	x(8)	x(8)	1.19	m
Turkey[3,4]	2.26	0.11	2.37	m	1.02	m	0.01	1.03	m
United Kingdom	3.54	0.25	3.79	m	0.64	n	0.40	1.04	0.09
United States[1]	3.74	0.14	3.87	0.02	2.26	0.16	0.29	2.71	0.11
Country mean	*3.21*	*0.22*	*3.62*	*0.31*	*0.96*	*0.05*	*0.33*	*1.29*	*0.21*

Note: x indicates that data are included in another column. The column reference is shown in brackets after "x". e.g., x(2) means that data are included in column 2.
1. Post-secondary non-tertiary is included in tertiary education and excluded from primary, secondary and post-secondary non-tertiary education.
2. Post-secondary non-tertiary included in both upper secondary and tertiary education.
3. Research and development expenditure and thus total expenditure are underestimated.
4. Ancillary services in public institutions only. Other ancillary services included in instructional services.
Source: OECD. See Annex 3 for notes (*www.oecd.org/edu/eag2003*).

OECD COUNTRIES

B6

Table B6.2
Expenditure per student on instruction, ancillary services and research and development (R&D) (2000)
Expenditure per student on educational institutions in US dollars converted using PPPs from public and private sources, by type of service and level of education

| | Primary, secondary and post-secondary non-tertiary education | | | Tertiary education | | | |
| | Direct expenditure on educational institutions | | | Direct expenditure on educational institutions | | | |
	Educational core services	Ancillary services (transport, meals, housing provided by institutions)	Total	Educational core services	Ancillary services (transport, meals, housing provided by institutions)	Research and development	Total
	(1)	(2)	(3)	(4)	(5)	(6)	(7)
Australia	5 671	210	5 881	8 835	672	3 347	12 854
Austria	x(3)	x(3)	7 883	7 148	x(4)	3 702	10 851
Belgium	x(3)	x(3)	5 732	7 098	x(4)	3 673	10 771
Belgium (Fl.)	5 421	369	5 790	7 118	511	4 153	11 782
Canada[1]	5 640	307	5 947	11 093	826	3 065	14 983
Czech Republic	2 258	398	2 656	4 151	259	1 022	5 431
Denmark[2]	x(3)	x(3)	7 436	8 553	x(4)	3 428	11 981
Finland	4 705	587	5 292	5 323	19	2 902	8 244
France	5 517	863	6 380	6 094	537	1 742	8 373
Germany	6 048	138	6 185	6 643	30	4 225	10 898
Greece[3]	3 475	49	3 524	2 359	109	933	3 402
Hungary[3]	2 120	290	2 410	5 140	779	1 106	7 024
Iceland[3]	x(3)	x(3)	6 373	x(7)	x(7)	x(7)	7 994
Ireland	3 851	83	3 934	9 552	x(5)	1 531	11 083
Italy[3]	6 489	250	6 739	7 717	348	x(4)	8 065
Japan[2]	x(3)	x(3)	5 913	x(7)	x(7)	x(7)	10 914
Korea	x(3)	x(3)	3 608	x(7)	x(7)	x(7)	6 118
Luxembourg	m	m	m	m	m	m	m
Mexico	x(3)	x(3)	1 415	3 918	x(5)	770	4 688
Netherlands	5 084	54	5 138	7 230	n	4 704	11934
New Zealand	x(3)	x(3)	m	x(7)	x(7)	x(7)	m
Norway[3]	x(3)	x(3)	7 399	x(7)	x(7)	x(7)	13 353
Poland[3]	1 869	119	1 988	2 443	n	779	3 222
Portugal	x(3)	x(3)	4 500	x(7)	x(7)	x(7)	4 766
Slovak Republic	1 579	153	1 732	4 105	432	412	4 949
Spain	4 474	162	4 636	5 182	x(4)	1 483	6 666
Sweden	5 701	620	6 321	7 869	a	7 228	15 097
Switzerland[3]	x(3)	x(3)	7 210	x(7)	x(7)	x(7)	18 450
Turkey[3]	m	m	822	4 071	m	50	4 121
United Kingdom	4 472	412	4 884	5 950	n	3 707	9 657
United States[1,4]	7 600	277	7 877	16 982	1 168	2 208	20 358
Country mean	*4 554*	*297*	*5 010*	*6 701*	*356*	*2 499*	*9 571*

Note: x indicates that data are included in another column. The column reference is shown in brackets after "x". *e.g.*, x(2) means that data are included in column 2.
1. Post-secondary non-tertiary included in tertiary education.
2. Post-secondary non-tertiary included in both upper secondary and tertiary education.
3. Public institutions only.
4. Public and independent private institutions only.
Source: OECD. See Annex 3 for notes (*www.oecd.org/edu/eag2003*).

Table B6.3
Expenditure on educational institutions, by resource category (2000)
Distribution of total and current expenditure on educational institutions from public and private sources, by resource category and level of education

	Primary, secondary and post-secondary non-tertiary education						Tertiary education					
	Percentage of total expenditure		Percentage of current expenditure				Percentage of total expenditure		Percentage of current expenditure			
	Current	Capital	Compensation of teachers	Compensation of other staff	Compensation of all staff	Other current	Current	Capital	Compensation of teachers	Compensation of other staff	Compensation of all staff	Other current
	(1)	(2)	(3)	(4)	(5)	(6)	(7)	(8)	(9)	(10)	(11)	(12)
Australia	93.5	6.5	56.1	16.0	72.2	27.8	91.3	8.7	32.6	28.1	60.8	39.2
Austria	94.7	5.3	69.7	8.5	78.2	21.8	96.2	3.8	47.3	19.7	67.1	32.9
Belgium	m	m	m	m	m	m	m	m	m	m	m	m
Belgium (Fl.)	96.5	3.5	68.1	13.7	81.8	18.2	95.9	4.1	46.5	21.3	67.8	32.2
Canada[1]	96.8	3.2	61.3	15.1	76.4	23.6	96.1	3.9	x(11)	x(11)	67.1	32.9
Czech Republic	92.2	7.8	46.5	16.4	62.9	37.2	89.7	10.4	26.8	23.5	50.3	49.7
Denmark[2]	93.6	6.4	52.3	26.1	78.4	21.6	85.9	14.1	52.0	25.4	77.4	22.6
Finland	93.2	6.8	56.3	12.1	68.4	31.6	93.9	6.1	33.9	25.5	59.4	40.6
France	91.3	8.7	x(5)	x(5)	78.8	21.2	89.1	10.9	x(11)	x(11)	70.1	29.9
Germany	92.7	7.3	x(5)	x(5)	85.7	14.3	89.2	10.8	x(11)	x(11)	75.9	24.1
Greece[3]	83.2	16.8	x(5)	x(5)	91.0	9.0	75.6	24.4	x(11)	x(11)	59.6	40.4
Hungary[1]	92.6	7.4	x(5)	x(5)	74.9	25.1	82.4	17.6	x(11)	x(11)	62.6	37.4
Iceland	85.2	14.8	x(5)	x(5)	m	m	94.4	5.6	x(11)	x(11)	87.4	12.6
Ireland[1]	91.0	9.0	76.3	5.5	81.9	18.1	85.3	14.7	45.7	23.4	69.1	30.9
Italy[3]	94.6	5.4	66.9	15.6	82.5	17.5	82.8	17.2	44.5	23.2	67.7	32.3
Japan[2]	88.8	11.2	x(5)	x(5)	88.1	11.9	80.9	19.1	x(11)	x(11)	67.5	32.5
Korea	84.2	15.8	75.0	8.5	83.5	16.5	72.2	27.8	37.3	12.8	50.0	50.0
Luxembourg	m	m	m	m	m	m	m	m	m	m	m	m
Mexico[3]	97.6	2.4	80.6	14.4	95.0	5.0	98.4	1.6	65.6	20.1	85.7	14.3
Netherlands	96.1	3.9	x(5)	x(5)	76.7	23.3	94.1	5.9	x(11)	x(11)	76.7	23.3
New Zealand	m	m	m	m	m	m	m	m	m	m	m	m
Norway	88.2	11.8	x(5)	x(5)	81.7	18.3	88.5	11.5	x(11)	x(11)	63.8	36.2
Poland[3]	92.9	7.1	x(5)	x(5)	77.0	23.0	92.5	7.5	x(11)	x(11)	95.8	4.2
Portugal	96.5	3.5	x(5)	x(5)	94.3	5.7	85.7	14.3	x(11)	x(11)	76.2	23.8
Slovak Republic	96.3	3.7	58.1	17.9	76.1	23.9	89.8	10.2	32.6	21.8	54.4	45.6
Spain	93.6	6.4	76.4	9.5	85.9	14.1	79.4	20.6	56.4	21.5	77.9	22.1
Sweden	m	m	46.3	15.0	61.6	38.4	m	m	x(11)	x(11)	57.8	42.2
Switzerland[1]	91.4	8.6	71.9	12.8	84.7	15.3	88.4	11.6	52.8	24.4	77.2	22.8
Turkey[3]	88.5	11.5	x(5)	x(5)	93.4	6.6	78.5	21.5	x(11)	x(11)	75.8	24.2
United Kingdom	94.3	5.7	53.1	20.5	73.6	26.4	98.2	1.8	33.0	24.8	57.8	42.2
United States[1,3]	88.4	11.6	55.9	26.3	82.1	17.9	92.8	7.2	x(11)	x(11)	61.7	38.3
Country mean	*92.2*	*7.8*	*63.0*	*14.9*	*80.3*	*19.7*	*88.3*	*11.7*	*43.7*	*22.7*	*68.8*	*31.2*
Argentina[3]	96.9	3.1	61.1	29.5	90.7	9.3	98.6	1.4	54.8	35.5	90.4	9.6
Brazil[3,4]	94.7	5.3	x(5)	x(5)	77.3	22.7	97.0	3.0	x(11)	x(11)	82.5	17.5
Chile[3]	84.7	15.3	x(1)	x(1)	x(1)	x(1)	92.0	8.0	x(7)	x(7)	x(7)	x(7)
India[1,3,4]	97.5	2.5	78.6	9.6	88.2	11.8	98.4	1.6	99.8	x(9)	99.8	0.2
Indonesia[3]	93.9	6.1	78.0	7.7	85.8	14.2	82.0	18.0	87.2	11.8	99.0	1.0
Israel	91.6	8.4	x(5)	x(5)	77.5	22.5	90.5	9.5	x(11)	x(11)	76.5	23.5
Jamaica[3]	95.4	4.6	48.4	8.8	57.2	42.8	93.5	6.5	56.9	21.9	78.8	21.2
Malaysia[3]	69.5	30.5	69.8	12.4	82.2	17.8	54.0	46.0	31.6	13.5	45.1	54.9
Paraguay[3]	93.0	7.0	65.6	12.9	78.5	21.5	92.3	7.7	59.8	15.2	75.0	25.0
Philippines[3]	91.6	8.4	85.6	m	85.6	14.4	95.4	4.6	75.2	m	75.2	24.8
Tunisia[3]	88.8	11.2	x(1)	x(1)	x(1)	x(1)	m	m	m	m	m	m
Uruguay[3]	95.3	4.7	66.7	18.9	85.6	14.4	94.9	5.1	63.8	22.7	86.5	13.5
Zimbabwe	98.2	1.8	60.2	m	60.2	39.8	m	m	m	m	m	m

Note: x indicates that data are included in another column. The column reference is shown in brackets after "x". *e.g.*, x(2) means that data are included in column 2.
1. Post-secondary non-tertiary education included in tertiary education.
2. Post-secondary non-tertiary included in both upper secondary and tertiary education.
3. Public institutions only.
4. Year of reference 1999.
Source: OECD. See Annex 3 for notes (*www.oecd.org/edu/eag2003*).

(left margin: OECD COUNTRIES / NON-OECD COUNTRIES)

*(right margin label: **B6**)*

ACCESS TO EDUCATION, PARTICIPATION AND PROGRESSION

OVERVIEW

Chapter C looks at access to education, participation and progression, in terms of…

…the expected duration of schooling, overall and at different levels of education, as well as entry to and participation in different types of educational programmes and institutions,…

…cross-border movements of students…

C

…and the transition from education to work.

INDICATOR C1: SCHOOL EXPECTANCY AND ENROLMENT RATES

- In 25 out of 28 OECD countries, individuals participate in formal education for between 16 and 20 years, on average. Most of the variation among countries on this measure derives from differences in enrolments in upper secondary education.

- School expectancy increased between 1995 and 2001 in 20 out of 21 OECD countries reporting comparable data.

- In half of the OECD countries, more than 70 per cent of children aged three to four are enrolled in either pre-primary or primary programmes. At the other end of the spectrum, a 17-year-old can expect to spend an average of 2.6 years in tertiary education.

- In the majority of OECD countries, females can expect to receive 0.5 more years, on average, of education than males.

Chart C1.1

School expectancy (2001)

Expected years of schooling under current conditions, excluding education for children under five years of age, by level of education

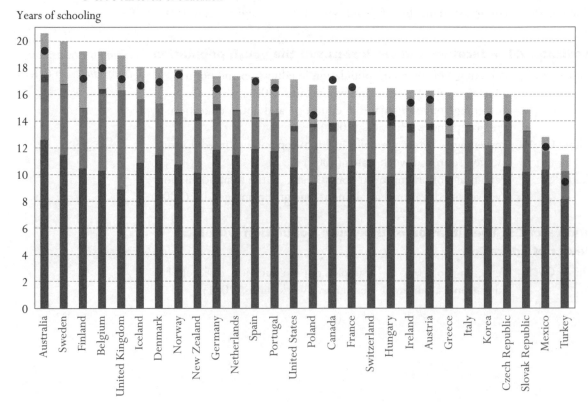

Countries are ranked in descending order of the total school expectancy for all levels of education in 2001.
Source: OECD. Table C1.1. See Annex 3 for notes *(www.oecd.org/edu/eag2003).*

C1

Policy context

A well-educated population is critical for a country's economic and social development, present and future. Societies therefore, have an intrinsic interest in ensuring broad access to a wide variety of educational opportunities for children and adults. Early childhood programmes prepare children for primary education. They can provide help to combat linguistic and social disadvantages and provide opportunities to enhance and complement home educational experiences. Primary and secondary education lay the foundations for a wide range of competencies and prepare young people to become lifelong learners and productive members of society. Tertiary education provides a range of options for acquiring advanced knowledge and skills, either immediately after school or later.

This indicator presents several measures of participation in education to elucidate levels of access to education in different OECD countries. Enrolment trends at different levels of education are also presented as an indicator of the evolution of access to education.

This indicator examines enrolments at all levels of education.

Evidence and explanations

Overall participation in education

One way of looking at participation in education is to estimate the number of years during which a five-year-old child can expect to be in either full-time or part-time education during his/her lifetime, given current enrolment rates. *School expectancy* is estimated by taking the sum of enrolment rates for each single year of age, starting at age five (Chart C1.1). In OECD countries, a child in Mexico and Turkey can expect to be in education for 12 years or less, compared to 19 or more years in Australia, Belgium, Finland, Sweden and the United Kingdom.

In 25 out of 28 OECD countries, individuals participate in formal education for between 16 and 20 years, on average.

C1

Most of the variation in school expectancy among OECD countries comes from differences in enrolment rates in upper secondary education. Relative differences in participation are large at the tertiary level, but apply to a smaller proportion of the cohort and therefore have less of an effect on school expectancy.

Most of the variation comes from differences in enrolment rates in upper secondary education.

Measures of the average length of schooling like *school expectancy* are affected by participation rates over the life cycle and therefore underestimate the actual number of years of schooling in systems where access to education is expanding. Nor does this measure distinguish between full-time and part-time participation. OECD countries with relatively large proportions of part-time enrolments will therefore tend to have relatively high values. In Australia, Belgium, Portugal, Sweden and the United Kingdom, part-time education accounts for three or more years of school expectancy (Table C1.1).

In OECD countries where school expectancy at a given level of education exceeds the number of grades at that level, repeating a level (or, in the case of Australia, the number of adults enrolling in those programmes) has a greater impact on school expectancy than the proportion of students leaving school before completing that level of education.

*Long school expectancy
does not necessarily
imply that all young
people have access
to higher levels of
education...*

Enrolment rates are influenced by entry rates to a particular level of education and by the typical duration of studies. A high number of expected years in education, therefore, does not necessarily imply that all young people will participate in education for a long time. Belgium and Sweden, where five-year-olds can expect to be in school for more than 19 years, have nearly full enrolment (rates over 90 per cent) for 15 and 13 years of education, respectively. Conversely, Australia and Finland, which have equally high school expectancy, have nearly full enrolment (rates over 90 per cent) for only 12 years of education (Table C1.2).

*...but in most OECD
countries, virtually all
young people receive at
least 12 years of formal
education.*

In most OECD countries, virtually all young people have access to 12 years of formal education. At least 90 per cent of students are enrolled in an age band spanning 14 or more years in Belgium, France and Japan. Mexico and Turkey, by contrast, have enrolment rates exceeding 90 per cent for a period of seven years or less (Table C1.2).

*In the majority of OECD
countries, females can
expect to receive 0.5
more years, on average,
of education than males.*

In the majority of OECD countries, females can expect to receive 0.5 more years, on average, of education than males. The variation in school expectancy is generally greater for females than for males. Some OECD countries show sizeable gender differences. In Korea, Switzerland and Turkey, males can expect to receive between 0.6 and 1.9 years more education than females. The opposite is true in Belgium, Finland, Iceland, New Zealand, Norway, Sweden and the United Kingdom, where the expected duration of enrolment for females exceeds that of males by more than one year (in Sweden by more than three years) (Table C1.1).

Trends in participation in education

*School expectancy
increased between 1995
and 2001 in 20 out of
21 OECD countries.*

School expectancy increased between 1995 and 2001 in 20 out of 21 OECD countries for which comparable trend data are available (Table C1.1). In Greece, Hungary, Poland and Turkey, the increase was 15 per cent or more over this relatively short period.

Participation in early childhood education

*In half of the OECD
countries, over 70 per
cent of children aged
three to four are enrolled
in either pre-primary or
primary programmes.*

In the majority of OECD countries, universal enrolment, which is defined here as enrolment rates exceeding 90 per cent, starts between the ages of five and six years. However, in Belgium, the Czech Republic, Denmark, France, Germany, Hungary, Iceland, Italy, Japan, New Zealand, Norway, Spain, Sweden and the United Kingdom, over 70 per cent of children aged three to four are already enrolled in either pre-primary or primary programmes (Table C1.2). Their enrolment rates range from under 22 per cent in Canada, Korea, Switzerland and Turkey, to over 90 per cent in Belgium, France, Iceland, Italy and Spain.

Given the impact of early childhood education and care on building a strong foundation for lifelong learning and on ensuring equitable access to learning opportunities later, pre-primary education is very important. However, institutionally based pre-primary programmes covered by this indicator are not the only form of quality early childhood education and care. Inferences about access to and quality of pre-primary education and care should therefore be made very carefully.

Participation towards the end of compulsory education and beyond

Several factors, including a higher risk of unemployment and other forms of exclusion for young people with insufficient education, influence the decision to stay enrolled beyond the end of compulsory education. In many OECD countries, the transition from education to employment has become a longer and more complex process that provides the opportunity or the obligation for students to combine learning and work to develop marketable skills (see Indicator C4).

Compulsory education in OECD countries ends between the ages of 14 (Korea, Portugal and Turkey) and 18 (Belgium, Germany and the Netherlands), and in most countries at age 15 or 16 (Table C1.2). However, the statutory age at which compulsory education ends does not always correspond to the age at which enrolment is universal.

Compulsory education ends between the ages of 14 and 18 in OECD countries, and in most countries at age 15 or 16.

While participation rates in most OECD countries are high until the end of compulsory education, they drop below 90 per cent before the age at which students are no longer legally required to be enrolled in school in Mexico, the Netherlands, Turkey and the United States. In the Netherlands and the United States, this may be due in part to the fact that compulsory education ends at age 18 and 17 respectively, which is comparatively high. By contrast, in 20 OECD countries, virtually all children remain in school beyond the age at which compulsory education ends (Table C1.2).

Participation in education tends to be high until the end of compulsory education, but in four OECD countries, more than 10 per cent of students never finish compulsory education.

In most OECD countries, enrolment rates gradually decline starting in the last years of upper secondary education. There are several noteworthy exceptions, however where enrolment rates remain relatively high until the age of 20 to 29. In Australia, Belgium, Poland and the Nordic countries, for example, enrolment rates for 20 to 29-year-olds still exceed 25 per cent (Table C1.2)

In Australia, Belgium, Poland and the Nordic countries, one out of four 20 to 29-year-olds participates in education.

The transition to post-secondary education

Graduates of upper secondary programmes who decide not to enter the labour market upon graduation and people who are already working and want to upgrade their skills can choose from a wide range of post-secondary programmes. In OECD countries, tertiary programmes vary in the extent to which they are theoretically based and designed to prepare students for advanced research programmes or professions with high skill requirements (tertiary-type A), or focus on occupationally specific skills so that students can directly enter the labour market (tertiary-type B). The institutional location of programmes used to give a relatively clear idea of their nature (*e.g.*, university versus non-university institutions of higher education), but these distinctions have become blurred and are therefore not applied in the OECD indicators.

Upper secondary graduates in many education systems can also enrol in relatively short programmes (less than two years) to prepare for trades or specific vocational fields. These programmes are offered as advanced or second upper secondary programmes in some OECD countries (*e.g.*, Austria, Germany, Hungary and Spain); in others they are offered in post-secondary education (*e.g.*,

Post-secondary non-tertiary programmes are offered in 25 out of 29 OECD countries.

Canada and the United States). From an internationally comparable point of view, these programmes straddle upper secondary and tertiary education and are therefore classified as a different level of education (post-secondary non-tertiary education). In 25 out of 29 OECD countries, these kinds of programmes are offered to upper secondary graduates (see Table C1.1).

Participation in tertiary education

On average in OECD countries, a 17-year-old can expect to receive 2.6 years of tertiary education.

On average in OECD countries, a 17-year-old can expect to receive 2.6 years of tertiary education. Both tertiary entry rates and the typical duration of study affect the expectancy of tertiary education. In Australia, Finland, Greece, Korea, New Zealand, Norway, Spain, Sweden and the United States, the figure is three years or more. In the Czech Republic, Mexico, the Slovak Republic and Turkey, by contrast, the expectancy of tertiary education is 1.6 years or less (see Table C1.1 and Indicator C2).

Policies to expand education have, in many OECD countries, increased pressure for greater access to tertiary education.

Policies to expand education have increased pressure for greater access to tertiary education in many OECD countries. Thus far, this pressure has more than compensated for declines in cohort sizes which had led, until recently, to predictions of stable or declining demand from school leavers in several OECD countries. Whereas some OECD countries are now showing signs of a levelling demand for tertiary education, the overall trend remains upward.

Definitions and methodologies

Data refer to 2000-2001 and are based on the UOE data collection on education statistics, which is administered annually by the OECD, and the 2002 World Education Indicators Programme.

Except where otherwise noted, figures are based on head counts, that is, they do not distinguish between full-time and part-time study. A standardised distinction between full-time and part-time participants is very difficult because in several OECD countries, the concept of part-time study is not recognised, although in practice, at least some students would be classified as part-time by other countries. For some OECD countries, part-time education is not completely covered by the reported data.

The average length of time a five-year-old can expect to be formally enrolled in school during his/her lifetime, or *school expectancy*, is calculated by adding the net enrolment percentages for each single year of age from five onwards. The average duration of schooling for the cohort will reflect any tendency to lengthen (or shorten) studies in subsequent years. When comparing data on school expectancy, however, it must be borne in mind that neither the length of the school year nor the quality of education is necessarily the same in each country.

Net enrolment rates expressed as percentages in Table C1.2 are calculated by dividing the number of students of a particular age group enrolled in all levels of education by the size of the population of that age group. Table C1.1 shows the index of change in school expectancy between 1995 and 2001. Enrolment data for 1994-1995 were obtained through a special survey in 2000 and follow the ISCED-97 classification.

C₁

Table C1.1
School expectancy (2001)
Expected years of schooling under current conditions, excluding education for children under the age of five

	2001							Full-time	Part-time	Index of change in school expectancy for all levels of education combined (1995=100)
	Full-time and part-time							All levels of education combined	All levels of education combined	
	All levels of education combined			Primary and lower secondary education	Upper secondary education	Post-secondary non-tertiary education	Tertiary education			
	M+F	Males	Females	M+F				M+F		M+F
	(1)	(2)	(3)	(4)	(5)	(6)	(7)	(8)	(9)	(10)
Australia*	20.6	20.3	20.9	11.9	4.3	0.6	3.1	15.5	5.0	107
Austria*	16.3	16.2	16.3	8.2	3.8	0.5	2.4	16.3	n	104
Belgium*	19.2	18.6	19.8	9.3	5.7	0.4	2.8	16.2	3.0	107
Canada	16.6	16.4	16.9	8.8	3.4	0.7	2.8	15.7	1.0	98
Czech Republic	16.0	15.9	16.1	9.1	3.6	0.2	1.6	15.8	0.2	112
Denmark	18.0	17.5	18.5	9.6	3.9	n	2.6	18.0	n	106
Finland*	19.2	18.5	20.0	9.1	4.5	0.1	4.2	19.2	n	112
France	16.6	16.4	16.8	9.5	3.3	n	2.6	16.6	n	101
Germany*	17.3	17.5	17.2	10.1	3.0	0.5	2.1	17.3	0.1	106
Greece	16.1	15.9	16.4	9.0	2.8	0.3	3.1	15.9	0.2	116
Hungary*	16.4	16.2	16.7	8.1	3.8	0.7	2.2	14.8	1.6	115
Iceland	18.0	17.3	18.8	9.9	4.7	0.1	2.4	16.2	1.8	108
Ireland*	16.3	15.8	16.8	10.8	2.2	0.7	2.5	15.3	1.0	106
Italy*	16.1	15.7	16.4	8.2	4.4	0.1	2.4	16.0	0.1	m
Japan	m	m	m	9.1	3.0	m	m	m	m	m
Korea	16.1	17.0	15.1	8.9	2.8	m	3.9	16.1	n	112
Luxembourg	m	m	m	9.1	3.6	0.1	m	m	m	m
Mexico	12.8	12.7	12.8	9.5	1.4	m	1.1	12.6	n	105
Netherlands	17.3	17.5	17.2	10.5	3.3	0.1	2.5	16.5	0.8	m
New Zealand	17.8	17.0	18.6	10.1	3.8	0.6	3.2	15.5	2.3	m
Norway	17.8	17.2	18.5	9.9	3.8	0.1	3.1	16.6	1.2	102
Poland	16.7	16.2	17.2	8.0	4.1	0.3	2.9	14.6	2.1	116
Portugal	17.1	16.7	17.6	10.8	2.9	m	2.5	13.8	3.3	104
Slovak Republic	14.9	14.8	15.0	9.0	3.0	0.1	1.6	14.2	0.6	m
Spain	17.3	16.9	17.7	10.9	2.3	0.1	3.0	16.7	0.6	102
Sweden	20.0	18.5	21.6	9.7	5.2	0.1	3.2	16.5	3.5	m
Switzerland	16.5	16.8	16.1	9.5	3.3	0.3	1.8	16.0	0.4	m
Turkey*	11.5	12.2	10.3	8.0	2.1	m	1.2	11.5	n	121
United Kingdom	18.9	17.9	19.9	8.9	7.4	m	2.6	14.6	4.3	110
United States	17.1	16.7	17.5	9.5	2.7	0.4	3.5	15.5	1.6	m
Country mean	*16.9*	*16.6*	*17.2*	*9.4*	*3.6*	*0.2*	*2.6*	*15.7*	*1.2*	*108*
Argentina[1]	17.0	16.3	17.6	10.8	2.2	m	3.0	14.7	2.2	m
Brazil[1]	15.7	15.4	15.9	10.8	2.7	m	0.9	15.7	n	m
Chile[1]	14.8	15.0	14.6	8.4	3.5	m	1.7	14.8	n	m
China	11.7	m	m	8.9	1.2	m	0.6	11.2	0.5	m
Egypt	11.3	11.6	10.9	8.0	2.0	0.1	1.1	11.2	0.1	m
Indonesia	11.2	11.4	11.0	8.9	1.2	pm	0.7	11.2	n	m
Israel	15.6	15.4	15.7	8.6	3.1	0.1	2.7	15.1	0.4	m
Jamaica	13.2	m	m	9.2	1.6	0.7	0.8	12.8	0.4	m
Malaysia[1]	12.6	12.3	12.9	8.6	1.8	0.2	1.3	12.4	0.1	m
Paraguay[1]	11.9	11.9	11.9	9.2	1.4	m	0.6	11.9	n	m
Peru[1]	13.5	13.4	13.6	10.3	1.4	0.5	0.6	13.5	n	m
Philippines[1]	11.9	11.8	12.0	9.3	0.7	0.2	1.4	11.9	n	m
Russian Federation	14.6	m	m	7.0	1.2	0.7	3.2	14.6	m	m
Thailand	13.2	13.2	13.2	9.6	2.4	n	2.0	13.2	m	m
Tunisia	13.7	m	m	9.9	2.3	n	1.0	13.7	n	m
Uruguay[1]	15.8	15.5	16.0	10.0	2.6	m	1.9	15.8	n	m
Zimbabwe	12.2	12.6	11.8	9.6	1.3	n	0.2	12.2	n	m

Note: x indicates that data are included in another column. The column reference is shown in brackets after "x". *e.g.*, x(2) means that data are included in column 2.
1. Year of reference 2000.
* See Annex 3 for notes (*www.oecd.org/edu/eag2003*).
Source: OECD.

OECD COUNTRIES

NON-OECD COUNTRIES

C1

Table C1.2
Enrolment rates (2001)
Full-time and part-time students in public and private institutions, by age

	Ending age of compulsory education	Number of years at which over 90% of the population are enrolled	Age range at which over 90% of the population are enrolled	Students aged:					
				4 and under as a percentage of the population of 3 to 4-year-olds	5-14 as a percentage of the population of 5 to 14-year-olds	15-19 as a percentage of the population of 15 to 19-year-olds	20-29 as a percentage of the population of 20 to 29-year-olds	30-39 as a percentage of the population of 30 to 39-year-olds	40 and over as a percentage of the population of over 40-year-olds
	(1)	(2)	(3)	(4)	(5)	(6)	(7)	(8)	(9)
Australia	15	12	5 - 16	38.1	100.1	81.1	28.3	14.4	6.6
Austria	15	12	5 - 16	62.1	98.7	76.9	18.6	4.1	0.4
Belgium*	18	15	3 - 17	119.4	100.2	91.0	26.5	7.3	2.9
Canada	16	12	6 - 17	20.8	97.2	75.0	21.2	4.3	1.1
Czech Republic	15	13	5 - 17	76.5	99.8	87.8	14.7	1.1	0.1
Denmark	16	11	4 - 15	84.6	97.2	82.9	31.5	5.7	0.9
Finland	16	12	6 - 17	38.7	93.5	85.3	39.2	10.4	2.1
France*	16	15	3 - 17	119.3	101.0	86.6	19.6	1.7	a
Germany	18	12	6 - 17	70.4	100.1	89.4	24.2	2.8	0.2
Greece	15	10	6 - 16	29.2	98.1	77.0	23.8	0.3	n
Hungary	16	12	5 - 16	80.7	99.4	79.0	20.0	3.8	0.4
Iceland*	16	13	4 - 16	122.7	98.9	79.2	30.1	6.8	1.9
Ireland*	15	12	5 - 16	26.1	100.6	80.9	16.6	3.0	x(8)
Italy*	15	13	3 - 15	98.9	99.4	72.2	17.1	2.0	x(8)
Japan	15	14	4 - 17	76.8	101.0	m	m	m	m
Korea	14	12	6 - 17	18.2	92.6	79.3	25.0	1.6	0.3
Luxembourg	15	11	4 - 15	68.8	92.2	78.1	6.0	0.3	n
Mexico	15	7	6 - 12	35.2	95.0	41.0	9.1	2.9	0.4
Netherlands	18	13	4 - 16	48.9	99.3	86.2	24.3	3.2	0.7
New Zealand	16	12	4 - 15	85.9	99.3	73.0	23.4	10.0	3.4
Norway	16	12	6 - 17	75.9	97.6	85.3	26.3	6.3	1.4
Poland	15	12	6 - 17	29.0	94.3	85.5	25.8	3.8	x(8)
Portugal	14	11	5 - 15	67.9	107.0	73.3	21.7	3.4	0.6
Slovak Republic	16	11	6 - 16	68.5	97.9	74.6	12.0	1.3	0.2
Spain*	16	12	4 - 16	107.5	103.6	80.1	23.5	2.5	0.4
Sweden*	16	13	6 - 18	73.1	98.1	86.4	33.0	14.6	3.6
Switzerland	15	11	6 - 16	21.5	98.7	83.3	19.7	3.5	0.2
Turkey*	14	6	7 - 12	n	83.5	30.0	5.4	0.3	n
United Kingdom*	16	12	4 - 15	81.0	98.7	74.7	23.3	13.0	5.7
United States	17	11	5 - 15	47.4	102.1	77.6	22.6	4.9	1.2
Country mean	*16*	*12*		*63.1*	*98.2*	*77.7*	*21.8*	*4.8*	*1.3*
Argentina[1]	14	10	5 - 14	39.1	105.6	65.8	23.3	5.4	1.4
Brazil[1]	14	9	7 - 15	25.4	89.8	74.6	20.8	6.7	1.8
Chile[1]	14	9	6 - 14	23.1	93.6	67.8	m	m	m
China	14	5	7 - 12	n	81.7	m	m	m	m
Egypt	13	6	6 - 12	6.7	85.3	32.4	m	n	n
India[1]	14	m	m	m	m	m	m	m	m
Indonesia	15	7	6 - 13	n	86.4	44.8	3.4	n	n
Israel	15	11	5 - 16	104.6	96.9	63.3	15.1	3.6	0.8
Jamaica	12	11	4 - 14	70.9	97.8	40.6	m	m	m
Malaysia[1]	12	8	6 - 13	12.7	93.1	46.9	8.6	0.5	0.1
Paraguay[1]	14	5	7 - 11	6.7	87.6	50.4	4.1	0.2	0.1
Peru[1]	16	9	6 - 14	54.1	99.3	53.8	9.1	1.8	0.4
Philippines[1]	12	7	7 - 13	0.4	85.1	35.6	m	m	m
Russian Federation	15	9	7 - 15	m	83.3	70.8	15.4	m	m
Thailand	14	8	4 - 11	60.3	96.5	54.1	m	m	m
Tunisia	16	5	6 - 10	26.0	86.7	53.9	m	n	n
Uruguay[1]	15	9	6 - 14	25.3	98.5	65.9	20.4	4.1	0.6
Zimbabwe	12	7	7 - 13	n	88.4	38.3	n	n	n

OECD COUNTRIES / *NON-OECD COUNTRIES*

C1

Note: Ending age of compulsory education is the age at which compulsory schooling ends. For example, an ending age of 18 indicates that all students under 18 are legally obliged to participate in education.
Note: x indicates that data are included in another column. The column reference is shown in brackets after "x". *e.g.,* x(2) means that data are included in column 2.
1. Year of reference 2000.
* See Annex 3 for notes (*www.oecd.org/edu/eag2003*).
Source: OECD.

INDICATOR C2: ENTRY TO AND EXPECTED YEARS IN TERTIARY EDUCATION AND PARTICIPATION IN SECONDARY EDUCATION

- Today, four out of ten school leavers are likely to attend tertiary programmes leading to the equivalent of a bachelor's or higher tertiary-type A degree. In some OECD countries, every second school leaver is likely to attend such a programme.

- On average in OECD countries, a 17-year-old can now expect to enrol in 2.6 years of tertiary-type A programmes, of which 2 years will be full-time.

- With the exception of France and Germany, participation in tertiary education grew in all OECD countries between 1995 and 2001.

- The majority of tertiary students are enrolled in public institutions, but in Belgium, Japan, Korea, the Netherlands and the United Kingdom, most students are enrolled in privately managed institutions.

- The majority of primary and secondary students are enrolled in public institutions. However, privately managed schools now enrol, on average, 10 per cent of primary students, 13 per cent of lower secondary students and 20 per cent of upper secondary students.

Chart C2.1
Entry rates to tertiary education (2001)
Sum of net entry rates for single year of age in tertiary-type A and tertiary-type B education

C₂

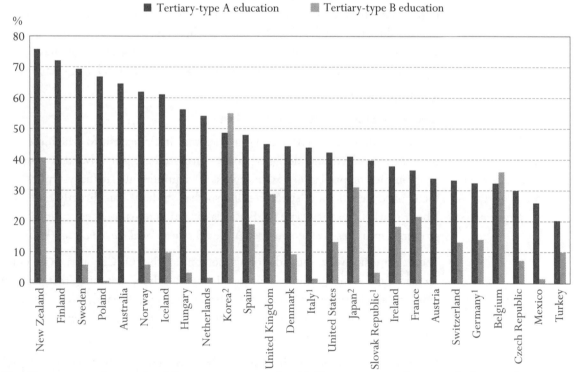

Note: Net entry rates for type A and B programmes cannot be added because some students enter both types of programmes.
1. Entry rate for type B programmes calculated as gross entry rate.
2. Entry rate for type A and B programmes calculated as gross entry rate.
Countries are ranked in descending order of the total entry rates for tertiary-type A education.
Source: OECD. Table C2.1. See Annex 3 for notes (*www.oecd.org/edu/eag2003*).

Policy context

This indicator shows the percentage of the youth cohort that will enter different types of tertiary education during their lives.

High tertiary entry and participation rates help to ensure the development and maintenance of a highly educated population and labour force. Tertiary education is associated with better access to employment and higher earnings (see Indicator A12). Rates of entry to tertiary education are a partial indication of the degree to which a population is acquiring high-level skills and knowledge that the labour market in knowledge societies values.

Entry and participation rates reflect both the accessibility of tertiary education and the perceived value of attending tertiary programmes.

As students have become more aware of the economic and social benefits of tertiary education, entry rates into tertiary type A and tertiary-type B programmes have risen. Continued growth in participation, and a widening diversity of backgrounds and interests of the people aspiring to tertiary studies, will require a new kind of provision. Tertiary institutions will need to meet growing demand by expanding the number of places that they offer and by adapting their programmes, teaching and learning to the diverse needs of new generations of students.

The indicator also shows patterns of participation at the secondary level of education.

Graduation from upper secondary education is becoming the norm in most OECD countries, but the curricular content in upper secondary programmes can vary, depending on the type of education or occupation for which the programmes are designed. Most upper secondary programmes in OECD countries are designed primarily to prepare students for tertiary studies, and their orientation can be general, pre-vocational or vocational. In addition to preparing students for further education, most OECD countries also have upper secondary programmes which prepare students to enter the labour market directly. Some OECD countries, however, delay vocational training until after graduation from upper secondary education, although these post-secondary programmes often resemble upper secondary level programmes.

Evidence and explanations

Overall access to tertiary education

47 per cent of today's young people in OECD countries will enter tertiary-type A programmes.

In OECD countries, tertiary programmes vary in the extent to which they are theoretically based and designed to prepare students for advanced research programmes or professions with high skill requirements (tertiary-type A), or focus on occupationally specific skills so that students can directly enter the labour market (tertiary-type B). For a classification of national educational programmes into these categories, see Annex 3 at *www.oecd.org/edu/eag2003*.

Today, almost every second young person in the OECD area will enter tertiary-type A programmes during his/her lifetime, assuming that current entry rates continue. In fact, in Australia, Finland, Iceland, New Zealand, Norway, Poland and Sweden, over 60 per cent of young people enter tertiary-type A programmes (Table C2.1).

In other OECD countries, the rates of first-time entry to tertiary-type A programmes are considerably lower: the estimated first-time entry rates for the Czech Republic, Mexico and Turkey are 30 per cent or below.

C₂

The proportion of people who enter tertiary-type B programmes is generally smaller than the proportion entering tertiary-type A programmes. In 24 OECD countries with available data, 15 per cent of young people, on average, will enter tertiary-type B programmes. The figures range from 1 per cent in Italy, Mexico and Poland to over 30 per cent in the Belgium, Japan and New Zealand, and 50 per cent in Korea (Table C2.1 and Chart C2.1).

In Belgium, wide access to tertiary-type B programmes counterbalances comparatively low rates of entry to tertiary-type A programmes. Other OECD countries, most notably Korea and the United Kingdom, have entry rates around the OECD average for tertiary-type A programmes, and comparatively high rates of entry to tertiary-type B programmes. New Zealand stands out as a country with entry rates at both levels that are the highest among OECD countries.

Net rates of entry to tertiary education should also be seen in the light of participation in post-secondary non-tertiary programmes, which are an important alternative to tertiary education in some OECD countries (Indicator C1).

People entering tertiary-type B programmes may also enter tertiary-type A programmes later in their lives. Tertiary-type A and B entry rates cannot be added together to obtain overall tertiary-level entry rates because entrants might be double counted.

Participation in tertiary education

Enrolment rates provide another perspective on participation in tertiary education. They reflect both the total number of individuals entering tertiary education and the duration of their studies. The sum of net enrolment rates for each single year of age, referred to as the *expectancy of tertiary education*, gives an overall measure of the amount of tertiary education undertaken by an age cohort rather than by individual participants. In contrast to entry rates, expectancy of tertiary education, which is based on enrolments in tertiary-type A and tertiary-type B programmes, can be summed.

On average in OECD countries, a 17-year-old can expect to receive 2.6 years of tertiary education, of which two years will, on average, be full-time. In Australia, Finland, Greece, Korea, New Zealand, Norway, Sweden and the United States, 17-year-olds can expect to receive at least three years of full-time or part-time tertiary education during their lifetimes. In Finland and Korea, students can expect to receive about four years of full-time studies. By contrast, the expectancy of tertiary education is less than two years in the Czech Republic, Mexico, the Slovak Republic, Switzerland and Turkey (Table C2.2).

On average in OECD countries, expectancy of enrolment in tertiary-type A programmes (2.1 years) is far higher than that in tertiary-type B programmes (0.4 years). Because tertiary-type A programmes tend to be longer, they dominate the stock of enrolments and therefore the volume of resources required, all other things being equal (see Indicator B1, Table B1.3).

Fifteen per cent of today's young people will enter tertiary-type B programmes.

C₂

In Australia, Finland, Greece, Korea, New Zealand, Norway, Sweden and the United States, young people can expect to receive at least three years of tertiary education during their lifetime.

The longer tertiary-type A programmes tend to increase the stock of enrolments, and therefore the volume of resources required.

The majority of tertiary students are enrolled in public institutions, but in some OECD countries the majority are in privately managed institutions.

In the majority of OECD countries, public institutions provide and manage tertiary-type A programmes. However, in Belgium, the Netherlands and the United Kingdom, the majority of students are enrolled in privately managed institutions that draw predominantly on public funds. In Japan and Korea, over 70 per cent of students are enrolled in institutions that are privately managed and financed predominantly from private sources. In Mexico, Poland, Portugal and the United States (Table C2.3), around 30 per cent of students are enrolled in such institutions.

Trends in participation

Participation in tertiary education grew in most OECD countries between 1995 and 2001.

With the exception of France and Germany, participation in tertiary education grew in all OECD countries between 1995 and 2001. In half of the OECD countries with available data, the number of students enrolled in tertiary education increased by over 25 per cent, and in the Czech Republic, Greece, Hungary, Korea and Poland, it grew by 54, 61, 94, 54 and 134 per cent, respectively (Table C2.2).

Chart C2.2

Change in the number of tertiary students in relation to changing participation rates and demography (2001)

Index of change in the number of students at the tertiary level between 1995 and 2001, and the relative contribution of demographic changes and changing enrolment rates (1995 = 100)

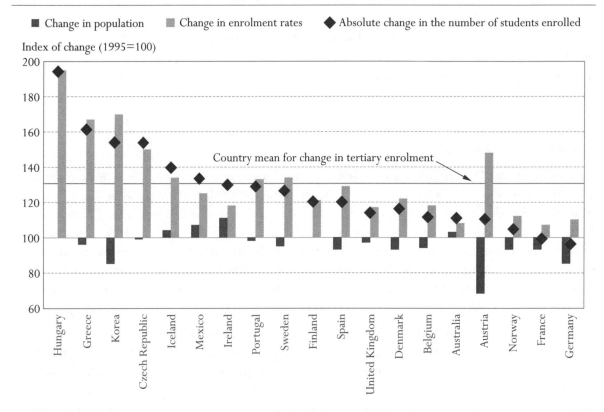

Countries are ranked in descending order of the absolute change in number of tertiary students.
Source: OECD. Table C2.2. See Annex 3 for notes *(www.oecd.org/edu/eag2003).*

At the tertiary level, changes in enrolment rates are less closely tied to changes in the size of the relevant age cohort than is true for primary and secondary education. Chart C2.2 breaks down the change in the number of students enrolled into two components: changes in cohort sizes and changes in enrolment rates. Growing demand, reflected in higher enrolment rates, is the main factor driving expansion in tertiary enrolments. Australia, Ireland and Mexico are the only OECD countries where population increases significantly contributed to higher tertiary enrolments, but in all cases, higher enrolment rates were even more significant. Conversely, the actual increase in tertiary students would have been significantly higher in many OECD countries (in particular Austria and Korea) had the population not decreased. In France and Germany, these decreases were actually more significant than increases in enrolment rates, meaning that overall, there was a slight drop in tertiary enrolment, despite a 7 and 10 per cent increase in enrolment rates, respectively.

Growing demand, reflected in higher participation rates, is the main factor driving expansion in tertiary enrolments.

Age of entrants

Traditionally, students typically enter tertiary-type A programmes immediately after having completed upper secondary education, and this remains true in many OECD countries. In Belgium, France, Ireland and the Slovak Republic, for example, more than 80 per cent of all first-time entrants are under 22 years of age (Table C2.1).

In Belgium, France, Ireland and the Slovak Republic, more than 80 per cent of all entrants to tertiary-type A programmes are under 22 years of age, whereas in Denmark, Iceland, New Zealand, Sweden and Switzerland, more than half the students enter this level for the first time after the age of 22.

In other OECD countries, the transition to the tertiary level is often delayed, in some cases by some time spent in the labour force. In these countries, first-time entrants to tertiary-type A programmes are typically older and show a much wider range of entry ages. In Denmark, Iceland, New Zealand, Sweden and Switzerland, for example, more than half the students enter this level for the first time after the age of 22 (Table C2.1). The proportion of older first-time entrants to tertiary-type A programmes may, among other factors, reflect the flexibility of these programmes and their suitability to students outside the typical or modal age cohort. It may also reflect a specific view of the value of work experience for higher education studies, which is characteristic of the Nordic countries and common in Australia and New Zealand, where a sizeable proportion of new entrants is much older than the typical age of entry. In Australia, New Zealand, Swizerland, the United States and the Nordic countries, more than 20 per cent of first-time entrants are 27 years of age or older.

Participation in and graduation from upper secondary vocational education

In most OECD countries, students do not follow a uniform curriculum at the upper secondary level. Programmes at the upper secondary level are subdivided into three categories based on the degree to which they are oriented towards a specific class of occupations or trades and lead to a labour-market relevant qualification:

Upper secondary programmes are classified based on whether they are...

• *Type 1 (general)* education programmes are not designed explicitly to prepare participants for specific occupations or trades, or for entry into further vocational or technical education programmes.

...general,...

...pre-vocational...

- **Type 2 (pre-vocational or pre-technical)** education programmes are mainly designed to introduce participants to the world of work and to prepare them for entry into further vocational or technical education programmes. Successful completion of such programmes does not lead to a labour-market relevant vocational or technical qualification. At least 25 per cent of the programme content should be vocational or technical.

...or vocational.

- **Type 3 (vocational)** education programmes prepare participants for direct entry into specific occupations without further training. Successful completion of such programmes leads to a labour-market relevant vocational qualification.

The degree to which a programme has a vocational or general orientation does not necessarily determine whether participants have access to tertiary education. In several OECD countries, vocationally oriented programmes are designed to prepare for further studies at the tertiary level, while in other countries, many general programmes do not provide direct access to further education.

In more than half of the OECD countries, the majority of upper secondary students attend vocational or apprenticeship programmes.

In all OECD countries, students can choose between vocational, pre-vocational and general programmes. In more than half of the OECD countries, the majority of upper secondary students attend vocational or apprenticeship programmes. In OECD countries with dual-system apprenticeship programmes (Austria, Germany, Luxembourg, the Netherlands and Switzerland), and in Australia, Belgium, the Czech Republic, Poland, the Slovak Republic and the United Kingdom, 60 per cent or more of upper secondary students are enrolled in vocational programmes. The exception is Iceland, where the majority of students are enrolled in general programmes even though dual-system apprenticeship programmes are offered (Table C2.5).

In most OECD countries, vocational education is school-based. In Austria, the Czech Republic, Iceland and the Slovak Republic, however, about half of the vocational programmes have combined school-based and work-based elements. In Denmark, Germany, Hungary and Switzerland, the majority of vocational programmes have both school-based and work-based elements.

Upper secondary enrolment by type of institution

The majority of upper secondary students are enrolled in public institutions...

Although the majority of primary and secondary students are enrolled in publicly managed and financed schools, in OECD countries, 20 per cent of upper secondary students on average are now enrolled in privately managed schools (Table C2.4 and Chart C2.3).

...but enrolments in privately managed upper secondary institutions account for the majority of students in Belgium, Korea, the Netherlands and the United Kingdom.

The majority of upper secondary students in Belgium, Korea, the Netherlands and the United Kingdom are enrolled in government-dependent private institutions (58, 54, 90 and 67 per cent respectively). Private educational institutions that are financed mainly by household payments are far less common at the upper secondary level and below, and are occasionally perceived as imposing barriers to the participation of students from low income families. However, in France, Mexico, Portugal and Spain, between 10 and 22 per cent of upper secondary students are enrolled in private institutions that are financed predominantly by unsubsidised household payments, and in Japan this figure is 30 per cent (Table C2.4).

Percentage of students enrolled in public and private institutions (2001)

■ Public institutions ■ Government-dependent private institutions ■ Independent private institutions

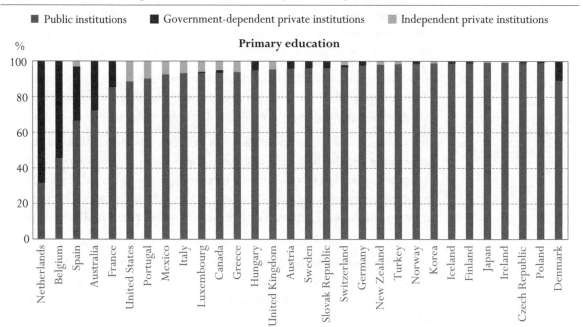

Primary education

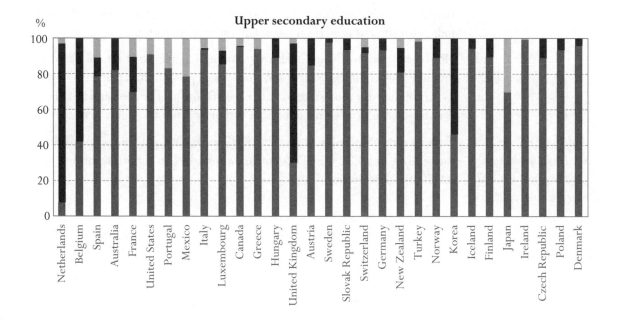

Upper secondary education

Countries are ranked in descending order of percentage of students enrolled in private institutions in primary education.
Source: OECD Table C2.4. See Annex 3 for notes *(www.oecd.org/edu/eag2003).*

C₂

Definitions and methodologies

Data refer to the school year 2000–2001 and are based on the UOE data collection on education statistics, which is administered annually by the OECD (for details, see Annex 3).

Table C2.1 shows, for all ages, the sum of net entry rates. The net entry rate of a specific age is obtained by dividing the number of first-time entrants of that age to each type of tertiary education by the total population in the corresponding age group (multiplied by 100). The sum of net entry rates is calculated by adding the rates for each single year of age. The result represents the proportion of people in a synthetic age-cohort who enter tertiary education, irrespective of changes in population sizes and of differences between OECD countries in the typical entry age. Table C2.1 shows also the 20th, 50th and 80th percentiles of the age distribution of first-time entrants, *i.e.*, the age below which 20 per cent, 50 per cent and 80 per cent of first-time entrants are to be found.

New (first-time) entrants are students who are enrolling at the relevant level of education for the first time. Foreign students enrolling for the first time in a post-graduate programme are considered first-time entrants.

Not all OECD countries can distinguish between students entering a tertiary programme for the first time and those transferring between different levels of tertiary education or repeating or re-entering a level after an absence. Thus, first-time entry rates for each level of tertiary education cannot be added up to total tertiary-level entrance rate because it would result in double-counting entrants.

Table C2.2 shows the expected number of years for which 17-year-olds will be enrolled in tertiary education, or the sum of net enrolment rates for people aged 17 and over (divided by 100). This measure is a function of the number of participants in tertiary education and the duration of tertiary studies. Since the denominator also includes those who have never participated in tertiary education, the indicator cannot be interpreted as the average number of years an individual student requires to complete tertiary education.

Pre-vocational and vocational programmes include both school-based programmes and combined school and work-based programmes that are recognised as part of the education system. Entirely work-based education and training that is not overseen by a formal education authority is not taken into account.

Data for 1994–1995 are based on a special survey carried out in OECD member countries in 2000.

Data on tertiary enrolment in 1994-1995 were obtained from a special survey carried out in 2000. OECD countries were asked to report according to the ISCED-97 classification.

C₂

Table C2.1
Entry rates to tertiary education and age distribution of new entrants (2001)
Sum of net entry rates for each year of age, by gender and programme destination

	Tertiary-type B			Tertiary-type A					
	Net entry rates			Net entry rates			Age at:		
	M+F	Males	Females	M+F	Males	Females	20th percentile[1]	50th percentile[1]	80th percentile[1]
	(1)	(2)	(3)	(4)	(5)	(6)	(7)	(8)	(9)
Australia	m	m	m	65	58	72	18.5	20.3	28.5
Austria	m	m	m	34	31	37	19.1	20.4	23.3
Belgium	36	29	43	32	32	33	18.3	18.8	21.1
Canada	m	m	m	m	m	m	m	m	m
Czech Republic	7	5	10	30	26	35	18.9	19.9	22.4
Denmark	9	12	7	44	33	56	21.1	22.8	27.0
Finland	a	a	a	72	62	83	19.9	21.6	27.0
France	22	22	21	37	30	43	18.3	18.9	20.3
Germany[2]	14	10	19	32	32	33	20.1	21.4	24.1
Greece	m	m	m	m	m	m	m	m	m
Hungary	3	3	4	56	50	63	19.3	21.0	26.2
Iceland	10	11	9	61	42	80	20.9	22.8	30.0
Ireland	18	18	19	38	33	43	18.3	19.0	19.9
Italy[2]	1	1	2	44	38	50	m	m	m
Japan[3]	31	22	41	41	48	33	m	m	m
Korea[3]	55	56	54	49	52	45	m	m	m
Luxembourg	m	m	m	m	m	m	m	m	m
Mexico	1	2	1	26	26	25	18.3	19.5	26.2
Netherlands	2	1	2	54	51	58	18.4	19.8	23.1
New Zealand	41	34	47	76	62	89	19.0	23.4	<40
Norway	6	7	5	62	48	76	20.1	21.7	<40
Poland	1	n	1	67	x(4)	x(4)	m	m	m
Portugal	m	m	m	m	m	m	m	m	m
Slovak Republic[2]	3	2	5	40	40	39	18.6	19.5	21.3
Spain	19	19	19	48	42	54	18.4	19.0	22.4
Sweden	6	6	6	69	55	84	20.3	22.6	<40
Switzerland	13	15	12	33	37	29	20.4	22.2	28.7
Turkey	10	11	9	20	23	18	18.3	19.5	22.9
United Kingdom	29	25	33	45	41	49	18.4	19.4	24.3
United States	13	12	15	42	36	49	18.4	19.3	28.3
Country mean	*15*	*13*	*16*	*47*	*41*	*51*			
Argentina[4]	35	21	48	59	53	64	m	m	m
Brazil[3]	m	m	m	31	27	35	m	m	m
Chile[3,4]	16	16	15	43	45	40	m	m	m
Indonesia	5	5	5	12	14	11	m	m	m
Israel	m	m	m	50	46	56	21.3	23.6	26.9
Paraguay[4]	10	6	14	m	m	m	m	m	m
Philippines[4]	x(4)	x(5)	x(6)	52	48	56	m	m	m
Thailand[3]	20	17	24	47	x(4)	x(4)	m	m	m
Tunisia[3]	m	m	m	28	x(4)	x(4)	m	m	m
Uruguay[3,4]	13	9	16	30	23	37	m	m	m

(left margin: OECD COUNTRIES / NON-OECD COUNTRIES)

(right margin box: C2)

Note: x indicates that data are included in another column. The column reference is shown in brackets after "x". *e.g.*, x(2) means that data are included in column 2.
1. 20/50/80 per cent of new entrants are below this age.
2. Entry rate for type B programmes calculated as gross entry rate.
3. Entry rate for type A and B programmes calculated as gross entry rate.
4. Year of reference 2000.
Source: OECD. See Annex 3 for notes (*www.oecd.org/edu/eag2003*).

Table C2.2
Expected years in tertiary education and changes in total tertiary enrolment (2001)
Expected years of tertiary education under current conditions, by gender and mode of study, and index of change in total enrolment in tertiary education (1995=100)

		Tertiary-type B education			Tertiary-type A education			Total tertiary education (type A, B and advanced research programmes)			Change in enrolment (1995=100)		
		Full-time and part-time		Full-time	Full-time and part-time		Full-time	Full-time and part-time		Full-time	Total tertiary education	Attributable to:	
												Change in population	Change in enrolment rates
		M + F	Females	M + F	M + F	Females	M + F	M + F	Females	M + F			
		(1)	(2)	(3)	(4)	(5)	(6)	(7)	(8)	(9)	(10)	(11)	(12)
OECD COUNTRIES	Australia	0.7	0.7	0.2	2.3	2.6	1.4	3.1	3.4	1.7	111	103	108
	Austria	0.2	0.3	0.2	2.0	2.1	2.0	2.4	2.5	2.4	110	68	148
	Belgium	1.4	1.6	1.1	1.3	1.3	1.3	2.8	3.0	2.4	112	94	118
	Canada	0.7	0.8	0.6	2.0	2.3	1.4	2.8	3.1	2.1	100	m	m
	Czech Republic	0.2	0.2	0.2	1.3	1.3	1.2	1.6	1.6	1.5	154	99	150
	Denmark	0.3	0.2	0.3	2.3	2.8	2.3	2.6	3.0	2.6	116	93	122
	Finland	0.1	0.1	0.1	3.8	4.2	3.8	4.2	4.6	4.2	120	100	121
	France	0.6	0.7	0.6	1.8	2.0	1.8	2.6	2.8	2.6	99	93	107
	Germany*	0.3	0.4	0.3	1.7	1.7	1.7	2.1	2.1	2.0	96	85	110
	Greece	1.0	1.0	1.0	2.0	2.2	2.0	3.1	3.3	3.1	161	96	167
	Hungary*	n	0.1	n	2.1	2.4	1.1	2.2	2.4	1.2	194	100	195
	Iceland	0.2	0.2	0.1	2.2	2.8	1.7	2.4	3.0	1.9	140	104	134
	Ireland	x(7)	x(8)	x(9)	x(7)	x(8)	x(9)	2.6	2.9	1.9	130	111	118
	Italy	n	0.1	n	2.3	2.7	2.3	2.4	2.7	2.4	106	m	m
	Japan	m	m	m	m	m	m	m	m	m	m	m	m
	Korea	1.6	1.2	1.6	2.3	1.7	2.3	3.9	2.9	3.9	154	85	170
	Luxembourg	m	m	m	m	m	m	m	m	m	m	m	m
	Mexico	n	n	n	1.0	1.0	1.0	1.1	1.0	1.1	134	107	125
	Netherlands	n	n	n	2.4	2.5	2.1	2.5	2.6	2.1	m	m	m
	New Zealand	0.8	1.0	0.4	2.4	2.8	1.7	3.2	3.8	2.1	m	m	m
	Norway	0.2	0.2	0.2	2.8	3.5	2.1	3.1	3.8	2.3	105	93	112
	Poland	n	n	n	2.8	3.3	1.4	2.9	3.4	1.5	234	m	m
	Portugal	0.1	0.1	a	2.3	2.7	a	2.5	2.9	a	129	98	133
	Slovak Republic	0.1	0.1	n	1.4	1.5	1.0	1.6	1.7	1.1	m	m	m
	Spain	0.3	0.3	0.3	2.5	2.8	2.3	3.0	3.2	2.7	120	93	129
	Sweden	0.1	0.1	0.1	2.9	3.5	1.6	3.2	3.8	1.8	126	95	134
	Switzerland	0.4	0.3	0.1	1.3	1.1	1.2	1.8	1.5	1.4	m	m	m
	Turkey*	0.3	0.3	0.3	1.0	0.8	1.0	1.3	1.1	1.3	137	m	m
	United Kingdom	0.8	0.9	0.2	1.7	1.9	1.4	2.6	2.9	1.7	114	97	117
	United States	0.7	0.8	0.3	2.7	3.0	1.7	3.5	3.9	2.1	m	m	m
	Country mean	*0.4*	*0.4*	*0.3*	*2.1*	*2.3*	*1.7*	*2.6*	*2.8*	*2.0*	*131*	*95*	*133*
NON-OECD COUNTRIES	Argentina[1]	0.7	1.1	0.7	2.3	2.4	m	3.0	3.5	0.7	m	m	m
	Brazil[1]	x(4)	x(5)	x(6)	0.9	1.0	0.9	0.9	1.0	0.9	m	m	m
	Indonesia	0.2	0.2	0.2	0.5	0.4	0.5	0.7	0.6	0.7	m	m	m
	Israel	m	m	m	2.1	2.4	1.6	2.9	3.3	2.5	m	m	m
	Malaysia[1]	0.6	0.6	0.5	0.7	0.7	0.6	1.3	1.3	1.1	m	m	m
	Paraguay[1]	0.2	0.3	0.2	x(7)	x(8)	x(9)	1.0	1.1	1.0	m	m	m
	Peru[1]	0.6	0.7	0.6	m	m	m	0.6	0.7	0.6	m	m	m
	Russian Federation[2]	1.0	1.1	1.0	2.1	2.4	2.1	3.2	3.6	3.2	m	m	m
	Thailand	m	m	m	1.5	1.3	0.7	1.9	1.7	1.1	m	m	m
	Uruguay[1,2]	0.5	0.7	0.5	1.4	1.7	1.4	1.9	2.4	1.9	m	m	m

1. Year of reference 2000.
2. Excludes advanced research programmes.
Note: x indicates that data are included in another column. The column reference is shown in brackets after "x". *e.g.*, x(2) means that data are included in column 2.
* See Annex 3 for notes (*www.oecd.org/edu/eag2003*).
Source: OECD.

C₂

Table C2.3
Students enrolled in public and private institutions and full-time and part-time programmes in tertiary education (2001)
Distribution of students, by mode of study, type of institution and programme destination

	Type of institution						Mode of study			
	Tertiary-type B education			Tertiary-type A and advanced research programmes			Tertiary-type B education		Tertiary-type A and advanced research programmes	
	Public	Government-dependent private	Independent private	Public	Government-dependent private	Independent private	Full-time	Part-time	Full-time	Part-time
	(1)	(2)	(3)	(4)	(5)	(6)	(7)	(8)	(9)	(10)
OECD COUNTRIES										
Australia	98.4	1.6	a	99.9	a	0.1	34.3	65.7	61.0	39.0
Austria	64.2	35.8	x(2)	95.1	4.9	x(6)	68.9	31.1	100.0	a
Belgium	47.5	52.5	m	41.1	58.9	m	73.3	26.7	95.5	4.5
Canada	100.0	n	n	100.0	n	n	87.4	12.6	68.3	31.7
Czech Republic	65.8	34.2	a	98.9	1.1	a	100.0	n	92.6	7.4
Denmark	100.0	a	a	99.8	0.2	a	100.0	a	100.0	a
Finland	83.1	16.9	a	85.1	14.9	a	100.0	a	100.0	a
France	73.0	11.5	15.5	88.6	0.8	10.6	100.0	a	100.0	a
Germany	64.3	35.7	x(2)	100.0	a	a	83.8	16.2	100.0	a
Greece	100.0	a	a	100.0	a	a	100.0	a	100.0	a
Hungary	86.4	13.6	a	86.6	13.4	a	88.1	11.9	55.9	44.1
Iceland	38.2	61.8	n	93.8	6.2	n	71.5	28.5	79.4	20.6
Ireland	96.5	a	3.5	93.7	a	6.3	64.1	35.9	82.9	17.1
Italy	63.5	a	36.5	93.6	a	6.4	100.0	a	100.0	a
Japan	9.5	a	90.5	27.5	a	72.5	96.9	3.1	90.6	9.4
Korea	13.8	a	86.2	22.9	a	77.1	100.0	a	100.0	a
Luxembourg	100.0	a	a	100.0	a	a	100.0	a	100.0	a
Mexico	95.2	a	4.8	67.1	a	32.9	100.0	a	100.0	a
Netherlands	9.2	90.8	m	31.3	68.7	m	58.2	41.8	81.4	18.6
New Zealand	79.3	20.1	0.5	98.8	1.2	n	46.4	53.6	69.1	30.9
Norway	82.8	17.2	x(2)	88.7	11.3	x(6)	86.1	13.9	72.3	27.7
Poland	86.5	11.5	2.0	71.5	a	28.5	76.0	24.0	53.8	46.2
Portugal	52.9	a	47.1	71.1	a	28.9	m	m	m	m
Slovak Republic	94.0	6.0	a	99.4	0.4	0.2	61.2	38.8	70.4	29.6
Spain	75.9	17.1	6.9	88.2	n	11.8	99.7	0.3	90.8	9.2
Sweden	71.5	0.9	27.6	94.4	5.6	a	92.0	8.0	53.8	46.2
Switzerland	37.3	40.5	22.2	91.2	6.6	2.2	31.5	68.5	92.0	8.0
Turkey*	98.6	a	1.4	96.3	a	3.7	100.0	a	100.0	a
United Kingdom	a	100.0	n	a	100.0	n	29.7	70.3	76.3	23.7
United States	92.6	a	7.4	68.9	a	31.1	42.5	57.5	63.0	37.0
Country mean	*69.3*	*18.9*	*14.1*	*79.8*	*9.8*	*12.0*	*79.0*	*21.0*	*84.5*	*15.5*
NON-OECD COUNTRIES										
Argentina[1]	58.7	29.8	11.6	85.2	a	14.8	100.0	a	m	m
Brazil[1]	m	a	m	34.6	a	65.4	m	m	100.0	m
Chile[1]	6.7	6.1	87.2	32.1	23.0	44.9	100.0	a	100.0	a
China	m	m	m	m	m	m	56.8	43.2	85.3	14.7
Egypt	m	m	m	m	m	m	m	m	94.5	5.5
India	m	m	m	m	m	m	100.0	a	85.5	14.5
Indonesia	49.8	a	50.2	33.5	a	66.5	100.0	a	100.0	a
Israel	m	m	m	12.1	80.5	7.3	100.0	n	80.4	19.6
Jamaica	79.3	a	20.7	66.1	a	33.9	57.9	42.1	55.7	44.3
Malaysia[1]	58.1	a	41.9	70.9	a	29.1	85.3	14.7	95.5	4.5
Paraguay[1]	45.9	x(3)	54.1	44.6	a	55.4	100.0	a	m	m
Peru[1]	46.1	1.1	52.8	m	a	m	100.0	a	m	m
Philippines[1]	40.5	a	59.5	30.3	a	69.7	100.0	a	100.0	a
Russian Federation	97.8	a	2.2	90.3	a	9.7	m	m	m	m
Thailand	57.7	a	42.3	87.7	a	12.3	100.0	n	64.5	35.5
Tunisia	m	a	m	m	a	m	100.0	a	100.0	a
Uruguay[1]	88.3	a	11.7	88.6	a	11.4	100.0	a	100.0	a
Zimbabwe	91.9	8.1	a	92.0	8.0	a	m	m	m	m

Note: x indicates that data are included in another column. The column reference is shown in brackets after "x". *e.g.*, x(2) means that data are included in column 2.
1. Year of reference 2000.
* See Annex 3 for notes (*www.oecd.org/edu/eag2003*).
Source: OECD.

Table C2.4
**Students enrolled in public and private institutions and full-time and part-time programmes
in primary and secondary education (2001)**
Distribution of students, by mode of study and type of institution

		Type of institution								Mode of study	
		Primary education			Lower secondary education			Upper secondary education			Primary and secondary education	
		Public	Government-dependent private	Independent private	Public	Government-dependent private	Independent private	Public	Government-dependent private	Independent private	Full-time	Part-time
		(1)	(2)	(3)	(4)	(5)	(6)	(7)	(8)	(9)	(10)	(11)
OECD COUNTRIES	Australia	72.4	27.6	a	70.2	29.8	a	81.9	18.1	a	75.9	24.1
	Austria	95.8	4.2	x(2)	92.5	7.5	x(5)	84.4	15.6	x(8)	99.4	0.6
	Belgium	45.6	54.4	m	43.1	56.9	m	41.6	58.4	m	81.3	18.7
	Canada	93.5	1.4	5.1	92.2	1.1	6.7	94.9	0.7	4.5	99.5	0.5
	Czech Republic	99.1	0.9	a	98.3	1.7	a	88.7	11.3	a	99.9	0.1
	Denmark	89.2	10.8	a	87.4	12.6	a	95.6	4.4	a	100.0	a
	Finland	98.8	1.2	a	95.8	4.2	a	89.3	10.7	a	100.0	a
	France	85.4	14.3	0.2	79.0	20.7	0.2	69.6	19.6	10.8	100.0	a
	Germany	97.6	2.4	x(2)	93.2	6.8	x(5)	93.0	7.0	x(8)	99.8	0.2
	Greece	93.7	a	6.3	94.7	a	5.3	93.7	a	6.3	98.1	1.9
	Hungary	94.9	5.1	a	94.5	5.5	a	88.6	11.4	a	96.6	3.4
	Iceland	98.6	1.4	n	99.0	1.0	n	94.0	6.0	n	93.2	6.8
	Ireland	99.1	n	0.9	100.0	n	n	98.9	n	1.1	99.9	0.1
	Italy	93.0	a	7.0	96.6	a	3.4	93.3	0.9	5.8	99.3	0.7
	Japan	99.1	a	0.9	94.3	a	5.7	69.6	a	30.4	98.9	1.1
	Korea	98.6	a	1.4	78.1	21.9	a	45.8	54.2	a	100.0	a
	Luxembourg	93.3	0.7	6.0	79.0	14.0	6.9	85.2	7.6	7.2	100.0	n
	Mexico	92.3	a	7.7	86.2	a	13.8	78.2	a	21.8	100.0	a
	Netherlands	31.6	68.4	a	23.8	75.8	0.4	7.3	89.5	3.2	97.2	2.8
	New Zealand	98.0	a	2.0	95.8	a	4.2	80.7	13.7	5.6	94.7	5.3
	Norway	98.4	1.6	x(2)	98.0	2.0	x(5)	88.8	11.2	x(8)	99.1	0.9
	Poland	99.1	0.9	a	98.9	1.1	a	93.3	6.6	0.1	95.3	4.7
	Portugal	90.0	a	10.0	89.8	a	10.2	82.9	a	17.1	92.5	7.5
	Slovak Republic	96.1	3.9	a	95.2	4.8	a	93.3	6.7	a	99.1	0.9
	Spain	66.6	30.2	3.2	66.5	30.3	3.2	78.3	10.5	11.2	96.2	3.8
	Sweden	96.1	3.9	a	96.5	3.5	a	97.4	2.6	a	84.5	14.3
	Switzerland	96.6	1.1	2.2	93.3	2.3	4.3	91.4	3.5	5.1	99.6	0.4
	Turkey*	98.2	a	1.8	a	a	a	97.9	a	2.1	100.0	a
	United Kingdom	95.2	a	4.8	93.5	0.3	6.1	30.0	67.0	3.0	76.8	23.2
	United States	88.4	a	11.6	90.1	a	9.9	90.6	a	9.4	100.0	n
	Country mean	*89.8*	*7.8*	*2.7*	*83.8*	*10.1*	*3.1*	*80.6*	*14.6*	*5.6*	*95.9*	*4.1*
NON-OECD COUNTRIES	Argentina	80.1	16.4	3.5	77.4	19.3	3.3	71.0	23.3	5.7	100.0	a
	Brazil	92.1	a	7.9	90.3	a	9.7	85.8	a	14.2	100.0	a
	China	m	m	m	m	m	m	m	m	m	97.3	2.7
	Chile	55.7	36.7	7.6	58.0	34.4	7.6	51.1	33.0	15.8	100.0	a
	Egypt	91.1	1.0	7.9	m	m	m	93.3	0.2	6.6	100.0	a
	Indonesia	84.1	a	15.9	63.0	a	37.0	47.3	a	52.7	100.0	a
	India	83.5	8.5	8.0	65.9	19.4	14.7	44.8	36.5	18.7	99.9	0.1
	Israel	100.0	a	a	100.0	a	a	100.0	a	a	99.0	1.0
	Jamaica	95.1	a	4.9	98.1	a	1.9	96.8	a	3.2	m	m
	Malaysia	97.1	a	2.9	94.3	a	5.7	94.0	a	6.0	m	m
	Paraguay[1]	85.3	9.5	5.2	75.7	11.5	12.8	67.0	10.1	22.9	100.0	a
	Peru	87.0	3.3	9.7	84.0	4.8	11.2	81.2	5.2	13.6	100.0	a
	Philippines	92.7	a	7.3	78.2	a	21.8	74.0	a	26.0	100.0	a
	Russian Federation	99.6	a	0.4	99.7	a	0.3	99.6	a	0.4	m	m
	Thailand	86.8	13.2	x(2)	95.4	4.6	x(5)	90.7	9.3	a	85.9	14.1
	Tunisia	99.2	a	0.8	97.2	a	2.8	85.6	a	14.4	100.0	a
	Uruguay	86.0	a	14.0	87.2	a	12.8	89.5	a	10.5	100.0	a
	Zimbabwe	12.7	87.3	a	26.8	73.2	a	30.8	69.2	a	100.0	a

Note: x indicates that data are included in another column. The column reference is shown in brackets after "x". *e.g.*, x(2) means that data are included in column 2.
1. Year of reference 2000.
Source: OECD. See Annex 3 for notes (*www.oecd.org/edu/eag2003*).

C2

Table C2.5
Upper secondary enrolment patterns (2001)
Enrolment in public and private upper secondary institutions by type of programme

	Distribution of enrolment by type of programme			
	General	Pre-vocational	Vocational	*of which:* combined school and work-based
	(1)	(2)	(3)	(4)
OECD COUNTRIES				
Australia	36.1	a	63.9	x(3)
Austria	21.4	6.8	71.8	36.2
Belgium	30.8	a	69.2	2.5
Canada	84.8	8.0	7.2	a
Czech Republic	19.3	0.8	79.9	37.9
Denmark	45.4	0.3	54.3	53.5
Finland	43.3	a	56.7	10.3
France	43.3	a	56.7	12.0
Germany	36.7	a	63.3	51.2
Greece	64.8	a	35.2	a
Hungary	49.8	38.7	11.5	11.5
Iceland	63.6	1.2	35.2	17.8
Ireland	74.2	25.8	a	a
Italy	35.7	38.4	25.9	a
Japan	74.1	0.8	25.1	a
Korea	65.9	a	34.1	a
Luxembourg	36.2	a	63.8	13.5
Mexico	87.8	a	12.2	x(3)
Netherlands	29.9	a	70.1	a
New Zealand	m	m	m	m
Norway	42.4	a	57.6	a
Poland	37.9	a	62.1	a
Portugal	71.7	a	28.3	m
Slovak Republic	22.4	a	77.6	42.5
Spain	64.4	a	35.6	5.1
Sweden*	48.3	a	51.7	n
Switzerland	35.0	a	65.0	57.3
Turkey	60.3	a	39.7	7.7
United Kingdom	33.1	x(3)	66.9	x(3)
United States	m	m	m	m
Country mean	*48.5*	*4.5*	*47.2*	*15.0*
NON-OECD COUNTRIES				
Argentina[1]	33.9	a	66.1	a
Brazil[1]	89.1	a	10.9	m
Chile[1]	58.6	a	41.4	a
Egypt	34.6	a	65.4	a
India[1]	99.5	a	0.5	a
Israel	67.0	a	33.0	3.9
Jamaica	99.4	a	0.6	m
Malaysia[1]	84.6	a	15.4	a
Paraguay[1]	80.4	a	19.6	a
Peru[1]	81.7	a	18.3	a
Philippines[1]	100.0	a	a	a
Russian Federation	100.0	a	a	a
Thailand	74.1	a	25.9	a
Tunisia	88.2	6.4	5.4	a
Uruguay[1]	81.6	a	18.4	a
Zimbabwe[2]	100.0	a	a	a

Note: x indicates that data are included in another column. The column reference is shown in brackets after "x". *e.g.,* x(2) means that data are included in column 2.
1. Year of reference 2000.
* See Annex 3 for notes (*www.oecd.org/edu/eag2003*).
Source: OECD.

C₂

INDICATOR C3: FOREIGN STUDENTS IN TERTIARY EDUCATION

- Five countries (Australia, France, Germany, the United Kingdom and the United States) receive 71 per cent of all foreign students studying in the OECD area.

- In absolute numbers, students from Greece, Japan, Korea and Turkey represent the largest sources of intakes from OECD countries. Students from China and Southeast Asia comprise the largest numbers of foreign students from non-OECD countries.

- In relative terms, the percentage of foreign students enrolled in OECD countries ranges from below one to almost 17 per cent in Switzerland. Proportional to their size, Australia, Austria, Belgium, Switzerland and the United Kingdom take in the most foreign students, when measured as a percentage of their tertiary enrolments.

C₃

Chart C3.1

Percentage of tertiary students enrolled who are not citizens of the country of study (2001)

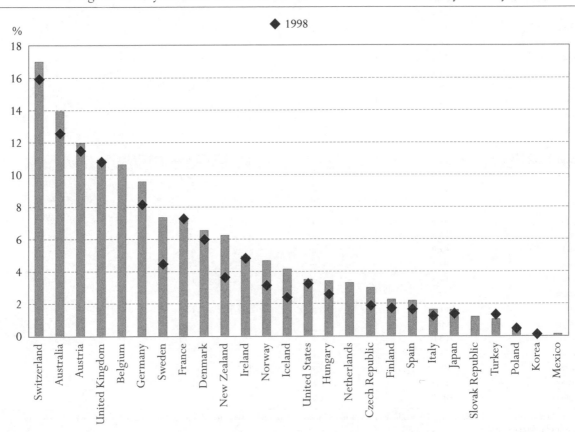

◆ 1998

Countries are ranked in descending order of the percentage of students enrolled who are not citizens of the country of study.
Source: OECD. Table C3.1. See Annex 3 for notes *(www.oecd.org/edu/eag2003).*

Policy context

The international dimension of higher education is receiving growing attention from multiple perspectives.

This indicator shows the mobility of students between countries ...

On the one hand, the general trend towards freely circulating capital, goods and services coupled with changes in the openness of labour markets have increased the demand for new kinds of educational provision in OECD countries. Governments as well as individuals are looking increasingly to higher education to play a role in broadening the horizons of students and allowing them to develop a deeper understanding of the multiplicity of languages, cultures and business methods in the world. One way for students to expand their knowledge of other societies and languages and hence to leverage their labour market prospects is to study in tertiary educational institutions in countries other than their own. As a matter of fact, several OECD governments have set up schemes and policies to promote such mobility.

The international mobility of students involves economic costs and benefits, that depend to a large extent on sending countries' policies regarding financial aid to students going overseas for study, and host countries' policies on tuition fees and financial support for overseas' students. While the direct short-term monetary costs and benefits of this mobility are relatively easy to measure, the long-term social and economic outcomes are far more difficult to quantify.

...in terms of sending and host country policies.

From the perspective of institutions, foreign enrolments may constrain the instructional settings and processes insofar as the curriculum and teaching methods sometimes have to be adapted to a culturally and linguistically diverse student body. These constraints are greatly outweighed, however, by numerous benefits to host institutions. Indeed, foreign enrolments can help to reach the critical mass needed to diversify the range of educational programmes offered, and may compensate for variations in domestic enrolment rates. They can also increase tertiary institutions' financial resources.

Internationalisation brings benefits and constraints to institutions,...

C3

Last but not least, international negotiations currently underway on trade liberalisation of services highlight the economic implications of the internationalisation of the provision of education services. The trend towards greater internationalisation of education is likely to have a growing impact on countries' balances of payments, and some OECD countries already show signs of specialisation in education exports. In this perspective, it is worth noting that in addition to student flows across borders, cross-border electronic delivery of highly flexible educational programmes and campuses abroad are also relevant to the internationalisation of higher education, although no comparable data exist yet.

...has an impact on countries' balance of payments...

The internationalisation of higher education, however, has many more economic outcomes in addition to those reflected in the trade balance. The internationalisation of education can also be seen as an opportunity for smaller and / or less developed educational systems to improve the cost efficiency of their education provision. Indeed, training opportunities abroad may constitute

... and may improve the cost efficiency of education provision.

a cost-efficient alternative to national provision, and allow countries to focus limited resources on educational programmes where economies of scale can be generated.

The numbers and trends in students studying in other countries can provide some idea of the extent of student mobility. In the future, it will also be important to develop ways to quantify and measure other components of the internationalisation of education.

Evidence and explanations

Distribution of foreign students by host countries

In 2001, 1.65 million students were enrolled outside their country of origin,

In 2001, 1.65 million students were enrolled outside their country of origin, of which 1.54 million (or 94 per cent) studied in the OECD area. This represented a 1.5 per cent increase in total student mobility since the previous year.

...a 16 per cent increase since 1998.

Although student flows into OECD countries increased by only 1.1 per cent between 2000 and 2001, comparison with 1998 figures shows that the absolute number of foreign students enrolled in the OECD area has increased by 16 per cent within four years. For data see Annex 3 at *www.oecd.org/edu/eag2003*.

Five OECD countries attract seven out of ten foreign students.

A relatively small number of countries enrols the vast majority of foreign students studying in the OECD area and in other non-OECD countries reporting such data. The United States receives the most foreign students (in absolute terms) with 28 per cent of the total of all foreign students, followed by the United Kingdom and Germany (14 and 12 per cent respectively), France and Australia (nine and seven per cent, respectively) (Chart C3.2). These five host countries account for about 71 per cent of all students studying abroad.

Among these countries, it is noteworthy that over one year, France and Germany both increased their share of all foreign students by about half a percentage point. Australia displayed the highest increase in the share of foreign students among OECD countries, with a year-to-year increase of 0.8 percentage point amounting to some 15,000 additional foreign students in absolute terms (see Indicator C3 from *Education at a Glance 2002*).

Not all non-national students came to the host country expressly with the intention to study.

This indicator defines a foreign student as someone who is not a citizen of the country of study. In most countries, it has not been possible to distinguish between foreign students who are residents in the country but who have immigrated (or whose parents have immigrated), and students who came to the country expressly to pursue their education. This leads to an overestimation of the foreign student body in countries with comparatively stringent naturalisation policies.

For example, Germany is a high-ranking destination for foreign students but the actual number of non-resident students registered in German tertiary education institutions accounts for only two-thirds of all foreign students. This is because a significant number of "domestic foreigners", that is mainly children of migrant workers, are considered foreign for the purposes of this indicator, despite having grown up in Germany and holding permanent residence in this country.

The language spoken is critical for selecting a foreign country in which to study. Countries whose language of instruction is widely spoken and read (*e.g.*, English, French, German) dominate in hosting foreign students, be it in absolute or relative terms.

Language of instruction is a critical factor in selecting a country in which to study.

The dominance of English-speaking countries such as Australia, the United Kingdom and the United States (in absolute numbers) may be largely attributable to the fact that students intending to study abroad are most likely to have learned English in their home country. As a matter of fact, an increasing number of institutions in non-English-speaking countries now offer courses in English to attract foreign students, especially so in Nordic countries, which

Chart C3.2

Distribution of foreign students by host country (2001)

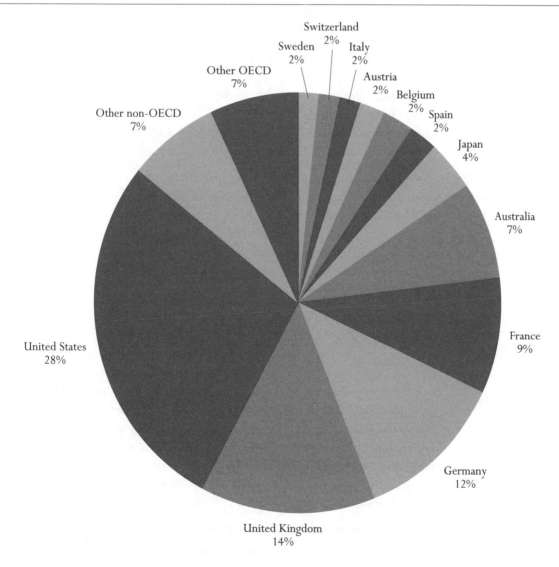

C3

Source: OECD.

may explain the comparatively large increase in the index of the proportion of foreign students enrolled in Finland, Norway and Sweden between 1998 and 2001 (Table C3.1).

Proportion of foreign students by countries of origin

The geographic composition of the foreign students' intake is fairly stable over time.

The increase over time in the number of foreign students was fairly balanced among the different world regions, as shown by the fairly stable geographic composition of the foreign students' intake.

Asian students form the largest group of foreign students studying in reporting OECD and non-OECD countries, with 42 per cent of the total, followed by Europeans (33 per cent), in particular citizens of the European Union (21 per cent). Students from Africa account for 11 per cent of all foreign students. Altogether, 41 per cent of foreign students enrolled in reporting OECD and non-OECD countries are citizens of an OECD country. For data, see Annex 3 at *www.oecd.org/edu/eag2003*.

Students from Greece, Japan and Korea represent the largest intakes from OECD countries...

The predominance of students from Asia and Europe among foreign intakes is also noticeable when focusing on OECD countries. Students from Korea and Japan comprise the largest groups of all foreign students, at 4.3 and 3.4 per cent respectively, followed by students from Germany (3.3 per cent), Greece (3.3 per cent), France (2.9 per cent), and Turkey (2.7 per cent). Together, these countries account for 20 per cent of all foreign students in reporting OECD and non-OECD countries. For data see Annex 3 at *www.oecd.org/edu/eag2003*.

C₃

...while students from China and Southeast Asia make up the largest proportion of foreign students from non-OECD countries.

With respect to foreign students originating from non-OECD countries, students from China represent 8.0 per cent of all foreign students (not including an additional 1.4 per cent from Hong Kong), followed by students from India (3.8 per cent), Morocco (2.7 per cent), Malaysia (2.0 per cent) and Indonesia (2.0 per cent). Another 3.8 per cent of all foreign students originate from Southeast Asia – Indonesia, Singapore and Thailand. For data see Annex 3 at *www.oecd.org/edu/eag2003*.

International trade, financial, economic and historical relations are important factors underlying student mobility. For example, the promotion of regional economic integration by organisations and treaties such as the European Union, NAFTA, ASEAN and APEC may provide incentives for students to develop their understanding of partner countries' cultures and languages, and to build bilateral or multilateral networks. Some national governments have made international student mobility an explicit part of their socio-economic development strategies. For example, several governments in the Asia-Pacific region, such as Australia, Japan and New Zealand, have initiated policies to attract foreign students to study in their higher education institutions, often on a revenue generating or at least self-financing basis.

Foreign student intakes as a proportion of total enrolments

The foregoing analysis has focused on the distribution of absolute numbers of foreign students by countries of destination and origin. One way to take the size of the national tertiary education systems into account is to examine the intake of tertiary students in a particular country as well as the number of students studying abroad relative to its tertiary enrolments.

Australia, Austria and Switzerland receive the largest proportion of foreign students relative to total tertiary enrolment in their countries (between 12 and 17 per cent), followed by Belgium, Germany and the United Kingdom. By contrast, in Italy, Japan, Korea, Mexico, Poland, the Slovak Republic and Turkey, the proportion of foreign students in tertiary enrolment remains below 2 per cent (Chart C3.1).

The percentage of foreign students enrolled in OECD countries ranges from below one to 17 per cent.

In comparison with OECD countries, non-OECD countries participating in the World Education Indicators project receive marginal numbers of foreign students relative to their size, with the exception of Malaysia and Uruguay where foreign students reach 3.4 and 2.2 per cent of enrolments respectively (Table C3.1).

Compared to 1998, several OECD countries have experienced a significant increase in the proportion of foreign students enrolled in their education system. This upward trend is especially noticeable in Germany, Italy, Spain, and the Nordic, Eastern European and Asian-Pacific OECD countries, with indexes of change ranging between 115 and 173.

Australia, Germany and New Zealand, which already play significant roles, might further increase their position on the international education market.

This trend is also visible in the case of three of the top receiving countries relative to their size, Australia, Germany and New Zealand, with indexes of change at 111, 117 and 170, respectively. This suggests that these countries might play an even greater role in the internationalisation of higher education in the future.

Students studying abroad relative to total enrolments

It is also possible to estimate the extent to which students study abroad by comparing the number of students of a particular nationality studying abroad to national tertiary enrolments. The measure used here only covers students leaving their country to study in OECD and non-OECD countries that report data; it does not cover students who study abroad in countries other than those reporting their intakes in Table C3.1. The indicator is thus likely to underestimate the proportion of students studying abroad. Another potential source of underestimation may be that the indicator is calculated on a full-year basis whereas many students study abroad for less than a full academic year. For example, more than half of the students from the United States who study abroad leave for half a year or less, and only 14 per cent stay in the host country for a full academic year.

The ratio of students studying abroad to total enrolment in the country of origin varies widely, from below 1 per cent in Australia (0.6 per cent), Mexico (0.7 per cent) and the United States (0.2 per cent), to as much as 24 per cent in Iceland and 228 per cent in Luxembourg (see Table 3.1, column 6). The latter case is specific, however, because Luxembourg only offers post-secondary non-tertiary programmes or the first year at the tertiary level. Since students in

Greece, Iceland, Ireland, Luxembourg and Norway send a large proportion of their students abroad, while Australia, Mexico and the United States send relatively few.

C3

Luxembourg must continue their studies abroad, a large number of students are enrolled outside the country.

Net balance of international student exchange

Proportional to their size, Australia, Switzerland and the United Kingdom show the largest net intake of foreign students.

Although the United States receives over 444,000 foreign students more than the total number of US students going abroad, other countries have much larger net intakes of students when the size of their tertiary systems is taken into account. In Australia, Switzerland and the United Kingdom, the net intake is between 4.4 and 6.9 per cent of their tertiary enrolment (see Table C3.1, column 7). Conversely, Iceland, Ireland, Norway and the Slovak Republic show the highest relative net outflow of students, at 20.5, 5.3, 5.1 and 6 per cent of total tertiary enrolments, respectively. The balances of student flows take only students to and from reporting OECD and non-OECD countries into account. The absolute balance of countries that accept a significant number of students from non-reporting countries or that send students to non-reporting countries may differ from these figures.

Various push–pull factors help to explain student mobility patterns.

Given the numerous benefits that foreign students may bring to their host countries, it is important to identify the factors likely to enhance student mobility.

Student mobility patterns can be attributed to a variety of push-pull factors, such as language barriers, the academic reputation of particular institutions or programmes, the flexibility of programmes with respect to counting time spent abroad towards degree requirements, the limitations of higher education provision in the home country, restrictive university admission policies at home, financial incentives and tuition costs.

These patterns also reflect geographical and historical links between countries, future job opportunities, cultural aspirations, and government policies to facilitate credit transfer between home and host institutions. The transparency and flexibility of courses and degree requirements also count.

Trade effects and economic benefits of the internationalisation of higher education

The net intake of foreign students indicates the magnitude of the benefits countries can potentially reap from the international exchange of tertiary students.

A first direct benefit of the intake of foreign students is the tuition fee revenue that is generated and most importantly the domestic consumption by foreign students, which both appear in the balance of current accounts as exports of educational services. The magnitude of this gain is highest when host countries adopt a full-fee tuition policy for overseas students, while in countries where tuition fees charged to foreign students are below the cost of education provision, the net gain depends on the extent of foreign students' domestic consumption. Exports of educational services were estimated at US$ 30 billion in 1998, or 3 per cent of total OECD trade in services. In a top receiving country such as Australia, exports of educational services were the third largest service sector export earner in 2000-2001, representing nearly 12 per cent of total service exports.

In addition to the direct benefits of internationalised higher education, a higher client-base of tertiary education may result in indirect gains, whereby net receiving countries generate economies of scale in tertiary education, and can therefore diversify their range of programmes and / or reduce their unit costs. This can be particularly important for host countries with a relatively small population (*e.g.* Switzerland).

The presence of a potential foreign student client-base also compels higher education institutions to offer quality programmes that stand out among competitors, which may contribute to the development of a highly reactive, client-driven higher education.

Finally, the intake of foreign students can to some extent involve technology transfers (especially in advanced research programmes), foster intercultural contacts and help to build social networks for the future.

Profile of foreign intake by host country

In some countries a comparatively large proportion of foreign students is enrolled in tertiary-type B programmes. This is the case in Belgium (44.3 per cent), New Zealand (24.3 per cent) and Korea (18.4 per cent) among OECD countries, and to a very large extent in Malaysia (79.4 per cent) among non-OECD countries. By contrast other countries see a large proportion of their foreign students choose highly theoretical advanced research programmes. This is most notably the case in Finland (19.6 per cent), Switzerland (18.1 per cent), Spain (17.1 per cent), the United States (16.6 per cent) and Sweden (15.1 per cent), suggesting that these countries offer attachive advanced programmes to prospective foreign graduate students. This latter group of countries is also likely to benefit from larger technology transfers and tuition revenue per foreign student (in the countries which charge foreign students full tuition costs) (Table C3.4).

The profile of the intake of foreign students varies significantly among countries, suggesting different specialisations on the international education market.

C₃

Definitions and methodologies

Students are classified as foreign students if they are not citizens of the country in which the data are collected. While pragmatic and operational, this classification may create inconsistencies resulting from differing national policies regarding the naturalisation of immigrants and the inability of several countries to report foreign students net of permanent resident students. Countries that naturalise immigrants stringently and which cannot identify non-resident foreign students therefore over-estimate the size of their foreign student body, compared to more lenient countries. Bilateral comparisons of the data on *foreign* students should therefore be made with caution, since some countries differ in the definition and coverage of their foreign students (see Annex 3 at *www.oecd.org / edu / eag2003*).

Data refer to the academic year 2000-2001 and are based on the UOE data collection on education statistics, which is administered annually by the OECD (see Annex 3).

Foreign student data are collected by host countries and therefore relate to students that are coming in rather than to students going abroad. Host countries covered by this indicator are OECD countries with the exception of Canada, Greece, Luxembourg and Portugal as well as the following non-OECD countries: Argentina, Chile, India, Indonesia, Malaysia, the Philippines, the Russian Federation, Thailand, Tunisia and Uruguay. This indicator does not include students studying in OECD countries that did not report foreign students nor in non-OECD countries other than those mentioned above. All statements on students studying abroad therefore underestimate the real number of students abroad.

The method of obtaining data on the number of foreign students is the same as that used for collecting data on total enrolments, *i.e.,* records of regularly enrolled students in an educational programme are used. Domestic and foreign students are usually counted on a specific day or period of the year. This procedure measures the proportion of foreign enrolments in an education system, but the actual number of individuals involved in foreign exchange may be much higher, since many students study abroad for less than a full academic year, or participate in exchange programmes that do not require enrolment (*e.g.,* inter-university exchange or advanced research short-term mobility).

Tables C3.1, C3.2 and C3.3 show foreign enrolment as a proportion of the total enrolment in the host country or country of origin. Total enrolment, used as a denominator, comprises all persons studying in the country (including all foreign students) but excludes all students from that country who study abroad.

The index of intensity of foreign students' intake shown in Table C3.1 compares the numbers of foreign students as a proportion of domestic enrolments with the average order of magnitude for OECD countries. This makes it possible to refine the scale of foreign students' intakes based on the size of the tertiary education system. An index higher (lower) than one reflects a higher (lower) intake as a proportion of enrolments compared with the OECD mean. Alternatively, this index can also be interpreted in terms of a comparison of the weight of a country in OECD foreign students' intakes with its weight in OECD enrolments. If so, an index higher (lower) than one reflects a higher (lower) foreign students' intake than the country's weight in OECD enrolments would suggest.

The proportions of students abroad given in Table C3.2 do not include the proportion of all students of a certain nationality studying abroad, but expresses the numbers of students of a given nationality as a proportion of the total domestic enrolment at the tertiary level, excluding students who are nationals of that country who are not studying in their home country.

Table C3.4 shows the distribution of foreign students enrolled in an education system according to the level and type of education in which they are enrolled.

Table C3.1
Exchange of students in tertiary education (2001)
Foreign students enrolled as a percentage of all students (foreign plus domestic), and exchange of students as a percentage of total tertiary enrolment

Reading the first column: 13.9 per cent of all students in tertiary education in Australia are foreign students (from throughout the world).
Reading the fourth column: Australia enrols 2.6 times more foreign tertiary students than the average OECD country, while Malaysia's proportion of foreign students is 0.6 times the OECD average.
Reading the fifth column: Foreign tertiary students from other countries that report foreign students, represent 6.9 per cent of all tertiary students in Australia.
Reading the sixth column: 0.6 per cent of all tertiary students in Australia study in other countries that report foreign students.
Column 7 represents the difference between column 5 and column 6.

	Foreign students from throughout the world as a percentage of all students (foreign and domestic students)			Index of intensity of foreign students' intake relative to OECD reference area[1]	Exchange of students with other reporting countries[2] (relative to total tertiary enrolment)			Foreign enrolment by gender	
			Index of change (1998=100)		Intake of students from other reporting countries	National students enrolled abroad in other reporting countries	Net intake of foreign students from other reporting countries		
	2001	1998						% males	% females
	(1)	(2)	(3)	(4)	(5)	(6)	(7)	(8)	(9)
OECD COUNTRIES									
Australia	13.9	12.6	111	2.6	6.9[3]	0.6[3]	6.3[3]	53.1	46.9
Austria	12.0	11.5	104	2.2	8.1	4.4	3.8	49.0	51.0
Belgium	10.6	m	m	2.0	5.7	2.8	2.9	50.9	49.1
Canada	m	2.8	m	m	m	m	m	m	m
Czech Republic	3.0	1.9	157	0.6	1.7	2.0	-0.3	55.1	44.9
Denmark	6.5	6.0	109	1.2	2.8	3.2	-0.4	45.3	54.7
Finland	2.2	1.7	130	0.4	0.8	3.5	-2.7	56.9	43.1
France	7.3	7.3	99	1.4	1.7	2.3	-0.6	m	m
Germany	9.6	8.2	117	1.8	4.7	2.6	2.0	52.2	47.8
Greece	m	m	m	m	m	11.4	m	m	m
Hungary	3.4	2.6	131	0.6	1.2	2.2	-1.0	56.2	43.8
Iceland	4.1	2.4	173	0.8	3.3	23.8	-20.5	35.2	64.8
Ireland	4.9	4.8	102	0.9	4.0	9.2	-5.3	47.7	52.3
Italy	1.6	1.2	130	0.3	0.2	2.3	-2.0	45.4	54.6
Japan	1.6	1.4	114	0.3	0.7	1.4	-0.7	54.6	45.4
Korea	0.1	0.1	128	n	n	2.3	-2.2	56.8	43.2
Luxembourg	m	30.5	m	m	m	228.5	m	m	m
Mexico	0.1	m	m	n	n	0.7	-0.7	m	m
Netherlands	3.3	m	m	0.6	2.0	2.3	-0.3	50.7	49.3
New Zealand	6.2	3.7	170	1.2	2.7	3.5	-0.8	49.6	50.4
Norway	4.7	3.2	147	0.9	2.3	7.4	-5.1	m	m
Poland	0.4	0.5	82	0.1	0.1	1.1	-1.0	m	m
Portugal	m	m	m	m	m	2.8	m	m	m
Slovak Republic	1.2	m	m	0.2	0.3	6.2	-6.0	61.3	38.7
Spain	2.2	1.7	131	0.4	1.4	1.4	n	45.0	55.0
Sweden	7.3	4.5	164	1.4	4.4	4.2	0.2	m	m
Switzerland	17.0	15.9	107	3.2	11.8	4.9	6.9	55.9	44.1
Turkey	1.0	1.3	78	0.2	n	2.8	-2.7	73.1	26.9
United Kingdom	10.9	10.8	101	2.0	5.6	1.2	4.4	52.2	47.8
United States	3.5	3.2	108	0.7	1.7	0.2	1.5	58.1	41.9
Country mean	*5.3*	*5.8*	*·*	*1.0*	*2.8*	*4.0[4]*		*52.6*	*47.4*
NON-OECD COUNTRIES									
Argentina	0.7	m	m	0.1	0.1	1.4	-1.2	m	m
Chile	0.8	m	m	0.1	0.3	1.1	-0.7	m	m
India	0.1	m	m	n	n	0.7	-0.7	m	m
Indonesia	n	m	m	n	n	1.1	-1.1	m	m
Malaysia	3.4	m	m	0.6	1.3	6.0	-4.7	m	m
Philippines	0.1	m	m	n	n	0.2	-0.2	m	m
Russian Federation	0.9	m	m	0.2	m	m	m	m	m
Thailand	0.1	m	m	n	n	0.9	-0.9	m	m
Tunisia	1.2	m	m	0.2	m	m	m	m	m
Uruguay	2.2	m	m	0.4	m	m	m	m	m

1. The index compares the numbers of foreign students as a proportion of domestic enrolements with the average order of magnitude for OECD countries. This makes it possible to refine the scale of foreign students' intakes based on the size of the tertiary education system. An index higher (lower) than one reflects a higher (lower) intake as a proportion of enrolements compared with the OECD mean.
2. Data in columns 5 to 7 do not show the exchange of students throughout the world. Coverage is limited to the OECD and non-OECD countries shown in the table that report data in column 1. Therefore data are not comparable to those reported in Column 1.
3. Tertiary-type A and advanced research programmes only.
4. Country mean excludes Luxembourg.
Source: OECD. See Annex 3 for notes (*www.oecd.org/edu/eag2003*).

Table C3.2
Proportion of foreign students in tertiary education in the country of study (2001)
Number of foreign students enrolled in tertiary education as a percentage of students in the country of destination, based on head counts

The table shows the share of students in each country that have citizenship of another country.
Example: Reading the second column: 0.03 per cent of Austrian tertiary students are Belgian citizens, 0.02 per cent of Austrian students are Canadian citizens, etc.
Reading the first row: 0.02 per cent of Danish tertiary students are Australian citizens, 0.05 per cent of Irish tertiary students are Australian citizens, etc.

Countries of destination

Countries of origin	Australia	Austria	Belgium	Czech Republic	Denmark	Finland	France	Germany	Iceland	Ireland	Italy	Japan
OECD COUNTRIES												
Australia	a	0.01	n	n	0.02	0.01	0.01	0.01	0.01	0.05	n	0.01
Austria	0.02	a	0.01	n	0.01	0.01	0.02	0.32	0.13	0.03	n	n
Belgium	0.01	0.03	a	n	0.01	0.01	0.10	0.05	0.01	0.04	0.01	n
Canada	0.15	0.02	0.02	0.01	0.02	0.03	0.05	0.02	0.05	0.11	n	0.01
Czech Republic	0.01	0.15	0.01	n	a	0.01	0.02	0.08	0.04	0.01	0.01	n
Denmark	0.02	0.02	0.01	n	n	0.02	0.01	0.03	0.48	0.02	n	n
Finland	0.01	0.06	0.02	n	0.06	a	0.01	0.05	0.29	0.06	n	n
France	0.04	0.16	2.95	n	0.06	0.04	a	0.31	0.27	0.33	0.03	0.01
Germany	0.14	2.30	0.14	0.01	0.30	0.09	0.26	a	0.35	0.30	0.04	0.01
Greece	0.01	0.12	0.17	0.16	0.01	0.01	0.13	0.38	n	0.03	0.49	n
Hungary	0.01	0.45	0.03	n	0.01	0.03	0.03	0.14	n	n	0.01	n
Iceland	n	0.01	n	n	0.39	0.01	n	0.01	n	a	n	n
Ireland	0.04	0.02	0.02	n	0.02	0.01	0.03	0.03	n	n	a	n
Italy	0.02	2.68	0.83	n	0.04	0.03	0.18	0.36	0.17	0.08	n	a
Japan	0.28	0.11	0.05	n	0.02	0.03	0.07	0.10	0.06	0.02	n	n
Korea	0.32	0.12	0.02	n	n	0.01	0.08	0.23	n	0.01	n	0.45
Luxembourg	n	0.11	0.39	n	n	n	0.07	0.08	0.01	0.01	n	n
Mexico	0.02	0.03	0.02	n	0.01	0.01	0.05	0.02	0.01	n	n	n
Netherlands	0.04	0.04	0.73	n	0.05	0.02	0.02	0.09	0.07	0.03	n	n
New Zealand	0.53	n	n	n	0.01	n	n	n	n	n	n	n
Norway	0.28	0.03	0.01	0.02	0.77	0.02	0.02	0.04	0.35	0.09	n	n
Poland	0.02	0.35	0.07	0.03	0.11	0.02	0.10	0.49	0.13	0.02	0.02	n
Portugal	0.01	0.02	0.18	n	0.01	0.01	0.14	0.09	n	0.03	n	n
Slovak Republic	0.01	0.41	0.01	1.42	n	0.01	0.01	0.05	0.02	n	n	n
Spain	0.01	0.13	0.36	n	0.05	0.03	0.18	0.28	0.13	0.13	0.01	n
Sweden	0.12	0.09	0.01	0.02	0.35	0.21	0.04	0.04	0.31	0.05	0.01	n
Switzerland	0.02	0.10	0.03	n	0.02	0.01	0.05	0.09	0.06	0.01	0.04	n
Turkey	0.02	0.49	0.12	n	0.10	0.01	0.10	1.28	0.01	n	0.01	n
United Kingdom	0.52	0.08	0.06	0.09	0.20	0.05	0.13	0.12	0.16	1.16	0.01	0.01
United States	0.46	0.14	0.05	0.02	0.12	0.07	0.12	0.17	0.26	1.10	0.01	0.03
Argentina	0.01	0.01	0.01	n	n	n	0.03	0.02	n	n	0.01	n
Brazil	0.03	0.03	0.04	n	0.02	0.01	0.07	0.07	n	n	0.01	n
Chile	0.02	0.01	0.03	n	0.01	n	0.02	0.02	n	n	n	n
China	0.92	0.15	0.20	n	0.08	0.36	0.15	0.44	0.09	0.06	0.01	0.80
Egypt	0.01	0.09	0.02	0.01	0.01	n	0.04	0.06	n	0.02	n	0.01
India	0.71	0.04	0.04	0.01	0.01	0.02	0.01	0.07	0.02	0.04	0.01	0.01
Indonesia	1.23	0.01	0.02	n	n	n	0.01	0.10	n	n	n	0.03
Jamaica	n	n	n	n	n	n	0.00	n	n	n	n	n
Jordan	0.01	0.03	n	0.01	n	n	0.01	0.05	0.02	0.01	0.01	n
Malaysia	1.49	n	n	n	n	n	0.01	0.01	n	0.36	n	0.04
Paraguay	n	n	n	n	n	n	0.00	n	n	n	n	n
Peru	0.01	0.03	0.02	n	0.01	0.01	0.02	0.04	n	n	0.01	n
Philippines	0.08	0.01	0.02	n	0.01	0.01	0.00	0.01	n	n	n	0.01
Russian Federation	0.03	0.13	0.06	0.06	0.06	0.27	0.08	0.36	0.12	0.03	0.01	0.01
Thailand	0.37	0.01	0.01	n	0.01	n	0.02	0.02	0.01	n	n	0.03
Tunisia	n	0.02	0.08	n	n	n	0.00	0.06	n	n	0.01	n
Uruguay	n	n	n	n	n	n	0.00	n	n	n	n	n
Zimbabwe	0.04	n	n	n	n	n	0.00	n	n	n	n	n
Total: Africa	*0.44*	*0.36*	*3.06*	*0.09*	*0.20*	*0.26*	*3.71*	*0.93*	*0.05*	*0.25*	*0.12*	*0.02*
Total: Asia	*8.96*	*1.47*	*0.73*	*0.28*	*0.53*	*0.60*	*0.98*	*3.25*	*0.28*	*0.84*	*0.19*	*1.46*
Total: Europe	*1.47*	*9.74*	*6.34*	*2.00*	*3.06*	*1.24*	*2.04*	*4.82*	*3.42*	*2.55*	*1.15*	*0.05*
Total: North America	*0.63*	*0.21*	*0.14*	*0.04*	*0.16*	*0.11*	*0.26*	*0.26*	*0.34*	*1.23*	*0.03*	*0.04*
Total: Oceania	*0.75*	*0.01*	*n*	*n*	*0.03*	*0.01*	*0.01*	*0.02*	*0.01*	*0.05*	*n*	*0.01*
Total: South America	*0.11*	*0.12*	*0.18*	*0.03*	*0.06*	*0.02*	*0.21*	*0.20*	*0.02*	*0.01*	*0.07*	*0.02*
Not specified	*0.39*	*0.06*	*0.17*	*0.54*	*2.49*	*0.02*	*0.05*	*0.08*	*0.01*	*n*	*0.05*	*n*
Total: All countries	**13.93**	**11.97**	**10.62**	**2.98**	**6.53**	**2.25**	**7.25**	**9.56**	**4.13**	**4.93**	**1.61**	**1.60**

Source: OECD. See Annex 3 for notes (*www.oecd.org/edu/eag2003*).

C3

Table C3.2 (continued)
Proportion of foreign students in tertiary education in the country of study (2001)
Number of foreign students enrolled in tertiary education as a percentage of students in the country of destination, based on head counts

The table shows the share of students in each country that have citizenship of another country.
Example: Reading the second column: 0.35 per cent of Dutch tertiary students are Belgian citizens, 0.01 per cent of Dutch students are Canadian citizens, etc.
Reading the first row: 0.01 per cent of Dutch tertiary students are Australian citizens, 0.05 per cent of Swedish tertiary students are Australian citizens, etc.

Countries of destination

Countries of origin	Korea	Netherlands	New Zealand	Norway	Poland	Slovak Republic	Spain	Sweden	Switzerland	Turkey	United Kingdom	United States
Australia	n	0.01	a	0.01	n	n	n	0.05	0.03	n	0.06	0.02
Austria	n	0.02	0.01	0.02	n	n	0.03	0.09	0.49	n	0.06	0.01
Belgium	n	0.35	0.00	0.01	n	n	0.07	0.05	0.17	n	0.12	0.01
Canada	n	0.01	0.06	0.03	0.01	0.01	n	0.08	0.11	n	0.15	0.16
Czech Republic	n	0.01	n	0.02	0.01	0.20	0.01	0.03	0.08	n	0.02	0.01
Denmark	n	0.01	0.02	0.40	n	n	0.02	0.23	0.05	n	0.08	0.01
Finland	n	0.02	0.01	0.12	n	n	0.02	1.00	0.04	n	0.12	0.01
France	n	0.07	0.04	0.06	n	n	0.27	0.27	1.88	n	0.60	0.05
Germany	n	0.63	0.17	0.24	0.01	0.01	0.23	0.57	3.52	0.01	0.65	0.06
Greece	n	0.02	n	0.01	n	0.18	0.02	0.07	0.16	0.08	1.39	0.02
Hungary	n	0.01	n	0.01	n	0.02	0.01	0.06	0.10	n	0.02	0.01
Iceland	n	n	n	0.14	n	n	n	0.09	0.01	n	0.01	n
Ireland	n	0.01	n	0.01	n	n	0.02	0.03	0.03	n	0.59	0.01
Italy	n	0.07	n	0.04	n	n	0.28	0.16	2.61	n	0.29	0.02
Japan	0.02	0.01	0.28	0.01	n	n	0.01	0.04	0.12	n	0.30	0.30
Korea	n	a	0.31	n	n	n	n	0.01	0.06	n	0.11	0.29
Luxembourg	n	n	n	n	n	n	n	n	0.12	n	0.03	n
Mexico	n	n	0.01	0.01	n	n	0.07	0.03	0.05	n	0.07	0.07
Netherlands	n	n	a	0.07	n	n	0.05	0.15	0.16	n	0.12	0.01
New Zealand	n	n	a	n	n	n	n	0.01	0.01	n	0.02	0.01
Norway	n	0.02	0.08	n	a	n	0.01	0.34	0.08	n	0.19	0.01
Poland	n	0.04	n	0.04	n	0.02	0.02	0.23	0.21	n	0.03	0.02
Portugal	n	0.03	0.01	0.01	n	n	a	0.03	0.30	n	0.11	0.01
Slovak Republic	n	n	n	0.01	n	n	0.00	a	0.06	n	0.01	0.00
Spain	n	0.19	n	0.03	n	n	n	0.21	0.93	n	0.35	0.03
Sweden	n	0.02	0.07	0.53	0.01	n	0.02	a	0.15	a	0.20	0.03
Switzerland	n	0.02	0.01	0.02	n	n	0.01	0.06	n	n	a	0.01
Turkey	n	0.20	n	0.02	n	n	n	0.04	0.34	a	0.09	a
United Kingdom	n	0.13	0.08	0.20	n	n	0.13	0.22	0.18	0.01	a	0.05
United States	0.01	0.05	0.29	0.16	0.02	0.01	0.03	0.25	0.21	n	0.57	a
Argentina	n	n	0.01	n	n	n	0.06	0.01	0.06	n	0.02	0.02
Brazil	n	0.01	0.02	0.02	n	n	0.05	0.02	0.11	n	0.05	0.06
Chile	n	0.01	0.01	0.03	n	n	0.04	0.07	0.04	n	0.01	0.01
China	0.05	0.08	1.88	0.11	n	n	0.01	0.17	0.26	0.01	0.50	0.38
Egypt	n	0.01	n	0.01	n	0.01	n	n	0.04	n	0.06	0.01
India	n	0.01	0.20	0.05	n	n	n	0.03	0.07	n	0.21	0.35
Indonesia	n	0.11	0.22	n	n	n	n	0.01	0.02	n	0.05	0.07
Jamaica	n	n	n	n	n	n	n	n	n	n	0.02	0.03
Jordan	n	n	n	n	n	0.01	n	n	0.01	0.01	0.04	0.01
Malaysia	n	n	0.60	n	n	n	n	0.01	n	n	0.44	0.05
Paraguay	n	n	n	n	n	n	n	n	n	n	n	n
Peru	n	0.01	n	0.01	n	n	0.05	0.02	0.10	n	0.01	0.02
Philippines	n	0.01	0.03	n	n	n	0.00	0.01	0.01	n	0.01	0.02
Russian Federation	n	0.05	0.02	0.18	0.02	0.02	0.01	0.15	0.23	0.06	0.07	0.04
Thailand	n	n	0.19	0.01	n	n	n	0.02	0.01	n	0.13	0.07
Tunisia	n	n	n	n	n	n	n	n	0.12	n	n	n
Uruguay	n	n	0.01	n	n	n	0.01	n	0.01	n	n	n
Zimbabwe	n	n	0.01	0.01	n	n	n	n	n	n	0.11	0.01
Total: Africa	n	0.51	0.08	0.39	0.02	0.09	0.22	0.18	1.10	0.03	0.88	0.22
Total: Asia	0.11	0.66	4.49	0.54	0.06	0.27	0.06	0.64	1.33	0.68	3.60	2.16
Total: Europe	n	1.83	0.56	2.67	0.26	0.79	1.39	4.51	12.90	0.33	5.29	0.51
Total: North America	0.01	0.07	0.36	0.21	0.03	0.01	0.14	0.39	0.43	n	0.90	0.36
Total: Oceania	n	0.01	0.68	0.01	n	n	0.00	0.06	0.04	n	0.09	0.03
Total: South America	n	0.21	0.06	0.08	n	0.01	0.36	0.16	0.53	n	0.14	0.21
Not specified	n	0.01	n	0.77	0.01	a	n	1.41	0.67	a	0.02	a
Total: All countries	0.12	3.29	6.23	4.65	0.38	1.17	2.18	7.35	16.99	1.04	10.92	3.50

OECD COUNTRIES

NON-OECD COUNTRIES

C₃

Source: OECD. See Annex 3 for notes (*www.oecd.org/edu/eag2003*).

Table C3.3
Proportion of citizens in tertiary education studying abroad (2001)
Number of students enrolled in tertiary education in other countries as a percentage of students enrolled in the country of origin, based on head counts

The table shows the share of students from each country that are studying in other countries.
Example: Reading the first column: 0.06 per cent of Japanese tertiary students study in Australia, 0.09 per cent of Korean students study in Australia, etc.
Reading the first row: 0.02 per cent of Australian students study in France, 0.03 per cent of Australian students study in Germany, etc.

	Countries of origin	Countries of destination												
		Australia	Austria	Belgium	Czech Republic	Denmark	Finland	France	Germany	Iceland	Ireland	Italy	Japan	Korea
OECD COUNTRIES	Australia	a	n	n	n	n	n	0.02	0.03	n	0.01	n	0.04	n
	Austria	0.05	a	0.02	n	0.01	0.01	0.16	2.49	n	0.02	0.03	0.01	n
	Belgium	0.02	0.02	a	n	0.01	0.01	0.56	0.27	n	0.02	0.03	0.01	n
	Czech Republic	0.03	0.15	0.01	n	a	0.01	0.14	0.66	n	0.01	0.04	0.01	n
	Denmark	0.09	0.03	0.03	n	n	a	0.14	0.35	0.03	0.01	0.02	0.01	n
	Finland	0.04	0.06	0.03	n	0.04	a	0.11	0.36	0.01	0.03	0.02	0.01	n
	France	0.02	0.02	0.52	n	0.01	0.01	a	a	n	0.03	0.02	0.01	n
	Germany	0.06	0.29	0.02	n	0.03	0.01	0.25	a	n	0.02	0.04	0.01	n
	Greece	0.01	0.06	0.13	0.09	n	0.01	0.54	1.68	n	0.01	1.86	n	n
	Hungary	0.02	0.36	0.03	n	0.01	0.02	0.16	0.87	n	n	0.03	0.02	n
	Iceland	0.05	0.24	0.06	0.03	7.43	0.33	0.40	1.64	n	a	0.05	0.09	n
	Ireland	0.21	0.03	0.03	0.01	0.03	0.01	0.34	0.32	n	n	a	0.01	n
	Italy	0.01	0.39	0.17	n	n	n	0.21	0.42	n	0.01	n	a	n
	Japan	0.06	0.01	n	n	n	n	0.04	0.05	n	n	n	n	0.02
	Korea	0.09	0.01	n	n	n	n	0.05	0.16	n	n	n	0.57	n
	Luxembourg	0.32	12.0	55.39	n	n	n	54.20	64.55	0.04	0.87	0.95	0.24	n
	Mexico	0.01	n	n	n	n	n	0.05	0.02	n	n	n	0.01	n
	Netherlands	0.08	0.02	0.52	n	0.02	0.01	0.09	0.38	n	0.01	0.01	0.01	n
	New Zealand	2.60	n	n	n	0.01	n	0.02	0.03	n	n	n	0.04	n
	Norway	1.29	0.04	0.01	0.03	0.77	0.03	0.18	0.49	0.02	0.08	0.02	0.01	n
	Poland	0.01	0.05	0.01	n	0.01	n	0.11	0.57	n	n	0.02	n	n
	Portugal	0.02	0.01	0.17	n	n	n	0.73	0.46	n	0.01	0.01	0.01	n
	Slovak Republic	0.04	0.75	0.03	2.57	n	0.01	0.18	0.72	n	n	0.05	0.01	n
	Spain	0.01	0.02	0.07	n	n	n	0.20	0.32	n	0.01	0.01	n	n
	Sweden	0.30	0.07	0.01	0.01	0.19	0.16	0.24	0.25	0.01	0.02	0.03	0.02	n
	Switzerland	0.11	0.17	0.07	n	0.03	0.02	0.64	1.20	n	0.01	0.44	0.02	n
	Turkey	0.01	0.08	0.03	n	0.01	n	0.13	1.65	n	n	0.01	0.01	n
	United Kingdom	0.22	0.01	0.01	0.01	0.02	0.01	0.13	0.12	n	0.09	0.01	0.02	n
	United States	0.03	n	n	n	n	n	0.02	0.03	n	0.01	n	0.01	n
NON-OECD COUNTRIES	Argentina	0.02	0.01	0.01	n	n	n	0.11	0.09	n	n	0.06	0.02	n
	Brazil	0.01	n	0.01	n	n	n	0.05	0.05	n	n	0.01	0.01	n
	Chile	0.04	n	0.03	n	0.01	n	0.08	0.10	n	n	0.01	0.01	n
	Egypt	n	0.01	n	n	n	n	0.05	0.07	n	n	n	0.01	n
	Indonesia	0.36	n	n	n	n	n	0.01	0.07	n	n	n	0.04	n
	Jamaica	0.01	0.01	n	n	n	n	0.03	0.03	n	n	n	0.01	n
	Malaysia	2.35	n	n	n	n	n	0.02	0.04	n	0.11	n	0.32	n
	Paraguay	n	n	0.01	0.01	n	n	0.04	0.05	n	n	0.01	0.04	0.02
	Philippines	0.03	n	n	n	n	n	n	0.01	n	n	n	0.02	n
	Russian Federation	n	n	n	n	n	0.01	0.02	0.10	n	n	n	n	n
	Thailand	0.15	n	n	n	n	n	0.02	0.02	n	n	n	0.05	n
	Tunisia	n	0.03	0.13	n	n	n	0.03	0.61	n	n	0.05	0.02	n
	Uruguay	0.02	0.01	0.01	n	n	n	0.05	0.04	n	n	0.01	0.01	n
	Zimbabwe	1.02	0.01	0.02	0.02	0.02	0.01	0.02	0.20	n	0.02	n	0.02	n

Source: OECD. See Annex 3 for notes (*www.oecd.org/edu/eag2003*).

C3

Table C3.3 (continued)
Proportion of citizens in tertiary education studying abroad (2001)
Number of students enrolled in tertiary education in other countries as a percentage of students enrolled in the country of origin, based on head counts

The table shows the share of students from each country that are studying in other countries.
Example: Reading the second column: 0.01 per cent of Japanese tertiary students study in New Zealand, 0.02 per cent of Korean students study in New Zealand, etc.
Reading the first row: 0.02 per cent of Australian students study in Sweden, 0.01 per cent of Australian students study in Switzerland, etc.

	Countries of destination												
Countries of origin	Netherlands	New Zealand	Norway	Poland	Portugal	Slovak Republic	Spain	Sweden	Switzerland	Turkey	United Kingdom	United States	Total
Australia	n	a	n	n	m	n	n	0.02	0.01	n	0.14	0.26	0.55
Austria	0.04	0.01	0.01	n	m	n	0.24	0.12	0.30	n	0.47	0.35	4.35
Belgium	0.49	n	0.01	n	m	n	0.35	0.05	0.08	n	0.67	0.21	2.80
Czech Republic	0.02	n	0.01	0.09	m	0.11	0.07	0.04	0.05	n	0.16	0.37	1.98
Denmark	0.03	0.02	0.40	0.01	m	n	0.17	0.43	0.04	n	0.91	0.45	3.18
Finland	0.03	n	0.08	n	m	n	0.12	1.28	0.03	n	0.91	0.28	3.45
France	0.02	n	0.01	n	m	n	0.24	0.05	0.15	n	0.62	0.31	2.02
Germany	0.15	0.01	0.02	0.01	m	n	0.20	0.10	0.28	n	0.64	0.42	2.59
Greece	0.02	n	n	0.01	m	0.05	0.07	0.05	0.05	0.27	5.99	0.50	11.42
Hungary	0.02	n	0.01	0.02	m	0.01	0.04	0.06	0.05	n	0.12	0.31	2.16
Iceland	0.21	n	2.63	0.01	m	n	0.18	3.30	0.13	n	2.19	4.75	23.71
Ireland	0.02	n	0.01	n	m	n	0.20	0.07	0.03	n	7.33	0.57	9.22
Italy	0.02	n	n	n	m	n	0.28	0.03	0.24	n	0.34	0.17	2.28
Japan	n	0.01	n	n	m	n	n	n	n	n	0.16	1.02	1.39
Korea	a	0.02	n	n	m	n	n	n	n	n	0.07	1.27	2.25
Luxembourg	0.71	n	n	n	m	n	0.99	0.16	8.05	n	27.52	2.50	228.48
Mexico	n	n	n	n	m	n	0.06	n	n	n	0.07	0.45	0.69
Netherlands	n	a	0.03	n	m	n	0.17	0.11	0.05	n	0.49	0.32	2.33
New Zealand	0.01	a	n	n	m	n	n	0.01	0.01	n	0.25	0.47	3.47
Norway	0.04	0.07	n	a	m	n	0.14	0.63	0.07	n	2.04	0.96	6.93
Poland	0.01	n	n	n	m	n	0.02	0.05	0.02	n	0.04	0.12	1.07
Portugal	0.04	n	0.01	n	m	a	0.38	0.03	0.13	n	0.59	0.2	2.80
Slovak Republic	0.01	n	0.01	0.05	m	n	a	0.02	0.06	n	0.09	0.32	4.94
Spain	0.05	n	n	n	m	n	n	0.04	0.08	n	0.40	0.20	1.43
Sweden	0.03	0.04	0.28	0.03	m	n	0.12	a	a	n	1.13	1.11	4.05
Switzerland	0.05	0.01	0.03	n	m	n	0.13	0.14	n	a	0.85	0.98	4.91
Turkey	0.06	n	n	n	m	n	n	0.01	0.03	a	a	0.59	2.64
United Kingdom	0.03	0.01	0.02	n	m	n	0.11	0.04	0.01	0.01	a	0.34	1.22
United States	n	n	n	n	m	n	n	0.01	n	n	0.09	a	0.21
Argentina	n	n	n	n	m	n	0.24	0.01	0.02	n	0.09	0.60	1.30
Brazil	n	n	n	n	m	n	0.04	n	0.01	n	0.04	0.28	0.50
Chile	0.01	0.01	0.01	n	m	n	0.17	0.06	0.02	n	0.07	0.30	0.92
Egypt	n	n	n	n	m	n	n	n	n	n	0.07	0.11	0.36
Indonesia	0.02	0.01	n	n	m	n	n	n	n	n	0.03	0.33	0.88
Jamaica	n	0.01	0.01	n	m	n	n	n	n	n	0.90	8.62	9.64
Malaysia	n	0.19	n	n	m	n	n	n	n·	n	1.67	1.23	5.96
Paraguay	n	n	n	n	m	n	0.05	n	n	n	0.02	0.39	0.65
Philippines	n	n	n	n	m	n	n	n	n	n	0.01	0.11	0.20
Russian Federation	n	n	n	n	m	n	n	0.01	0.01	0.01	0.02	0.08	0.30
Thailand	n	0.02	n	n	m	n	n	n	n	n	0.13	0.46	0.87
Tunisia	0.01	n	n	0.01	m	n	0.01	n	0.10	n	0.02	0.16	1.18
Uruguay	n	0.01	n	n	m	n	0.16	0.01	0.02	n	0.04	0.35	0.75
Zimbabwe	0.01	0.06	0.08	0.02	m	0.01	0.02	0.03	0.01	0.01	6.93	4.42	12.98

OECD COUNTRIES

NON-OECD COUNTRIES

C3

Source: OECD. See Annex 3 for notes (*www.oecd.org/edu/eag2003*).

Table C3.4
Foreign students by level and type of tertiary education (2001)
Distribution of tertiary foreign students by level and type of education

	Tertiary-type B	Tertiary-type A	Advanced research programmes	Tertiary-type A and advanced research programmes	Total tertiary
	(1)	(2)	(3)	(4)	(5)
Australia	8.4	86.2	5.4	91.6	100.0
Austria	2.3	86.5	11.2	97.7	100.0
Belgium	44.3	50.8	5.0	55.7	100.0
Czech Republic	3.4	81.7	14.9	96.6	100.0
Denmark	11.7	88.3	a	88.3	100.0
Finland	1.1	79.3	19.6	98.9	100.0
France	8.8	91.2	m	m	100.0
Germany	6.1	93.9	m	93.9	100.0
Iceland	2.6	96.0	1.4	97.4	100.0
Italy	9.2	90.3	0.5	90.8	100.0
Japan	5.8	x(4)	x(4)	94.2	100.0
Korea	18.4	68.4	13.2	81.6	100.0
Mexico	1.7	93.3	5.0	98.3	100.0
Netherlands	0.8	99.2	a	99.2	100.0
New Zealand	24.3	73.0	2.7	75.7	100.0
Norway	4.9	87.3	7.9	95.1	100.0
Poland	1.4	98.6	m	98.6	100.0
Slovak Republic	0.3	92.3	7.4	99.7	100.0
Spain	4.2	78.6	17.1	95.8	100.0
Sweden	2.3	82.6	15.1	97.7	100.0
Switzerland	14.2	67.7	18.1	85.8	100.0
Turkey	6.6	93.4	m	93.4	100.0
United Kingdom	14.6	73.8	11.6	85.4	100.0
United States	x(2)	83.4	16.6	m	100.0
Chile	10.1	m	m	89.9	100.0
Malaysia	79.4	m	m	20.6	100.0
Philippines	n	m	m	100.0	100.0
Russian Federation	8.0	m	m	92.0	100.0

Note: x indicates that data are included in another column. The column reference is shown in brackets after "x". *e.g.*, x(2) means that data are included in column 2.
Source: OECD. See Annex 3 for notes (*www.oecd.org/edu/eag2003*).

OECD COUNTRIES

C₃

NON-OECD COUNTRIES

INDICATOR C4: EDUCATION AND WORK STATUS OF THE YOUTH POPULATION

- In 22 out of 27 OECD countries, more female than male 20 to 24-year-olds are in education. 20 to 24-year-old males are more likely to be employed.

- The percentage of 20 to 24-year-olds not in education ranges from 50 to 70 per cent, in most OECD countries.

- In some countries, education and work largely occur consecutively, while in other countries they are concurrent.

- Work-study programmes, relatively common in European countries, offer coherent vocational education routes to recognised occupational qualifications. In other countries, initial education and work are rarely associated.

Chart C4.1
Percentage of 20 to 24-year-olds in education and not in education
(employed and not employed), by gender (2001)

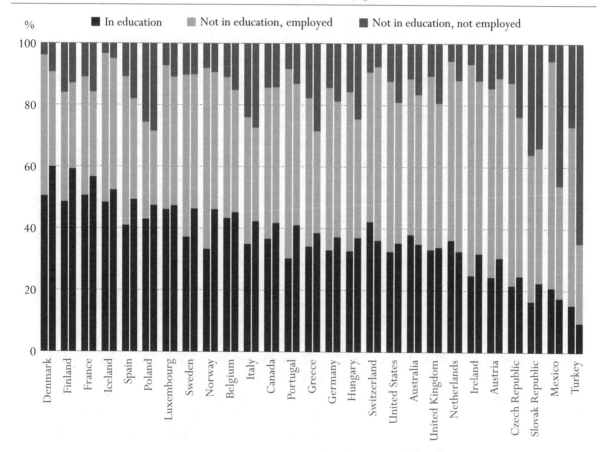

Note: The first bar represents males, the second bar represents females.
Countries are ranked in descending order of the percentage of 20 to 24-year-old females in education.
Source: OECD. Tables C4.1a and C4.1b. See Annex 3 for notes *(www.oecd.org/edu/eag2003).*

C4

Policy context

This indicator examines the education and employment status of young males and females.

All OECD countries are experiencing rapid social and economic changes that are making the transition to working life more uncertain. In some OECD countries, education and work largely occur consecutively, while in other OECD countries they may be concurrent. The ways in which education and work are combined can significantly affect the transition process. Of particular interest, for example, is the extent to which working -beyond the usual "summer jobs" for students- while studying may facilitate entry into the labour force. On the other hand, many hours of work while studying may result in dropping out of education rather than contribute to a successful transition to the labour market.

Evidence and explanations

Combining work and education

Work-study programmes and other ways of combining work and education are common in some OECD countries, but rare in others.

Table C4.1 reveals the education and work status of young people in the age groups 15 to 19, 20 to 24 and 25 to 29. Working while studying can occur as part of work-study programmes or in the form of part-time jobs out of school hours. Work-study programmes are relatively common in European countries such as Austria, the Czech Republic, Germany and Switzerland, and offer coherent vocational education routes to recognised occupational qualifications. Many young people also combine paid work out of school hours with education. This form of initial contact with the labour market between the ages of 15 and 19 is a major feature of the transition from education to work in Australia, Canada, Denmark, Iceland, the Netherlands, Norway, the United States and, to a lesser extent, Finland, Sweden, Switzerland and the United Kingdom. Finally, in Belgium, France, Ireland and the Mediterranean and Eastern European countries, initial education and work are rarely associated.

During the years spent in education, the employment status of males and females is broadly similar in most OECD countries.

The employment status of males and females is broadly similar during the years spent in education, with the exception of Austria and Germany, where noticeably more males participate in work-study programmes. In Australia, Canada, Denmark, Finland, Iceland, the Netherlands, Norway and Sweden, noticeably more females than males in the 15 to 29-year-old age group combine work outside school hours with education (Tables C4.1a and C4.1b).

Entry into the labour market after initial education

The transition from education to work occurs at different points of time in different OECD countries, depending on various educational and labour market factors.

As they grow older, young people participate decreasingly in education and increasingly in the labour force. The percentage of young people not in education in most OECD countries is between 10 and 30 per cent for 15 to 19-year-olds, rises to between 50 and 70 per cent for 20 to 24-year-olds and reaches 80 to 95 per cent for 25 to 29-year-olds (Chart C4.2). However, in many OECD countries young people begin their transition to work later, and in some cases over a longer period. This trend reflects not only the demand for education, but also the general state of the labour market, the length and orientation of educational programmes in relation to the labour market and the prevalence of part-time education.

Chart C4.2

Percentage of the youth population in education and not in education,
by age group and work status (2001)

■ Employed, not in education   ■ Students in work-study programmes   ■ Non-employed, in education
■ Non-employed, not in education   ■ Employed, in education

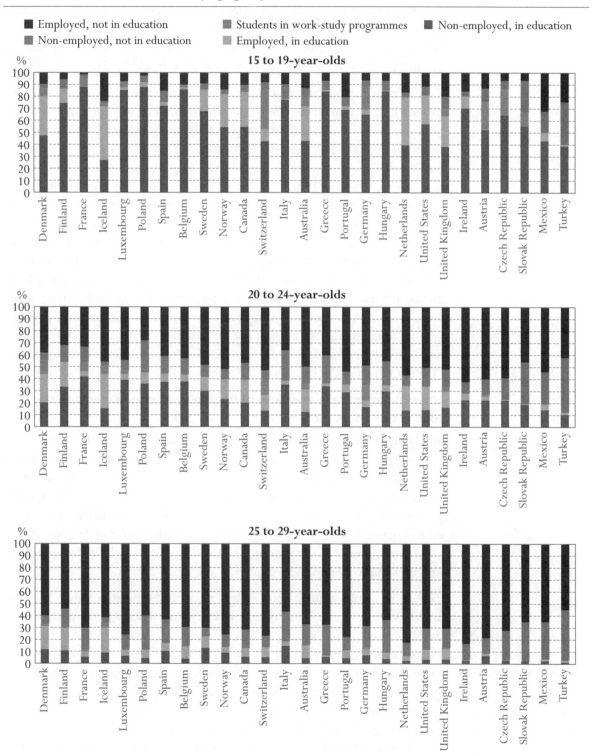

C4

Countries are ranked in descending order of the percentage of 20 to 24-year-olds in education.
Source: OECD. Table C4.1. See Annex 3 for notes (*www.oecd.org/edu/eag2003*).

The age at which people enter the labour market after completing initial education has consequences for employment. Overall, older non-students are more likely to be employed than non-students in the age group 15 to 19 years, while a higher percentage of male than female non-students are working. In relative terms, more females than males are out of the labour force, particularly during the years associated with child-bearing and child-rearing, captured by the age group 25 to 29 years in this indicator (Tables C4.1a and C4.1b).

Employment-to-population ratios among young adults who are not in education provide information on the effectiveness of transition frameworks and thus help policy-makers to evaluate transition policies. In two-thirds of OECD countries, fewer than 65 (and in some even fewer than 50) per cent of 15 to 19-year-olds not in education are working, which may suggest that because these young people have left school early, they are not viewed by employers as having the skills necessary for productive employment. Employment-to-population ratios for 20 to 24-year-olds generally exceed 70 per cent, but ratios in some OECD countries such as Greece, Italy, Poland and Turkey are still around or below 65 per cent. For the 25 to 29 age group, most OECD countries have ratios of between 70 and 80 per cent, with the exception of Italy, Mexico, Poland, the Slovak Republic and Turkey. Employment-to-population ratios for young males tend to be higher than for young females after leaving education, probably because of family-related reasons and because the social acceptability of being unemployed is still higher for females than for males in many OECD countries (Tables C4.1a and C4.1b).

Unemployment rate and ratio of unemployed non-students to the total youth population

Young people represent the principal source of new skills in OECD countries. In most OECD countries, education policy seeks to encourage young people to complete at least upper secondary education. Since jobs on offer in the labour market require ever higher general skill levels and more flexible learning skills, persons with low attainment are often severely penalised. Differences in the ratio of unemployed non-students to the total youth population by level of educational attainment are an indicator of the degree to which further education improves the economic opportunities of any young person.

Traditional unemployment measures overestimate unemployment in the transition period and are insensitive to different systems of combining education and work in the transition period.

The youth unemployment rate by age group is the most common measure available for describing the labour market status of young people. However, unemployment rates do not take educational circumstances into account. Consequently, an unemployed young person counted in the numerator may, in some OECD countries, be enrolled in education. The denominator may include young people in vocational training, provided they are apprenticed, but not those in school-based vocational courses. Hence, if almost all young people in a particular age group are still in education, the unemployment rate will reflect only the few in the labour market and may therefore appear very high, particularly among the youngest cohort who have usually left the education system with very low qualifications.

The ratio of unemployed non-students to the total age cohort is therefore a more appropriate way to reflect the likelihood of youth unemployment. This is because young people who are looking for a job while still in education are usually seeking part-time or temporary work while studying, unlike those entering the labour market after leaving school.

On average, completing upper secondary education reduces the unemployment-to-population ratio (*e.g.*, unemployment among non-students as a percentage of the entire age cohort) of 20 to 24-year-olds by about 6 percentage points, and that of 25 to 29-year-olds by about 4 percentage points (Table C4.2). In 19 out of 26 OECD countries, the unemployment-to-population ratio among 20 to 24-year-olds not in education is less than 8 per cent for those with upper secondary or post-secondary non-tertiary education. This proportion remains below 8 per cent for people without upper secondary education in only seven OECD countries. Since it has become the norm in most OECD countries to complete upper secondary education, many young persons who do not are much more likely to have employment difficulties during their working lives.

The ratio of unemployed people who have not completed upper secondary education to the total youth population is 1.5 times higher on average than for upper secondary graduates.

Chart C4.3

Ratio of unemployed non-students to the population of 20 to 24-year-olds, by level of educational attainment (2001)

■ Below upper secondary education
■ Upper secondary and post-secondary non-tertiary education
■ Tertiary education

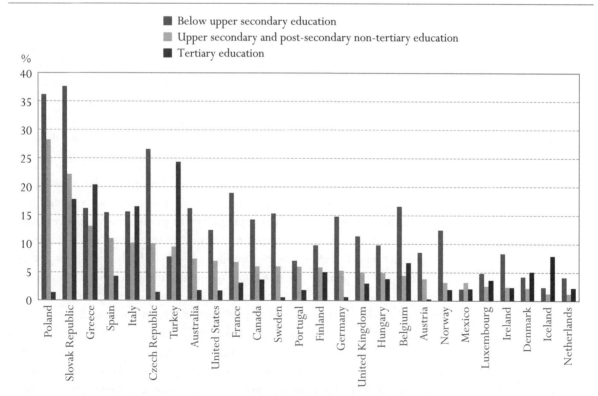

Countries are ranked in descending order of the ratio of unemployed non-students to the population of 20 to 24-year-olds having attained upper secondary and post-secondary non-tertiary education.
Source: OECD. Table C4.2. See Annex 3 for notes (*www.oecd.org/edu/eag2003*).

Upper secondary education, and even tertiary-level education, does not guarantee a job.

Nevertheless, in a number of OECD countries, for upper secondary graduates aged 20 to 24, the ratio of unemployed non-students to the total youth population is above 7 per cent (Chart C4.3). In a few OECD countries, even young people who have completed tertiary-level education are subject to considerable unemployment risk when they enter the labour market. The ratio of unemployed non-students to the total youth population among this age group is 16 per cent or more in Greece, Italy, the Slovak Republic and Turkey, and higher than 12 per cent for 25 to 29-year-olds in Greece and Italy (Table C4.2).

Definitions and methodologies

Data for this indicator were obtained from a special OECD data collection on the first quarter of the year.

Data for this indicator, which were obtained from a special OECD data collection, usually refer to the first quarter or the average of the first three months of the calendar year, and therefore exclude summer employment. The labour force status categories shown in this section are defined according to ILO guidelines, with one exception. For the purposes of these indicators, persons in work-study programmes (see below) have been classified separately as *in education* and *employed*, without reference to their ILO labour force status during the survey reference week, since they may not necessarily be in the work component of their programmes during the reference week, and may therefore not be employed then. *"Other employed"* includes individuals employed according to the ILO definition, but excludes those attending work-study programmes who are already counted as employed. Finally, *"not in the labour force"* includes individuals who are not working and who are not unemployed, *i.e.* individuals who are not looking for a job.

Work-study programmes combine work and education as parts of an integrated, formal education or training activity, such as the dual system in Germany; *apprentissage* or *formation en alternance* in France and Belgium; internship or co-operative education in Canada; and apprenticeship in Ireland. Vocational education and training take place in school settings and working environments. Students or trainees can be paid or not, usually depending on the type of job and the course or training.

The enrolment rates shown in Table C4.1 are estimated on the basis of self-reports collected during labour force surveys that often correspond only imprecisely with enrolment counts obtained from administrative sources shown elsewhere in this publication, for several reasons. First, age may not be measured in the same way. For example, in administrative data, both enrolment and age are measured on January 1st in OECD countries in the northern hemisphere, whereas in some labour force surveys, enrolment is measured in the reference week, while the age recorded is the age that will be attained at the end of the calendar year, even if the survey is conducted in the early part of the year. This means that recorded enrolment rates may occasionally reflect a population that is almost one year younger than the specified age range. At ages when movements out of education may be significant, this affects enrolment rates. Second, young people may be enrolled in several programmes and can sometimes be counted twice in administrative statistics but only once in a labour force survey.

C4

Moreover, not all enrolments may be captured in administrative statistics, particularly in profit-making institutions. Third, the programme classification used in the self-reports in labour force surveys do not always correspond to the qualification standards used for administrative data collections.

C₄

Table C4.1
Percentage of the *youth population* in education and not in education, by age group and work status (2001)

		In education					Not in education				Total in education and not in education
	Age group	Students in work-study programmes[1]	Other employed	Unemployed	Not in the labour force	Sub-total	Employed	Unemployed	Not in the labour force	Sub-total	
Australia	15-19	7.3	29.0	6.4	36.7	79.5	13.0	4.3	3.3	20.5	100
	20-24	5.1	18.8	2.3	10.2	36.5	49.6	6.9	7.0	63.5	100
	25-29	0.8	10.6	0.9	3.6	15.8	67.0	4.5	12.7	84.2	100
Austria	15-19	22.7	0.6	0.4	52.2	75.8	12.9	2.2	9.1	24.2	100
	20-24	1.6	3.3	0.4	22.1	27.4	59.8	3.4	9.4	72.6	100
	25-29	0.1	2.1	0.2	6.4	8.7	78.5	3.0	9.8	91.3	100
Belgium	15-19	2.0	1.7	0.3	85.7	89.7	4.1	1.8	4.5	10.3	100
	20-24	0.9	5.4	0.9	36.9	44.2	42.8	6.9	6.1	55.8	100
	25-29	0.9	10.2	0.4	3.5	15.0	69.5	7.3	8.1	85.0	100
Canada	15-19	a	29.1	5.2	49.5	83.9	10.2	2.6	3.3	16.1	100
	20-24	a	19.0	1.5	18.7	39.1	46.6	6.3	8.0	60.9	100
	25-29	a	7.2	0.2	5.4	12.8	71.4	6.1	9.7	87.2	100
Czech Republic	15-19	21.9	0.2	n	64.8	87.0	6.2	4.1	2.8	13.0	100
	20-24	0.1	0.6	0.2	22.2	23.1	58.9	9.3	8.7	76.9	100
	25-29	n	0.3	n	2.6	3.0	72.1	7.2	17.7	97.0	100
Denmark	15-19	6.6	32.9	3.4	44.0	86.8	9.4	1.2	2.5	13.2	100
	20-24	11.4	23.6	3.5	16.8	55.3	38.1	2.9	3.6	44.7	100
	25-29	1.0	19.8	1.0	10.5	32.4	60.0	1.9	5.7	67.6	100
Finland	15-19	a	11.6	5.9	68.7	86.3	5.7	2.1	5.9	13.7	100
	20-24	a	20.6	4.4	28.9	53.9	31.7	6.1	8.3	46.1	100
	25-29	a	19.0	1.8	8.9	29.8	54.5	6.3	9.4	70.2	100
France	15-19	6.2	0.4	n	88.2	94.9	1.7	1.8	1.6	5.1	100
	20-24	7.3	4.4	0.6	41.3	53.6	33.1	8.5	4.9	46.4	100
	25-29	1.6	4.4	0.4	5.0	11.4	70.3	9.1	9.2	88.6	100
Germany	15-19	19.4	4.0	0.6	64.5	88.5	6.4	1.4	3.7	11.5	100
	20-24	12.6	5.5	0.3	16.7	35.0	48.7	5.6	10.8	65.0	100
	25-29	1.4	5.0	0.2	6.8	13.5	68.5	5.8	12.2	86.5	100
Greece	15-19	0.2	1.1	0.6	83.8	85.7	6.8	3.9	3.6	14.3	100
	20-24	0.1	2.4	1.3	32.8	36.5	40.2	14.0	9.3	63.5	100
	25-29	0.1	1.2	0.5	5.0	6.7	67.4	12.7	13.2	93.3	100
Hungary	15-19	a	0.6	0.2	84.3	85.1	6.5	2.1	6.3	14.9	100
	20-24	a	4.8	0.5	29.5	34.8	45.0	5.5	14.7	65.2	100
	25-29	a	5.3	0.2	3.7	9.1	63.4	5.3	22.1	90.9	100
Iceland	16-19	2.8	44.6	3.7	23.4	74.4	23.7	1.6	0.3	25.6	100
	20-24	6.5	28.3	1.0	14.6	50.3	45.6	2.0	2.1	49.7	100
	25-29	3.9	21.0	n	8.9	33.8	61.5	1.4	3.4	66.2	100
Ireland	15-19	a	9.9	0.5	69.8	80.3	15.5	1.9	2.2	19.7	100
	20-24	a	5.5	0.4	22.4	28.3	62.4	3.3	6.0	71.7	100
	25-29	a	0.5	n	2.7	3.3	83.1	2.8	10.7	96.7	100
Italy	15-19	n	0.6	0.8	76.8	78.2	9.6	4.9	7.3	21.8	100
	20-24	0.1	3.1	1.8	33.6	38.6	35.8	11.8	13.8	61.4	100
	25-29	0.1	3.6	1.2	13.5	18.4	56.4	9.9	15.3	81.6	100
Luxembourg	15-19	3.6	2.3	0.2	85.2	91.2	7.0	0.6	1.2	8.8	100
	20-24	2.6	4.9	0.3	38.9	46.7	44.2	3.5	5.5	53.3	100
	25-29	0.4	5.0	0.2	5.9	11.6	75.9	1.8	10.7	88.4	100
Mexico	15-19	a	7.1	0.3	42.8	50.2	32.0	1.6	16.3	49.8	100
	20-24	a	4.7	0.2	14.1	19.1	53.8	2.0	25.1	80.9	100
	25-29	a	1.6	n	2.5	4.1	64.8	1.6	29.4	95.9	100
Netherlands	15-19	m	40.1	3.5	36.0	79.6	16.3	1.4	2.7	20.4	100
	20-24	m	20.5	1.0	12.9	34.4	56.9	2.1	6.6	65.6	100
	25-29	m	3.9	0.2	2.3	6.4	82.3	1.5	9.8	93.6	100
Norway	16-19	a	27.6	6.9	47.5	82.0	14.1	1.6	2.3	18.0	100
	20-24	a	16.4	2.1	21.1	39.6	51.7	3.2	5.5	60.4	100
	25-29	a	5.0	0.7	8.2	13.9	75.9	3.2	7.0	86.1	100
Poland	15-19	a	3.9	1.2	86.7	91.8	2.4	3.4	2.4	8.2	100
	20-24	a	9.4	6.7	29.2	45.2	27.7	18.9	8.2	54.8	100
	25-29	a	7.1	1.5	2.9	11.4	59.9	15.7	13.0	88.6	100
Portugal	15-19	a	2.9	0.4	68.7	72.0	20.3	2.8	4.9	28.0	100
	20-24	a	6.5	0.6	28.5	35.6	53.7	5.1	5.6	64.4	100
	25-29	a	6.3	0.4	4.4	11.0	77.6	3.6	7.8	89.0	100
Slovak Republic	15-19	11.4	0.1	n	55.7	67.3	6.3	11.0	15.5	32.7	100
	20-24	a	0.4	0.6	18.5	19.4	45.7	22.8	12.1	80.6	100
	25-29	a	0.1	n	2.2	2.3	65.0	16.9	15.7	97.7	100
Spain	16-19	0.5	3.0	1.6	70.7	75.8	15.1	5.4	3.6	24.2	100
	20-24	0.7	6.8	2.6	34.9	45.0	40.7	8.7	5.6	55.0	100
	25-29	0.2	6.4	2.2	8.2	17.0	63.1	8.6	11.2	83.0	100
Sweden	16-19	a	17.9	4.4	63.4	85.8	9.1	1.9	3.3	14.2	100
	20-24	a	11.6	2.0	28.0	41.6	48.2	5.1	5.1	58.4	100
	25-29	a	9.9	1.2	11.8	22.9	70.2	3.2	3.8	77.1	100
Switzerland	15-19	32.5	10.3	3.9	38.9	85.7	7.5	m	6.2	14.3	100
	20-24	12.1	13.2	m	13.7	39.3	52.3	2.8	5.6	60.7	100
	25-29	m	7.7	m	4.8	13.5	75.1	m	9.5	86.5	100
Turkey	15-19	a	1.4	38.5	0.3	40.3	24.3	5.8	29.7	59.7	100
	20-24	a	1.9	9.5	0.9	12.2	41.9	9.2	36.7	87.8	100
	25-29	a	1.6	1.2	0.3	3.0	54.7	7.3	35.0	97.0	100
United Kingdom	15-19	4.8	20.4	2.2	48.7	76.1	15.7	4.4	3.7	23.9	100
	20-24	3.8	13.2	1.2	15.3	33.5	51.7	5.0	9.7	66.5	100
	25-29	1.0	8.7	0.4	3.2	13.3	70.6	3.6	12.5	86.7	100
United States	15-19	a	23.9	3.5	53.7	81.2	11.4	2.8	4.7	18.8	100
	20-24	a	19.5	1.3	13.1	33.9	50.5	5.4	10.2	66.1	100
	25-29	a	8.4	0.5	2.9	11.8	70.5	4.1	13.5	88.2	100
Country mean	*15-19*	*5.3*	*12.1*	*3.5*	*58.9*	*79.8*	*11.6*	*2.9*	*5.7*	*20.2*	*100*
	20-24	*2.4*	*10.2*	*1.7*	*22.8*	*37.1*	*46.6*	*6.9*	*9.4*	*62.9*	*100*
	25-29	*0.4*	*6.7*	*0.6*	*5.4*	*13.2*	*68.5*	*5.7*	*12.5*	*86.8*	*100*

1. Students in work-study programmes are considered to be both in education and employed, irrespective of their labour market status according to the ILO definition.
Source: OECD. See Annex 3 for notes (*www.oecd.org/edu/eag2003*).

Table C4.1a
Percentage of *young males* in education and not in education, by age group and work status (2001)

		In education					Not in education				Total in education and not in education
	Age group	Students in work-study programmes[1]	Other employed	Unemployed	Not in the labour force	Sub-total	Employed	Unemployed	Not in the labour force	Sub-total	
Australia	15-19	10.8	25.2	5.8	37.6	79.4	12.8	5.2	2.7	20.6	100
	20-24	7.9	16.5	2.5	11.1	38.1	50.5	7.8	3.6	61.9	100
	25-29	1.1	10.3	1.0	3.5	15.8	74.7	5.3	4.1	84.2	100
Austria	15-19	28.2	0.3	0.4	46.3	75.2	11.8	2.2	10.9	24.8	100
	20-24	2.2	2.9	0.2	19.0	24.3	61.2	4.3	10.2	75.7	100
	25-29	0.1	2.6	n	7.6	10.4	81.6	3.4	4.7	89.6	100
Belgium	15-19	3.1	1.3	0.3	83.5	88.2	5.7	2.2	3.8	11.8	100
	20-24	1.6	6.2	1.1	34.3	43.3	45.8	7.4	3.5	56.7	100
	25-29	1.0	12.6	0.6	3.0	17.2	73.4	6.3	3.1	82.8	100
Canada	15-19	a	27.0	5.3	49.3	81.6	11.7	3.5	3.2	18.4	100
	20-24	a	16.6	1.7	18.3	36.6	49.0	8.6	5.8	63.4	100
	25-29	a	6.2	n	5.0	11.3	76.4	7.2	5.1	88.7	100
Czech Republic	15-19	27.6	0.2	n	58.5	86.3	7.3	4.1	2.3	13.7	100
	20-24	0.2	0.6	n	20.7	21.6	65.8	10.5	2.2	78.4	100
	25-29	a	0.2	n	3.0	3.3	88.5	6.2	2.0	96.7	100
Denmark	15-19	9.6	30.7	2.3	44.8	87.4	7.9	2.0	2.7	12.6	100
	20-24	12.6	21.2	3.2	13.5	50.5	45.7	2.6	1.2	49.5	100
	25-29	0.6	22.8	1.1	8.4	32.8	62.8	1.5	2.8	67.2	100
Finland	15-19	a	9.2	4.8	68.8	82.7	5.3	2.5	9.5	17.3	100
	20-24	a	17.7	4.3	26.5	48.5	35.6	7.3	8.7	51.5	100
	25-29	a	19.6	1.6	8.1	29.3	61.6	4.8	4.3	70.7	100
France	15-19	8.6	0.2	n	85.6	94.5	2.1	1.9	1.5	5.5	100
	20-24	8.0	3.1	0.5	38.9	50.5	38.5	8.2	2.7	49.5	100
	25-29	1.5	3.8	0.5	4.7	10.5	78.4	8.3	2.8	89.5	100
Germany	15-19	21.6	3.7	0.7	61.6	87.6	7.5	1.6	3.3	12.4	100
	20-24	12.0	5.0	0.3	15.6	32.9	52.8	7.0	7.3	67.1	100
	25-29	1.7	5.9	0.3	8.1	16.1	72.3	6.7	4.9	83.9	100
Greece	15-19	0.4	1.4	0.6	83.4	85.8	8.6	3.2	2.4	14.2	100
	20-24	n	2.2	0.6	31.3	34.2	48.2	11.8	5.9	65.8	100
	25-29	n	1.3	0.3	5.6	7.2	79.4	10.5	2.8	92.8	100
Hungary	15-19	a	0.9	n	83.4	84.3	6.9	2.6	6.2	15.7	100
	20-24	a	4.6	0.6	27.5	32.7	51.7	7.3	8.3	67.3	100
	25-29	a	5.3	0.2	2.6	8.1	76.0	7.0	8.9	91.9	100
Iceland	16-19	3.8	36.7	4.2	24.5	69.2	28.4	2.0	0.5	30.8	100
	20-24	7.4	26.0	0.9	13.9	48.3	48.3	2.4	0.9	51.7	100
	25-29	3.7	18.8	n	5.7	28.2	70.3	1.0	0.5	71.8	100
Ireland	15-19	a	9.2	0.6	65.6	75.4	20.3	2.4	1.9	24.6	100
	20-24	a	4.9	0.4	19.5	24.8	68.5	3.7	3.0	75.2	100
	25-29	a	0.4	n	2.7	3.2	89.0	3.3	4.5	96.8	100
Italy	15-19	n	0.6	0.5	75.6	76.7	11.5	5.0	6.8	23.3	100
	20-24	n	2.9	1.4	30.6	34.9	41.1	11.7	12.2	65.1	100
	25-29	0.2	3.5	0.9	13.3	17.9	65.7	9.5	6.9	82.1	100
Luxembourg	15-19	4.3	3.1	0.3	83.7	91.3	7.1	0.8	0.8	8.7	100
	20-24	3.4	5.0	0.3	37.5	46.1	46.7	4.4	2.8	53.9	100
	25-29	0.6	6.3	0.5	6.8	14.1	80.5	2.1	3.3	85.9	100
Mexico	15-19	a	9.4	0.3	40.5	50.1	42.7	1.8	5.4	49.9	100
	20-24	a	5.9	0.2	14.7	20.8	73.6	2.6	3.0	79.2	100
	25-29	a	2.0	n	2.8	4.8	90.5	2.1	2.6	95.2	100
Netherlands	15-19	m	37.2	3.0	36.4	76.6	19.6	1.5	2.3	23.4	100
	20-24	m	20.8	1.0	14.4	36.3	58.1	1.9	3.8	63.8	100
	25-29	m	5.2	0.2	2.6	7.9	86.6	1.5	4.1	92.1	100
Norway	16-19	a	25.1	6.6	47.7	79.5	16.3	1.8	2.4	20.5	100
	20-24	a	12.2	1.9	19.2	33.3	58.7	3.9	4.1	66.7	100
	25-29	a	4.7	0.8	6.3	11.7	80.7	3.8	3.8	88.3	100
Poland	15-19	a	4.5	1.1	85.2	90.9	2.9	3.9	2.4	9.1	100
	20-24	a	9.3	6.7	27.0	43.0	31.4	20.6	5.0	57.0	100
	25-29	a	7.1	1.3	2.6	11.0	69.9	15.0	4.1	89.0	100
Portugal	15-19	a	2.7	0.3	66.4	69.5	25.0	1.5	4.0	30.5	100
	20-24	a	6.8	0.4	23.1	30.2	61.5	4.2	4.1	69.8	100
	25-29	a	6.5	0.3	4.7	11.5	82.1	2.3	4.0	88.5	100
Slovak Republic	15-19	15.3	0.1	n	52.6	68.0	4.1	10.6	17.3	32.0	100
	20-24	a	0.2	0.5	15.8	16.5	47.6	28.4	7.5	83.5	100
	25-29	a	0.1	n	2.3	2.4	72.7	20.0	4.9	97.6	100
Spain	16-19	0.7	3.3	1.3	64.8	70.2	21.2	5.4	3.2	29.8	100
	20-24	0.7	6.5	2.1	31.7	40.9	48.3	7.4	3.3	59.1	100
	25-29	n	6.0	1.8	7.9	15.8	72.1	7.3	4.8	84.2	100
Sweden	16-19	a	15.3	3.7	66.4	85.4	8.1	1.8	4.6	14.6	100
	20-24	a	10.4	1.9	24.9	37.2	52.6	5.8	4.4	62.8	100
	25-29	a	9.0	1.2	10.6	20.8	74.1	3.6	1.5	79.2	100
Switzerland	15-19	34.7	9.0	m	38.8	86.8	6.8	m	5.7	13.2	100
	20-24	15.3	14.6	m	11.8	42.2	48.5	m	6.9	57.8	100
	25-29	m	10.1	m	5.0	16.4	79.2	m	m	83.6	100
Turkey	15-19	a	2.0	43.2	0.3	45.5	31.4	7.8	15.3	54.5	100
	20-24	a	2.3	11.7	1.2	15.2	57.9	12.6	14.3	84.8	100
	25-29	a	2.1	1.2	0.3	3.6	78.4	10.5	7.6	96.4	100
United Kingdom	15-19	7.0	17.4	2.3	48.2	75.0	16.7	5.7	2.7	25.0	100
	20-24	4.6	11.4	1.6	15.6	33.1	56.4	6.1	4.4	66.9	100
	25-29	0.6	7.5	0.3	2.5	10.9	79.6	4.2	5.3	89.1	100
United States	15-19	a	21.9	3.8	54.6	80.3	12.7	3.0	4.0	19.7	100
	20-24	a	17.7	1.2	13.5	32.5	55.3	6.3	5.8	67.5	100
	25-29	a	7.8	0.5	2.2	10.5	79.3	4.4	5.8	89.5	100
Country mean	*15-19*	*6.5*	*11.0*	*3.4*	*57.6*	*78.6*	*13.4*	*3.2*	*4.7*	*21.4*	*100*
	20-24	*2.8*	*9.4*	*1.8*	*21.2*	*35.1*	*51.8*	*7.6*	*5.4*	*64.9*	*100*
	25-29	*0.4*	*7.0*	*0.5*	*5.1*	*13.1*	*76.9*	*5.8*	*4.1*	*86.9*	*100*

1. Students in work-study programmes are considered to be both in education and employed, irrespective of their labour market status according to the ILO definition.
Source: OECD. See Annex 3 for notes *(www.oecd.org/edu/eag2003)*.

Table C4.1b
Percentage of *young females* in education and not in education, by age group and work status (2001)

	Age group	In education					Not in education				Total in education and not in education
		Students in work-study programmes[1]	Other employed	Unemployed	Not in the labour force	Sub-total	Employed	Unemployed	Not in the labour force	Sub-total	
Australia	15-19	3.7	33.0	7.1	35.8	79.7	13.2	3.3	3.9	20.3	100
	20-24	2.3	21.2	2.2	9.2	34.9	48.6	6.0	10.5	65.1	100
	25-29	0.4	10.9	0.8	3.7	15.7	59.3	3.7	21.2	84.3	100
Austria	15-19	16.9	0.9	0.3	58.3	76.5	14.1	2.2	7.2	23.5	100
	20-24	1.0	3.6	0.6	25.3	30.5	58.4	2.6	8.5	69.5	100
	25-29	0.0	1.7	0.3	5.1	7.1	75.5	2.7	14.7	92.9	100
Belgium	15-19	0.9	2.1	0.2	88.0	91.1	2.4	1.3	5.2	8.9	100
	20-24	0.2	4.6	0.8	39.6	45.1	39.7	6.4	8.8	54.9	100
	25-29	0.8	7.8	0.3	4.0	12.9	65.5	8.4	13.3	87.1	100
Canada	15-19	a	31.4	5.1	49.7	86.2	8.7	1.7	3.3	13.8	100
	20-24	a	21.4	1.3	19.0	41.8	44.1	4.0	10.2	58.2	100
	25-29	a	8.2	0.2	5.9	14.3	66.4	4.9	14.3	85.7	100
Czech Republic	15-19	15.9	0.2	0.2	71.3	87.7	5.0	4.1	3.2	12.3	100
	20-24	a	0.7	0.3	23.7	24.6	51.7	8.1	15.6	75.4	100
	25-29	a	0.3	n	2.3	2.6	55.1	8.3	34.1	97.4	100
Denmark	15-19	3.4	35.2	4.5	43.2	86.3	11.0	0.4	2.3	13.7	100
	20-24	10.1	26.0	3.7	20.1	59.9	30.8	3.3	6.0	40.1	100
	25-29	1.6	16.7	1.0	12.8	32.0	57.0	2.3	8.7	68.0	100
Finland	15-19	a	14.3	7.2	68.7	90.2	6.0	1.6	2.1	9.8	100
	20-24	a	23.5	4.5	31.2	59.2	27.9	5.0	7.9	40.8	100
	25-29	a	18.4	2.1	9.8	30.3	46.6	8.1	15.1	69.7	100
France	15-19	3.7	0.5	n	90.9	95.3	1.2	1.8	1.7	4.7	100
	20-24	6.5	5.8	0.7	43.6	56.6	27.6	8.7	7.1	43.4	100
	25-29	1.7	4.9	0.4	5.3	12.3	62.3	9.9	15.5	87.7	100
Germany	15-19	17.0	4.3	0.6	67.5	89.3	5.3	1.3	4.0	10.7	100
	20-24	13.2	6.0	0.3	17.7	37.2	44.1	4.1	14.6	62.8	100
	25-29	1.1	4.1	0.2	5.3	10.7	64.6	4.7	20.0	89.3	100
Greece	15-19	n	0.7	0.6	84.2	85.6	4.8	4.7	4.9	14.4	100
	20-24	n	2.5	1.9	34.1	38.5	33.1	16.0	12.4	61.5	100
	25-29	n	1.0	0.7	4.5	6.3	55.0	14.9	23.9	93.7	100
Hungary	15-19	a	0.4	0.3	85.2	85.9	6.1	1.6	6.3	14.1	100
	20-24	a	5.1	0.3	31.5	37.0	38.5	3.7	20.8	63.0	100
	25-29	a	5.2	0.2	4.8	10.2	51.3	3.7	34.8	89.8	100
Iceland	16-19	1.8	52.7	3.2	22.2	79.9	18.8	1.3	0.0	20.1	100
	20-24	5.5	30.6	1.1	15.3	52.4	42.6	1.6	3.3	47.6	100
	25-29	4.1	23.4	n	12.3	39.8	52.0	1.8	6.4	60.2	100
Ireland	15-19	a	10.7	0.5	74.3	85.6	10.5	1.4	2.6	14.4	100
	20-24	a	6.1	0.3	25.4	31.8	56.2	3.0	9.0	68.2	100
	25-29	a	0.5	n	2.8	3.4	77.1	2.4	17.1	96.6	100
Italy	15-19	n	0.7	1.0	78.1	79.8	7.7	4.7	7.8	20.2	100
	20-24	n	3.3	2.1	36.7	42.3	30.4	11.9	15.4	57.7	100
	25-29	n	3.8	1.4	13.8	19.0	47.0	10.2	23.8	81.0	100
Luxembourg	15-19	2.9	1.4	n	86.7	91.1	6.8	0.4	1.6	8.9	100
	20-24	1.9	4.8	0.2	40.3	47.3	41.8	2.7	8.1	52.7	100
	25-29	n	3.7	n	5.1	9.2	71.3	1.5	18.0	90.8	100
Mexico	15-19	a	4.8	0.3	45.2	50.3	21.4	1.3	27.0	49.7	100
	20-24	a	3.7	0.2	13.6	17.5	36.4	1.6	44.5	82.5	100
	25-29	a	1.2	n	2.2	3.5	42.3	1.2	53.0	96.5	100
Netherlands	15-19	m	43.1	4.0	35.5	82.7	12.8	1.3	3.1	17.3	100
	20-24	m	20.1	1.1	11.4	32.6	55.6	2.3	9.5	67.4	100
	25-29	m	2.6	0.2	2.1	4.9	78.0	1.5	15.7	95.1	100
Norway	16-19	a	30.1	7.2	47.3	84.7	11.9	1.3	2.2	15.3	100
	20-24	a	20.7	2.3	23.1	46.1	44.5	2.5	6.9	53.9	100
	25-29	a	5.3	0.6	10.2	16.1	70.9	2.7	10.3	83.9	100
Poland	15-19	a	3.3	1.3	88.2	92.8	1.8	2.8	2.5	7.2	100
	20-24	a	9.4	6.6	31.4	47.4	24.1	17.3	11.2	52.6	100
	25-29	a	7.0	1.6	3.2	11.9	49.6	16.5	22.0	88.1	100
Portugal	15-19	a	3.0	0.5	71.0	74.5	15.5	4.1	5.9	25.5	100
	20-24	a	6.2	0.8	34.0	41.0	46.0	5.9	7.1	59.0	100
	25-29	a	6.1	0.5	4.0	10.6	73.0	4.8	11.5	89.4	100
Slovak Republic	15-19	7.4	0.1	n	58.9	66.5	8.6	11.3	13.6	33.5	100
	20-24	a	0.5	0.6	21.2	22.4	43.8	16.9	16.9	77.6	100
	25-29	a	0.2	n	2.0	2.2	57.2	13.8	26.9	97.8	100
Spain	16-19	0.3	2.7	1.9	76.9	81.8	8.7	5.5	4.0	18.2	100
	20-24	0.7	7.2	3.2	38.2	49.3	32.8	10.0	7.9	50.7	100
	25-29	0.4	6.9	2.7	8.5	18.4	53.8	10.0	17.9	81.6	100
Sweden	16-19	a	20.7	5.2	60.3	86.1	10.1	1.9	1.8	13.9	100
	20-24	a	12.8	2.1	31.4	46.3	43.6	4.3	5.8	53.7	100
	25-29	a	10.8	1.1	13.1	25.0	66.1	2.8	6.1	75.0	100
Switzerland	15-19	30.4	11.5	m	39.0	84.5	8.3	m	6.7	15.5	100
	20-24	8.6	11.8	m	15.7	36.2	56.3	m	m	63.8	100
	25-29	m	5.3	m	m	10.5	71.0	m	16.1	89.5	100
Turkey	15-19	a	0.8	33.2	0.2	34.2	16.1	3.5	46.2	65.8	100
	20-24	a	1.4	7.4	0.6	9.4	25.9	5.8	59.0	90.6	100
	25-29	a	1.0	1.1	0.2	2.3	26.7	3.5	67.5	97.7	100
United Kingdom	15-19	2.6	23.6	2.1	49.1	77.3	14.7	3.1	4.8	22.7	100
	20-24	2.9	15.1	0.8	15.1	33.9	46.9	3.9	15.2	66.1	100
	25-29	1.3	9.9	0.5	4.0	15.8	61.4	2.9	19.9	84.2	100
United States	15-19	a	26.0	3.2	52.8	82.0	9.9	2.6	5.4	18.0	100
	20-24	a	21.2	1.3	12.8	35.3	45.7	4.5	14.4	64.7	100
	25-29	a	9.0	0.6	3.5	13.0	62.2	3.9	20.9	87.0	100
Country mean	*15-19*	*4.0*	*13.3*	*3.3*	*60.3*	*81.0*	*9.7*	*2.6*	*6.6*	*19.0*	*100*
	20-24	*2.0*	*10.9*	*1.7*	*24.5*	*39.1*	*41.4*	*6.0*	*13.2*	*60.9*	*100*
	25-29	*0.4*	*6.5*	*0.6*	*5.6*	*13.3*	*59.9*	*5.6*	*21.1*	*86.7*	*100*

1. Students in work-study programmes are considered to be both in education and employed, irrespective of their labour market status according to the ILO definition.
Source: OECD. See Annex 3 for notes *(www.oecd.org/edu/eag2003)*.

C4

Table C4.2
Percentage of unemployed non-students in the total population,
by level of educational attainment, age group and gender (2001)

		Below upper secondary education			Upper secondary and post-secondary non-tertiary education			Tertiary education		All levels of education			
		15-19	20-24	25-29	15-19	20-24	25-29	20-24	25-29	15-19	20-24	25-29	15-29
Australia	Males	7.6	17.5	11.0	3.3	8.1	4.1	1.8	2.9	5.8	7.8	5.3	6.3
	Females	3.9	14.7	6.6	4.2	6.3	4.5	1.7	1.5	4.0	6.0	3.7	4.6
	M+F	5.8	16.1	8.7	3.7	7.3	4.3	1.7	2.1	5.0	6.9	4.5	5.5
Austria	Males	9.1	11.8	5.4	0.6	4.2	3.4	0.2	1.9	2.3	4.3	3.4	3.3
	Females	11.3	5.2	4.0	0.6	3.3	2.9	0.3	0.8	2.4	2.6	2.7	2.6
	M+F	10.1	8.4	4.6	0.6	3.8	3.2	0.2	1.4	2.4	3.4	3.0	3.0
Belgium	Males	2.3	17.9	10.9	1.9	3.7	5.3	8.4	4.9	2.2	7.4	6.3	5.4
	Females	1.2	14.2	13.0	1.7	5.0	10.2	5.6	4.4	1.3	6.4	8.4	5.5
	M+F	1.8	16.5	11.9	1.8	4.3	7.6	6.6	4.6	1.8	6.9	7.4	5.4
Canada	Males	2.7	17.1	15.5	6.1	7.7	7.5	5.1	4.7	3.5	8.6	7.2	6.5
	Females	1.4	9.3	6.0	2.6	4.0	6.5	2.6	3.7	1.7	4.0	4.9	3.6
	M+F	2.1	14.2	11.4	4.3	6.0	7.1	3.6	4.1	2.7	6.3	6.1	5.1
Czech Republic	Males	9.1	33.0	19.7	2.9	10.5	5.7	1.5	1.9	4.2	10.5	6.2	7.2
	Females	7.6	18.7	18.7	3.5	9.2	8.1	1.4	1.7	4.2	8.1	8.3	7.1
	M+F	8.5	26.5	19.2	3.2	9.9	6.9	1.4	1.8	4.2	9.3	7.2	7.1
Denmark	Males	0.4	4.6	5.7	m	2.6	1.8	1.8	1.6	0.4	3.3	2.3	2.1
	Females	1.9	3.6	1.8	m	1.7	0.6	7.9	3.9	2.0	2.6	1.5	2.0
	M+F	1.2	4.1	3.7	6.7	2.2	1.1	5.0	2.6	1.2	2.9	1.9	2.0
Finland	Males	2.0	11.8	10.6	5.8	6.4	4.5	7.6	2.0	2.5	7.3	4.8	4.8
	Females	0.7	5.8	15.4	7.7	5.1	8.5	4.1	6.0	1.6	5.0	8.1	4.8
	M+F	1.4	9.7	12.3	6.7	5.7	6.2	4.9	4.3	2.1	6.1	6.3	4.8
France	Males	1.8	20.0	15.3	3.0	5.5	7.3	2.3	5.6	1.9	8.2	8.3	6.1
	Females	1.5	17.4	16.4	4.1	8.0	10.7	3.6	6.1	1.8	8.7	9.9	6.8
	M+F	1.6	18.9	15.9	3.6	6.7	8.9	3.1	5.9	1.9	8.4	9.1	6.5
Germany	Males	2.5	18.6	17.1	0.5	6.4	6.7	0.4	1.5	1.5	7.1	6.7	5.1
	Females	2.0	10.9	7.4	0.6	3.6	5.0	0.7	2.4	1.3	4.1	4.7	3.4
	M+F	2.3	14.7	12.0	0.5	5.2	5.8	0.5	1.9	1.4	5.7	5.7	4.3
Greece	Males	2.5	14.3	9.0	5.4	11.2	10.6	9.2	12.8	3.2	11.8	10.5	8.5
	Females	2.9	18.7	13.9	9.3	14.4	14.4	27.3	16.8	4.7	16.0	14.9	12.2
	M+F	2.7	16.1	10.9	7.5	13.0	12.5	20.3	15.2	3.9	14.0	12.7	10.4
Hungary	Males	1.7	14.4	15.2	6.4	6.0	6.0	6.0	0.3	2.6	7.3	7.0	5.8
	Females	0.8	5.1	5.7	4.4	3.6	4.0	2.3	0.5	1.6	3.7	3.7	3.1
	M+F	1.3	9.7	10.3	5.3	4.8	5.0	3.8	0.4	2.1	5.5	5.3	4.5
Iceland [1]	Males	1.3	1.2	3.6	a	2.2	a	a	2.2	1.3	1.6	1.8	1.6
	Females	2.0	3.2	1.4	a	a	a	20.0	2.6	2.0	2.4	1.0	1.8
	M+F	1.7	2.3	2.4	a	1.2	a	7.8	2.3	1.6	2.0	1.4	1.7
Ireland	Males	2.3	10.0	7.3	2.3	2.0	2.8	2.1	1.4	2.3	3.7	3.3	3.1
	Females	1.2	5.6	4.6	1.7	2.8	2.5	2.3	1.4	1.3	3.0	2.4	2.2
	M+F	1.8	8.3	6.1	1.9	2.4	2.7	2.3	1.4	1.8	3.3	2.8	2.7
Italy	Males	4.7	15.5	11.0	8.0	9.6	8.2	13.9	10.9	5.0	11.7	9.5	9.0
	Females	4.0	15.5	10.2	9.5	10.5	9.2	17.9	14.2	4.7	11.9	10.2	9.3
	M+F	4.3	15.5	10.6	8.8	10.1	8.7	16.5	12.9	4.9	11.8	9.9	9.1
Luxembourg	Males	0.6	2.3	2.1	a	3.2	0.0	3.1	2.4	0.5	2.8	1.4	1.6
	Females	0.9	7.2	3.5	a	1.7	0.5	4.1	2.2	0.8	4.3	2.1	2.4
	M+F	0.8	4.8	2.8	a	2.5	0.3	3.5	2.3	0.7	3.5	1.8	2.0
Mexico	Males	1.9	2.6	1.8	0.9	5.9	4.2	2.0	2.8	1.9	2.5	2.1	2.1
	Females	1.2	1.4	1.0	4.2	2.1	1.2	2.1	2.3	1.3	1.6	1.2	1.4
	M+F	1.5	2.0	1.4	3.1	3.1	1.8	2.0	2.5	1.6	2.0	1.6	1.7
Netherlands	Males	1.3	3.9	3.6	2.4	1.0	0.7	0.0	0.8	1.5	1.9	1.5	1.6
	Females	1.4	4.3	2.6	1.1	1.3	1.1	3.3	1.3	1.4	2.3	1.5	1.7
	M+F	1.4	4.1	3.1	1.7	1.2	0.9	2.2	1.1	1.4	2.1	1.5	1.7
Norway [1]	Males	3.1	14.6	9.2	1.3	3.8	4.1	1.3	2.2	1.9	3.9	3.7	3.3
	Females	1.7	9.1	6.9	1.1	2.4	3.3	2.3	1.6	1.3	2.6	2.7	2.3
	M+F	2.5	12.3	8.1	1.2	3.2	3.8	1.9	1.8	1.6	3.2	3.2	2.8
Poland	Males	7.3	39.1	25.9	3.2	27.9	16.1	1.0	6.1	4.0	20.6	15.0	13.3
	Females	4.7	31.6	27.5	2.7	28.5	18.8	1.5	7.8	3.0	17.3	16.5	12.6
	M+F	6.1	36.1	26.6	2.9	28.2	17.4	1.3	7.1	3.5	18.9	15.7	12.9
Portugal	Males	2.7	6.0	2.9	0.3	4.2	1.2	0.4	2.2	1.7	4.3	2.5	2.9
	Females	8.1	8.3	5.6	1.2	7.4	4.3	2.6	3.7	4.5	5.9	4.9	5.2
	M+F	5.1	6.9	4.2	0.8	5.9	2.7	1.8	3.0	3.0	5.1	3.7	4.0
Slovak Republic	Males	3.7	50.7	43.8	32.2	27.3	19.5	17.5	12.4	10.6	28.4	20.0	19.9
	Females	1.5	18.9	19.3	37.1	16.7	15.0	17.9	4.8	11.3	16.9	13.8	14.1
	M+F	2.6	37.5	30.0	34.8	22.1	17.4	17.7	8.2	11.0	22.8	16.9	17.0
Spain [1]	Males	10.7	13.1	9.1	1.5	8.2	8.5	2.8	5.4	6.2	7.6	7.6	7.3
	Females	14.8	18.7	13.9	2.0	13.7	10.7	5.5	8.0	7.1	10.5	10.6	9.8
	M+F	12.3	15.3	11.1	1.7	10.8	9.6	4.2	6.8	6.6	9.0	9.0	8.5
Sweden [1]	Males	18.6	17.5	9.8	1.0	6.4	4.1	0.1	0.5	1.9	5.9	3.7	3.9
	Females	21.2	12.2	9.0	1.1	5.4	3.3	0.8	0.8	2.0	4.4	2.9	3.1
	M+F	19.8	15.2	9.5	1.0	5.9	3.7	0.5	0.7	1.9	5.2	3.3	3.5
Switzerland	Males	m	m	m	m	m	m	m	m	m	m	m	m
	Females	m	m	m	m	m	m	m	m	m	m	m	m
	M+F	m	m	m	m	m	m	m	m	m	m	m	1.7
Turkey	Males	6.7	13.6	10.8	11.4	10.0	11.4	23.3	7.6	7.8	12.6	10.5	10.1
	Females	2.4	2.7	2.1	8.5	8.5	6.4	25.1	8.4	3.5	5.8	3.5	4.3
	M+F	4.6	7.6	6.3	10.2	9.4	9.6	24.3	7.9	5.8	9.2	7.3	7.4
United Kingdom	Males	4.8	15.2	13.9	5.9	5.8	4.1	3.2	2.0	5.5	6.1	4.3	5.3
	Females	1.8	7.2	6.3	3.8	3.9	3.0	2.7	1.4	3.1	3.9	2.8	3.3
	M+F	3.4	11.3	10.1	4.9	4.9	3.5	3.0	1.7	4.3	5.0	3.5	4.3
United States	Males	9.7	12.5	7.1	1.8	7.7	4.4	2.3	3.5	3.2	6.3	4.4	4.6
	Females	9.0	12.0	9.0	1.9	6.1	5.3	1.1	1.3	2.8	4.5	3.9	3.8
	M+F	9.4	12.3	8.0	1.8	6.9	4.8	1.7	2.3	3.0	5.4	4.1	4.2
Country mean	Males	4.5	14.8	11.0	4.0	7.3	5.6	4.3	3.8	3.1	7.5	5.9	5.6
	Females	4.1	10.5	8.6	4.2	6.5	5.9	6.2	4.1	2.8	6.1	5.6	4.9
	M+F	4.3	12.8	9.7	4.4	6.9	5.8	5.3	4.0	3.0	6.8	5.8	5.3

1. Data refer to 16 to 19-year-olds.

Source: OECD. See Annex 3 for notes *(www.oecd.org/edu/eag2003)*.

C4

INDICATOR C5: THE SITUATION OF THE YOUTH POPULATION WITH LOW LEVELS OF EDUCATION

- Most persons aged 15 to 19 are still in school. In many OECD countries, a high percentage of those who are not still in school are either unemployed or not in the labour force.

- In Austria, Italy, Mexico, the Slovak Republic and Turkey over 10 per cent of persons aged 15 to 19 are neither at school nor in the workforce.

- In Austria, Finland, the Slovak Republic and Sweden, more young males than females are neither at school nor in the workforce, and the reverse is true in Greece, Mexico, Portugal and Turkey.

C5

Chart C5.1

Percentage of 15 to 19-year-olds who are not in education or work, by gender (2001)

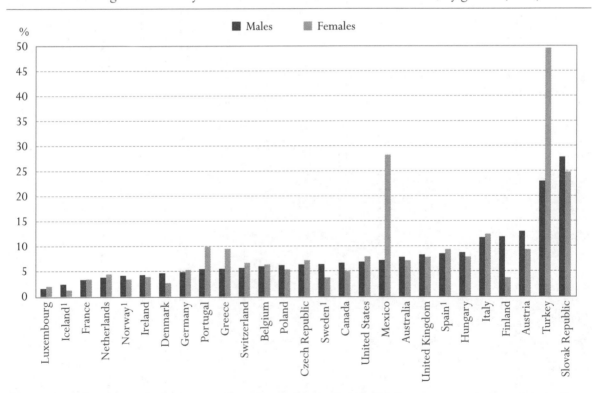

1. 16 to 19-year-olds.
Countries are ranked in ascending order of 15 to 19-year-old males not in education or work.
Source: OECD. Tables C4.1a and C4.1b. See Annex 3 for notes *(www.oecd.org/edu/eag2003).*

Policy context

Entering the labour market is often a difficult period of transition. While the length of time spent in education has increased, a significant proportion of young people still remain in a bad position as if they are neither in education nor working, *i.e.*, they are either unemployed or in non-employment. This situation gives particular cause for concern for younger age groups, many of whom have no unemployment status or welfare coverage (see *A Caring World*, OECD, 1999).

As the interrelationships between education, the economy and the well-being of nations become ever closer, providing for effective educational careers of young people and for successful transitions from initial education to working life become major policy concerns. Rising skill demands in OECD countries have made upper secondary diplomas a minimum for successfully entering the labour market and a basis for further participation in lifelong learning. Young people with lower qualifications run a higher risk of long-term unemployment or unstable or unfulfilling employment, which can have additional consequences such as social exclusion.

Evidence and explanations

Young people not in education or work

Over 80 per cent of persons between the ages of 15 and 19 are in education in most OECD countries. A small proportion of this age group is employed after having left school, although this figure is as high as 10 per cent for nine OECD countries and even more than 20 per cent in four others (Table C4.1).

There is, however, a group of young people who are no longer in education but not yet at work. Some are officially unemployed if they are actively seeking work, while those who are not doing so for some reason are considered to be in non-employment. Their reasons may be many and varied, such as discouragement because of the difficulty of finding work or voluntary withdrawal because of family circumstances. In 18 out of 27 OECD countries, the proportion of these young people is higher than the proportion of those with unemployment status.

To be out of education and out of employment is very uncommon in Denmark, France, Iceland, Ireland, Luxembourg, the Netherlands and Norway yet common in Austria, Italy, Mexico, the Slovak Republic and Turkey. In these countries, over 10 per cent of young people aged 15 to 19 are neither at school nor in work (Table C4.1). In other OECD countries, the proportion is lower but not insignificant, ranging from 4 to 10 per cent. The problem affects more young males than females in Austria, Finland, the Slovak Republic and Sweden, and the reverse is true in Greece, Mexico, Portugal and Turkey (Chart C5.1), differences between the sexes remain small in the other countries.

Young people with low qualifications may run an increased risk of long-term unemployment or of unstable, unfulfilling employment, which can have other negative consequences such as social exclusion. Early drop-out has become

This indicator reflects on the situation of young people who are no longer in education but who are not yet in employment.

Most 15 to 19-year-olds are still at school. In many OECD countries, a high percentage of those who are not are either unemployed or not in the labour force.

C5

Between the ages of 20 and 24, the scale of the problem grows

and changes since most young people enter the labour market at that age.

one of the most important educational policy problems. For students between 20 and 24 years, the scale of the problem grows compared to the age group 15 to 19 years and changes since most young people are entering the labour market at that age for the first time after having completed education. There is often a period of unemployment and adjustment before finding a secure and satisfying job (Chart C5.3).

In seven OECD countries including the Nordic and Eastern European countries as well as Switzerland and the United Kingdom, the proportion of young people without upper secondary education in the age group remains under 10 per cent. This is a limited group, but one that is certainly in a difficult position. In 12 out of 27 OECD countries, this potentially "at risk" group represents between 10 and 20 per cent of the age group. The challenge in terms of increasing upper secondary graduation rates is significant here. For the remaining eight OECD countries, more than 20 per cent of the age group falls under this category.

The consequences of having left school without an upper secondary qualification can be observed by comparing the work status of those with and those without an upper secondary qualification. In all OECD countries except one, higher educational attainment is associated with an increase in the employment

Chart C5.2

Percentage of 20 to 24-year-olds who are not in education and who have not attained upper secondary education, by gender (2001)

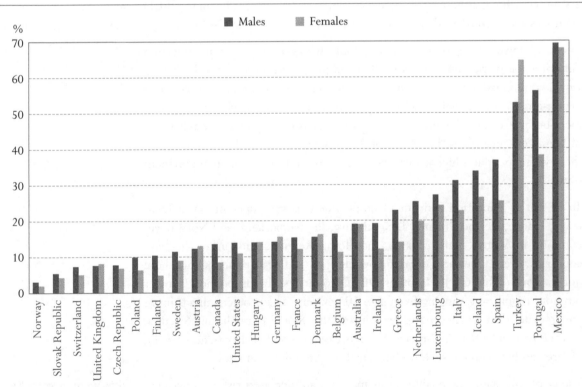

Countries are ranked in ascending order of the percentage of 20 to 24-year-old males who are not in education and who have not completed upper secondary education.
Source: OECD. Table C5.1. See Annex 3 for notes *(www.oecd.org/edu/eag2003).*

rate on average of 19 percentage points. The comparison also reveals some patterns related to the specific organisation of the labour market. The gap between those with upper secondary qualifications and those without is remarkably small in all Mediterranean countries, which suggests a good match between qualifications - even if these are low - and employment. The United Kingdom is an interesting case in that the prevalence of low qualifications is one of the lowest among OECD countries, but the unemployment differentials are particularly high, suggesting that the few persons who have not obtained an upper secondary qualification are particularly disadvantaged.

Definitions and methodologies

The indicator is based on labour force survey data on age-specific proportions of young people in each of the specified categories. The definitions of the labour force statuses of those not in education (and not enrolled in work-study programmes) are based on ILO guidelines. Data for this indicator were calculated from the special OECD data collection on transition from education to work (see Indicator A11).

Data for this indicator were calculated from the special OECD data collection on transition from education to work.

An "early school leaver" could broadly be defined as "a young person who has not attained upper secondary education and is not in education, or in a work-study programme leading to an upper secondary qualification or higher". However,

Chart C5.3

Employment rates for 20 to 24-year-olds who are not in education, by level of educational attainment (2001)

C5

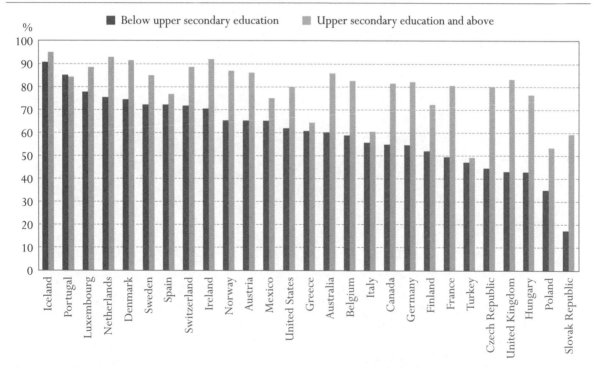

Countries are ranked in descending order of the employment rate of 20 to 24-year-olds who are not in education and who have not completed upper secondary education.
Source: OECD Table C5.1. See Annex 3 for notes *(www.oecd.org/edu/eag2003).*

such a definition needs to include the specification of an age group within which very few people can still be attending school at the primary or secondary level. Young people aged 18 and 19, in a significant number of OECD countries, are still enrolled in upper secondary education. Very early leavers may eventually return to school. Moreover, labour market outcomes at early ages may not be representative of outcomes at later ages. The OECD therefore defines a young adult with low level of education as "a person aged 20-24 years who has not attained upper secondary education and who is not enrolled in education nor in a work-study programme".

C₅

Table C5.1
Percentage of 20 to 24-year-olds not in education, by level of educational attainment, gender and work status (2001)

| | | Below upper secondary education | | | | Upper secondary education and above | | | | | |
		Employed	Unemployed	Not in the labour force	Sub-total	Employed	Unemployed	Not in the labour force	Sub-total	In education	Total 20 to 24-year-olds
Australia	Males	13.4	4.0	1.6	18.9	37.1	3.9	2.0	43.0	38.1	100
	Females	9.2	3.2	6.4	18.9	39.4	2.8	4.1	46.2	34.9	100
	M+F	11.3	3.6	4.0	18.9	38.2	3.3	3.0	44.6	36.5	100
Austria	Males	8.6	1.4	2.2	12.2	52.6	2.8	8.0	63.5	24.3	100
	Females	7.8	0.7	4.5	12.9	50.6	1.9	4.1	56.6	30.5	100
	M+F	8.2	1.1	3.3	12.6	51.6	2.4	6.0	60.0	27.4	100
Belgium	Males	10.9	3.9	1.5	16.2	35.0	3.5	2.0	40.5	43.3	100
	Females	5.2	2.0	4.0	11.1	34.5	4.4	4.8	43.8	45.1	100
	M+F	8.0	2.9	2.7	13.7	34.8	4.0	3.4	42.1	44.2	100
Canada	Males	8.4	2.7	2.4	13.5	40.6	5.9	3.4	49.9	36.6	100
	Females	3.5	0.9	3.9	8.3	40.6	3.1	6.3	49.9	41.8	100
	M+F	6.0	1.8	3.1	10.9	40.6	4.5	4.8	49.9	39.1	100
Czech Republic	Males	4.2	2.5	1.0	7.7	61.6	7.9	1.2	70.7	21.6	100
	Females	2.2	1.3	3.3	6.7	49.5	6.9	12.3	68.6	24.6	100
	M+F	3.2	1.9	2.1	7.2	55.7	7.4	6.6	69.7	23.1	100
Denmark	Males	13.6	1.2	0.5	15.4	32.1	1.4	0.7	34.2	50.4	100
	Females	9.8	1.6	4.7	16.1	20.9	1.7	1.4	23.9	60.0	100
	M+F	11.7	1.4	2.6	15.7	26.4	1.5	1.0	29.0	55.3	100
Finland	Males	5.8	1.8	2.7	10.4	29.8	5.4	5.9	41.1	48.5	100
	Females	2.1	0.5	2.2	4.8	25.8	4.5	5.6	36.0	59.2	100
	M+F	3.9	1.2	2.5	7.6	27.8	5.0	5.8	38.6	53.9	100
France	Males	8.9	4.5	1.9	15.2	29.6	3.7	0.8	34.2	50.6	100
	Females	4.5	3.3	4.2	12.0	23.0	5.4	2.9	31.4	56.7	100
	M+F	6.7	3.9	3.0	13.6	26.3	4.6	1.9	32.8	53.6	100
Germany	Males	9.1	2.8	2.2	14.1	44.0	4.4	4.4	52.8	33.1	100
	Females	6.8	1.8	6.9	15.4	37.9	2.4	7.0	47.2	37.4	100
	M+F	8.0	2.3	4.4	14.7	41.1	3.4	5.6	50.1	35.2	100
Greece	Males	17.4	3.4	1.9	22.8	30.7	8.4	3.9	43.0	34.2	100
	Females	5.1	2.8	6.0	13.9	27.5	13.2	6.5	47.2	38.9	100
	M+F	10.9	3.1	4.0	18.1	29.0	10.9	5.3	45.2	36.7	100
Hungary	Males	7.8	2.2	3.9	13.9	43.9	5.1	4.5	53.4	32.7	100
	Females	4.1	0.8	9.0	14.0	34.3	2.9	11.8	49.1	37.0	100
	M+F	6.0	1.5	6.5	14.0	39.0	4.0	8.2	51.2	34.8	100
Iceland	Males	31.8	1.9	0.0	33.7	16.8	0.5	0.5	17.7	48.6	100
	Females	22.5	0.5	3.3	26.4	19.8	1.1	0.0	20.9	52.7	100
	M+F	27.3	1.3	1.6	30.1	18.3	0.8	0.2	19.3	50.6	100
Ireland	Males	15.3	2.0	1.8	19.1	53.2	1.6	1.2	56.1	24.8	100
	Females	6.5	0.8	4.8	12.0	49.7	2.2	4.2	56.1	31.8	100
	M+F	10.9	1.4	3.3	15.6	51.5	1.9	2.7	56.1	28.3	100
Italy	Males	20.3	5.6	5.2	31.1	20.8	6.2	7.0	34.0	34.9	100
	Females	9.5	4.1	9.1	22.6	20.9	7.8	6.4	35.1	42.3	100
	M+F	14.9	4.8	7.1	26.9	20.8	7.0	6.7	34.6	38.6	100
Luxembourg	Males	22.4	3.1	1.6	27.1	26.1	1.2	1.3	28.6	44.3	100
	Females	17.4	0.5	6.2	24.2	25.1	2.3	2.0	29.3	46.5	100
	M+F	19.9	1.8	4.0	25.6	25.6	1.8	1.6	29.0	45.4	100
Mexico	Males	64.7	1.9	2.7	69.3	8.9	0.6	0.3	9.9	20.8	100
	Females	26.9	1.0	40.0	68.0	9.5	0.6	4.5	14.5	17.5	100
	M+F	44.6	1.5	22.5	68.6	9.2	0.6	2.5	12.4	19.1	100
Netherlands	Males	21.7	1.3	2.3	25.2	36.5	0.6	1.5	38.5	36.3	100
	Females	12.1	1.1	6.6	19.7	43.6	1.3	3.0	47.8	32.6	100
	M+F	16.9	1.2	4.4	22.5	40.0	0.9	2.2	43.1	34.4	100
Norway	Males	2.1	0.5	0.4	3.0	56.6	3.4	3.7	63.7	33.3	100
	Females	1.1	0.2	0.6	1.9	43.6	2.3	5.9	51.8	46.3	100
	M+F	1.6	0.4	0.5	2.5	50.2	2.9	4.8	57.9	39.7	100
Poland	Males	4.0	3.8	2.0	9.8	27.4	16.7	3.0	47.2	43.0	100
	Females	1.6	2.0	2.6	6.2	22.5	15.3	8.6	46.4	47.4	100
	M+F	2.8	2.9	2.3	8.0	24.9	16.0	5.9	46.8	45.2	100
Portugal	Males	49.6	3.4	3.0	56.0	12.9	0.9	0.4	14.2	29.8	100
	Females	30.3	3.2	4.6	38.0	16.9	2.8	1.6	21.2	40.7	100
	M+F	39.9	3.3	3.8	47.0	14.9	1.8	1.0	17.7	35.3	100
Slovak Republic	Males	0.8	3.1	1.4	5.3	46.7	25.3	6.1	78.2	16.5	100
	Females	0.8	0.9	2.4	4.2	43.0	16.0	14.4	73.4	22.4	100
	M+F	0.8	2.1	1.9	4.8	44.9	20.7	10.2	75.8	19.4	100
Spain	Males	29.5	4.9	2.3	36.7	20.3	2.7	1.2	24.3	39.1	100
	Females	14.9	4.9	5.5	25.3	19.6	5.6	2.8	28.0	46.7	100
	M+F	22.4	4.9	3.8	31.2	20.0	4.1	2.0	26.1	42.8	100
Sweden	Males	8.4	2.0	1.0	11.4	45.1	3.9	3.5	52.5	36.1	100
	Females	6.1	1.1	1.6	8.8	38.3	3.3	4.3	45.9	45.3	100
	M+F	7.3	1.6	1.3	10.2	41.8	3.6	3.9	49.3	40.6	100
Switzerland	Males	4.7	m	m	7.3	43.9	m	m	50.1	42.6	100
	Females	m	m	m	m	51.9	m	m	58.3	36.7	100
	M+F	4.4	m	m	6.2	47.8	m	4.1	54.1	39.8	100
Turkey	Males	38.5	7.3	7.0	52.8	19.5	5.3	7.3	32.1	15.2	100
	Females	16.8	1.8	46.0	64.6	9.1	4.0	13.0	26.0	9.4	100
	M+F	27.6	4.5	26.6	58.7	14.3	4.7	10.1	29.1	12.2	100
United Kingdom	Males	4.5	1.3	1.7	7.6	52.4	4.8	2.5	59.7	32.8	100
	Females	2.1	0.6	5.3	8.1	45.3	3.3	9.5	58.1	33.8	100
	M+F	3.4	1.0	3.5	7.8	48.9	4.0	6.0	58.9	33.3	100
United States	Males	10.3	1.8	1.8	13.9	45.0	4.6	4.1	53.6	32.5	100
	Females	5.0	1.3	4.6	10.8	40.8	3.2	9.9	53.9	35.3	100
	M+F	7.6	1.5	3.2	12.3	42.8	3.9	7.0	53.7	33.9	100
Country mean	*Males*	*16.2*	*2.8*	*2.1*	*21.1*	*35.9*	*4.8*	*3.0*	*44.0*	*35.0*	*100*
	Females	*8.7*	*1.6*	*7.3*	*17.6*	*32.7*	*4.4*	*5.8*	*43.2*	*39.0*	*100*
	M+F	*12.5*	*2.2*	*4.7*	*19.4*	*34.3*	*4.7*	*4.5*	*43.6*	*37.0*	*100*

Note: Students in work-study programmes are considered to be both in education and employed, irrespective of their labour market status according to the ILO definition.

Source: OECD. See Annex 3 for notes *(www.oecd.org/edu/eag2003)*.

THE LEARNING ENVIRONMENT AND ORGANISATION OF SCHOOLS

OVERVIEW

Chapter D reviews the learning environment and organisation of schools, in terms of…

…student learning conditions…

…teachers' and students' use of information and communication technology,…

…teacher training and professional development…

D

D

INDICATOR D1: TOTAL INTENDED INSTRUCTION TIME FOR STUDENTS IN PRIMARY AND SECONDARY EDUCATION

- Students between the ages of 9 and 11 receive, on average among OECD countries, 813 hours per year of compulsory instruction time and 840 hours per year of intended instruction time in the classroom, while students between the ages of 12 and 14 receive nearly 100 hours more per year. However, these figures vary significantly among countries.

- On average among countries, reading and writing in the language of instruction, mathematics and science comprise about half of the compulsory curriculum for 9 to 11-year-olds and 41 per cent for 12 to 14-year-olds.

- The degree to which schools and local and regional authorities can specify curricular content and timetables varies widely from country to country.

D1

Intended instruction time in public institutions, by school subject (2001)

Percentage of total intended instruction time allocated for the compulsory core curriculum, by subject, compulsory flexible curriculum and non-compulsory curriculum, for 9 to 11-year-olds and 12 to 14-year-olds

Intended instruction time for 9 to 11-year-olds (average total intended instruction time 840 hours)

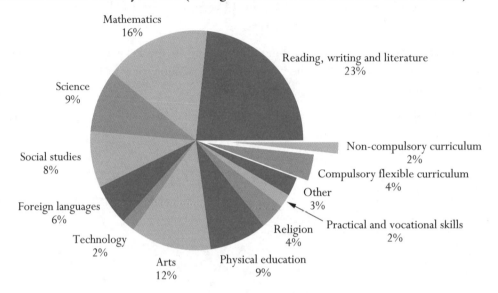

Intended instruction time for 12 to 14-year-olds (average total intended instruction time 939 hours)

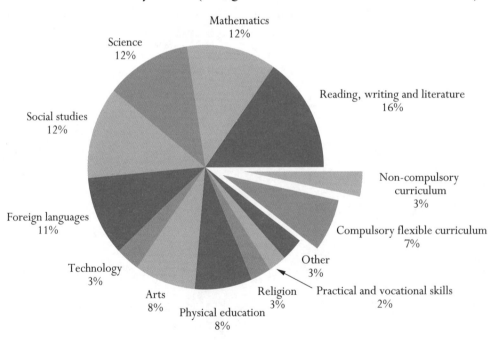

Source: OECD. Tables D1.2a and D1.2b. See Annex 3 for notes *(www.oecd.org/edu/eag2003)*.

D1

Policy context

The amount and quality of the time that people spend learning between early childhood and the start of their working lives are decisive for shaping their lives, socially and economically. Instruction time in formal classroom settings comprises a large part of the public investment in student learning. Matching resources with students' needs and using time in an optimal manner, from the perspective of the learner and of public investment, are major challenges for education policy. The costs of resources depend primarily on the costs of teacher labour, of institutional maintenance, and of other educational resources. The length of time during which resources are made available to students, as shown in this indicator on instruction time in classroom settings in the formal education system, are therefore important.

This indicator shows intended instruction time in classroom settings in the formal education system.

Evidence and explanations

What this indicator shows

This indicator captures intended instruction time as a measure of exposure to learning in formal classroom settings as per public regulations. It also shows how instruction time is allocated to different curricular areas. The indicator is calculated as the intended net hours of instruction for the grades in which the majority of students are 7 to 15 years of age. Although such data are difficult to compare among countries because of different curriculum policies, they nevertheless provide an indication of how much contact time countries consider students need in order to achieve the educational goals that have been set for them.

Intended instruction time is an important indicator of the public resources invested in education…

In some countries, intended instruction time varies considerably among regions or different types of school. In many countries, local education authorities or schools can determine the number and allocation of hours. Additional teacher time is often planned for individual remedial teaching or enhancement of the curriculum. On the other hand, time may be lost because too few qualified substitutes exist to replace absent teachers or because students are absent.

…but needs to be interpreted in the context of often considerable variation among regions and schools…

Annual instruction time should also be seen together with the length of compulsory education, which measures the time during which young people receive full-time educational support from public resources, or during which more than 90 per cent of the population participates in education (see Indicator C1). Intended instruction time also does not capture the quality of learning opportunities being provided or the level or quality of human and material resources involved. Other indicators in this section tackle the issue of the availability of educational resources (Indicator D3, D4 and D7) and of teachers relative to the student population (Indicator D2).

…and in the context of other forms of learning time and of the quality of teaching that are not captured by this indicator.

D1

Curriculum policies

Decision-making responsibilities for planning students' programmes of learning vary greatly from country to country. Two basic models exist in OECD countries, with several variants.

Responsibilities for curriculum provision are distributed in different ways.

In some OECD countries, subjects and content are defined, and time is allocated at a national (or sub-national) level...

In one model of curriculum regulation, national or regional authorities specify subject areas, the time allocated to them and the content, and schools must respect with a greater or lesser degree of flexibility these national or sub-national curricular specifications. In Austria, England, France, Germany, Greece, Portugal and Spain, the national authorities (German *Länder*, Spanish Autonomous Communities) establish curricula for all types of schools, grades and subjects. Typically, the documents define subjects, the time allocated to them and the content in more or less detail by grade level and type of programme, while the school is responsible for managing and delivering the curriculum.

Curriculum regulation in Greece

In Greece the Pedagogical Institute draws up detailed curricula and timetables for primary and secondary education. All subjects are compulsory for all pupils and of equal importance.

...while in others, local school authorities, or the schools themselves, are primarily responsible for providing the curricula, with attainment targets set at the national level.

In the second model of curriculum regulation, national authorities establish attainment targets or standards, while local authorities or schools are responsible for planning and implementing curricula. For example, in both the Flemish and French Communities of Belgium, the Czech Republic, Denmark, the Netherlands, New Zealand and Scotland, national policy documents describe the targets, and local authorities or schools specify the subjects, content and time allocated to them. National policy documents, in these countries often provide a frame for planning by specifying minimum requirements for subjects to be taught, time to be devoted to study areas, and/or desirable content for studies thereby giving guidance to schools for curriculum planning.

The secondary education curriculum in Scotland (Grades 7-10)

The curriculum in Scottish secondary schools in not laid down by law, but advice on the secondary school curriculum is given to all schools by Learning and Teaching Scotland (formerly the Scottish Consultative Council on the Curriculum) in the document: Curriculum Design for the Secondary Stages (last updated in 1999). In the first two years of secondary education all pupils undertake a common course with a wide range of subjects, from within the five curriculum areas of the 5-14 curriculum but with some subjects that are new to pupils. Schools vary in the number of subjects or courses they offer in the first two years, but the following subjects are common to all secondary schools: English, a modern foreign language, mathematics, science, geography, history, home economics, technical education, art, music, physical education, and religious and moral education. In the next two years of secondary education, curriculum guidance is given within the framework of eight 'modes of study and activity' into which all subjects fit: language and communication, mathematical studies and applications, scientific studies and applications, social and environmental studies, technological activities and applications, creative and aesthetic activities, physical education and, religious and moral education.

Compulsory curriculum regulations in Denmark

In Denmark, the Ministry of Education issues the regulations pertaining to the aims of teaching in each subject and topic, as well as curriculum guidelines for individual subjects and the distribution of lessons. Within this framework, schools and municipalities are permitted to work out their own curricula.

National curriculum documents play an important role in shaping school curricula irrespective of the legal status of the curriculum documents. Combined with graduation requirements and examinations they serve the purpose of harmonising the content of education within countries. Recent developments in curriculum policies show a tendency towards decentralisation of curriculum decisions in countries where centralised prescriptive syllabi were in use for many decades (*e.g.* in the German speaking European countries and Eastern Europe). At the same time, in countries with traditionally decentralised curriculum policies (like Australia, New Zealand, the United Kingdom and the United States), national standards of competence levels have been negotiated in the past 20 years. As a result of cross-fertilization, national curriculum documents have become more similar among countries, and an international 'core curriculum' appears to be emerging with similar study areas and more similar descriptions of desired competence levels.

Development of curriculum policies in different countries suggests that countries seek a balance between national standards and local autonomy in curriculum decisions.

Total intended instruction time in classroom settings in the formal education system

Total intended instruction time is an estimate of the number of hours during which students are taught both the compulsory and non-compulsory parts of the curriculum.

The total number of intended instruction hours between ages 7 and 14 averages 6 896 hours among OECD countries. However, formal requirements range between 5 472 hours in Finland and 8 058 hours in Italy. These hours comprise compulsory and non-compulsory hours that the school is obliged to offer to students. Whereas the total intended instruction time within this age range is a good indicator of students' theoretical workload, it cannot be interpreted as actual instruction students receive over the years they spend in initial education. Often in countries with greater student workload, the age band of compulsory education is less and students drop out of the school system earlier, whereas in other countries a more even distribution of study time over more years amounts in the end to a larger number of total instruction hours for all. Table D1.1 shows the age range at which over 90 per cent of the population is in education and Chart D1.2 shows the total number of intended instruction time students receive between ages 7 and 14.

Students receive, on average, 6 896 hours of instruction between the ages of 7 and 14.

D1

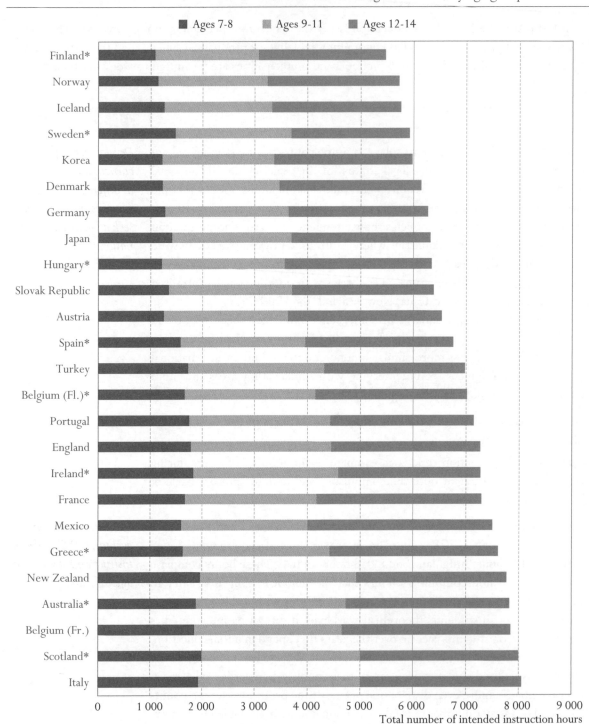

Chart D1.2

Total number of intended instruction hours between ages 7 and 14, by age group

■ Ages 7-8   ■ Ages 9-11   ■ Ages 12-14

Total number of intended instruction hours

Countries are ranked in ascending order of total number of intended instruction hours.
* See Annex 3 for notes on specific countries.
Source: OECD. Table D1.1. See Annex 3 for notes on methodology *(www.oecd.org/edu/eag2003).*

On average, the non-compulsory part of the curriculum comprises 2 per cent of the total intended instruction time for 9 to 11-year-old students and 4 per cent for 12 to 14-year-old students. However, a considerable amount of additional non-compulsory instruction time can sometimes be provided. In primary schools, all intended instruction time is compulsory for students in most OECD countries, but the additional non-compulsory part is as high as 20 per cent in Turkey, 15 per cent in Hungary and 11 per cent in the French Community of Belgium. In lower secondary education, non-compulsory instruction time is a feature in Australia, the French Community of Belgium, Denmark, England, France, Hungary, Ireland, the Slovak Republic and Turkey, and ranges from 4 per cent in the Slovak Republic to 28 per cent in Hungary (Tables D1.2a and D1.2b and Chart D1.1).

On average, the non-compulsory part of the curriculum accounts for 3 per cent of total intended instruction time, but this varies greatly among countries.

Compulsory instruction time in classroom settings in the formal education system

Total compulsory instruction time is an estimate of the number of hours during which students are taught both the compulsory core and compulsory flexible parts of the curriculum.

For 7 to 8-year-olds and 9 to 11-year-olds, total intended instruction time equals total compulsory instruction time in most countries. For 12 to 14-year-olds, the average number of hours of total intended instruction time is equal to the total compulsory instruction time in Austria, Finland, Germany, Greece, Iceland, Italy, Japan, Korea, Mexico, Norway, Portugal, Scotland, the Netherlands and Sweden.

Within the formal education system, the annual amount of total compulsory instruction time in classroom settings averages 747 hours for 7 to 8-year-olds, 813 hours for 9 to 11-year-olds and 900 hours for 12 to 14-year-olds. For 15-year-old students, the average number of compulsory instruction hours per year is 908 hours for the typical programme in which most 15-year-olds are enrolled (Table D1.1).

For students aged 9 to 11 years, 49 per cent of the compulsory curriculum on average is devoted to the three basic subject areas: reading and writing (24 per cent), mathematics (16 per cent) and science (9 per cent). On average, 9 per cent of the compulsory curriculum is devoted to social studies and 6 per cent to modern foreign languages. The arts account for 12 per cent and physical education accounts for 9 per cent of the total compulsory curriculum time. These seven study areas form part of the curriculum in all OECD countries for these age cohorts. At this level, classroom activities in the study areas are not necessarily organised as separate subject classes (Table D1.2a).

The teaching of reading and writing, mathematics and science form almost half the compulsory instruction time for all students aged 9 to 11 years …

D1

For 12 to 14-year-old students in OECD countries, an average of 41 per cent of the compulsory curriculum, is devoted to three basic subject areas: reading and writing (16 per cent), mathematics (13 per cent) and science (12 per cent). In these age cohorts, a relatively larger part of the curriculum is devoted to social studies (13 per cent) and modern foreign languages (11 per cent), whereas

…and 41 per cent for students aged 12 to 14 years.

somewhat less time is devoted to the arts (9 per cent). Physical education accounts for 8 per cent. These seven study areas form part of the curriculum in all OECD countries for lower secondary students. Technology is included in about half of the countries, and religion is included in over half of the OECD countries as part of the compulsory curriculum (Table D1.2b).

On average, 4 per cent of compulsory instruction time belongs to the flexible part of the curriculum in the grades where most students are 9 to 11 years of age while the corresponding proportion is 7 per cent for students aged 12 to 14.

In most OECD countries, the number of hours of compulsory instruction is defined. Within the compulsory part of the curriculum, students have varying degrees of freedom to choose the subjects they want to learn. On average, the flexible part of the curriculum comprises 4 per cent of compulsory instruction time in the grades where most students are 9 to 11 years of age, and 7 per cent for students 12 to 14 years of age. However, for 9 to 11- year-olds, Australia stands out as operating 61 per cent of the compulsory curriculum on a flexible basis. Scotland has the second highest degree of flexibility (20 per cent). For 12 to 14-year-olds, Australia and Scotland again have the highest degree of flexibility in the compulsory curriculum (23 and 27 per cent respectively), although for several other countries there is more than 10 per cent of flexibility in the compulsory curriculum (the French Community of Belgium, Finland, Iceland, Korea, the Netherlands, Portugal and Spain) (Tables D1.2a and D1.2b).

Definitions and methodologies

Data on instruction time are from the 2002 OECD-INES survey on Teachers and the Curriculum and refer to the school year 2000-2001.

Instruction time for 7 to 15-year-olds refers to the formal number of class 60 minute-hours per school year organised by the school for instructional activities for students in the reference school year 2000-2001. For countries with no formal policy on instruction time, the number of hours was estimated from survey data. Hours lost when schools are closed for festivities and celebrations, such as national holidays, are excluded. Intended instruction time does not include non-compulsory time outside the school day, homework, individual tutoring, or private study done before or after school.

• *Compulsory curriculum* refers to the amount and allocation of instruction time that every school must provide and all students must attend. The measurement of the time devoted to specific study areas (subjects) focuses on the minimum common core rather than on the average time spent on study areas, since the data sources (policy documents) do not allow more precise measurement. Total compulsory curriculum comprises the compulsory core curriculum as well as the compulsory flexible curriculum.

• *The compulsory core curriculum* refers to the set or groups of subjects (study areas) that are common to all students such as mathematics, science, social studies, language of instruction and, in some cases, a foreign language, and which can be considered core study areas. Even if all students must study all core study areas, choices may be made within a study area. For example, there may be a choice between an integrated science subject and separate science subjects like biology or physics, or between foreign languages.

• *Compulsory flexible curriculum* refers to the part of the compulsory curriculum where there is flexibility in time spent on a subject and/or a

D1

choice can be made between study areas. For example, a school may be able to choose between offering religious education or more science, or art, but to offer one of these is considered compulsory within the compulsory time framework.

• ***The non-compulsory part of the curriculum*** refers to the average time to which students are entitled above the compulsory hours of instruction. These subjects often vary from school to school or from region to region, and may take the form of "non-compulsory elective" subjects.

• ***Intended instruction time*** refers to the number of hours per year during which students receive instruction in the compulsory and non-compulsory parts of the curriculum.

For 15-year-olds, typical instruction time refers to the programme in which most 15-year-olds are enrolled. This can be a programme in lower or upper secondary education, and in most countries it refers to a general programme. If the system channels students into different programme types at this age, an estimation of the average instruction time may have been necessary for the most important mainstream programmes weighted by the proportion of students in the grade level where most 15-year-olds are enrolled. Where vocational programmes are also calculated, in typical instruction time, only the school-based part of the programme should be included in the calculations.

The instruction time for the least demanding programme refers to programmes stipulated for students who are least likely to continue studying beyond mandatory school age or beyond lower secondary education. Such programmes may or may not exist in a country depending on streaming and selection policies. In many countries students are offered the same amount of instruction time in all or most programmes but there is flexibility in the choice of study areas or subjects. Often such choices have to be made quite early if programmes are long and differ substantially.

For the classification of subject areas and specific notes on countries, see *www.oecd.org/edu/eag2003*.

D1

Table D1.1
Compulsory and non-compulsory instruction time in public institutions (2001)
Average number of hours per year of total compulsory and non-compulsory instruction time in the curriculum for 7 to 8, 9 to 11, 12 to 14 and 15-year-olds

	Age range at which over 90% of the population are enrolled	Average number of hours per year of total compulsory instruction time					Average number of hours per year of total intended instruction time				
		Ages 7-8	Ages 9-11	Ages 12-14	Age 15 (typical programme)	Age 15 (minimum required programme)	Ages 7-8	Ages 9-11	Ages 12-14	Age 15 (typical programme)	Age 15 (minimum required programme)
Australia*	5 - 16	920	928	978	964	944	945	946	1 033	1 029	1 021
Austria	5 - 16	678	833	997	1 095	1 048	678	833	997	1 095	1 048
Belgium (Fl.)*	3 - 17	a	a	a	a	a	831	831	955	955	448
Belgium (Fr.)	3 - 17	840	840	1 005	m	m	930	930	1 065	m	m
Czech Republic*	5 - 17	648	720	806	886	338	m	m	m	886	m
Denmark	4 - 15	615	750	800	720	720	615	750	890	900	900
England	4 - 15	854	843	821	893	m	890	890	940	940	m
Finland*	6 - 17	542	665	798	855	a	542	665	798	855	a
France	3 - 17	835	835	946	1 027	m	835	835	1 038	1 131	m
Germany	6 - 17	642	788	878	900	m	642	788	878	900	m
Greece*	6 - 16	816	928	1 064	1 186	1 003	816	928	1 064	1 429	1 246
Hungary*	5 - 16	555	680	722	833	m	611	784	925	1 207	m
Iceland	4 - 16	630	692	809	817	a	630	692	809	817	a
Ireland*	5 - 16	915	915	839	802	713	915	915	899	891	891
Italy	3 - 15	969	1 020	1 020	m	m	969	1 020	1 020	m	m
Japan	4 - 17	709	761	875	m	a	709	761	875	m	a
Korea	6 - 17	612	718	867	963	a	612	718	867	963	a
Mexico	6 - 12	800	800	1167	m	m	800	800	1 167	m	m
Netherlands*	4 - 16	m	1 000	1067	m	a	m	1 000	1 067	m	a
New Zealand	4 - 15	m	m	m	m	m	985	985	948	930	m
Norway	6 - 17	570	703	827	855	a	570	703	827	855	a
Portugal	5 - 15	875	894	904	827	a	875	894	904	827	a
Scotland*	4 - 15	1 000	1 000	1 000	1 000	1 000	1 000	1 000	1 000	1 000	1 000
Slovak Republic	6 - 16	645	750	860	870	a	679	784	894	904	a
Spain*	4 - 16	792	792	929	963	963	792	792	932	963	963
Sweden*	6 - 18	741	741	741	741	a	741	741	741	741	a
Switzerland	6 - 16	m	m	m	m	m	m	m	m	m	m
Turkey	7 - 12	720	720	791	959	a	864	864	887	959	a
United States	5 - 15	m	m	m	m	m	m	m	m	m	m
Country mean		*747*	*813*	*900*	*908*	*841*	*779*	*840*	*939*	*962*	*940*
Argentina[1]	5 - 14	m	m	m	m	m	m	729	928	m	m
Brazil	7 - 15	m	m	m	m	m	m	800	800	m	m
Chile	6 - 14	m	m	m	m	m	m	1 140	1 080	m	m
Egypt	6 - 12	m	m	m	m	m	m	1 035	675	m	m
India	m	m	m	m	m	m	m	1 051	1 176	m	m
Indonesia	6 - 13	m	m	m	m	m	m	1 120	1 274	m	m
Jamaica	4 - 14	m	m	m	m	m	m	950	950	m	m
Malaysia	6 - 13	m	m	m	m	m	m	964	1230	m	m
Paraguay	7 - 11	m	m	m	m	m	m	854	1 148	m	m
Peru[1]	6 - 14	m	m	m	m	m	m	783	914	m	m
Philippines	7 - 13	m	m	m	m	m	m	1 067	1 467	m	m
Russian Federation	7 - 15	m	m	m	m	m	m	814	989	m	m
Thailand	4 - 11	m	m	m	m	m	m	1 160	1 167	m	m
Tunisia	6 - 10	m	m	m	m	m	m	960	880	m	m
Uruguay	6 - 14	m	m	m	m	m	m	455	913	m	m
Zimbabwe	7 - 13	m	m	m	m	m	m	871	1 102	m	m

OECD COUNTRIES

NON-OECD COUNTRIES

D1

1. Year of reference 2000.
* See Annex 3 for notes (*www.oecd.org/edu/eag2003*).
Source: OECD.

Table D1.2a

Intended instruction time per subject as a percentage of total compulsory instruction time for 9 to 11-year-olds (2001)

Percentage of intended instruction time devoted to various subject areas within the total compulsory curriculum

	Compulsory core curriculum											TOTAL compulsory core curriculum	Compulsory flexible curriculum	TOTAL compulsory curriculum	Non-compulsory curriculum
	Reading, writing and literature	Mathematics	Science	Social studies	Modern foreign languages	Technology	Arts	Physical education	Religion	Practical and vocational skills	Other				
	(1)	(2)	(3)	(4)	(5)	(6)	(7)	(8)	(9)	(10)	(11)	(12)	(13)	(14)	(15)
OECD COUNTRIES															
Australia[1]	12	8	3	4	2	2	3	4	1	n	n	39	61	100	2
Austria	23	15	10	2	7	n	20	12	7	x(12)	2	100	n	100	n
Belgium (Fl.)	a	a	a	a	a	a	a	a	a	a	a	a	a	a	a
Belgium (Fr.)[1]	x(11)	x(11)	x(11)	x(11)	5	x(11)	x(11)	7	7	x(11)	81	100	m	100	11
Czech Republic[2]	24	19	16	4	12	n	15	8	n	3	n	100	n	100	m
Denmark	25	16	8	4	7	n	21	11	4	n	4	100	n	100	n
England	29	23	11	8	n	10	8	7	4	n	n	100	n	100	6
Finland	21	17	15	x(3)	9	n	13	11	6	9	n	100	n	100	n
France	28	20	5	10	9	3	8	15	n	n	n	100	n	100	n
Germany	21	17	6	6	8	1	15	11	7	n	5	97	3	100	n
Greece	29	14	11	11	10	n	8	7	7	n	2	100	n	100	n
Hungary	27	17	5	7	7	n	15	12	n	7	3	100	n	100	15
Iceland	20	13	6	9	2	n	17	10	3	3	n	84	16	100	n
Ireland	30	12	12	4	n	n	12	4	10	n	17	100	n	100	n
Italy	17	10	8	11	10	3	13	7	6	n	n	84	16	100	n
Japan	23	17	10	10	n	5	14	10	n	n	10	100	n	100	n
Korea	19	15	12	12	5	n	13	9	n	2	3	89	11	100	n
Mexico	30	25	15	20	n	n	5	5	n	n	n	100	n	100	n
Netherlands[3]	30	19	x(4)	15	2	2	10	7	4	n	12	100	n	100	n
New Zealand	m	m	m	m	m	m	m	m	m	m	m	m	m	m	m
Norway	22	15	7	8	6	n	16	7	9	n	9	100	n	100	n
Portugal[4]	16	13	10	10	13	16	10	10	3	n	n	100	n	100	n
Scotland	20	15	5	5	x(1)	5	10	5	15	x(13)		80	20	100	n
Slovak Republic	31	20	8	8	5	n	12	11	1	4	n	100	n	100	5
Spain	21	17	9	9	12	n	12	11	x(13)	n	n	92	8	100	n
Sweden	22	14	12	13	12	x(12)	7	8	x(12)	7	n	94	6	100	n
Switzerland	m	m	m	m	m	m	m	m	m	m	m	m	m	m	m
Turkey	19	13	10	10	9	n	7	6	7	10	1	91	9	100	20
United States	m	m	m	m	m	m	m	m	m	m	m	m	m	m	m
Country mean[1]	*24*	*16*	*9*	*9*	*6*	*2*	*12*	*9*	*4*	*2*	*3*	*96*	*4*	*100*	*2*
NON-OECD COUNTRIES															
Argentina[5]	19	19	15	15	7	4	7	7	a	a	n	93	7	100	m
Chile	m	m	m	m	m	m	m	m	m	m	m	75	25	100	m
Egypt	30	15	9	6	9	2	5	7	7	5	5	100	a	100	m
India	19	17	12	12	19	a	4	12	a	a	a	96	4	100	m
Indonesia	22	22	13	11	a	a	5	5	5	13	5	100	a	100	m
Jamaica	24	21	11	11	a	a	8	8	8	a	9	100	a	100	m
Malaysia	21	15	11	9	15	n	4	4	13	4	4	100	a	100	m
Paraguay	26	13	8	10	xr	7	10	7	3	xr	10	93	7	100	m
Peru[5]	m	m	m	m	m	m	m	m	m	m	m	70	30	100	m
Philippines	13	13	13	13	13	a	8	4	a	13	13	100	a	100	m
Russian Federation	31	15	4	9	6	6	6	6	a	m	m	85	15	100	m
Thailand	14	10	m	m	m	m	m	m	m	23	39	86	14	100	m
Tunisia	27	13	5	7	n	2	3	3	4	n	36	100	n	100	m
Uruguay	28	29	13	19	a	a	9	3	a	a	a	100	a	100	m
Zimbabwe	19	13	8	8	17	8	4	4	8	8	n	100	n	100	m

1. Australia and Belgium (Fr.) are not included in the country means.
2. For 9 to 10-year-olds, social studies is included in science.
3. Includes 9 and 11-year-olds only.
4. Includes 10 to 11-year-olds only.
5. Year of reference 2000.

Source: OECD. See Annex 3 for notes *(www.oecd.org/edu/eag2003)*.

D1

Table D1.2b
Intended instruction time per subject as a percentage of total compulsory instruction time for 12 to 14-year-olds (2001)
Percentage of intended instruction time devoted to various subject areas within the total compulsory curriculum

	Compulsory core curriculum											TOTAL compulsory core curriculum	Compulsory flexible curriculum	TOTAL compulsory curriculum	Non-compulsory curriculum
	Reading, writing and literature	Mathematics	Science	Social studies	Modern foreign languages	Technology	Arts	Physical education	Religion	Practical and vocational skills	Other				
	(1)	(2)	(3)	(4)	(5)	(6)	(7)	(8)	(9)	(10)	(11)	(12)	(13)	(14)	(15)
OECD COUNTRIES															
Australia	12	12	10	9	5	8	8	8	1	2	3	77	23	100	6
Austria	12	15	14	12	10	n	18	11	6	n	n	100	n	100	n
Belgium (Fl.)	a	a	a	a	a	a	a	a	a	a	a	a	a	a	a
Belgium (Fr.)[1]	15	13	6	12	12	3	3	9	6	n	6	85	15	100	6
Czech Republic	14	14	21	14	11	n	11	7	n	7	n	100	n	100	n
Denmark	23	15	14	13	11	n	10	8	4	n	4	100	n	100	11
England	14	14	14	14	11	10	9	9	5	n	n	100	n	100	15
Finland[2]	12	12	13	8	13	n	7	8	4	10	n	86	14	100	n
France	17	15	12	13	12	6	7	11	n	n	n	93	7	100	10
Germany	14	13	11	12	16	4	10	9	5	1	2	97	3	100	n
Greece	12	11	10	10	15	5	6	8	6	1	16	100	n	100	n
Hungary	13	13	13	15	9	4	12	9	n	8	5	100	n	100	28
Iceland	15	12	8	7	15	n	14	9	3	6	n	88	12	100	n
Ireland[3]	29	13	11	16	7	x(15)	4	5	9	x(15)	6	100	n	100	7
Italy[1]	22	10	10	15	10	10	13	7	3	n	n	100	n	100	n
Japan	14	12	11	12	13	7	11	10	n	n	7	98	2	100	n
Korea	15	12	11	11	11	5	7	9	n	3	6	88	12	100	n
Mexico	14	14	17	26	9	n	6	6	n	9	n	100	n	100	n
Netherlands	10	10	8	11	14	5	7	9	n	3	n	78	22	100	n
New Zealand	m	m	m	m	m	m	m	m	m	m	m	m	m	m	m
Norway	16	13	9	11	10	n	8	10	7	n	16	100	n	100	n
Portugal	13	13	15	17	10	n	10	10	3	n	n	90	10	100	n
Scotland	19	10	9	9	x(1)	8	8	5	5	x(13)	n	73	27	100	n
Slovak Republic	15	16	16	17	10	n	7	7	3	3	n	97	3	100	4
Spain	15	11	11	10	11	8	12	7	x(13)	x(13)	3	87	13	100	n
Sweden	22	14	12	13	12	x(12)	7	8	x(12)	7	n	94	6	100	n
Switzerland	m	m	m	m	m	m	m	m	m	m	m	m	m	m	m
Turkey[1]	15	14	16	10	15	n	4	4	5	6	3	91	9	100	12
United States	m	m	m	m	m	m	m	m	m	m	m	m	m	m	m
Country mean	*16*	*13*	*12*	*13*	*11*	*3*	*9*	*8*	*3*	*3*	*3*	*93*	*7*	*100*	*4*
NON-OECD COUNTRIES															
Argentina[4]	13	13	13	15	8	8	8	8	a	a	5	90	10	100	m
Chile	m	m	m	m	m	m	m	m	m	m	m	92	8	100	m
Egypt	24	13	11	8	13	5	5	5	5	5	4	100	a	100	m
India	11	15	15	13	13	a	4	13	a	a	a	83	17	100	m
Indonesia	16	16	14	13	6	a	5	5	5	15	5	100	a	100	m
Jamaica	16	13	13	13	5	16	5	5	5	3	4	100	a	100	m
Malaysia	13	11	11	13	11	n	4	4	9	9	13	100	a	100	m
Paraguay	20	12	14	13	x(13)	12	10	5	2	x(7)	7	95	5	100	m
Peru[4]	14	14	12	23	6	a	6	6	6	7	a	93	7	100	m
Philippines	9	9	9	9	9	18	6	3	a	a	9	82	18	100	m
Russian Federation	23	13	14	13	8	6	4	5	a	a	m	87	13	100	m
Thailand	11	6	9	11	x(13)	x(13)	3	9	x(11)	6	14	69	31	100	m
Tunisia	17	14	5	15	5	5	7	10	5	n	17	100	n	100	m
Uruguay	13	13	19	18	8	a	5	5	a	a	a	81	19	100	m
Zimbabwe	13	11	11	8	13	11	10	5	7	11	n	100	n	100	m

1. Includes 12 to 13-year-olds only.
2. For 12-year-olds, social studies is included in science.
3. For 13 to 14-year-olds, arts is included in non-compulsory curriculum.
4. Year of reference 2000.
Source: OECD. See Annex 3 for notes (*www.oecd.org/edu/eag2003*).

D1

INDICATOR D2: CLASS SIZE AND RATIO OF STUDENTS TO TEACHING STAFF

- The average class size in primary education is 22, but varies among countries from 36 students per class in Korea to less than half of that number in Greece, Iceland and Luxembourg.

- The number of students per class increases by an average of two students between primary and lower secondary education, but ratios of students to teaching staff tend to decrease with increasing levels of education due to more annual instruction time.

- Teaching and non-teaching staff employed in primary and secondary schools ranges from less than 80 persons per 1 000 students enrolled in Canada, Japan, Korea and Mexico to 119 persons or more per 1 000 students in France, Hungary, Iceland and Italy.

Chart D2.1

Average class size in public and private institutions, by level of education (2001)

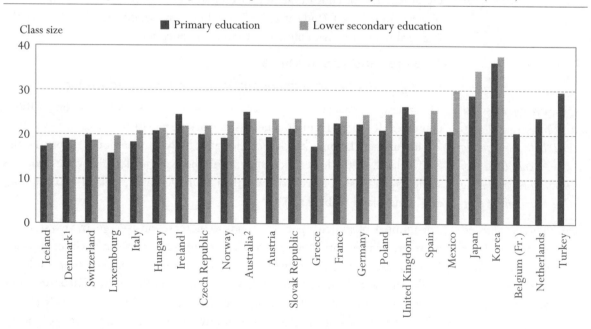

D2

Countries are ranked in ascending order of average class size in lower secondary education.
1. Public institutions only.
2. Year of reference 2000.
Source: OECD. Table D2.1. See Annex 3 for notes *(www.oecd.org/edu/eag2003).*

Policy context

This indicator shows class sizes and ratios of students to teaching staff...

Class sizes are widely debated in many OECD countries. Smaller classes are valued because they may allow students to receive more individual attention from their teachers and reduce the disadvantage of managing large numbers of students and their work. Smaller class sizes may also influence parents when they choose schools for their children. However, the predominance of teacher costs in educational expenditure means that reducing class sizes leads to sharp increases in the costs of education.

Another important indicator of the resources devoted to education is the ratio of students to teaching staff. Because of the difficulty of constructing direct measures of educational quality, especially at higher levels of education, this indicator is often used as a proxy for quality, on the assumption that a smaller ratio of students to teaching staff means better student access to teaching resources. However, a smaller ratio of students to teaching staff may have to be weighed against higher salaries for teachers, greater investment in teaching technology, or more widespread use of assistant teachers and other paraprofessionals whose salaries are often considerably lower than those of qualified teachers. Moreover, as larger numbers of children with special educational needs are integrated into normal classes, more use of specialised personnel and support services may limit the resources available for reducing the ratio of students to teaching staff.

...and the proportion of teaching and non-teaching staff employed in education.

The number of teaching and non-teaching staff employed in education per 1 000 students is an indicator of the proportion of a country's human resources that is devoted to educating the population. The number of persons employed as either teachers or educational support personnel, and the level of compensation of educational staff (Indicator D5), are both important factors affecting the financial resources that countries commit to education.

Evidence and explanations

Average class size in primary and lower secondary education

The average class size in primary education is 22, but varies among countries from 36 students per class to less than half of that.

The average class size in primary education varies widely among OECD countries. It ranges from 36 students per primary class in Korea to fewer than 20 in Austria, Denmark, Greece, Iceland, Italy, Luxembourg, Norway and Switzerland. At the lower secondary level, the average class size varies from 38 students per class in Korea to fewer than 20 in Denmark, Iceland, Luxembourg and Switzerland (Table D2.1).

D2

The number of students per class increases by an average of two between primary and lower secondary education.

The number of students per class tends to increase, on average, by two students between primary and lower secondary education. In Austria, Greece, Japan, Mexico and Spain, the increase in average class size exceeds four students, while Australia, Denmark, Ireland, Switzerland and the United Kingdom show a drop in the number of students per class between these two levels (Chart D2.1). The indicator on class size is limited to primary and lower secondary education because class sizes are difficult to define and compare at higher levels of education, where students often attend several different classes, depending on the subject area.

In nine out of the 20 countries with comparable data, the difference in class sizes between public and private institutions exceeds three students at the primary level. Public institutions at primary level have at least three students more per class than private institutions in the Czech Republic, Norway, Poland, Switzerland and Turkey. Differences tend to be smaller at the lower secondary level but the average class size in private lower secondary schools is still lower than in public schools in eight out of the 18 countries with comparable data (Table D2.1).

Public institutions at the primary level have at least three students more per class than private institutions in the Czech Republic, Norway, Poland, Switzerland and Turkey.

Ratio of students to teaching staff

The indicator also provides the ratio of students to teaching staff, which is obtained by dividing the number of full-time equivalent "students" at a given level of education by the number of full-time equivalent "teachers" at that level and in similar types of institutions. The relationship between the ratio of students to teaching staff and average class size is influenced by many factors, including the number of hours during which a student attends class each day, the length of a teacher's working day, the number of classes or students for which a teacher is responsible, the subject taught, the division of the teacher's time between teaching and other duties, the grouping of students within classes and the practice of team-teaching.

Many factors contribute to differences in the ratio of students to teaching staff.

In primary education, the ratio of students to teaching staff, expressed in full-time equivalents, ranges from around 30 students per teacher in Korea and Turkey to 10 in Denmark. The country mean in primary education is 17 students per teacher. There is slightly more variation among countries in the ratio of students to teaching staff at the secondary level, ranging from more than 20 students per full-time equivalent teacher in Korea and Mexico to below 11 in Austria, Belgium, Greece, Italy, Luxembourg, Norway and Portugal. On average among countries, the ratio of students to teaching staff at the secondary level of education is 14, which is close to the ratios in the Czech Republic (14), Finland (14), Germany (15), Japan (15), Poland (15), the Slovak Republic (14), Sweden (15) and the United Kingdom (15) (Table D2.2).

In Korea and Turkey, the ratio of students to teaching staff in primary education is approximately three times as high as in Denmark.

As the difference in the mean ratios of students to teaching staff between primary and secondary education indicates, there are fewer students per teacher as the level of education rises. With the exception of Denmark, Hungary, Mexico, Poland and Sweden, the ratio of students to teaching staff in every OECD country decreases between primary and secondary levels of education, despite a tendency for class sizes to increase. This is mostly because instruction time tends to increase with the level of education.

Between primary and secondary education, there are fewer students per teacher as the level of education rises.

D2

In France, Korea and Turkey, the decrease in the ratio of students to teaching staff from the primary to the secondary levels is between seven and 13 students per full-time equivalent teacher, which is more marked compared to other countries. In France and Korea, this mainly reflects differences in the annual instruction time, but it may also result from delays in matching the teaching force to demographic changes, or from differences in teaching hours for teachers at different levels of education. The general trend is consistent among countries, but it is not obvious from an educational perspective why a smaller ratio of students to teaching staff should be more desirable at higher levels of education (Table D2.2).

In general, the ratio of students to teaching staff at the tertiary level tends to be higher than that in secondary education.

The ratio of students to teaching staff in public and private tertiary institutions ranges from 54 students per teacher in Korea to 12 or below in Germany, Iceland, Japan, Norway, the Slovak Republic and Sweden (Table D2.2). Such comparisons in tertiary education, however, should be made with caution since it is still difficult to calculate full-time equivalent students and teachers on a comparable basis at this level.

In 12 out of the 17 countries for which data are available for both tertiary-type A and advanced research programmes and tertiary-type B education, the ratio of students to teaching staff is lower in the generally more occupationally specific tertiary-type B programmes than in tertiary-type A and advanced research programmes (Chart D2.2). Germany, Hungary, Korea, the Slovak Republic and Turkey are the only countries with a higher ratio in tertiary-type B programmes.

The ratio of students to teaching staff in pre-primary education tends to be between that in primary and secondary education.

The ratio of students to teaching staff in pre-primary education tends to be lower than in primary education, but slightly higher than in secondary education. In pre-primary education, the ratio ranges from fewer than eight students per teacher in Denmark, Iceland and New Zealand to 22 students or more per teacher in Germany, Korea, Mexico and the United Kingdom. There is little apparent relationship between the ratio of students to teaching staff in pre-primary and primary education, suggesting that the staffing requirements or emphases at these levels differ within countries (Table D2.2).

Teaching staff and non-teaching staff employed in education

Average class sizes, total instruction time and teachers' working time contribute to country variation.

The variation among countries in the relative size of the teaching force cannot be explained solely by differences in the size of the school-age population, but is also affected by the average class size, the total instruction time of students (Indicator D1), teachers' average working time (Indicator D6), and the division of teachers' time between teaching and other duties.

The relative proportions of teachers and other educational personnel differ widely from one country to another.

There are significant differences among OECD countries in the distribution of educational staff between teaching and other categories, reflecting differences among countries in the organisation and management of schooling. Teaching and non-teaching staff employed in primary and secondary schools ranges from less than 80 persons per 1 000 students enrolled in Canada, Japan, Korea and Mexico to 119 persons or more per 1 000 students in France, Hungary, Iceland and Italy (Chart D2.3).

Non-teaching staff represent on average 30 per cent of the total teaching and non-teaching staff in primary and secondary schools.

Among the 13 OECD countries for which data are available for each category of personnel employed in education, the staff not classified as instructional personnel represent on average 30 per cent of the total teaching and non-teaching staff in primary and secondary schools. In seven of these countries, these staff represent between 30 and 40 per cent of total teaching and non-teaching staff. This proportion exceeds 40 per cent in the Czech Republic and France. Compared to the number of students enrolled in primary and

D₂

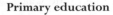

Ratio of students to teaching staff in public and private institutions, by level of education (2001)

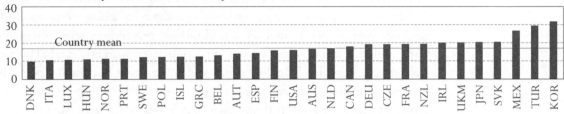

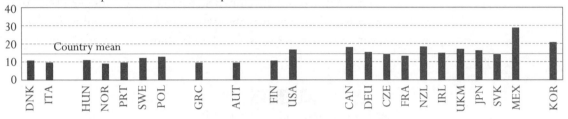

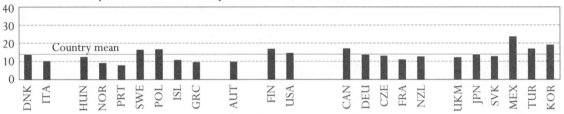

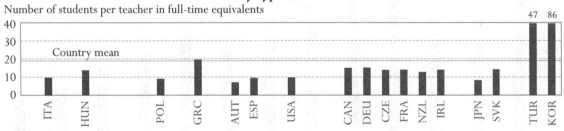

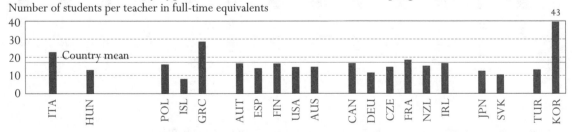

D₂

Note: Please refer to the Reader's Guide for list of country codes and country names used in this chart.
Countries are ranked in ascending order of number of students per teacher in primary education.
Source: OECD. Table D2.2. See Annex 3 for notes *(www.oecd.org/edu/eag2003).*

secondary schools, non-teaching staff employed in education represents more than 40 persons per 1 000 students in the Czech Republic, France, Iceland and the United States (Table and Chart D2.3).

These differences reflect the numbers of staff that countries employ in non-teaching capacities, *e.g.*, principals without teaching responsibilities, guidance counsellors, school nurses, librarians, researchers without teaching responsibilities, bus drivers, janitors and maintenance workers, etc. In Hungary, Iceland, Italy, Poland and the United States, maintenance and operations personnel working in primary and secondary schools represent more than 20 persons per 1 000 students enrolled in these schools. Administrative personnel represent between 9 and 10 persons per 1 000 students enrolled in primary and secondary schools in Italy, Mexico and the United States and 19 persons per 1 000 students in the Czech Republic, whereas the staff employed in school and higher level management exceed 6 persons per 1 000 students in the Czech Republic,

Chart D2.3

Teaching staff and non-teaching staff (2001)
Teaching staff and non-teaching staff in primary and secondary schools per 1 000 students, calculations based on full-time equivalents

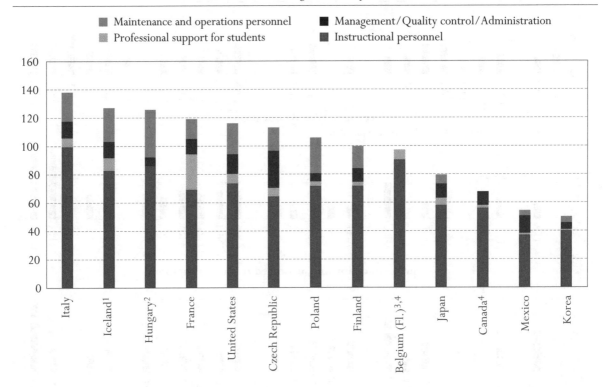

D2

Countries are ranked in descending order of the proportion of instructional personnel per 1 000 students.
1. Data on higher level management and administrative personnel are missing.
2. Data on professionnal support for students are missing.
3. Data on management/quality control/administration personnel are missing.
4. Data on maintenance and operations personnel are missing.
Source: OECD. Table D2.3. See Annex 3 for notes *(www.oecd.org/edu/eag2003).*

EDUCATION AT A GLANCE © OECD 2003

France, Iceland and the Slovak Republic, and 10 persons in Norway (Chart D2.3). Finally, the staff employed to provide professional support for students are relatively numerous in France (25 persons per 1 000 students enrolled in primary and secondary schools) and to a lesser extent in Iceland and the United States (9 and 7 persons per 1 000 students enrolled respectively in primary and secondary schools).

Definitions and methodologies

Class sizes have been calculated by dividing the number of students enrolled by the number of classes. In order to ensure comparability among countries, special needs programmes have been excluded. Data include only regular programmes at primary and lower secondary levels of education and exclude teaching in sub-groups outside the regular classroom setting.

Data refer to the school year 2000–2001, and are based on the UOE data collection on education statistics that is administered annually by the OECD.

Instructional personnel comprise:

- *Teaching staff* refers to professional personnel directly involved in teaching students. The classification includes classroom teachers; special education teachers; and other teachers who work with a whole class of students in a classroom, in small groups in a resource room, or in one-to-one teaching situations inside or outside a regular classroom. Teaching staff also includes department chairpersons whose duties include some teaching, but excludes non-professional personnel who support teachers in providing instruction to students, such as teachers' aides and other paraprofessional personnel.

- *Teachers' aides and teaching / research assistants* include non-professional personnel or students who support teachers in providing instruction to students. This type of personnel is not included in tables D2.1 and D2.2.

Non-instructional personnel comprises four categories:

- *Professional support for students* includes professional staff who provide services to students that support their learning. In many cases, these staff originally qualified as teachers but then moved into other professional positions within the education system. This category also includes all personnel employed in education systems who provide health and social support services to students, such as guidance counsellors, librarians, doctors, dentists, nurses, psychiatrists and psychologists and other staff with similar responsibilities.

- *School and higher level management* includes professional personnel who are responsible for school management and administration and personnel whose primary responsibility is the quality control and management of higher levels of the education system. This category covers principals, assistant principals, headmasters, assistant headmasters, superintendents of schools, associate and assistant superintendents, commissioners of education and other management staff with similar responsibilities.

- *School and higher level administrative personnel* includes all personnel who support the administration and management of schools and of higher levels of the education system. The category includes: receptionists, secretaries, typists and word processing staff, book-keepers and clerks,

D2

analysts, computer programmers, network administrators, and others with similar functions and responsibilities.

• *Maintenance and operations personnel* includes personnel who support the maintenance and operation of schools, the transportation of students to and from school, school security and catering. This category includes the following types of personnel: masons, carpenters, electricians, maintenance repairers, painters and paperhangers, plasterers, plumbers and vehicle mechanics. It also includes bus drivers and other vehicle operators, construction workers, gardeners and ground staff, bus monitors and crossing guards, cooks, custodians, food servers and others with similar functions.

D₂

Table D2.1
Average class size, by type of institution and level of education (2001)
Calculations based on number of students and number of classes

	Primary education				Lower secondary education			
	Public institutions	Government-dependent private institutions	Independent private institutions	TOTAL: Public and private institutions	Public institutions	Government-dependent private institutions	Independent private institutions	TOTAL: Public and private institutions
	(1)	(2)	(3)	(4)	(5)	(6)	(7)	(8)
Australia[1]	24.9	25.9	a	25.0	23.6	22.2	a	23.5
Austria	19.4	20.9	x(2)	19.4	23.5	24.2	x(6)	23.6
Belgium	m	m	m	m	m	m	m	m
Belgium (Fr.)	20.1	21.1	m	20.5	21.4	m	m	m
Canada	m	m	m	m	m	m	m	m
Czech Republic	20.1	11.3	a	20.0	22.0	19.0	a	22.0
Denmark	19.0	m	m	19.0	18.6	m	m	18.6
Finland	m	m	a	m	m	m	a	m
France	22.3	23.9	n	22.6	24.1	25.0	12.8	24.2
Germany	22.4	24.0	x(2)	22.4	24.5	26.0	x(6)	24.6
Greece	17.2	a	20.6	17.4	23.6	a	26.9	23.7
Hungary	20.9	19.7	a	20.8	21.2	25.4	a	21.4
Iceland	17.3	16.5	n	17.3	17.8	15.0	n	17.8
Ireland	24.5	m	m	24.5	21.9	m	m	21.9
Italy	18.2	a	20.4	18.3	20.8	a	21.4	20.8
Japan	28.8	a	34.5	28.8	34.3	a	37.3	34.5
Korea	36.3	a	35.9	36.3	37.9	37.2	a	37.7
Luxembourg	15.5	21.8	20.3	15.8	19.4	20.7	20.3	19.7
Mexico	20.6	a	24.2	20.9	30.1	a	28.8	30.0
Netherlands	m	m	m	23.9	m	m	m	m
New Zealand	m	m	m	m	m	m	m	m
Norway	19.3	15.6	x(2)	19.2	23.2	19.7	x(6)	23.1
Poland	21.2	12.4	a	21.1	24.8	13.7	a	24.6
Portugal	m	m	m	m	m	m	m	m
Slovak Republic	21.3	21.0	n	21.3	23.6	24.2	n	23.6
Spain	19.5	24.8	21.6	20.9	24.5	28.6	22.6	25.6
Sweden	m	m	m	m	m	m	m	m
Switzerland	19.9	14.1	15.4	19.8	18.8	17.7	16.1	18.7
Turkey	29.9	a	20.5	29.6	a	a	a	a
United Kingdom	26.4	a	m	m	24.7	m	m	m
United States	m	m	m	m	m	m	m	m
Country mean	*22.0*	*19.5*	*23.7*	*22.0*	*23.8*	*22.8*	*23.3*	*24.0*
Brazil	26.7	a	18.8	25.8	34.5	a	27.4	33.6
Chile	33.3	36.6	23.6	33.3	32.3	35.8	24.3	32.5
Egypt	41.7	35.7	36.0	41.1	44.6	42.8	32.8	43.9
India	40.1	x(1)	x(1)	40.1	38.5	x(5)	x(5)	38.5
Indonesia	25.7	23.1	m	25.2	40.5	35.5	m	38.5
Israel	25.6	a	a	25.6	31.1	a	a	31.1
Jamaica	33.8	a	m	34.2	32.4	a	m	32.4
Paraguay	18.1	21.7	17.4	18.4	29.5	28.4	20.2	27.7
Philippines	42.2	a	32.9	41.4	48.5	a	44.9	47.6
Thailand	23.2	37.5	a	24.5	34.9	25.4	a	34.1
Tunisia	29.0	a	25.9	28.9	33.7	a	19.2	33.2
Uruguay	18.9	a	m	18.9	29.9	a	26.4	29.4

(left margin: OECD COUNTRIES / NON-OECD COUNTRIES)

1. Year of reference 2000.
Source: OECD. See Annex 3 for notes (*www.oecd.org/edu/eag2003*).

D2

Table D2.2
Ratio of students to teaching staff in public and private institutions (2001)
by level of education, calculations based on full-time equivalents

	Pre-primary education	Primary education	Lower secondary education	Upper secondary education	All secondary education	Post secondary non-tertiary education	Tertiary-type B	Tertiary-type A & advanced research programmes	All tertiary education
	(1)	(2)	(3)	(4)	(5)	(6)	(7)	(8)	(9)
OECD COUNTRIES									
Australia[1]	m	17.0	m	m	m	m	m	15.0	m
Austria	18.1	14.3	9.8	9.9	9.8	9.9	7.3	16.9	15.8
Belgium	16.7	13.4	x(5)	x(5)	9.8	x(5)	x(9)	x(9)	18.1
Canada	11.5	18.3	18.4	17.2	17.8	x(7)	15.2	17.0	16.2
Czech Republic	12.7	19.4	14.5	13.1	13.8	10.0	14.1	15.0	14.9
Denmark	6.9	10.0	11.1	13.9	12.4	m	m	m	m
Finland	13.0	16.1	10.9	17.0	14.0	x(4)	x(4)	16.8	16.8
France	19.2	19.5	13.5	11.2	12.3	a	14.2	18.9	18.1
Germany	24.6	19.4	15.7	13.7	15.2	15.0	15.4	11.9	12.3
Greece	14.5	12.7	9.8	9.7	9.7	m	19.8	28.9	25.2
Hungary	11.4	11.3	11.2	12.5	11.8	9.1	14.0	13.2	13.3
Iceland	5.2	12.6	x(2)	10.9	m	x(5,9)	m	8.3	8.0
Ireland	14.5	20.3	15.2	x(3)	x(3)	x(3)	14.2	17.1	16.0
Italy	12.8	10.8	9.9	10.4	10.2	m	10.0	23.1	22.4
Japan	18.5	20.6	16.6	14.0	15.1	x(4,9)	8.5	12.8	11.3
Korea	22.2	32.1	21.0	19.3	20.1	a	86.1	42.8	53.9
Luxembourg[2]	17.4	11.0	x(5)	x(5)	9.1	m	m	m	m
Mexico	21.9	27.0	29.2	23.8	27.3	a	x(9)	x(9)	15.2
Netherlands	x(2)	17.2	x(5)	x(5)	17.1	x(5)	x(9)	x(9)	12.6
New Zealand	7.6	19.6	18.7	12.8	15.7	12.5	13.0	15.7	15.0
Norway	m	11.6	9.3	9.2	9.3	x(4)	x(9)	x(9)	11.5
Poland	12.8	12.5	13.1	16.8	15.4	16.4	9.3	16.3	16.2
Portugal	16.9	11.6	9.9	8.0	8.9	m	x(9)	x(9)	m
Slovak Republic	10.0	20.7	14.5	12.9	13.8	14.1	14.5	10.7	10.8
Spain	16.0	14.7	x(5)	x(5)	11.0	x(5)	9.8	14.2	13.4
Sweden	10.3	12.4	12.4	16.6	14.6	m	x(9)	x(9)	9.3
Switzerland[2]	m	m	m	m	m	m	m	m	m
Turkey	15.6	29.8	a	17.2	17.2	a	46.7	13.6	16.1
United Kingdom[1]	22.1	20.5	17.3	12.3	14.5	m	x(9)	x(9)	17.6
United States	14.9	16.3	17.0	14.8	15.9	a	10.1	14.9	13.7
Country mean	*14.9*	*17.0*	*14.5*	*13.8*	*13.9*	*12.4*	*19.0*	*17.2*	*16.5*
NON-OECD COUNTRIES									
Argentina[2,3]	19.9	22.7	13.2	9.0	11.2	a	12.1	8.0	9.3
Brazil[4]	18.7	24.8	20.7	19.0	20.1	a	x(9)	x(9)	15.2
Chile[4]	24.9	33.4	33.0	28.4	30.1	a	m	m	m
China[4]	32.8	19.9	18.6	20.7	19.1	8.5	32.4	12.7	16.9
Egypt	22.1	22.3	21.2	13.2	17.0	m	m	m	m
India[2,4]	34.3	40.0	36.1	30.4	34.1	40.0	29.0	21.9	21.9
Indonesia	23.2	25.6	19.2	17.0	18.4	a	x(9)	x(9)	17.5
Israel	m	20.1	12.9	12.7	12.8	m	m	m	m
Jamaica	23.7	33.6	19.4	17.3	19.3	10.6	17.1	11.4	14.6
Malaysia[4]	26.7	18.8	x(5)	x(5)	18.4	12.0	15.1	17.5	16.9
Paraguay[4]	x(2)	18.8	x(5)	x(5)	21.5	a	22.1	m	m
Philippines[4]	30.1	35.2	43.4	22.4	36.4	45.0	x(9)	x(9)	25.9
Russian Federation	7.0	17.3	m	m	m	10.2	14.6	15.3	15.0
Thailand	30.3	20.4	20.6	33.2	25.4	a	24.9	27.9	27.1
Tunisia[2]	m	22.7	13.3	199.1	21.0	8.8	x(9)	x(9)	18.2
Uruguay[4]	28.3	20.8	11.8	21.1	14.6	a	x(9)	x(9)	8.7
Zimbabwe	m	38.1	x(5)	x(5)	31.5	17.6	0.0	0.0	10.8

1. Includes only general programmes in lower and upper secondary education.
2. Public institutions only.
3. Year of reference 1999.
4. Year of reference 2000.
Source: OECD. See Annex 3 for notes *(www.oecd.org/edu/eag2003).*

D2

Table D2.3
Teaching staff and non–teaching staff employed in public and private institutions (2001)
Teaching staff and non-teaching staff in primary and secondary schools per 1 000 students, calculation based on full-time equivalents

| | Instructional personnel | | Professional support for students | Management/Quality Control/ Administration | | Maintenance and operations personnel | TOTAL teaching and non-teaching staff |
	Classroom teachers, academic staff and other teachers	Teacher aides and teaching/research assistants		School and higher level management	School and higher level administrative personnel		
Australia	m	m	m	m	m	m	m
Austria	89.9	m	m	m	m	m	m
Belgium	89.6	m	m	m	m	m	m
Belgium (Fl.)	90.4	a	6.9	m	m	m	97.3
Canada	55.5	0.5	2.0	4.9	4.7	m	67.7
Czech Republic	64.2	0.1	5.9	6.9	19.4	16.4	113.0
Denmark	89.4	m	m	m	m	m	m
Finland	67.4	4.3	2.6	2.3	7.5	15.8	99.9
France	69.3	m	25.0	6.9	3.9	13.8	119.0
Germany	61.4	m	m	m	m	m	m
Greece	91.5	m	m	m	m	m	m
Hungary	86.0	m	m	m	6.2	33.6	125.8
Iceland[1]	82.8	n	8.9	7.4	4.2	23.7	127.0
Ireland	59.5	m	m	2.0	m	m	m
Italy	96.2	3.5	6.3	1.8	9.9	20.4	138.0
Japan	58.1	m	5.0	5.3	4.8	6.4	79.5
Korea	40.1	a	0.8	2.5	2.2	4.4	50.0
Luxembourg	87.6	m	m	m	m	m	m
Mexico	36.9	0.3	1.1	3.4	8.8	3.9	54.4
Netherlands	58.3	m	m	m	m	m	m
New Zealand	57.9	m	m	m	m	m	m
Norway	97.1	m	m	10.9	m	m	m
Poland	71.7	a	3.2	5.5	m	25.4	105.8
Portugal	99.2	m	m	m	m	m	m
Slovak Republic	64.8	m	m	6.3	m	m	m
Spain	80.5	m	m	m	m	m	m
Sweden	74.2	m	m	4.6	m	m	m
Switzerland	m	m	m	m	m	m	m
Turkey	38.2	m	m	m	m	m	m
United Kingdom	52.3	m	m	m	m	m	m
United States	62.1	11.5	6.6	5.1	8.9	21.9	116.2
Country mean	*71.4*	*3.4*	*6.2*	*5.1*	*7.3*	*16.9*	*99.5*

1. Data on higher level management and administrative personnel are missing.
Source: OECD. See Annex 3 for notes (*www.oecd.org/edu/eag2003*).

D₂

INDICATOR D3: TEACHERS' AND STUDENTS' USE OF INFORMATION AND COMMUNICATION TECHNOLOGY IN UPPER SECONDARY EDUCATION

• Among the 14 countries with comparable data represented in this indicator, a typical student in upper secondary education attends schools where there is one computer for every 9 students. This ratio varies widely among countries; from three students per computer in Denmark and Sweden to more than 15 students per computer in Mexico and Spain.

• On average, 63 per cent of students attend schools where principals reported that teachers' lack of knowledge and skills was an obstacle to successful ICT implementation: More than three-quarters of students attend schools where the principal reported this in France and Norway.

• On average, one-third of teachers participated in ICT-related professional development in the school year 2000/2001, compared to one-half of teachers who participated in non-ICT related professional development in the same period.

• From a list of 22 obstacles to the use of ICT in teaching - including obstacles related to computer hardware and infrastructure, computer software, teachers and school and classroom organisation – insufficient number of computers for students to use tended to be reported by the principals of upper secondary students as the *most serious obstacle* to the use of ICT in teaching. A shortage of maintenance and technical support, as well as teachers' lack of knowledge/skills in using computers for instructional purposes were other frequently reported obstacles.

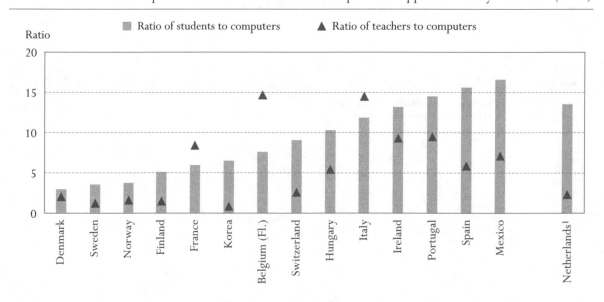

Chart D3.1

Ratio of students to computers and ratio of teachers to computers in upper secondary education (2001)

■ Ratio of students to computers ▲ Ratio of teachers to computers

Countries are ranked in ascending order of the ratio of students to computers.
1. Country did not meet international sampling requirements. The reported data are unweighted.
Source: OECD ISUSS database, 2003. Tables D3.1 and D3.3. See Annex 3 for notes *(www.oecd.org/edu/eag2003)*.

Policy context

OECD economies depend increasingly on technological knowledge and skills in the labour force. Thus, schools have an important role to play in providing students with the necessary skills to succeed in today's competitive technology-based labour market. But the successful integration of information and communications technologies in schooling requires more than investment in hardware and software for schools. Information and communication technology must be incorporated into national policies and school curricula as a tool to achieve educational objectives. Teachers must receive appropriate training to understand how to effectively assimilate computer technology in the teaching and learning process and in their administrative duties. The organisation of instruction time and use of teaching and learning strategies must be sufficiently flexible to allow for the most effective use of ICT in lesson time. Finally, the successful use of information technology in schools demands adequate technical support and a global perspective that encourages information sharing among schools and other educational institutions and organisations.

OECD's International Survey of Upper Secondary Schools (ISUSS) asked school principals about the use of information technology in their schools.

In 2001, OECD conducted the International Survey of Upper Secondary Schools (ISUSS), in which several aspects of the use of information technology by teachers and students in upper secondary education were explored. School principals were asked about the number of computers in their schools; the use of technology for educational purposes and more specifically in students' assignments; the use of computers by teachers; professional development of teachers in computer technology; the nature of ICT-related co-operation among schools and other institutions; and the perceived teacher, software, hardware and organisation-related obstacles to attaining goals involving information technology. (For a description of the survey see Annex 3 on *www.oecd.org/edu/eag2003*.)

Evidence and explanations

Provision of information and communication technology in schools

Availability of computers for students in upper secondary education

The average number of students per computer is often used as a proxy for the extent to which technologies are accessible to students. In ISUSS, principals in upper secondary schools were asked to specify the total number of computers available for all students in their school. A ratio of students to computers was then calculated by dividing the total number of computers available to students in the school by the total number of students enrolled in the school. On average in OECD countries participating in the survey, a typical student in upper secondary education attends schools where there is one computer for every nine students. This ratio varies widely between countries; from three students per computer in Denmark and Sweden to more than 15 students per computer in Mexico and Spain.

A typical student in upper secondary education attends a school where there is one computer for every 9 students, although this ratio varies widely among countries.

D3

It is important to note when interpreting these data that the availability of hardware does not guarantee its use by students and teachers, nor does it indicate how easily the technology can be accessed when needed, either in the classroom or other locations. Nor does the ratio guarantee that the quality of hardware

Although availability does not guarantee the effective use of computers,...

(e.g., compatibility, memory, speed, attached peripheral devices and software) is appropriate for classroom use. Finally, average ratios may hide variation between schools due to such factors as the geographical or socio-economic location of the school and the type of educational institution (Table D3.1).

…network technologies have considerably improved accessibility of electronic information over the past 5 years.

While in many countries the use of computers in schools is by no means a recent phenomenon, the World Wide Web and e-mail have only been introduced in most schools over the last five years. In the International Survey of Upper Secondary Schools, school principals were asked in which year technologies such as word processing and spreadsheet applications, the World Wide Web and e-mail were first used in the school for educational purposes. By 1985, over 19 per cent of upper secondary students in the Flemish Community of Belgium, Denmark, Finland and Switzerland attended schools where word processing and spreadsheet applications were used for educational purposes. By 2000, all students in upper secondary education in Finland, France, Hungary, Ireland, and Norway attended schools where this software was in use. Between 1995 and 2000, use of word processing and spreadsheet packages increased by 20 percentage points or more in Hungary, Italy, Mexico and Spain; and by almost 50 percentage points in Korea. By contrast, in 1995 an average of 24 per cent of students attended schools which were using the Internet and only 13 per cent of students attended schools which had an e-mail system available for teachers and students. However, by 2000 on average, 4 out of 5 upper secondary students attended schools where the Internet and intranet were in use (Table D3.1 and Chart D3.2).

Software and hardware-related obstacles to the use of information and communication technology in teaching

On average for all countries, lack of computers for students' use was perceived by school principals as the most serious obstacle to the use of ICT in teaching in their schools.

School principals were also asked to report the *most serious* obstacle to the use of ICT in teaching from a list of 22 potential obstacles concerning computer hardware and infrastructure, computer software, teachers and organisation. On average, of all the obstacles listed, insufficient numbers of computers for students' use was perceived by school principals as the *most serious* obstacle to the use of ICT in teaching. The principals of more than 20 per cent of upper secondary students in Mexico, Portugal and Spain reported this as the *most serious* obstacle. Mexico has the highest ratio of students to computers, while Denmark and Sweden have the lowest ratio, so these results must be interpreted within the context of the ICT policies and expectations in each school and country. Outdated computers were also reported to be the *most serious* obstacle to the use of ICT by many principals, particularly in Hungary, Mexico, Spain and Sweden, where the principals of 10 per cent of students reported this. Shortage of maintenance and technical support was perceived as *the most serious obstacle* to the use of ICT in teaching by the principals of more than 25 per cent of students in the Flemish Community of Belgium and France but less than five per cent in Hungary, Italy, Mexico and Norway (Table D3.2).

Other hardware and infrastructure-related obstacles, such as the lack of Internet connection, lack of space to store computers and weak infrastructure

D3

Introduction of information and communication technology (ICT) in schools (1980-2000)
Percentage of upper secondary students attending schools where computer applications, the Internet and E-mail were introduced by 1980, 1985, 1990, 1995 and 2000

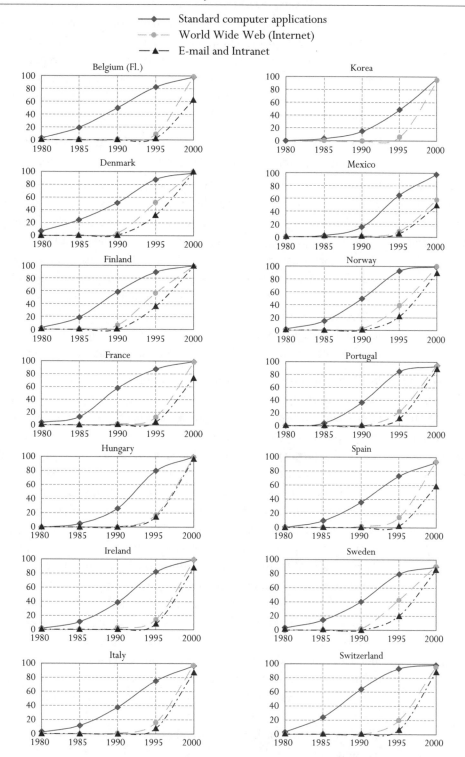

Note: The Netherlands did not meet international sampling requirements and is therefore excluded from this chart.
Source: OECD ISUSS database, 2003. Table D3.1. See Annex 3 for notes *(www.oecd.org/edu/eag2003).*

D3

(*i.e.*, electricity, telecommunications), were not perceived by school principals as serious threats to using ICT in the classroom (Table D3.2).

While quality and quantity of hardware were reported by many school principals as posing *the most serious* threat to the integration of ICT into teaching and learning, few school principals reported software-related issues as *the most serious* obstacle to using computers in the classroom. However, 10 per cent of students in Korea attend schools where the principal reported insufficient number of copies of software for instructional purposes as *the most serious* obstacle; and 12 per cent where the principal indicated that the lack of variety of software was a problem (Table D3.2).

Teachers and information and communications technologies

Availability of computers for teachers in upper secondary education

In three-quarters of countries, teachers have better access to computers than students.

Computers are an important tool for both teachers and school administrators, who use computers to complete everyday tasks such as updating student records, writing letters to parents and committees, completing electronic student assessment, preparing lessons and updating school and class Web sites. Thus, information and communications technologies can improve the quality and effectiveness of teachers' work, and can also be used to achieve effective learning outcomes. In order to achieve these objectives, schools need to invest in hardware, software and training resources to equip teachers to effectively use ICT in their daily work. Despite these efforts, some teachers may find it difficult to adapt these new technologies to their working and teaching methods.

In Denmark, Finland, Korea, Norway and Sweden, there are two teachers or less for every computer and more than 49 per cent of teachers use computer applications and the Internet for educational purposes.

In ISUSS, school principals in upper secondary schools were asked the total number of computers available only for teachers' use in their school. A ratio of teachers to computers was then calculated by dividing the total number of computers available only to teachers in the school by the total number of full-time equivalent teachers in the school. Chart D3.1 shows that in three-quarters of countries, teachers have better access to computers than students. In Denmark, Finland, Korea, Norway and Sweden, two teachers or less share a computer, although these countries also have small ratios of students to computers. School principals were also asked to report the percentage of teachers in upper secondary education who use computer applications, the World Wide Web and e-mail for educational purposes at least once a month. In the same five countries, school principals reported that more than 49 per cent of teachers use computer applications and the Internet for educational purposes. This indicates that teachers in these countries are using the ICT resources at their disposal (Table D3.3). In contrast, in Ireland and Mexico, less than one-third of teachers use computer applications, one-quarter or less use the Internet, and 13 per cent or less use e-mail for educational purposes at least once a month. In these countries, more than 10 per cent of students attend schools where school principals also reported that insufficient numbers of computers for teachers' use was the *most serious* obstacle to the use of ICT in teaching (Table D3.2).

D3

Teachers' professional development in ICT

Making teachers comfortable with using ICT and encouraging them to integrate ICT into their lesson plans is a key objective of providing professional development to teachers. Well-planned, ongoing professional development that is linked to the school's curriculum goals is essential if teachers are to use technology appropriately to promote learning for all students in the classroom. In ISUSS, school principals were asked the percentage of teachers in upper secondary education who participated in ICT-related professional development in the school year 2000/2001. On average, one-third of teachers participated in ICT-related professional development, compared to one-half of teachers who were reported to have participated in non-ICT related professional development. In Denmark, Finland and Norway, more than 40 per cent of teachers participated in ICT-related professional development, while participation of teachers in non-ICT related professional development was more than 56 per cent in these countries (Table D4.3).

Although one-third of teachers participated in ICT-related professional development in the school year 2000/2001…

School principals were also asked to report whether the lack of training opportunities for teachers was an obstacle to reaching the school's information technology-related goals. On average, 40 per cent of students in upper secondary education attended schools where school principals reported that insufficient training opportunities for teachers were an obstacle to attaining ICT-related goals. In Ireland, Norway and Spain, this figure was more than 55 per cent. Although insufficient opportunities for professional development was reported to hinder the use of ICT in teaching, few school principals reported that this was the *most serious* obstacle to the use of ICT in teaching (Table D3.2 and D3.3).

School principals also reported on other teacher-related obstacles to ICT implementation. On average, 63 per cent of students attended schools where principals reported that teachers' lack of knowledge and skills was an obstacle to successful ICT implementation; three-quarters of students did in France and Norway (Chart D3.3 and Table D3.3). Teachers' lack of knowledge and skills in using computers for instructional purposes was reported as the *most serious* obstacle to using ICT in teaching by the principals of an average of 10 per cent of upper secondary students (Table D3.2).

…63 per cent of students attended schools where principals reported that teachers' lack of knowledge and skills was an obstacle to successful ICT implementation,…

Only 37 per cent of students attended schools where principals reported that teachers' lack of willingness to use a computer was an obstacle to reaching the schools' ICT-related goals. These results indicate that while schools have made provision for professional development of teachers in ICT and many teachers are willing and able to use these resources, more support is required to ensure that teachers are fully equipped to use modern technology in their professional activities (Table D3.3 and Chart 3.3).

…and 37 per cent attended schools where principals thought teachers were not willing to use computers.

D3

Integrating computers into classroom teaching

Information and communication technology can be used to facilitate a broad range of teaching and learning methodologies. They can be used in both independent and group learning situations, allow students to work at their own individual pace, develop students' research and analytical skills, and provide

In many schools, computers are mainly used for educational purposes by obtaining information from the Internet...

additional opportunities for learning by simulation. Teachers can also integrate computer-related activities into students' homework.

In ISUSS, school principals were asked the extent to which computers are used for various educational purposes. On average among countries, more than two-thirds of students attend schools where computers are used "a lot" to obtain information from the Internet, but only one third attend schools where computers are used to promote independent learning and only one student in five or less attends schools where computers are used to provide additional instruction or practicing opportunities, or to enhance synergy between different study areas. Notably, however, in the Nordic countries, where higher percentages of teachers participate in professional development than elsewhere (both in ICT related and in other professional development activities), computers are used more regularly for purposes other than just gathering information from the Internet: The main purposes reported are to develop skills of independent learning (39, 42 and 58 per cent in Denmark, Norway and Sweden respectively), and to provide additional instruction and practice (52 and 49 per cent in Norway and Sweden respectively).

Chart D3.3

Teacher-related obstacles to reaching ICT goals in upper secondary education (2001)
Percentage of upper secondary students whose principals reported certain teacher-related obstacles to reaching the school's ICT-related goals

■ Percentage of teachers using computer applications (first axis)
■ Insufficient time for teachers to prepare lessons in which computers are used (second axis)
◆ Lack of interest/willingness of teachers to use computers (second axis)
▲ Teachers' lack of knowledge/skills in using computers for instructional purposes (second axis)

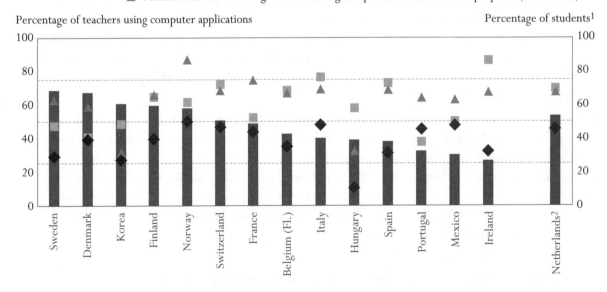

D3

Countries are ranked in descending order of the percentage of teachers using computer applications as reported by the principal.
1. Percentage of students attending schools with various teacher-related obstacles to ICT development.
2. Country did not meet international sampling requirements. The reported data are unweighted.
Source: OECD ISUSS database, 2003. Tables D3.2 and D3.3. See Annex 3 for notes *(www.oecd.org/edu/eag2003).*

On average, between 52 and 61 per cent of students attend schools where computers are used "a little" to support independent learning, to promote learning by simulation, to provide additional instructional opportunities and to combine school subjects. The frequency of these responses calls attention to the fact that in spite of large investments in computer technology in schools, less progress has been achieved to integrate this into instruction and education. The popularity of Internet use in schools indicates that computers are most easily used as 'mass media'. Compared to more labour intensive uses, surfing on the Internet is interesting and self rewarding. There is limited evidence on the extent to which this contributes to knowledge acquisition. No doubt, some students can find a way to learn faster with the Internet and they should be given the opportunity to do so. In Mexico, 41 per cent of students attend schools where principals report that computers are used a lot to allow students to learn/work at their own pace during lessons. However, time and effort has to be spent on more intensive uses of computers if they are to be worth the investment (Table D3.4).

Inflexible organisation of classrooms and instruction time can be an obstacle to the effective implementation of ICT-related goals in schools. Of the 22 obstacles to the use of information and communication technology in teaching listed in Table D3.2, more than 10 per cent of students attend schools in Finland, Hungary, and Switzerland where school principals reported that insufficient time for teachers to prepare lessons in which computers are used was the *most serious* obstacle to the use of information and communication technology in

…but school principals reported that not enough time is allowed for teachers to prepare lessons in which computers are used and to integrate computers in classroom instruction.

Chart D3.4

Use of computers to reach different educational goals in upper secondary education (2001)

Distribution of means for upper secondary students attending schools where principals reported that computers are used a lot to reach various educational goals, by country

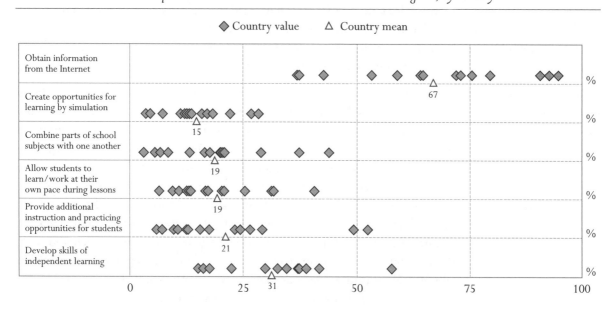

D3

Source: OECD ISUSS database, 2003. Table D3.4. See Annex 3 for notes *(www.oecd.org/edu/eag2003)*.

EDUCATION AT A GLANCE © OECD 2003

339 ■

teaching. The principals of more than 10 per cent of students in Italy and Sweden reported that difficulties integrating computers into classroom instruction was the *most serious* obstacle. Few school principals reported scheduling problems in computer and Internet time between classes as the *most serious* obstacle (Table D3.2).

Increasingly, students are using computers to help them to complete their schoolwork. Results in ISUSS indicate that students are regularly using computers as a word processing and as a research tool to complete their school assignments. School principals were asked if certain computer-related activities comprised a regular part of students' assignments in upper secondary education. In all countries, more than 85 per cent of students attend schools where operating a computer (saving files, printing, etc.) and writing documents with a word processor form a regular part of their assignments. On average, more than three-quarters of students attend schools where using spreadsheet programmes and sending, searching for and using electronic forms of communication are regularly used in students' assignments. Other activities such as making illustrations with graphics programmes, writing programmes, communicating via e-mail with teachers and other students, and using educational software are used less frequently (Table D3.5). It should be noted, however, that 'regular part of students' assignments' was defined quite liberally by setting 'at least once a month' as a criterion. It is very likely, that a criterion of 'at least once a week' would have yielded different results.

Co-operation in the development of information and communication technology

Co-operation among various stakeholders in technological development in schools is vital to ensure efficiency and cost effectiveness.

The provision of technical support from both inside and outside the school is vital to ensure the successful functioning of computer hardware and software systems in schools. Technical problems must be addressed as soon as they arise to avoid disruption of lessons; new hardware and software must be purchased, installed and maintained on a regular basis; and advice on instructional materials, information exchange, teacher training courses and software and hardware must be sought from specialists and institutions inside or outside the school.

Many schools are more likely to share knowledge and information on ICT with other educational institutions, rather than with private companies or public organisations.

Results from ISUSS show that in most countries, schools are more likely to share knowledge and information on ICT development with other educational institutions, rather than seek the advice of private companies or other stakeholders. In ISUSS, school principals were asked whether schools co-operate with educational institutions, private companies or other organisations like school authorities, ministries, municipal libraries, etc. in matters of purchasing, exchanging software, hardware and electronic learning material, professional development and the development of learning materials, maintenance or delivery of instruction related to computer technology. In most countries, school principals reported most co-operation with other educational institutions on issues such as ICT-related joint education experience through ICT (*e.g.,* communication and exchange of information, joint research projects) and professional development. More than 50 per cent of students

D3

in Denmark, Finland, Korea and Norway attend schools where principals reported co-operation with other educational institutions through sharing educational experience; and more than 70 per cent of students attended schools in Denmark and Sweden where principals reported co-operation with other educational institutions on ICT-related professional development of teachers. In most countries, particularly Hungary, schools are more likely to co-operate with private companies in more specialised matters of development of software, computer networks, learning environments and learning materials (Table D3.6).

The major obstacles to developing the use of information and communication technology in upper secondary schools

School principals were asked to report the three most serious obstacles to reaching the school's goals related to information and communication technology development. Earlier in this indicator, percentages of students were reported who attend schools where one of a list of 22 potential obstacles were reported as the most serious obstacle to development of the school's ICT-related goals (Table D3.2). To calculate the seriousness of each obstacle in a country, a weight of 3, 2, and 1 was assigned to the obstacles mentioned as the most serious, the second most serious and the third most serious obstacle. Chart D3.5 summarises the obstacles weighted by seriousness in each country.

The overall picture among countries shows that only nine out of 22 problems appear in the international list of most serious problems. Insufficient number of student computers has the highest score of being a problem even in the countries where computers are used in the most versatile way (or just because it is so).

Insufficient student access to computers still appears to be the most serious obstacle to the integration of ICT...

The second most serious problem seems to be teachers' lack of knowledge and skills in using computers in instruction. The policy implications of this finding are not simple and straightforward. Should countries develop teachers' ICT skills and their skills in using ICT in the classroom? Or is it more important to deploy school computers in the system 'en masse'? Should countries rely upon the Internet for educational software since that is what is most used? Or should they develop co-operation in educational software development to provide material for schools at an acceptable price? What kind of professional development and what blend of development activities and investments into computers and computer-related educational resources would ensure the most cost-effective ways of improving the e-learning environment?

...followed by teachers' lack of knowledge and skills in using computers in instruction.

D3

The data on hindering factors (Table D3.2 and Chart D3.5), on the timeline of introducing ICT (Table D3.1) and the variety of use of computers in different countries (Table D3.4) indicate that the integration of new technology and a new technological environment in schools requires both a generally higher level of expenditure on quickly outdating equipment, educational material and skills of using them and innovative approaches to organising teaching and learning in schools.

Chart D3.5

Most serious obstacles to using ICT in teaching in upper secondary education (2001)
Country level 'problem score' of perceived obstacles to reaching computer-related goals based on responses of principals

■ The most serious obstacle
◆ The second most serious obstacle
▲ The third most serious obstacle

	Ratio of students to computers	Ratio of teachers to computers	Hardware and software-related obstacles					Teacher-related obstacles			
			Insufficient number of computers for teachers	Insufficient number of computers for students	Outdated (older than 3 years) computers	Not enough variety of software	Shortage of maintenance and technical support	Insufficient time for teachers to prepare lessons	Difficulties to integrate computers into classroom instruction	Lack of interest/ willingness of teachers to use computers	Teachers' lack of knowledge/ skills in using computers in instruction
Belgium (Fl.)	7.5	14.7					■		▲		◆
Denmark	2.8	2.1	▲	■							◆
Finland	5.0	1.6		▲				◆			■
France	5.8	8.5		▲			■				◆
Hungary	10.2	5.5	▲		◆			■			
Ireland	13.1	9.4		■			◆				▲
Italy	11.7	14.6		◆					■	▲	
Korea	6.4	0.8			■	◆	▲				
Mexico	16.5	7.2	▲	■	◆						
Norway	3.7	1.7	◆	▲							■
Portugal	14.4	9.6	▲	■							◆
Spain	15.5	5.9		■	▲					◆	
Sweden	3.4	1.3		■	▲						◆
Switzerland	9.0	3.2		▲				■			◆
Netherlands[1]	13.5	2.3						◆		■	▲

1. Country did not meet international sampling requirements. The reported data are unweighted.
Source: OECD ISUSS database, 2003. See Annex 3 for notes *(www.oecd.org/edu/eag2003).*

Data on use of ICT in schools derive from the OECD's International Survey of Upper Secondary Schools (ISUSS) in 2001.

Definitions and methodologies

Data in this indicator are drawn from the OECD's International Survey of Upper Secondary Schools (ISUSS), a study of mainstream upper secondary education implemented in 4 400 schools of 15 countries in the school year 2001/2002. For more detail see Annex 3 at *www.oecd.org/edu/eag2003.*

Computer includes computers capable of supporting other multimedia equipment such as a CDROM or a sound card and which are used for educational purposes in the school. Computers used only for recreation purposes are excluded.

Information and communication technology (ICT) represents the set of activities and technologies that involve the electronic display, processing and storage of information and communication technology. Global industry, international media and academics increasingly now use ICT to describe this set.

ICT is characterized by unprecedented global flows in information, products, people, capital and ideas.

Educational purpose means the use of computers in planning, organising and evaluating student learning, and the use of computers as a teaching and learning tool by, for example, retrieving demonstration material from the Internet, editing information, preparing documentation material, preparing tasks and tests, correcting student work, etc.

Most serious obstacle to reaching a school's goals related to information and communication technology is the obstacle that principals ranked as first from the three most serious obstacles they were asked about in the ISUSS questionnaire.

Data for Chart D3.5 were calculated from the mean 'difficulty' score of the various obstacles in each country. In the questionnaire, principals were asked to name the three most serious problems they see as obstacles to reaching goals of development of information and communication technology in their school. These responses were weighted by the order of difficulty, *i.e.* they were assigned a value of 3, 2, and 1 to the obstacles named as the most serious obstacles, the second more serious obstacle and the third most serious obstacle, respectively. These school level difficulty scores for each item were aggregated on the country level weighted by the enrolment of upper secondary students. The obstacles having the largest, second largest and third largest aggregate value in the country are shown in Table D3.5.

D3

Table D3.1

Introduction of basic computer applications in upper secondary education (1980–2000)

Cumulative percentages of upper secondary students attending schools where the following information technologies were introduced, by year and total number of upper secondary students enrolled in the school divided by the total number of computers available for all students in the school

	Percentage of upper secondary students attending schools where standard word processing and spreadsheet applications were introduced by...					Percentage of upper secondary students attending schools where the Internet was introduced by...					Percentage of upper secondary students attending schools where an e-mail system accessible for teachers and students was introduced by...					Ratio of students to computers
	1980	1985	1990	1995	2000	1980	1985	1990	1995	2000	1980	1985	1990	1995	2000	
Belgium (Fl.)	3	20	50	83	98	n	n	n	9	99	n	n	n	3	62	8
Denmark	7	25	52	88	98	1	1	4	52	100	n	1	1	32	99	3
Finland	2	19	59	90	100	n	1	6	57	99	n	n	n	36	98	5
France	4	13	58	88	100	n	n	2	12	98	n	n	n	4	73	6
Hungary	n	5	26	80	100	n	n	1	18	100	n	n	n	14	97	10
Ireland	2	11	39	82	100	n	n	2	14	98	n	1	1	8	88	13
Italy	3	12	38	75	97	n	n	1	16	99	n	n	n	8	87	12
Korea	1	4	15	49	97	n	n	n	7	94	n	n	n	6	91	6
Mexico	n	2	15	65	98	n	n	1	9	58	n	n	n	5	49	17
Norway	2	15	49	93	100	n	n	2	39	100	n	n	n	22	90	4
Portugal	n	4	37	85	94	n	n	n	22	95	n	n	n	11	89	14
Spain	n	10	36	73	93	n	n	2	14	94	n	n	n	2	59	16
Sweden	3	14	40	80	90	n	n	2	43	91	n	n	n	20	85	3
Switzerland	3	25	64	93	99	n	n	n	20	96	n	n	n	6	88	9
Country mean	*2*	*13*	*41*	*80*	*97*	*n*	*n*	*2*	*24*	*94*	*n*	*n*	*n*	*13*	*83*	*9*
Netherlands [1]	2	12	40	65	100	n	n	n	15	95	n	n	n	n	60	13

1. Country did not meet international sampling requirements. The reported data are unweighted.

Source: OECD ISUSS database, 2003. See Annex 3 for notes (*www.oecd.org/edu/eag2003*).

Table D3.2

Most serious obstacle to using ICT in teaching in upper secondary education (2001)

Percentage of upper secondary students attending schools where the principal reported that the most serious obstacle to the use of ICT in teaching is one of the following

	Hardware and infrastructure-related obstacles						Software-related obstacles			Teacher-related obstacles							Organisation/planning-related obstacles (school-related obstacles)					Other
	Insufficient number of computers for teachers' use	Insufficient number of computers for students' use	Outdated (older than 3 years) computers	Internet connection is not available	Not enough space to locate computers appropriately	Weak infrastructure (telecommunications, electricity)	Not enough copies of software for instructional purposes	Not enough variety (types) of software	Poor quality of available software	Insufficient time for teachers to prepare lessons in which computers are used	Difficult to integrate computers into classroom instruction	Difficult to use with low achieving students	No time in teachers' schedule to explore opportunities for using the Internet	Lack of interest/willingness of teachers to use computers	Teachers' lack of knowledge/skills in using computers for instructional purposes	Not enough training opportunities for teachers	Problems in scheduling enough computer time for different classes	No time in the school schedule for using the Internet	Insufficient plans and/or resources to prevent theft and vandalism of computers	Not enough staff to supervise students using computers	Shortage of maintenance and technical support	Lack of support from the governing body or community
Belgium (Fl.)	8	9	8	n	4	2	2	1	1	4	9	n	1	8	6	n	3	n	n	2	28	4
Denmark	13	18	3	3	5	n	1	7	1	4	3	n	1	3	18	1	5	1	1	3	10	n
Finland	8	10	6	n	6	n	n	2	2	11	4	n	1	12	14	4	5	n	n	3	8	3
France	7	11	4	n	3	4	2	n	n	2	5	n	2	8	10	1	2	1	n	5	30	1
Hungary	13	9	14	n	4	7	6	2	n	14	8	1	2	1	3	1	3	n	n	2	2	6
Ireland	11	19	7	n	4	1	n	n	n	4	6	n	4	4	9	4	6	3	n	1	16	n
Italy	12	14	7	n	8	2	2	1	1	7	11	n	3	14	8	1	n	3	n	2	3	1
Korea	1	10	m	n	3	n	10	12	1	7	6	1	1	5	3	2	2	1	3	1	9	n
Mexico	13	38	11	2	5	2	2	3	n	1	5	1	2	5	4	n	1	n	1	1	n	4
Norway	17	16	5	1	4	3	n	1	1	2	8	n	3	7	15	4	4	n	n	2	4	2
Portugal	14	24	5	1	3	4	3	4	n	2	7	n	1	6	14	n	1	1	n	5	5	2
Spain	8	28	10	1	4	4	1	1	1	5	9	1	2	4	10	1	2	n	1	1	5	n
Sweden	8	18	11	n	5	1	5	n	1	5	11	n	1	4	12	n	7	1	n	3	9	4
Switzerland	6	13	1	1	4	1	1	n	n	18	5	1	5	7	10	3	8	1	n	2	13	1
Country mean	*10*	*17*	*8*	*1*	*4*	*2*	*2*	*3*	*1*	*6*	*7*	*n*	*2*	*6*	*10*	*2*	*3*	*1*	*n*	*2*	*10*	*2*
Netherlands[1]	5	11	3	n	1	4	2	3	1	20	4	n	1	10	17	1	2	n	1	3	10	2

1. Country did not meet international sampling requirements. The reported data are unweighted.

Source: OECD ISUSS database, 2003. See Annex 3 for notes (*www.oecd.org/edu/eag2003*).

Table D3.3

Teachers' access to information and communication technology in upper secondary education, as reported by school principals (2001)

Ratio of full-time equivalent teachers to computers available only to teachers, percentage of teachers using computer applications, the Internet and e-mail for educational purposes at least once per month, percentage of upper secondary students whose principals reported teacher-related obstacles to reaching the school's ICT-related goals, and percentage of teachers who participated in ICT-related professional development activities in the school year 2000/2001, as reported by school principals

	Availability of computers to teachers	Use of computers by teachers for educational purposes at least once per month [1]			Percentage of upper secondary students whose principals reported the following teacher-related obstacles to reaching the school's information technology-related goals:							Percentage of teachers who participated in ICT-related professional development activities [1]
	Ratio of teachers to computers [1]	Percentage of teachers using computer applications	Percentage of teachers using the Internet	Percentage of teachers using e-mail system	Insufficient time for teachers to prepare lessons in which computers are used	Difficult to integrate computers into classroom instruction	Difficult to use with low achieving students	No time in teachers' schedule to explore opportunities for using the Internet	Lack of interest/willingness of teachers to use computers	Teachers' lack of knowledge/skills in using computers for instructional purposes	Not enough training opportunities for teachers	
OECD COUNTRIES												
Belgium (Fl.)	15	42	33	14	69	76	22	41	35	67	25	30
Denmark	2	67	63	33	41	48	26	29	39	59	38	52
Finland	2	59	56	33	65	74	27	35	39	66	31	43
France	9	49	34	13	52	62	26	40	44	75	44	20
Hungary	5	39	32	15	58	61	23	36	10	33	14	19
Ireland	9	26	24	12	87	93	20	83	32	67	63	28
Italy	15	40	28	12	76	80	28	71	48	69	47	23
Korea	1	60	77	41	49	25	14	9	27	32	25	35
Mexico	7	30	21	13	50	62	47	65	48	63	42	31
Norway	2	58	49	16	61	87	9	29	50	87	55	44
Portugal	10	32	29	14	38	66	43	47	45	64	36	26
Spain	6	38	30	11	73	81	44	69	31	69	56	29
Sweden	1	68	62	43	48	70	14	29	29	63	41	37
Switzerland	3	51	44	29	72	57	32	61	46	68	39	28
Country mean	*6*	*47*	*42*	*21*	*60*	*67*	*27*	*46*	*37*	*63*	*40*	*32*
Netherlands [2]	2	53	50	20	74	70	15	38	46	68	19	45

1. Weighted by upper secondary enrolments.
2. Country did not meet international sampling requirements. The reported data are unweighted.
Source: OECD ISUSS database, 2003. See Annex 3 for notes (*www.oecd.org/edu/eag2003*).

D3

Table D3.4
Use of computers to reach different educational goals in upper secondary education (2001)
Percentage of upper secondary students attending schools where principals reported the use of computers to reach various educational goals

	Develop skills of independent learning			Provide additional instruction and practicing opportunities for students			Allow students to learn/work at their own pace during lessons			Combine parts of school subjects with one another			Create opportunities for learning by simulation			Obtain information from the Internet		
	Not at all	A little	A lot	Not at all	A little	A lot	Not at all	A little	A lot	Not at all	A little	A lot	Not at all	A little	A lot	Not at all	A little	A lot
Belgium (Fl.)	11	71	18	16	69	15	23	64	13	36	59	6	51	42	7	3	33	64
Denmark	4	57	39	7	70	23	3	66	32	3	53	44	6	72	22	n	7	93
Finland	1	76	22	12	76	13	19	71	9	27	66	7	49	47	4	1	24	75
France	4	61	35	35	59	6	33	55	13	22	57	21	32	52	16	2	34	65
Hungary	16	66	18	80	13	7	41	42	17	28	52	21	29	44	27	4	23	73
Ireland	11	74	15	19	57	24	44	50	6	42	55	3	61	35	4	4	54	43
Italy	5	58	37	14	57	29	31	52	17	12	51	37	23	49	28	7	40	53
Korea	5	58	37	64	25	11	11	58	31	16	68	17	22	61	17	2	18	80
Mexico	13	50	37	27	46	26	17	42	41	21	50	29	51	37	11	39	23	37
Norway	1	57	42	2	45	52	4	76	20	11	69	20	23	64	14	1	5	95
Portugal	8	62	30	18	65	18	25	54	21	23	64	13	28	54	18	8	33	59
Spain	25	59	16	48	43	10	51	38	11	54	38	8	49	38	13	12	51	37
Sweden	3	40	58	2	49	49	9	66	25	8	72	20	17	70	13	3	6	91
Switzerland	7	61	33	18	70	12	18	68	13	12	70	18	30	57	12	5	23	72
Country mean	*8*	*61*	*31*	*26*	*53*	*21*	*23*	*57*	*19*	*22*	*59*	*19*	*34*	*52*	*15*	*6*	*27*	*67*
Netherlands [1]	14	53	33	12	76	12	22	58	19	44	47	9	20	53	26	1	16	83

1. Country did not meet international sampling requirements. The reported data are unweighted.
Source: OECD ISUSS database, 2003. See Annex 3 for notes (*www.oecd.org/edu/eag2003*).

Table D3.5
Computer-related activities in upper secondary education (2001)
Percentage of upper secondary students attending schools where various computer-related activities form a regular part of students' assignments at least once a month

	Operating a computer (saving files, printing, etc.)	Writing documents with a word processor	Making illustrations with graphical programmes	Calculating with spreadsheets programmes	Writing programmes	Communicating via e-mail with teachers and other students	Sending, searching for and using electronic forms of information	Using educational software (e.g., taking tests, exercises)
Belgium (Fl.)	99	95	42	75	27	38	85	60
Denmark	99	99	68	88	14	74	96	70
Finland	97	96	64	61	19	79	96	63
France	94	91	58	88	13	44	86	71
Hungary	97	96	70	86	44	53	92	85
Ireland	87	87	66	62	13	34	67	49
Italy	90	89	56	78	47	39	68	81
Korea	90	92	46	68	14	86	91	74
Mexico	93	93	84	84	60	44	49	74
Norway	99	99	66	82	21	67	88	66
Portugal	94	94	82	81	38	48	75	76
Spain	86	87	60	60	18	23	61	46
Sweden	96	97	61	73	30	87	91	67
Switzerland	93	91	57	70	14	52	82	60
Country mean	*94*	*93*	*63*	*75*	*27*	*55*	*80*	*67*
Netherlands [1]	99	99	39	63	9	48	82	87

1. Country did not meet international sampling requirements. The reported data are unweighted.
Source: OECD ISUSS database, 2003. See Annex 3 for notes (*www.oecd.org/edu/eag2003*).

EDUCATION AT A GLANCE © OECD 2003

Table D3.6
Schools' co-operation with other organisations in ICT in upper secondary education (2001)
Percentage of upper secondary students attending schools where principals reported co-operation with various types of organisations

	Other educational institutions in…						Private companies in …						Other organisations in…					
OECD COUNTRIES	Donation, exchange and/or joint purchase of ICT-related items	Joint educational experience through ICT (e.g., communication and exchange of information, joint research projects)	Professional development with regard to ICT	Development of software, computer networks, learning environments, learning materials	Joint computer network and/or joint system/network maintenance	Delivery of instruction (e.g., on-line courses)	Donation, exchange and/or joint purchase of ICT-related items	Joint educational experience through ICT (e.g., communication and exchange of information, joint research projects)	Professional development with regard to ICT	Development of software, computer networks, learning environments, learning materials	Joint computer network and/or joint system/network maintenance	Delivery of instruction (e.g., on-line courses)	Donation, exchange and/or joint purchase of ICT-related items	Joint educational experience through ICT (e.g., communication and exchange of information, joint research projects)	Professional development with regard to ICT	Development of software, computer networks, learning environments, learning materials	Joint computer network and/or joint system/network maintenance	Delivery of instruction (e.g., on-line courses)
Belgium (Fl.)	26	39	31	26	22	12	13	5	8	9	12	1	21	13	23	13	7	9
Denmark	43	71	71	55	42	36	15	1	7	14	8	6	16	14	24	14	27	12
Finland	43	60	48	54	58	37	8	5	13	9	4	3	15	10	16	18	21	5
France	32	48	59	36	50	17	9	4	4	7	5	1	10	3	7	4	5	2
Hungary	23	42	43	25	11	10	21	7	15	24	6	3	24	19	33	37	12	8
Ireland	8	25	43	17	6	8	16	3	5	7	9	2	4	5	14	8	4	3
Italy	16	49	22	32	12	31	8	9	11	6	4	4	5	9	11	8	6	18
Korea	58	54	48	53	42	43	9	6	4	5	29	6	6	9	12	13	11	11
Mexico	18	23	21	17	14	19	6	3	3	3	7	2	7	3	5	3	2	4
Norway	37	56	59	43	54	31	12	3	8	10	4	9	14	15	20	15	24	8
Portugal	18	44	27	22	7	9	12	4	14	14	17	0	16	14	11	15	5	1
Spain	26	36	43	28	21	23	9	4	6	7	10	4	9	6	8	6	2	5
Sweden	24	48	72	32	33	28	10	5	5	12	7	7	14	10	19	11	31	5
Switzerland	28	38	48	33	29	15	10	3	6	11	10	2	9	5	14	14	12	3
Country mean	*29*	*45*	*45*	*34*	*29*	*23*	*11*	*4*	*8*	*10*	*9*	*4*	*12*	*10*	*16*	*13*	*12*	*7*
Netherlands [1]	40	63	62	50	34	23	13	6	6	14	1	1	6	9	12	13	5	1

1. Country did not meet international sampling requirements. The reported data are unweighted.
Source: OECD ISUSS database, 2003. See Annex 3 for notes (*www.oecd.org/edu/eag2003*).

D3

INDICATOR D4: TEACHER TRAINING AND PROFESSIONAL DEVELOPMENT OF TEACHERS

- All OECD countries now require a tertiary-type A or tertiary-type B qualification (ISCED 5A or 5B) in order to enter the teaching profession at the primary level and beyond.

- The duration of pre-service training for primary teachers varies from three years in Austria, the Flemish and French Communities of Belgium, Iceland, Ireland, New Zealand and Spain to five years or more in Finland, France and Germany.

- For lower secondary education, the duration of pre-service training is higher than for primary education in slightly more than half of the countries.

Chart D4.1

Level of teacher participation in professional development activities (2000/2001)
Percentage of teachers in upper secondary education who have participated in professional development activities

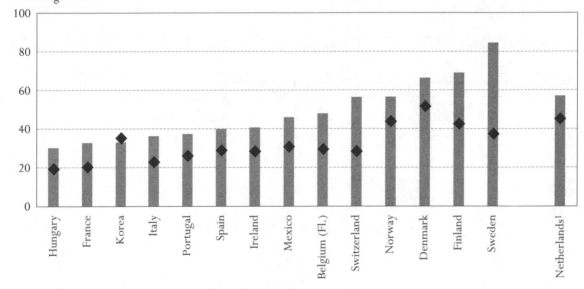

■ Professional development activities (other than ICT-related)   ◆ ICT-related professional development activities

Countries are ranked in ascending order of the percentage of upper secondary students whose principals reported that at least one teacher participated in ICT-related (or non-ICT-related) professional development activities during the school year 2000/2001.
Note: Data are weighted by upper secondary student enrolments.
1. Country did not meet international sampling requirements. The reported data are unweighted.
Source: OECD ISUSS database, 2003. Table D4.3.

D4

Policy context

Increasing expectations of schools and teachers, with in addition the current development of knowledge-based societies and economies, require a highly skilled teacher workforce. Ensuring a sufficient number of skilled teachers to educate all children is therefore an important policy concern for all OECD countries.

This indicator shows the current subject matter and qualifications for teachers in public education.

Although a wide range of external factors influence teaching effectiveness, both initial and continuing professional development of individual teachers are linked to their ability to provide quality instruction. Opportunities for professional development can help existing classroom teachers to maintain or improve their teaching skills.

This indicator focuses on the qualification requirements for new teachers for pre-primary, primary, lower secondary and upper secondary education (general programmes) in the public sector. It examines the type of educational qualifications (*e.g.* ISCED 3, 5B, 5A), the number of full-time equivalent years of pre-service teacher training, and alternative study paths to become a teacher. Where available, the percentage of the current stock of teachers with the required qualification level is also provided.

Evidence and explanations

Pre-service teacher training

For primary education and beyond, a tertiary qualification is required for entry to the teaching profession in all OECD countries for which data are available. In Austria and Belgium (both Flemish and French Communities), a tertiary-type B qualification is sufficient for entry to the profession in primary education, while in Japan, Korea and Portugal both tertiary-type A and tertiary-type B qualification are possible. In lower secondary education, a tertiary-type B qualification is sufficient in Belgium (and Austria for one programme), while both tertiary type-A and tertiary-type B qualification are accepted in Japan. In the other OECD countries a tertiary-type A qualification is required in lower secondary education. At the upper secondary level (general programmes) almost all OECD countries require a tertiary-type A qualification. The only exception at this level is the Flemish Community of Belgium where both tertiary-type A and B qualifications are possible to enter the teaching profession (Tables D4.1a, D4.1b, D4.1c and D4.1d).

All OECD countries now require a tertiary qualification for entry to the teaching profession at the primary level and beyond.

D4

Initial teacher training in the Flemish Community of Belgium

In the Flemish Community of Belgium, initial teacher training is provided at institutes of higher education for pre-primary, primary and lower secondary school teachers teaching specific subjects to children in the first stage and second stage of secondary education (group 1). Initial teacher training for upper secondary school teachers teaching subjects to pupils aged 14-21 in the second, third and fourth stage of secondary education (group 2) is provided at universities and for some disciplines partly at an institute of higher education. Qualified upper secondary school teachers – group 2 – always have a university or Master's degree.

D4

Pre-service teacher training in Austria

In Austria general compulsory education teachers at the pre-primary, primary and general secondary level (Hauptschule) are trained at teacher training institute colleges (Pädagogische Akademien). Teachers for primary school and the pre-school level have to qualify in all subjects taught at these schools, teachers for general secondary schools qualify for two subjects. Teachers for the academic secondary schools (Allgemeinbildende höhere Schulen) and the medium and higher level secondary and vocational school (Berufsbildende Mittlere und Höhere Schulen) are trained at universities.

Teacher education in Finland

In Finland, university faculties of education and equivalent units called teacher education units provide the pre-service training of all new teachers in public education. This includes the training of kindergarten teachers, class teachers, which mainly provide instruction for grades 1–6 and, subject teachers, who teach one or several subjects in grade 7-9 in basic education and/or in general upper secondary education.

Chart D4.2

Number of years of post-secondary education required to become a teacher (2001)

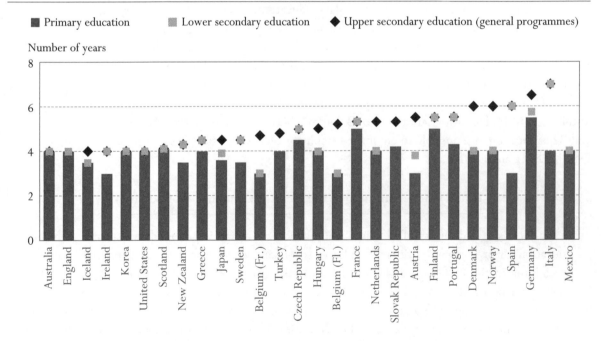

■ Primary education   ■ Lower secondary education   ◆ Upper secondary education (general programmes)

Countries are ranked in ascending order of the number of years of post-secondary education required to become a teacher in upper secondary education.
Source: OECD. Tables D4.1b-d. See Annex 3 for notes on methodology *(www.oecd.org/edu/eag2003).*

Teaching as an all graduate profession in Ireland

Since 1975, all teachers in Ireland are required to be graduates. The great majority of pre-primary and primary teachers qualify via a Bachelor of Education degree, obtained on the concurrent mode in which both content and teaching methodology are covered. Trainees for secondary teaching, after graduation with a primary degree, follow a one-year course in a university, leading to a Higher Diploma in Teaching.

For primary teachers the average length of pre-service training varies between three years in Austria, Belgium, Iceland, Ireland, New Zealand and Spain to five years or more in Finland, France and Germany (Table D4.1). For lower secondary teachers, the average duration of pre-service training is longer than that in primary education in slightly more than half of the countries, whereas it is the same for all other countries. Moreover, the average duration of teacher training ranges from below four years in the Flemish Community of Belgium and Iceland to six years or more in Spain and Italy. At the upper secondary level of education (general programmes), it varies from three years in Belgium to six years or more in Germany and Italy.

On average, pre-service training for teachers in secondary education tends to be longer than in primary education.

Teacher training programmes typically consist of subject specific studies, pedagogical studies and assisted teaching practice, which can be pursued consecutively or concurrently. In the concurrent model the pedagogical and practical training is provided at the same time as the subject matter, while in the consecutive structure the pedagogical and practical training follows the subject matter course. Under this model students usually first obtain a higher education degree (tertiary-type A or B) in one or more subjects before entering pedagogical and practical training.

The organisational structure of teacher training varies among and within OECD countries.

In primary education, the concurrent model of pre-service training is adopted in the majority of OECD countries. In France and Germany, pre-service training is organised according to the consecutive model; in Australia, England, Iceland, Ireland, New Zealand, Portugal, Scotland and the Slovak Republic pedagogical studies can be taken either concurrently with or following completion of subject-matter studies (often following a tertiary-type A degree in a particular subject).

In primary education, the concurrent model of pre-service training is predominant …

D4

In lower secondary education, in Belgium, Denmark, Greece, Hungary, Ireland, Italy, Japan, Korea, Mexico, the Netherlands, Turkey and the United States pre-service training is organised according the concurrent model. In Australia, Austria, the Czech Republic, England, Finland, Iceland, New Zealand, Norway, Portugal, Scotland, the Slovak Republic and Sweden pre-service training can be followed either concurrently or consecutively. In France, Germany and Spain, pre-service training is organised according to the consecutive model.

… while in lower secondary education, pre-service training is equally organised concurrently and consecutively …

Teacher education in Sweden

In Sweden, a new, integrated teaching degree was established on 1 July 2001, replacing eight of the previous 11 teaching degrees. The new structure means that all future teachers will have a common basic competence, combined with a chosen specialisation in particular subjects/subject areas and/or age groups. The new teaching degree comprises a programme of a minimum of 120 credits (equal to three years of full-time studies) and a maximum of 220 credits, depending on the chosen area and education level.

The teacher-training programme will consist of three well-integrated education areas:

- a general education area, common for all students, covering key topics such as learning, special pedagogy, socialisation and fundamental values, as well as interdisciplinary subject studies (at least 60 credits)

- an education area covering the subject(s) the future teacher intends to teach (at least 40 credits)

- an education area with a specialisation, complementing earlier acquired knowledge (at least 20 credits)

Some phases of the education involve practical activities. At least 10 credits (*i.e.* study weeks) in the general education area and at least 10 credits per orientation should be located at a school.

Within the teacher-training programme there is an alternative route, where the student takes at least 60 credits of subject studies for teaching in a core or programme specific subject and then takes 60 credits in the general education area (see above).

Teacher education in Finland

Both kindergarten teachers and class teachers are educated at the teacher education departments of faculties of education at the universities.

Students in kindergarten teacher education complete the Bachelor of Education degree consisting of 120 credits. The majority of kindergarten teachers work in day-care centres as teachers and educators of children under school age.

Students in class teacher education take a Master's degree (160 credits) at a faculty of education, with education as their main subject. Class teachers may provide instruction in all subjects in forms 1–6 in basic education.

Subject teachers who teach forms 7-9 in basic education as well as general upper secondary education have a Master's degree (160-180 credits). Most subject teachers take a degree in their respective faculties, with the subject of instruction as their major. The department of teacher education is responsible for organising their studies in education. These studies are completed at the same time and in interaction with each other. The 35-credit pedagogical studies are specific for the subject matter.

D4

In upper secondary education (general programmes), the organisation of pre-service training varies more widely among countries. In Austria, Denmark, France, Germany, Iceland, the Netherlands, Norway and Spain pre-service training is organised according to the consecutive model, while in the Flemish Community of Belgium, Greece, Hungary, Ireland, Italy, Japan, Korea, Turkey and the United States, students typically follow the concurrent model. In all other countries, both pre-service training models are in use.

... and in upper secondary education the model used varies widely among countries.

The consecutive model in Germany

In Germany, pre-service training for all levels of education is long. Depending on the ISCED level the first phase takes 7 to 9 semesters study of subjects, didactics and educational science. In the second phase prospective teachers are required to spend between 18 and 24 months in a practical and professional training period (Vorbereitungsdienst).

Three parallel models in Korea

Teachers for primary education are trained at regional teacher training colleges. The primary teacher training course is a four-year course organised according to the concurrent model with an emphasis on foundation skills, general courses in education and the methodology of primary education and skills development.

Teachers for secondary education are trained at universities.

Students can choose between two programmes of study both of the same length (four years) leading to the same level of qualification. They can take the teacher training course organised by the faculty of teacher training. This course follows the concurrent model, *i.e.* students take the subject courses, subject methodology courses and courses in educational science as part of an integrated curriculum.

Students also have the option to follow another concurrent model: while taking a degree course in their area of specialisation, they can also take foundation courses for teacher training to meet teacher qualification requirements. The difference between the two types of programmes is mainly in emphasis: while the former type offers more education and education policy-related courses, the latter type offers more in-depth courses in the specialisation area.

Both programmes can be completed in four years and give a qualification that entitles the holder to teach at the secondary level.

Primary teacher diplomas and secondary teacher diplomas entitle the holder to teach only at the relevant level. To become a primary teacher, a person with a secondary teacher diploma has to complete a second degree course in primary education.

D4

The concurrent and consecutive model of pre-service training in the Netherlands

In the Netherlands initial training for pre-primary, primary and lower secondary education (grade two) teachers is organised according to the concurrent model. In this model, teaching practice is an important component of the pre-service training.

Prospective teachers for upper secondary education (grade one teachers) must have either a first university degree or a grade two qualification in the subject to be studied. For the first option the training consists of university study (four years), followed by postgraduate university teaching training courses (one year). For the second option the training is based on the combination of a grade two teacher training programme followed by a grade one teacher training programme.

Three models of teacher education in Scotland

In Scotland, three models of teacher education exist:

1. The consecutive model: prospective teachers who already hold a university degree and wish to teach in either a primary or a secondary school can follow a one-year course for a Post-Graduate Certificate in Education (PGCE) at a teacher education institution.

2. The concurrent model: to become a primary teacher or a secondary teacher of technology, physical education or music it is possible to take a 4-year course leading to a Bachelor of Education at a teacher education institution. In this route teaching practice is provided throughout the training.

3. The combined model: to become a secondary teacher in certain subjects it is possible to take a combined degree, including subject study, study of education and school experience. In this model most of the teaching practice takes place in the final six months.

D4

In some countries, teachers with a qualification for teaching may also need a licence to access a permanent post in public education.

The licensing status is a measure of teacher qualifications that combines aspects of knowledge about subject matter and about teaching and learning. Obtaining a licence might also depend on passing a (competitive) teacher examination and/ or having a short teaching experience. In the latter, licensing typically involves a probation period of at least one school year. The examinations may include in-depth interviews, observation of the candidate's teaching, or a portfolio with records of achievement and work experience.

In France, Germany, Greece, Italy, Japan, Korea, Spain, and depending on the State in Mexico, a competitive examination is necessary to obtain a licence for teaching in public institutions. Mandatory work experience for licensing is required in England, Ireland, Italy, New Zealand, Portugal, Scotland, Spain, Turkey and the United States and can last between one and three years.

Competitive examinations in France

Since 1992, new pre-elementary, elementary and secondary teachers are required to be holders of at least a first degree or equivalent diploma. Students who want to prepare for either the competition for primary school teachers or one of the competitive recruitment examinations for secondary teaching are required to take a one-year teacher training course at an *Institut Universitaire de Formation de Maître* (IUFM).

Examination for public school teachers in Japan

Public school teachers are public officials and are appointed by the prefectural board of education in which the schools are located. Teachers are employed through the teacher appointment examination administered by each prefectural board of education. Procedure and content of the examination differ according to the boards of education, but the examination is generally composed of written tests of teaching subjects and general education subjects, an interview test, and a practical examination.

Mandatory work experience in Spain

The probation period in Spain is part of the requisites to become a civil servant teacher in public education. It takes place immediately after teachers have passed the competitive examinations. It lasts for one school year when the new teacher has to teach in a school taking charge of real groups of pupils and has to prove his/her professional aptitude in practice

---

Probationary period in the United States

Individuals who successfully complete a 4-year programme of teacher education will generally obtain either a state or local teaching license. However, they usually have a probationary period of up to about three years before they obtain a permanent, tenured position.

D4

Professional development of teachers

Pre-service teacher training is only the first step to become a teaching professional. School practice and further professional development are equally important elements in teacher education. Maintenance of teaching skills, development of new skills, updating knowledge in the subject matter and in teaching methodology as well as in the theory of learning and teaching are all essential elements of professional development.

Given that there are rapid changes in the knowledge base as well as in the knowledge technologies in institutional education, a regular update of professional knowledge and skills for teachers is more important than ever. Education policy makers are increasingly aware of the need for more efficient professional development policies. However, information about professional development for teachers is very limited: it is difficult to know how these activities should be planned, supported and required to support the growing demand for quality in all educational aspects.

With the International Survey of Upper Secondary Schools (ISUSS), OECD attempted for the first time to examine the intensity and variety of professional development activities among countries (for a brief description of the study see Annex 3 at *www.oecd.org/edu/eag2003.)* The following questions were addressed to school principals: how does the school support professional development of teachers; what is the percentage of teachers who participate in professional development activities, and what are the more common types of activities for professional development (Tables D4.2 and D4.3).

A budget for teachers' professional development is provided to all or most schools in the Flemish Community of Belgium, Denmark, Finland, Hungary, Italy, Norway, Sweden and Switzerland ...

On average, about 60 per cent of the students attend schools where a separate budget is available for professional development. However, there are some systematic differences between countries: in France, Korea, Portugal and Spain, professional development of teachers is budgeted and organised by professional authorities. By contrast, all schools in the Flemish Community Belgium, Denmark, Hungary and Sweden, and most schools in Finland, Italy, Norway, and Switzerland are provided a budget allocated for professional development. In most countries, the majority of schools provide time for teachers for professional development (Table D4.2). In Portugal, teachers are entitled to a certain number of days of professional development activities.

...and over 90 per cent of students attend schools where the school principal reported that the school organises staff development activities (including research) in Denmark, Norway and Sweden.

Professional development in its wider sense includes research and co-operation of teachers in curriculum development and evaluation projects. Such activities are often organised by the schools themselves. Over 90 per cent of students attend schools where school principals reported such activities in Denmark, Norway and Sweden. By contrast, this type of activity seems less common in France and Korea, where the school principals of about half of upper secondary students or less reported that staff development activities are organised in their schools.

Professional development activities are characteristic of the school as a learning community.

The modern concept of professional development covers a wide range of professional activities. Some theorists suggest that professional development should be seen as a growth process that involves the acquisition of new knowledge, accumulation of experience, and the art of combining these into creative solutions. In this context, they argue, professional development activities should be seen as an inherent part of school culture.

In ISUSS principals were asked about types of teachers' professional development activities.

In ISUSS, principals were asked about types of professional development activities in which teachers (at least one teacher) had participated during the school year 2000/2001. In the questionnaire the list of types of activities includes the more traditional in-service training and mentoring activities as

D4

well as activities related to exchange of experience, collaborative research and networking activities. Although the actual intensity of the different types of activities could not be assessed within the framework of a school survey, the responses concerning the preferred type and the variety of professional development activities differ significantly among countries.

In-service teacher training is the mostly used mode of professional development and includes, in general, (short) courses or workshops on subject matter, methodology and other education-related topics. In-service teacher training is usually organised by professional bodies attached to education authorities and, recently, by more and more teacher associations, trade unions and private consulting bodies as well. In 10 out of the 14 countries that participated in ISUSS, more than 90 per cent of students attended schools where the principal reported teacher participation in course-type professional development activities (Chart D4.3 and Table D4.3).

Courses and workshops appear to be the most frequent types of professional development activities…

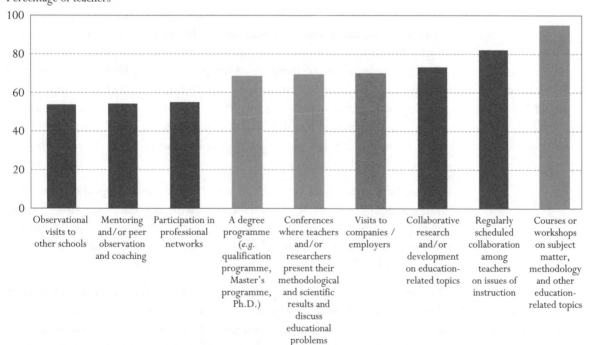

Chart D4.3

Common types of professional development activities (2001)
Country mean percentage of upper secondary students attending schools where principals reported that at least one teacher participated in various professional development activities

■ Participation in ***mentoring and peer observation*** types of professional development
■ Participation in ***other*** types of professional development
■ Participation in ***course-type*** professional development

Percentage of teachers

Subjects are ranked in ascending order of the country mean percentage of upper secondary students attending schools where principals reported that at least one teacher had participated in a professional development activity during the school year 2000/2001.
Source: OECD ISUSS database, 2003. Table D4.3.

D4

...and some teachers participate in degree courses as part of their career strategy.

From the individual teacher's point of view, participation in degree programmes can also be considered as in-service training. Participation in courses resulting in a higher or a specific qualification is usually voluntary, and initiated by teachers themselves as part of their career strategies. Sometimes, participation in a degree programme is recommended or required of teachers: such cases may occur when teachers are temporarily allowed to teach with a qualification lower than normally required because of permanent teacher shortages. The principals of more than 90 per cent of upper secondary students in Hungary, Korea and Sweden, (as opposed to only 28 per cent in Italy) reported that at least one of the teachers had participated in a degree programme during the school year 2000/2001 (Chart D4.4 and Table D4.3).

Observational visits to other schools are a frequent practice in Denmark, Finland, Korea, Norway, Portugal and Sweden. Formal peer observation or mentoring is more often used in Denmark, France, Italy, Korea, Mexico and Switzerland.

There are great differences between countries in the frequency of observational visits to other schools. This type of peer reviewing and exchange of experience has an important role in maintaining and improving professional standards among schools. On average among countries, about 50 per cent of students attend schools where some form of peer reviewing or peer observation of classes is practiced. Observational visits to other schools appear to be most frequent in Korea, Portugal and Sweden, where over 80 per cent of students attend schools where the principal reported that at least one teacher participated in such activities. By contrast one quarter or less of students in France and Ireland attend schools where the principal reported the same. More formal peer observation including mentoring and coaching is arranged, recognised and supported in the schools of 80 per cent or more of upper secondary students in Korea and Switzerland (Chart D4.4 and Table D4.3).

There is regularly scheduled collaboration among teachers on issues of instruction in the overwhelming majority of schools in most of the 14 countries with comparable data.

There is regularly scheduled collaboration among teachers on issues of instruction in the majority of schools in almost all countries with available data. On average, four out of five students attend schools where the principal reported scheduled collaboration among teachers. Often, the context of collaboration is a school research or development project (*e.g.,* curriculum development, introduction of a quality management system, action research, etc.). The principals of less than half of upper secondary students reported that at least one teacher had participated in collaborative research and innovation efforts in Ireland.

Networking of teachers beyond the walls of the school appears to be a less frequent practice in most of the countries with available data. However, the principals of 60 per cent or more of students in Denmark, Finland, Korea, Norway and Sweden reported that teachers had participated in teacher networks outside the school.

In countries for which professional development activities comprise a wide range of different possibilities, participation rates

To what extent do teachers participate in the various types of professional development activities? A large section of professional development activities is related to information and communication technology. According to the assessment from school principals, one third of all upper secondary teachers participated in ICT-related professional activities in the school year 2000/2001 and around one half participated in professional development activities

D4

related to other topics. Participation rates are the highest in Denmark, Finland, Norway, and Sweden; in these countries, more than 35 per cent of teachers participated in ICT-related professional development and between 55 and 85 per cent participated in other professional development activities. By contrast, in France, Hungary, Ireland, Italy, Portugal and Spain, participation rates range from 20 to 30 per cent for ICT-related activities and from 30 to 40 per cent for other professional activities. It should be noted that the actual level of participation may be higher than school principals report. Teachers may attend courses without the knowledge of school management, which indeed is the case in France and Spain, where professional development activities are organised by educational authorities via direct contact with teachers (Chart D4.1 and Table D4.3).

are high, especially in Denmark, Finland, Norway and Sweden.

Chart D4.4

Teachers' participation in professional development activities (2001)
Percentage of upper secondary students attending schools where the principal reported that at least one teacher participated in professional development activities (including ICT-related activities) during the school year 2000/2001, by type of activity

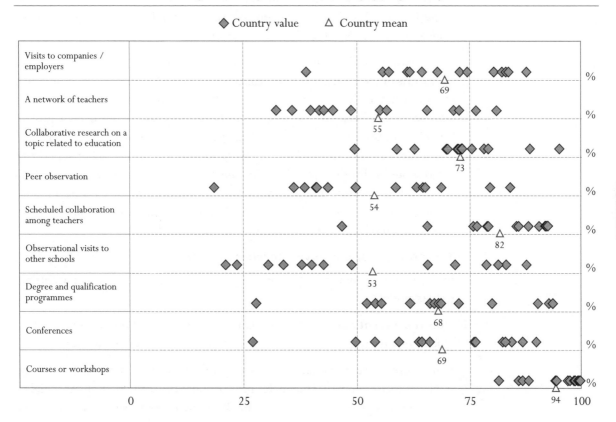

D4

Definitions and methodologies

Data on pre-service training are from the 2002 OECD-INES survey on Teachers and the Curriculum and refer to the school year 2000-2001.

The duration of pre-service training for new teachers refers to the typical number of full-time equivalent years of teacher training required to become a fully qualified teacher according to the formal policy of the country. In systems where the teacher has to work before being fully qualified, these years of practice do not have to be included. Deviations from this definition are reported in Annex 3.

Probation period refers to the employment status of starting teachers who get tenure on condition of satisfactory performance during a certain period defined by law or regulations. This mandatory work experience is required to be a licensed teacher in some countries.

Competitive examination refers to teacher examinations organised by local, regional or national authorities in order to select teachers for the public education system.

Parts of pre-service studies

Pre-service teacher training typically consists of three parts:

- ***subject specific studies*** covering general studies and theoretical and in-depth studies of the subject(s) to be taught;

- ***pedagogical studies*** covering the theoretical foundations of education and teaching as well as studies of subject matter methodology and other education specific studies (*e.g.* education of special needs students, educational measurement, educational planning, etc.).

- ***assisted teaching practice*** covering the teaching practice under the supervision of a teacher trainer which is required to obtain a teacher diploma. It does not include, however, post-qualification teaching practice required to become a licensed teacher (*e.g.* to be able to take a permanent post in public education). An important distinction may be that student teachers have typically partial responsibility or part-time jobs (*e.g.* their teacher supervisor is responsible for the class). Typically student teachers are not salaried teachers even if they receive some allowance for the (usually part-time) work they are doing at school. By contrast, teachers in their probation year(s) are typically salaried, fully qualified and have jobs of full responsibility.

The structure of pre-service teacher training

In most OECD countries, pre-service teacher training is organised according to two models:

- the ***concurrent model*** in which theoretical and practical training in education pedagogy is provided at the same time as study of the subject matter

- the ***consecutive model*** in which theoretical and practical training follows the subject matter course. Under this model students usually first obtain a higher education degree (tertiary-type A or B) in one or more subjects before they train in the theory and practice of education.

D4

Professional development of teachers

Professional development in this indicator refers to any activity that develops an individual's skills, knowledge, expertise and other characteristics as a teacher. These include personal study and reflection, collaborative development of new approaches, as well as formal courses.

Data are drawn from OECD's International Survey of Upper Secondary Schools implemented in the 2001/2002 school year in 15 countries. For a brief description of the survey see Annex 3 at *www.oecd.org/edu/eag2003*.

Data on the professional development of teachers are from OECD's International Survey of Upper Secondary Schools (ISUSS).

D4

Table D4.1a
Pre-service teacher training requirements in pre-primary education (2001)
System-level information on types of teacher training programmes and percentage of teachers with different types of qualifications

	Cumulative years of education required for entry into the training programme	Duration of training programme in years	Consecutive (—) or concurrent (‖)	Mandatory work experience as licensing requirement in years	Competitive examination to enter the public education system	Year of introduction	Percentage of current teacher stock with this type of qualification	ISCED type of final qualification	Valid for programme level/type
Australia	12-13	4	‖	a	No	1994-1998	65%	5A	0
Austria	8	5	‖	a	No	a	80%	3A	0
	12	3	‖	a	No	1999	73%	5B	0,1,2,3 voc
Belgium (Fl.)	12	3	‖	a	No	1997-1998	98%	5B	0
Belgium (Fr.)	12	3	‖	a	No	a	a	5B	0
Czech Republic	9	4	‖	a	No	m	m	3A	0
	13	3	‖	a	No	1998	m	5A	0
	13	5	‖	a	No	m	m	5A	0
	13	3	‖	a	No	1995	m	5B	0
Denmark	12	3.5	‖	a	No	a	a	5A	0
England	13	3-4	‖	1	No	1969	m	5A	0,1,2,3
	13	4	—	1	No	1973	m	5A	0,1,2,3
Finland	12	3	‖	a	No	2000	a	5A	0
	12	5	‖	a	No	1998	a	5A	0
France	12	5	—	a	Yes	1992	a	5A	0,1
Germany	10	2-3	‖	a	Yes	m	m	5B	0
Greece	12	4	‖	a	Yes	2000	m	5A	0
Hungary	12	3	‖	a	No	a	80%	5A	0
Iceland	14	3	‖	m	No	a	m	5A	0
Ireland	12	3	‖	1	No	1975	m	5A	0,1
	12	4	—	a	No	m	m	5A	0,1
Italy	13	4	‖	1	Yes	1996	a	5A	0
Japan	12	2	‖	a	Yes	1949	75%	5A,5B	0
	12	4	‖	a	Yes	1949	19%	5A	0
	12	6	‖	a	Yes	1988	n	5A	0
Korea	12	2	‖	a	Yes	a	m	5B	0
	12	4	‖	a	Yes	a	m	5A	0
Mexico	12	4	‖	a	Yes/No	1999	m	5A	0
Netherlands	11	4	‖	a	No	1986	a	5A	0,1
New Zealand	12	3	‖	2	No	1988	m	5B	0
	13	4	‖	2	No	1996	m	5A	0,1
Norway	m	m	m	m	m	m	m	m	m
Portugal	12	3	‖	a	No	1997	m	5B	0,1 (1st c)
Scotland	12	3.75-4.75	—	≥ 1	No	m	m	5A	0,1,2,3
	12	4	‖	≥ 1	No	m	m	5A	0,1,2,3
Slovak Republic	8-9	4	‖	a	No	m	98%	3A	0
	12	5	‖	a	No	1996	1%	5A	0
	12	4	‖	a	No	1996	1%	5A	0
Spain	12	3	‖	1	Yes	1991	95%	5A	0,1
Sweden	12	3.5	‖	a	No	2001	a	5A	0,1
Switzerland	m	m	m	m	m	m	m	m	m
Turkey	11-13	4	‖	1	No	1992	a	5A	0
United States	12	4	‖	≤ 3	No	a	90%	5A	0,1

Source: OECD. See Annex 3 for notes (*www.oecd.org/edu/eag2003*).

Table D4.1b
Pre-service teacher training requirements in primary education (2001)
System-level information on types of teacher training programmes and percentage of teachers with different types of qualifications

	Cumulative years of education required for entry into the training programme	Duration of training programme in years	Consecutive (—) or concurrent (||)	Mandatory work experience as licensing requirement in years	Competitive examination to enter the public education system	Year of introduction	Percentage of current teacher stock with this type of qualification	ISCED type of final qualification	Valid for programme level/type
Australia	12-13	4	||	a	No	1994-1998	53%	5A	1
	13	4	—	a	No	1994-1995	8%	5A	1
Austria	12	3	||	a	No	1999	73%; 91%	5B	0 ,1,2,3 voc
Belgium (Fl.)	12	3	||	a	No	1997-1998	86%	5B	1
Belgium (Fr.)	12	3	||	a	No	a	a	5B	1
Czech Republic	13	4	||	a	No	m	m	5A	1
Denmark	12	4	||	a	No	a	a	5A	1,2
England	13	3-4	||	1	No	1969	m	5A	0,1,2,3
	13	4	—	1	No	1973	m	5A	0,1,2,3
Finland	12	5	||	a	No	1995	a	5A	1
France	12	5	—	a	Yes	1992	a	5A	0,1
Germany	12-13	5.5	—	a	Yes	m	m	5A	1
	12-13	5.5-6.5	—	a	Yes	m	m	5A	1,2
Greece	12	4	||	a	Yes	2000	m	5A	1
Hungary	12	4	||	a	No	a	80%	5A	1, 2 (Gr 5-6)
Iceland	14	3	||	m	No	a	m	5A	1,2
	14	4	—	m	No	a	m	5A	1,2
Ireland	12	3	||	1	No	1975	m	5A	0,1
	12	4.5	—	a	No	m	m	5A	0,1
Italy	13	4	||	1	Yes	1996	a	5A	1
Japan	12	2	||	a	Yes	1949	18%	5A,5B	1
	12	4	||	a	Yes	1949	78%	5A	1
	12	6	||	a	Yes	1988	1%	5A	1
Korea	12	4	||	a	Yes	a	m	5B	1
	12	4	||	a	Yes	a	m	5A	1
Mexico	12	4	||	a	Yes/No	1997	m	5A	1
Netherlands	11	4	||	a	No	1986	a	5A	0,1
New Zealand	13	3	||	2	No	1997	m	5A	0,1
	13	4	—	2	No	1996	m	5A	1,2
Norway	13	4	||	a	No	1998	79%	5A	1,2
Portugal	12	3	||	a	No	1997	m	5B	0,1 (1st c)
	12	4	||	1	No	1997	m	5B	1 (2nd c)
	12	6	—	1	No	1988	m	5A	1 (2nd c)
Scotland	12	3.75-4.75	—	≥ 1	No	m	m	5A	0,1,2,3
	12	4	||	≥ 1	No	m	m	5A	0,1,2,3
Slovak Republic	12-13	4	||	a	No	m	93%	5A	1
	12-13	7	—	a	No	m	7%	5A	1
Spain	12	3	||	1	Yes	1991	90%	5A	0,1
Sweden	12	3.5	||	a	No	2001	a	5A	0,1
Switzerland	m	m	m	m	m	m	m	m	m
Turkey	11-13	4	||	1	No	1992	m	5A	1 (6-10 yrs)
	11-13	4	||	1	No	1982	m	5A	1 (9-13 yrs)
United States	12	4	||	≤ 3	No	a	90%	5A	1

Source: OECD. See Annex 3 for notes (*www.oecd.org/edu/eag2003*).

D4

(OECD COUNTRIES)

Table D4.1c
Pre-service teacher training requirements in lower secondary education (2001)
System-level information on types of teacher training programmes and percentage of teachers with different types of qualifications

	Cumulative years of education required for entry into the training programme	Duration of training programme in years	Consecutive (—) or concurrent (||)	Mandatory work experience as licensing requirement in years	Competitive examination to enter the public education system	Year of introduction	Percentage of current teacher stock with this type of qualification	ISCED type of final qualification	Valid for programme level/type
Australia	12-13	4	||	a	No	1976-1998	>41%	5A	2
	12	4	||	a	No	1998	5%	5A	2,3
	13-15	4	—	a	No	Varies	>17%	5A	2
Austria	12	3	||	a	No	1999	91%	5B	0,1,2,3 voc
	12	5.5	—	a	No	a	100%	5A	2,3
Belgium (Fl.)	12	3	||	a	No	1997-1998	47%	5B	2
	a	2-4	||	a	No	1988-1989	20%	5B	2,3
Belgium (Fr.)	12	3	||	a	No	a	a	5B	2
Czech Republic	13	5	||	a	No	m	m	5A	2
	13	7	—	a	No	m	m	5A	2
Denmark	12	4	||	a	No	a	a	5A	1,2
England	13	3-4	||	1	No	1969	m	5A	0,1,2,3
	13	4	—	1	No	1973	m	5A	0,1,2,3
Finland	12	5	||	a	No	1980	a	5A	2
	12	6	—	a	No	1980	a	5A	2
France	12	5	—	a	Yes	1991	a	5A	2,3
	12	5	—	a	Yes	1991	a	5A	2,3
	12	6	—	a	Yes	1988	a	5A	2,3
Germany	12-13	5.5-6.5	—	a	Yes	m	m	5A	1,2
	12-13	6.5	—	a	Yes	m	m	5A	2,3
Greece	12	4	||	a	Yes	2000	m	5A	2,3
	12	5	||	a	Yes	2000	m	5A	2,3
Hungary	12	4	||	a	No	a	80%	5A	2
Iceland	14	3	||	m	No	a	m	5A	1,2
	14	4	—	m	No	a	m	5A	1,2
Ireland	12	4	||	1	No	1922	m	5A	2,3
Italy	13	6-8	||	1	Yes	1996	a	5A	2
Japan	12	2	||	a	Yes	1949	7%	5A,5B	2
	12	4	||	a	Yes	1949	91%	5A	2
	12	6	||	a	Yes	1988	2%	5A	2
Korea	12	4	||	a	Yes	a	m	5A	2,3
	12	4	||	a	Yes	a	m	5A	2,3
	16	2-2.5	||	a	Yes	a	m	5A	2,3
Mexico	12	4	||	a	Yes/No	a	m	5A	2
	12	6	||	a	Yes/No	a	m	5A	2
Netherlands	11	4	||	a	No	1986	a	5A	2
New Zealand	13	4	—	2	No	1996	m	5A	1,2,3
	13	5	||	2	No	1998	m	5A	2,3
	13	4	||	2	No	1975	m	5A	2,3
Norway	13	4	||	a	No	1998	61%	5A	1,2
	13	4	—	a	No	1998	25%	5A	2,3
Portugal	12	5	||	a	No	m	m	5A	2,3
	12	6	—	a	No	1988	m	5A	2,3
Scotland	12	3.75-4.75	—	≥ 1	No	m	m	5A	0,1,2,3
	12	4	||	≥ 1	No	m	m	5A	0,1,2,3
	12	3.5-4.5	||	≥ 1	No	m	m	5A	1,2,3
Slovak Republic	12-13	5	||	a	No	m	91%	5A	2,3
	12-13	7	—	a	No	m	9%	5A	2,3
Spain	12	6	—	1	Yes	1991	80%	5A	2,3
	12	4	—	1	Yes	1991	20%	5A	2
Sweden	12	4.5	||	a	No	2001	a	5A	2,3
	12	4.5	—	a	No	2001	a	5A	2,3
Switzerland	m	m	m	m	m	m	m	m	m
Turkey	a	a	a	a	a	a	a	a	a
	11-13	4	||	1	No	1982	m	5A	1
United States	12	4	||	≤ 3	No	a	90%	5A	2,3

OECD COUNTRIES

Source: OECD. See Annex 3 for notes (*www.oecd.org/edu/eag2003*).

Table D4.1d
Pre-service teacher training requirements in upper secondary education, general programmes (2001)
System-level information on types of teacher training programmes and percentage of teachers with different types of qualifications

OECD COUNTRIES	Cumulative years of education required for entry into the training programme	Duration of training programme in years	Consecutive (—) or concurrent (| |)	Mandatory work experience as licensing requirement in years	Competitive examination to enter the public education system	Year of introduction	Percentage of current teacher stock with this type of qualification	ISCED type of final qualification	Valid for programme level/type
Australia	12-13	4	| |	a	No	1976-1998	49%	5A	3
	12-13	4	—	a	No	1976-1994	19%	5A	3
	12	4	| |	a	No	1998	5%	5A	2,3
Austria	12	5.5	—	a	No	a	100%	5A	2,3
Belgium (Fl.)	12	4.6-5.8	| |	a	No	1997-1998	n	5A	3
	12	4.6-5.8	| |	a	No	1997-1998	29%	5A	3
	a	2-4	| |	a	No	1988-1989	20%	5B	2,3
Belgium (Fr.)	12	4.24	– or | |	a	No	a	m	5A	3
	12	5.24	– or | |	a	No	a	m	5A	3
Czech Republic	13	5	| |	a	No	m	m	5A	3
	13	7	—	a	No	m	m	5A	3
Denmark	12	4	—	a	No	a	a	5A	3
England	13	3-4	| |	1	No	1969	m	5A	0,1,2,3
	13	4	—	1	No	1973	m	5A	0,1,2,3
Finland	12	5	| |	a	No	1984	a	5A	3
	12	6	—	a	No	1984	a	5A	3
France	12	5	—	a	Yes	1991	a	5A	2,3
	12	5	—	a	Yes	1991	a	5A	2,3
	12	6	—	a	Yes	1988	a	5A	2,3
Germany	12-13	6.5	—	a	Yes	m	m	5A	3
Greece	12	4	| |	a	Yes	2000	m	5A	2,3
	12	5	| |	a	Yes	2000	m	5A	2,3
Hungary	12	5	| |	a	No	a	80%	5A	3
Iceland	14	4	—	m	No	a	m	5A	3
Ireland	12	4	| |	1	No	1922	m	5A	2,3
Italy	13	6-8	| |	1	Yes	1996	a	5A	3
Japan	12	4	| |	a	Yes	1949	72%	5A	3
	12	6	| |	a	Yes	1988	28%	5A	3
Korea	12	4	| |	a	Yes	a	m	5A	2,3
	12	4	| |	a	Yes	a	m	5A	2,3
	16	2-2.5	| |	a	Yes	a	m	5A	2,3
Mexico	m	m	m	m	m	m	m	m	m
Netherlands	11	5.5	—	a	No	1986	m	5A	3
	11	5	—	a	No	1987	m	5A	3
New Zealand	13	4	—	2	No	1996	m	5A	1,2,3
	13	5	| |	2	No	1998	m	5A	2,3
	13	4	| |	2	No	1975	m	5A	2,3
Norway	13	4	—	a	No	1998	m	5A	2,3
	13	6	—	a	No	1998	m	5A	3
Portugal	12	5	| |	a	No	m	m	5A	2,3
	12	6	—	a	No	1988	m	5A	2,3
Scotland	12	3.75-4.75	—	≥ 1	No	m	m	5A	0,1,2,3
	12	4	| |	≥ 1	No	m	m	5A	0,1,2,3
	12	3.5-4.5	| |	≥ 1	No	m	m	5A	1,2,3
Slovak Republic	12-13	5	| |	a	No	m	87%	5A	2,3
	12-13	7	—	a	No	m	13%	5A	2,3
Spain	12	6	—	1	Yes	1991	a	5A	2,3
Sweden	12	4.5	| |	a	No	2001	a	5A	2,3
	12	4.5	—	a	No	2001	a	5A	2,3
Switzerland	m	m	m	m	m	m	m	m	m
Turkey	11-13	4	| |	1	No	1992	m	5A	3 (14-16 yrs)
	11-13	5	| |	1	No	1998	m	5A	3 (14-16 yrs)
	11-13	5.5	| |	1	No	1998	m	5A	3 (14-16 yrs)
United States	12	4	| |	≤ 3	No	a	90%	5A	2,3

Source: OECD. See Annex 3 for notes (*www.oecd.org/edu/eag2003*).

D4

Table D4.2
Schools supporting professional development (2001)
Percentage of upper secondary students whose school principals reported that the school supports professional development of teachers, by type of support provided

	The school has a separate budget for the professional development of teachers	The school provides time for teachers for professional development	The school organises staff development activities (*e.g.*, research)	The school collects and circulates information on professional development courses in the school district
Belgium (Fl.)[1]	98	90	88	98
Denmark	96	100	97	92
Finland	79	96	73	95
France	19	69	59	89
Hungary	84	89	81	98
Ireland	45	90	74	83
Italy	81	83	90	84
Korea	29	59	40	90
Mexico	37	80	87	94
Norway	80	95	94	91
Portugal	8	34	75	96
Spain	17	33	72	99
Sweden	98	85	94	97
Switzerland	86	91	87	90
Country mean	*61*	*78*	*79*	*93*
Netherlands[2]	92	90	94	99

Note: Weighted by upper secondary enrolments.
1. Every school in Belgium (Fl.) receives a budget for the professional development of teachers from the Education Department.
2. Country did not meet international sampling requirements. The reported data are unweighted.
Source: OECD ISUSS database 2003. See Annex 3 for notes (*www.oecd.org/edu/eag2003*).

D4

Table D4.3

Teachers' participation in professional development activities in upper secondary education (2001)

Percentage of teachers in upper secondary education who participated in professional development activities.
Pecentage of upper secondary students attending schools where principals reported that at least one teacher participated in professional developement activities (including ICT-related activities) during the school year 2000/2001, by type of activity

	Percentage of upper secondary teachers who participated in professional development activities in the school year 2000/2001		Participation in course-type professional development			Participation in mentoring and peer observation types of professional development					Participation in other types of professional development
	ICT-related professional development activities	Other professional development activities	Courses or workshops on subject matter, methodology and other education-related topics	Conferences where teachers and/or researchers present their methodological and scientific results and discuss educational problems	A degree programme (e.g., qualification programme, Master's programme, Ph.D.)	Observational visits to other schools	Regularly scheduled collaboration among teachers on issues of instruction	Mentoring and/or peer observation and coaching as part of a formal arrangement recognised or supported by the school or educational authorities	Collaborative research and/or development on a topic related to education	A network of teachers (e.g., one organised by an outside agency or over the Internet)	Visits to companies/ employers
OECD COUNTRIES											
Belgium (Fl.)	29.6	47.6	98.8	64.3	67.1	30.6	85.6	43.7	73.4	42.9	72.9
Denmark	51.7	66.1	100.0	86.9	72.6	78.8	92.9	68.8	95.3	76.7	74.6
Finland	42.7	68.7	99.6	76.5	61.7	71.9	65.6	38.6	88.7	71.5	87.9
France	20.2	32.5	86.0	27.1	52.3	23.6	79.4	64.7	72.3	44.8	61.7
Hungary	19.5	29.9	94.3	84.5	93.7	42.8	90.7	58.6	58.8	40.0	57.2
Ireland	28.4	40.4	94.5	66.0	68.1	21.1	46.8	18.6	49.6	55.3	55.8
Italy	22.9	35.9	88.2	63.6	27.9	38.0	92.5	65.1	79.5	56.6	61.2
Korea	35.3	32.8	98.5	83.1	92.9	87.8	88.3	84.2	69.9	72.8	39.0
Mexico	30.8	45.7	97.6	59.4	68.7	40.2	86.0	63.2	72.6	35.8	64.4
Norway	43.9	56.2	99.4	82.5	66.1	65.8	92.2	41.2	78.5	65.6	82.4
Portugal	26.1	36.9	81.7	54.0	80.2	81.5	76.0	49.9	62.7	41.9	83.8
Spain	28.8	39.7	86.8	49.9	55.4	33.9	79.2	36.3	75.7	32.4	68.0
Sweden	37.4	84.3	97.0	90.0	90.4	83.3	76.8	41.4	73.6	81.2	83.3
Switzerland	28.3	56.1	97.5	76.1	54.1	48.9	92.8	79.8	70.0	48.9	80.6
Country mean	*31.8*	*48.1*	*94.3*	*68.8*	*67.9*	*53.4*	*81.8*	*53.9*	*72.9*	*54.7*	*69.5*
Netherlands[1]	45.2	56.8	98.3	73.3	43.9	22.2	85.1	44.7	76.8	42.8	61.3

Note: Weighted by upper secondary enrolments.
1. Country did not meet international sampling requirements. The reported data are unweighted.
Source: OECD ISUSS database, 2003. See Annex 3 for notes (*www.oecd.org/edu/eag2003*).

D4

INDICATOR D5: SALARIES OF TEACHERS IN PUBLIC PRIMARY AND SECONDARY SCHOOLS

- The mid-career salaries of lower secondary teachers range from less than US$ 10 000 in Hungary and the Slovak Republic to US$ 40 000 and more in Germany, Japan, Korea, Switzerland and the United States.

- An upper secondary teacher's salary per teaching hour is, on average, 40 per cent higher than that of a primary teacher, but the difference varies from 10 per cent or less in Australia, New Zealand, Scotland, the Slovak Republic, Turkey and the United States to around 60 per cent or more in the Flemish Community of Belgium, France, Hungary, Iceland, Korea, the Netherlands and Spain.

- In lower secondary education, teachers in Australia, Denmark, England, New Zealand and Scotland reach the highest step on the salary scale in 11 years or less, while a teacher in Austria, the Czech Republic, France, Greece, Hungary, Italy, Japan, Korea and Spain must teach for more than 30 years before reaching the maximum.

- In most countries, allowances are paid to all or most teachers for taking on management responsibilities; teaching more classes or hours than are required under a full-time contract (*e.g.*, acting duties); and involvement in special tasks such as guidance counselling or training student teachers.

Chart D5.1

Teachers' salaries in lower secondary education (2001)
Annual statutory teachers' salaries in public institutions in lower secondary education, in equivalent US dollars converted using PPPs, and the ratio of salary after 15 years of experience to GDP per capita

■ Salary after 15 years of experience/minimum training
● Salary at the top of scale/minimum training
● Starting salary/minimum training

Equivalent US dollars converted using PPPs

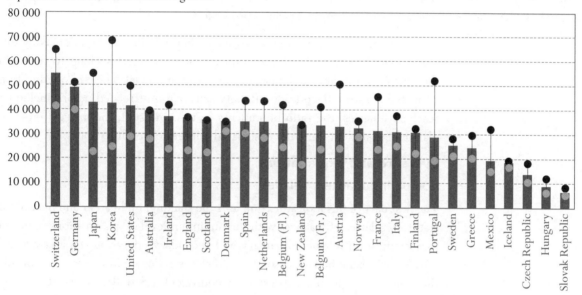

Ratio of salary after 15 years of experience to GDP per capita

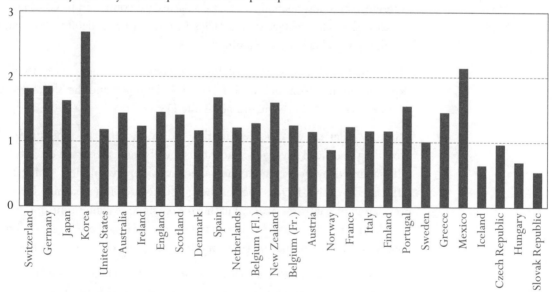

D5

Countries are ranked in descending order of teachers' salaries in lower secondary education after 15 years of experience and minimum training.
Source: OECD. Table D5.1. See Annex 3 for notes *(www.oecd.org/edu/eag2003).*

*This indicator shows
the starting, mid-career
and maximum statutory
salaries of teachers in
public primary and
secondary education, as
well as various incentive
schemes used in teacher
rewards systems.*

Policy context

Education systems employ a large number of professionals in an increasingly competitive market. Ensuring that there are a sufficient number of skilled teachers is a key concern in all OECD countries. Salaries and working conditions of teachers, including starting salaries and pay scales, and the costs incurred by individuals in becoming teachers, compared to salaries and costs in other high-skill occupations are key factors in determining the supply of qualified teachers. Both affect the career decisions of potential teachers and the types of people who are attracted to the teaching profession.

Teachers' salaries are the largest single cost in providing education, making this compensation a critical consideration for policy-makers seeking to maintain the quality of teaching and a balanced education budget. The size of education budgets naturally reflects trade-offs between many interrelated factors, including teachers' salaries, the ratio of students to teaching staff, the instruction time planned for students, and the designated number of teaching hours.

Evidence and explanations

Comparing teachers' salaries

The first part of this indicator compares the starting, mid-career and maximum statutory salaries of teachers with the minimum level of qualifications required for certification in public primary and secondary education. First, teachers' salaries are examined in absolute terms at starting, mid-career and top-of-the-scale salary points, expressed in equivalent US dollars converted using purchasing power parities. This provides information on the influence of teaching experience on national salary scales, and on the cost of teaching time in different countries. Second, teachers' salaries are compared to GDP per capita to assess the value of teachers' salaries in terms of affordability for countries. Third, bonus schemes are examined.

The annual statutory salaries of lower secondary teachers with 15 years of experience range from below US$ 10 000 in Hungary and the Slovak Republic, to over US$ 50 000 in Switzerland (Table D5.1).

Statutory salaries, as reported in this indicator, refer to scheduled salaries according to official pay scales. These must be distinguished from the actual wage bills incurred by governments and teachers' average salaries, which are also influenced by other factors such as the age structure of the teaching force or the prevalence of part-time work. Furthermore, since teaching time and teachers' workload can vary considerably between countries, these factors should be considered when comparing statutory salaries for teachers in countries.

An alternative measure of salaries and the cost of teaching time is the statutory salary for a full-time classroom teacher relative to the number of hours per year which that teacher is required to spend teaching students (Indicator D6). Although this measure does not adjust salaries for the amount of time that teachers spend in various teaching-related activities, it can nonetheless provide a rough estimate of the cost of the actual time teachers spend in the classroom.

D5

The average statutory salary per teaching hour after 15 years of experience is US$ 37 in primary, US$ 45 in lower secondary, and US$ 52 in upper secondary general education. In primary education, Hungary, Mexico, the Slovak Republic and Turkey have relatively low salary costs per teaching hour (US$ 19 or less). By contrast, costs are relatively high in Denmark, Germany, Japan and Korea (US$ 50 or more). There is even more variation in salary cost per teaching hour in general upper secondary schools, ranging from US$ 20 or less in Hungary, the Slovak Republic and Turkey to US$ 80 or more in Japan and Korea (Table D5.1).

The average statutory salary per teaching hour after 15 years of experience is US$ 37 in primary, US$ 45 in lower secondary, and US$ 52 in upper secondary general education.

Among other considerations, countries invest in teaching resources relative to their ability to fund educational expenditure. Comparing statutory salaries to GDP per capita is, therefore, another way of assessing the relative value of teachers' salaries among countries.

Comparing statutory salaries relative to GDP per capita reveals that…

Mid-career salaries for teachers in basic (primary and lower secondary) education relative to GDP per capita are lowest in Hungary (0.69), Iceland (0.64), Norway (0.88) and the Slovak Republic (0.55) and highest in Korea (2.69) and Turkey (2.12). In upper secondary general education, the lowest ratios are found in Hungary (0.87), Norway (0.88) and the Slovak Republic (0.55), and mid-career salaries relative to the GDP are highest in Korea (2.69) and Switzerland (2.11) (Table D5.1).

…mid-career salaries for teachers in basic education are low in Hungary, Iceland, Norway and the Slovak Republic, but relatively high in Korea and Turkey.

Some countries, such as the Czech Republic, Hungary, the Slovak Republic and Turkey have both relatively low GDP per capita and low teachers' salaries. Others there have a relatively low GDP per capita and teachers' salaries that are comparable to those in countries with much higher GDP (*e.g.,* Greece, Korea, Mexico and Portugal). Iceland has relatively high GDP per capita and lower than OECD average teachers' salaries, whereas Switzerland and the United States have a high GDP per capita and high teachers' salaries (Chart D5.1 and Table D5.1).

Some countries make a major investment in human resources despite lower levels of national income.

When comparing an index of change between 1996 and 2001 for teachers' salaries and GDP per capita, teachers' salaries have, in general, grown more slowly than GDP per capita but the inverse situation is prevailing in some countries such as the Czech Republic, Germany, Italy, Japan, Mexico and New Zealand. In the French Community of Belgium, France, Ireland, the Netherlands and Switzerland, the index of change between 1996 and 2001 in teachers' salaries is even decreasing related to GDP per capita over the same period (Chart D5.2).

D5

The International Standard Classification of Occupations (ISCO-88) identifies ten occupational groups, each of which is defined by a set of tasks and duties. Occupational groups are further defined in ISCO-88 by the skills needed by an individual to carry out the tasks and duties in a given job. Such skills could be acquired through formal education or through informal training and experience, and are divided into four broad skill levels. Skill levels 3 and 4 require tertiary-level qualifications (ISCED 5 and 6). These skill levels are required in occupations classified as ISCO Category 1 (legislators, senior officials and managers), Category 2 (professionals) and Category 3 (technicians

Comparing the average salaries of teachers with those in other professions in the public sector allows to gauge the competitiveness of the teaching profession in relation to other public sector professions.

and associated professionals). Twelve public sector occupations were selected from ISCO categories 1 to 3 in order to compare the salaries of teachers with those in other public sector professions.

Teachers in secondary education tend to earn less than executive officials with a tertiary-type A qualification, town planners and civil engineers.

In half or more of the OECD countries, town planners, civil engineers, executive officials with tertiary qualifications and agricultural scientists earn more than secondary teachers. But secondary teachers tend to earn more than draughtspersons, pre-primary teachers, librarians or social workers. The data suggest two obvious career options for secondary teachers: for those who excel in their subject field university posts offer an alternative. For those who are more engaged in pedagogy and management, becoming a head teacher (principal) may be a career goal (Table D5.3). These data, however, consider

Chart D5.2.

Changes in annual statuary teachers' salaries in lower secondary education, in equivalent US dollars converted using PPPs, and national income

Change between 1996 and 2001 in annual statutory teachers' salaries after 15 years of experience in public institutions in lower secondary education compared with GDP per capita (2001 constant US dollars and 2001 constant PPPs)

────▶ Index of change between 1996 and 2001in teachers' salaries is higher than in GDP per capita over the same period

────▶ Index of change between 1996 and 2001in GDP per capita is higher than in teachers' salaries over the same period

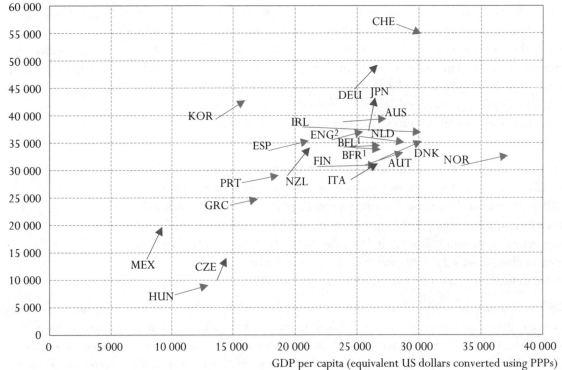

Note: Please refer to the Reader's Guide for list of country codes and country names used in this chart.
The beginning of the arrow indicates spending per student and GPD per capita in 1996. The end of the arrow indicates the corresponding values for 2001.
1. Data on teachers' salaries (1996) and GDP per capita (1996, 2001) refer to Belgium as a whole.
2. Data on GDP per capita (1996, 2001) refer to the United Kingdom.
Source: OECD. Table D5.4 and Annex 2. See Annex 3 for notes on methodology *(www.oecd.org/edu/eag2003)*.

only employees in the public sector. The private sector offers a much bigger range of opportunities, and therefore plays a more important role in shaping the labour market for professionals qualified to teach in upper secondary education.

In Australia, England, Greece, Ireland, Japan, Korea, New Zealand, Norway, Portugal, Scotland, Turkey and the United States, upper secondary and primary teachers' salaries are comparable, while in the remaining OECD countries, teachers' salaries increase with the level of education in absolute terms. For example, in Belgium, Hungary, Iceland, the Netherlands and Switzerland, the mid-career salary of an upper secondary teacher is at least 25 per cent higher than that of a primary school teacher (Table D5.1).

In most countries, salaries increase with the level of education.

Even in countries where statutory salaries are the same in primary and secondary education, salaries per teaching hour are usually higher in upper secondary education than in primary education, since in most countries, secondary teachers are required to teach fewer hours than primary teachers. On average among countries, upper secondary teachers' salary per teaching hour exceeds that of primary teachers by 40 per cent. However, in Australia, New Zealand, Scotland, the Slovak Republic, Turkey and the United States, this difference is only 10 per cent or less, whereas it is around 60 per cent or more in the Flemish Community of Belgium, France, Hungary, Iceland, Korea, the Netherlands and Spain (Table D5.1).

An upper secondary teacher's salary per contact hour is, on average, 40 per cent higher than that of a primary teacher.

Comparing gross teachers' salaries between countries at the point of entry into the teaching profession, after 15 years of experience, and at the top of the salary scale, provides information on the extent to which teaching experience influences salary scales within countries. The difference between statutory starting salaries and subsequent increases is an indication of the financial return to experience. On average, among OECD countries, statutory salaries for primary and lower secondary teachers with 15 years of experience are 37 to 38 per cent higher than starting salaries.

Teaching experience and qualifications influence teachers' salary scales in many OECD countries.

Teachers in Australia, Denmark, England, New Zealand and Scotland reach the highest step on the salary scale within 7 to 11 years. In Belgium, Finland, Germany, Ireland, the Netherlands, Norway, Portugal, the Slovak Republic, Switzerland and Turkey the curve flattens after 20 to 28 years. In Austria, the Czech Republic, France, Greece, Hungary, Italy, Japan, Korea and Spain, teachers reach the top of the salary scale after more than 30 years of service (Table D5.1).

Teachers in Austria, Japan, Korea, Mexico and Portugal start with a relatively low salary level, but the ratio of the top to the starting salary is 2 to 1 or more. By contrast, top salaries of teachers in Denmark, Iceland and Norway are less than 30 per cent higher than starting salaries. In Iceland, long service is rewarded by a reduction in the number of statutory teaching hours rather than by higher salaries. In Greece, salary increments and reduced teaching time are both used to reward long service (Table D5.1).

D5

In addition, bonus schemes can compensate for permanent or temporary special duties and responsibilities that teachers take on.

In addition to basic pay scales, many school systems have developed incentive schemes for teachers, which may take the form of financial remuneration and/or a reduction in the number of teaching hours. Together with the starting salary, such incentive schemes affect a person's decision to enter into and stay in the teaching profession. Initial incentives for graduate teachers may include family allowances and bonuses for working in certain locations, higher initial salaries for higher than minimum teaching certification or qualifications, and additional compensation for those holding educational qualifications in multiple subjects or with certification to teach students with special educational needs.

Reduction of required teaching hours is a compensation often used instead of additional pay.

A specific type of bonus is the reduction of required teaching hours. In some countries, this bonus is used to reward experience or long service (*e.g.* in Greece and Iceland), in others, rather than being paid for special duties, teachers are compensated by a reduction of teaching hours for carrying out special tasks or activities (e.g. leading a drama club, or acting as teacher supervisor of student teachers, etc.).

Reduction of teaching time in Greece

When a secondary education teacher is appointed the teaching time is 21 teaching hours per week. After 6 years the teaching time is 19 teaching hours per week. After 12 years the teaching time is 18 teaching hours per week and finally after 20 years the teaching time is 16 teaching hours per week. The remaining hours of the working time of teachers' obligation have to be spent within school

---

D5

In about half of the OECD countries, schools have at least some responsibility in deciding on levels and extent of compensation for special tasks and additional activities undertaken by teachers…

In most countries, allowances are paid to all or most teachers for taking on management responsibilities; teaching more classes or hours than are required under a full-time contract (*e.g.*, acting duties); and involvement in special tasks such as guidance counselling or training student teachers. Although in many countries, there are country level regulations for payment of allowances for overtime work, management responsibilities, and special tasks and activities, in about half of the OECD countries with comparable data (Australia, Austria, the Czech Republic, Denmark, England, Finland, France, Greece, Hungary, Iceland, Italy, New Zealand, Portugal, Scotland, the Slovak Republic and Sweden), schools have at least some responsibility in deciding on the levels and extent of compensation for such activities.

…but in many countries, there are fixed rates of compensation for management positions and administrative tasks…

In most countries management positions are filled by local, regional or national authorities depending on the type of school involved; and the appointee has a statutory right to a reduction of the teaching load (or exemption from teaching obligation) and to an allowance depending on the salary scale, seniority and the size of the school (with a supplement for long term exercise of the function). Teachers entrusted with more limited administrative or co-ordinating functions are remunerated by a flat-rate compensation or a reduction of teaching load, which are fixed centrally and apply whenever such a function is assigned (normally by the principal). There is a certain pool of extra pay (flat rate remuneration) for extra duties available for assignment by the principal. For specific projects the Ministry for Education, Science and Culture may grant a reduction of the teaching load.

In England, from 1 September 2000 additional points on the scale for responsibility were replaced by flat-rate allowances for taking on significant specified management responsibilities beyond those common to the majority of classroom teachers. There were separate pay scales for head teachers and deputy heads.

In Portugal principals receive an increase in salary for the duration of their assignment, while heads of curricular departments, class tutors' co-ordinators and class tutors have their teaching time reduced, during the time they hold the position. The school board makes the decision regarding the reduction of teaching time for middle managers.

In Spain, in lower and upper secondary education there should be a head in each Didactical Department. When there is a teacher with a recognised senior teaching position (Catedrático condition), he/she is the Head of the Department. If there are more than one "catedrático", the Department may suggest to the school principal that one of these teachers be the Head but, in any case, the school principal makes the definitive nomination and the high local education authority makes the final decision. If there is not a teacher with the "catedrático condition" in a certain Department, any of the other teachers can become Head of Department (usually teachers rotate in this position). All the Department Heads receive a fixed salary supplement during the time they hold that responsibility. The standard duration of each "mandate" as Department Head is four years. In primary education any teacher can be the co-ordinator of the teachers in the cycle, but no salary supplement is awarded for this position (Table D5.2 and Annex 3 at *www.oecd.org/edu/eag2003*).

Once in the teaching profession, teaching personnel must be recognised and rewarded for good teaching. Schools can provide incentives by awarding additional remuneration for completing professional development activities, for involvement in special activities, for taking on extra management responsibilities or for outstanding performance in teaching (Table D5.2).

…while school principals tend to have more authority in awarding additional remuneration for professional development or outstanding performance.

D5

In England, extra points on the main scale are awarded for excellent performance. Experienced teachers are also able to apply for the performance threshold, in which they are assessed against national standards. If successful, they are moved to the 'upper pay scale', with the prospect of further pay increases based on performance. In the Czech Republic, Denmark, Hungary, Mexico, New Zealand, Portugal, the Slovak Republic, Sweden, Turkey and the United States, allowances are also paid for outstanding performance. In Mexico bonuses awarded to teachers for outstanding performance are based on evaluations of learning achievement of students in the class or subject. In Portugal, after 15 years of teaching, and after receiving an appraisal of "Good" given by the head teacher, teachers may apply for a special appraisal of their curriculum vitae and

---

Promotion awarded for further qualification

In the Slovak Republic, two teacher qualification examinations exist, which are organised with the aim to promote the professional development of teachers. The first examination is designed for fully qualified teachers with a university degree who can show at least 5 years of professional teaching experience. The requirement for the second teacher qualification examination is a university degree and at least 10 years of professional teaching experience. To pass the qualification examination, teachers have to sit for an oral examination and write and defend a thesis. The holders of the certificate of the first examination have the right to be shifted into a higher salary grade. The completion of the second teacher qualification examination can be acknowledged by an increase in personal bonus to the basic salary. The examinations are organised by regional centres of methodology and the State Institute of Pedagogy.

---

receive an increase of two years in their career progression, although this rarely occurs. In Turkey extra salary for teachers with excellent performance are based on evaluations by the Provincial Directorate of Education and the Ministry (Table D5.2 and Annex 3 at *www.oecd.org/edu/eag2003*).

Differences in tax schemes, social benefit systems, allowances and entitlements may enhance basic salaries of all teachers differently in OECD countries.

Pay scales are based on the simple principles of qualification levels and years of service but in reality, the structure of the teacher compensation system is far more complex. Many countries include regional allowances for teaching in remote regions, or a family allowance as part of the annual gross salary. Entitlements may include reduced rates on public transportation, tax allowances on purchasing cultural goods, and other quasi-pecuniary entitlements that contribute to teacher's basic income. There are large differences between the taxing and social benefit systems in OECD countries. This makes it important to compare teachers' salaries with caution.

Definitions and methodologies

Data are from the 2002 OECD-INES survey on Teachers and the Curriculum and refer to the school year 2000-2001.

Data on statutory teachers' salaries and bonuses (Table D5.1) are derived from the 2002 OECD-INES Survey on Teachers and the Curriculum. Data refer to the school year 2000-2001, and are reported in accordance with formal policies for public institutions.

Statutory salaries (Table D5.1) refer to scheduled salaries according to official pay scales. The salaries reported are gross (total sum of money paid by the employer) less the employer's contribution to social security and pension (according to existing salary scales). Salaries are "before tax", *i.e.*, before deductions for income taxes.

Gross teachers' salaries were converted using GDP and Purchasing Power Parities (PPPs) exchange rate data from the OECD National Accounts database. The reference date for GDP per capita is the calendar year 2000, while the

D5

period of reference for teachers' salaries is 30 June 2000 to 30 June 2001. The reference date for PPPs is 2000-2001. Data are adjusted for inflation with reference to January 2001. For countries with different financial years (*i.e.*, Australia and New Zealand) and countries with slightly different salary periods (*e.g.*, Hungary, Iceland, Norway and Spain) to the general OECD norm, a correction to the deflator is made only if this results in an adjustment of over 1 percent. Small adjustments have been discounted because even for salaries referring to 2000-2001, the exact period for which they apply will only be slightly different. Reference statistics and reference years for teachers' salaries are provided in Annex 2.

Starting salaries refer to the average scheduled gross salary per year for a full-time teacher with the minimum training necessary to be fully qualified at the beginning of the teaching career.

Salaries after 15 years of experience refer to the scheduled annual salary of a full-time classroom teacher with the minimum training necessary to be fully qualified and have 15 years of experience. The maximum salaries reported refer to the scheduled maximum annual salary (top of the salary scale) of a full-time classroom teacher with the minimum training to be fully qualified for the job.

An adjustment to base salary is defined as any difference in salary between what a particular teacher actually receives for work performed at a school and the amount that he or she would be expected to receive on the basis of level of experience (*i.e.*, number of years in the teaching profession). Adjustments may be temporary or permanent, and they can effectively move a teacher "off-scale", on to a different salary, or to a higher step on the same salary scale.

The index used to compare primary teachers' salaries with those of other employees derives from a 1999 Survey of Compensation of Employees for Selected Occupations in General Government conducted by the EUROSTAT-OECD PPP Programme (Table D5.3). The compensation costs of the selected occupations are intended to be representative of the compensation of employees recorded in the national accounts under government expenditure on general public services and education. Definitions of selected occupations have been taken form the 1988 version of the International Standard Classification of Occupations (ISCO) of the International Labour Office.

D5

Table D5.1
Teachers' salaries (2001)
Annual statutory salaries of teachers in public institutions at starting salary, after 15 years of experience and at the top of the scale by level of education, in equivalent US dollars converted using PPPs

	Primary education				Lower secondary education				Upper secondary education, general programmes			
	Starting salary/ minimum training	Salary after 15 years of experience /minimum training	Salary at top of scale /minimum training	Ratio of salary after 15 years of experience to GDP per capita	Starting salary/ minimum training	Salary after 15 years of experience /minimum training	Salary at top of scale /minimum training	Ratio of salary after 15 years of experience to GDP per capita	Starting salary/ minimum training	Salary after 15 years of experience /minimum training	Salary at top of scale /minimum training	Ratio of salary after 15 years of experience to GDP per capita
Australia	27 980	39 715	39 715	1.45	28 025	39 668	39 668	1.44	28 024	39 668	39 668	1.44
Austria	23 384	31 124	46 833	1.09	24 251	33 187	50 428	1.16	24 742	34 516	52 692	1.21
Belgium (Fl.)	24 618	33 047	39 127	1.23	24 618	34 475	42 028	1.29	30 544	44 085	52 990	1.65
Belgium (Fr.)	23 430	31 984	38 380	1.19	23 865	33 684	41 264	1.26	29 741	43 328	52 263	1.62
Czech Republic	10 704	13 941	18 429	0.97	10 704	13 941	18 429	0.97	12 200	15 520	21 045	1.08
Denmark	31 165	35 297	35 297	1.17	31 165	35 297	35 297	1.17	30 103	40 019	42 734	1.33
England	23 297	36 864	36 864	1.46	23 297	36 864	36 864	1.46	23 297	36 864	36 864	1.46
Finland	19 835	27 175	28 075	1.03	22 320	30 945	32 429	1.17	23 104	32 429	34 314	1.23
France	21 702	29 193	43 073	1.14	24 016	31 507	45 501	1.23	24 016	31 507	45 501	1.23
Germany	38 412	46 459	49 839	1.75	39 853	49 053	51 210	1.84	43 100	52 839	55 210	1.99
Greece	20 422	24 716	29 798	1.46	20 422	24 716	29 798	1.46	20 422	24 716	29 798	1.46
Hungary	6 340	8 957	12 200	0.69	6 340	8 957	12 200	0.69	7 704	11 260	14 809	0.87
Iceland	16 883	18 717	19 373	0.64	16 883	18 717	19 373	0.64	23 282	29 546	32 306	1.02
Ireland	22 727	36 837	41 580	1.23	23 861	37 234	41 977	1.24	23 861	37 234	41 977	1.24
Italy	23 537	28 483	34 339	1.07	25 400	31 072	37 798	1.17	25 400	31 959	39 561	1.20
Japan	22 800	43 043	54 921	1.63	22 800	43 043	54 921	1.63	22 800	43 069	56 580	1.63
Korea	25 177	42 845	68 581	2.69	25 045	42 713	68 449	2.69	25 045	42 713	68 449	2.69
Mexico	11 703	15 455	25 565	1.69	14 993	19 588	32 240	2.14	m	m	m	m
Netherlands	27 464	32 750	39 645	1.14	28 498	35 055	43 552	1.22	28 773	48 889	57 808	1.70
New Zealand	17 544	33 941	33 941	1.61	17 544	33 941	33 941	1.61	17 544	33 941	33 941	1.61
Norway	28 942	32 621	35 502	0.88	28 942	32 621	35 502	0.88	28 942	32 621	35 502	0.88
Portugal	19 585	28 974	52 199	1.56	19 585	28 974	52 199	1.56	19 585	28 974	52 199	1.56
Scotland	22 388	35 872	35 872	1.42	22 388	35 872	35 872	1.42	22 388	35 872	35 872	1.42
Slovak Republic	5 319	6 604	7 581	0.55	5 319	6 604	8 377	0.55	5 319	6 604	9 267	0.55
Spain	26 875	31 357	39 123	1.50	30 228	35 215	43 790	1.68	31 345	36 500	45 345	1.74
Sweden	21 498	25 722	28 489	1.01	21 498	25 722	28 489	1.01	23 070	27 535	29 653	1.08
Switzerland	35 059	46 048	54 900	1.52	41 358	54 852	64 707	1.81	49 484	63 893	74 949	2.11
Turkey	10 014	12 031	17 325	2.12	a	a	a	a	9 162	11 180	16 473	1.97
United States	28 681	41 595	50 636	1.19	28 693	41 595	49 728	1.19	28 806	41 708	49 862	1.19
Country mean	*21 982*	*30 047*	*36 455*	*1.31*	*23 283*	*31 968*	*38 787*	*1.34*	*24 350*	*34 250*	*41 344*	*1.43*
Argentina	8 181	11 362	13 568	0.92	10 617	15 249	18 454	1.23	10 617	15 249	18 454	1.23
Brazil	7 922	10 695	11 628	1.45	14 900	17 263	18 800	2.35	16 701	17 777	20 326	2.42
Chile	11 631	12 902	17 310	1.37	11 631	12 902	17 310	1.37	11 631	13 487	18 107	1.43
Egypt	2 222	4 961	m	1.37	2 222	4 961	m	1.37	2 222	4 961	m	1.37
Indonesia	1 172	1 855	3 535	0.61	1 172	1 855	3 535	0.61	1 219	2 234	3 535	0.73
Jamaica	7 345	8 751	8 751	2.38	7 345	8 751	8 751	2.38	7 345	8 751	8 751	2.38
Malaysia[1]	9 344	14 280	17 650	1.59	13 647	21 936	29 513	2.49	13 647	21 936	29 513	2.49
Paraguay	9 146	9 146	9 146	2.07	14 266	14 266	14 266	3.22	14 266	14 266	14 266	3.22
Peru[1]	5 597	5 597	5 597	1.22	5 536	5 536	5 536	1.20	5 536	5 536	5 536	1.20
Philippines	10 777	11 896	12 811	3.06	10 777	11 896	12 811	3.06	10 777	11 896	12 811	3.06
Thailand	6 057	14 886	28 390	2.49	6 057	14 886	28 390	2.49	6 057	14 886	28 390	2.49
Tunisia[2]	13 418	13 564	15 409	2.14	17 073	17 236	19 500	2.72	20 782	20 977	23 482	3.31
Uruguay[3]	5 734	6 872	8 295	0.76	5 734	6 872	8 295	0.76	6 240	7 378	8 801	0.82

Side labels: OECD COUNTRIES; NON-OECD COUNTRIES

1. Year of reference 2000.
2. Including additional bonuses.
3. Salaries for a position of 20 hours per week. Most teachers hold two positions.
See Annex 2 for reference statistics used in the calculation of teachers' salaries.
Source: OECD. See Annex 3 for notes (*www.oecd.org/edu/eag2003*).

D5

Table D5.1 (continued)
Teachers' salaries (2001)
*Annual statutory salaries of teachers in public institutions at starting salary, after 15 years of experience and at the top of the scale by level of education,
in equivalent US dollars converted using PPPs*

	Ratio of salary after 15 years of experience to starting salary				Salary per hour of net contact (teaching) time after 15 years of experience			Ratio of salary per teaching hour of upper secondary and primary teachers (after 15 years of experience)
	Primary education	Lower secondary education	Upper secondary education, general programmes	Years from starting to top salary (lower secondary education)	Primary education	Lower secondary education	Upper secondary education, general programmes	
OECD COUNTRIES								
Australia	1.42	1.42	1.42	10	44	48	49	1.09
Austria	1.33	1.37	1.40	34	39	53	57	1.47
Belgium (Fl.)	1.34	1.40	1.44	27	40	48	66	1.65
Belgium (Fr.)	1.37	1.41	1.46	27	45	47	66	1.47
Czech Republic	1.30	1.30	1.27	32	23	23	27	1.17
Denmark	1.13	1.13	1.33	8	55	55	71	1.30
England	1.58	1.58	1.58	8	a	a	a	a
Finland	1.37	1.39	1.40	20	41	56	60	1.44
France	1.35	1.31	1.31	34	32	49	52	1.60
Germany	1.21	1.23	1.23	28	59	67	77	1.30
Greece	1.21	1.21	1.21	33	32	39	39	1.24
Hungary	1.41	1.41	1.46	40	12	16	20	1.76
Iceland	1.11	1.11	1.27	18	30	30	53	1.79
Ireland	1.62	1.56	1.56	22	40	51	51	1.26
Italy	1.21	1.22	1.26	35	38	51	52	1.37
Japan	1.89	1.89	1.89	31	68	77	90	1.33
Korea	1.70	1.71	1.71	37	52	77	82	1.59
Mexico	1.32	1.31	m	14	19	17	m	m
Netherlands	1.19	1.23	1.70	22	35	40	56	1.60
New Zealand	1.93	1.93	1.93	7	34	35	36	1.04
Norway	1.13	1.13	1.13	28	46	52	65	1.41
Portugal	1.48	1.48	1.48	26	38	45	54	1.45
Scotland	1.60	1.60	1.60	11	38	40	40	1.06
Slovak Republic	1.24	1.24	1.24	27	10	10	11	1.05
Spain	1.17	1.16	1.16	39	36	62	67	1.87
Sweden	1.20	1.20	1.19	a	a	a	a	a
Switzerland	1.31	1.33	1.29	24	m	m	m	m
Turkey	1.20	a	1.22	27	19	a	20	1.05
United States	1.45	1.45	1.45	m	37	37	37	1.02
Country mean	*1.37*	*1.38*	*1.41*	*25*	*37*	*45*	*52*	*1.38*
NON-OECD COUNTRIES								
Argentina	1.39	1.44	1.44	21-24	16	19	21	1.37
Brazil	1.35	1.16	1.06	25	m	m	m	m
Chile	1.11	1.11	1.16	30	16	16	16	1.05
Egypt	2.23	2.23	2.23	m	8	8	8	1.00
Indonesia	1.58	1.58	1.83	32	1	3	3	2.20
Jamaica	1.19	1.19	1.19	12	9	9	9	1.00
Malaysia[1]	1.53	1.57	1.64	22	16	29	29	1.87
Paraguay	1.00	1.00	1.00	a	11	16	14	1.25
Peru[1]	1.00	1.00	1.00	22	9	m	10	1.19
Philippines	1.10	1.10	1.10	22	10	10	12	1.20
Thailand	2.46	2.46	2.46	37	20	23	23	1.17
Tunisia[2]	1.01	1.01	1.01	30	24	41	50	2.09
Uruguay[3]	1.20	1.20	1.18	24	a	a	a	a

1. Year of reference 2000.
2. Including additional bonuses.
3. Salaries for a position of 20 hours per week. Most teachers hold two positions.
See Annex 2 for reference statistics used in the calculation of teachers' salaries.
Source: OECD. See Annex 3 for notes (*www.oecd.org/edu/eag2003*).

D5

Table D5.2
Adjustments to base salary for teachers in public schools (2001)
Types of adjustments to base salary awarded to teachers in public schools, by authority responsible for making the decision regarding the adjustment

■ Decision for additional bonus made by the head teacher/ school principal
▲ Decision for additional bonus made by the local or regional authority
● Decision for additional bonus made by the national authority

OECD COUNTRIES	Holding an initial educational qualification higher than the minimum qualification required to enter the teaching profession	Reaching high scores in the qualification examination	Holding an educational qualification in multiple subjects (e.g., history and mathematics)	Successful completion of professional development activities	Management responsibilities in addition to teaching duties (e.g., serving as a head of department or co-ordinator of teachers in a particular class/grade)	Holding a higher than minimum level of teacher certification or training obtained during professional life (e.g., master teacher; holding an advanced certificate rather than an ordinary certificate)	Outstanding performance in teaching (e.g. based on higher student achievement, independent assessment of teaching skills, etc.)	Teaching courses in a particular field (e.g., mathematics or science)
Australia	▲				■ ▲	▲		
Austria					■ ▲ ●			
Belgium (Fl.)					●			
Belgium (Fr.)								
Czech Republic					■ ●		■	
Denmark	■		■	■	■ ▲ ●	■		
England		●			■	●	■	■
Finland	▲ ●				▲ ●			
France					●			
Germany					▲			
Greece		●					●	
Hungary		●		●	■ ●	●	■	■ ●
Iceland	▲ ●		●	▲ ●	■ ▲ ●	▲ ●		▲ ●
Ireland		●	●		●	●		
Italy								
Japan					▲			
Korea					●			
Mexico	■ ▲		●	■ ▲		▲ ●	●	
Netherlands								
New Zealand					■	●	■	■ ●
Norway		●			●	●		
Portugal		●		●	■ ●	●	▲	
Scotland	▲ ●				■ ▲			
Slovak Republic							▲	
Spain				▲	▲			
Sweden	■	■	■	■	■	■	■	■
Switzerland					▲			
Turkey		●		●			●	
United States	▲			▲	▲	▲	▲	▲

Source: OECD. See Annex 3 for notes (*www.oecd.org/edu/eag2003*).

D5

Table D5.2 (continued)
Adjustments to base salary for teachers in public schools (2001)
Types of adjustments to base salary awarded to teachers in public schools, by authority responsible for making the decision regarding the adjustment

■ Decision for additional bonus made by the head teacher/ school principal
▲ Decision for additional bonus made by the local or regional authority
● Decision for additional bonus made by the national authority

	Teaching students with special educational needs (in regular schools)	Teaching more classes or hours than required by full-time contract (*e.g.*, overtime compensation)	Special activities (*e.g.*, sports and drama clubs, homework clubs, Summer school, etc.)	Special tasks (*e.g.*, training student teachers, guidance counseling)	Teaching in a disadvantaged, remote or high cost area (location allowance)	Family status (*e.g.*, married, number of children)	Age (independent of years of teaching experience)	Other
Australia	▲			■ ▲	■ ▲ ●	▲		
Austria		■ ●	■ ●	■ ●		●	●	●
Belgium (Fl.)		●						●
Belgium (Fr.)								●
Czech Republic	■ ●	●		●			■	
Denmark		●	■	■				
England	■	■	■		■ ●			
Finland		▲ ●	■ ▲	■ ▲	▲ ●			▲ ●
France	●	●	■	●	●	●		
Germany		▲			●	●	▲ ●	
Greece		■		●	●	●		
Hungary	■ ●	■ ▲ ●	●	■ ▲ ●	●		●	■ ●
Iceland	■ ▲ ●	■ ▲ ●	■ ▲ ●	■ ▲ ●	▲		▲ ●	▲ ●
Ireland								
Italy		■	■	■	▲	●	▲	
Japan	▲	▲	▲		▲	▲		▲
Korea	●	●			●	●		
Mexico					●			■ ▲
Netherlands	●							
New Zealand	●		■	■ ●	●			●
Norway		●			●			●
Portugal	●	●	■	●		●		
Scotland					▲			
Slovak Republic		■						
Spain					▲	▲		
Sweden	■	■	■	■	■			
Switzerland	▲	▲ ●	▲	▲		●		▲
Turkey		●	●		●	●		●
United States	▲	▲		▲	▲			

Source: OECD. See Annex 3 for notes (*www.oecd.org / edu / eag2003*).

D5

Table D5.3
Comparison of average secondary teachers' salaries with those of other public sector employees (1999)
Average compensation of employees for selected occupations in the public sector (secondary teacher =100)

Comparison with a secondary teacher's salary
- ■ Between -10 and +10 per cent of a secondary teacher's salary
- ▼ More than 10 but less than 30 per cent lower than a secondary teacher's salary
- ▽ More than 30 per cent lower than a secondary teacher's salary
- ▲ More than 10 but less than 30 per cent higher than a secondary teacher's salary
- △ More than 30 per cent higher than a secondary teacher's salary

	Draughts-person	Pre-primary teacher	Computer operator	Librarian	Social worker	Executive official II[1]	University lecturer	Town planner	Civil engineer	Executive official I[1]	Head teacher	Agricultural scientist	Primary teacher
Australia	■	▼	■	▼	▼	■	■	■	■	▲			▼
Austria	▽	▽	▽	▽	▼	▼	▲	△	△	▲	▲	■	▼
Canada	■	▼	▼	■	■	▼	△	▲	△	▲	△	▲	▼
Czeh Republic	■	▽	▼	▼	■	■	△	△	△	▲	△	△	▼
Denmark	▼	▼	■	■	▼	▼	▲	▲	▲	▼	△	▲	■
Finland	▽	▼	▽	▼	▼	▽	▲	■	▲	▽	△	■	▼
France	▼	▼	■	▲	▼	▼	△	▲	△	▲	△	▲	▼
Germany	▽	▽	▽	■	■	▼	■		■	■	▲	■	▼
Greece	▼	▼	■	▼	▼	▽	△	■	■	▼	▲	▼	▼
Hungary	▼	▽	▼	▼	▽	▼	▲	△	△	△	△	△	▼
Iceland	▼	▼	■	■	▲	▼	△	△	△	▼	▲	■	■
Ireland	■		▽	■	△	▽	△	△	■	■	△	▼	■
Italy		■	■			■					▲		■
Japan	△	■	▼			△	△	△	△	△	△	△	■
Korea		■	▲	▲	▽	△	▲	△	△	△	△	△	■
Luembourg	▽	▼	▽		▼	▽			■	▼	▲		▼
Mexico	▽	▽	▼	▽	▽	△	△	△	△	△	△	■	▼
Netherlands	▼	■	■			■	△		△	△	■		■
New Zealand	▽	▽	▼	■	▼		△	■	▼		△		■
Norway	■	▼		■	■		△	▲	▲	▲	▲		■
Poland	■	▼	■	▼	■		△	▲	△		△	▲	■
Portugal	■	■	■	△	△	■	△	△	△	△	△	△	■
Spain	▽	▼	▼	▲	▼	△	△	▼	△	△	△	△	▼
Sweden	■	▼	■	■	■	▼	▲		▲	■	△	▲	■
Turkey	▽	■	▽	▽	▼	▽	△	▼	▼	▽	▲	△	■
United Kingdom						▽				▼	△		■
United States	▼	▼	▽	■	■	△	△	△	△	△		▲	■

Note: Occupations are classified according to ISCO-88 (Categories 1 to 3).
1. Unlike Executive Official I, Executive Official II does not require a tertiary-type A qualification and sometimes works to an Executive Official I.
Source: EUROSTAT-OECD Purchasing Power Parities Programme (1999). See Annex 3 for notes (*www.oecd.org/edu/eag2003*).

D5

Table D5.4
Change in teachers' salaries (1996 and 2001)
Index of change[1] between 1996 and 2001 in teachers' salaries at starting salary, after 15 years of experience and at the top of the salary scale, by level of education, converted to 2001 price levels using GDP deflators (1996=100)

	Primary education			Lower secondary education			Upper secondary education, general programmes		
	Starting salary/ minimum training	Salary after 15 years of experience/ minimum training	Salary at top of scale/ minimum training	Starting salary/ minimum training	Salary after 15 years of experience/ minimum training	Salary at top of scale/ minimum training	Starting salary/ minimum training	Salary after 15 years of experience/ minimum training	Salary at top of scale/ minimum training
Australia	131	102	102	131	102	102	131	102	102
Austria	102	106	101	102	107	102	98	102	95
Belgium (Fl.)[2]	103	103	102	101	101	101	101	101	101
Belgium (Fr.)[2]	98	99	100	98	98	99	98	99	99
Czech Republic	140	140	155	140	140	155	141	138	156
Denmark	119	111	108	119	111	108	106	99	101
England	98	103	103	98	103	103	98	103	103
Finland	101	105	105	101	101	101	102	101	101
France	m	m	m	m	m	m	m	m	m
Germany	119	114	113	113	111	109	115	113	102
Greece	106	108	110	103	105	107	103	105	107
Hungary	118	123	129	118	123	129	112	124	131
Iceland	m	m	m	m	m	m	m	m	m
Ireland	98	103	98	98	98	98	98	98	98
Italy	111	111	110	110	110	110	110	110	109
Japan	105	116	103	105	116	103	105	116	103
Korea	115	110	110	113	109	110	113	109	110
Mexico	136	136	137	137	141	144	m	m	m
Netherlands	101	98	97	99	97	97	99	97	97
New Zealand	103	117	117	103	117	117	103	117	117
Norway	115	106	114	115	106	114	106	103	105
Portugal	106	104	109	106	104	109	106	104	109
Scotland	103	99	99	m	m	m	103	99	99
Slovak Republic	m	m	m	m	m	m	m	m	m
Spain	94	93	91	106	105	102	94	94	93
Sweden	m	m	m	m	m	m	m	m	m
Switzerland	99	97	100	99	97	101	99	97	102
Turkey	m	m	m	m	m	m	m	m	m
United States	m	m	m	m	m	m	m	m	m

1. The index is calculated as teacher salary 2001 in national currency * 100 / Teacher salary 1996 in national currency * GDP deflator 2001 (1996=100).
2. The data for Belgium in 1996 are based on Belgium as a whole.
See Annex 2 for reference statistics used in the calculation of this indicator.
Source: OECD. See Annex 3 for notes (*www.oecd.org/edu/eag2003*).

D5

INDICATOR D6: TEACHING TIME AND TEACHERS' WORKING TIME

- The number of teaching hours per year in public primary schools averages 792 hours but ranges from 605 to 1 139 hours among OECD countries.

- The average number of teaching hours in lower secondary education is 714 hours but ranges from 553 to 1 182 hours among OECD countries.

- The average number of teaching hours in upper secondary education is 656 hours but ranges from 478 to 1 121 hours among OECD countries.

- Regulations of teachers' working time vary among countries. In most countries, teachers are formally required to work a specific number of hours; while in others just teaching time in lessons per week is specified.

D6

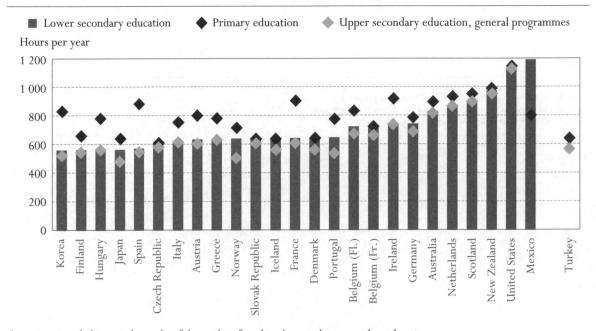

Chart D6.1

Number of teaching hours per year (2001)

Net contact time in hours per year in public institutions, by level of education

■ Lower secondary education ◆ Primary education ◆ Upper secondary education, general programmes

Hours per year

Countries are ranked in ascending order of the number of teaching hours in lower secondary education.
Source: OECD. Table D6.1. See Annex 3 for notes *(www.oecd.org/edu/eag2003).*

Policy context

In addition to class size and the ratio of students to teaching staff (Indicator D2), students' hours of instruction (Indicator D1) and teachers' salaries (Indicator D5), the amount of time teachers spend teaching influences the financial resources which countries need to invest in education. Teaching hours and the extent of non-teaching duties are also important elements of teachers' working conditions and are related to the attractiveness of the teaching profession.

This indicator shows the number of hours per year that a full-time teacher is required to spend teaching according to formal policy in his/her country.

Evidence and explanations

Teaching time

A primary school teacher teaches an average of 792 hours per year but this varies from 650 hours or less in the Czech Republic, Denmark, Iceland, Japan, the Slovak Republic and Turkey to 950 hours or more in New Zealand, Scotland and the United States (Chart D6.1 and Table D6.2).

A public primary school teacher teaches an average of 792 hours per year.

In lower secondary education, a teacher teaches on average 714 hours per year. The teaching load here ranges from between 553 and 564 hours in Finland, Hungary, Japan, Korea and Spain to over 900 hours in Mexico, New Zealand and the United States (Chart D6.1 and Table D6.2).

A lower secondary teacher teaches an average of 714 hours per year, but this figure ranges from 553 hours to 1 182 hours.

An upper secondary teaching load is equal to or less than that in lower secondary education. A teacher of general subjects has an average statutory load of 656 hours per year among OECD countries. Teaching loads range from less than 500 hours in Japan to over 900 hours in New Zealand and the United States (Chart D6.1 and Table D6.2).

In France, Korea and Spain, a primary teacher is required to teach almost more than 300 hours more than an upper secondary teacher (general programmes). By contrast, in Australia, the French Community of Belgium, the Czech Republic, Denmark, Germany, Iceland, the Netherlands, New Zealand, Scotland, the Slovak Republic, Turkey and the United States the difference is 100 hours or less (Chart D6.1).

In most countries, a primary school teacher teaches for more hours than a lower and upper secondary teacher, but the differentials vary widely between countries.

In interpreting the differences in teaching hours between countries, it needs to be taken into account that net contact time, as used for the purpose of this indicator, does not correspond to the number of lessons a teacher has during the week. Whereas contact time in itself is a substantial component of workload, the preparation for classes and necessary follow-up (including correcting students' work) relates more closely to the number of lessons per week. Other elements of teaching load (like the number of subjects taught, the number of students taught, and the number of years a teacher teaches the same students) should also be taken account when establishing the average teaching load of teachers within a country. These factors, however, can often only be assessed at school level.

D6

With the exception of Austria, the French Community of Belgium, Hungary, Korea and Spain, teaching time did not change substantially between 1996 and 2001.

With the exception of Austria (primary education), the French Community of Belgium (primary education), Hungary, Korea (secondary education) and Spain (upper secondary education), teaching time in most OECD countries was about the same in 1996 and 2001. However, in Korea, teachers in secondary education were required to teach 21 per cent more in 2001 than in 1996, while in Spain net contact time dropped by 13 per cent in upper secondary education (Table D6.2).

Teachers' working time

Regulations of teachers' working time vary widely among countries.

The regulations of teachers' working time vary widely among countries. While some countries formally regulate contact time only, others establish working hours as well. In some countries, time is allocated for teaching and non-teaching activities within the formally established working time. Within the framework of statutory working time and teaching time, teachers' actual workload may vary widely.

In most countries, teachers are formally required to work a specified number of hours...

In most countries, teachers are formally required to work a specified number of hours per week to earn their full-time salary including teaching and non-teaching time. Within this framework, however, countries vary regarding what they specify in terms of allocating time to teaching and non-teaching activities. Typically, the number of hours for teaching is specified, but some countries also regulate at national level the time that a teacher has to be present in the school.

...in some, working time at school is also specified while ...

In Australia, the French Community of Belgium (primary education), the Czech Republic, England, Greece, Iceland, Ireland, Mexico (primary and lower secondary education), New Zealand, Norway, Portugal, Scotland, Spain, Sweden, Turkey and the United States, the working time for which teachers are required to be available at school, for both teaching time and non-teaching time, is specified.

Working time in Australia

Teachers in Australia have to spend a certain number of working hours at school, which includes teaching and non-teaching activities. In addition to this there are other not defined (additional) non-teaching duties undertaken outside these specified hours. Therefore most Australian teachers work longer hours than those reported.

D6

... in others, just the total statutory working time in hours per year is defined.

In Denmark, Germany, Greece, Hungary, Iceland, Ireland (primary education), Japan, Korea, the Netherlands, Norway, Portugal, Scotland, the Slovak Republic, Spain, Sweden and Turkey, the total working time that teachers have to work per year is specified. In addition, in some countries the number of hours to be spent on non-teaching activities is also (partly) specified. However, it is not specified whether the teachers have to spend the non-teaching hours at school or outside school.

Allocation of working time in the Netherlands

In the Netherlands at all education levels, 10 per cent of the total annual required 1 659 working hours are available for professional development. In lower secondary and upper secondary (general programmes) education for example, in addition to 867 teaching hours per year, 173 hours per year are allowed for preparation, 166 hours for professional development, and 452 hours for other tasks.

In Australia, Austria, Belgium, the Czech Republic, England, Finland, France, Ireland (secondary education), Italy, Mexico, New Zealand and the United States there are no formal requirements for how much time should be spent on non-teaching duties. However, this does not mean that teachers are totally free in carrying out the other tasks. In Austria, provisions concerning teaching time are based on the assumption that the duties of the teacher (including preparing lessons and tests, marking and correcting papers, examinations, and administrative tasks) amount to a total working time of 40 hours per week. In the Flemish Community of Belgium, the additional non-teaching hours within the school are set at the school level. There are no regulations regarding lesson preparation, correction of tests and marking students' papers, etc. The government just defines the minimum and maximum number of teaching periods (of 50 minutes each) per week at each level of education. In Finland, although not formally set, teachers in primary and lower secondary education are, in addition to their teaching load, required to spend two hours per week on planning, meetings or co-operation with the homes. In upper secondary education Finnish teachers are required to reserve two to five hours per week on meetings and other tasks.

In 12 out of 27 OECD countries for which data are available there are no formal requirements on non-teaching time.

In the Czech Republic, Japan and Korea, teachers are required to work the same number of hours as civil servants. No further regulations are provided at the national level concerning teaching or non-teaching hours. However, in Korea, teachers are required to work during the school vacation on their own schedule on professional development (Table D6.1).

... while in the Czech Republic, Japan and Korea, teachers' working time is specified only in the general regulations on civil servants' working time.

D6

Teaching and working time in Korea

There is no policy on how many hours teachers should teach in a week or a month or a year. The data on teaching time is based on the annual administrative data collection and refer to the time teachers usually teach per week during the school year. Teachers are civil servants and their working time is regulated within that framework. Whereas there are national regulations on the length of the school year and on the working hours of civil servants, which apply to teachers during the school year period, during the summer and winter vacations teachers work on self-regulated schedules of professional development training.

Working time in the Czech Republic

In the Czech Republic teachers are public employees and their working time is set accordingly. Teachers are supposed to work 42 hours a week (excluding lunch breaks) over 40.2 weeks, of which only teaching time is further specified.

Definitions and methodologies

Teaching time

Data are from the 2002 OECD-INES Survey on Teachers and the Curriculum and refer to the school year 2000-2001.

The number of teaching hours is defined as net contact hours calculated on the basis of the annual number of weeks of instruction multiplied by the minimum/maximum number of periods that a teacher is supposed to spend teaching a class or a group, multiplied by the length of a period in minutes and divided by 60. This excludes break periods between lessons and days when schools are closed for public holidays and festivities. In primary education, however, short breaks that teachers spend with the class are typically included.

Working time

Working time refers to the normal working hours of a full-time teacher. According to the formal policy in a given country, working time can refer:

- only to the time directly associated with teaching (and other curricular activities for students such as assignments and tests, but excluding annual examinations);

- or to time directly associated with teaching and to hours devoted to other activities related to teaching, such as lesson preparation, counselling students, correcting assignments and tests, professional development, meetings with parents, staff meetings and general school tasks.

Working time does not include paid overtime.

Working time in school

Working time in school refers to the working time teachers are supposed to be at school, including teaching time and non-teaching time.

Number of teaching weeks and days

The number of teaching weeks refers to the number of weeks of instruction excluding holiday weeks, and is calculated as the number of teaching weeks less the days that the school is closed for festivities.

D6

Table D6.1
The organisation of teachers' working time (2001)
Number of teaching weeks, teaching days, net teaching hours, and teacher working time over the school year

	Number of weeks of instruction		Number of days of instruction		Net teaching time in hours			Working time required at school in hours			Total statutory working time in hours		
	Primary education	Lower secondary education	Primary education	Lower secondary education	Primary education	Lower secondary education	Upper secondary education, general pro-grammes	Primary education	Lower secondary education	Upper secondary education, general pro-grammes	Primary education	Lower secondary education	Upper secondary education, general pro-grammes
Australia	40	40	198	198	893	825	816	1 023	1 087	1 087	a	a	a
Austria	38	38	184	184	799	627	602	a	a	a	a	a	a
Belgium (Fl.)	37	37	178	179	831	716	671	m	m	m	a	a	a
Belgium (Fr.)	37	37	162	180	717	720	661	962	m	m	a	a	a
Czech Republic	39	39	192	192	605	605	576	1 746	1 746	1 746	a	a	a
Denmark	42	42	200	200	640	640	560	m	m	m	1 680	1 680	1 680
England	38	38	190	190	a	a	a	1 265	1 265	1 265	a	a	a
Finland	38	38	190	190	656	555	542	a	a	a	a	a	a
France	35	35	m	m	905	637	609	a	a	a	a	a	a
Germany	40	40	189	189	784	735	684	a	a	a	1 708	1 708	1 708
Greece	40	38	195	185	780	629	629	1 500	1 425	1 425	1 762	1 762	1 762
Hungary	37	37	185	185	777	555	555	a	a	a	1 864	1 864	1 864
Iceland	35	35	170	170	634	634	560	1 650	1 650	1 720	1 800	1 800	1 800
Ireland	37	33	183	167	915	735	735	915	735	735	915	a	a
Italy	34	34	m	m	748	612	612	a	a	a	a	a	a
Japan	35	35	193	193	635	557	478	a	a	a	1 940	1 940	1 940
Korea	37	37	220	220	828	553	519	a	a	a	1 613	1 613	1 613
Mexico	42	42	200	200	800	1182	m	800	1 182	m	a	a	a
Netherlands	40	40	195	195	930	867	867	a	a	a	1 659	1 659	1 659
New Zealand	39	39	197	194	985	968	950	985	968	950	a	a	a
Norway	38	38	190	190	713	633	505	903	823	695	1 718	1 718	1 718
Portugal	36	36	175	175	772	641	533	875	770	640	1 526	1 526	1 526
Scotland	38	38	190	190	950	893	893	1 075	1 075	1 075	1 153	1 153	1 153
Slovak Republic	40	40	192	192	634	634	605	a	a	a	1 736	1 736	1 736
Spain	37	36	176	171	880	564	548	1 140	1 140	1 140	1 425	1 425	1 425
Sweden	a	a	a	a	a	a	a	1 360	1 360	1 360	1 800	1 800	1 800
Switzerland	m	m	m	m	m	m	m	m	m	m	m	m	m
Turkey	38	a	180	a	639	a	567	870	a	756	1 816	1 816	1 816
United States	36	36	180	180	1 139	1 127	1 121	1 353	1 371	1 371	a	a	a
Argentina[1]	38	38	161	161	725	805	710	m	m	m	m	m	m
Brazil	40	40	200	200	800	800	800	m	m	m	m	m	m
Chile	40	40	191	191	860	860	860	m	m	m	m	m	m
Egypt	36	36	187	187	748	748	748	m	m	m	m	m	m
India	52	52	225	225	1 013	1 125	1 125	m	m	m	m	m	m
Indonesia	44	44	252	164	1 260	738	738	m	m	m	m	m	m
Jamaica	38	38	190	190	950	950	950	m	m	m	m	m	m
Malaysia[1]	41	41	192	192	758	768	768	m	m	m	m	m	m
Paraguay	41	42	203	203	812	903	1 015	m	m	m	m	m	m
Peru[1]	36	36	174	174	783	626	626	m	m	m	m	m	m
Philippines	40	40	196	196	1 176	1 176	980	m	m	m	m	m	m
Russian Federation	45	45	215	215	860	774	774	m	m	m	m	m	m
Sri Lanka	40	40	200	200	960	1 200	1 200	m	m	m	m	m	m
Thailand	40	40	181	181	760	652	652	m	m	m	m	m	m
Tunisia	36	32	147	137	735	548	548	m	m	m	m	m	m
Uruguay[2]	38	38	183	183	732	488	488	m	m	m	m	m	m
Zimbabwe	37	37	180	180	954	954	954	m	m	m	m	m	m

OECD COUNTRIES / *NON-OECD COUNTRIES*

1. Year of reference 2000.
2. Teaching time for a position of 20 hours per week. Most teachers hold two positions.
Source: OECD. See Annex 3 for notes (*www.oecd.org/edu/eag2003*).

D6

Table D6.2
Number of teaching hours per year (1996, 2001)
Net contact time in hours per year in public institutions by level of education, and index of change from 1996 to 2001

		Primary education		Lower secondary education			Upper secondary education general programmes		
		2001	1996	Index of change 1996-2001 (1996=100)	2001	1996	Index of change 1996-2001 (1996=100)	2001	1996	Index of change 1996-2001 (1996=100)
OECD COUNTRIES	Australia	893	m	m	825	m	m	816	m	m
	Austria	799	684	117	627	658	95	602	623	97
	Belgium (Fl.)	831	841	99	716	724	99	671	679	99
	Belgium (Fr.)	717	858	84	720	734	98	661	677	98
	Czech Republic	605	635	95	605	607	100	576	580	99
	Denmark	640	640	100	640	640	100	560	560	100
	England	a	780	m	a	720	m	a	m	m
	Finland	656	m	m	555	m	m	542	m	m
	France	905	900	101	637	647	98	609	m	m
	Germany	784	772	102	735	715	103	684	671	102
	Greece	780	780	100	629	629	100	629	629	100
	Hungary	777	m	m	555	473	117	555	473	117
	Iceland	634	m	m	634	m	m	560	m	m
	Ireland	915	915	100	735	735	100	735	735	100
	Italy	748	748	100	612	612	100	612	612	100
	Japan	635	m	m	557	m	m	478	m	m
	Korea	828	m	m	553	456	121	519	428	121
	Mexico	800	800	100	1182	1182	100	m	m	m
	Netherlands	930	930	100	867	867	100	867	867	100
	New Zealand	985	985	100	968	968	100	950	950	100
	Norway	713	713	100	633	633	100	505	505	100
	Portugal	772	783	99	641	644	99	533	574	93
	Scotland	950	975	97	893	m	m	893	917	97
	Slovak Republic	634	m	m	634	m	m	605	m	m
	Spain	880	900	98	564	a	m	548	630	87
	Sweden	a	624	m	a	576	m	a	528	m
	Switzerland	m	871	m	m	850	m	m	669	m
	Turkey	639	m	m	a	a	a	567	m	m
	United States	1139	m	m	1127	m	m	1121	m	m
	Country mean	*792*	*807*		*714*	*703*		*656*	*648*	
NON-OECD COUNTRIES	Argentina[1]	725	m	m	805	m	m	710	m	m
	Brazil	800	m	m	800	m	m	800	m	m
	Chile	860	m	m	860	m	m	860	m	m
	Egypt	748	m	m	748	m	m	748	m	m
	India	1013	m	m	1125	m	m	1125	m	m
	Indonesia	1260	m	m	738	m	m	738	m	m
	Jamaica	950	m	m	950	m	m	950	m	m
	Malaysia[1]	758	m	m	768	m	m	768	m	m
	Paraguay	812	m	m	903	m	m	1015	m	m
	Peru[1]	783	m	m	626	m	m	626	m	m
	Philippines	1176	m	m	1176	m	m	980	m	m
	Russian Federation	860	m	m	774	m	m	774	m	m
	Sri Lanka	960	m	m	1200	m	m	1200	m	m
	Thailand	760	m	m	652	m	m	652	m	m
	Tunisia	735	m	m	548	m	m	548	m	m
	Uruguay[2]	732	m	m	488	m	m	488	m	m
	Zimbabwe	954	m	m	954	m	m	954	m	m

1. Year of reference 2000.
2. Teaching time for a position of 20 hours per week. Most teachers hold two positions.
Source: OECD. See Annex 3 for notes (*www.oecd.org/edu/eag2003*).

D6

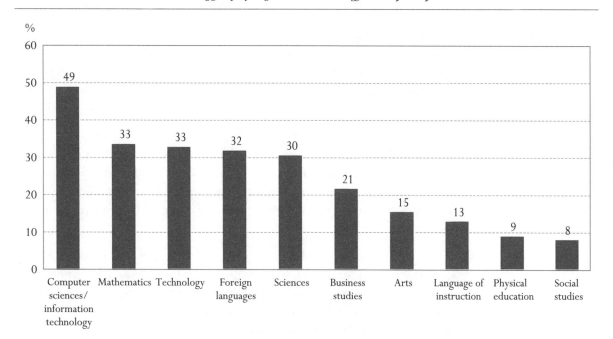

INDICATOR D7: TEACHER SUPPLY AND DEMAND

- The percentages of less than fully qualified teachers employed full-time ranges from 0.4 per cent in Ireland to 20 per cent or more in Mexico, Norway, Portugal, and Sweden.

- On average, about 12 per cent of teaching posts (full-time equivalent) were vacant and were to be covered at the beginning of school year 2001/2002 in the countries for which upper secondary schools were surveyed.

- Nearly two thirds of the teachers in Mexico and Switzerland, but only less than 1 per cent in Korea are employed on a part-time basis.

- In upper secondary education, teacher shortage is most pressing in computer science, mathematics, foreign languages, science, and technology, whereas it appears less problematic in the arts, physical education, social studies and language of instruction.

Chart D7.1

Average perceived difficulty of hiring qualified teachers in various study areas (2001)
Cross-country mean percentage of upper secondary students attending schools where the principal reported that hiring fully qualified teachers is difficult, by study area

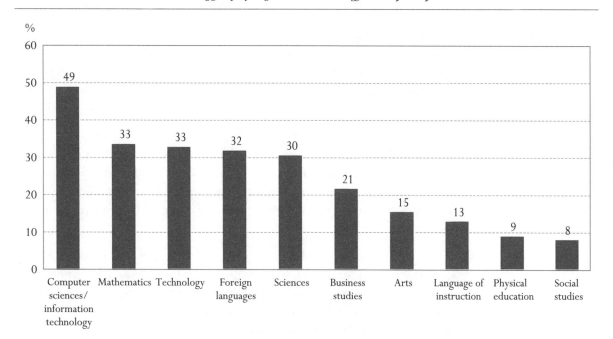

Subjects are ranked in descending order of the cross-country mean percentage of upper secondary students attending schools where the principal reported that hiring fully qualified teachers is difficult.
Note: Proportions by study area are calculated for cross-country means.
Source: OECD ISUSS database, 2003. Table D7.3.

Policy context

Teachers are the key actors of school and classroom processes. Supply of sufficiently qualified teachers for each course is a major task school managers and school authorities are facing. On the system level, provisions for teacher training and teacher licensing, recruitment policies, statutory salary and bonus schemes, and statutory work conditions constitute the basic policy framework for teacher supply.

However, at the local level, demand for and supply of teachers with specific subject matter expertise depends on a series of other factors as well. Local labour market conditions influence teachers' career decisions, *e.g.* industries competing for skills and expertise that teachers dispose of can play a role in the 'brain drain' from schools and conversely, the absence of other local labour opportunities may influence the choice of a teaching career. Teacher flow in a school may also depend on the age composition of the teaching staff, and on the social composition of the student population as well as on the school's working climate.

Evidence and explanations

This indicator presents school level data on teacher supply and demand in 15 OECD countries. In the International Survey of Upper Secondary Schools (ISUSS), principals were asked about vacancies and modes of covering vacancies in their schools. Responses show that there are large differences among systems in the size of the teacher shortage problem. Also, besides evident similarities regarding relative shortages across study areas, countries appear to have characteristic national difficulties in certain areas of teacher expertise.

Less than fully qualified teachers constitute a substantial part of the teaching staff in several OECD countries at the upper secondary level.

Schools are sometimes compelled to assign to classes teachers who are less than fully qualified. This may be the case in subject areas where there is a chronic shortage of specific expertise. Also, in the case of longer leave, *e.g.* sick leave or study leave, the principal may temporarily have to assign classes to other teachers who have a different qualification area to cover a temporary vacancy (out of field teaching).

D7

Lack of full qualification does not mean that a person is teaching without any qualification. It can mean that a person has a qualification in teaching but not a qualification required at the upper secondary level, or a qualification in the subject matter but not a qualification in teaching. (For qualification requirements see Indicator D4.)

ISUSS data show that a substantial part of the teaching staff is less than fully qualified in several OECD countries. Except for Korea, where only fully qualified teachers are allowed to teach, the percentage of teachers who are not fully qualified ranges from 0.4 per cent in Ireland to 20 per cent or more in Mexico, Norway, Portugal and Sweden, if only full-time posts are considered (Chart D7.2 and Table D7.1).

In all 15 countries with available data, a distinction is made between tenured and temporary employment. Often, a tenure means civil servant status, which is awarded on condition of a probation period (*e.g.*, Italy, Spain). Temporary employment is, therefore, a characteristic mode of the employment for starting teachers in these countries. Another reason for temporary employment is when a school hires a teacher who has less than full qualification for teaching at the upper secondary level. Such emergency solutions are usually accepted only on a temporary basis. Further, the labour cost of fixed term employment may be lower, if side benefits and favourable pension schemes are tied to tenure and the school or the local authority bears the cost of employing teachers.

On average among countries, 12 per cent of all full-time teachers are employed through temporary contracts. However, the frequency of this practice differs from country to country: according to the ISUSS study, 4 per cent or less of full-time teachers in the schools of upper secondary students are temporary staff in Denmark and Korea, whereas more than one out of five teachers is employed on a temporary basis in the Flemish Community of Belgium and Portugal.

Many teachers are hired on a part-time basis among OECD countries, but this practice depends very much on the education system and on practical circumstances as well. The employment of part-time teachers may have organisational reasons: for example in small schools there may not be a

On average among countries, 12 per cent of all full-time teachers are employed as temporaries, whereas four per cent or less are temporaries in Denmark and Korea.

Nearly two-thirds of the teachers in Mexico and Switzerland, but only less than 1 per cent

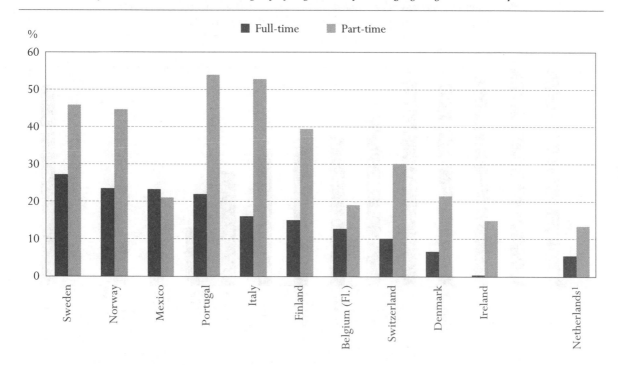

Chart D7.2

Teachers who are not fully qualified (2001)

Full-time and part-time teachers who are not fully qualified as a percentage of all full-time and part-time teachers

Countries are ranked in descending order of percentage of full-time not fully qualified teachers.
Note: The number of teachers is calculated as head counts.
1. Country did not meet international sampling requirements. The reported data are unweighted.
Source: OECD ISUSS database, 2003. Table D7.1.

D7

in Korea are employed on a part-time basis.

sufficient number of classes in an area of specialisation to cover a full-time job. Another reason may be that it is difficult to find a qualified teacher who would take on a full-time post (for financial or family reasons for example), while it is possible to find applicants for part-time work. Employing part-time teachers may have financial reasons as well in countries where full-time employment and/or civil servant status offers higher wages or substantial side benefits that part-time teachers do not enjoy. The percentage of part-time teachers ranges between 0.6 per cent in Korea and over 60 per cent in Mexico and Switzerland (Table D7.1).

Hiring teachers is mostly the responsibility of schools in the Flemish Community of Belgium, Denmark, Hungary, Ireland, Mexico, Norway and Sweden. By contrast, in other countries, teachers are hired and placed in schools by professional authorities.

The ability to recruit and retain highly qualified teachers is one of the crucial school policy issues determining the quality of education. Teachers' morality, expertise and willingness to co-operate with each other and with their students (often referred to as the ethos of the school), appear to be the most important source of the social and human capital available in an institution. To be effective school leaders, principals may need at least some responsibility for appointing and dismissing teachers. At the upper secondary level, hiring teachers is a school responsibility in the schools of 9 out of 10 students in the Flemish Community of Belgium, Denmark, Hungary, Norway and Sweden. More than three quarters of students in Ireland, two thirds or more in Finland, Mexico and Switzerland, and about half of students or less in Italy, Korea, Portugal and Spain go to schools where the responsibility of hiring teachers lies with the school (Chart D7.3 and Table D7.2).

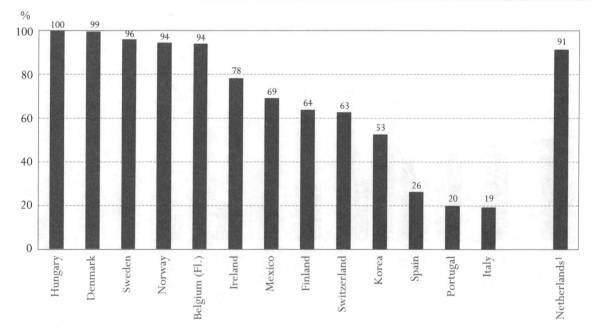

Chart D7.3

The school's responsibility in hiring teachers (2001)
Percentage of upper secondary students attending schools where principals reported that hiring new teachers is the school's responsibility

Countries are ranked in descending order of the percentage of upper secondary students attending schools where principals reported that hiring new teachers is the school's responsibility.
1. Country did not meet international sampling requirements. The reported data are unweighted.
Source: OECD ISUSS database, 2003. Table D7.2.

D7

In a balanced school staff there are young, mid-career and elder teachers, males and females and a wide range of expertise and personal characteristics. Teacher flow is a natural part of a school's life: elder teachers retire, young teachers enter the profession, teachers change school or leave the profession, new teachers are hired. Problems occur when the normal speed of turnover is upset, *i.e.* there is no teacher mobility at all or many teachers retire at the same time (this can happen, when members of a school staff are of similar age). Fluctuation of the teaching staff can be an equally distressing problem, because it endangers the school's professional integrity. External factors including labour market conditions and local social climate may cause anomalies in the normal teacher flow threatening the age and gender balance of teachers in a school besides causing shortages in specific kinds of expertise. Within a school's life such situations call for emergency solutions.

On average among the 14 countries with comparable data, the ratio of vacant posts to the total number of full-time equivalent teachers is equal to 12.3 per cent. At a constant level of teacher flow, this would mean that, theoretically, a full staff turnover could be expected in every 8 years. Aggregated on the country level, the percentage of vacant posts ranges from 2 per cent in Korea to 4 per cent in Denmark to around 30 per cent in Italy indicating that there is a considerable fluctuation of the teacher force in this latter country (Table D7.2).

Compared to the number of full-time equivalent teachers, on average about 12 per cent of vacancies were to be filled at the beginning of school year 2001/2002 in schools where upper secondary education was provided.

How did schools fill the vacant posts? Over 90 per cent of students attend schools where the principal reported that a fully qualified teacher could be hired in the Flemish Community of Belgium, Denmark, Ireland, Italy, Mexico, Norway, Portugal, Spain and Sweden. This, however, was not always possible, and schools had to find other solutions to provide staff for all scheduled classes as well. Principals reported that they had employed a less than fully qualified teacher, extended class size, cancelled planned courses, or added to the workload of teachers with more or less frequency.

About one third of students attended schools where the principal reported having hired a teacher with less than a full qualification. The principals of more than 50 per cent of upper secondary students in the Flemish Community of Belgium, Finland, Norway, Sweden and Switzerland, but only of 1 per cent in Korea and virtually none in Spain reported that they had hired a less than fully qualified teacher. Compared to the former practices, expanding class size appeared to be a relatively rare practice. Adding sections to other teachers' normal teaching hours is another common practice in dealing with vacancies. This practice in most common in Hungary, where this is done in almost all schools, and in Denmark and Switzerland, where it is practiced in the schools of more than half of the upper secondary students. By contrast, adding sections to other teachers' normal teaching hours is relatively rarely done in the Flemish Community of Belgium, Ireland, Portugal and Spain, where the principals of less than 20 per cent of upper secondary students reported this practice (Chart D7.4 and Table D7.2).

When in need, schools often hire teachers with less than a full qualification or add to qualified teachers' workload to cover vacancies....

D7

...whereas cancelling courses or expanding class size are relatively rare practices.

Schools rarely cancel courses due to the absence of the assigned teacher. On average among countries, the principals of hardly more than 3 per cent of students reported that a planned course had been cancelled because of vacant posts, ranging between nil in Italy and Hungary and 9 per cent in Denmark. More frequently than cancelling courses, school management decided to expand class size to be able to assign a teacher. On average, 9 per cent of students attend schools where this practice was reported, ranging between 3 per cent in Italy and 20 per cent in Mexico (Chart D7.4 and Table D7.2).

The actual frequency of these practices can be better estimated if one compares also the percentage of vacant posts that needed to be filled. Thus, for example, in Denmark, adding sections to other teachers' teaching hours should be interpreted in the light of the information that only 4 per cent of vacant posts had to be filled compared to the 30 per cent vacant posts in Italy (Table D7.2).

Frequency of teacher absence is an important indicator of school quality.

Absence of a teacher on duty has consequences both for students and the teaching staff: either classes have to be cancelled or classes have to be covered by other teachers who may or may not take over all functions of the originally assigned teacher with respect to the scheduled learning tasks. Frequency of

Chart D7.4

Methods used to respond to teacher vacancies (2001)
Percentage of upper secondary students attending schools that use different methods to respond to teacher vacancies, as reported by principals

■ Hire a teacher with less than a full qualification   ■ Add sections (courses) to other teachers' normal teaching hours
■ Expand the size of some of the classes   ■ Cancel a planned course

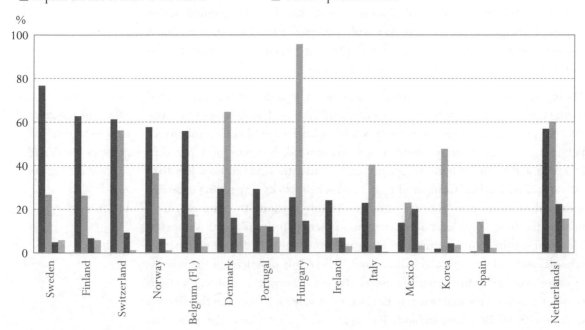

D7

Countries are ranked in descending order of the percentage of upper secondary students attending schools that hire a teacher with less than a full qualification to cover teaching vacancies, as reported by principals.
1. Country did not meet international sampling requirements. The reported data are unweighted.
Source: OECD ISUSS database, 2003. Table D7.2.

teacher absence is one indicator of school discipline, but may depend on outside constraints (*e.g.,* teacher shortages) as well as school leadership and work conditions in the school.

Principals in the ISUSS study were asked about the percentage of classes cancelled or covered by another teacher during the second month of the school year 2001/2002. Data suggest that schools rarely cancel classes because of the absence of the assigned teacher. On average among countries, principals reported that 3.5 per cent of classes had been cancelled and 6.6 per cent were covered by another teacher. However, the average number of classes cancelled ranges between 1 per cent in Finland and 6 per cent in Portugal, and the percentage of classes covered by another teacher ranges between 2 per cent in Portugal and 14 per cent in Ireland (Table D7.2). Taken together, in the 12 countries where data are available, on average, 10 per cent of classes were cancelled or covered by another teacher, ranging between 6 per cent in Finland and Sweden and 18 per cent in Ireland (Chart D7.5 and Table D7.2).

The percentage of classes cancelled or covered by another teacher ranges from six per cent in Finland and Sweden to 18 per cent in Ireland.

The shortage of qualified teachers has been a concern of education policy makers in many OECD countries. Policy makers name the aging of the teaching force and unattractiveness of teaching as a job as the most frequent causes of teacher shortages. Teacher supply and demand from the point of

The ISUSS study made a first attempt to assess relative teacher shortages by subject areas.

Chart D7.5

Percentage of class periods cancelled or covered by another teacher
because of the absence of the assigned teacher (2001)

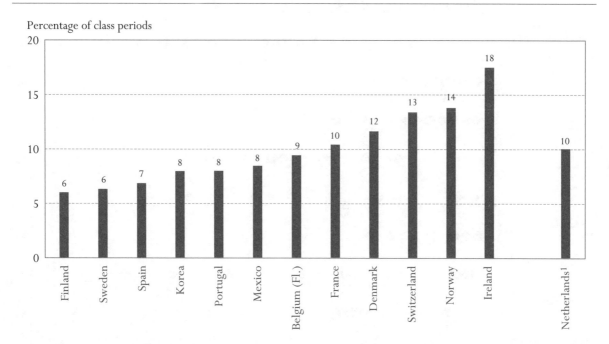

Percentage of class periods

Countries are ranked in ascending order of the percentage of class periods cancelled or covered by another teacher because of the absence of the assigned teacher.
1. Country did not meet international sampling requirements. The reported data are unweighted.
Source: OECD ISUSS database, 2003. Table D7.2.

D7

view of the school depends on a complex set of conditions and constraints, including system-wide, regional and local conditions of the labour market, status of the profession, social conditions of the school's environment, teachers' work conditions and career structure, as well as school climate. Teacher shortages, therefore, rarely affect the whole system to an equal extent. Shortages usually appear at particular levels of education and in particular subject areas in most countries. How do countries compare in the level of the teacher shortage problem and in what areas are shortages most pressing? The ISUSS Study attempted to shed some light on these questions by asking school principals of upper secondary schools to indicate subject areas where they perceive difficulties in hiring fully qualified teachers.

Among countries, teacher shortage appears to be most pressing in computer science,

On average among the 14 countries with comparable data, every second student attends schools reporting that it is difficult to hire a fully qualified teacher in computer science and information technology, and every third student attends schools reporting that it is difficult to hire teachers of mathematics, science,

Chart D7.6

Perceived difficulty of hiring qualified teachers in various study areas (2001)
Percentage of upper secondary students attending schools where the principal reported that hiring fully qualified teachers is difficult, by study area

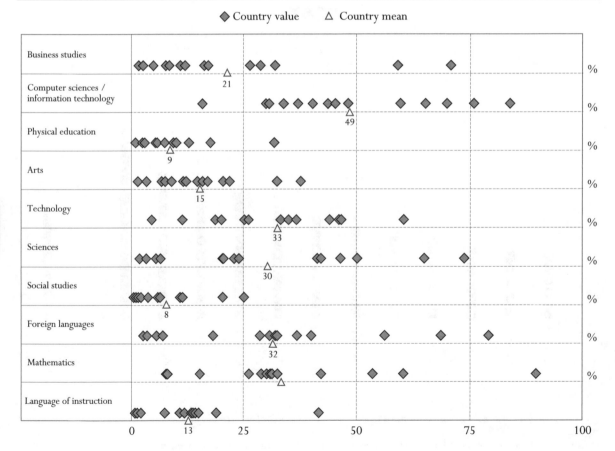

Source: OECD ISUSS database, 2003. Table D7.3

technology and foreign languages. In all these areas, the labour market was expanding with the development of knowledge industries, internationalisation and political integration. However, on average, less than one student in ten attends a school where the principal thinks it is difficult to hire a qualified teacher for physical education or social studies (Chart D7.1, Chart D7.6 and Table D7.3).

There are differences between countries both in the level of perceived teacher shortage and the study areas in which teacher shortages are perceived to be most pressing. In seven of the ten listed study areas in the Flemish Community of Belgium, the schools of more than half of the upper secondary students report difficulties in hiring qualified teachers. By contrast, less than 20 per cent of students attend schools where the principal perceived shortages in any of the ten listed study areas in Italy (Table D7.3).

As indicated in Chart D7.6, countries experience different levels of difficulties in the same subject area. Shortage of teachers for business studies appears to be gravest in Switzerland, whereas principals in Italy or Korea do not report such difficulties. Principals in Finland reported higher than average difficulties in finding teachers for arts (38 per cent). Ireland reported shortages of technology teachers; science teachers were most sought after in the Flemish Community of Belgium and Ireland. There was a shortage in foreign language teachers in the Flemish Community of Belgium, Hungary and Mexico and in mathematics teachers in the Flemish Community of Belgium, Denmark, and Switzerland. Principals of more than half of the students reported difficulties hiring qualified teachers in these subjects (Chart D7.6 and Table D7.3).

Research suggests that the decision to become a teacher is the result of a complex set of considerations related to job alternatives, relative earnings, career structure, merit based incentives, status of the profession, and personal circumstances. The policy implications of the findings of OECD's International Survey of Upper Secondary Schools vary for different countries. Further analysis is required to find out how sufficient supply of teachers and relative shortages are related to the quality of the teacher force and how this can be influenced through teacher policies.

Definitions and methodologies

Data are derived from OECD's International Survey of Upper Secondary Schools implemented in the 2001/2002 school year in 15 countries. For a brief description of the study see Annex 3 at *www.oecd.org/edu/eag2003*.

School in this indicator refers to 'school site' *i.e.* the education unit where service is provided. In the majority of cases school and school site is the same. However, in countries where schools as administrative units have several school sites, school refers only to one sampled school site within the school as an administrative unit.

Shortage of teachers in different study areas. ISUSS respondents (school principals) participants were asked to indicate whether they perceive difficulties in hiring fully qualified teachers in the following study areas: language of

mathematics, foreign languages, science and technology whereas it appears least problematic in social studies.

Shortage of qualified secondary teachers appears to be more extensive in the Flemish Community of Belgium, whereas the scope of the problem appears less in Italy.

D7

Data on teacher supply and demand are derived from OECD's International Survey of Upper Secondary Schools implemented in the school year 2001/2002 in 15 countries.

instruction, mathematics, foreign languages, sciences, computer science and information technology, technology, business studies, social studies, the arts, and physical education.

Temporary employment. Fixed term employment not extended longer than one school year.

Teacher with less than a full qualification. Full qualification means that a teacher has fulfilled all the training requirements for teaching a certain subject at the upper secondary level and meets all other administrative requirements.

Vacant posts were calculated as full-time post, since no distinction could be made between full-time and part-time vacancies. This may mean an overestimation of the proportion of vacancies in countries where part-time posts are customary.

D7

Table D7.1

Percentage of temporary, not fully qualified and part-time teachers in upper secondary education (2001)

Percentage of full-time and part-time teachers who are temporaries or not fully qualified, as reported by school principals

		Full-time temporaries as a percentage of full-time teachers	Full-time teachers who are not fully qualified as a percentage of full-time teachers	Part-time temporaries as a percentage of part-time teachers	Part-time teachers who are not fully qualified as a percentage of part-time teachers	Part-time teachers as a percentage of total teachers
OECD COUNTRIES	Belgium (Fl.)	20.9	12.8	27.8	19.2	34.9
	Denmark	4.0	6.6	37.0	21.6	11.8
	Finland	18.6	15.1	41.9	39.5	21.1
	France	m	m	m	m	m
	Hungary	12.1	m	76.8	m	10.2
	Ireland	8.6	0.4	100.0	15.0	19.0
	Italy	16.1	16.1	16.5	52.9	6.6
	Korea	3.0	n	38.8	n	0.6
	Mexico	14.4	23.3	32.0	21.1	63.1
	Norway	6.8	23.6	13.1	44.8	24.0
	Portugal	21.9	22.0	40.7	54.0	19.3
	Spain	m	m	m	m	m
	Sweden	12.3	27.3	31.7	45.9	22.1
	Switzerland	10.8	10.2	32.1	30.3	62.4
	Country mean	*12.4*	*14.3*	*40.7*	*31.3*	*24.6*
	Netherlands [1]	3.1	5.5	7.3	13.5	50.5

1. Country did not meet international sampling requirements. The reported data are unweighted.
Source: OECD ISUSS database, 2003. See Annex 3 for notes *(www.oecd.org/edu/eag2003)*.

Table D7.2

Teaching vacancies and teacher absenteeism (2001)

Percentage of upper secondary students attending schools with no teaching vacancies, percentage of FTE vacant posts to total number of full-time equivalent teachers, percentage of upper secondary students attending schools which are responsible for hiring teachers, use of various methods to cover teaching vacancies, and percentage of class periods cancelled or covered by another teacher because of the absence of the assigned teacher, as reported by school principals

		Percentage of students attending schools where there are no teaching vacancies to be filled	Percentage of FTE teaching posts that needed to be filled in the 2001/2002 school year	Percentage of upper secondary students attending schools which are responsible for hiring teachers	Percentage of upper secondary students attending schools that use the following methods to cover teaching vacancies:					Percentage of class periods cancelled because of the absence of the assigned teacher	Percentage of class periods covered by another teacher because of the absence of the assigned teacher
					Hire a fully qualified teacher	Hire a teacher with less than a full qualification	Cancel a planned course	Expand the size of some of the classes	Add sections (courses) to other teachers' normal teaching hours		
OECD COUNTRIES	Belgium (Fl.)	5.3	10.0	94.0	95.0	55.7	2.8	9.1	17.4	4.6	4.9
	Denmark	3.4	3.9	99.5	91.4	29.2	8.9	15.9	64.5	3.5	8.2
	Finland	3.4	12.3	63.8	87.8	62.6	5.7	6.6	26.1	1.0	5.0
	France	m	m	m	m	m	m	m	m	5.4	5.0
	Hungary	3.6	7.8	99.8	80.7	25.2	n	14.5	95.6	4.4	m
	Ireland	3.5	9.3	78.2	98.6	23.8	2.8	6.8	6.6	3.4	14.1
	Italy	10.3	29.9	19.4	98.0	22.6	0.3	3.2	40.1	4.2	m
	Korea	1.2	2.0	52.6	56.6	1.5	3.5	4.1	47.6	1.5	6.5
	Mexico	6.1	16.0	69.1	90.8	13.5	3.1	20.0	22.7	4.2	4.3
	Norway	6.4	11.0	94.4	96.8	57.5	1.1	6.2	36.4	2.5	11.3
	Portugal	12.8	18.2	20.1	94.2	29.1	7.0	11.9	12.0	6.0	2.0
	Spain	7.7	14.9	26.4	97.5	0.3	2.1	8.5	14.0	3.4	3.4
	Sweden	7.9	10.4	95.9	98.2	76.5	5.7	4.7	26.5	2.4	3.9
	Switzerland	10.4	13.9	62.7	85.5	61.1	1.0	9.1	56.1	3.3	10.1
	Country mean	*6.3*	*12.3*	*67.4*	*90.1*	*35.3*	*3.4*	*9.3*	*35.8*	*3.5*	*6.6*
	Netherlands [1]	2.9	5.7	91.4	86.8	56.7	15.5	22.3	60.0	6.1	3.9

1. Country did not meet international sampling requirements. The reported data are unweighted.
Source: OECD ISUSS database, 2003. See Annex 3 for notes *(www.oecd.org/edu/eag2003)*.

D7

Table D7.3
Perceived difficulty of hiring qualified teachers in various study areas (2001)
Percentage of upper secondary students attending schools where principals reported that hiring fully qualified teachers is difficult, by study area

	Language of instruction	Mathematics	Foreign languages	Social studies	Sciences	Technology	Arts	Physical education	Computer sciences/ information technology	Business studies
Belgium (Fl.)	41.8	89.9	68.7	20.5	73.8	46.3	11.7	2.4	84.0	59.2
Denmark	1.3	53.7	5.8	3.8	41.6	25.3	3.4	13.0	48.3	4.8
Finland	11.9	30.2	28.9	6.7	24.1	35.1	37.9	17.7	65.4	16.4
France	19.0	26.4	32.2	25.2	46.6	36.9	20.6	6.0	34.0	26.5
Hungary	14.6	31.5	79.2	6.1	23.0	4.6	9.1	5.5	70.1	32.1
Ireland	10.9	42.2	40.1	11.9	65.1	60.5	17.1	31.9	45.5	28.9
Italy	15.3	15.4	2.7	1.2	3.3	18.8	1.5	0.9	15.8	2.6
Korea	7.6	8.2	37.0	11.4	6.6	11.5	15.8	3.0	30.3	1.6
Mexico	13.6	29.2	56.3	11.0	20.6	33.3	32.5	10.2	30.8	8.7
Norway	13.9	31.1	18.3	1.7	20.5	20.1	7.8	5.9	40.5	7.9
Portugal	0.9	8.2	3.6	2.1	5.6	46.8	22.1	5.8	44.0	12.0
Spain	2.3	7.9	7.2	0.6	1.8	26.3	14.8	2.5	37.2	11.1
Sweden	11.9	32.7	30.9	1.2	42.3	44.2	12.4	9.5	59.8	17.3
Switzerland	13.5	60.5	32.6	6.1	50.4	46.8	7.0	7.6	76.0	70.9
Country mean	*12.7*	*33.4*	*31.7*	*7.8*	*30.4*	*32.6*	*15.3*	*8.7*	*48.7*	*21.4*
Netherlands[1]	41.7	55.6	37.5	14.2	32.5	5.8	7.8	9.1	16.7	28.6

OECD COUNTRIES

1. Country did not meet international sampling requirements. The reported data are unweighted.
Source: OECD ISUSS database, 2003. See Annex 3 for notes (*www.oecd.org/edu/eag2003*).

D7

INDICATOR D8: AGE AND GENDER DISTRIBUTION OF TEACHERS, AND STAFF EMPLOYED IN EDUCATION

- In 15 out of 19 OECD countries, most primary teachers are at least 40 years old, and in Germany, Italy and Sweden, more than one third of teachers are older than 50 years.

- Compared with 1998, the average proportion of teachers aged 50 years or over increased on average by 6.2 per cent (1.8 percentage points) in secondary education. In Finland, Germany, Ireland and the United Kingdom, this proportion rose by more than 4 percentage points.

- The proportion of young teachers increased in 10 out of 14 OECD countries for which data are available. In France, Korea, Luxembourg, New Zealand and Sweden, the proportion of teachers aged under 30 years increased by more than 3 percentage points whereas Ireland and Japan are the only two countries showing a significant decrease between 1998 and 2001 in the proportion of teachers under 30 years.

Chart D8.1

Change in the age distribution of teachers (1998 and 2001)
*Change in the age distribution of secondary teachers in public and private institutions
between 1998 and 2001 (1998=0), based on head counts*

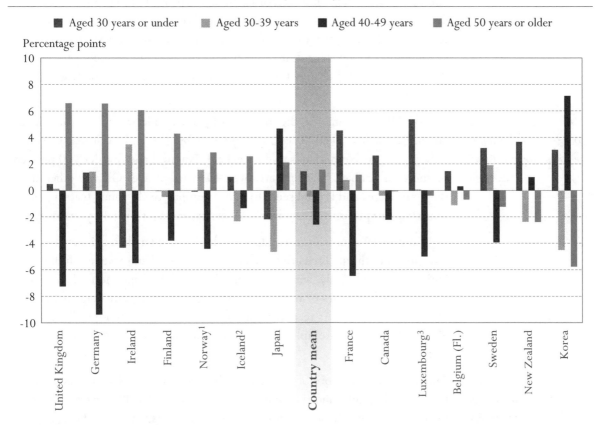

Countries are ranked in descending order of the difference between 1998 and 2001 in the percentage of teachers aged 50 years or older.
1. Including primary education.
2. Excluding lower secondary education.
3. Public institutions only.
Source: OECD. Table D8.3. See Annex 3 for notes *(www.oecd.org/edu/eag2003).*

D8

Policy context

The demography of teachers is becoming a major concern in many OECD countries, particularly in those countries where student enrolment is expected to expand further. Ensuring that there will be enough skilled teachers to educate all children is an important policy issue. If a large proportion of teachers are concentrated in the older age cohorts, countries may have to develop effective policies to replace retired teachers and attract newly qualified teachers to the teaching profession (Indicator D7). With seniority as an important criterion in teachers' pay scales and additional financial incentives required to attract new teachers to the teaching profession (Indicator D5), the age distribution of teachers can also have a considerable impact on educational budgets.

Evidence and explanations

Age

General demographic trends, as well as the attractiveness of teaching relative to other professions at different points in time, can influence the age distribution of the teaching force. In many countries, the post-war baby boom, combined with increasing tertiary participation rates, created a large concentration of teachers between the ages of 40 and 50 during the 1990s. On one hand, in countries where the population of school age is projected to grow over the next decade (see Indicator A1), there is increasing concern that a large proportion of teachers will reach retirement age at a time when enrolments are continuing to expand. On the other hand, in countries where enrolment is about to decrease due to demographic change for instance, there is a risk that some teachers may lose their jobs.

In most OECD countries, the majority of primary and secondary students are taught by teachers aged 40 years or older (Table D8.1). In Canada, Germany, Italy, Japan, the Netherlands, New Zealand, Portugal and Sweden, 60 per cent or more of primary teachers are over 40 years of age. On the other hand, Belgium, Korea and Poland seem to have a comparatively young teaching force; more than 50 per cent of primary teachers are younger than 40 years of age.

In 15 out of 19 countries, secondary teachers are older than primary teachers. Exceptions to this pattern are France, Japan, Portugal and Sweden. In Belgium, Finland, Iceland, Italy and the Netherlands, the proportion of secondary teachers aged 40 years or over is at least 13 percentage points higher than that of primary teachers. As teachers' salaries (Indicator D5) are typically linked to either age or years of employment, these countries are likely to face relatively high wage bills.

About one fifth or more of primary teachers in Belgium, Korea, Luxembourg, the Slovak Republic and the United Kingdom are under 30 years of age; fewer than 10 per cent of teachers in Germany, Italy and Japan are in this age group. Differences between countries in the proportion of young teachers can be explained in part by the typical completion ages of tertiary education (Annex 1), by prior retirement of older teachers and by entry requirements for the teaching profession (Chart D8.2).

D8

Chart D8.2

Age distribution of teachers (2001)
Distribution of teachers in public and private institutions, by level of education and age group

■ Aged 30 years or under   ▨ Aged 30-39 years   ■ Aged 40-49 years   ■ Aged 50 years or older

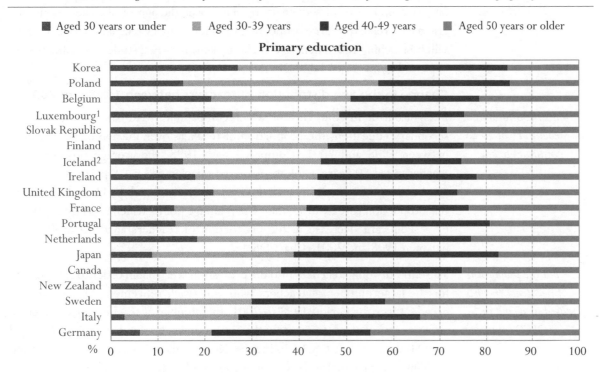

Primary education

Korea
Poland
Belgium
Luxembourg[1]
Slovak Republic
Finland
Iceland[2]
Ireland
United Kingdom
France
Portugal
Netherlands
Japan
Canada
New Zealand
Sweden
Italy
Germany

% 0   10   20   30   40   50   60   70   80   90   100

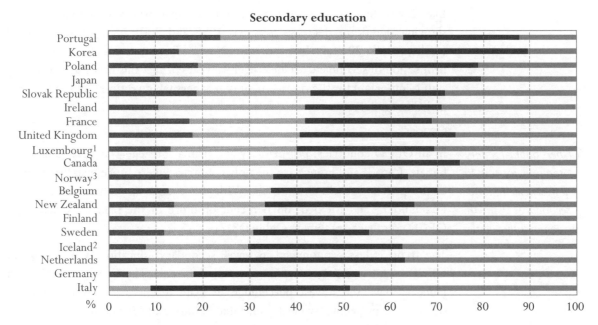

Secondary education

Portugal
Korea
Poland
Japan
Slovak Republic
Ireland
France
United Kingdom
Luxembourg[1]
Canada
Norway[3]
Belgium
New Zealand
Finland
Sweden
Iceland[2]
Netherlands
Germany
Italy

% 0   10   20   30   40   50   60   70   80   90   100

D8

Countries are ranked in ascending order of the percentage of teachers aged 40 years or older.
1. Public institutions only.
2. Excluding lower secondary education.
3. Including primary education.
Source: OECD. Tables D8.1 and D8.3. See Annex 3 for notes *(www.oecd.org/edu/eag2003).*

Several countries have a large proportion of teachers within a decade of retirement.

The potential for teacher shortage is highest in countries with the largest proportion of older teachers combined with projections of stable or growing enrolment. Germany, Italy and Sweden have with more than 40 per cent the largest proportions of secondary teachers over the age of 50. These countries also have a relatively large proportion of older primary teachers. These teachers will be reaching retirement age at about the time when student enrolments are expected to increase (Table D8.1).

Change in the age distribution of teachers between 1998 and 2001

In most countries, the teaching workforce continues to age…

In eight out of 14 countries for which comparable trend data are available for secondary education, the proportion of teachers over the age of 50 increased between 1998 and 2001. Compared with 1998, the average proportion of teachers aged 50 years or older increased on average by 1.8 percentage points in secondary education. In Finland, Germany, Ireland and the United Kingdom, this proportion rose by more than 4 percentage points which is partly explained by a significant decrease in the proportion of teachers aged 40 to 49 years between 1998 and 2001 (Chart D8.1).

…but the proportion of new teachers also increased in 10 out of 14 OECD countries

The entry of young teachers into the profession is crucial in order to compensate for the large number of teachers who will reach retirement age in the next decade. Over the period 1998 to 2001, the number of teachers aged under 30 years increased at approximately the same rate as the number of teachers aged over 50 years (Chart D8.1). In France, Korea, Luxembourg, New Zealand and Sweden, the proportion of teachers aged under 30 years increased by more than 3 percentage points whereas Ireland and Japan are the only two countries showing significant decrease between 1998 and 2001 in the proportion of teachers under 30 years. In Sweden and New Zealand, two countries with a high proportion of secondary teachers over 40 years of age, this renewal of teaching staff is important for the replacement of teachers taking retirement (Table D8.3 and Chart D8.1).

Gender

Teachers of pre-primary and primary and, to a lesser extent, lower secondary classes are predominantly female.

In all OECD countries, pre-primary and primary teachers are predominantly female. Canada and France are the only countries where more than 20 per cent of pre-primary teachers are male. With the exceptions of Denmark, Japan, Luxembourg and Mexico, 68 per cent or more of the primary teachers in OECD countries are female (Table D8.2).

The trend is less pronounced in lower secondary education. On average in OECD countries, one out of three teachers is male. The Czech Republic and Hungary have the lowest percentage of male teachers in lower secondary schools (16 per cent), while Japan, Luxembourg and Mexico have the highest (60, 59 and 50 per cent respectively).

The higher the level of education, the higher the proportion of male teachers.

Although females tend to dominate the profession in pre-primary and primary education, and less so in lower secondary education, in upper secondary education the percentages of male and female teachers are similar. In general, females are less well represented at higher levels of education than at lower levels. At the

D8

upper secondary level, the proportion of teachers who are female ranges from 40 per cent or less in Denmark, Germany, Japan and Korea to between 59 and 68 per cent in Canada, Hungary, Italy, Poland, Portugal, the Slovak Republic and the United Kingdom. At the tertiary-type A and advanced research programmes level, male teachers are in the majority in all countries for which data are available. At this level, the proportion of female teachers ranges from less than 15 per cent in Japan to over 40 per cent in Finland, France, Iceland, Ireland, New Zealand and the United States (Table D8.2).

Definitions and methodologies

Data on age and gender derive from the UOE Questionnaire 2002, reference year 2000/2001. Characteristics are measured as the percentage of teachers in each of the five age groups, by level of education. Data for 1998 included in Chart D8.1 derive from the UOE Questionnaire 2001 and refer to the school year 1997/1998.

Teachers are defined as "persons whose professional activity involves the transmitting of knowledge, attitudes and skills that are stipulated in a formal curriculum to students enrolled in formal educational institutions". This definition includes chairpersons of departments whose duties include some amount of teaching. The category does not include personnel with other titles, (e.g., dean, director, associate dean, assistant dean, chair or head of department), even if their principal activity is instruction or research. This definition of teachers does not include student teachers or teaching/research assistants.

Data refer to the school year 2000/2001 and are based on the UOE data collection on education statistics administered in 2002 (for details see Annex 3).

D8

Table D8.1
Age distribution of teachers (2001)
Percentage of teachers in public and private institutions by level of education and age group, based on head counts

	Primary education					Lower secondary education					Upper secondary education				
	< 30 years	30-39 years	40-49 years	50-59 years	>= 60 years	< 30 years	30-39 years	40-49 years	50-59 years	>= 60 years	< 30 years	30-39 years	40-49 years	50-59 years	>= 60 years
	(1)	(2)	(3)	(4)	(5)	(6)	(7)	(8)	(9)	(10)	(11)	(12)	(13)	(14)	(15)
Australia	m	m	m	m	m	m	m	m	m	m	m	m	m	m	m
Austria	m	m	m	m	m	m	m	m	m	m	m	m	m	m	m
Belgium	21.5	29.5	27.7	20.7	0.7	x(11)	x(12)	x(13)	x(14)	x(15)	12.7	21.8	35.6	27.7	2.2
Canada	11.8	24.4	38.7	24.0	1.1	11.8	24.4	38.7	24.0	1.1	11.8	24.4	38.7	24.0	1.1
Czech Republic	m	m	m	m	m	m	m	m	m	m	m	m	m	m	m
Denmark	m	m	m	m	m	m	m	m	m	m	m	m	m	m	m
Finland	13.2	32.9	29.3	24.0	0.6	9.4	27.3	29.2	33.0	1.1	5.8	23.6	32.7	32.6	5.2
France	13.5	28.1	34.7	23.3	0.3	18.9	23.0	26.2	30.9	1.0	15.4	26.2	28.1	29.1	1.1
Germany	6.1	15.3	33.7	39.3	5.6	4.2	10.7	34.6	44.0	6.5	3.3	21.9	37.5	31.8	5.4
Greece	m	m	m	m	m	m	m	m	m	m	m	m	m	m	m
Hungary	m	m	m	m	m	m	m	m	m	m	m	m	m	m	m
Iceland	15.4	29.2	30.2	19.0	6.2	x(1)	x(2)	x(3)	x(4)	x(5)	7.7	21.9	32.8	26.0	11.5
Ireland	18.1	25.9	34.1	17.5	4.4	10.5	31.3	29.2	24.0	4.9	x(6)	x(7)	x(8)	x(9)	x(10)
Italy	2.8	24.3	38.7	29.8	4.3	n	5.0	39.2	51.7	4.1	0.1	11.5	45.0	39.2	4.3
Japan	8.8	30.1	43.9	17.0	0.2	11.6	35.8	39.0	13.0	0.5	10.3	29.0	34.0	24.0	2.7
Korea	27.2	31.6	26.1	14.5	0.6	17.6	45.0	28.8	8.3	0.4	12.7	38.9	36.7	11.2	0.5
Luxembourg[1]	26.0	22.5	27.0	23.7	0.8	13.1	26.8	29.5	29.1	1.6	x(6)	x(7)	x(8)	x(9)	x(10)
Mexico	m	m	m	m	m	m	m	m	m	m	m	m	m	m	m
Netherlands	18.4	21.1	37.4	21.7	1.5	x(11)	x(12)	x(13)	x(14)	x(15)	8.3	17.2	37.5	34.5	2.6
New Zealand	16.0	20.1	32.0	26.0	5.9	15.0	19.7	31.6	27.3	6.4	12.4	18.9	32.2	29.5	7.0
Norway	x(6)	x(7)	x(8)	x(9)	x(10)	15.8	23.3	27.7	27.3	5.9	5.4	19.1	31.2	35.7	8.6
Poland	15.5	41.3	28.6	13.4	1.2	23.1	36.0	30.0	10.0	0.9	16.6	26.0	30.2	22.5	4.7
Portugal	13.8	25.8	41.2	16.5	2.7	24.2	38.3	25.4	10.0	2.2	23.5	39.3	25.2	9.8	2.2
Slovak Republic	22.1	24.9	24.8	22.6	5.7	22.1	24.9	24.8	22.6	5.7	14.4	23.4	33.9	22.5	5.8
Spain	m	m	m	m	m	m	m	m	m	m	m	m	m	m	m
Sweden	12.7	17.3	28.2	35.5	6.2	16.8	21.5	23.3	31.2	7.2	7.2	16.9	25.8	40.9	9.2
Switzerland[1]	m	m	m	m	m	m	m	m	m	m	m	m	m	m	m
Turkey	m	m	m	m	m	m	m	m	m	m	m	m	m	m	m
United Kingdom	21.9	21.3	30.8	25.3	0.7	17.8	22.8	33.4	25.1	0.9	17.8	22.8	33.4	25.1	0.9
United States	m	m	m	m	m	m	m	m	m	m	m	m	m	m	m
Country mean	*16.2*	*26.0*	*32.4*	*22.8*	*2.6*	*14.5*	*26.0*	*30.7*	*25.7*	*3.2*	*11.1*	*23.7*	*33.7*	*27.3*	*4.3*
Argentina[2]	30.3	31.2	27.5	10.1	0.9	24.3	34.5	27.2	11.7	2.3	24.4	34.6	26.9	11.7	2.4
Brazil[2]	35.1	36.5	21.3	6.7	0.3	26.2	37.5	26.2	9.1	1.0	23.2	36.1	26.7	12.3	1.8
Chile[2]	8.8	22.3	33.5	28.5	6.9	8.8	22.3	33.5	28.5	6.9	9.6	28.3	35.0	21.1	6.0
China	34.1	25.4	26.3	14.1	0.1	45.6	33.4	13.4	7.5	0.1	37.9	41.0	12.1	8.5	0.6
Indonesia	51.6	34.9	9.8	3.7	a	14.1	50.2	21.6	12.7	1.4	16.5	48.5	24.6	9.0	1.5
Israel	21.1	30.6	33.1	14.1	1.1	14.5	30.2	34.3	19.1	2.0	10.6	27.9	32.9	23.9	4.8
Jamaica	28.3	20.4	35.1	15.3	0.9	32.4	29.8	27.6	9.3	0.9	22.4	30.6	36.7	10.2	n
Malaysia[2]	20.1	46.7	22.2	9.8	1.2	x(11)	x(12)	x(13)	x(14)	x(15)	12.1	48.0	31.3	8.5	n
Philippines[2]	10.4	28.8	19.4	33.6	7.8	13.5	35.9	28.2	18.8	3.5	13.5	35.9	28.2	18.9	3.5

OECD COUNTRIES / NON-OECD COUNTRIES

D8

Note: x indicates that data are included in another column. The column reference is shown in brackets after «x», *e.g.*, x(2) means that data are included in column 2.
1. Public institutions only.
2. Year of reference 2000.
Source: OECD. See Annex 3 for notes (*www.oecd.org/edu/eag2003*).

Table D8.2
Gender distribution of teachers (2001)
Percentage of females among teaching staff in public and private institutions by level of education, based on head counts

	Pre-primary education	Primary education	Lower secondary education	Upper secondary education (all programmes)	Upper secondary education (general programmes)	Upper secondary education (vocational programmes)	Post-secondary non-tertiary education	Tertiary-type B	Tertiary-type A and advanced research programmes	All levels of education
	(1)	(2)	(3)	(4)	(5)	(6)	(7)	(8)	(9)	(10)
OECD COUNTRIES										
Australia	m	m	m	m	m	m	m	m	37.3	m
Austria	99.0	90.3	65.3	48.1	56.8	44.3	50.2	45.5	26.5	63.0
Belgium	92.4	78.1	x(4)	58.0	x(4)	x(4)	x(4)	x(9)	38.0	65.3
Canada	68.1	68.1	68.1	68.4	68.1	70.1	x(8)	47.6	33.9	60.2
Czech Republic	99.7	84.4	84.1	53.2	54.5	52.9	50.3	56.4	33.4	70.9
Denmark	84.0	64.0	64.1	34.1	39.3	27.8	m	m	m	65.6
Finland	96.5	73.2	71.1	57.3	68.2	51.4	x(4)	x(4)	44.9	66.9
France	79.8	79.8	64.5	55.4	58.3	50.6	m	50.6	44.7	65.0
Germany	95.0	82.0	59.2	40.3	40.7	39.9	37.3	46.5	27.4	58.3
Greece	m	m	m	m	m	m	m	m	m	m
Hungary	99.9	86.2	84.2	60.1	60.1	60.1	60.1	49.9	37.1	75.3
Iceland	98.1	78.3	x(2)	46.6	x(4)	x(4)	x(4,8,9)	50.4	49.2	74.2
Ireland	94.0	82.2	58.6	x(3)	x(3)	x(3)	x(3)	35.0	48.2	63.4
Italy	98.1	94.8	73.1	59.0	x(4)	x(4)	a	27.5	40.0	75.8
Japan	98.0	65.0	40.0	24.6	x(4)	x(4)	x(4,8,9)	36.1	14.1	45.3
Korea	99.6	71.6	61.0	32.0	31.4	33.0	a	30.9	25.3	49.5
Luxembourg[1]	97.2	66.5	41.1	x(3)	x(3)	x(3)	m	a	a	58.1
Mexico	94.4	65.8	49.7	40.6	39.5	46.3	a	m	m	60.9
Netherlands	m	77.6	x(4)	41.1	38.5	46.0	a	x(9)	31.6	57.1
New Zealand	98.8	83.9	65.8	56.1	58.5	50.7	50.5	50.9	43.4	68.0
Norway	m	x(3)	72.6	45.0	x(4)	x(4)	x(9)	x(9)	36.2	60.3
Poland	96.6	83.5	73.9	60.9	69.5	56.1	69.0	62.7	47.7	76.7
Portugal	99.1	82.1	70.0	67.3	m	m	m	m	m	76.3
Slovak Republic	100.0	93.3	76.5	67.3	70.8	66.4	68.8	67.7	37.6	75.8
Spain	93.0	70.8	x(4)	52.2	x(4)	x(4)	x(4)	48.0	35.9	59.2
Sweden	97.2	79.9	62.6	50.3	55.6	46.2	23.6	x(9)	39.1	68.7
Switzerland[1]	m	m	m	m	m	m	m	m	26.6	m
Turkey	m	m	m	m	m	m	m	m	m	m
United Kingdom	97.2	81.8	59.4	59.2	59.4	59.0	x(4)	33.9	x(8)	65.3
United States	94.7	86.5	60.3	50.8	50.8	a	41.4	41.4	41.4	65.8
Country mean	*94.8*	*78.6*	*64.8*	*51.4*	*54.1*	*50.1*	*50.1*	*45.9*	*36.0*	*65.0*
NON-OECD COUNTRIES										
Argentina[2]	96.0	89.1	71.2	65.5	65.5	65.5	a	67.4	46.4	75.7
Brazil[2]	98.1	92.6	84.3	69.9	69.9	x(5)	a	x(9)	40.8	83.1
Chile[2]	99.0	74.4	74.4	53.3	56.6	47.6	a	m	m	m
China	97.5	52.2	43.8	40.2	37.5	48.8	m	m	45.4	50.6
India[2]	84.0	35.6	34.8	33.5	33.5	46.3	40.0	40.0	37.0	39.4
Indonesia	98.1	52.2	41.6	38.0	39.8	34.3	a	x(9)	40.8	48.3
Israel	m	83.1	78.1	68.2	68.2	x(5)	m	m	m	77.2
Jamaica	98.1	91.0	66.8	m	x(3)	42.9	x(8)	62.9	46.3	76.3
Malaysia[1,2]	100.0	64.6	x(4)	61.5	61.8	20.0	41.7	38.7	44.0	64.2
Philippines[2]	96.9	87.3	76.4	76.4	76.4	a	m	m	m	m
Russian Federation	m	98.7	89.3	x(3)	x(3)	x(3)	61.4	72.1	47.7	76.8
Tunisia	95.8	49.8	42.4	m	x(3)	n	n	35.2	x(8)	46.4
Zimbabwe	m	48.2	38.5	x(3)	x(3)	x(3)	17.4	26.2	m	m

Note: x indicates that data are included in another column. The column reference is shown in brackets after «x», *e.g.*, x(2) means that data are included in column 2.
1. Public institutions only.
2. Year of reference 2000.
Source: OECD. See Annex 3 for notes (*www.oecd.org/edu/eag2003*).

D8

Table D8.3
Age distribution of teachers (1998, 2001)
Percentage of teachers in public and private institutions in secondary education, based on head counts

		Secondary education (2001)				Secondary education (1998)				
		< 30 years	30-39 years	40-49 years	50-59 years	>= 60 years	< 30 years	30-39 years	40-49 years	50-59 years	>= 60 years
OECD COUNTRIES	Australia	m	m	m	m	m	m	m	m	m	m
	Austria	m	m	m	m	m	8.1	30.4	41.1	19.5	0.9
	Belgium	12.7	21.8	35.6	27.7	2.2	m	m	m	m	m
	Belgium (Fl.)	15.0	23.2	35.7	24.5	1.6	13.5	24.3	35.4	24.9	1.9
	Canada	11.8	24.4	38.7	24.0	1.1	9.1	24.8	40.9	24.0	1.2
	Czech Republic	m	m	m	m	m	m	m	m	m	m
	Denmark	m	m	m	m	m	m	m	m	m	m
	Finland	7.5	25.4	31.1	32.8	3.2	7.5	25.9	34.8	29.2	2.6
	France	17.1	24.6	27.1	30.0	1.1	12.6	23.8	33.6	29.1	0.8
	Germany	4.0	14.0	35.4	40.5	6.2	2.6	12.5	44.8	36.6	3.5
	Greece	m	m	m	m	m	m	m	m	m	m
	Hungary	m	m	m	m	m	m	m	m	m	m
	Iceland [1]	7.7	21.9	32.8	26.0	11.5	6.7	24.2	34.2	23.9	11.1
	Ireland	10.5	31.3	29.2	24.0	4.9	14.8	27.8	34.7	19.1	3.7
	Italy	0.1	8.7	42.5	44.5	4.2	m	m	m	m	m
	Japan	10.9	32.2	36.4	18.8	1.7	13.1	36.8	31.7	16.8	1.6
	Korea	15.0	41.7	33.0	9.9	0.5	11.9	46.2	25.9	12.6	3.5
	Luxembourg [2]	13.1	26.8	29.5	29.1	1.6	7.7	26.7	34.5	28.2	2.9
	Mexico	m	m	m	m	m	m	m	m	m	m
	Netherlands	8.3	17.2	37.5	34.5	2.6	m	m	m	m	m
	New Zealand	13.8	19.4	31.9	28.2	6.7	10.1	21.7	30.9	28.9	8.4
	Norway [3]	12.9	22.1	28.7	29.7	6.6	12.9	20.5	33.1	27.7	5.8
	Poland	19.0	29.7	30.1	17.8	3.3	m	m	m	m	m
	Portugal	23.8	38.8	25.3	9.9	2.2	m	m	m	m	m
	Slovak Republic	18.7	24.2	28.8	22.5	5.7	m	m	m	m	m
	Spain	m	m	m	m	m	m	m	m	m	m
	Sweden	11.7	19.1	24.6	36.4	8.3	8.4	17.1	28.6	38.1	7.8
	Switzerland [2]	m	m	m	m	m	10.1	27.1	35.1	24.2	3.5
	Turkey	m	m	m	m	m	m	m	m	m	m
	United Kingdom	17.8	22.8	33.4	25.1	0.9	17.3	22.6	40.7	18.5	0.9
	United States	m	m	m	m	m	m	m	m	m	m
	Country mean	*12.6*	*24.5*	*32.4*	*26.8*	*3.8*	*10.4*	*25.8*	*35.0*	*25.1*	*3.7*
NON-OECD COUNTRIES	Argentina [4]	24.3	34.5	27.0	11.7	2.4	m	m	m	m	m
	Brazil [4]	25.1	37.0	26.3	10.2	1.3	m	m	m	m	m
	Chile [4]	9.3	26.2	34.5	23.7	6.3	m	m	m	m	m
	China	43.7	35.3	13.1	7.8	0.2	m	m	m	m	m
	Indonesia	15.1	49.5	22.8	11.2	1.4	m	m	m	m	m
	Israel	12.2	28.8	33.4	21.9	3.7	30.6	1.1	33.3	12.2	28.8
	Jamaica	32.4	29.8	27.6	9.3	0.9	m	m	m	m	m
	Malaysia [2,4]	12.1	48.0	31.3	8.5	n	m	m	m	m	m
	Philippines [4]	13.5	35.9	28.2	18.8	3.5	m	m	m	m	m

1. Excluding lower secondary education.
2. Public institutions only.
3. Including primary education.
4. Year of reference 2000.
Source: OECD. See Annex 3 for notes *(www.oecd.org/edu/eag2003).*

D8

TYPICAL GRADUATION AGES

The typical graduation age is the age at the end of the last school/academic year of the corresponding level and programme when the degree is obtained. The typical age is based on the assumption of full-time attendance in the regular education system without grade repetition. (Note that at some levels of education the term "graduation age" may not translate literally and is used here purely as a convention.)

Table X1.1a
Typical graduation ages in upper secondary education

	Programme orientation		Educational/labour market destination			
	General programmes	Pre-vocational or vocational programmes	ISCED 3A programmes	ISCED 3B programmes	ISCED 3C short programmes[1]	ISCED 3C long programmes[1]
OECD COUNTRIES						
Australia	m	m	17	m	m	m
Austria	18	18	18	18	18	a
Belgium	18	18	18	a	18	18
Czech Republic	18	18	18	18	17	a
Denmark	19-20	19-20	19-20	a	a	19-20
Finland	19	19	19	a	a	a
France	18-19	17-20	18-19	19-20	17-20	18-21
Germany	19	19	19	19	a	a
Greece	17-18	17-18	17-18	a	a	17-18
Hungary	18-20	16-17	18-20	20-22	16-17	18
Iceland	19	19	19	18	17	19
Ireland	17-18	17-18	17-18	a	a	17-18
Italy	19	19	19	19	17	a
Japan	18	18	18	18	16	18
Korea	17-18	17-18	17-18	a	a	17-18
Luxembourg	19	17-19	17-19	19	n	17-19
Mexico	18	19	18	a	19	19
Netherlands	17-18	18-20	17-18	a	18-19	18-20
New Zealand	m	a	18	17	17	17
Norway	18-19	18-19	18-19	a	m	16-18
Poland	19	20	19-20	a	18	a
Slovak Republic	18	16-18	18	a	17	16
Spain	17	17	17	a	17	17
Sweden	19	19	19	19	a	19
Switzerland	18-20	18-20	18-20	18-20	17-19	17-19
Turkey	16	16	16	a	a	m
United States	m	m	m	m	m	m
NON-OECD COUNTRIES						
Argentina	17	17	17	a	a	a
Brazil	17	17	17	17	a	17
Chile	18	18	18	18	a	a
China	18	18	18	a	17-18	18
Egypt[2]	17	17	17	17	a	17
India	18	18	18	a	m	m
Indonesia	18	18-19	18	18	a	a
Israel	18	18	18	18	18	18
Jamaica	17	17	17	17	a	a
Jordan[2]	18	18	18	a	18	18
Malaysia[3]	17-19	17	19	a	a	17
Paraguay[2]	17	17	17	a	a	17
Peru	17	17	17	17	a	a
Philippines[2]	16	a	16	a	a	a
Russian Federation[2]	17	17-18	17	a	m	m
Thailand	17	17	17	17	a	a
Tunisia[2]	19	19	19	19	a	19
Uruguay[2]	17	18	18	18	a	a
Zimbabwe[2]	19	17	19	a	a	17

1. Duration categories for ISCED 3C - Short: at least one year shorter than ISCED 3A/3B programmes; Long: of similar duration to ISCED 3A or 3B programmes.
2. OECD estimate.
3. OECD estimate for general and pre-vocational/vocational programmes.
Source: OECD.

Table X1.1b
Typical graduation ages in post-secondary non-tertiary education

		Educational/labour market destination		
		ISCED 4A programmes	ISCED 4B programmes	ISCED 4C programmes
OECD COUNTRIES	Austria	19	20	20
	Belgium	19	a	19-21
	Czech Republic	20	a	20
	Denmark	21-22	a	21-22
	Finland	a	a	25-29
	France	18-21	a	19-21
	Germany	22	22	a
	Hungary	20-22	a	19-22
	Iceland	a	a	20
	Ireland	a	a	19
	Italy	a	a	20
	Korea	a	a	a
	Luxembourg	a	a	20-25
	Mexico	a	a	a
	Netherlands	a	a	18-20
	New Zealand	18	18	18
	Norway	20-25	a	20-25
	Poland	a	a	21
	Slovak Republic	20-21	a	a
	Spain	18	18	a
	Sweden	m	m	19-20
	Switzerland	19-21	21-23	a
	Turkey	a	a	a
	United States	a	a	20
NON-OECD COUNTRIES	Argentina	a	a	a
	Brazil	a	a	a
	China	a	20	20
	Indonesia	a	a	a
	Jordan[1]	a	a	a
	Malaysia[1]	20	18	19
	Paraguay	a	a	a
	Peru	a	a	m
	Philippines[1]	19	19	17
	Russian Federation	a	a	18
	Thailand[1]	a	a	19
	Tunisia	a	21	a

1. OECD estimate.
Source: OECD.

Annex 1

Table X1.1c
Typical graduation ages in tertiary education

| | Tertiary-type B (ISCED 5B) | Tertiary-type A (ISCED 5A) | | | | Advanced research programmes (ISCED 6) |
		All programmes	3 to less than 5 years	5 to 6 years	More than 6 years	
Australia	m	a	20-21	22-23	24	25-29
Austria	m	a	22	23	a	25
Belgium	m	a	m	m	m	25-29
Czech Republic	22	a	22	24	a	26
Denmark	21-25	a	22-24	25-26	27-30	30
Finland	21-22	a	25-29	25-29	30-34	29
France	20-21	a	21-22	23-24	25	25-26
Germany	21	a	25	26	a	28
Greece	m	a	m	m	m	24-28
Hungary	m	a	m	m	m	30
Iceland	22-24	a	23	25	27	29
Ireland	20	a	21	23	24	27
Italy	22-23	a	22	23-25	25-27	27-29
Japan	20	a	22	23	a	27
Korea	m	a	m	m	m	26
Mexico	m	a	m	m	m	24-28
Netherlands	m	a	m	m	m	25
New Zealand	20	21	m	m	m	28
Norway	m	a	m	m	m	29
Poland	m	24	m	m	m	m
Slovak Republic	20-21	a	m	m	m	27
Spain	19	20-22	m	m	m	25-27
Sweden	22-23	a	23-25	25-26	a	27-29
Switzerland	23-29	a	23-26	23-26	28	29
Turkey	m	m	m	m	m	28-29
United Kingdom	20	a	21	23	24	24
United States	m	m	m	m	m	28

Note: Where tertiary-type A data are available by duration of programme, the graduation rate for all programmes is the sum of the graduation rates by duration of programme.
Source: OECD.

Table X1.2a.

School year and financial year used for the calculation of indicators

■ Financial year   ■ School year

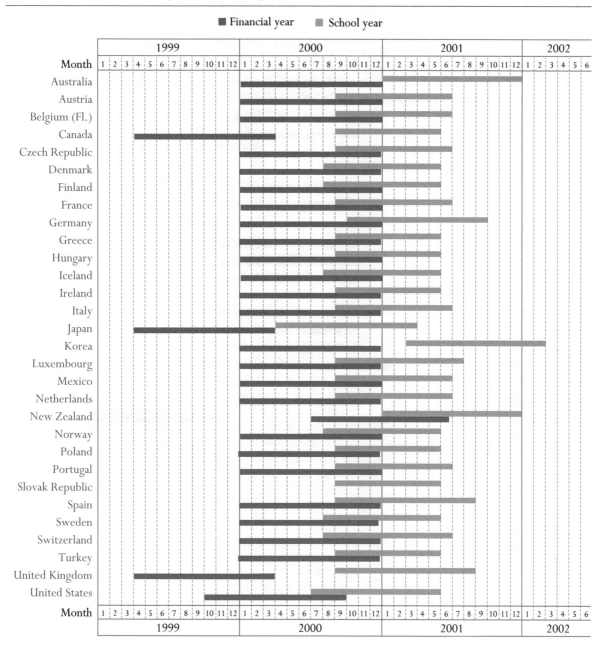

Source: OECD.

Table X1.2b.
School year and financial year used for the calculation of indicators

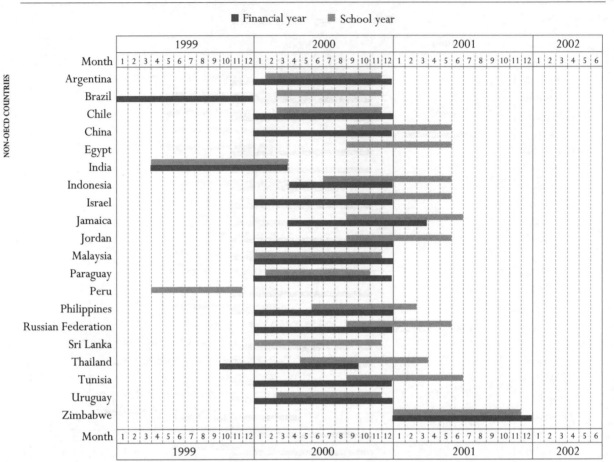

Source: OECD.

Annex

2

BASIC REFERENCE STATISTICS

Table X2.1
Overview of the economic context using basic variables (reference period: calendar year 2000, 2000 current prices)

	Total public expenditure as a percentage of GDP	GDP per capita (in equivalent US dollars converted using PPPs)	GDP deflator (1995 =100)	Labour force participation rates	Unemployment rates
Australia[1]	35.3	26 325	109.77	74.9	6.2
Austria	52.5	28 070	104.91	71.2	3.5
Belgium	49.5	26 392	106.93	65.6	6.6
Belgium (Fl.)	m	26 871	m	m	m
Canada	39.9	28 130	108.14	77.3	6.8
Czech Republic	45.1	13 806	135.27	72.4	8.8
Denmark	54.7	28 755	111.02	80.6	4.5
Finland	48.9	25 357	107.65	74.7	9.8
France[2]	51.1	25 090	104.76	68.3	10.0
Germany	45.9	26 139	103.07	72.9	8.1
Greece	43.3	15 885	128.59	64.5	11.1
Hungary	35.0	12 204	192.37	60.6	6.4
Iceland	41.5	28 143	116.99	86.6	2.3
Ireland	32.2	28 285	122.60	68.8	4.3
Italy	46.5	25 095	114.80	61.2	10.5
Japan	33.9	26 011	96.11	78.2	4.8
Korea	24.4	15 186	109.07	67.5	4.1
Luxembourg	39.5	48 239	113.56	64.5	2.3
Mexico	20.6	9 117	229.16	65.0	2.2
Netherlands	45.3	27 316	111.05	75.2	3.3
New Zealand[1]	m	20 372	107.01	76.5	6.0
Norway	41.1	36 242	131.51	82.0	3.4
Poland	42.9	9 547	172.95	67.3	16.1
Portugal	45.3	16 780	117.98	75.2	4.0
Slovak Republic	27.5	11 278	132.72	70.1	18.8
Spain	39.5	20 195	115.31	67.1	13.9
Sweden	55.1	26 161	105.62	80.2	5.8
Switzerland	35.9	29 617	102.03	82.7	2.7
Turkey	m	6 211	1 322.55	53.5	6.6
United Kingdom	38.9	24 964	114.57	77.9	5.5
United States	31.6	34 602	109.01	79.6	4.0

OECD COUNTRIES

1. Australia and New Zealand: GDP per capita, total public expenditure as a percentage of GDP and GDP deflator calculated for the fiscal year.
2. Excluding Over Sea Departments (DOM).
Source : OECD.

Annex
2

Table X2.2
Basic reference statistics (reference period: calendar year 2000, 2000 current prices)[1]

	Gross Domestic Product (in millions of local currency)	Gross Domestic Product (adjusted to financial year)[3]	Total public expenditure (in millions of local currency)	Total population in thousands (mid-year estimates)	Purchasing Power Parity (PPP)
Australia[2]	669 307	648 964	236 267	19 157	1.3272
Austria	207 037	a	108 658	8 110	0.90942
Belgium	247 469	a	122 417	10 246	0.91515
Belgium (Fl.)	150 905	a	m	6 137	0.91515
Canada	1 049 448	986 442	418 575	30 770	1.21247
Czech Republic	1 984 833	a	895 971	10 272	13.99567
Denmark	1 279 585	a	700 172	5 338	8.33624
Finland	130 234	a	63 738	5 176	0.99228
France[4]	1 402 687	a	717 100	59 373	0.94161
Germany	2 030 000	a	930 760	82 188	0.94493
Greece	121 652	a	52 687	10 920	0.70131
Hungary	13 150 766	a	4 607 797	10 211	105.53243
Iceland	658 247	a	272 951	281	83.19
Ireland	102 910	a	33 100	3 799	0.95764
Italy	1 166 548	a	541 944	57 762	0.80478
Japan[5]	513 534 000	512 261 325	174 240 275	126 926	155.54866
Korea	521 959 212	a	127 416 694	47 008	731.19353
Luxembourg	20 815	a	8 223	439	0.98404
Mexico	5 485 372	a	1 131 197	97 379	6.17846
Netherlands	402 599	a	182 218	15 922	0.92567
New Zealand[2]	112 316	a	m	3 831	1.43914
Norway	1 465 096	a	602 619	4 491	9.00148
Poland	684 982	a	294 012	38 646	1.85656
Portugal	115 546	a	52 286	10 231	0.67308
Slovak Republic	908 801	a	249 956	5 401	14.91982
Spain	609 319	a	240 560	39 927	0.75566
Sweden	2 196 764	a	1 211 269	8 871	9.46586
Switzerland	405 530	a	145 394	7 184	1.90599
Turkey	124 583 458 275	a	m	67 461	297337.1047
United Kingdom	950 415	914 448	369 288	58 655	0.64907
United States	9 762 100	9 624 775	3 080 259	282 128	1

OECD COUNTRIES (side label)

1. Data on GDP, PPPs and total public expenditure in countries in the Euro zone are provided in Euros.
2. Australia and New Zealand: GDP and total public expenditure calculated for the fiscal year.
3. For countries where GDP is not reported for the same reference period as data on educational finance, GDP is estimated as: wt-1 (GDPt - 1) + wt (GDPt), where wt and wt-1 are the weights for the respective portions of the two reference periods for GDP which fall within the educational financial year. Adjustments were made in Chapter B for Australia, Canada, Japan, the United Kingdom and the United States.
4. Excluding Over Sea Departments (DOM).
5. Total public expenditure adjusted to financial year.
Source: OECD.

Annex **2**

Table X2.3
Basic reference statistics (reference period: calendar year 1995, 1995 current prices)[1]

	Gross Domestic Product (in millions of local currency)	Gross Domestic Product (adjusted to financial year)[3]	Gross Domestic Product (2000 constant prices, base year=1995)[2]	Total public expenditure (in millions of local currency)	Total population in thousands (mid-year estimates)	Purchasing Power Parity (PPP)
Australia[2]	502 828	487 088	609 739	189 446	18 072	1.28709
Austria	172 287	a	197 352	98 676	8 047	0.99802
Belgium	202 174	a	231 433	106 823	10 137	0.91083
Belgium (Fl.)	m	a	m	m	m	m
Canada	798 300	768 883	970 488	381 542	29 354	1.18256
Czech Republic	1 381 049	a	1 467 285	783 678	10 327	10.81133
Denmark	1 009 756	a	1 152 532	608 853	5 222	8.41666
Finland	95 251	a	120 981	56 546	5 108	0.98583
France[4]	1 168 124	a	1 338 909	625 707	58 020	0.98485
Germany	1 801 300	a	1 969 500	1 010 030	81 661	1.03058
Greece	79 927	a	94 606	37 026	10 454	0.59599
Hungary	5 614 042	a	6 836 059	2 327 299	10 329	60.55234
Iceland	442 256	a	562 638	186 846	267	75.87188
Ireland	52 641	a	83 937	21 876	3 601	0.80588
Italy	923 052	a	1 016 192	492 878	57 301	0.80067
Japan[5]	497 739 400	493 311 250	534 311 798	153 063 675	125 570	169.94188
Korea	377 349 800	a	478 532 887	84 022 000	45 093	730.50462
Luxembourg	13 215	a	18 329	6 023	410	0.96362
Mexico	1 837 019	a	2 393 720	380 924	90 164	2.95733
Netherlands	302 233	a	362 552	170 327	15 460	0.92001
New Zealand[2]	92 679	a	104 961	36 441	3 656	1.46721
Norway	937 445	a	1 114 028	457 033	4 358	9.14417
Poland	308 104	a	396 050	147 561	38 588	1.13714
Portugal	80 827	a	97 933	36 403	10 027	0.59394
Slovak Republic	568 923	a	684 751	190 290	5 364	11.8966
Spain	437 787	a	528 439	192 600	39 223	0.7337
Sweden	1 772 021	a	2 079 780	1 158 840	8 827	9.7281
Switzerland	363 329	a	397 470	133 827	7 041	2.01088
Turkey	7 762 456 069	a	9 419 920 522	m	61 646	22334.21004
United Kingdom	719 176	690 789	829 517	317 455	57 958	0.65391
United States	7 338 400	7 252 125	8 955 100	2 516 240	266 327	1

1. Data on GDP, PPPs and total public expenditure in countries in the Euro zone are provided in Euros.
2. Australia and New Zealand: GDP and total public expenditure calculated for the fiscal year.
3. For countries where GDP is not reported for the same reference period as data on educational finance, GDP is estimated as: wt-1 (GDPt - 1) + wt (GDPt), where wt and wt-1 are the weights for the respective portions of the two reference periods for GDP which fall within the educational financial year. Adjustments were made in Chapter B for Australia, Canada, Japan, the United Kingdom and the United States.
4. Excluding Over Sea Departments (DOM).
5. Total public expenditure adjusted to financial year.
Source: OECD.

Annex 2

Table X2.4a
Reference statistics used in the calculation of teachers' salaries (1996, 2001)[1]

	Teachers' salaries in national currency (1996)[2]								
	Primary education			Lower secondary education			Upper secondary education, general programmes		
	Starting salary/ minimum training	Salary after 15 years of experience / minimum training	Salary at top of scale / minimum training	Starting salary/ minimum training	Salary after 15 years of experience / minimum training	Salary at top of scale / minimum training	Starting salary/ minimum training	Salary after 15 years of experience / minimum training	Salary at top of scale / minimum training
Australia	25 693	46 781	46 781	25 693	46 781	46 781	25 693	46 781	46 781
Austria	273 982	351 193	552 278	283 432	368 653	590 454	301 229	403 649	663 299
Belgium (Fl.)[3]	826 125	1 111 024	1 319 954	845 118	1 183 834	1 443 412	1 048 768	1 514 107	1 820 112
Belgium (Fr.)[3]	826 125	1 111 024	1 319 954	845 118	1 183 834	1 443 412	1 048 768	1 514 107	1 820 112
Czech Republic	83 855	108 624	130 015	83 855	108 624	130 015	94 669	122 739	147 160
Denmark	200 000	244 000	250 000	200 000	244 000	250 000	218 000	310 000	325 000
England	13 182	20 145	20 145	13 053	20 145	20 145	13 053	20 145	20 145
Finland	105 000	139 000	143 000	118 000	165 000	172 000	122 000	172 000	182 000
France	m	m	m	m	m	m	m	m	m
Germany	57 900	73 200	78 950	63 100	79 200	84 500	67 300	83 800	96 900
Greece	3 670 410	4 379 874	5 161 802	3 796 212	4 505 676	5 287 604	3 796 212	4 505 676	5 287 604
Hungary	341 289	462 618	597 402	341 289	462 618	597 402	435 279	574 067	717 756
Iceland	m	m	m	m	m	m	m	m	m
Ireland	14 361	22 201	26 275	15 075	23 526	26 524	15 075	23 526	26 524
Italy	28 926 072	34 910 707	42 335 570	31 392 416	38 330 149	46 921 350	31 392 416	39 523 876	49 262 026
Japan	3 462 000	5 917 000	8 475 000	3 462 000	5 917 000	8 475 000	3 462 000	5 917 000	8 733 000
Korea	14 928 000	26 679 000	42 469 000	15 108 000	26 859 000	42 529 000	15 108 000	26 859 000	42 529 000
Mexico	29 105	38 606	63 264	37 092	47 174	76 196	m	m	m
Netherlands	47 980	58 480	71 900	50 520	63 570	78 980	50 950	88 750	105 240
New Zealand	23 000	39 220	39 220	23 000	39 220	39 220	23 000	39 220	39 220
Norway	165 228	201 446	204 211	165 228	201 446	204 211	178 752	207 309	222 078
Portugal	1 998 800	3 007 500	5 192 800	1 998 800	3 007 500	5 192 800	1 998 800	3 007 500	5 192 800
Scotland	12 510	20 796	20 796	m	m	m	12 510	20 796	20 796
Slovak Republic	m	m	m	m	m	m	m	m	m
Spain	3 096 257	3 631 038	4 648 785	3 096 257	3 631 038	4 648 785	3 590 887	4 214 139	5 287 728
Sweden	m	m	m	m	m	m	m	m	m
Switzerland	65 504	87 585	100 847	76 772	104 350	117 629	92 163	121 937	136 001
Turkey	m	m	m	m	m	m	m	m	m
United States	m	m	m	m	m	m	m	m	m

OECD COUNTRIES (side label)

1. Data on salaries in countries in the Euro zone are provided in the old national currencies to enable comparisons between 1996 and 2001 data.
2. Teachers' salaries in national currencies (1996) are converted to US dollars using GDP deflators (1996, 2001), PPPs (January 2001) and correction for inflation (2001).
3. Data on teachers' salaries for 1996 refer to Belgium.
Source: OECD.

Table X2.4a (continued)
Reference statistics used in the calculation of teachers' salaries (1996, 2001)[1]

		Teachers' salaries in national currency (2001)[2]								
		Primary education			**Lower secondary education**			**Upper secondary education, general programmes**			
		Starting salary / minimum training	**Salary after 15 years of experience / minimum training**	**Salary at top of scale / minimum training**	**Starting salary / minimum training**	**Salary after 15 years of experience / minimum training**	**Salary at top of scale / minimum training**	**Starting salary / minimum training**	**Salary after 15 years of experience / minimum training**	**Salary at top of scale / minimum training**	**GDP deflator 2001 (1996=100)**
OECD COUNTRIES	Australia	37 135	52 709	52 709	37 195	52 648	52 648	37 194	52 648	52 648	110
	Austria	293 364	390 454	587 532	304 238	416 334	632 629	310 398	433 010	661 035	105
	Belgium (Fl.)[3]	916 528	1 230 325	1 456 670	916 528	1 283 477	1 564 691	1 137 153	1 641 278	1 972 790	108
	Belgium (Fr.)[3]	872 308	1 190 743	1 428 867	888 505	1 254 061	1 536 231	1 107 248	1 613 095	1 945 737	108
	Czech Republic	153 341	199 718	264 009	153 341	199 718	264 009	174 778	222 333	301 485	131
	Denmark	264 000	299 000	299 000	264 000	299 000	299 000	255 000	339 000	362 000	111
	England	15 141	23 958	23 958	15 141	23 958	23 958	15 141	23 958	23 958	113
	Finland	118 900	162 900	168 300	133 800	185 500	194 400	138 500	194 400	205 700	112
	France	134 432	180 835	266 817	148 766	195 169	281 857	148 766	195 169	281 857	105
	Germany	71 390	86 346	92 628	74 067	91 167	95 175	80 103	98 202	102 609	104
	Greece	4 818 952	5 832 446	7 031 622	4 818 952	5 832 446	7 031 622	4 818 952	5 832 446	7 031 622	124
	Hungary	691 692	977 280	1 331 064	691 692	977 280	1 331 064	840 552	1 228 536	1 615 776	172
	Iceland	1 480 272	1 641 162	1 698 641	1 480 272	1 641 162	1 698 641	2 041 400	2 590 600	2 832 600	125
	Ireland	17 796	28 844	32 558	18 684	28 844	32 869	18 684	29 155	32 869	126
	Italy	35 923 289	43 472 039	52 411 123	38 767 304	47 424 304	57 689 387	38 767 304	48 777 387	60 380 387	112
	Japan	3 478 000	6 566 000	8 378 000	3 478 000	6 566 000	8 378 000	3 478 000	6 570 000	8 631 000	96
	Korea	18 302 750	31 146 750	49 855 800	18 206 750	31 050 750	49 759 800	18 206 750	31 050 750	49 759 800	106
	Mexico	73 336	96 846	160 197	93 954	122 746	202 027	m	m	m	185
	Netherlands	55 754	66 485	80 482	57 853	71 163	88 413	58 411	99 248	117 353	116
	New Zealand	26 000	50 300	50 300	26 000	50 300	50 300	26 000	50 300	50 300	109
	Norway	243 100	274 000	298 200	243 100	274 000	298 200	243 100	274 000	298 200	128
	Portugal	2 542 400	3 761 200	6 776 100	2 542 400	3 761 200	6 776 100	2 542 400	3 761 200	6 776 100	120
	Scotland	14 550	23 313	23 313	14 550	23 313	23 313	14 550	23 313	23 313	113
	Slovak Republic	81 000	100 560	115 440	81 000	100 560	127 560	81 000	100 560	141 120	134
	Spain	3 371 421	3 933 670	4 907 865	3 791 978	4 417 574	5 493 269	3 932 164	4 578 875	5 688 403	116
	Sweden	205 100	245 400	271 800	205 100	245 400	271 800	220 100	262 700	282 900	106
	Switzerland	66 597	87 470	104 286	78 562	104 195	122 914	93 998	121 368	142 369	103
	Turkey	3 130 218 000	3 760 938 000	5 415 618 000	a	a	a	2 864 088 000	3 494 808 000	5 149 488 000	1 151
	United States	28 681	41 595	50 636	28 693	41 595	49 728	28 806	41 708	49 862	109

1. Data on salaries in countries in the Euro zone are provided in the old national currencies to enable comparisons between 1996 and 2001 data.
2. Teachers' salaries in national currencies (2001) are converted to US dollars using PPPs (January 2001) and correction for inflation (2001). These data are available in this table.
3. Data on teachers' salaries for 1996 refer to Belgium.
Source: OECD.

Table X2.4b
Reference statistics used in the calculation of teachers' salaries (1996, 2001)

	Purchasing Power Parity (PPP) (2000)[1]	Purchasing Power Parity (PPP) (2001)[1]	Purchasing Power Parity (PPP) (January 2001)[1]	Gross Domestic Product (in millions of local currency, calendar year 2001)[1]	Gross Domestic Product (in millions of local currency, calendar year 1996)[1]
Australia	1.32	1.33	1.33	713 627	529 886
Austria	12.57	12.52	12.55	2 915 216	2 449 959
Belgium (Fl.)[2]	37.21	37.25	37.23	10 257 710	8 349 916
Belgium (Fr.)[2]	37.21	37.25	37.23	10 257 710	8 349 916
Czech Republic	14.08	14.57	14.33	2 157 828	1 566 968
Denmark	8.30	8.34	8.32	1 344 488	1 060 887
England[3]	0.65	0.65	0.65	987 735	762 214
Finland	5.90	5.90	5.90	808 477	586 897
France	6.22	6.17	6.19	9 601 387	7 951 366
Germany	1.87	1.85	1.86	4 050 915	3 586 405
Greece	238.76	241.15	239.96	44 613 035	29 935 228
Hungary	105.60	112.61	109.10	14 823 932	6 893 934
Iceland	84.80	90.56	87.68	750 031	474 586
Ireland	0.75	0.78	0.77	90 160	45 742
Italy	1 522.88	1 529.65	1 526.26	2 355 848 091	1 902 275 700
Japan	155.28	149.81	152.55	503 303 500	510 802 400
Korea	729.93	724.01	726.97	545 013 252	418 478 988
Mexico	6.17	6.36	6.27	5 765 922	2 525 575
Netherlands	2.00	2.06	2.03	945 771	694 299
New Zealand	1.44	1.48	1.46	120 231	96 911
Norway	9.07	9.05	9.06	1 510 866	1 026 924
Portugal	128.09	131.54	129.81	24 600 144	17 287 603
Scotland[3]	0.65	0.65	0.65	987 735	762 214
Slovak Republic	14.77	15.21	14.99	989 297	628 588
Spain	126.49	128.67	127.58	108 423 939	77 244 867
Sweden	9.55	9.53	9.54	2 167 196	1 817 149
Switzerland	1.90	1.90	1.90	414 882	365 833
Turkey	302 272.28	465 131.47	383 701.87	181 408 563 151	14 772 110 189
United States	1.00	1.00	1	10 019 700	7 751 100

1. Data on PPPs and GDP in countries in the Euro zone are provided in the old national currencies to enable comparisons between 1996 and 2001 data.
2. Data on Gross Domestic Product (1996 and 2001) refer to Belgium.
3. Data on Gross Domestic Product (1996 and 2001) refer to the United Kingdom.
Source: OECD.

Table X2.4b (continued)
Reference statistics used in the calculation of teachers' salaries (1996, 2001)

	Total population in thousands (calendar year 2001)	Total population in thousands (calendar year 1996)	GDP per capita (in equivalent US dollars, calendar year 2001)[1]	GDP per capita (in equivalent US dollars, calendar year 1996)[2]	Reference year for 2001 salary data	Adjustments for inflation (2000)
Australia	19 470 000	18 420 000	27 474	23 982	2000/2001	1.00
Austria	8 131 953	8 059 385	28 626	25 551	2000/2001	1.00
Belgium (Fl.)[3]	10 281 000	10 155 000	26 782	23 789	2000/2001	1.00
Belgium (Fr.)[3]	10 281 000	10 155 000	26 782	23 789	2000/2001	1.00
Czech Republic	10 260 408	10 315 300	14 433	13 648	2000/2001	1.00
Denmark	5 357 000	5 256 000	30 082	26 747	April 1, 2000	0.98
England[4]	60 012 000	58 075 800	25 294	22 883	Oct 2000/Sep 2001	1.00
Finland	5 188 000	5 125 000	26 434	21 726	2001	0.98
France	60 908 000	59 634 345	25 538	22 694	2000/2001	1.00
Germany	82 340 000	81 896 000	26 587	24 496	2000/2001	1.00
Greece	10 954 982	10 475 878	16 887	14 673	2000	1.02
Hungary	10 187 000	10 311 000	12 922	10 235	2000/2001	1.00
Iceland	284 600	268 927	29 101	24 375	Jan 2001	1.00
Ireland	3 852 552	3 626 082	30 052	20 476	2001	0.98
Italy	57 927 000	57 397 000	26 587	24 293	2000/2001	1.00
Japan	127 210 000	125 864 000	26 410	25 880	2000/2001	1.00
Korea	47 342 828	45 524 681	15 901	13 509	2001	1.00
Mexico	99 109 143	92 159 259	9 141	7 955	2000/2001	1.00
Netherlands	16 043 000	15 526 000	28 685	25 142	Jan 2001	1.00
New Zealand	3 850 000	3 714 000	21 119	19 298	2001	0.98
Norway	4 513 000	4 381 000	37 008	33 284	2000	1.08
Portugal	10 061 000	10 055 580	18 589	15 672	2000/2001	1.00
Scotland[4]	60 012 000	58 075 800	25 294	22 883	2000/2001	1.00
Slovak Republic	5 379 000	5 374 000	12 089	10 301	Jan-Jun 2001	0.98
Spain	40 265 500	39 278 800	20 928	17 732	2000	1.02
Sweden	8 896 000	8 841 000	25 551	22 957	2000	1.00
Switzerland	7 231 000	7 072 000	30 266	28 131	2001	1.00
Turkey	68 610 000	62 695 000	5 685	5 832	2000	1.23
United States	285 908 000	269 448 000	35 045	31 492	2000/2001	1.00

1. GDP per capita in national currencies (2001) are converted to US dollars using PPPs (2001), total population (2001) and total GDP current expenditure (2001). These data are available in this table.
2. GDP per capita in national currencies (1996) are converted to US dollars using GDP deflators (1996, 2001), PPPs (2001), total population (1996) and total GDP current expenditure (1996). These data are available in this table.
3. Data on Gross Domestic Product (1996 and 2001) refer to Belgium.
4. Data on Gross Domestic Product (1996 and 2001) refer to the United Kingdom.
Source: OECD.

General notes

Definitions

Gross Domestic Product (GDP) refers to the producers' value of the gross outputs of resident producers, including distributive trades and transport, less the value of purchasers' intermediate consumption plus import duties. GDP is expressed in local money (in millions). For countries which provide this information for a reference year that is different from the calendar year (such as Australia and New Zealand), adjustments are made by linearly weighting their GDP between two adjacent national reference years to match the calendar year.

The **GDP deflator** is obtained by dividing the GDP expressed at current prices by the GDP expressed at constant prices. This provides an indication of the relative price level in a country. Data are based on the year 1995.

GDP per capita is the Gross Domestic Product (in equivalent US dollars converted using PPPs) divided by the population.

Purchasing Power Parity exchange rates (PPP) are the currency exchange rates that equalise the purchasing power of different currencies. This means that a given sum of money when converted into different currencies at the PPP rates will buy the same basket of goods and services in all countries. In other words, PPPs are the rates of currency conversion which eliminate the differences in price levels among countries. Thus, when expenditure on GDP for different countries is converted into a common currency by means of PPPs, it is, in effect, expressed at the same set of international prices so that comparisons between countries reflect only differences in the volume of goods and services purchased.

Total public expenditure as used for the calculation of the education indicators, corresponds to the non-repayable current and capital expenditure of all levels of government. Current expenditure includes final consumption expenditure (*e.g.,* compensation of employees, consumption intermediate goods and services, consumption of fixed capital, and military expenditure), property income paid, subsidies, and other current transfers paid (*e.g.,* social security, social assistance, pensions and other welfare benefits). Capital expenditure is spending to acquire and/or improve fixed capital assets, land, intangible assets, government stocks, and non-military, non-financial assets, and spending to finance net capital transfers.

The **unemployment rate** is calculated as the percentage of unemployed people in the labour force, where unemployment is defined according to the guidelines of the International Labour Office (ILO). The **labour force participation** rate for a particular age group relates to the percentage of individuals in the population of that age group who are either employed or unemployed, where these terms are defined according to the ILO guidelines. Rates for age groups are defined correspondingly.

Sources

The 2003 edition of the National Accounts of OECD countries: Main Aggregates, Volume I

The theoretical framework underpinning national accounts has been provided for many years by the United Nations' publication *A System of National Accounts*, which was released in 1968. An updated version was released in 1993 (commonly referred to as SNA93).

OECD Analytical Data Base, January 2003

SOURCES, METHODS AND TECHNICAL NOTES

Annex 3 on sources and methods is available in electronic form only. It can be found at *www.oecd.org/edu/eag2003*.

GLOSSARY

Additional bonuses to base salary: Additional bonuses to base salary refer to additional payments that teachers may acquire in addition to the amount received on the basis of educational qualification and experience (salary scale). These bonuses may be awarded for teaching in remote areas, for participating in school improvement projects or special activities or for excellence in teaching performance. See also *Teacher's salaries.*

Advanced Research Qualifications (ISCED 6): Advanced Research Qualifications refer to tertiary programmes that lead directly to the award of an advanced research qualification, *e.g.,* Ph.D. The theoretical duration of these programmes is three years full-time in most countries (for a cumulative total of at least seven years full-time at the tertiary level), although the actual enrolment time is typically longer. The programmes are devoted to advanced study and original research. See also *International Standard Classification of Education (ISCED).*

Age: See *Theoretical age, Typical age, Typical ending age, Typical graduation age* and *Typical starting age.*

Ancillary services: See *Expenditure on ancillary services.*

Capital expenditure: Capital expenditure represents the value of educational capital acquired or created during the year in question, that is, the amount of capital formation regardless of whether the capital outlay was financed from current revenue or by borrowing. Capital expenditure includes outlays on construction, renovation, and major repair of buildings and expenditure for new or replacement equipment. Although capital investment requires a large initial expenditure, the plant and facilities have a lifetime that extends over many years.

Civic knowledge scale: This was derived as part of the IEA's Civic Knowledge Study through the administration of a civic knowledge test to 14-year olds. The test was designed to measure students' knowledge of fundamental democratic principles and their skills in interpreting material with civic and political content.

Class size: Class size is the average number of students per class, calculated by dividing the number of students enrolled by the number of classes. In order to ensure comparability between countries, special needs programmes have been excluded. Data include only regular programmes at these two levels of education and also exclude teaching in sub-groups outside the regular classroom setting.

Combined school and work-based programmes: In combined school and work-based programmes, instruction is shared between school and the workplace, although instruction may take place primarily in the workplace. Programmes are classified as combined school and work-based if less than 75 per cent of the curriculum is presented in the school environment or through distance education. Programmes that are more than 90 per cent work-based are excluded. See also *General programmes, Programme orientation, School-based programmes* and *Vocational programmes.*

Comprehensive private internal rate of return: See *Private internal rate of return.*

Compulsory core curriculum: Compulsory core curriculum is the minimum required time devoted to core subjects and study areas within the compulsory curriculum. See also *Compulsory curriculum, Compulsory flexible curriculum, Intended instruction time* and *Non-compulsory curriculum.*

Compulsory curriculum: Compulsory curriculum refers to the amount and allocation of instruction time that has to be provided in every school and must be attended by all students. See also *Compulsory core curriculum, Compulsory flexible curriculum, Intended instruction time* and *Non-compulsory curriculum.*

Compulsory education: The legal age from which children are no longer compelled to attend school (*e.g.,* 15th birthday). The ending age of compulsory schooling is thus different from the ending age of an educational programme.

Compulsory flexible curriculum: Compulsory flexible curriculum refers to the part of the compulsory curriculum in which there is flexibility or choice for schools or students. For example, a school may choose to offer more classes than the minimum in science and only the minimum required number of classes in art within the compulsory time frame. See also *Compulsory core curriculum, Compulsory curriculum, Intended instruction time* and *Non-compulsory curriculum.*

Computer: As used in the indicator on the availability and use of computers this refers to computers capable of supporting other multimedia equipment such as a CDROM or a soundcard and which are used for educational purposes in the school. Computers used only for recreation purposes are excluded.

Continuing education and training: For the purpose of these indicators, continuing education and training for adults is defined as all kinds of general and job-related education and training that is organised, financed or sponsored by authorities, provided by employers or self- financed.

Core services: See *Expenditure on educational core services.*

Country of birth: See *Native students, First-generation students* and *Non-native students.*

Current expenditure: Current expenditure is expenditure on goods and services consumed within the current year, which needs to be made recurrently to sustain the production of educational services. Minor expenditure on items of equipment, below a certain cost threshold, is also reported as current spending. Current expenditure includes final consumption expenditure, property income paid, subsidies and other current transfers (*e.g.,* social security, social assistance, pensions and other welfare benefits). See also *Final consumption expenditure, Property income paid,* and *Other current transfers.*

Direct expenditure on educational institutions: Direct expenditure on educational institutions are purchases by a government agency of educational resources to be used by educational institutions (*e.g.,* direct payments of teachers' salaries by a central or regional education ministry, direct payments by a municipality to building contractors for the construction of school buildings, and procurement of textbooks by a central or regional authority for subsequent distribution to local authorities or schools) and payments by a government agency to educational institutions that have the responsibility for purchasing educational resources themselves (*e.g.,* a government appropriation or block grant to a university, which the university then uses to pay staff salaries and to buy other resources; government allocations of funds to fiscally autonomous public schools; government subsidies to private schools; and government payments under contract to private companies conducting educational research). Direct expenditure by a government agency does not include tuition payments received from students (or their families) enrolled in public schools under that agency's jurisdiction, even if the tuition payments flow, in the first instance, to the government agency rather than to the institution in question. See also *Instructional educational institutions* and *Non-instructional educational institutions.*

Dropouts: Dropouts are defined as those students who leave the specified level in the educational system without obtaining a first qualification. See also *Survival rates.*

Duration of programme: Programme duration refers to the standard number of years in which a student can complete the education programme.

Earnings: Earnings are annual money earnings as direct payment for labour services provided, before taxes. Income from other sources, such as government social transfers, investment income, net increase in the value of an owner operated business and any other income not directly related to work are not to be included. See also *Relative earnings.*

Educational attainment: Educational attainment is expressed by the highest completed level of education, defined according to the International Standard Classification of Education (ISCED).

Educational institution: An educational institution is an entity that provides instructional services to individuals or education-related services to individuals and other educational institutions. See *Private institution* and *Public institution.*

Educational personnel: The classification is based on function and organises staff into four main functional categories. The classification is: *i)* Instructional personnel; *ii)* Professional support for students; *iii)* Management/Quality control/Administration; and *iv)* Maintenance and operations personnel. Teaching staff (teachers) and teachers' aides make up the category instructional personnel. For the purposes of Indicator D2, only teaching staff is taken into account. See also *Full-time teacher, Full-time equivalent teacher, Instructional personnel, Maintenance and operations personnel, Management/Quality control/Administration, Part-time teacher, Professional support for students, Ratio of students to teaching staff, Teaching staff* and *Teaching time.*

Employed: The employed, which is defined according to the guidelines of the International Labour Office (ILO), are those who during the survey reference week: work for pay (employees) or profit (self-employed and unpaid family workers) for at least one hour or; have a job but are temporarily not at work (through injury, illness, holiday or vacation, strike or lock-out, educational or training leave, maternity or parental leave, etc.) and have a formal attachment to their job. See also *Labour force, Participation rate, Unemployed, Unemployment rate* and *Work status.*

Enrolment rate: Enrolment rates are expressed as net enrolment rates, which are calculated by dividing the number of students of a particular age group enrolled in all levels of education by the number of people in the population in that age group.

Entry rates: Entry rates are expressed as net entry rates, which represent the proportion of people of a synthetic age-cohort who enter the tertiary level of education, irrespective of changes in the population sizes and of differences between OECD countries in the typical entry age. The net entry rate of a specific age is obtained by dividing the number of first-time entrants to each type of tertiary education of that age by the total population in the corresponding age group (multiplied by 100). The sum of net entry rates is calculated by adding the net entry rates for each single year of age. See also *New entrants.*

Expected percentage: The percentage that one would expect to see in a cell in a table if the percentages in the cells were evenly distributed according to the parameters of the categories in the row and column totals. The observed percentage is the actual recorded percentage for that cell.

Expected years of schooling: See *School expectancy.*

Expenditure on Research and Development (R&D): Expenditure on Research and Development (R&D) refers to all expenditure on research performed at universities and at other institutions of tertiary education, regardless of whether the research is funded from general institutional funds or through separate grants or contracts from public or private sponsors. This includes all research institutes and experimental stations operating under the direct control of, or administered by, or associated with, higher education institutions. See also *Expenditure on ancillary services* and *Expenditure on educational core services.*

Expenditure on ancillary services: Ancillary services are services provided by educational institutions that are peripheral to the main educational mission. The two main components of ancillary services are student welfare services and services for the general public. At ISCED levels 0-3, student welfare services include such things as meals, school health services, and transportation to and from school. At the tertiary level, they include halls of residence (dormitories), dining halls, and health care. Services for the general public include such things as museums, radio and television broadcasting, sports, and recreational or cultural programmes. Day or evening childcare provided by pre-primary and primary institutions is not included as an ancillary service. Entities providing ancillary services cover separate organisations that provide such education-related services as vocational and psychological counselling, placement, transportation of students, and student meals and housing. See also *Expenditure on educational core services* and *Expenditure on Research and Development (R&D).*

Expenditure on educational core services: Expenditure on educational core services includes all expenditure that is directly related to instruction and education. This should cover all expenditure on teachers, school buildings, teaching materials, books, tuition outside schools, and administration of schools. See also *Expenditure on ancillary services* and *Expenditure on Research and Development (R&D).*

Expenditure on educational institutions: Expenditure on educational institutions includes expenditure on instructional educational institutions as well as expenditure on non-instructional educational institutions. See also *Direct expenditure on educational institutions*, *Instructional educational institutions* and *Non-instructional educational institutions.*

Expenditure on non-instruction: Expenditure on non-instruction is all expenditure broadly related to student living costs.

Expenditure outside educational institutions: Expenditure outside educational institutions is expenditure on educational services purchased outside institutions, *e.g.,* books, computers, external tuition, etc. It also deals with student living costs and costs of student transport not provided by institutions.

Expenditure over the average duration of tertiary studies: Expected expenditure over the average duration of tertiary studies is calculated by multiplying current annual expenditure by the typical duration of tertiary studies.

Field of study: Field of study, as defined in International Standard Classification of Education (ISCED), is as the subject matter taught in an education programme. For details and implementation, see the *Fields of Education and Training - Manual* (EUROSTAT, 1999).

Final consumption expenditure: Final consumption expenditure of government services is the value of goods and services produced for their own use on current account, *i.e.,* the value of their gross output less the value of their commodity and non-commodity sales and the value of their own-account capital formation which is not segregated as an industry. The value of their gross output is equal to the sum of the value of their intermediate consumption of goods and services (including indirect taxes paid), compensation of employees, and consumption of fixed capital (*i.e.,* its depreciation due to normal wear and tear and to foreseen obsolescence). See also *Current expenditure*, *Property income paid* and *Other current transfers.*

Financial aid to students: Financial aid to students comprises: *i)* Government scholarships and other government grants to students or households. These include, in addition to scholarships and similar grants (fellowships, awards, bursaries, etc.), the following items: the value of special subsidies provided to students, either in cash or in kind, such as free or reduced-price travel on public transport systems; and family allowances or child allowances that are contingent on student status. Any benefits provided to students or households in the form of tax reductions, tax subsidies, or other special tax provisions are not included; *ii*) Student loans, which are reported on a gross basis, that is, without subtracting or netting out repayments or interest payments from the borrowers (students or households).

First-generation students: "First-generation" are those students who reported in PISA that they were born in the country of assessment but whose parents were born in another country. See *Native students* and *Non-native students*.

Foreign students: Foreign students are students who do not hold the citizenship of the country for which the data are collected. While pragmatic and operational, this classification may give rise to inconsistencies resulting from national policies regarding naturalisation of immigrants, combined with the inability of several countries to report separately foreign students net of those holding permanent residence permits. As a result, countries where naturalisation of immigrants is stringent and identification of non-resident foreign students impossible over-estimate the size of the foreign student body, compared to countries granting citizenship to their immigrants more easily.

Full-time equivalent student: A full-time equivalent (FTE) measure attempts to standardise a student's actual course load against the normal course load. Calculating the full-time/part-time status requires information on the time periods for actual and normal course loads. For the reduction of head-count data to FTEs, where data and norms on individual participation are available, course load is measured as the product of the fraction of the normal course load for a full-time student and the fraction of the school/academic year. [FTE = (actual course load/normal course load) * (actual duration of study during reference period/normal duration of study during reference period).] When actual course load information is not available, a full-time student is considered equal to one FTE. See also *Full-time student, Mode of study, Part-time student, Student* and *Study load*.

Full-time equivalent teacher: A full-time equivalent (FTE) attempts to standardise a full-time teacher's teaching load against that of a part-time teacher. The basis for the calculation are the "statutory working hours" and not the "total or actual working hours" or "total or actual teaching hours". The full-time equivalence of part-time educational personnel is then determined by calculating the ratio of hours worked by part-time personnel over the statutory hours worked by a full-time employee during the school year. See also *Educational personnel, Full-time teacher, Instructional personnel, Part-time teacher, Ratio of students to teaching staff, Teaching staff, Working time* and *Teaching time*.

Full-time student: Students enrolled in primary and secondary level educational programmes are considered to participate full-time if they attend school for at least 75 per cent of the school day or week (as locally defined) and would normally be expected to be in the programme for the entire academic year. This includes the work-based component in combined school and work-based programmes. At the tertiary level, an individual is considered full-time if he or she is taking a course load or educational programme considered requiring at least 75 per cent of a full-time commitment of time and resources. Additionally, it is expected that the student will remain in the programme for the entire year. See also *Full-time equivalent student, Mode of study, Part-time student, Student* and *Study load*.

Full-time teacher: A teacher employed for at least 90 per cent of the normal or statutory number of hours of work for a full-time teacher over a complete school year is classified as a full-time teacher. See also *Educational personnel, Full-time equivalent teacher, Instructional personnel, Part-time teacher, Ratio of students to teaching staff* and *Teaching staff* and *Working time*.

Fully qualified teacher: refers to teachers who have fulfilled all the training requirements for teaching a certain subject at the upper secondary level according to the qualification requirements of the country and further meets all other administrative requirements to fill a permanent post in the school (*e.g.* probation period).

General programmes: General programmes are programmes that are not designed explicitly to prepare participants for a specific class of occupations or trades or for entry into further vocational or technical education programmes. Less than 25 per cent of the programme content is classified as vocational or technical. See also *Pre-vocational programmes, Programme orientation, Upper secondary education (ISCED 3)* and *Vocational programmes*.

Government-dependent private institution: A government-dependent private institution is an institution that receives more than 50 per cent of its core funding from government agencies. The term "government dependent" refers only to the degree of a private institution's dependence on funding from government sources; it does not refer to the degree of government direction or regulation. See also *Educational institution, Government-dependent private institution, Private institution* and *Public institution*.

Graduates: Graduates are those students who were enrolled in the final year of a level of education (*e.g.,* upper secondary education) and who completed it successfully during the reference year, regardless of their age. However, there are exceptions (especially in tertiary education) where graduation can also be recognised by the awarding of a certificate without the requirement that the participants are enrolled. See also *Graduation/Successful completion, Gross graduation rates, Net graduation rates* and *Unduplicated total count of graduates*.

Graduation/Successful completion: Successful completion is defined by each country. In some countries, completion is defined in terms of passing an examination or a series of examinations. In other countries, completion occurs after a requisite number of course hours have been accumulated (although completion of some or all of the course hours may also involve examinations). See also *Graduates, Gross graduation rates, Net graduation rates* and *Unduplicated total count of graduates*.

Graduation rate: See *Gross graduation rates* and *Net graduation rates*.

Gross Domestic Product (GDP): Gross Domestic Product (GDP) refers to the producers' value of the gross outputs of resident producers, including distributive trades and transport, less the value of purchasers' intermediate consumption plus import duties. GDP is expressed in local money (in millions). For countries which provide this information for a reference year that is different to the calendar year (*e.g.,* Australia and New Zealand), adjustments are made by linearly weighting GDP between two adjacent national reference years to match the calendar year. Data for GDP are provided in Annex 2.

Gross graduation rates: Gross graduation rates refer to the total number of graduates (the graduates themselves may be of any age) at the specified level of education divided by the population at the typical graduation age from the specified level. In many countries, defining a typical age of graduation is difficult, however, because graduates are dispersed over a wide range of ages. See also *Graduates, Graduation/Successful completion, Net graduation rates* and *Unduplicated total count of graduates*.

Head count: This refers to the method of data collection: the number of individuals are counted, regardless of the intensity of participation/length of their programme. See also *Full-time student, Part-time student, Full-time teacher* and *Part-time teacher*.

Human capital: Human capital is productive wealth embodied in labour, skills and knowledge.

IEA's Civic Education Study: The International Association for the Evaluation of Educational of Achievement's (IEA) Civic Education Study tested 14-year-olds in 28 countries, including 17 OECD countries, on their knowledge of civic-related content, their skills in understanding political communication, their concepts and attitudes towards civics, and their participation or practice in this area. The test was designed to identify and examine the ways in which young people are prepared to undertake their role as citizens in democracies, both inside and outside the school.

Independent private institution: An independent private institution is an institution that receives less than 50 per cent of its core funding from government agencies. The term "independent" refers only to the degree of a private institution's dependence on funding from government sources; it does not refer to the degree of government direction or regulation. See also *Educational institution, Government-dependent private institution, Private institution* and *Public institution.*

Index of intensity of foreign students' intake: The index of intensity of foreign students' intake compares the numbers of foreign students as a proportion of domestic enrolments with the average order of magnitude for OECD countries. This makes it possible to refine the scale of foreign students' intakes based on the size of the tertiary education system. The ratio calculated is as follows:

$$\text{Index of intensity, country } i = \frac{\dfrac{\textit{foreign students country } i}{\textit{foreign students OECD}}}{\dfrac{\textit{enrolments country } i}{\textit{enrolments OECD}}} = \frac{\dfrac{\textit{foreign students country } i}{\textit{enrolments country } i}}{\dfrac{\textit{foreign students OECD}}{\textit{enrolments OECD}}}$$

An index higher (lower) than one reflects a higher (lower) intake as a proportion of enrolments compared with the OECD mean. Alternatively, this index can also be interpreted in terms of a comparison of the weight of a country in OECD foreign students' intakes with its weight in OECD enrolments. If so, an index higher (lower) than one reflects a higher (lower) foreign students' intake than the country's weight in OECD enrolments would suggest.

Instruction time: See *Intended instruction time.*

Instructional educational institutions: Instructional educational institutions are educational institutions that directly provide instructional programmes (*i.e.,* teaching) to individuals in an organised group setting or through distance education. Business enterprises or other institutions providing short-term courses of training or instruction to individuals on a "one-to-one" basis are not included. See also *Expenditure on educational institutions* and *Non-instructional educational institutions.*

Instructional personnel: Instructional Personnel comprises two sub-categories: Classroom teachers at ISCED 0-4 and academic staff at ISCED 5-6; and teacher aides at ISCED 0-4 and teaching / research assistants at ISCED 5-6. See also *Educational personnel, Maintenance and operations personnel, Management / Quality control / Administration, Professional support for students, Ratio of students to teaching staff, Teaching staff* and *Teaching time.*

Intended instruction time: Intended instruction time refers to the number of hours per year for which students receive instruction in both the compulsory and non-compulsory parts of the curriculum. For countries that have no formal policy on instruction time, the number of hours was estimated from survey data. Hours lost when schools are closed for festivities and celebrations, such as national holidays, are excluded. Intended instruction time does not include non-compulsory time outside the school day. It does not include homework, individual tutoring or private study taken before or after school. See also *Compulsory core curriculum, Compulsory curriculum, Compulsory flexible curriculum* and *Non-compulsory curriculum.*

Intergovernmental transfers: Intergovernmental transfers are transfers of funds designated for education from one level of government to another. The restriction to funds earmarked for education is very important in order to avoid ambiguity about funding sources. General-purpose intergovernmental transfers are not included (*e.g.,* revenue sharing grants, general fiscal equalisation grants, or distributions of shared taxes from a national government to provinces, states, or Länder), even where such transfers provide the funds that regional or local authorities draw on to finance education.

International Standard Classification of Education (ISCED): The International Standard Classification of Education (ISCED-97) is used to define the levels and fields of education used in this publication. For details on ISCED 1997 and how it is nationally implemented see *Classifying Educational Programmes: Manual For ISCED-97 Implementation in OECD Countries* (Paris, 1999). See also *Pre-primary education (ISCED 0), Primary education (ISCED 1), Lower secondary education (ISCED 2), Upper secondary education (ISCED 3), Post-secondary non-tertiary level of education (ISCED 4), Tertiary-type A education (ISCED 5A), Tertiary-type B education (ISCED 5B)* and *Advanced Research Qualifications (ISCED 6).*

International Standard Classification of Occupations (ISCO): The International Standard Classification of Occupations (1998) classifies persons according to their actual and potential relation with jobs. Jobs are classified with respect to the type of work performed or to be performed. The basic criteria used to define the system of major, sub-major, minor and unit groups is the "skill" level and "skill specialisation" required to carry out the tasks and duties of the occupations, with separate major groups for "Legislators, senior officials and managers" and for "Armed forces".

Internet: The Internet is an electronic communications network that connects computer networks and organisational computer facilities around the world. See also *Local Area Network* and *World Wide Web.*

International Survey of Upper Secondary Schools (ISUSS): A questionnaire survey carried out in 4 400 upper secondary schools in 15 countries during the school year 2000/2001. The survey asked school principals about staffing, admission and grouping policies, support of professional development, teachers' participation in professional development activities, the availability and use of computers in the school, the school's contacts, feedback on the school's functioning, and career counselling.

Job-related continuing education and training: Job-related continuing education and training refers to all organised, systematic education and training activities in which people take part in order to obtain knowledge and/or learn new skills for a current or a future job, to increase earnings, to improve job and/or career opportunities in a current or another field and generally to improve their opportunities for advancement and promotion.

Labour force: The total labour force or currently active population, which is defined according to the guidelines of the International Labour Office (ILO), comprises all persons who fulfil the requirements for inclusion among the employed or the unemployed as defined in *OECD Labour Force Statistics.* See also *Work status.*

Labour productivity: GDP divided by the numbers in employment.

Language spoken at home: In PISA, students were asked if the language spoken at home most of the time is the language of assessment, another official national language, other national dialect or language, or another language. The responses were then grouped into two categories: the language spoken at home most of the time is different from the language of assessment, from other official national languages, and from other national dialects or languages, and; the language spoken at home most of the time is the language of assessment, other official national languages, or other national dialects or languages.

Local area network (LAN): A Local Area Network is a network of personal computers in a small area (as an office) that are linked by cable, can communicate directly with other devices in the network, and can share resources. See also *Internet* and *World Wide Web*.

Lower secondary education (ISCED 2): Lower secondary education (ISCED 2) generally continues the basic programmes of the primary level, although teaching is typically more subject-focused, often employing more specialised teachers who conduct classes in their field of specialisation. Lower secondary education may either be "terminal" *(i.e.,* preparing students for entry directly into working life) and/or "preparatory" *(i.e.,* preparing students for upper secondary education). This level usually consists of two to six years of schooling (the mode of OECD countries is three years). See also *International Standard Classification of Education (ISCED).*

Maintenance and operations personnel: Maintenance and operations personnel refers to personnel who support the maintenance and operation of schools, school security and ancillary services, such as the transportation of students to and from school and food services operations. This category includes the following types of personnel: masons, carpenters, electricians, locksmiths, maintenance repairers, painters and paperhangers, plasterers, plumbers, and vehicle mechanics. It also includes bus drivers and other vehicle operators, construction workers, gardeners and groundskeepers, bus monitors and crossing guards, cooks/food carers, custodians, food servers, dormitory supervisors, and security guards. See also *Educational personnel, Instructional personnel, Management/Quality control/Administration, Professional support for students, Ratio of students to teaching staff* and *Teaching staff.*

Management/Quality control/Administration: Management/Quality control/Administration comprises four categories: School Level Management, Higher Level Management, School Level Administrative Personnel and Higher Level Administrative Personnel at all ISCED levels. See also *Educational personnel, Instructional personnel, Maintenance and operations personnel, Professional support for students, Ratio of students to teaching staff* and *Teaching staff.*

Mathematical literacy: Mathematical literacy is defined in PISA as the capacity to identify, understand and engage in mathematics, and to make well-founded judgements about the role that mathematics plays in an individual's current and future private life, occupational life, social life with peers and relatives, and life as a constructive, concerned and reflective citizen. See also *Reading literacy* and *Scientific literacy.*

Mode of study: Mode of study refers to the study load of the student, whether full-time or part-time. See also *Full-time student, Full-time equivalent student, Part-time student, Student* and *Study load.*

Native students: "Native" students are those students who reported in PISA that they were born in the country of assessment and who had at least one parent born in that country. See *First-generation students* and *Non-native students.*

Net capital transfers paid: Net capital transfers paid are capital transfers to the resident private sector and to the rest of the world minus capital transfers received from the resident private sector and the rest of the world.

Net contact hours of teaching: See *Teaching time.*

Net graduation rates: Net graduation rates is the percentage of persons within a virtual age cohort who obtain a tertiary qualification, thus being unaffected by changes in population size or typical graduation age. The net graduation rate is calculated by dividing the number of graduates by the population for each single year of age. See also *Graduates, Graduation / Successful completion, Gross graduation rates* and *Unduplicated total count of graduates.*

New entrants: New entrants to a level of education are students who are entering any programme leading to a recognised qualification at this level of education for the first time, irrespective of whether the students enter the programme at the beginning or at an advanced stage of the programme. See also *Entry rates.*

Non-compulsory curriculum: The non-compulsory curriculum is that which is defined entirely at the school level or eventually at the programme level if various programme types exist. See also *Compulsory core curriculum, Compulsory curriculum, Compulsory flexible curriculum* and *Intended instruction time.*

Non-instructional educational institutions: Non-instructional educational institutions are educational institutions that provide administrative, advisory or professional services to other educational institutions, although they do not enrol students themselves. Examples include national, state, and provincial ministries or departments of education; other bodies that administer education at various levels of government or analogous bodies in the private sector; and organisations that provide such education-related services as vocational or psychological counselling, placement, testing, financial aid to students, curriculum development, educational research, building operations and maintenance services, transportation of students, and student meals and housing. See also *Expenditure on educational institutions* and *Instructional educational institutions.*

Non-native students: "Non-native" students are those students who reported in PISA that they were born outside the country of assessment and whose parents were also born in another country. See also *Native students* and *First-generation students.*

Non-salary compensation: Non-salary compensation includes expenditure by employers or public authorities on retirement programmes, health care or health insurance, unemployment compensation, disability insurance, other forms of social insurance, non-cash supplements (*e.g.,* free or subsidised housing), maternity benefits, free or subsidised child care, and such other fringe benefits as each country may provide. This expenditure does not include contributions made by the employees themselves, or deducted from their gross salaries. See also *Salaries* and *Staff compensation.*

Other current transfers: Other current transfers paid are net casualty insurance premiums, social security benefits, social assistance grants, unfunded employee pension and welfare benefits (paid directly to former or present employees without having special funds, reserves or insurance for this purpose), current transfers to private non-profit institutions serving households and current transfers to the rest of the world. See also *Current expenditure, Final consumption expenditure* and *Property income paid.*

Participation rate: The labour force participation rate, which is defined according to the guidelines of the International Labour Office (ILO), refers to the percentage of individuals in the population of the same age group who are either employed or unemployed. See also *Employed, Labour force, Unemployed* and *Unemployment rate.*

Part-time student: Students enrolled in primary and secondary-level educational programmes are considered to participate part-time if they attend school for less than 75 per cent of the school day or week (as locally defined) and would normally be expected to be in the programme for the entire academic year. At the tertiary level, an individual is considered part-time if he or she is taking a course load or educational programme that requires less than 75 per cent of a full-time commitment of time and resources. See also *Full-time equivalent student, Full-time student, Mode of study, Student* and *Study load.*

Part-time teacher: A teacher employed for less than 90 per cent of the normal or statutory number of hours of work for a full-time teacher over a complete school year is classified as a part-time teacher. See also *Educational personnel, Full-time equivalent teacher, Full-time teacher, Instructional personnel, Ratio of students to teaching staff* and *Teaching staff, Teaching time* and *Working time.*

PIRLS: Progress in Reading Literacy Study that was undertaken by the International Association for the Evaluation of Educational Achievement (IEA) during 2001 focussing on the acquisition of reading literacy of 4th-grade students.

PIRLS target population: The PIRLS target population was students in the upper of the two adjacent grades that contained the largest proportion of 9-year-old students at the time of testing. Beyond the age criterion embedded in the definition, the target population should represent that point in the curriculum where students have essentially finished learning the basic reading skills and will focus more on "reading to learn" in the subsequent grades. Thus the PIRLS target grade was expected to be 4th grade.

PISA index on control strategies: The PISA index on control strategies was derived from the frequency with which students used the following strategies when studying: I start by figuring out exactly what I need to learn; I force myself to check to see if I remember the most important things; and, when I study and don't understand something, I look for additional information to clarify this. A four-point scale with the response categories 'almost never', 'sometimes', 'often' and 'almost always' was used.

PISA index on co-operative learning: The PISA index on co-operative learning was derived from students' level of agreement with the following statements: I like to work with other students; I like to help other people do well in a group; and, it is helpful to put together everyone's ideas when working on a project. A four-point scale with the response categories 'disagree', 'disagree somewhat', 'agree somewhat' and 'agree' was used. Similarly, the PISA index on *competitive learning* was derived from students' level of agreement with the following statements: I like to try to be better than other students; trying to be better than others makes me work well; I would like to be the best at something; and, I learn faster if I'm trying to do better than the others. A four-point scale with the response categories 'disagree', 'disagree somewhat', 'agree somewhat' and 'agree' was used.

PISA index of elaboration: The PISA index on elaboration was derived from the frequency with which students used the following strategies when studying: I try to relate new material to things I have learned in other subjects; I chart out how the information might be useful in the real world; I try to understand the material better by relating it to things I already know; and, I chart out how the material fits in with what I have already learned. A four-point scale with the response categories 'almost never', 'sometimes', 'often' and 'almost always' was used.

PISA index on interest in mathematics: PISA index on interest in mathematics was derived from students' level of agreement with the following statements: when I do mathematics, I sometimes get totally absorbed; mathematics is important to me personally; and because doing mathematics is fun, I wouldn't want to give it up. A four-point scale with the response categories 'disagree', 'disagree somewhat', 'agree somewhat' and 'agree' was used.

PISA index on interest in reading: PISA index on interest in reading was derived from students' level of agreement with the following statements: because reading is fun, I wouldn't want to give it up; I read in my spare time; and, when I read, I sometimes get totally absorbed. A four-point scale with the response categories 'disagree', 'disagree somewhat', 'agree somewhat' and 'agree' was used.

PISA index on memorisation: The PISA index on memorisation was derived from the frequency with which students used the following strategies when studying: I memorise everything that might be covered; I memorise as much as possible; I memorise all new material so I that I can recite it; and I practice saying the material to myself over and over. A four-point scale with the response categories 'almost never', 'sometimes', 'often' and 'almost always' was used.

PISA index of reading engagement: The PISA index of reading engagement is built on three components: frequency of reading, diversity and content of reading, and interest in reading. To assess the first component, students were asked about how much time they usually spent on reading for enjoyment each day. To assess the second component, students were asked to indicate the kinds of materials they choose to read (*e.g.* newspapers, magazines, fiction, non-fiction, comics, e-mails and web pages) and the frequency with which they read each type of material. To assess the third component, a reading attitude scale comprising nine statements about reading, either positive or negative, were included in the questionnaire. Students were asked to indicate their degree of agreement with each statement. Based on these questions, an index of reading engagement was created. The index scale ranges from −1 to 1, with 0 as the mean value for the combined OECD student population.

PISA index on student self-concept in reading: PISA index on student self-concept in reading was derived from students' level of agreement with the following statements: I'm hopeless in <classes of the language of assessment>; I learn things quickly in the <classes of the language of assessment>; and, I get good marks in the <language of assessment>. A four-point scale with the response categories 'disagree', 'disagree somewhat', 'agree somewhat' and 'agree' was used. Similarly, the PISA index on *self-concept in mathematics* was derived from students' level of agreement with the following statements: I get good marks in mathematics; mathematics is one of my best subjects; and, I have always done well in mathematics. A four-point scale with the response categories 'disagree', 'disagree somewhat', 'agree somewhat' and 'agree' was used.

PISA International Socio-Economic Index of Occupational Status (ISEI): The PISA International Socio-Economic Index of Occupational Status (ISEI) was derived from students' responses on parental occupation. The index captures the attributes of occupations that convert parents' education into income. The index was derived by the optimal scaling of occupation groups to maximise the indirect effect of education on income through occupation and to minimise the direct effect of education on income, net of occupation (both effects being net of age). For more information on the methodology, see Ganzeboom *et al.* (1992). The PISA International Socio-Economic Index of Occupational Status is based on either the father or mother's occupations, whichever is the higher.

PISA mean score: To facilitate the interpretation of the scores assigned to students in PISA, the PISA mean score for combined reading, mathematical and scientific literacy performance across OECD countries was set at 500 and the standard deviation at 100, with the data weighted so that each OECD country contributed equally. The mean score in the PIRLS analysis was similarly calculated.

PISA Reading Profile Cluster: In PISA, students were asked to rate how frequently they chose to read different kinds of print materials, including magazines, newspapers, comics, and fiction and non-fiction books. Based on their responses, students were grouped into four distinct reading profiles, or *clusters*. The distribution into these clusters relies on two dimensions: the frequency of reading on the one hand, and the diversity of reading on the other hand. This twofold dimension is reflected in the expressions such as "involved in diversified reading" or "diversified reader". For the cluster analysis in this indicator, reading one kind of material 'several times a month' or 'several times a week' is considered as frequent reading, 'a few times a year' and 'once a month' as moderate reading, and 'never or hardly ever' as no reading.

PISA population: The PISA population refer to 15-year-old students, or students who were from 15 years and 3 (completed) months to 16 years and 2 (completed) months at the beginning of the testing period, and who were enrolled in an educational institution, regardless of the grade level or type of institution in which they were enrolled and of whether they participated in school full-time or part-time. See also *Population*.

Population: Population refers to all nationals present in or temporarily absent from the country and aliens permanently settled in the country. For further details, see *OECD Labour Force Statistics*. See also *PISA population*.

Post-secondary non-tertiary level of education (ISCED 4): Post-secondary non-tertiary education straddles the boundary between upper secondary and post-secondary education from an international point of view, even though it might clearly be considered upper secondary or post-secondary programmes in a national context. Although their content may not be significantly more advanced than upper secondary programmes, they serve to broaden the knowledge of participants who have already gained an upper secondary qualification. The students tend to be older than those enrolled at the upper secondary level. See also *International Standard Classification of Education (ISCED)*.

Pre-primary education (ISCED 0): Pre-primary education (ISCED 0) is defined as the initial stage of organised instruction, designed primarily to introduce very young children to a school-type environment, that is, to provide a bridge between home and a school-based atmosphere. ISCED level 0 programmes should be centre or school-based, be designed to meet the educational and developmental needs of children at least three years of age, and have staff that are adequately trained (*i.e.,* qualified) to provide an educational programme for the children. See also *International Standard Classification of Education (ISCED)*.

Pre-vocational programmes: Pre-vocational education is mainly designed to introduce participants to the world of work and to prepare them for entry into further vocational or technical programmes. Successful completion of such programmes does not lead to a labour-market relevant vocational or technical qualification. See also *General programmes, Programme orientation, Upper secondary education (ISCED 3)* and *Vocational programmes*.

Primary education (ISCED 1): Primary education (ISCED 1) usually begins at ages five, six or seven and lasts for four to six years (the mode of the OECD countries being six years). Programmes at the primary level generally require no previous formal education, although it is becoming increasingly common for children to have attended a pre-primary programme before entering primary education. The boundary between pre-primary and primary education is typically the beginning of systematic studies characteristic of primary education, *e.g.,* reading, writing and mathematics. It is common, however, for children to begin learning basic literacy and numeracy skills at the pre-primary level. See also *International Standard Classification of Education (ISCED)*.

Private expenditure: Private expenditure refers to expenditure funded by private sources, *i.e.,* households and other private entities. "Households" means students and their families. "Other private entities" include private business firms and non-profit organisations, including religious organisations, charitable organisations, and business and labour associations. Private expenditure comprises school fees; materials such as textbooks and teaching equipment; transport to school (if organised by the school); meals (if provided by the school); boarding fees; and expenditure by employers on initial vocational training. Note that private educational institutions are considered service providers, not funding sources.

Private institution: An institution is classified as private if it is controlled and managed by a non-governmental organisation (*e.g.,* a Church, Trade Union or business enterprise), or if its Governing Board consists mostly of members not selected by a public agency. See also *Educational institution, Government-dependent private institution, Independent private institution* and *Public institution.*

Private internal rate of return: The private internal rate of return is equal to the discount rate that equalises the real costs of education during the period of study to the real gains from education thereafter. In its most comprehensive form, the costs equal tuition fees, foregone earnings net of taxes adjusted for the probability of being in employment minus the resources made available to students in the form of grants and loans. See also *Social rate of return.*

Professional activity: Any activity that develops an individual's skills, knowledge, expertise and other characteristics as a teacher. These include personal study and reflection, collaborative development of new approaches, as well as formal courses.

Professional support for students: Professional support for students comprises pedagogical support at ISCED 0-4 and academic support at ISCED 5-6; and health and social support at ISCED 0-6. See also *Educational personnel, Instructional personnel, Maintenance and operations personnel, Management / Quality control / Administration, Ratio of students to teaching staff* and *Teaching staff.*

Programme destination: Programme destination, which is defined according to International Standard Classification of Education (ISCED), refers to the destination for which programmes have been designed to prepare students, such as tertiary education, the labour market or other programmes at the same or other levels of education.

- A programmes are designed to prepare students for direct access to the next level of education;

- B programmes are designed to prepare students for access to certain types of but not all programmes at the next level of education; and

- C programmes are designed to prepare students for direct access to the labour market or other programmes at the same level of education.

Programme duration: See *Duration of programme.*

Programme for International Student Assessment (PISA): The Programme for International Student Assessment is an international study conducted by the OECD which measures how well young adults, at age 15 and therefore approaching the end of compulsory schooling, are prepared to meet the challenges of today's knowledge societies.

Programme orientation: Programme orientation, which is defined according to International Standard Classification of Education (ISCED), refers to the degree to which a programme is specifically oriented towards a certain class of occupations or trades and leads to a labour-market relevant qualification. See also *General programmes, Pre-vocational programmes* and *Vocational programmes.*

Property income paid: Property income paid is defined as interest, net land rent and royalties paid. See also *Current expenditure, Final consumption expenditure* and *Other current transfers.*

Public expenditure: Public expenditure refers to spending of public authorities at all levels. Expenditure that is not directly related to education (*e.g.,* culture, sports, youth activities, etc.) is, in principle, not included. Expenditure on education by other ministries or equivalent institutions, for example Health and Agriculture, is included.

Public institution: An institution is classified as public if it is controlled and managed directly by a public education authority or agency or; is controlled and managed either by a government agency directly or by a governing body (Council, Committee etc.), most of whose members are appointed by a public authority or elected by public franchise. See *Educational institution* and *Public institution.*

Purchasing Power Parities (PPP): Purchasing Power Parities (PPP) are the currency exchange rates that equalise the purchasing power of different currencies. This means that a given sum of money, when converted into different currencies at the PPP rates, will buy the same basket of goods and services in all countries. In other words, PPPs are the rates of currency conversion, which eliminate the differences in price levels among countries. Thus, when expenditure on GDP for different countries is converted into a common currency by means of PPPs, it is, in effect, expressed at the same set of international prices so that comparisons between countries reflect only differences in the volume of goods and services purchased. The purchasing power parities used in this publication are given in Annex 2.

Ratio of students to computers: In ISUSS, the ratio of students per computer was calculated by dividing the total number of computers in each school by the total number of students enrolled in each school.

Ratio of students to teaching staff: The ratio of students to teaching staff is calculated as the total number of full-time equivalent students divided by the total number of full-time equivalent educational personnel. See also *Educational personnel, Full-time equivalent student, Full-time equivalent teacher, Instructional personnel, Maintenance and operations personnel, Management / Quality control / Administration, Professional support for students, Teaching staff* and *Teaching time.*

Reading literacy: Reading literacy is defined in PISA as the ability to understand, use and reflect on written texts in order to achieve one's goals, to develop one's knowledge and potential, and to participate effectively in society. See also *Mathematical literacy* and *Scientific literacy.* Reading literacy is defined similarly in PIRLS as the ability to understand and use those written language forms required by society and/or valued by the individual.

Relative earnings: Relative earnings from work are the mean annual earnings from employment of individuals with a certain level of educational attainment divided by the mean annual earnings from employment of individuals whose highest level of education is the upper secondary level. See also *Earnings.*

Research and development: See *Expenditure on Research and Development (R&D).*

Retirement expenditure: Retirement expenditure is the cost incurred currently, exclusive of any contribution by employees, in providing future retirement benefits for persons currently employed in education. This cost can be measured by actual or imputed employers (or third party) contributions to retirement systems. The reason for not counting employee's contributions is that they are already counted in the gross salary component of total compensation.

Salaries: Salaries means the gross salaries of educational personnel, before deduction of taxes, contributions for retirement or health care plans, and other contributions or premiums for social insurance or other purposes. See also *Non-salary compensation* and *staff compensation.*

School expectancy: School expectancy is the average duration of formal education in which a five-year-old child can expect to enrol over his or her lifetime. It is calculated by adding the net enrolment percentages for each single year of age from the age of five onwards.

School location: In PISA, school location refers to the community in which the school is located, such as a <village, hamlet or rural area> (fewer than 3 000 people), a <small town> (3 000 to about 15 000 people), a <town> (15 000 to about 100 000 people), a <city> (100 000 to about 1 000 000 people), close to the centre of a <city> with over 1 000 000 people or elsewhere in a <city> with over 1 000 000 people.

School site: The unit of analysis in indicators drawing data from the International Survey of Upper Secondary Schools. School site refers to an establishment where education is provided according to one or more educational programme(s). A school site usually consists of a single building although it may comprise two or more buildings within a few minutes walking distance. A school site has permanent teaching staff and permanent student population. Although in many countries schools do not have more than one site (and thus the distinction between school and school site is not needed, there are countries where the classical image of a school housed in a single building is no longer valid for all schools. Quite often a school as an administrative or budgetary unit consists of several school sites located far apart (even in different municipalities).

School-based programmes: In school-based (vocational and technical) programmes, instruction takes place (either partly or exclusively) in educational institutions. This includes special training centres for vocational education run by public or private authorities or enterprise-based special training centres if these qualify as educational institutions. These programmes can have an on-the-job training component, *i.e.,* a component of some practical experience in the workplace. See also *Combined school and work-based programmes*, *General programmes, Programme orientation* and *Vocational programmes.*

Scientific literacy: PISA defines scientific literacy as the capacity to use scientific knowledge, to identify questions, and to draw evidence-based conclusions in order to understand and help make decisions about the natural world and the changes made to it through human activity. See also *Mathematical literacy* and *Reading literacy.*

Secondary education (ISCED 23): See *Lower secondary education* and *Upper secondary education.*

Social internal rate of return: The social internal rate of return refers to the costs and benefits to society of investment in education, which includes the opportunity cost of having people not participating in the production of output and the full cost of the provision of education rather than only the cost borne by the individual. The social benefit includes the increased productivity associated with the investment in education and a host of possible non-economic benefits, such as lower crime, better health, more social cohesion and more informed and effective citizens. See also *Private rate of return.*

Spending on educational services other than instruction: Spending on educational services other than instruction includes public spending on ancillary services such as meals, transport to schools, or housing on the campus; private spending on fees for ancillary services; subsidised private spending on student living costs or reduced prices for transport; and private spending on student living costs or transport. See also *Expenditure on ancillary services, Expenditure on educational core services* and *Expenditure on Research and Development (R&D).*

Staff compensation: Expenditure on staff compensation includes gross salaries plus non-salary compensation (fringe benefits). See also *Non-salary compensation* and *Salaries.*

Standard error: The standard errors are expressions of the degree of uncertainty of an estimate, which are estimates of national performance based on samples of students rather than the values that could be calculated if every student in every country had answered every question. Consequently, it is important to know the degree of uncertainty inherent in the estimates.

Statistical significance: Differences are reported as statistically significant when a difference of that size, or larger, would be observed less than 5 per cent of the time, if there was actually no difference in corresponding population values. Similarly, the risk of reporting as significant if there is, in fact, no correlation between two measures is contained at 5 per cent.

Statutory teacher's salaries: See *Teacher's salaries.*

Student: A student is defined as any individual participating in educational services covered by the data collection. The number of students enrolled refers to the number of individuals (head count) who are enrolled within the reference period and not necessarily to the number of registrations. Each student enrolled is counted only once. See also *Full-time student, Full-time equivalent student, Part-time student* and *Study load.*

Study load: There are two basic measures of study load: time in the classroom and progress towards a qualification. Time in classroom attempts to measure the amount of instruction time that a student receives and can be counted as hours of instruction per day or year, counts of the number of courses taken, or a combination of the two. These measures are based on characteristics of the course or on patterns of attendance, not on the programme in which the student is enrolled. Because of this, such measures of study load will be useful when there is no programme structure or when programme structures are not comparable. The second measure of study load is the unit used to measure progress towards a qualification. Such measures focus less on the amount of instruction and more on the "academic value" of that instruction. It is conceivable, therefore, those courses with the same quantity of instruction may have different academic values and they would only be the same if measures of academic progress were made in amounts of instruction. See also *Full-time equivalent student, Full-time student, Mode of study* and *Part-time student.*

Support services: Entities providing support services to other educational institutions include institutions that provide educational support and materials as well as operation and maintenance services for buildings. These are commonly part of the general-purpose units of public authorities.

Survival rates: Survival rate at the tertiary level is defined as the proportion of new entrants to the specified level of education who successfully complete a first qualification. It is calculated as the ratio of the number of students who are awarded an initial degree to the number of new entrants to the level n years before, *n* being the number of years of full-time study required to complete the degree. See also *Dropout.*

Teachers' salaries: Teachers' salaries are expressed as statutory salaries, which are scheduled salaries according to official pay scales. The salaries reported are defined as gross salaries (total sum of money that is paid by the employer for the labour supplied) minus the employer's contribution to social security and pension (according to existing salary scales).

- Starting salaries refer to the average scheduled gross salary per year for a full-time teacher with the minimum training necessary to be fully qualified at the beginning of his or her teaching career.

- Salaries after 15 years of experience refer to the scheduled annual salary of a full-time classroom teacher with the minimum training necessary to be fully qualified and with 15 years' experience.

- Maximum salaries reported refer to the scheduled maximum annual salary (top of the salary scale) of a full-time classroom teacher with the minimum training to be fully qualified for his or her job.

Salaries are "before tax", *i.e.,* before deductions for income taxes. See also *Additional bonuses to base salary.*

Teaching days: The number of teaching days is the number of teaching weeks minus the days when the school is closed for festivities. See also *Teaching time, Teaching weeks, Working time* and *Working time in school.*

Teaching staff: Teaching staff refer to professional personnel directly involved in teaching students, including classroom teachers; special education teachers; and other teachers who work with students as a whole class in a classroom, in small groups in a resource room, or in one-to-one teaching inside or outside a regular classroom. Teaching staff also includes chairpersons of departments whose duties include some amount of teaching, but it does not include non-professional personnel who support teachers in providing instruction to students, such as teachers' aides and other paraprofessional personnel. See also *Educational personnel, Full-time teacher, Full-time equivalent teacher, Instructional personnel Maintenance and operations personnel, Management/Quality control/Administration, Part-time teacher, Professional support for students, Ratio of students to teaching staff* and *Teaching time.*

Teaching time: Teaching time is defined as the net contact hours of teaching. It is calculated on the basis of the annual number of weeks of instruction multiplied by the minimum/maximum number of periods, which a teacher is supposed to spend teaching a class or a group, multiplied by the length of a period in minutes and divided by 60. Periods of time formally allowed for breaks between lessons or groups of lessons, and days when schools are closed for public holidays and festivities, are excluded. In primary education, however, short breaks that teachers spend with the class are typically included. See also *Teaching days, Teaching weeks, Working time* and *Working time in school.*

Teaching weeks: The number of teaching weeks is defined as the number of weeks of instruction not counting holiday weeks. See also *Teaching days, Teaching time, Working time* and *Working time in school.*

Temporary teacher: Teacher who has no tenure, or 'a person employed for a fixed term not longer than one school year'.

Tertiary education (ISCED 56): See *Tertiary-type A education (ISCED 5A)* and *Tertiary-type B education (ISCED 5B).*

Tertiary-type A education (ISCED 5A): Tertiary-type A programmes (ISCED 5A) are largely theory-based and are designed to provide sufficient qualifications for entry to advanced research programmes and professions with high skill requirements, such as medicine, dentistry or architecture. Tertiary-type A programmes have a minimum cumulative theoretical duration (at tertiary level) of three years' full-time equivalent, although they typically last four or more years. These programmes are not exclusively offered at universities. Conversely, not all programmes nationally recognised as university programmes fulfil the criteria to be classified as tertiary-type A. Tertiary-type A programmes include second degree programmes like the American Master. First and second programmes are sub-classified by the cumulative duration of the programmes, *i.e.,* the total study time needed at the tertiary level to complete the degree. See also *International Standard Classification of Education (ISCED)* and *Tertiary-type B education (ISCED 5B).*

Tertiary-type B education (ISCED 5B): Tertiary-type B programmes (ISCED 5B) are typically shorter than those of tertiary-type A and focus on practical, technical or occupational skills for direct entry into the labour market, although some theoretical foundations may be covered in the respective programmes. They have a minimum duration of two years full-time equivalent at the tertiary level. See also *International Standard Classification of Education (ISCED)* and *Tertiary-type A education (ISCED 5A).*

Theoretical age: Theoretical ages refer to the ages as established by law and regulation for the entry and ending of a cycle of education. Note that the theoretical ages may differ significantly from the typical ages. See also *Typical age, Typical ending age, Typical graduation age* and *Typical starting age.*

Third International Mathematics and Science Study (TIMSS): The Third International Mathematics and Science Study, conducted by the IEA, measured the mathematics and science achievement of fourth and eighth-grade students in 1995, 1999 and 2003.

Transfer and payments to other private entities: Transfer and payments to other private entities are government transfers and certain other payments (mainly subsidies) to other private entities (commercial companies and non-profit organisations). These transfers and payments can take diverse forms, *e.g.,* transfers to business or labour associations that provide adult education; subsidies to companies or labour organisations (or associations of such entities) that operate apprenticeship programmes; and interest rate subsidies or defaults guarantee payments to private financial institutions that provide student loans.

Typical age: Typical ages refer to the ages that normally correspond to the age at entry and ending of a cycle of education. These ages relate to the theoretical duration of a cycle assuming full-time attendance and no repetition of a year. The assumption is made that, at least in the ordinary education system, a student can proceed through the educational programme in a standard number of years, which is referred to as the theoretical duration of the programme. See also *Theoretical age, Typical ending age*, *Typical graduation age and Typical starting age,*.

Typical ending age: The typical ending age should be the age at the beginning of the last school/academic year of the corresponding level and programme. See also *Theoretical age, Typical age, Typical graduation age* and *Typical starting age.*

Typical graduation age: The typical graduation age should be the age at the end of the last school/ academic year of the corresponding level and programme when the degree is obtained. Note that at some levels of education the term "graduation age" may not translate literally and would be equivalent to a "completion age"; it is used here purely as a convention. See also *Theoretical age, Typical age, Typical ending age* and *Typical starting age.*

Typical starting age: The typical starting age should be the age at the beginning of the first school/academic year of the corresponding level and programme. See also *Theoretical age, Typical age, Typical ending age* and *Typical graduation age.*

Unduplicated total count of graduates: Unduplicated total count of graduates is calculated by netting out those students who graduated from programmes in a previous year and/or who are earning more than one qualification at the specified level during the reference period. It represents therefore a count of individuals graduating and not certificates being awarded. See also *Graduates,* **Graduation/Successful completion,** *Gross graduation rates and Net graduation rates.*

Unemployed: The unemployed, which is defined according to the guidelines of the International Labour Office (ILO), refers to individuals who are without work, actively seeking employment and currently available to start work. See also *Employed, Labour force, Participation rate, Unemployment rate* and *Work status.*

Unemployment rate: The unemployment rate (expressed as a percentage), which is defined according to the guidelines of the International Labour Office (ILO), is the number of unemployed persons divided by the number of labour force participants. See also *Employed, Labour force, Participation rate* and *Unemployed.*

Upper secondary education (ISCED 3): Upper secondary education (ISCED 3) corresponds to the final stage of secondary education in most OECD countries. Instruction is often more organised along subject-matter lines than at ISCED level 2 and teachers typically need to have a higher level, or more subject-specific, qualifications than at ISCED 2. The entrance age to this level is typically 15 or 16 years. There are substantial differences in the typical duration of ISCED 3 programmes both across and between countries, typically ranging from two to five years of schooling. ISCED 3 may either be "terminal" (*i.e.,* preparing the students for entry directly into working life) and/or "preparatory" (*i.e.,* preparing students for tertiary education). Programmes at level 3 can also be subdivided into three categories based on the degree to which the programme is specifically oriented towards a specific class of occupations or trades and leads to a labour-market relevant qualification: General, Pre-vocational or pre-technical, and Vocational or technical programmes. See also *General programmes, International Standard Classification of Education (ISCED), Pre-vocational programmes* and *Vocational programmes.*

Vocational programmes: Vocational education prepares participants for direct entry, without further training, into specific occupations. Successful completion of such programmes leads to a labour-market relevant vocational qualification. Some indicators divide vocational programmes into school-based programmes and combined school and work-based programmes on the basis of the amount of training that is provided in school as opposed to training in the workplace. See also *Combined school and work-based programmes, General programmes, Pre-vocational programmes, Programme orientation, School-based programmes* and *Upper secondary education (ISCED 3).*

Work status: Work status, which is defined according to the guidelines of the International Labour Office (ILO), refers to the position of the population within the labour force as defined in *OECD Labour Force Statistics.* See also *Employed, Labour force* and *Unemployed.*

Work study programmes: 'Work-study programmes' are combinations of work and education in which periods of both form part of an integrated, formal education or training activity. Examples of such programmes include the 'dual system' in Germany; 'apprentissage' or 'formation en alternance' in France and Belgium; internship or co-operative education in Canada; apprenticeship in Ireland; and "youth training" in the United Kingdom.

Working time: Teacher's working time refers to the normal working hours of a full-time teacher. According to the formal policy in a given country, working time can refer only to the time directly associated with teaching (and other curricular activities for students such as assignments and tests, but excluding annual examinations); or to time directly associated with teaching and to hours devoted to other activities related to teaching, such as lesson preparation, counselling of students, correction of assignments and tests, professional development, meetings with parents, staff meetings and general school tasks. Working time does not include paid overtime. See also *Educational personnel, Full-time equivalent teacher, Full-time teacher, Instructional personnel, Part-time teacher, Ratio of students to teaching staff, Teaching days, Teaching staff, Teaching time, Teaching weeks* and *Working time in school.*

Working time in school: Working time in school refers to the working time teachers are supposed to be at school including teaching time and non-teaching time. See also *Teaching days, Teaching time, Teaching weeks* and *Working time.*

World Wide Web (WWW): The World Wide Web is a part of the Internet designed to allow easier navigation of the network through the use of graphical user interfaces and hypertext links between different addresses. See also *Internet* and *Local Area Network.*

CONTRIBUTORS TO THIS PUBLICATION

Many people have contributed to the development of this publication. The following lists the names of the country representatives, researchers and experts who have actively taken part in the preparatory work leading to the publication of this edition of Education at a Glance - Indicators. The OECD wishes to thank them all for their valuable efforts.

National Co-ordinators

Mr. Dan ANDERSSON (Sweden)

Ms. Ikuko ARIMATSU (Japan)

M. Dominique BARTHÉLÉMY (Belgium)

Mr. H.H. DALMIJN (Netherlands)

Mr. Antonio Manuel Pinto FAZENDEIRO (Portugal)

Mr. Michael FEDEROWICZ (Poland)

Mr. Guillermo GIL (Spain)

Mr. Heinz GILOMEN (Switzerland)

Ms. Margrét HARÐARDÓTTIR (Iceland)

Mr. G. Douglas HODGKINSON (Canada)

Mr. Gregory KAFETZOPOULOS (Greece)

Mr. Hojin HWANG (Korea)

Mr. Matti KYRÖ (Finland)

Mr. Antonio Giunta LA SPADA (Italy)

Ms. Kye Young LEE (Korea)

Mr. Jérôme LEVY (Luxembourg)

Ms. Teresa LEMOS (Portugal)

Mr. Dittrich MAGERKURTH (Germany)

Mr. Victor MANUEL VELÁZQUEZ CASTAÑEDA (Mexico)

Mr. Lubomir MARTINEC (Czech Republic)

Mr. Gerardo MUÑOZ SANCHEZ-BRUNETE (Spain)

Ms. Marion NORRIS (New Zealand)

Mr. Torlach O CONNOR (Ireland)

Mr. Brendan O'REILLY (Australia)

Mr. Laurence OGLE (United States)

Ms. Hyun-Jeong PARK (Korea)

Mr. Elin PEDERSEN (Norway)

Mr. Mark NEMET (Austria)

Mr. Vladimir POKOJNY (Slovak Republic)

Mr. Imre RADÁCSI (Hungary)

Ms. Janice ROSS (United Kingdom)

Mr. Ingo RUSS (Germany)

Mr. Claude SAUVAGEOT (France)

Mr. Yasuyuki SHIMOTSUMA (Japan)

Mr. Ole-Jacob SKODVIN (Norway)

Mr. Ken THOMASSEN (Denmark)

Ms. Ann VAN DRIESSCHE (Belgium)

Ms. Angela VEGLIANTE (European Commission)

Mr. Arturo VILLARUEL (Mexico)

Mr. I. ZKARABIYIK (Turkey)

Technical Group on Education Statistics and Indicators

Mr. R.R.G. ABELN (Netherlands)

Mr. Paul AMACHER (Switzerland)

Ms. Birgitta ANDREN (Sweden)

Ms. Karin ARVEMO-NOTSTRAND (Sweden)

Ms. Alina BARAN (Poland)

Ms. Eva BOLIN (Sweden)

Mr. Fernando CELESTINO REY (Spain)

Mr. Fernando CORDOVA CALDERON (Mexico)

Mr. Eduardo DE LA FUENTE (Spain)

Ms. Gemma DE SANCTIS (Italy)

Ms. Ritsuko DOKO (Japan)

Ms. Maria DOKOU (Greece)

Mr. J. Douglas DREW (Canada)

Mr. Douglas LYND (UNESCO)

Mr. Dittrich MAGERKURTH (Germany)

Mr. Robert MAHEU (Canada)

Mr. Joaquim MAIA GOMES (Portugal)

Ms. Sabine MARTINSCHITZ (Austria)

Ms. Giuliana MATTEOCCI (Italy)

Mr. Konstantinos MITROGIANNIS (Greece)

Mr. Geir NYGARD (Norway)

Mr. Muiris O'CONNOR (Ireland)

Mr. Brendan O'REILLY (Australia)

Ms. Hyun-Jeong PARK (Korea)

Mr. Wolfgang PAULI (Austria)

Mr. João PEREIRA DE MATOS (Portugal)

Ms. Mary DUNNE (EUROSTAT)

Mr. Michele EGLOFF (Switzerland)

Mr. Timo ERTOLA (Finland)

Mr. Pierre FALLOURD (France)

Ms. Alzbeta FERENCICOVA (Slovak Republic)

Mrs. Esin FENERCIOGLU (Turkey)

Mr. Paul GINI (New Zealand)

Mr. Bengt GREF (Sweden)

Ms. Yonca GUNDUZ-OZCERI (Turkey)

Mr. Heikki HAVEN (Finland)

Mr. Walter HÖRNER (Germany)

Ms. Maria HRABINSKA (Slovak Republic)

Mr. Jesus IBANEZ MILLA (Spain)

Mr. Klaus Fribert JACOBSEN (Denmark)

Ms. Michèle JACQUOT (France)

Ms. Nathalie JAUNIAUX (Belgium)

Mr. Felix KOSCHIN (Czech Republic)

Mr. Karsten KUHL (Denmark)

Ms. Kye Young LEE (Korea)

Mr. Steve LEMAN (United Kingdom)

Mr. Jérôme LEVY (Luxembourg)

Ms. Judit KOZMA LUKACS (Hungary)

Ms. Michaela KLENHOVÁ (Czech Republic)

Mr. Spyridon PILOS (EUROSTAT)

Ms. Elena REBROSOVA (Slovak Republic)

Mr. Jean Paul REEFF (Luxembourg)

Mr. Ron ROSS (New Zealand)

Mr. Jean-Claude ROUCLOUX (Belgium)

Mr. Ingo RUSS (Germany)

Mr. Joel SHERMAN (United States)

Mr. Thomas SNYDER (United States)

Ms. Maria Pia SORVILLO (Italy)

Mr. Konstantinos STOUKAS (Greece)

Mr. Dick TAKKENBERG (Netherlands)

Mr. Ken THOMASSEN (Denmark)

Mr. Mika TUONONEN (Finland)

Mr. Shuichi UEHARA (Japan)

Ms. Ásta URBANCIC (Iceland)

Mr. Matti VAISANEN (Finland)

Ms. Erika VALLE BUTZE (Mexico)

Ms. Liselotte VAN DE PERRE (Belgium)

Ms. Ann VAN DRIESSCHE (Belgium)

Ms. Elisabetta VASSENDEN (Norway)

Mr. Rik VERSTRAETE (Belgium)

Mr. Yoshihiro NAKAYA (Japan)

Network A on Educational Outcomes

Lead Country: United States

Network Leader: Mr. Eugene OWEN

Mr. Helmut BACHMANN (Austria)

Ms. Anna BARKLUND (Sweden)

Ms. Lorna BERTRAND (United Kingdom)

Ms. Iris BLANKE (Luxembourg)

Ms. Christiane BLONDIN (Belgium)

Mr. Fernando CORDOVA CALDERON (Mexico)

Ms. Chiara CROCE (Italy)

Mr. Guillermo GIL (Spain)

Mr. Jürgen HORSCHINEGG (Austria)

Mr. Sevki KARACA (Turkey)

Ms. Anne-Berit KAVLI (Norway)

Mr. Myungioon LEE (Korea)

Ms. Mariann LEMKE (United States)

Mrs. Jacqueline LEVASSEUR (France)

Mr. Pirjo LINNAKYLA (Finland)

Mr. Jay MOSKOWITZ (United States)

Ms. Glória RAMALHO (Portugal)

Mr. Erich RAMSEIER (Switzerland)

Mr. Jean-Paul REEFF (Luxembourg)

Mr. Thierry ROCHER (France)

Mr. Vladislav ROSA (Slovak Republic)

Ms. Eva SCHOEYEN (Norway)

Mr. Jochen SCHWEITZER (Germany)

Mr. Gerry SHIEL (Ireland)

Mr. Joern SKOVSGAARD (Denmark)

Mr. Arnold A. J. SPEE (Netherlands)

Ms. Maria STEPHENS (United States)

Mr. P. Benedek TÓTA (Hungary)

Mr. Luc VAN DE POELE (Belgium)

Ms. Evangelia VARNAVA-SKOURA (Greece)

Mr. Ryo WATANABE (Japan)

Ms. Anita WESTER (Sweden)

Mr. Jerry MUSSIO (Canada)

Mr. Michael O'GORMAN (Canada)

Mr. Jules PESCHAR (Netherlands)

Ms. Wendy WHITHAM (Australia)

Ms. Lynne WHITNEY (New Zealand)

Network B on Student Destinations

Lead country: Sweden

Network Leader: Mr. Jonas BÖRJESSON (2002) / Ms. Ann-Caroline NORDSTRÖM (2003)

Ms. Yupin BAE (United States)

Ms. Ariane BAYE (Belgium)

Ms. Irja BLOMQVIST (Finland)

Ms. Anna BORKOWSKY (Switzerland)

Mr. Richard BRIDGE (Australia)

Mr. Fernando CELESTINO REY (Spain)

Ms. Jihee CHOI (Korea)

Mr. Erik DAHL (Norway)

Mr. H.H. DALMIJN (Netherlands)

Mr. Patrice DE BROUCKER (Canada)

Ms. Pascaline DESCY (CEDEFOP)

Mr. Kjetil DIGRE (Norway)

Ms. Isabelle ERAUW (Belgium)

Ms. Lisa HUDSON (United States)

Mr. Evangelos INTZIDIS (Greece)

Mr. Olof JOS (Sweden)

Ms. Christiane KRÜGER-HEMMER (Germany)

Mr. Pavel KUCHAR (Czech Republic)

Mr. Karsten KÜHL (EUROSTAT)

Mr. Jérôme LEVY (Luxembourg)

Ms. Anne-France MOSSOUX (CEDEFOP)

Mr. Philip O'CONNELL (Ireland)

Ms. Simona PACE (Italy)

Mr. Ali PANAL (Turkey)

Mr. Kenny PETERSSON (Sweden)

Mr. Spyridon PILOS (EUROSTAT)

Ms. Cheryl REMINGTON (New Zealand)

Ms. Aila REPO (Finland)

Ms. Véronique SANDOVAL (France)

Ms. Emilia SAO PEDRO (Portugal)

Ms. Astrid SCHORN (Luxembourg)

Mr. Peter SCRIMGEOUR (United Kingdom)

Mr. Dan SHERMAN (United States)

Ms. Irena SKRZYPCZAK (Poland)

Ms. Maria-Pia SORVILLO (Italy)

Mr. Ken THOMASSEN (Denmark)

Ms. Mariá THURZOVÁ (Slovak Republic)

Ms. Éva TÓT (Hungary)

Ms. Paola UNGARO (Italy)

Ms. Stina UTTERSTRÖM (Sweden)

Mr. Johan VAN DER VALK (Netherlands)

Mr. Jaco VAN RIJN (Netherlands)

Network C on School Features and Processes

Lead Country: Netherlands

Network Leader: Mr. Jaap SCHEERENS

Ms. Bodhild BAASLAND (Norway)

Ms. Giovanna BARZANO (Italy)

Ms. Kathryn CHANDLER (United States)

Mr. Vassilios CHARISMIADIS (Greece)

Ms. Maria do Carmo CLÍMACO (Portugal)

Mr. H.H. DALMIJN (Netherlands)

Mr. Philippe DELOOZ (Belgium)

Mr. Gunnar ENEQUIST (Sweden)

Ms. Esin FENERCIOGLU (Turkey)

Mr. Heikki LYYTINEN (Finland)

Ms. Nelly MCEWEN (Canada)

Mr. Lubomir MARTINEC (Czech Republic)

Mr. Gerd MÖLLER (Germany)

Mr. Mario OLIVA RUIZ (Mexico)

Ms. Hyun-Jeong PARK (Korea)

Mr. Jørgen Balling RASMUSSEN (Denmark)

Ms. Olga ROMERO HERNANDEZ (Mexico)

Ms. Marie-Claude RONDEAU (France)

Ms. Flora GIL TRAVER (Spain)

Mr. Paul GINI (New Zealand)

Mr. Sean GLENNANE (Ireland)

Mrs. Kerry GRUBER (United States)

Ms. Maria HENDRIKS (Netherlands)

Ms. Maria HRABINSKA (Slovak Republic)

Ms. Anna IMRE (Hungary)

Mr. Christian KRENTHALLER (Austria)

Mr. Raynald LORTIE (Canada)

Mr. Ingo RUSS (Germany)

Ms. Astrid SCHORN-BUCHNER (Luxembourg)

Mr. Joel SHERMAN (United States)

Ms. Pavlina STASTNOVA (Czech Republic)

Mr. Eugene STOCKER (Switzerland)

Mr. Jason TARSH (United Kingdom)

Ms. Erika VALLE BUTZE (Mexico)

Mr. Peter VAN PETEGEM (Belgium)

World Education Indicators

Mr. Mark AGRANOVITCH (Russian Federation)

Mr. Ma'moun AL-MA'AYTA (Jordan)

Mr. Ramon BACANI (Philippines)

Mr. C. BALAKRISHNAN (India)

Ms. Valerie BEEN (Jamaica)

Mr. Ade CAHYANA (Indonesia)

Mr. Farai CHOGA (Zimbabwe)

Mr. Manuel COK APARCANA (Peru)

Ms. Jehad Jamil Abu EL-SHAAR (Jordan)

Mr. Otaviano HELENE (Brazil)

Ms. Vivian HEYL (Chile)

Mr. Mohsen KTARI (Tunisia)

Ms. Zhi-Hua LIN (China)

Ms. Khalijah MOHAMMAD (Malaysia)

Ms. Irene OIBERMAN (Argentina)

Ms. Mara PEREZ TORRANO (Uruguay)

Mr. Mohammed RAGHEB (Egypt)

Mrs. Sirivarn SVASTIWAT (Thailand)

Ms. Dalia Noemi ZARZA PAREDES (Paraguay)

Others contributors to this publication

Mr. Kai v. AHLEFELD (Layout)

Mr. Gilles BURST (Layout)

Ms. Manuela DE SOUSA (OECD)

Mr. John FLINT (Editor)

Mr. Stéphane GUILLOT (OECD)

Mr. Philippe HERVE (OECD)

Ms. Katja HETTLER (Layout)

Mr. Thomas KRÄHENBÜHL (Layout)

Ms. Gala MARCHAL (Layout)

Ms. Cécile SLAPE (OECD)

RELATED OECD PUBLICATIONS

Classifying Educational Programmes: Manual for ISCED-97 implementation in OECD countries (1999)
ISBN 92-64-17037-5   41.00   US$ 43.00   £ 26.00   ¥ 5,050.00

From Initial Education to Working Life: Making transitions work (2000)
ISBN 92-64-17631-4   39.00   US$ 37.00   £ 23.00   ¥ 3,900.00

Literacy in the Information Age: Final report of the International Adult Literacy Survey (OECD and Statistics Canada) (2000)
ISBN 92-64-17654-3   33.00   US$ 31.00   £ 19.00   ¥ 3,250.00

Measuring Student Knowledge and Skills: The PISA 2000 assessment of reading, mathematical and scientific literacy (2000)
ISBN 92-64-17646-2   20.00   US$ 20.00   £ 12.00   ¥ 2,100.00

Where are the Resources for Lifelong Learning? (2000)
ISBN 92-64-17677-2   26.00   US$ 26.00   £ 16.00   ¥ 2,700.00

Knowledge and Skills for Life: First Results from PISA 2000 (2001)
ISBN 92-64-19671-4   21.00   US$ 19.00   £ 13.00   ¥ 2,110.00

Starting Strong: Early Childhood Education and Care (2001)
ISBN 92-64-18675-1   45.00   US$ 40.00   £ 28.00   ¥ 4,550.00

Teachers for Tomorrow's Schools: Analysis of the 2000 World Education Indicators (2001)
ISBN 92-64-18699-9   22.00   US$ 20.00   £ 14.00   ¥ 2,200.00

Education Policy Analysis (2002)
ISBN 92-64-1 9930-6   20 .00   US$ 20.00   £ 1 3 .00   ¥ 2,350 .00

Financing Education: Investments and returns - Analysis of the World Education Indicators (2002)
ISBN 92-64-19971-3   25.00   US$25.00   £16.00   ¥3,050.00

PISA 2000 Technical Report (2002)
ISBN 92-64-19951-9   30.00   US$30.00   £19.00   ¥3,500.00

Manual for the PISA 2000 Database (2002)
ISBN 92-64-19822-9   20.00   US$19.00   £12.00   ¥2,300.00

Sample Tasks from the PISA 2000 Assessment: Reading, Mathematical and Scientific Literacy (2002)
ISBN 92-64-19765-6   20.00   US$ 19.00   £ 12.00   ¥ 2,300.00

Reading for Change: Performance and Engagement across Countries (2003)
ISBN 92-64-09926-3   24.00   US$ 24.00   £ 15.00   ¥ 2,800.00

Literacy Skills for the World of Tomorrow: Further results from PISA 2000 (2003)
ISBN 92-64-10286-8   21.00   US$ 24.00   £ 14.00   ¥ 2,700.00

The PISA 2003 Assessment Framework: Mathematics, Reading, Science and Problem Solving Knowledge and Skills (2003)
ISBN 92-64-10172-1   24.00   US$ 28.00   £ 16.00   ¥ 3,100.00

Learners for Life: Student Approaches to Learning: Results from PISA 2000
ISBN 92-64-10390-2   PRICE NOT YET DEFINED

Education Policy Analysis (2003)
To be published in November 2003

These titles are available at the OECD Online Bookshop: *www.oecd.org/bookshop*.

OECD PUBLICATIONS, 2, rue André-Pascal, 75775 PARIS CEDEX 16
PRINTED IN FRANCE
(96 2003 06 1 P) ISBN 92-64-10233-7 – No. 53175 2003